TEMAS

SPANISH FOR THE GLOBAL COMMUNITY

TEMAS

SPANISH FOR THE GLOBAL COMMUNITY

SECOND EDITION

JORGE H. CUBILLOS
University of Delaware

EDWIN M. LAMBOY
Montclair University

THOMSON
™
HEINLE

Australia • Brazil • Canada • Mexico • Singapore • Spain • United Kingdom • United States

Temas
Spanish for the Global Community
Second Edition
Cubillos | Lamboy

Executive Editor: Carrie Brandon
Acquisitions Editor: Helen Alejandra Richardson
Development Editor: Mercedes Roffé
Senior Project Manager, Editorial Production: Esther Marshall
Marketing Manager: Lindsey Richardson
Marketing Assistant: Marla Nasser
Advertising Project Manager: Stacey Purviance
Managing Technology Project Manager: Sacha Laustsen
Manufacturing Manager: Marcia Locke
Compositor: Pre-Press Company, Inc.
Project Management: Katy Faria, Pre-Press Company, Inc.

Photo Manager: Sheri Blaney
Photo Reseacher: Jill Engebretson
Text Permissions Editor: Lianca Letelier
Text Designer: Brian Salisbury
Senior Art Director: Bruce Bond
Cover Designer: Yvo Riezebos
Illustrator: Dave Sullivan
Cover Printer: C&C Offset Printing Co., Ltd
Printer: C&C Offset Printing Co., Ltd

Cover image: ©Photodisc/GETTY IMAGES; *inside cover endpaper:* © Diana Ong/Superstock

Thomson Higher Education
25 Thomson Place
Boston, MA 02210-1202
USA

For more information about our products, contact us at:
Thomson Learning Academic Resource Center
1-800-423-0563
For permission to use material from this text or product, submit a request online at **http://www.thomsonrights.com**
Any additional questions about permissions can be submitted by e-mail to **thomsonrights@thomson.com**

Printed in China
2 3 4 5 6 7   09 08 07
Library of Congress Control Number: 2005931889

Student Edition ISBN-13: 978-1-4130-1049-7
            ISBN-10: 1-4130-1049-0

Credits appear on pages xxiii–xxv, which constitute a continuation of the copyright page.

América del Sur

MAR CARIBE

Barranquilla
Cartagena
Maracaibo
Caracas
R. Orinoco
Puerto de España
TRINIDAD Y TOBAGO

OCÉANO ATLÁNTICO

Medellín
Manizales
Cali
Bogotá
COLOMBIA

VENEZUELA

Georgetown
GUYANA
Paramaribo
SURINAM
Cayenne
GUAYANA
FRANCESA

ECUADOR

Quito
Guayaquil
ECUADOR
Iquitos
PERÚ

Manaus
R. Amazo
Belem

R. Madeira

Cajamarca

Recife

Machu
Picchu
Lima
Ayacucho
Cuzco
BOLIVIA
L. Titicaca
Arequipa
La Paz
Arica
Sucre
Iquique
Potosí

BRASIL

Brasilia

Salvador

Belo Horizonte

OCÉANO PACÍFICO
Antofagasta
Salta
PARAGUAY
Asunción
Tucumán
CHILE

São Paulo
Santos
Río de Janeiro

Córdoba
Mendoza
Valparaíso
Rosario
Santiago
Buenos Aires
Concepción
ARGENTINA
La Plata
Río de la Plata

R. Paraná
R. Uruguay
Porto Alegre
URUGUAY
Montevideo

ECUADOR

TRÓPICO DE CAPRICORNIO

Bahía Blanca

Puerto Montt

CORDILLERA DE LOS ANDES

ISLAS MALVINAS

| 0 | 200 | 400 | 600 | 800 millas |
| 0 | 200 | 400 | 600 | 800 kilómetros |

Punta Arenas
TIERRA DEL FUEGO
Cabo de Hornos
Estrecho de Magallanes

México, América Central y El Caribe

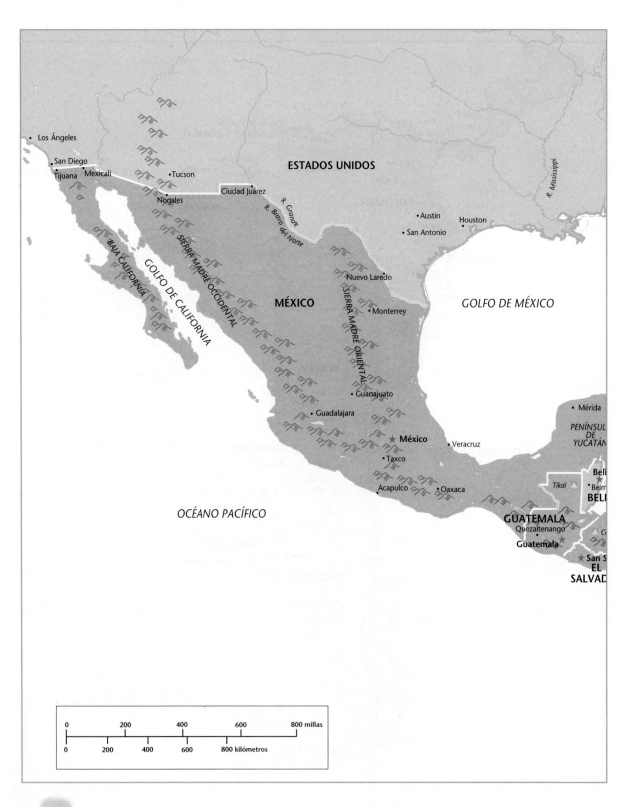

Los Ángeles

San Diego

Tijuana Mexicali

Tucson

Nogales

Ciudad Juárez

ESTADOS UNIDOS

R. Mississippi

R. Grande

R. Bravo del Norte

Austin

Houston

San Antonio

BAJA CALIFORNIA

GOLFO DE CALIFORNIA

SIERRA MADRE OCCIDENTAL

Nuevo Laredo

SIERRA MADRE ORIENTAL

MÉXICO

Monterrey

GOLFO DE MÉXICO

Guanajuato

Guadalajara

México

Veracruz

Taxco

Acapulco

Oaxaca

OCÉANO PACÍFICO

Mérida

PENÍNSUL
DE
YUCATÁN

Tikal

Beli

Belm

BELI

GUATEMALA

Quezaltenango

Guatemala

San S

EL
SALVAD

0	200	400	600	800 millas

0	200	400	600	800 kilómetros

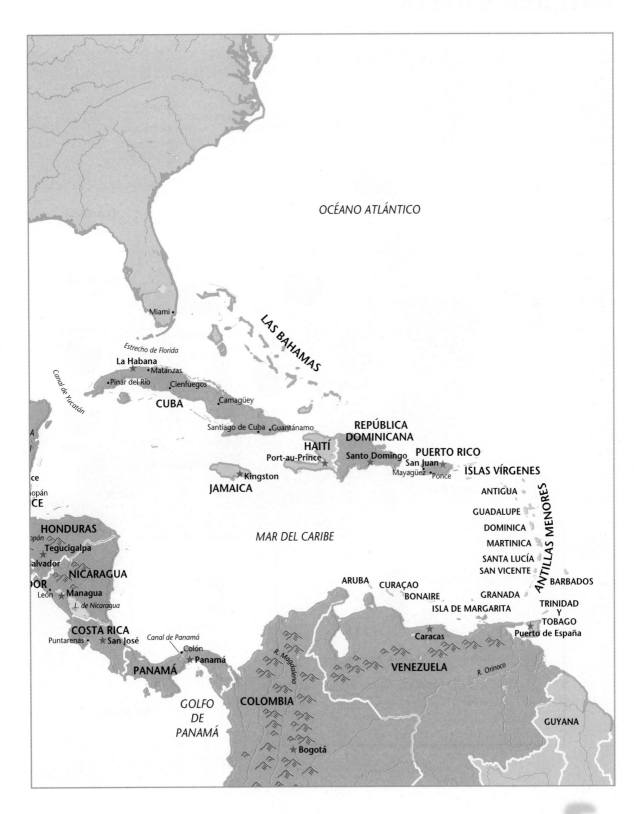

OCÉANO ATLÁNTICO

LAS BAHAMAS

Miami •

Estrecho de Florida

La Habana
★ •Matanzas
•Pinar del Río •Cienfuegos
CUBA •Camagüey

Canal de Yucatán

Santiago de Cuba •Guantánamo

REPÚBLICA
DOMINICANA

HAITÍ
Port-au-Prince ★ Santo Domingo•

PUERTO RICO
San Juan
★
Mayagüez• •Ponce

ISLAS VÍRGENES

•★Kingston

JAMAICA

ANTIGUA

GUADALUPE

DOMINICA

MARTINICA

SANTA LUCÍA
SAN VICENTE

ANTILLAS MENORES

BARBADOS

MAR DEL CARIBE

HONDURAS

opán Tegucigalpa
★
alvador ★

NICARAGUA
OR León• ★ Managua
L. de Nicaragua

COSTA RICA
Puntarenas • ★San José

PANAMÁ

Canal de Panamá
•Colón
★ Panamá

ARUBA CURAÇAO
BONAIRE

GRANADA

ISLA DE MARGARITA

TRINIDAD
Y
TOBAGO
Puerto de España

Caracas
★

R. Magdalena

VENEZUELA

R. Orinoco

GOLFO
DE
PANAMÁ

COLOMBIA

GUYANA

Bogotá
★

ce

opán

CE

Los hispanohablantes en los Estados Unidos

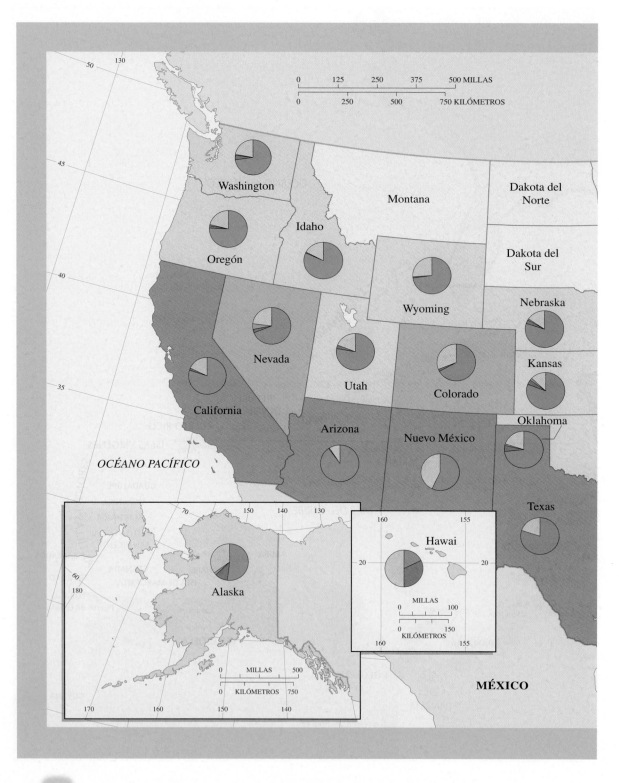

Maps

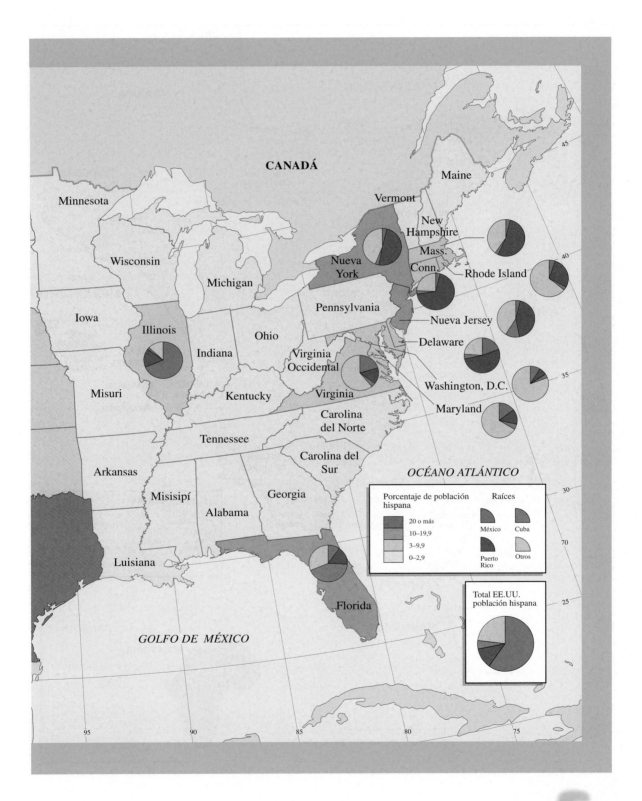

CANADÁ

Minnesota

Wisconsin

Michigan

Maine

Vermont

New Hampshire

Mass.

Conn.

Rhode Island

Nueva York

Iowa

Illinois

Indiana

Ohio

Pennsylvania

Nueva Jersey

Delaware

Misuri

Kentucky

Virginia Occidental

Virginia

Washington, D.C.

Maryland

Arkansas

Tennessee

Carolina del Norte

Carolina del Sur

OCÉANO ATLÁNTICO

Misisipí

Georgia

Alabama

Luisiana

Florida

GOLFO DE MÉXICO

Porcentaje de población hispana

Raíces

20 o más

10–19,9

3–9,9

0–2,9

México

Cuba

Puerto Rico

Otros

Total EE.UU. población hispana

Maps   ix

España

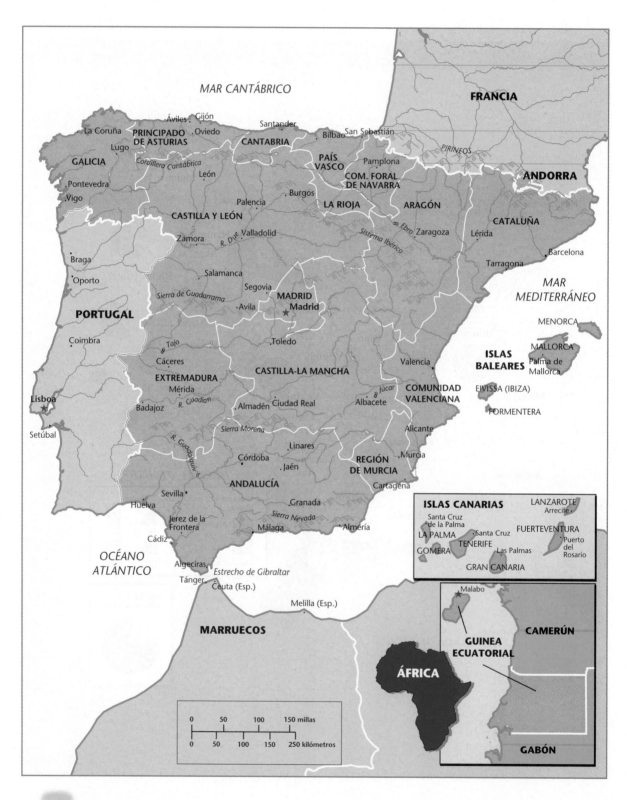

MAR CANTÁBRICO

FRANCIA

Áviles • Gijón
La Coruña • • Oviedo • Santander
• Lugo **PRINCIPADO** **CANTABRIA** • Bilbao San Sebastián
DE ASTURIAS *Cordillera Cantábrica* **PAÍS** • Pamplona
GALICIA • León **VASCO** **ANDORRA**
• Pontevedra **COM. FORAL**
• Vigo • Burgos **DE NAVARRA**
• Palencia **LA RIOJA** **ARAGÓN**
CASTILLA Y LEÓN *Sistema Ibérico* • Ebro Zaragoza **CATALUÑA**
• Zamora R. Due Valladolid • Lérida
• Braga • Barcelona
• Oporto • Salamanca Tarragona
• Segovia **MAR**
Sierra de Guadarrama **MADRID** **MEDITERRÁNEO**
PORTUGAL • Avila • Madrid ★
MENORCA
• Coimbra • Toledo MALLORCA
& Tajo **ISLAS** Palma de
• Cáceres **CASTILLA-LA MANCHA** • Valencia **BALEARES** Mallorca
EXTREMADURA EIVISSA (IBIZA)
• Mérida Júcar
Lisboa R. Guadian • Almadén Ciudad Real • Albacete **COMUNIDAD** FORMENTERA
★ • Badajoz **VALENCIANA**
• Setúbal *Sierra Morena* • Alicante
R. Guadalquivir • Linares
• Córdoba **REGIÓN** • Murcia
• Jaén **DE MURCIA**
ANDALUCÍA Cartagena
• Sevilla • Granada **ISLAS CANARIAS** LANZAROTE
• Huelva *Sierra Nevada* Santa Cruz Arrecife
Jerez de la • Málaga • Almería de la Palma FUERTEVENTURA
Frontera **LA PALMA** Santa Cruz Puerto
• Cádiz **OCÉANO** **GOMERA** TENERIFE Las Palmas del
ATLÁNTICO Algeciras • Rosario
Tánger • *Estrecho de Gibraltar* **GRAN CANARIA**
Ceuta (Esp.)

Melilla (Esp.) Malabo
★
MARRUECOS **GUINEA** **CAMERÚN**
ECUATORIAL
ÁFRICA

0   50   100   150 millas

0   50   100   150   250 kilómetros **GABÓN**

Scope and Sequence

Capítulo preparatorio
¡A empezar!   2

Vocabulario
El salón de clase; Los saludos; Las despedidas y las expresiones de cortesía
Los cursos
Los días y los meses; Los números; Los colores

Funciones y estructuras
Personal pronouns
Gender, number, and definite articles
Indefinite articles and the invariable impersonal verbal **hay**

	Vocabulario	Funciones y estructuras	Lecturas y vídeo
Unidad 1: La identidad			
Capítulo 1 Éste soy yo 22			**Enfoque:** Latin America
Tema 1: Datos personales 24	Los formularios	Providing information with the verb **ser** Describing people with adjectives	Perspectivas: Los documentos de identificación
Tema 2: Ocupaciones 34	Profesiones y ocupaciones	Talking about daily activities with simple present tense **-ar** verbs Talking about daily activities with simple present tense **-er** and **-ir** verbs	Vídeo: La llegada a Puerto Rico y a la Hacienda Vista Alegre
Tema 3: Intereses personales 45	Los pasatiempos	Expressing negation Exchanging information and asking questions with interrogative words	Lectura: Mi página personal en la Red
Capítulo 2 En familia 58			**Enfoque:** México
Tema 1: Ésta es mi familia 60	Los miembros de la familia	Describing physical appearance with adjectives and the verbs **ser** and **tener** Expressing possession	Perspectivas: La familia de José Miguel
Tema 2: La personalidad 70	Los rasgos personales	Talking about location, condition, and emotional states with the verbs **estar** and **tener** Talking about likes and dislikes with **gustar**	Vídeo: Los compañeros se conocen mejor
Tema 3: Nuestro hogar 83	Los espacios y los muebles de una casa	Talking about location with prepositions Expressing obligation with **tener que...** and **hay que...**	Lectura: La casa en Mango Street
Puesta en acción 1/2: Hosting a Mexican exchange student 96			

	Vocabulario	Funciones y estructuras	Lecturas y vídeo
Unidad II: La vida diaria			
Capítulo 3 Dónde y cuándo 100			**Enfoque:** Puerto Rico
Tema 1: Orientándonos en la ciudad 102	Lugares de interés	Talking about location and destination with the verbs **estar** and **ir** Telling time	Perspectivas: Turismo en Puerto Rico
Tema 2: De compras 113	Las compras y las formas de pago	Talking about daily activities with irregular **yo** form verbs Adverbs of frequency	Vídeo: El día de la primera excursión en Puerto Rico
Tema 3: La comida 124	Vamos a comer	Talking about daily activities with $e \rightarrow i$ stem-changing verbs Talking about future plans	Lectura: La dieta mediterránea
Capítulo 4 Preferencias y prioridades 140			**Enfoque:** España
Tema 1: El tiempo 142	El estado del tiempo y las estaciones	Talking about ongoing actions and events with the present progressive Comparing and contrasting with comparatives and superlatives	Perspectivas: Las variaciones climáticas en el mundo hispano
Tema 2: La ropa 153	Ropa de diario y accesorios	Talking about daily activities with $e \rightarrow ie$ and $o \rightarrow ue$ stem-changing verbs Talking about daily routines with reflexive verbs	Vídeo: Una charla sobre la ropa
Tema 3: La diversión 163	Los deportes	Talking about daily activities with irregular present tense verbs Describing people and objects with the verbs **ser** and **estar**	Lectura: De vacaciones
Puesta en acción 3/4: Organizing a business meeting in Puerto Rico 174			

	Vocabulario	Funciones y estructuras	Lecturas y vídeo
Unidad V: Interacciones			
Capítulo 9 Acuerdos y desacuerdos 352			**Enfoque:** Guatemala, Honduras y El Salvador
Tema 1: Las amistades 354	Un buen amigo	Giving advice with the subjunctive (regular verbs) Giving advice with the subjunctive (irregular verbs)	Perspectivas: La timidez
Tema 2: Relaciones laborales 369	Los compañeros y los jefes	Expressing wishes and requests Expressing emotions and feelings	Vídeo: ¿Algo más que una amistad?
Tema 3: Relaciones de pareja 381	Amor, noviazgo y matrimonio	Expressing doubt and denial Talking about hypothetical situations with the subjunctive	Lectura: La hija del caníbal
Capítulo 10 ¿Qué quieres hacer? 394			**Enfoque:** Argentina y Uruguay
Tema 1: A mantenernos en forma 396	La buena salud y las enfermedades	Giving suggestions and instructions (review of formal commands and advice) Giving instructions with informal commands	Perspectivas: Una buena figura
Tema 2: La diversión en la ciudad 409	Los deportes urbanos	Expressing opinion and emotion (review of the subjunctive) Expressing purpose, stipulation, or future time frame with the subjunctive in adverbial clauses	Vídeo: Un desastre en la cocina
Tema 3: Panorama cultural 420	Las bellas artes	Giving directives and advice (review of formal and informal commands and introduction of **nosotros** commands) Talking about the future with the future tense	Lectura: El túnel
Puesta en acción 9/10: Designing programs for workers in a corporate setting 436			

	Vocabulario	Funciones y estructuras	Lecturas y vídeo
Unidad VI: Expectativas			
Capítulo 11 Mirando hacia el futuro 442			**Enfoque:** Chile y Paraguay
Tema 1: Proyectos personales 444	Mis aspiraciones	Talking about aspirations (review of the future tense) Expressing conjecture and probability with the conditional tense	Perspectivas: Las claves de la ilusión
Tema 2: Un futuro tecnificado 456	Las comodidades de la era electrónica	Expressing opinion, emotion, wishes, doubt, stipulation, purpose and future time frame with the subjunctive and the infinitive Talking about the past using the imperfect subjunctive (regular verbs)	Vídeo: Aspiraciones y planes para el futuro
Tema 3: Utopías 470	Un mundo mejor	Talking about the past using the imperfect subjunctive (irregular verbs) Expressing condition (**si** clauses)	Lectura: El albergue de las mujeres tristes
Capítulo 12 La herencia hispana 486			**Enfoque:** Los hispanos en los Estados Unidos
Tema 1: Historia de la presencia hispana en los Estados Unidos 488		Talking about the past with the preterite, the imperfect, and the present perfect (review)	Lectura: Los antecedentes (Partes 1 y 2)
Tema 2: Abriendo caminos 498		Giving commands, advice, and opinions (review)	Vídeo: Se les fue volando el mes
Tema 3: Desafíos 504		Indicating probability with the future and conditional tenses (review)	Lectura: Entró y se sentó
Puesta en acción 11/12: Hispanic heritage 512			

Preface to the Student

*¡Bienvenidos a **Temas!*** This textbook is designed to give you the opportunity to discover the Spanish language through **active learning.** Its basic philosophy is that language acquisition results from participating in **meaningful interactions** with other language learners and/or native speakers. With this program, active learning takes place through classroom and independent learning tasks with the help of multimedia and the Internet.

As you proceed through this course, keep in mind the following principles, which have helped many learners achieve proficiency in a foreign language:

- **Practice.** Seek every opportunity to use the language in and out of the classroom. Take advantage of all the human and technological resources at hand.

- **Be adventurous.** Don't be afraid to take risks. Mistakes are a natural part of the learning process.

- **Be patient.** Learning a language takes time and effort. Don't expect it to happen overnight.

- **Be flexible.** Accept that you won't always understand everything or be able to say exactly what you want to say. There are many ways to get your point across.

- **Discover.** Appreciate the uniqueness of other cultures. Bridge the gap between your culture and others.

- **Expand your horizons.** Consider studying abroad and interacting with Spanish speakers in your area.

We hope that these words of advice will help you and that your experience learning the Spanish language and exploring the diverse cultures of the Spanish-speaking world is an enriching and rewarding one.

Acknowledgments

Writing a textbook is always a team effort, especially in the case of a project of this magnitude. For this reason, we would like to express our most sincere gratitude to Heinle Publishers for its leadership in the development of quality foreign language materials. Our deepest appreciation to Helen Alejandra Richardson (Senior Acquisitions Editor) for believing in the *Temas* program and in the promise of a second edition; to Mercedes Roffé (Developmental Editor), whose experience and pedagogical knowledge guided us toward the completion of this project; to Stasie Harrington for her incredible talent to create outstanding video activities; and to Esther Marshall (Senior Production Project Manager) for her creativity and vision. Our thanks also go to the other people at Heinle without whom we would not have successfully concluded this project: Heather Bradley (Associate Development Editor) and Caitlin McIntyre (Editorial Assistant). And finally, our thanks to all the free-lancers involved with the different stages of the production and in particular, Katy Faria (Project Manager on behalf of Pre-Press Company, Inc.), Linda Beaupré (Interior Designer), Margaret Hines (Copyeditor and Proofreader), Luz Galante (Native Reader), Lucy de la Cruz Gibbs and Soledad Phelan (Proofreaders).

We wish to especially thank the authors of the *Temas,* **Second Edition,** ancillaries:

Kimberley Sallee, *University of St. Louis,* for her work on the IRM.

Jennifer Rogers, *Blue River Community College,* for her work on the Testing Program.

Andy Noverr, *University of Michigan,* for his work on the CDROM and iLrn.

Bridgette Gunnels, *State University of West Georgia,* for her work on the website.

Our deepest gratitude to all the reviewers, whose ideas and feedback oriented and shaped the development of this Second Edition in many important ways.

Lee Abraham, *Villanova University*
Joseph A. Agee, *Morehouse College*
Pilar Alcade, *University of Memphis*
Aranxta Alegre-González, *Ohio State University*
Eileen M. Angelini, *Philadelphia University*
Barbara Avila-Shah, *University at Buffalo, SUNY*
Liliana Castro, *Front Range Community College*
Ana García Chicester, *University of Mary Washington*
Sarah DeSmet, *Wesleyan College*
Conxita Domenech, *Front Range Community College*
Linda Elliott-Nelson, *Arizona Western College*
Addison Everett, *Dixie State College*
Mary Fatora-Tumbaga, *Kauai Community College*
Hector Garza, *Southern Utah University*
Donald Gibbs, *Creighton University*

Pamela Gill, *Gaston College*
Peg Haas, *Kent State University*
Denise Hatcher, *Aurora University*
Tia Huggins, *Iowa State University*
Hans Jöerg-Busch, *University of Delaware*
Herman Johnson, *Xavier University*
David Julseth, *Belmont University*
Sofia Kearns, *Furman University*
Paula Luteran, *Hutchinson Community College*
Jeffrey R. Marks, *Ohio University*
Don Miller, *California State University, Chico*
Lilijana Milojevic, *Ocean County College*
Bill Monds, *Trinity Valley Community College*
Oscar Moreno, *Georgia State University*
Denise Overfield, *University of West Georgia*
Kay E. Raymond, *Sam Houston State University*
Marcie Rinka, *University of San Diego*
Regina Roebuck, *University of Louisville*
Jennifer Rogers, *Blue River Community College*
Tara Rojas, *University of Hawaii*
Patricia Rubio, *Skidmore College*
Jacqueline Sandone, *University of Missouri-Columbia*
Carmen Schlig, *Georgia State University*
Nancy Smith, *Allegheny College*
Elizabeth Vargas Dowdy, *Manatee Community College*
Susan Villar, *University of Minnesota*
Kathleen Wheatley, *University of Wisconsin- Milwaukee*
Jonnie Wilhite, *Kalamazoo Community College*
Nancy Whitman, *Los Medanos College*

Finally, we wish to thank our family, our friends, and all the people in Latin America and Spain who offered insights about their countries and their lives. Their contributions give this book its real-life flavor.

To all, our sincere thanks.

Jorge H. Cubillos and Edwin M. Lamboy

Student Components

Workbook/Lab Manual: Packaged with the Lab Audio CDs, it follows the organization of the main text, providing additional reading, writing, listening, and pronunciation pactice out of class. The writing activities, correlated to the latest version of **Atajo: Writing Assistant for Spanish,** direct you to the main points of information essential to the writing task, and guide you in the writing process.

Lab Audio CDs: Intended to use in conjunction with the **Workbook/Lab Manual**. These CDs provide listening comprehension reinforcement of structures and vocabulary, and also help improve pronunciation.

Student Multimedia CD-ROM: Provides you with fun, interactive practice of the vocabulary and grammar from each *Tema*. In addition to a variety of practice activities, the CD-ROM also offers audio- and video-enhanced sections that focus on pronunciation and culture and a reading section that describes on-going service learning projects to think about opportunities in your own community.

Atajo 4.0 CD-ROM: Writing Assistant for Spanish: This powerful program combines the features of a word processor with databases of language reference material, a searchable dictionary featuring the entire contents of Merriam-Webster's® Spanish English Dictionary, a verb conjugating reference, and audio recordings of vocabulary, example sentences, and authentic samples of the language. This will help you develop critical thinking skills as you learn to read, analyze, make word associations, and understand the link between language functions and linguistics structures.

Text Credits

This page constitutes an extension of the copyright page. We have made every effort to trace the ownership of all copyrighted material and to secure permission from copyright holders. In the event of any question arising as to the use of any material, we will be pleased to make the necessary corrections in future printings. Thanks are due to the following authors, publishers, and agents for permission to use the material indicated.

pp. 424–425: "La floreciente industria del cuerpo", reprinted by permission of *El País*, Montevideo, UY.

pp. 453–454: "El Tunel" by Ernesto Sabato.

pp. 505–506: "El albergue de las mujeres tristes" by Marcela Serrano.

pp. 530–531: "Entró y se sentó" by Rosaura Sanchez is reprinted with permission from the publisher of *Cuentos hispanos de los Estados Unidos* (Houston: *Arte Publico Press*–University of Houston, 1993)

p. 93: "La Casa en Mango Street", © 1984, Sandra Cisneros.

pp. 134–135: "La dieta mediterranea tambien reduce cancer y mortalidad general". Source: *EFE* 26/jun/2003, Association for the Advancement of the Mediterranean Diet.

pp. 171–172: "Las Vacaciones" from "La Familia no hay mas que una y al perro lo encontramos en calle". Reprinted by permission of *Gomaespuma Producciones S.L.*

pp. 214–215: "Historia de los incas", Pedro Sarmiento. Gamboa (1572)

pp. 229–230: Reprinted by permission of *El Nuevo Diario*, Martes, 18 de Marco, 2004.

pp. 290–291: "Dirección: el sur de la Florida", December 1997. Reprinted by permission of *Latin Trade*.

pp. 315–316: "Soñar en Cubano" by Christina Garcia.

pp. 331–332: "Encontrar trabajo vía cibernética" by Jay Dougtherty. Reprinted by permission of *El Universal Digital*, 14 de julio 1997. © dpa, 1997.

pp. 357–358: "Mi Amigo, Germán Cuervo", *Ediciones de la Universidad del Valle*.

pp. 406–407: "La hija del cannibal by Rosa Montero".

p. 111: Officina del Gobernador de Puerto Rico, © 1998.

Photo Credits

All photographs not otherwise credited are owned by © The Thomson Corporation or © Thomson/Heinle Image Resource Bank.

This book is dedicated to all those who seek to learn about the cultures and people of Spanish-speaking countries and to use this knowledge and the Spanish language in the context of the global community.

Capítulo preparatorio

¡A empezar!

Vocabulario	El salón de clase; Los saludos, las despedidas y las expresiones de cortesía	Los cursos	Los días y los meses; Los números; Los colores
Funciones y estructuras	Personal pronouns	Gender, number, and definite articles	Indefinite articles and the invariable impersonal verbal form **hay**

I. Vocabulario: El salón de clase

el profesor — la ventana — la profesora — el libro

Español 101 — Buenos días

el borrador la pizarra — la puerta

la mesa — la tiza — el cuaderno — el escritorio — el estudiante — la mochila — la estudiante

la silla — el bolígrafo

el lápiz — el cuaderno de ejercicios

Vocabulario práctico

Lo que dice el profesor
Abran el libro en la página...
Cierren sus libros.
Escriban...
Lean...

What the instructor says
Open your books on page . . .
Close your books.
Write . . .
Read . . .

Lo que dicen los estudiantes
Más despacio, por favor.
¿Qué significa... ?
¿Cómo se dice... ?
Repita, por favor.
No comprendo.

What students say
More slowly, please.
What does . . . mean?
How do you say . . . ?
Repeat, please.
I do not understand.

SABOR REGIONAL

A notebook is called a **carpeta** in Cuba and a **libreta** in the Dominican Republic and in Puerto Rico. Expect significant regional variations in the Spanish language, particularly in the area of vocabulary.

■ Aplicaciones

CD1-2

P-1 ¿Qué dice el (la) profesor(a)? *(What does the instructor say?)* Match the statements made by the instructor with the following pictures.

_____   _____

_____   _____

P-2 ¿Qué dices? *(What do you say?)* Provide an expression that you can use in each of the following cases.

    a. When you do not understand what the instructor is saying.
    b. When you do not know how to say something in Spanish.
    c. When you want your instructor to repeat a key point.
    d. When you do not know the meaning of a Spanish word.

II. Vocabulario: Los saludos, las despedidas y las expresiones de cortesía

—Buenos días, Julio.
—Buenos días, profesor Rodríguez. ¿Cómo está Ud.?
—Muy bien, gracias.

Good morning, Julio.
Good morning, Professor Rodríguez. How are you?
Very well, thank you.

—Hola, Pedro.
—Buenas noches, Marta. ¿Cómo te va?
—Muy bien, ¿y a ti?
—¡De maravilla!
—Aquí está el libro.
—Muchas gracias.
—De nada.

Hello, Pedro.
Good evening, Marta. How are you?
Very well, and you?
Wonderful!
Here is the book.
Thanks a lot.
You're welcome.

—Buenas tardes, ¿cómo te llamas?
—Me llamo Julián, ¿y tú?
—Me llamo Alicia. Mucho gusto.
—Encantado.

Good afternoon, what is your name?
My name is Julián, and yours?
My name is Alicia. Pleased to meet you.
My pleasure.

SABOR REGIONAL

Other equivalent expressions used in different parts of the Spanish-speaking world for **De nada** are **A la orden, No hay de qué,** and **Con gusto.**

The following are other expressions you can use to indicate how you are doing: **más o menos/regular** *(so-so)*; **mal** *(bad)*; **pésimo** *(terrible).*

Notice that physical contact is often part of a greeting in Hispanic culture. This contact ranges from a firm handshake among men, to a kiss on the cheek for close friends. Greetings accompanied by kissing are quite common among young men and women (and among women) in both Latin America and Spain.

—Adiós, Sr. Grisales.
—Bueno, hasta luego,
  Sr. González.

Good-bye, Mr. Grisales.
O.K., see you later,
  Mr. González.

Vocabulario práctico

¡Hasta pronto! *See you soon!*
¡Hasta la vista! *See you around!*

Chao. *Bye.*
Nos vemos el lunes. *I'll see you*
  on Monday.

Títulos de respeto

Doctor (Dr.)
Licenciado (Lic.)
Señor (Sr.)
Señora (Sra.)
Señorita (Srta.)

Titles of respect

Doctor
(For various professions)
Sir/Mr.
Madam/Mrs.
Miss

These titles are usually followed by the person's last name: **Dr. Jiménez, Sr. Gómez, Sra. Alarcón. Don** and **Doña,** which are used with older people as a sign of respect, are followed by the person's first name: **Don Juan, Doña María.**

■ Aplicaciones

P-3 Diálogos Complete the dialogues with appropriate comments and responses.

1. La Sra. Díaz: Buenos días, doctor.

   El Dr. Fernández: _____

   La Sra. Díaz: Pues no muy bien, doctor. Mire Ud.,...

2. Juan: _____

   Ana: Hola, Juan ¿Cómo estás?

   Juan: _____

3. Esteban: _____

   La profesora Ruiz: Mucho gusto, Esteban. Yo soy la profesora Ruiz.

   Esteban: _____

4. Julio: _____

   Elvira: Adiós, Julio. ¡Nos vemos el viernes!

When reporting on someone else's name, use the expression **Se llama...**

P-4 Saluda a tus compañeros Greet two or three of the people around you in Spanish. Learn their names and later introduce them to the rest of the class.

III. Funciones y estructuras: Personal pronouns

PERSON	SINGULAR	PLURAL
First	**yo** *(I)*	**nosotros, nosotras** *(we,* masculine/feminine)
Second	**tú** *(you,* informal) **usted** *(you,* formal)	**ustedes** *(you,* formal/informal) **vosotros, vosotras** *(you,* masculine/feminine, informal, Spain)
Third	**él** *(he)* **ella** *(she)*	**ellos, ellas** *(they,* masculine/feminine)

As you noticed in the previous section, the distinction between formal and informal ways of addressing a person is at the essence of effective social communication. While in English the level of formality of an exchange finds its expression mainly in the tone and the type of language used, in Spanish this influence extends also to the verb forms and pronouns selected.

The informal personal pronouns in Spanish are **tú** for the singular and **ustedes** (or **vosotros** in Spain) for the plural.

Note that in Spanish there is no equivalent of the English subject pronoun *it.*

Es mi escritorio.	*It is my desk.*
Es una clase difícil.	*It is a difficult class.*

In Spanish there is a gender distinction when it comes to groups made exclusively of women (**nosotras, vosotras, ellas**). The masculine form is used in the case of male only or mixed groups.

Nosotras somos profesoras.	***We** are professors.*
Vosotras sois responsables.	***You** are responsible.*
Ellas son mis hermanas.	***They** are my sisters.*

Since Spanish verbs have different endings for each person, personal pronouns are often omitted. The verb itself can indicate what the subject is.

Soy estudiante.	*I am a student.*
Trabaja en una oficina.	*He/She works in an office.*
Estudiamos español.	*We study Spanish.*

However, personal pronouns may be included in a sentence for clarification or emphasis.

Yo soy estudiante.	*I **(myself)** am a student.* (emphasis)
Él trabaja en una oficina.	*He works in an office.* (clarification)

■ Aplicaciones

P-5 ¿De quién habla? Complete the sentences with the appropriate pronoun according to the picture.

1. _____ soy Marta.

2. _____ son mis compañeras.

3. _____ es mi amigo Juan Ortega.

4. _____ somos estudiantes.

P-6 Completa las frases Make the following sentences more emphatic by adding the appropriate personal pronoun.

_____ *(I)* soy estudiante.

_____ *(You,* informal) eres profesora.

_____ *(He)* es Juan.

_____ *(We)* somos amigos.

_____ *(They,* feminine) son mis hermanas.

IV. Vocabulario: Los cursos

Humanidades	*Humanities*		Ciencias sociales	*Social Sciences*
literatura	*literature*		economía	*economics*
filosofía	*philosophy*		historia	*history*
lenguas	*languages*		sicología	*psychology*
			ciencias políticas	*political sciences*

Los cursos (Courses)

Matemáticas	*Mathematics*		Artes	*Arts*
álgebra	*algebra*		baile	*dance*
cálculo	*calculus*		música	*music*
geometría	*geometry*		pintura	*painting*

Ciencias naturales	*Natural Sciences*
biología	*biology*
geografía	*geography*
geología	*geology*
química	*chemistry*

Vocabulario práctico

Las especializaciones

administración de empresas	*business administration*
antropología	*anthropology*
comunicaciones	*communications*
derecho	*law*
educación física	*physical education*
informática	*computer science*
ingeniería	*engineering*
medicina	*medicine*
periodismo	*journalism*
fisioterapia	*physical therapy*
trabajo social	*social work*
veterinaria	*veterinary*

The major and minor system does not exist in Latin America or Spain. The institutions of higher education typically offer programs leading to professional degrees instead.

■ Aplicaciones

P-7 Su especialidad es... *(His/Her concentration is . . .)* List six people you know and their concentration (major).

V. Vocabulario: Los días y los meses

Months are not capitalized in Spanish. Dates are often expressed in the following order: day, month, year (10 de enero de 2007 = 10/01/07).

lunes	martes	miércoles	jueves	viernes	sábado	domingo

diciembre, enero, febrero

marzo, abril, mayo

junio, julio, agosto

septiembre, octubre, noviembre

P-8 ¿Comprendiste bien? Look at the following ads and answer the questions that follow.

Gran Concierto de Juanes. Coliseo Cubierto El Campín: sábado, 26 de febrero a las 6:00 p.m.

Vuele LAN a los Estados Unidos. Siempre con los mejores horarios. Santiago–Miami: dos vuelos diarios a las 10:00 y 11:00 p.m. Santiago–Nueva York: lunes, miércoles, viernes y domingos. Santiago–Los Ángeles: martes, jueves y sábados.

DE VUELTA AL COLEGIO, AHORRE EN SUS SUPERTIENDAS **MAKRO**: GRANDES DESCUENTOS EN ARTÍCULOS ESCOLARES. HORARIO ESPECIAL: LUNES A VIERNES: 7:00 A.M. A 10:00 P.M., SÁBADOS: 8:00 A.M. A 8:00 P.M., DOMINGOS: 12:00 A 6:00 P.M.

1. What days of the week is the Makro store open?
2. When does LAN fly to Miami? How about Los Angeles? And New York?
3. When is Juanes's concert?

P-9 ¿Cuándo es... ? Indicate in Spanish the month when the following events take place.

1. La independencia de los Estados Unidos
2. La Navidad *(Christmas)*
3. El Año Nuevo *(New Year)*
4. La Pascua *(Easter)*
5. El Día de Acción de Gracias *(Thanksgiving)*
6. El comienzo *(beginning)* de las clases
7. El examen final de la clase de español
8. El fin *(end)* del curso
9. Tu cumpleaños *(birthday)*

> To find out what classes your friend is taking this semester/trimester, you can ask: **¿Qué clases tomas este (semestre/trimestre)?**
>
> To reply you may say:
> **Tomo matemáticas, inglés y español.**

P-10 Horario *(Schedule)* **de clases** Interview a classmate and complete his/her schedule of classes.

	lunes	martes	miércoles	jueves	viernes	sábado	domingo
por la mañana *(in the morning)*							
por la tarde *(in the afternoon)*							
por la noche *(in the evening)*							

VI. Guía para la pronunciación: El alfabeto y las vocales

CD1–3

Letra	Nombre	Ejemplos	
A	a	Ana	Panamá
B	be	baile	Nubia
C	ce	casa, poco	César, Alicia
	che	chévere	derecho
D	de	día	todo
E	e	enero	empresas
F	efe	Fernando	elefante
G	ge	Gabriel	elegante
		Gertrudis	elegido
H	hache	hola	almohada
I	i	infante	estudiante
J	jota	junio	mejor
K	ka	kiosco	polka
L	ele	lápiz	helado
	elle	lluvia	silla
M	eme	mamá	Guatemala
N	ene	nada	Honduras
Ñ	eñe	ñato	señor
O	o	Óscar	doctor
P	pe	Pedro	España
Q	cu	queso	porque
R	ere	arpa	pero
	erre (or doble ere)	Ramón	perro
S	ese	Sandra	pasado
T	te	televisión	atuendo
U	u	uva	cuaderno
V	ve (or uve)	verano	Flavio
W	doble v (or doble uve)	Wilson	
X	equis	xilófono	exacto
Y	i griega	Yolanda	mayo
Z	ceta (or zeta)	Zapata	Mazatlán

Las vocales *a, e, i, o, u* The pronunciation of vowels in Spanish does not vary.

/a/	/e/	/i/	/o/	/u/
casa	café	tiza	sofá	uso
mamá	bebé	iglesia	bobo	útil
papá	jefe	inglés	lobo	uno

In English there is a tendency to diphthongize words ending in vowels such as **o** or **e**. In Spanish those letters retain their original sound (/o/ or /e/).

libro   por qué

vivo   Santa Fe

amigo   porque

VII. Vocabulario: Los números

Tiene **dos** lápices.
*She has **two** pencils.*

Éstas son mis **tres** hermanas.
*These are my **three** sisters.*

Es un edificio de **quince** pisos.
*It is a building of **fifteen** floors.*

Tengo **ochenta** dólares.
*I have **eighty** dollars.*

Hay **veinticinco** estudiantes.
*There are **twenty-five** students.*

Contiene **cincuenta** chocolates.
*It contains **fifty** chocolates.*

cero	**0**		
uno	1	once	11
dos	2	doce	12
tres	3	trece	13
cuatro	4	catorce	14
cinco	5	quince	15
seis	6	dieciséis	16
siete	7	diecisiete	17
ocho	8	dieciocho	18
nueve	9	diecinueve	19
diez	**10**		

veinte	**20**	treinta	**30**
veintiuno	21	treinta y uno	31
veintidós	22	treinta y dos	32
veintitrés	23	cuarenta	**40**
veinticuatro	24	cincuenta	50
veinticinco	25	sesenta	60
veintiséis	26	setenta	70
veintisiete	27	ochenta	80
veintiocho	28	noventa	90
veintinueve	29	cien	**100**

■ **Aplicaciones**

CD1–4 **P-11 Una fiesta** Listen to a phone message someone has left in your answering machine. How many items does he/she want you to bring to the class party? Circle the correct figure in each case.

1. mesas: 2, 4, 6
2. sillas: 10, 20, 30
3. pizzas: 5, 15, 25
4. refrescos *(soft drinks):*   11, 21, 31
5. platos *(dishes):*   44, 74, 94
6. servilletas *(napkins):*   50, 80, 100

P-12 ¿Cuánto es? In pairs, take turns completing the following calculations and expressing the results in Spanish.

Vocabulario útil: **más** = +   **menos** = −
            por = ×   **dividido por** = ÷

1. $11 + 6 =$ _____
2. $35 + 9 =$ _____
3. $55 + 23 =$ _____
4. $66 - 34 =$ _____
5. $71 - 17 =$ _____
6. $90 - 82 =$ _____
7. $4 \times 12 =$ _____
8. $3 \times 9 =$ _____
9. $25 \times 3 =$ _____
10. $20 \div 2 =$ _____
11. $72 \div 3 =$ _____
12. $96 \div 6 =$ _____

VIII. Vocabulario: Los colores

Los colores

- negro
- azul
- marrón/café
- dorado
- rojo
- gris
- verde
- anaranjado/color naranja
- rosado
- morado
- plateado
- blanco
- amarillo

■ Aplicaciones

P-13 ¿De qué color es... ? Look at the drawing of the class on page 3 and indicate the color of each of the following items.

Opciones: anaranjado, azul, verde, blanco, marrón

1. la tiza _____
2. la pizarra _____
3. la puerta _____
4. el bolígrafo _____
5. el lápiz _____

P-14 Las banderas *(The flags)* Indicate in Spanish the colors of the following national flags:

Colombia

México

Bolivia

España

Panamá

P

IX. Funciones y estructuras: Gender, number, and definite articles

Nouns are words that designate objects, animals, or persons such as *rock, cat,* or *mother.* All Spanish nouns have number and gender. Number refers to quantity (singular or plural). Gender indicates whether the word is considered to be masculine or feminine.

	MASCULINE	FEMININE
Singular	libro	puerta
Plural	libros	puertas

▪ A. Número

To form the plural of a noun, simply add **-s** to the end of the word. If it ends in a consonant, add **-es.**

cuaderno — cuadernos	borrador — borradores
tiza — tizas	profesor — profesores

To form the plural of words ending in **-z,** change the **z** to a **c** and add **-es.**

lápiz — lápices   voz *(voice)* — voces

If the word ends in **-s,** then the singular and plural forms are the same.

el lunes *(Monday)* — **los** lunes   **el** cumpleaños *(birthday)* — **los** cumpleaños

▪ B. Género

Nouns that end in **-o** typically are **masculine.**

el bolígrafo   el escritorio

Most nouns ending in **-a, -dad, -tad, -ión,** and **-sis** are **feminine.**

la mochila	la nación *(nation)*
la crisis	la libertad *(freedom)*

The following are notable exceptions:

la mano *(hand)*	el sistema *(system)*
el clima *(climate/weather)*	el tema *(theme)*
el día *(day)*	el análisis *(analysis)*
el problema *(problem)*	

To help you identify the gender of all nouns, the vocabulary entries in **Temas** include the words and their corresponding *definite articles* (**el, la, los,** or **las).**

▪ C. Definite articles

	MASCULINE	FEMININE
Singular	**el** libro	**la** puerta
Plural	**los** libros	**las** puertas

Definite articles are typically used to refer to nouns in a concrete or specific manner.

El juego comienza a las cinco.   *The game begins at five.*
Quiero **las** zapatillas rojas.   *I want the red sneakers.*

Definite articles are also used to refer to classes or categories.

Los abogados ganan   *Lawyers earn a lot of money.*
  mucho dinero.
El fútbol es un deporte   *Soccer is a very popular sport.*
  muy popular.

Definite articles also accompany titles of respect such as **Dr. (Dra.)** and **Sr. (Srta./Sra.)**.

¿Vas al cine con **la** Sra. Gómez?   *Do you go to the movies with*
                                      Mrs. Gómez?
El Dr. Silva trabaja aquí   *Dr. Silva works here in the*
  en la tarde.   *afternoon.*

■ Aplicaciones

P-15 ¿Cuántos quiere? *(How many do you want?)* You and your classmate are in line at a cafeteria in a Spanish-speaking country. How many of the following food items are you going to order?

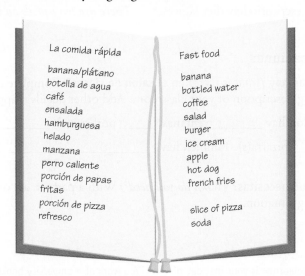

To order food you can use the following expression: **Queremos <u>dos</u> refrescos.** *We want <u>two</u> sodas.*

La comida rápida / Fast food

banana/plátano — banana
botella de agua — bottled water
café — coffee
ensalada — salad
hamburguesa — burger
helado — ice cream
manzana — apple
perro caliente — hot dog
porción de papas fritas — french fries
porción de pizza — slice of pizza
refresco — soda

P-16 ¿Una palabra masculina o femenina? Guess the gender of the following words and supply the corresponding definite article.

1. nacionalidad
2. inscripción
3. dirección
4. enfermera
5. secretaria
6. natación
7. atletismo
8. problema
9. mano
10. amigo

X. Funciones y estructuras: Indefinite articles and the invariable impersonal verbal form *hay*

A. Indefinite articles

In Spanish, much like in English, indefinite articles are used when referring to nouns in a general sense.

Tengo **una** mesa.	*I have a table.*
Necesito **unos** bolígrafos rojos.	*I need some red pens.*

Indefinite articles agree in number and gender with the nouns they refer to.

	MASCULINE	FEMININE
Singular	**un** cuaderno	**una** silla
Plural	**unos** cuadernos	**unas** sillas

B. The impersonal verbal form *hay*

To express *there is* and *there are*, use the impersonal verbal form **hay**. Note that this verbal form is used with both singular and plural nouns.

Hay una estudiante que se llama Helen.	*There is a student whose name is Helen.*
En el escritorio **hay** diez lápices.	*There are ten pencils on the desk.*

Aplicaciones

P-17 ¿Qué hay *(What is there)* **en el salón de clases?** Complete the following description of your classroom. Add other details if applicable.

En el salón hay _____ ventanas, _____ profesor(a), _____ sillas y _____ pizarra(s). También hay _____.

P-18 ¿Qué necesitas? *(What do you need?)* With a partner, act out the following situation.

Greet the clerk and thank him/her after the transaction. Remember that a helpful expression to indicate what you want is **Quiero...** *(I want)* . . . Look at the vocabulary you studied in this chapter to decide what you may need and the number of items you need to purchase.

Do not forget to greet the customer and to thank him/her after the transaction in a polite manner. A helpful expression to indicate price is: **Son veinte dólares.** *(It is twenty dollars.)*

Estudiante A	Estudiante B
Since tomorrow is your first day of class as an exchange student in a Spanish-speaking country, you have to stop by a bookstore to get a few things for your semester. Tell the shopkeeper what you need.	You work at a university bookstore in a Spanish-speaking country. Help this exchange student get what he/she needs.

Objetos en el salón de clase / Classroom objects

el bolígrafo	*pen*
el borrador	*eraser*
el cuaderno	*notebook*
el cuaderno de ejercicios	*workbook*
el escritorio	*desk*
el (la) estudiante	*student*
el lápiz	*pencil*
el libro	*book*
la mesa	*table*
la mochila	*backpack*
la pizarra	*chalkboard*
el profesor	*teacher (male)*
la profesora	*teacher (female)*
la puerta	*door*
la silla	*chair*
la tiza	*chalk*
la ventana	*window*

Lo que dice el profesor / What the instructor says

Abran el libro en la página…	*Open your books on page . . .*
Cierren sus libros.	*Close your books.*
Escriban…	*Write . . .*
Lean…	*Read . . .*

Lo que dicen los estudiantes / What the students say

Más despacio, por favor.	*More slowly, please.*
¿Qué significa… ?	*What does . . . mean?*
¿Cómo se dice… ?	*How do you say . . . ?*
Repita, por favor.	*Repeat, please.*
No comprendo.	*I do not understand.*

Saludos / Greetings

Buenos días.	*Good morning.*
Buenas (tardes/noches).	*Good (afternoon/evening).*
Me llamo…	*My name is . . .*
¿Cómo está Ud.?	*How are you? (formal)*
Bien, ¿y Ud.?	*Fine, and you? (formal)*
Muy bien, gracias.	*Very well, thank you.*
Mucho gusto. Encantado(a).	*Pleased to meet you.*
Hola.	*Hi. Hello.*
¿Cómo te va?	*How are you? (informal)*
Bien, ¿y a ti?	*Fine, and you? (informal)*
De maravilla.	*Great.*
De nada.	*You are welcome.*

Despedidas / Farewells

Adiós.	*Good-bye.*
Hasta luego.	*See you later.*
Hasta pronto.	*See you soon.*
Hasta la vista.	*See you around.*
Chao.	*Bye.*
Nos vemos el lunes.	*I'll see you on Monday.*

Títulos / Titles

Doctor(a)/Dr(a).	*Doctor (For various professions)*
Licenciado(a)/Lic(a).	
Señor/Sr.	*Sir/Mr.*
Señora/Sra.	*Madam/Mrs.*
Señorita/Srta.	*Miss*

Humanidades / Humanities

la literatura	*literature*
la filosofía	*philosophy*
las lenguas/los idiomas	*languages*

Ciencias sociales / Social sciences

las ciencias políticas	*political science*
la economía	*economics*
la historia	*history*
la sicología	*psychology*

Ciencias naturales / Natural sciences

la biología	*biology*
la geografía	*geography*
la geología	*geology*
la química	*chemistry*

Artes / Arts

el baile	*dance*
la música	*music*
la pintura	*painting*

Matemáticas / Mathematics

la álgebra	*algebra*
el cálculo	*calculus*
la geometría	*geometry*

Las especialidades / Majors

la administración de empresas	*business administration*
la antropología	*anthropology*
las comunicaciones	*communications*
el derecho	*law*
la educación física	*physical education*
la fisioterapia	*physical therapy*
la informática	*computer science*
la ingeniería	*engineering*
la medicina	*medicine*
el periodismo	*journalism*

el trabajo social	*social work*	**Los colores**	*Colors*
la veterinaria	*veterinary*	amarillo	*yellow*
		anaranjado/	*orange*
Los días de la semana	***Days of the week***	color naranja	
lunes	*Monday*	azul	*blue*
martes	*Tuesday*	blanco	*white*
miércoles	*Wednesday*	dorado	*gold*
jueves	*Thursday*	gris	*gray*
viernes	*Friday*	marrón/café	*brown*
sábado	*Saturday*	morado	*purple*
domingo	*Sunday*	negro	*black*
		plateado	*silver*
Los meses	***Months***	rojo	*red*
enero	*January*	rosado	*pink*
febrero	*February*	verde	*green*
marzo	*March*		
abril	*April*		

Funciones y estructuras
Personal pronouns, p. 7
Gender, number, and definite articles, pp. 16–17
Indefinite articles and the invariable impersonal
   verbal form **hay,** p. 18

mayo	*May*
junio	*June*
julio	*July*
agosto	*August*
septiembre	*September*
octubre	*October*
noviembre	*November*
diciembre	*December*

Unidad 1

La identidad

El mundo hispano

In this unit you will learn how to express basic information about yourself, your family, and people you know such as occupation, personal interests, and family background. In turn, the readings and videos will introduce you to Spanish-speakers who will share similar information about themselves. You will also learn basic information about the Spanish-speaking world, its geography, and its people. At the end of the unit you will exchange emails with José Francisco Reyes Galindo from Guanajuato, Mexico, who will be an exchange student in your home. You will also be able to connect with your community through diverse service tasks such as researching Latino student organizations, employment agencies, and local government initiatives to promote positive and healthy pastimes.

Éste soy yo

Para comenzar

With a classmate, indicate the appropriate caption for each photograph.

- En el mundo hispano existen diversas tradiciones culturales.
- La geografía de Latinoamérica es rica y variada.
- Los hispanos son amables y hospitalarios.

In this chapter you will learn . . .

- how to exchange information
- how to describe people and objects
- how to talk about professions, daily activities, and pastimes
- how to create a personal profile
- the extent and general characteristics of the Spanish-speaking world
- about leisure time activities in the Spanish-speaking world

	TEMA 1 Datos personales	TEMA 2 Ocupaciones	TEMA 3 Intereses personales
Vocabulario	Los formularios	Profesiones y ocupaciones	Los pasatiempos
Funciones y estructuras	Providing information with the verb **ser** Describing people with adjectives	Talking about daily activities with simple present tense **-ar** verbs Talking about daily activities with simple present tense **-er** and **-ir** verbs	Expressing negation Exchanging information and asking questions with interrogative words
Lecturas y vídeo	Perspectivas: Los documentos de identificación	Vídeo: La llegada a Puerto Rico y a la Hacienda Vista Alegre	Lectura: Mi página personal en la Red

Foto 1

Foto 2

Foto 3

 # Enfoque

A. ¿Qué más sabes del mundo hispano? *(What else do you know about the Spanish-speaking world?)* Before you watch the video, state what you think the following cognates (Spanish words that look like English words), taken from the video segment, mean in English.

centros administrativos   Península Ibérica   influencia africana
héroe importante   grupos indígenas   independencia

Check your answers with a partner. Then, choose **one** of the topics above and, based on what you both already know about the Spanish-speaking world, write down as much information as you can about it.

B. ¿En qué orden? *(In what order?)* As you watch the video, listen for the cognates from activity A and determine in what order they are presented in the video.

____ centros administrativos   ____ Península Ibérica
____ influencia africana   ____ héroe importante
____ grupos indígenas   ____ independencia

C. ¿Cierto o falso? Watch the video one more time and, with a partner, decide if the following statements are true **(ciertos)** or false **(falsos).** (If the information is incorrect, make the necessary changes.)

____ 1. There is great cultural and ethnic variety in the Spanish-speaking world.

____ 2. The Spanish language originated in the Iberian Peninsula.

____ 3. One of the most important indigenous groups in Latin America was the Aztec, which inhabited Perú.

____ 4. Most Latin American countries became independent from Spain in the nineteenth century.

____ 5. Simón Bolívar is one of the most prominent Argentinean heroes.

For more info, you may want to check the **Temas** site:
http://temas.heinle.com

Datos personales

I. Vocabulario: Los formularios (application forms)

Notice that the words in **Vocabulario práctico** are accompanied by the masculine definite article **el** or the feminine one **la**. These articles are presented here to help you identify the gender of the noun that follows. For the sake of brevity, these definite articles are usually omitted in forms and other official documents.

FORMULARIO DE INSCRIPCIÓN

APELLIDOS: *Jones*　　　　　　NOMBRES: *Susan Jane*

FECHA DE NACIMIENTO (dd-mm-aa) *23–05–72*

SEXO: *F*　　　　　　　　　　　PASAPORTE nº *4562339996*

DOMICILIO: *10 Savoy Road*　　　CIUDAD: *Chicago*

CÓDIGO POSTAL: *60681*　　　　PAÍS: *Estados Unidos*

TELÉFONO: (312) 555-3251　　　FAX: (312) 555-3252

CORREO ELECTRÓNICO: *sjjones @ aol.com*

NACIONALIDAD: *estadounidense*　　LENGUA MATERNA: *inglés*

Nivel de conocimiento del español (autoevaluación):

PRINCIPIANTE　　(INTERMEDIO)　　AVANZADO　　SUPERIOR

Desea inscribirse en el/los ciclo/s:

julio (1-25)　　　　agosto (3-28)　　　(septiembre (2-27))

Alojamiento:

• DESEA ALOJAMIENTO EN LA RESIDENCIA UNIVERSITARIA

en habitación doble　　　　en habitación individual

(• DESEA ALOJAMIENTO CON UNA FAMILIA)

• NO DESEA ALOJAMIENTO

Vocabulario práctico

el alojamiento *lodging*　　　　　la fecha de nacimiento *date of birth*

el apellido *last name*　　　　　hasta *until*

el correo electrónico *e-mail*　　la nacionalidad *nationality*

desde *since*　　　　　　　　el nombre *name*

el domicilio/la dirección *address*　el teléfono *phone (number)*

In the Spanish-speaking world your full name often includes a first name **(primer nombre)** and a middle name **(segundo nombre)** followed by the last name of your father **(primer apellido)** and your mother's maiden name **(segundo apellido).**

Juan José Pérez Caballero
Ana María Restrepo Gómez

■ Dates are indicated in Spanish beginning with the day of the week, followed by the number and the name of the month, and ending with the year.

Hoy es jueves, 27 <u>de</u> septiembre <u>de</u> 2008 (27/09/08).
Today is Thursday, September 27, 2008 (09/27/08).

- Note that in Spanish the components of the date are linked by the preposition **de** *(of)*. If the day of the week is not expressed, the date begins with the definite article **el.**

  Mi madre regresa **el** diez de octubre.
  My mother returns on October 10.

- The first day of the month is indicated with the ordinal number **primero.** Cardinal numbers (**dos, tres, cuatro,** etc.) are used for all other days.

  Las clases comienzan el **primero** de febrero y terminan el **quince** de mayo.
  Classes start on February first and end on May 15.

■ Asimilación

1-1 Información clave *(Key information)* Look at the application form on page 24 and answer the following questions.

1. What is the name of the applicant?
2. Where is she from?
3. What is she applying for?
4. When does she plan to begin her course?
5. How proficient is she in Spanish already?
6. What option did she select for lodging?
   a. with a family   c. at a hotel
   b. at a university dorm   d. at a youth hostel
7. What do you think the form means by **lengua materna?**
   a. her native language
   b. her mother's maiden name
   c. her mother's full name

■ Aplicaciones

1-2 ¿Qué falta? *(What is missing?)* Complete the form by adding the category name for each type of information supplied.

FORMULARIO DE INSCRIPCIÓN

_____ *Rodríguez*	_____ *Calle * Sol #125*
SEGUNDO APELLIDO: *Gil*	CIUDAD: *Málaga*
PRIMER NOMBRE: *Juan*	CÓDIGO POSTAL: *13421*
_____ *Guillermo*	PAÍS: *España*
_____ (dd-mm-aa) *18-02-70*	_____ *638-2311*
SEXO: *M*	FAX: *621-8833*
PASAPORTE nº: *F1-1262358*	CORREO ELECTRÓNICO: *gil12 @espa.com.es*
_____ *español*	LENGUA MATERNA: *español*

*The Spanish word **calle** means **street**.

■ Integración

1-3 El club de español Imagine that you have been asked to design the application form for the Spanish club in your school. With a partner, discuss what information you want the form to request from prospective applicants. Then prepare the form and submit it to your instructor for feedback.

Begin the conversation by saying **¿Qué información necesitamos?** *(What information do we need?)*

II. Funciones y estructuras: Providing personal information with the verb *ser*

The verb **ser** *(to be)* is used to talk about nationality and place of origin.

Ellos **son** dominicanos. **Son** de Santo Domingo, la capital. *They **are** Dominican. They **are** from Santo Domingo, the capital.*

Nosotros **somos** chilenos. Yo **soy** de Santiago y ella **es** de Valparaíso. *We **are** Chilean. I **am** from Santiago and she **is** from Valparaíso.*

Notice that the preposition **de** *(of)* is used before the name of the country or city, but not before the adjective of nationality.

Mi amigo es **de** <u>Caracas</u>. Es venezolano.

*My friend is **from** <u>Caracas</u>. He is Venezuelan.*

These are the forms of the verb **ser**:

SUBJECT PRONOUN	ser	MEANING(S)
yo	soy	*I am*
tú	eres	*you (informal, singular) are*
él/ella/usted	es	*he/she is*
		you (formal, singular) are
nosotros(as)	somos	*we are*
vosotros(as)	sois	*you (informal, plural, Spain) are*
ellos(as)/ustedes	son	*they/you (plural, Latin America) are*

REMEMBER

Tú is used to address someone informally and **usted** is used to address someone formally. Note that the form of the verb **ser** used with **usted** is the same form used with **él** and **ella**. Also remember that **vosotros(as)** is used in Spain while **ustedes** is the preferred form in Latin America. The latter is used with the same form of **ser** as **ellos(as)**.

The form of **ser** changes if you wish to find out where other people are from: **¿De dónde <u>es</u> el profesor?** *(Where <u>is</u> the professor from?)* **¿De dónde <u>son</u> ellos?** *(Where <u>are</u> they from?)* etc.

To find out where someone is from, ask **¿De dónde eres?** If you want to find out someone's nationality, ask **¿Cuál es tu nacionalidad?**

—¿Cuál es tu nacionalidad, Clarisa? *What is your nationality, Clarisa?*

—Soy uruguaya. *I am Uruguayan.*

—Y tú, Ramón, ¿de dónde eres? *And you, Ramón, where are you from?*

—Soy de Ecuador. *I am from Ecuador.*

■ Asimilación

1-4 Personalidades famosas Match the items on the left with the phrases on the right.

_____ Salma Hayek...

_____ Nicole Kidman y
       Russell Crowe...

_____ Fidel Castro: «Yo...»

_____ Barbara Walters a _(to)_
       Diane Sawyer: «Tú...»

_____ Derek Jeter y Alex Rodríguez:
       «Nosotros...»

a. eres de los Estados Unidos.

b. es de México.

c. somos de Nueva York.

d. son de Australia.

e. soy cubano.

CD1-6 **1-5 Información personal** Listen to the information provided by Carmen Delia and complete the chart below.

	Carmen Delia	**los hermanos**	**el amigo**
Nombre(s) Apellidos País _(country)_ de origen	Carmen Delia		Gómez Rivera

■ Aplicaciones

1-6 En mi clase de español With a partner, complete the following sentences using the correct form of the verb **ser** and the information requested.

1. ¿De dónde es tu compañero(a)?
   Mi compañero(a) _____ _(nombre)_ _____ de _____ _(ciudad)._

2. ¿De dónde eres tú?
   Yo _____ de _____ _(ciudad)._

3. ¿Cómo se llama tu profesor(a)? ¿De dónde es?
   Mi profesor(a) se llama _____; él/ella _____ de _____ _(country of origin)._

CD1-7 **1-7 Haciendo amigos** _(Making friends)_ Listen to and practice the following dialogue. Then personalize it by substituting the underlined words with your own information.

—Hola, me llamo <u>Steve</u>. ¿Cómo te llamas?
—Me llamo <u>Lauren</u>.
—Mucho gusto, <u>Lauren</u>.
—Igualmente. ¿De dónde eres, <u>Steve</u>?
—Soy de <u>Seattle</u>, ¿y tú?
—Soy de <u>Birmingham</u>.
—<u>Encantado</u> de conocerte.
—<u>Encantada</u>, <u>Steve</u>.

1-8 ¡Conózcanse mejor! *(Get to know each other better!)* Gather the necessary information from a classmate to fill in the blanks. Then introduce him/her to the rest of the class.

Ask appropriate questions such as **¿Cómo te llamas? ¿De dónde eres? ¿Cuál es tu nacionalidad? ¿Cuál es tu especialidad?** and **¿De dónde es tu familia originalmente?**

Mi compañero(a) se llama _____. Es de _____ *(ciudad)*. Es estudiante de _____ *(especialidad)*. Su *(His/Her)* familia es originalmente de _____.

■ Integración

1-9 Un(a) estudiante de intercambio *(exchange)* Act out the following situation with a classmate.

The American student	The exchange student
There is an exchange student from Bolivia in one of your classes. He/She seems a bit overwhelmed because it is the first day of classes and you want to help. Strike up a conversation with him/her and show him/her how friendly everyone is at this institution! (Find out his/her name, where he/she is from, and his/her major).	You are an exchange student from Bolivia. This is your first day of classes at this institution and you just came across a friendly face. Greet him/her and introduce yourself. Also, find out your classmate's name, where he/she is from, and his/her major.

1-10 Un correo electrónico Complete the following e-mail to tell your Spanish professor about the exchange student in one of your classes.

Fecha: _____

Para: Profesor(a) _____

De: _____

Re: Un(a) estudiante de intercambio

Estimado(a) profesor(a):

En mi clase de _____ hay un(a) estudiante de intercambio hispano(a).

Él/Ella _____ *(nombre y especialidad)*.

¡Hasta pronto!

_____ *(tu nombre)*

III. Funciones y estructuras: Describing people with adjectives

As you learned in **Capítulo preparatorio,** Spanish nouns have gender (masculine or feminine) and number (singular or plural). When a noun is being described by an adjective, the adjective shares the same gender and number with the noun. This is called *noun-adjective agreement.*

¿Cómo es **Nina**? Ella es **buena** y **simpática.**

¿Y tus **amigos**? Ellos son **divertidos** y muy **amistosos.**

The interrogative word **cómo** followed by a form of **ser** is used to find out what someone or something is like: ¿**Cómo eres**, Rogelio? Soy inteligente. *(What are you like, Rogelio? I am intelligent.)*

■ Spanish adjectives that end in **-o** in the masculine singular form (**activo, famoso, rico,** etc.) have four endings.

	MASCULINE	FEMININE
SINGULAR	**-o** José es buen**o.**	**-a** Rita es buen**a.**
PLURAL	**-os** José y Manuel son buen**os.** José y Rita son buen**os.**	**-as** Rita y Sara son buen**as.**

Adjectives that describe both masculine and feminine people (or things) take the masculine plural ending: Mi **padre** y mi **madre** son **estrictos**. Mi **coche** y mi **casa** son **nuevos** *(new).*

■ Adjectives that **do not** end in **-o** in the masculine singular form (**alegre, débil, mayor,** etc.) only have two endings: singular and plural.

	MASCULINE	FEMININE
SINGULAR	Mario es inteligent**e.**	Serena es inteligent**e.**
PLURAL	Mario y Carlos son inteligent**es.** Mario y Serena son inteligent**es.**	Serena y Lidia son inteligent**es.**

■ If an adjective ends in a vowel, add **-s** to show agreement of number; if it ends in a consonant, add **-es.**

Los chicos son muy **diligentes.**   *The guys are very **diligent.***
Zelma y Paco son **mayores.**   *Zelma and Paco are **mature (old).***

■ Adjectives are usually placed *after* the nouns they describe.

La Sra. López es una dentista **estupenda.**   *Mrs. López is a **stupendous** dentist.*
Víctor es un escritor **prolífico.**   *Víctor is a **prolific** writer.*

The following are some common adjectives you can use to describe objects and people.

activo *active*	fuerte *strong*
alegre *happy*	inteligente *intelligent*
amistoso/amigable *friendly*	joven *young*
antipático *unpleasant*	mayor/viejo *mature/old*
bueno *good*	pobre *poor*
débil *weak*	rico *rich*
diligente *diligent*	serio *serious*
divertido *fun*	simpático *nice*
estricto *strict*	tonto *foolish, dull*
famoso *famous*	trabajador *hard-working*

Adjectives of nationality that end in a consonant in the masculine singular form add an **-a** for the feminine.

Here is a list of other nationalities:

alemán (alemana) *German*
australiano *Australian*
canadiense *Canadian*
chino *Chinese*
estadounidense *American* (USA)
francés (francesa) *French*
griego *Greek*
inglés (inglesa) *English*
irlandés (irlandesa) *Irish*
italiano *Italian*
japonés (japonesa) *Japanese*
polaco *Polish*
ruso *Russian*

Adjectives of nationality can also be used to describe people. Here is a list of nationalities of Spanish-speaking countries.

argentino *Argentinean*	hondureño *Honduran*
boliviano *Bolivian*	mexicano *Mexican*
chileno *Chilean*	nicaragüense *Nicaraguan*
colombiano *Colombian*	panameño *Panamanian*
costarricense *Costa Rican*	paraguayo *Paraguayan*
cubano *Cuban*	peruano *Peruvian*
dominicano *Dominican*	puertorriqueño *Puerto Rican*
ecuatoriano *Ecuadorian*	salvadoreño *Salvadorian*
español(a) *Spanish*	uruguayo *Uruguayan*
guatemalteco *Guatemalan*	venezolano *Venezuelan*

To talk about origin you can also use the expression **ser** + **de origen (africano/estadounidense/europeo/...).**

La familia de James **es de origen asiático.**

James's family **is of Asian origin.**

■ Asimilación

CD1-8 **1-11 ¿Quién es?** Listen to what Minerva says about some of her friends and choose the name of the person(s) she is describing. Then compare your answers with those of a partner.

1. ____ Andrés y Lorena ____ Felicia ____ Sandra y Gabriela
2. ____ Jaime ____ Nora y Verónica ____ Alberto y Humberto
3. ____ Gloria ____ David y Jorge ____ Rigoberto
4. ____ Marta y Linda ____ Pamela y Wilberto ____ Juan
5. ____ Yolanda ____ Vivian y Cristóbal ____ Felipe

1-12 ¿Cierto o falso? Indicate whether the following sentences are true (**cierto-C**) or false (**falso-F**).

   ____ 1. Sammy Sosa es de origen europeo.

   ____ 2. La familia Kennedy es de origen irlandés.

   ____ 3. Julia Roberts es inglesa.

   ____ 4. Gloria Estefan es de origen colombiano.

   ____ 5. Enrique Iglesias es español.

   ____ 6. Venus y Serena Williams son australianas.

▨ Aplicaciones

1-13 Descripciones Provide two logical adjectives to complete each sentence.

1. Eminem es ___ y ___.
2. Britney Spears y Christina Aguilera son ___ y ___.
3. Bill Gates es ___ y ___.
4. Oprah Winfrey es ___ y ___.
5. Justin Timberlake y Celine Dion son ___ y ___.
6. El Presidente y la Primera Dama *(First Lady)* son ___ y ___.

1-14 ¿Cómo son y de dónde son? Complete the first blank with a logical adjective. Then, complete the second blank with an adjective of nationality. Use the clues provided!

> MODELO   La Sra. Ramos no es antipática. Es *simpática*. Ella es de San Salvador. Es *salvadoreña*.

1. Estela y Mónica no son tontas; son _____. Ellas son de Santo Domingo. Son _____.
2. El Sr. Vega no es rico; es _____. Él es de Montevideo; por lo tanto *(therefore)*, es _____.
3. Los amigos de Lupe no son mayores, sino *(but)* _____. Ellos son _____; son de San José.
4. Liliana es una niña muy mala. Ella no es _____. Es de Quito. Ella es _____.
5. Eduardo y Ángela son muy serios; no son _____. Ellos son _____; son de Lima.
6. Paula y Victoria no son fuertes, sino _____. Ellas son _____, de la Ciudad de México.

EN TU COMUNIDAD

Meet with the directors of a Hispanic or Latino student organization to find out what nationalities are represented in it and the most popular fields of study of its members. If your institution does not have such an organization, perhaps you can obtain information from the office of international affairs. Then, share with the class or write a short summary about your findings.

1-15 Firma aquí, por favor (*Sign here, please*)

Paso 1: Use the given clues to form questions and find six classmates who answer affirmatively. Pay attention to the endings of the adjectives and to the forms of the verb **ser!**

> MODELO   tú - activo
>
> E1: *¿Eres activo(a)?*
> E2: *Sí, soy activo(a).*
> E1: *Firma aquí, por favor. Gracias.*
>   o...
> E2: *No, no soy activo(a).*
> E1: *Gracias. Hasta luego.*

                                          Firma

1. tus amigos(as)—joven   _____
2. tú—trabajador(a)   _____
3. tus padres—estricto   _____
4. tu profesor(a) de español—amistoso   _____
5. tú—de origen...   _____

Paso 2: Now share the information with the rest of the class.

> MODELO   *Chris es activo. / Jennifer es activa.*

■ Integración

1-16 Los profesores de mi compañero(a) Find out what classes your partner is taking this semester and ask him/her to describe his/her professors.

> MODELO   E1: *¿Qué cursos tienes* (do you have) *este semestre?*
> E2: *Matemáticas, sociología, ...*
> E1: *¿Cómo es el profesor o la profesora de matemáticas?*
> E2: *La profesora es...*

1-17 Un resumen (*summary*) Write a summary of the answers you provided in activity 1-16. When you finish, hand it in to your professor for feedback.

IV. Perspectivas. Los documentos de identificación

■ Antes de leer

Su identificación, por favor What forms of identification are commonly used in the United States? What information do they provide? (Make a list in Spanish of the pieces of information typically found on an American ID.)

■ A leer

Look now at the following national IDs from Colombia and Spain. List the similarities and differences between those pieces of ID and the one you have in your wallet.

■ ¿Entendiste bien?

Indicate which country's ID . . .

1. includes information about the owner's blood type _____
2. includes the owner's home address _____
3. provides information about the owner's place of birth _____
4. includes the names of the owner's parents _____
5. provides information about the owner's height _____

Ocupaciones

I. Vocabulario: Profesiones y ocupaciones

*The masculine form is **el hombre de negocios**.

la cocinera   **el ingeniero**   **el policía**   **la mujer de negocios***

la peluquera   **el enfermero**   **la mesera**   **el abogado**   **el obrero**

Many professions in Spanish have English cognates: **el (la) profesor(a)**, **el (la) secretario(a)**, **el (la) dentista**, **el (la) científico(a)**, **el (la) doctor(a)**, **el actor/la actriz**, **el (la) músico(a)**, **el (la) director(a)**, **el (la) atleta**, **el (la) veterinario(a)**, **el (la) biólogo(a)**, **el (la) recepcionista**, etc.

SABOR REGIONAL

As you may expect, names of occupations vary. For example, *hairdresser* is **estilista** in Mexico and Panama, while *waiter/waitress* is **mozo(a)** in Argentina, Bolivia, Costa Rica, the Dominican Republic, and Uruguay.

Vocabulario práctico

el ama de casa *housewife*

el (la) arquitecto(a) *architect*

el (la) contable *accountant*

el (la) chofer *driver*

el (la) empleado(a) doméstico(a) *maid*

el (la) gerente *manager*

el (la) periodista *journalist*

el (la) programador(a) de computadoras *computer programmer*

el (la) vendedor(a) *salesperson*

■ Asimilación

1-18 Herramientas de trabajo *(Work tools)* Working with a classmate, indicate the name of the profession that requires the following work tools.

OPCIONES: recepcionista   mujer de negocios   empleada doméstica   obrero

1   **2**   **3**   **4**

CD1-9 **1-19 ¿De qué profesión se trata?** *(What occupation are we talking about?)* Indicate the name of the profession or occupation described.

    1. obrero, ingeniero, empleada doméstica

    2. profesora, abogado, arquitecto

    3. artista, recepcionista, peluquera

    4. policía, enfermera, periodista

LISTENING STRATEGY

Don't be upset if you do not understand every word you hear. Efficient listeners often guess the meaning of unfamiliar terms based on information provided by other contextual clues (words or phrases coming before or after unknown/unfamiliar words).

■ Aplicaciones

 1-20 ¿Quién trabaja aquí? *(Who works here?)* Indicate the profession of at least two people who work in each of the following places.

    1. una oficina

    2. una estación de televisión

    3. un hospital

    4. un restaurante

    5. una universidad

MODELO   *Una recepcionista y un gerente trabajan en un hotel.*

1-21 Intereses

Paso 1: Complete the chart with a list of at least four professions or occupations that appeal to you (on the left) and four that are of little or no interest to you (on the right).

Profesiones y ocupaciones que me interesan	Profesiones y ocupaciones que **no** me interesan

Paso 2: When finished, compare your list with that of other members of your group. What are the most popular professions in your group? What are the least popular? Present a summary of your findings to the rest of the class.

Sugerencia 1-21, Paso 2: Use the following model:

Preguntas para la discusión: ¿Qué profesiones te interesan más? ¿Qué profesiones no te interesan?

Informe *(Report)*: Las profesiones más populares son ____. Las profesiones menos populares son ____.

1-22 ¿Qué ocupación recomiendan? *(What occupation do you recommend?)* Complete the chart with the ideal profession or occupation for the following people.

Nombre	Descripción	Cursos o actividades favoritos	Ocupación ideal
María	inteligente	la física y las matemáticas	
Julio	fuerte, honesto	los deportes	
Esteban	creativo	visitar los museos de arte	
Josefina	diligente	la biología y la anatomía	
Antonio	independiente	los idiomas	

MODELO   E1: *María es inteligente. Ella estudia física y matemáticas.*
                  ¿Cuál es una profesión ideal para ella?
             E2: *Una profesión ideal para ella es...*

■ Integración

1-23 ¡Adivina! *(Guess!)* Take turns describing a profession or an occupation to one of your classmates by creating short sentences or by listing words and phrases that could be associated with that profession. Have him/her guess what profession or occupation you are talking about. Use only Spanish!

MODELO   E1: *Hospital, no es un doctor.*
             E2: *¡Enfermera! Pizarra, tiza.*
             E1: *¡Profesor!*

1-24 Mi familia Write a brief report about the profession or occupation of at least five members of your immediate family.

MODELO   *Mi padre es vendedor y mi madre es abogada. Mi tío John es abogado y mis tías Juana y Raquel son estudiantes. Mi hermana...*

II. Funciones y estructuras: Talking about daily activities with simple present tense -*ar* verbs

La enfermera **cuida** a las personas enfermas.
*The nurse **takes care of** the sick.*

Los cocineros **preparan** la comida en un restaurante.
*Cooks **prepare** food at a restaurant.*

Spanish verbs belong to one of three groups: those that end in **-ar** (**escuchar**), those that end in **-er** (**comprender**), and those that end in **-ir** (**escribir**). This form of the verb is called the *infinitive*. The first part of the infinitive, which carries the meaning of the verb (**escuch-, comprend-, escrib-**), is called the *stem* of the verb.

When we want to say that someone is actually carrying out a particular action, the ending of the verb changes to agree with the subject. This is called *conjugating a verb*.

Ella **trabaja** en una oficina, pero yo **trabajo** en un hospital.
Los arquitectos **diseñan** casas.

*She **works** in an office, but I **work** in a hospital.*
*Architects **design** houses.*

Verbs ending in **-ar** are conjugated by dropping the **-ar** from the infinitive and attaching the appropriate ending to the stem of the verb. These are the endings to be used with **-ar** verbs.

SUBJECT	-ar VERBS ENDING	escuchar *(to listen)*
yo	**-o**	escuch**o**
tú	**-as**	escuch**as**
él/ella/usted	**-a**	escuch**a**
nosotros(as)	**-amos**	escuch**amos**
vosotros(as)	**-áis**	escuch**áis**
ellos(as)/ustedes	**-an**	escuch**an**

Think of this classification of verbs as "families" (**-ar** family, **-er** family, and **-ir** family) that sometimes behave differently and sometimes behave similarly.

Do not confuse noun-adjective agreement (agreement of gender and number) with subject-verb agreement (agreement of person [first, second, or third] and number).

Here are some **-ar** verbs that can be used to talk about daily activities.

administrar *to administer, to manage*	informar *to inform*
bailar *to dance*	investigar *to investigate*
caminar *to walk*	limpiar *to clean*
cantar *to sing*	manejar *to drive*
cenar *to have dinner*	mirar *to look at, to see, to watch*
cocinar *to cook*	organizar *to organize*
comprar *to buy*	pintar *to paint*
contestar *to answer*	practicar *to practice*
cuidar *to take care of*	preparar *to prepare*
desayunar *to have breakfast*	programar *to program*
diseñar *to design*	representar *to represent*
enseñar *to teach*	tocar *to touch, to play an instrument*
escuchar *to listen*	tomar *to take, to drink*
estudiar *to study*	trabajar *to work*
hablar *to speak*	viajar *to travel*

SABOR REGIONAL

The verb **conducir** is the preferred term for *to drive* in Chile, Colombia, Panama, and Spain. In Puerto Rico people use **guiar**.

The present tense is used to talk about actions that:

■ are happening at the present time

Estudio para un examen.   *I am studying for a test.*

■ happen on a regular basis

Simón **camina** por el parque todos los días.   *Simon walks in the park every day.*

■ will happen in the near future

Viajamos a España el jueves.   *We are traveling to Spain on Thursday.*

Here are some expressions that will help you indicate how frequently an action takes place.

casi nunca *almost never*	nunca *never*
casi siempre *almost always*	siempre *always*
los... *on (day[s] of the week)*	todos los días *every day*

■ Asimilación

1-25 Las responsabilidades laborales *(work responsibilities)* Match the professions listed on the left with the responsibilities listed on the right. Then, compare your answers with those of a classmate.

_____ 1. el (la) policía   a. contesta el teléfono

_____ 2. el (la) cocinero(a)   b. investiga crímenes

_____ 3. el (la) gerente   c. prepara la comida en un restaurante

_____ 4. el (la) periodista   d. administra una compañía

_____ 5. el (la) secretario(a)   e. informa a las personas

_____ 6. el (la) chofer   f. maneja un autobús o un taxi

CD1–10 **1-26 La profesora Gutiérrez** Listen to a series of sentences about Professor Gutiérrez and write their numbers below the correct pictures. Careful! There is an extra picture!

A _____   B _____   C _____   D _____   E _____

■ Aplicaciones

1-27 Actividades rutinarias

Paso 1: Fill in the blanks with different activities that you do.

Regularmente, yo _____ y _____ por la mañana. Por la tarde, (yo) _____ y _____. Por la noche, (yo) _____ y _____.

Paso 2: Now share the information with the rest of the class. What are the most popular and least popular activities?

1-28 ¿Con qué frecuencia? Form complete sentences about the people listed on the left. Include an expression of frequency and a different activity in each sentence. Conjugate the verbs correctly.

MODELO   nosotros   casi siempre   hablar español en clase
            Nosotros casi siempre hablamos español en clase.

1. nosotros(as)   siempre   cenar en restaurantes caros (*expensive*)
2. los estudiantes típicos   casi siempre   viajar a países de habla española
3. nuestros amigos   casi nunca   hablar por teléfono
4. el (la) profesor(a)   escuchar la música de los Rolling Stones
              nunca   limpiar la casa los sábados
                           comprar en Banana Republic
                           tomar café de Starbucks
                           usar productos biodegradables

1-29 Los fines de semana

Paso 1: Find out if two of your classmates do some of these activities on weekends. Keep track of the answers.

MODELO   E1: *Mary Anne, ¿estudias español los fines de semana?*
E2: *Sí, estudio español los fines de semana. (o No, no estudio...)*
E1: *Y tú, Roger, ¿estudias... ?*
...

estudiar español
desayunar en un café
bailar en un club
escuchar música
hablar por teléfono

limpiar la casa
mirar la televisión
trabajar en una oficina
practicar un deporte

To make your writing flow naturally you can use connectors such as **pero** *(but)*, **y** *(and)*, **también** *(also)*, **por otro lado** *(on the other hand)*, and **finalmente** *(finally)* in **Paso 2**.

Paso 2: Use the information you gathered in **Paso 1** to prepare a brief summary and share it with the class.

MODELO   *Mary Anne y Roger estudian español los fines de semana, pero yo no estudio. Por otro lado, ...*

◼ Integración

1-30 El estilo de vida *(lifestyles)* **de los famosos** Act out the following situation with a partner. When you are finished, switch roles.

The journalist may ask direct questions like **¿Usted desayuna con amigos los sábados? ¿Usted siempre cena en...? ¿Usted maneja un carro...?** etc.

El (La) periodista	La persona famosa
You are a journalist interested in finding out what a famous person does on a regular basis. Take into consideration this person's occupation and what you know about his/her life (or what you would like to know!) when asking questions. Be creative!	You are a famous person being interviewed by a journalist. (Your partner and you must decide who you are first [a singer, an actor/actress, a scientist, a TV personality, a well-known business mogul, etc.].) He/She wants to know what you do on a regular basis. Be creative in your answers!

1-31 Un día en la vida de... Now write a summary about the lifestyle of the famous person you interviewed in activity 1-30. When you are ready, read your summary to the class without mentioning the person's name. Can your classmates guess the name of the celebrity you interviewed?

III. Funciones y estructuras: Talking about daily activities with simple present tense -er and -ir verbs

Somos atletas y **corremos** cinco millas todos los días.
*We are athletes and we **run** five miles every day.*

Soy periodista. Yo **escribo** artículos para un periódico.
*I am a journalist. I **write** articles for a newspaper.*

Verbs ending in **-er** and **-ir** are conjugated by dropping the **-er/-ir** from the infinitive and attaching the appropriate ending to the stem of the verb. These are the endings to be used with these verbs.

	-er/-ir verbs		
SUBJECT	ENDING	correr *(to run)*	escribir *(to write)*
yo	**-o**	corr**o**	escrib**o**
tú	**-es**	corr**es**	escrib**es**
él/ella/usted	**-e**	corr**e**	escrib**e**
nosotros(as)	**-emos/-imos***	corr**emos***	escrib**imos***
vosotros(as)	**-éis/-ís***	corr**éis***	escrib**ís***
ellos(as)/ustedes	**-en**	corr**en**	escrib**en**

✳Note that the only differences between the present tense conjugation of **-er** and **-ir** verbs are in the **nosotros(as)** and **vosotros(as)** forms.

Here are some common **-er** and **-ir** verbs that can be used to talk about daily activities.

-er VERBS

aprender *to learn*
beber *to drink*
comer *to eat*
comprender *to understand*
correr *to run*
creer (que) *to think/believe (that)*
deber *should, must* (do something)
leer *to read*
responder *to respond*
vender *to sell*

-ir VERBS

abrir *to open*
asistir (a) *to attend*
compartir *to share, to spend time*
discutir *to discuss*
escribir *to write*
recibir *to receive*
vivir *to live*

SABOR REGIONAL

Another Spanish word for **beber** is **tomar**.

The verb **creer** is commonly used in sentences that require the use of a second conjugated verb: Yo **creo** que su madre **es** ama de casa. *(I **think** [that] her mother **is** a housewife.)* While the use of *that* is optional in English, the use of **que** is obligatory in Spanish.

Deber is followed by a verb in the infinitive form: **Debes visitar** a María el sábado. *(You **should visit** María on Saturday.)* As you can see, **deber** is the verb that agrees with the subject.

■ **Asimilación**

1-32 ¿Lógica o ilógica? First, match the occupations on the left with the phrases on the right. Then, indicate whether the sentences you created are **lógicas (L)** or **ilógicas (I).** When you finish, compare your answers with those of your partner.

____ 1. Los buenos actores...

____ 2. Los escritores...

____ 3. Los buenos ingenieros...

____ 4. Las recepcionistas...

____ 5. Los vendedores...

____ 6. Los atletas...

a. escriben novelas de ciencia ficción. ____

b. venden productos a los consumidores. ____

c. creen que Al Pacino es mediocre. ____

d. no corren frecuentemente. ____

e. deben aprender a diseñar. ____

f. responden al teléfono. ____

CD1-11 **1-33 ¿Cómo es un día típico de tu profesor(a)?** Mark the activities that you think make up a typical day in the life of your professor. Then listen to the description to see which ones you guessed right.

____ asiste a reuniones

____ escribe informes

____ vende libros por el Internet

____ come con su familia

____ bebe refrescos *(soft drinks)*

____ comparte la computadora con sus hijos

____ lee el periódico

____ responde a los mensajes *(messages)* electrónicos

■ **Aplicaciones**

1-34 Por lo general... *(Generally . . .)*

Paso 1: Indicate whether or not the following phrases apply to you. If they do not, change the underlined words to make the sentence correct.

MODELO　aprender mucho en la clase de biología
Por lo general, (yo) aprendo mucho en la clase de biología. o
Por lo general, (yo) aprendo mucho en la clase de español.

1. escribir <u>buenas</u> monografías *(papers)*
2. creer que esta universidad es <u>buena</u>
3. comprender a las personas <u>mayores</u>

4. asistir a conciertos de música <u>popular</u>
5. comer en restaurantes <u>chinos</u>
6. discutir <u>mis problemas</u> con mis amigos

Paso 2: Turn the phrases in **Paso 1** into questions and find out if they apply to a partner. How similar or different are you?

MODELO　E1: *Noreen, ¿aprendes mucho en la clase de biología?*
E2: *Sí, aprendo mucho en la clase de biología.*
o　*No, aprendo mucho en la clase de cálculo.*

1-35 Creemos que... With a partner, choose two classmates and write five sentences about different things you think they do and do not do. Use some of the verbs on page 41 and follow the model. When you are ready, read the sentences and have the two classmates you chose react by saying **cierto** or **falso.** How well do you know them?

> MODELO   *Creemos que... y ...*

 1-36 ¿Con qué frecuencia? Write sentences about the people listed on the left. Include an expression of frequency and a different activity in each sentence. Conjugate the verbs correctly and follow the model.

> MODELO   nosotros   casi nunca   comprender las decisiones del gobierno
> *Nosotros casi nunca comprendemos las decisiones del gobierno.*

1. nosotros(as)
2. ustedes (la clase)
3. el (la) profesor(a)
4. nuestra familia

siempre
casi siempre
casi nunca
nunca

vender los libros al final *(end)* del semestre
responder a comentarios tontos
beber vino *(wine)* con la cena
comer vegetales
leer novelas románticas
escribir poemas de amor *(love)*

■ **Integración**

 1-37 Conociéndonos mejor *(Getting to know each other better)* Take a few minutes to think about the questions you need to ask to talk about the topics listed below. Then, in groups of two or three students, interview each other. Take notes.

- when, where, and how often you drink . . . /eat . . . /read . . .
- where you live
- whether or not you run, where and how often
- whether or not you believe certain things (*que el [la] profesor[a] es... , que la clase de español es... , que... ,* etc.)

You may have to use the following interrogative words and phrases: **cuándo** *(when),* **dónde** *(where),* and **con qué frecuencia** *(how often).*

1-38 Una persona admirable Think about a person you would like to emulate (a friend, a relative, a celebrity, etc.). What is this person like? What does he/she do and not do that makes you like him/her so much? Write a short paragraph about this person beginning with the following phrase: **Creo que** *(name)* **es una persona admirable.** When you finish, share it with your professor.

Retratos del mundo hispano As you complete **Tema 2,** you will get to know five Spanish speakers who share a unique intercultural experience in San Juan, Puerto Rico. Pre-viewing activities **(Preparación)** incorporate specific strategies to help you better comprehend what you will see and hear. Post-viewing activities **(¿Entendiste bien?)** will allow you to demonstrate both your comprehension and ability to actively use vocabulary, linguistic structures, and functions presented in each video segment.

COMPREHENSION STRATEGY

Anticipating Trying to guess the content of a message based on what we know about its context (who is involved, why, etc.) is a very helpful strategy to deal with authentic, native-speaker speech.

IV. Vídeo: La llegada a Puerto Rico y a la Hacienda Vista Alegre

■ Preparación

A. Expectativas What type of personal information do you think that the new roommates will share as they meet each other for the first time?

1. Place an X next to the **three** topics you expect to hear discussed.
   ____ a. sus nombres y apellidos
   ____ b. su edad
   ____ c. su fecha de nacimiento
   ____ d. su nacionalidad/país de origen
   ____ e. sus actividades rutinarias
   ____ f. sus estudios/especialidades

2. Compare your selections with those of a classmate. For each topic that you have chosen in common, write questions and responses that you expect to hear used in the video segment, for example: —*¿Cómo te llamas?* —*Me llamo...*

3. Watch the video and check your predictions. Were you correct? Did you hear any of the questions and responses you wrote?

■ ¿Entendiste bien?

B. Más detalles sobre los compañeros Complete the table below with information about the roommates. First, complete the first row with the three correct topics from activity A. Then, watch the video again and fill in the information for each roommate.

	NOMBRE	NACIONALIDAD	INTERESES

C. ¿Cómo son los compañeros? Write a brief description of each roommate using descriptive adjectives. Compare your descriptions with those of a classmate. Are your initial impressions of each person similar or different?

D. Enfoque comunitario In the video you saw how Spanish speakers introduce themselves and ask questions in order to get to know each other. Imagine that you meet a Spanish-speaking visitor in your town. How would you introduce yourself? How would you find out his/her name, country of origin, or profession? With a partner, create a brief self-introduction and a couple of questions you would ask the new aquaintance. Consider practicing this new language skill by actually introducing yourself to a native Spanish-speaking person in your community.

Intereses personales

I. Vocabulario: Los pasatiempos

Juliana **charla** constantemente **por teléfono** con sus amigas.

David **escucha música** mientras estudia.

Pancho **navega por la Red** todas las tardes.

Paco **toca la guitarra** frecuentemente.

Los Merino **ven televisión** por la noche después de cenar.

Vocabulario práctico

charlar por teléfono *to chat on the phone*
escuchar música *to listen to music*
leer un libro *to read a book*
(mirar/ver) televisión *to watch TV*
navegar por (la Red/el Internet) *to surf the Net*
pasear *to take a short trip, to go for a walk*
pasar (tiempo libre/los ratos libres) *to spend free time*
tocar un instrumento *to play an instrument*

The verbs **mirar** and **ver** are used in different parts of the Spanish-speaking world to refer to the act of watching TV. Both verbs are understood by all Spanish-speakers, and the rationale for selecting one or the other is mostly regional (or national).

■ Asimilación

1-39 Los pasatiempos de los españoles Look at the charts below and answer the questions that follow, on page 46.

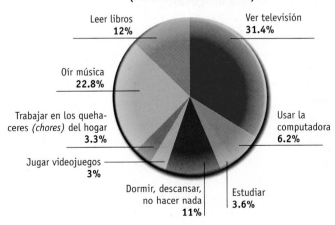

ACTIVIDADES DENTRO DE CASA (JÓVENES DE 15 A 29 AÑOS)

Leer libros 12%
Ver televisión 31.4%
Oír música 22.8%
Trabajar en los quehaceres (chores) del hogar 3.3%
Jugar videojuegos 3%
Dormir, descansar, no hacer nada 11%
Estudiar 3.6%
Usar la computadora 6.2%

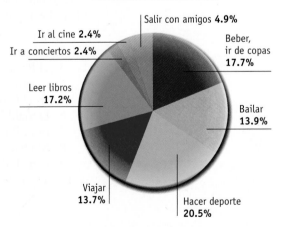

ACTIVIDADES FUERA DE CASA

Salir con amigos 4.9%
Ir al cine 2.4%
Ir a conciertos 2.4%
Leer libros 17.2%
Viajar 13.7%
Hacer deporte 20.5%
Bailar 13.9%
Beber, ir de copas 17.7%

Fuente: INJUVE, Calidad de vida de los jóvenes, 1998

1. ¿Cuál es el pasatiempo favorito de los jóvenes españoles dentro *(inside)* de casa?
2. ¿Cuál es el pasatiempo favorito de los jóvenes españoles fuera *(outside)* de casa?
3. ¿Son similares o diferentes los pasatiempos de los jóvenes españoles y los pasatiempos de los estadounidenses?
4. Selecciona dos actividades que haces dentro de casa y dos actividades que haces fuera de casa.

CD1-12 **1-40 ¿Cómo pasa el (la) profesor(a) su tiempo libre?** Listen and check your professor's pastimes. When finished, compare your answers with those of a classmate.

_____ Charla por teléfono.

_____ Escucha música.

_____ Lee un libro.

_____ Mira televisión.

_____ Navega por la Red.

_____ Toca un instrumento.

_____ Pasea.

_____ Escribe cartas.

■ Aplicaciones

1-41 En mis ratos libres... Complete the paragraph with the correct form of the verb in parentheses.

Me llamo Rosa. Trabajo en una oficina de abogados y también estudio en la universidad. En mis pocos ratos libres, _____ (leer). Casi nunca _____ (mirar) televisión. A veces mi esposo *(husband)* y yo _____ (escuchar) música o _____ (pasear). Los fines de semana (yo) _____ (charlar) con mis amigas, mientras mi esposo y sus amigos _____ (mirar) los partidos de fútbol por televisión.

1-42 ¿Cómo pasan sus ratos libres? List three likely pastime activities of the following personalities. Use your imagination!

1. la reina de Inglaterra
2. Bill Gates
3. el Papa
4. Martha Stewart
5. Fidel Castro
6. Donald Trump
7. Brad Pitt y Antonio Banderas
8. Michael Jordan
9. Paris Hilton
10. Tiger Woods

1-43 ¡A dibujar y a adivinar! *(Let's draw and guess!)* Think of a pastime and then draw on a piece of paper something related to that activity (the equipment used, the place where it is carried out, etc.). Your classmate must guess in 20 seconds or less.

■ Integración

1-44 Tus pasatiempos favoritos Talk to your partner about his/her pastimes and write down the answers.

- ¿Cuándo tienes tiempo libre? (los fines de semana, por las noches, un día en particular,...)
- ¿Lees mucho? ¿Cuál es tu autor(a) favorito(a)?
- ¿Miras la televisión? ¿Qué programas? ¿Cuál es tu actor/actriz favorito(a)?

1-45 Los pasatiempos de mi compañero(a) Based on the previous conversation, prepare a brief report about your classmate's pastimes.

Paso 1: Begin your report by writing the name of the person you interviewed and one statement that describes the person based on how he/she spends his/her free time.

Paso 2: List the main activities he/she does in his/her spare time. Remember to use connectors such as **y** *(and)*, **pero** *(but)*, and **también** *(also)*.

Paso 3: Close your report with an additional summary statement about your classmate or your personal opinion about his/her pastimes. Introduce this statement with one of the following expressions: **en conclusión** *(in conclusion)*, **en resumen** *(in summary)*, or **en mi opinión** *(in my opinion)*.

II. Funciones y estructuras: Expressing negation

¿Habla Ud. francés?

No, no hablo ni leo francés.

To make a negative statement, place the word **no** before the conjugated verb.

Matilde **no** ve televisión por la noche.

*Matilde does **not** watch TV at night.*

Nosotros **no** escuchamos música rap.

*We do **not** listen to rap music.*

There are other Spanish words you can use to express negation.

nada *nothing*	ni... ni *neither . . . nor*
nadie *nobody*	nunca *never*
ningún/ninguno(a) *no, none, any*	tampoco *either, neither*

Nadie pasea durante la semana.

***Nobody** goes for a walk during the week.*

Clara **nunca** charla por teléfono por la noche.

*Clara **never** talks on the phone at night.*

As you can see in the previous examples, these negative words can be used before the conjugated verb. However, if they are used after the conjugated verb, the word **no** must precede the verb. The result is a double-negative statement, which is correct and quite frequent in Spanish.

No pasea **nadie** durante la semana.

***Nobody** goes for a walk during the week.*

Carla **no** charla **nunca** por teléfono por la noche.

*Clara **never** talks on the phone at night.*

The word **ninguno** becomes **ningún** before masculine singular nouns, while **ninguna** is used before feminine singular nouns.

Esmeralda no toca **ningún** instrumento.

*Esmeralda does not play **any** instrument.*

The words **ninguno, ninguna,** and **ningún** normally function as adjectives and agree in gender (masculine/feminine) and number (singular/plural) with the noun to which they refer. Since they literally mean *not one*, they are usually used in the singular.

Mi primo no tiene **ningún** pasatiempo.	*My cousin does not have **any** pastimes.*
Ninguna de mis hermanas toca el piano.	***None** of my sisters plays the piano.*

The expression **ni... ni** can be used with nouns and with verbs. Nouns: *Mi madre no toca **ni** la guitarra **ni** la flauta.* Verbs: *Mi padre **ni** navega por la Red **ni** pasea.*

■ Asimilación

1-46 Mis fines de semana Think about the things you normally do and not do during the weekend and indicate whether or not the following statements apply to you. When you finish, compare your answers with those provided by your partner. Do you have similar routines?

_____ 1. No navego por la Red los fines de semana.

_____ 2. Nunca miro la televisión por la mañana.

_____ 3. No escucho música ni el sábado ni el domingo.

_____ 4. Nunca toco un instrumento.

_____ 5. Tampoco paseo con mi familia.

_____ 6. No leo ningún libro los domingos.

_____ 7. No charlo por teléfono con nadie.

_____ 8. No paso mi tiempo libre ni en mi casa ni en la universidad.

CD1–13 **1-47 ¿Y Sabrina?** Now listen to what Sabrina says about her weekends. Write **sí** next to the activities she does and **no** next to the activities she does not do.

_____ charlar por teléfono   _____ tocar un instrumento

_____ pasear   _____ leer libros

_____ escuchar música   _____ mirar la televisión

■ Aplicaciones

1-48 Situaciones Use the given negative words to complete the blanks. Pay attention to the use of double negatives!

1. Bianca _____ desea pasear y _____ desea ver televisión _____ . ¡Ella _____ es así *(like that)*! (no, nunca, tampoco, ni)

2. _____ Paco _____ Valentín escuchan música popular. En realidad, creo que ellos _____ escuchan _____ tipo de música. (no, ni, ningún, ni)

3. Nosotras _____ leemos libros de Danielle Steel. _____ leemos libros de John Grisham _____ . ¡_____ de mis amigos lee esos libros! (tampoco, no, nunca, ninguno)

1-49 Sopa de palabras *(Word soup)* Put the given words and phrases in logical order.

1. toca / ni Sonia / el piano / ni Nancy
2. ¿navegas / no / por la Red / los fines de semana / tú?
3. los programas / nadie / de Nickelodium / mira
4. miramos / no / los lunes / nosotros / la televisión / y / paseamos / tampoco
5. nunca / por teléfono / ellos / charlan / durante / la semana

1-50 Comparaciones First, make a list of four activities you do on a regular basis and four activities you never do. Then, take turns with your partner to read your activities and react by saying whether you do or do not do the same things. Do you have anything in common?

MODELOS
    E1: *Yo practico fútbol y fútbol americano.*
    E2: *Pues* (Well) *yo nunca practico ni fútbol ni fútbol americano.*
            o...
        Yo también practico fútbol y fútbol americano.

    E1: *Yo nunca desayuno en la universidad.*
    E2: *Yo tampoco desayuno en la universidad.*

■ Integración

1-51 Manteniendo las apariencias con *(keeping up appearances with)* **los Jones** Your partner and you are very rich. You are always competing for the title of the most spoiled millionaire in the world. Talk about the things you do not do using negative words (**no, nunca, ni... ni..., tampoco, nada, nadie,** etc.) and try to outdo each other! Be creative!

1-52 Los buenos amigos What do good friends do and not do? Think about the answer to this question and write a paragraph using most of the negative words you just learned.

III. Funciones y estructuras: Exchanging information and asking questions with interrogative words

In Spanish, to ask a *yes/no* question you can (1) raise your voice at the end of a sentence, (2) invert the position of the subject and the verb in the sentence, or (3) add the tag question **¿verdad?**, **¿cierto?**, or **¿no?** at the end of the sentence.

(1) ¿Gustavo lee libros de historia?
(2) ¿Lee Gustavo libros de historia? (Sí,/No, no) lee libros de historia.
(3) Gustavo lee libros de historia, ¿verdad?

Note that Spanish questions do not include an equivalent for the auxiliary verbs *do* and *does*. You may simply use a conjugated form of the main verb: ¿José **toca** la guitarra? (*Does José **play** the guitar?*)

To ask questions that request specific information and require more than a *yes* or *no* answer, you may use the following interrogative words.

INTERROGATIVE WORDS	EXAMPLES
¿cómo? *(how?/what . . . like?)*	**¿Cómo** estás, Lola? **¿Cómo** es este libro?
¿cuál(es)? *(what?/which?)* Note that **cuál** is singular and **cuáles** is plural.	**¿Cuál** es tu artista favorito? **¿Cuáles** son tus discos?
¿cuándo? *(when?)*	**¿Cuándo** es la clase de música?
¿cuánto(a)? *(how much?)*	**¿Cuánto** tiempo toma el paseo? **¿Cuánta** agua hay?
¿cuántos(as)? *(how many?)* **Cuánto(s)** refers to masculine nouns and **cuánta(s)** to feminine nouns.	**¿Cuántos** instrumentos toca ella? **¿Cuántas** sillas hay?
¿dónde? *(where?)*	**¿Dónde** está la biblioteca? **¿De dónde** son tus padres?
¿por qué? *(why?)* Questions that contain **por qué** are generally answered with **porque** *(because)*.	**¿Por qué** estudias español? **Porque** es la lengua de mis abuelos.
¿qué? *(what?)*	**¿Qué** es el Internet?
¿quién(es)? *(who?)* **Quién** is used to inquire about one person while **quiénes** is used to inquire about more than one person.	**¿Quién** es el Dr. Suárez? **¿Quiénes** son esas señoras?

■ Asimilación

CD1–14 **1-53 Preguntas personales** Answer the questions you will hear in complete sentences.

   1. ...   4. ...
   2. ...   5. ...
   3. ...

1-54 ¡Y más preguntas personales! For each question, choose the appropriate interrogative word. When you finish, compare your answers with the answers provided by your partner.

1. —¿(Cuántos/Cuánto) cursos tomas por semestre?
   —Tomo cinco cursos.
2. —¿(Qué/Cuál) es tu curso favorito?
   —Mi favorito es el curso de historia medieval.
3. —¿(Cuándo/Dónde) vives?
   —Vivo en la casa de mis padres, en los suburbios.
4. —¿(Cómo/Qué) son tus padres?
   —Mis padres son estrictos, pero son muy buenos.
5. —¿(Por qué/Quién) es tu mejor amiga?
   —Mi mejor amiga es Moraima.

■ Aplicaciones

1-55 Al revés *(Backwards)* Make up the questions you would have to ask to get the following answers.

MODELO   Es mi prima. → *¿Quién es?*

1. Ella es Lisa.
2. Ella es de Miami.
3. Es inteligente y un poco antipática.
4. Su pasatiempo favorito es leer.
5. No, ella no es amiga de Norberto.
6. Estudia comunicaciones.
7. Porque desea ser reportera de televisión.
8. Sí, ella es muy atractiva.

1-56 ¡Más detalles, por favor! Your partner and you always ask people to provide more details. React to the following statements by asking at least one logical question. Take turns asking and reacting to the statements.

MODELO   Anita no escucha música clásica.
           ¿Por qué no escucha música clásica? ¿Qué música escucha?
           ¿Cuál es su música favorita?

1. Alejandro es muy joven.
2. La familia de Margarita es grande.
3. Ni Petra ni Gisela estudian filosofía.
4. Nunca como en la cafetería universitaria.
5. Raúl es muy activo los fines de semana.
6. Vivimos en un apartamento precioso.
7. Mi horario es muy ajetreado *(busy)*.
8. Mi amigo se llama Federico.

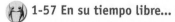

 1-57 En su tiempo libre...

Paso 1: Take a few minutes to write at least six questions you want to ask a classmate to find out more information about what he/she does in his/her free time. Use a different interrogative word in each question. Then, ask the questions and take notes.

Paso 2: Share the information with the rest of the class. Does he/she enjoy doing the things you thought he/she would enjoy? How similar or different are you?

■ Integración

1-58 Un nuevo miembro del club Act out the following situation in groups of three or four.

Los miembros de la comisión directiva	El nuevo miembro	El (La) amigo(a)
You are members of the board of directors of a club in your school. A new member brought one of his/her friends to a meeting because the friend is interested in joining the club as well. You want to find out as much as possible about him/her. Take turns asking questions related to his/her life, interests, studies/work, family, home, etc.	You have brought a friend to a meeting of a school club you recently joined because he/she wants to become a member too. Two of the members of the board of directors want to talk to him/her. As you expected, they will ask many questions to get to know him/her better. Try to help him/her make a good impression!	You are at a meeting of a school club your friend recently joined because you want to join as well. Two of the members of the board of directors want to meet you and they have many questions for you. They want to get to know as much as possible about you before accepting you as a new member of the club. Make a good impression! You may ask them questions as well.

 1-59 En busca de un(a) nuevo(a) empleado(a) *(In search of a new employee)* You are the director of an after-school program for adolescents and you need to hire a new employee. This person must be dynamic, reliable, and very special. Create the application form you will use to get as much information as possible about potential candidates for this position. Include varied and pertinent questions. Be creative!

EN TU COMUNIDAD

Find out and share later with the class what the most popular leisure activities are among the Spanish-speaking members (if any) of your community, how often they get to enjoy doing these activities, and what the day-to-day things are that stop them from doing them more often. Also, ask about what the local government is doing to promote positive and healthy pastimes among citizens (building parks, creating after-school programs, providing low-cost child care, etc.).

IV. Lectura: Mi página personal en la Red

■ Antes de leer

A. Para conversar en grupos What information do you expect to find on a personal home page on the World Wide Web? Make a list of those items in Spanish.

B. Cognados Circle the cognates you find on this home page.

C. Vocabulario nuevo Connect each word with its definition. Use your dictionary if necessary.

_____ 1. la derecha   a. historia, antecedentes

_____ 2. disfrutar   b. el lado opuesto al del corazón (usualmente las personas escriben con esta mano)

_____ 3. la izquierda   c. pasar un buen rato, pasarlo bien

_____ 4. novia   d. lo opuesto de la derecha

_____ 5. trayectoria   e. amiga especial con quien se tiene una relación romántica

VOCABULARIO PRÁCTICO

nombre, información personal, fotografías, conexiones favoritas

READING STRATEGY

Skimming Remember that when you skim a reading the first time, you are looking for cognates and the main ideas of the text.

Mi página en la Red

Fabián Pérez León

overview

I enjoy

¡Hola y bienvenido! Mi nombre es Fabián Pérez León. Soy de Medellín, Colombia. A continuación te presento mi **trayectoria** académica y personal, así como algunas de las actividades que **disfruto** hacer. Mi domicilio permanente es Calle 45 #20-31, Barrio Caldas, Medellín, Colombia. ¡Espero que disfrutes con la visita! ¡Gracias!

Datos personales Éste soy yo. Tengo veintitrés años y vivo en Medellín. Aquí incluyo fotos de mi familia y de Nubia, mi novia.

Trayectoria académica y laboral Soy ingeniero de sistemas y trabajo para IBM en esta ciudad.

equipment
weightlifting

I love

Pasatiempos Me interesa todo lo referente a **equipo** y programas de PCs. También practico **levantamiento de pesas** y, desde luego, fútbol. En el cine **me encanta** la trilogía de «Star Wars» y las películas de Steven Spielberg, de Arnold Schwarzenegger y Sylvester Stallone.

With regard to

eagles

En cuanto a la música, me gusta especialmente la música romántica. Para leer siempre busco revistas sobre deportes y ciencia y también me gustan algunas novelas. ¿Escribir? En ocasiones. Mis animales favoritos son los leones, los tigres y las **águilas**.

A leer

D. ¿Qué dice? *(What does it say?)* Answer the following questions in Spanish about this home page. Use the glossary and cognate recognition to make associations for meaning.

1. ¿De dónde es Fabián?
2. ¿Cuál es su profesión?
3. ¿Dónde trabaja?
4. ¿Cuáles son sus pasatiempos favoritos?

____ charlar por teléfono
____ navegar por la Red
____ escuchar música
____ tocar un instrumento
____ leer libros
____ pasear
____ mirar la televisión
____ otro(s): ____

E. Para conversar What information is missing in this home page? Prepare a list with your ideas and share it with the rest of the class.

F. Mi propia página web Imagine how you would like to represent yourself on a web page. Start by writing information that characterizes you. Prepare your own home page in Spanish for the web.

READING STRATEGY

Scanning Remember that during the second reading you are looking for specific information and comprehension of details. Also try to guess the meaning of words based on their context.

Formulario / *Application form*

el alojamiento	*lodging*
el apellido	*last name*
desde	*since*
el domicilio/la dirección	*address*
la fecha de nacimiento	*date of birth*
hasta	*until*
la nacionalidad	*nationality*
el nombre	*name*
el teléfono	*phone number*
el correo electrónico	*e-mail*

Características

activo	*active*
alegre	*happy*
amistoso/amigable	*friendly*
antipático	*unpleasant*
bueno	*good*
débil	*weak*
diligente	*diligent*
divertido	*fun*
estricto	*strict*
famoso	*famous*
fuerte	*strong*
inteligente	*intelligent*
joven	*young*
mayor	*mature, old*
pobre	*poor*
rico	*rich*
serio	*serious*
simpático	*nice*
tonto	*foolish, dull*
trabajador(a)	*hardworking*
viejo	*old*

Nacionalidades / *Nationalities*

argentino	*Argentinean*
boliviano	*Bolivian*
chileno	*Chilean*
colombiano	*Colombian*
costarricense	*Costa Rican*
cubano	*Cuban*
dominicano	*Dominican*
ecuatoriano	*Ecuadorian*
español	*Spanish*
estadounidense	*American (from the U.S.)*
guatemalteco	*Guatemalan*
hondureño	*Honduran*
mexicano	*Mexican*
nicaragüense	*Nicaraguan*
panameño	*Panamanian*
paraguayo	*Paraguayan*
puertorriqueño	*Puerto Rican*
salvadoreño	*Salvadorian*
uruguayo	*Uruguayan*
venezolano	*Venezuelan*

Mi familia es de origen...

africano	*African*
asiático	*Asian*
europeo	*European*

Expresiones de frecuencia

casi nunca	*almost never*
casi siempre	*almost always*
los...	*on (day[s] of the week)*
nunca	*never*
siempre	*always*
todos los días	*every day*

Conectores

en (conclusión/mi opinión/resumen)	*in (conclusion/my opinion/summary)*
finalmente	*finally*
pero	*but*
por otro lado	*on the other hand*
también	*also*
tampoco	*either, neither*
y	*and*

Profesiones

el (la) abogado(a)	*attorney, lawyer*
el (la) gerente	*manager*
el ama de casa	*housewife*
el (la) arquitecto(a)	*architect*
el (la) cocinero(a)	*cook*
el (la) contable	*accountant*
el (la) chofer	*driver*
el (la) empleado(a) doméstico(a)	*maid*
el (la) enfermero(a)	*nurse*
el hombre/la mujer de negocios	*businessman (woman)*
el (la) ingeniero(a)	*engineer*
el (la) obrero(a)	*construction worker*
el (la) peluquero(a)	*hairdresser*
el (la) periodista	*journalist*
el (la) policía	*policeman/woman*
el (la) programador(a) de computadoras	*computer programmer*
el (la) vendedor(a)	*salesperson*

Pasatiempos
charlar por teléfono
escuchar música
leer un libro
(mirar/ver) televisión
navegar por (la Red/el
    Internet)
pasear

pasar tiempo libre/los
    ratos libres
tocar un instrumento

Leisure time
to chat on the phone
to listen to music
to read a book
to watch TV
to surf the Net

to take a short trip;
    to go for a walk
to spend free time

to play an instrument

Funciones y estructuras
Verbos que terminan en **-ar**, p. 37
Verbos que terminan en **-er**, p. 41
Verbos que terminan en **-ir**, p. 41
Palabras negativas, p. 48
Palabras interrogativas, p. 51

Capítulo

2

Para comenzar

- ¿Quiénes son? *(Who are these people?)*
- ¿Dónde están? *(Where are they?)*
- ¿Qué hacen? *(What are they doing?)*

En familia

In this chapter you will learn . . .

- how to describe individuals
- how to describe a person's emotional state or condition
- how to talk about your home
- how to express possession and obligation
- how to talk about likes and dislikes
- about Spanish-speaking family values

	TEMA 1 Ésta es mi familia	**TEMA 2** La personalidad	**TEMA 3** Nuestra casa
Vocabulario	Los miembros de la familia	Los rasgos personales	Los espacios y los muebles de una casa
Funciones y estructuras	Describing physical appearance with adjectives and the verbs **ser** and **tener** Expressing possession	Talking about location, conditions, and emotional states with the verbs **estar** and **tener** Talking about likes and dislikes with **gustar**	Talking about location with prepositions Expressing obligation with **tener que...** and **hay que...**
Lecturas y vídeo	Perspectivas: La familia de José Miguel	Vídeo: Los compañeros se conocen mejor	Lectura: *La casa en Mango Street*

Foto 1

Foto 2

Foto 3

Enfoque

A. ¿Qué sabes ya de México? Before you watch the video, look at the phrases below and decide if they refer to Mexico's economy, government, tourism, or capital city. Write the letter of the corresponding category in the space provided. When you finish, check your answers with a partner.

E = la economía   **G** = el gobierno   **T** = el turismo   **C** = la capital

_____ 1. una república federal

_____ 2. la producción industrial y agrícola

_____ 3. playas famosas

_____ 4. la Ciudad de México

_____ 5. el petróleo

_____ 6. los sitios arqueológicos y pueblos coloniales

B. ¿Dónde está... ? As you watch the video for the first time, focus your attention on the video images and identify the places on the map on page vi.

_____ el Océano Pacífico   _____ los Estados Unidos   _____ Belice   _____ Veracruz

_____ la Ciudad de México   _____ Guatemala   _____ Teotihuacán

C. Un viaje para dos a México As you are reading a travel magazine, you come across the following sweepstakes that is offering all-inclusive getaway packages to Mexico. Read the description and follow the instructions to enter the contest.

> **Los encantos de México** Tenemos tres paquetes de vacaciones «todo incluido» diferentes para Ud.:
>
> 1. Celebre **El Día de la Independencia de México**, 16 de septiembre, visitando tres famosos sitios arqueológicos: Uxmal, Tula y Teotihuacán (14–19 de septiembre).
> 2. Celebre **El Día de Nuestra Señora de Guadalupe**, el 12 de diciembre, en el Distrito Federal (10–15 de diciembre).
> 3. Celebre el **Carnaval** en Veracruz (22–27 de febrero).

For more info, you may want to check the **Temas** site:
http://temas.heinle.com

Ésta es mi familia

I. Vocabulario: Los miembros de la familia

La **abuela** de Pedro se llama Berta. Tiene 63 años y es ama de casa.

La **madre** de Pedro se llama Marta. Tiene 46 años y es enfermera.

El **padre** de Pedro se llama Juan. Tiene 47 años y es electricista.

El **hermano mayor** de Pedro se llama Esteban. Tiene 26 años y es psicólogo.

Pedro tiene 18 años y es estudiante.

Pedro

La **hermana** de Pedro se llama Gabriela. Tiene 15 años y es estudiante.

Vocabulario práctico

La familia inmediata

el (la) abuelo(a) *grandfather/ grandmother*

el (la) esposo(a) *husband/wife*

el (la) hermano(a) *brother/sister*

el (la) hijo(a) *son/daughter*

la madre/mamá *mother*

el (la) nieto(a) *grandson/ granddaughter*

el padre/papá *father*

Otros parientes (*relatives*)

el (la) cuñado(a) *brother-in-law/ sister-in-law*

el (la) hermanastro(a) *stepbrother/ stepsister*

la madrastra *stepmother*

el padrastro *stepfather*

el (la) primo(a) *cousin*

el (la) sobrino(a) *nephew/niece*

el (la) suegro(a) *father-in-law/ mother-in-law*

el (la) tío(a) *uncle/aunt*

- Notice that **parientes** *(relatives)* is a false cognate. The Spanish word for *parents* is **padres.** Similarly, **parentesco** means *relationship.*

- Masculine plural terms (**padres, abuelos,** etc.) are often used in Spanish to refer to entire categories. For instance, the word **tíos** can be used to designate either *uncles* or both *uncles and aunts;* the word **sobrinos** can refer to *nephews* or to both *nephews and nieces,* etc.

- Use **mayor(es)** to talk about *older* siblings or children and **menor(es)** to talk about *younger* siblings or children.

- A negative statement such as **No tengo hermanas** *(I don't have any sisters)* can be used to indicate your lack of family members under a given category.

- If a family member has already passed away, you can say **falleció** *(passed away).* Use **fallecieron** if two or more family members have passed away (e.g., **Mis abuelos fallecieron.**).

- **Don** and **doña** are titles of respect often used when referring to older people. These titles are used only with first names and are not capitalized unless they begin a sentence (e.g., **Don Jorge es muy simpático. Él y doña María son los padres de Graciela.**).

■ Asimilación

2-1 ¿Cierto o falso? Indica si las oraciones *(sentences)* son **ciertas (C)** o **falsas (F)** según *(according to)* el gráfico en la página 60. Luego *(Then),* compara tus respuestas con las de un(a) compañero(a).

_____ 1. Pedro tiene dos hermanas.

_____ 2. La madre de Pedro se llama Matilde.

_____ 3. El esposo de Marta es electricista.

_____ 4. La nieta de Berta se llama Gabriela.

_____ 5. La abuela de Pedro es dentista.

_____ 6. La hija de Marta se llama Gabriela.

_____ 7. Doña Berta es la suegra de Juan.

_____ 8. Esteban es el sobrino de doña Berta.

_____ 9. Esteban y Gabriela son primos.

_____ 10. Gabriela es la cuñada de doña Berta.

CD1–16 **2-2 La familia del profesor Vargas** Escucha *(Listen to)* la descripción de la familia del profesor Vargas. Luego, copia el siguiente *(the following)* árbol genealógico *(family tree)* y complétalo con **los nombres** de sus familiares *(family members).*

La familia del profesor Vargas

■ Aplicaciones

2-3 Información personal Completa las oraciones con el nombre y la ocupación de los familiares indicados. Indica también *(also)* una de sus características personales.

MODELO   Mi padre *se llama Thomas y es abogado. Él es muy simpático.*

1. Mi madre _____.
2. Mi padre _____.
3. Mi primo(a) _____.
4. Mi hermano(a) menor _____.
5. Mi abuelo(a) _____.

2-4 La familia de Raúl Completa el párrafo con la palabra *(word)* más apropiada según el contexto.

Raúl es mexicano, tiene 36 años *(is 36 years old)* y vive en Veracruz. Su _____ (esposa / hija) se llama Alicia, tiene 32 años y trabaja en el puerto. Esteban es su _____ (padre / hijo mayor) y está en sexto grado *(sixth grade)*. Gonzalo es su _____ (hermano mayor / hijo menor) y va al jardín infantil *(kindergarten)*. Raúl tiene solamente un _____ (hijo menor / hermano) que es ingeniero y vive en la capital. Doña Teresa, la _____ (madre / hija menor), es ama de casa y vive con su hijo y sus nietos en Veracruz.

2-5 Entrevista Hazle preguntas *(Ask questions)* a tu compañero(a) y elabora *(draw)* su árbol genealógico. **Nota:** Recuerda *(Remember)* que puedes dar información real o imaginaria.

MODELO   *¿Cómo se llama tu padre?*

■ Integración

 2-6 Entrevista Representa la siguiente situación con un(a) compañero(a).

Estudiante A	Estudiante B
Imagine that you have decided to host a Mexican exchange student in your home. He/She is calling you from his/her home in Puebla. Find out as much information as possible about his/her family (their names, profession, personality, etc.). Be prepared to answer questions about your family.	You are a student from Puebla, Mexico, who is planning to participate in an exchange program in the U.S. Your host family is on the phone and they would like to have more information about you and your family. Be prepared to answer their questions, and ask some questions of your own (names of the different family members, profession, personality, etc.).

2-7 Mi familia Prepare a description of your family (include pictures, if possible). Be sure to provide information about the age, profession, place of residence, and personality of your closest relatives. Keep in mind that you will be exchanging compositions with other class members.

II. Funciones y estructuras: Describing physical appearance with adjectives and the verbs *ser* and *tener*

Mi tío Felipe es **gordo,** pero mi primo José es **delgado.**

Mi cuñada Beatriz es **rubia,** pero mi cuñada Ligia **tiene pelo negro.**

The verb **ser** is used to describe physical appearance. Following is a list of adjectives you can use to describe yourself and others, as well as objects.

alto *tall*	flaco *skinny*
bajo *short* (in height)	gordo *fat, overweight*
bonito *pretty*	grande *big*
calvo *bald*	guapo *handsome*
corto *short* (in length)	largo *long*
delgado *thin*	moreno *dark-haired*
difícil *difficult*	nuevo *new*
fácil *easy*	pequeño *small*
feo *ugly, unattractive*	rubio *blond(e)*

These adjectives, like other adjectives you have already learned, must agree in number and gender with the noun(s) they describe.

Mi **esposa** es **morena** y yo soy **rubio.**
*My **wife** is **dark-haired** and I am **blond(e)**.*

Los **exámenes** de filosofía son **difíciles.**
*Philosophy **exams** are **difficult**.*

The verb **tener** *(to have)* can also be used in descriptions. Like **ser**, **tener** is an irregular verb.

yo **tengo**	nosotros(as) **tenemos**
tú **tienes**	vosotros(as) **tenéis**
él/ella/usted **tiene**	ellos(as)/ustedes **tienen**

Tener can be used to talk about:

■ hair color

Mis parientes **tienen pelo rojo,** pero yo **tengo pelo negro.**
*My relatives **have red hair**, but I have **black hair**.*

REMEMBER

Ser is also used to describe objects and people and to talk about someone's nationality and origin.

SABOR REGIONAL

Other words for *dark-haired* are **morocho(a)** (Argentina and Uruguay) and **trigueño(a)** (Colombia, Cuba, and the Dominican Republic). The adjective **moreno(a)**, on the other hand, refers to skin color in places like Puerto Rico. Finally, other words for *blond* are **güero(a)** (Mexico) and **catire(a)** (Venezuela).

To describe a good-looking man, use the adjective **guapo** instead of **bonito.**

When talking about hair color **(tener pelo...)**, you may use the following words: **blanco** *(gray),* **castaño** *(brown),* **negro** *(black),* **rojo** *(red),* and **rubio** *(blond).*

■ features of different body parts

Mi cuñada Tatiana **tiene** ojos azules.

*My sister-in-law Tatiana **has** blue eyes.*

■ age

—**¿Cuántos años tiene** tu hermano?
—Mi hermano menor **tiene** quince años.

How old is your brother?
My younger brother is fifteen years old.

■ Asimilación

CD1-17 **2-8 ¿Qué familia es?** La familia Roldán Mercado y la familia Vera Cintrón viven en Guadalajara, México. Escucha las descripciones e indica a cuál de las dos familas se refieren. **¡OJO!** Las descripciones pueden *(may)* referirse a ambas *(both)* familias.

Familia Roldán Mercado

Familia Vera Cintrón

1. ____ Familia Roldán Mercado ____ Familia Vera Cintrón ____ ambas familias
2. ____ Familia Roldán Mercado ____ Familia Vera Cintrón ____ ambas familias
3. ____ Familia Roldán Mercado ____ Familia Vera Cintrón ____ ambas familias
4. ____ Familia Roldán Mercado ____ Familia Vera Cintrón ____ ambas familias
5. ____ Familia Roldán Mercado ____ Familia Vera Cintrón ____ ambas familias

2-9 ¿Quiénes son así *(like that)***?** Completen las oraciones con el nombre de personas famosas que cumplan con *(fit)* las descripciones.

1. ____ y ____ son morenos.
2. ____ tiene pelo gris.
3. ____ y ____ son bajas.
4. ____ es guapo.
5. ____ no es vieja.
6. ____ tiene ojos verdes.
7. ____ y ____ son bonitas.
8. ____ tiene aproximadamente veinte años.

■ Aplicaciones

2-10 Descripciones Completa las oraciones con una palabra lógica.

MODELO   La Sra. Bermúdez no es baja. Ella es muy *alta*.

1. Mis hermanas no tienen pelo corto. Ellas tienen pelo _____.
2. La casa *(house)* de Nicolás no es _____; es vieja.
3. Carlota y Doris son _____. Ellas no son bonitas.
4. El primo de Mauricio sólo *(only)* tiene doce años. Él es _____.
5. Mi familia es muy _____; no es nada grande.
6. Mi sobrina no es rubia. Ella tiene pelo _____.

2-11 Una persona de la clase Escojan *(Choose)* a una persona de la clase y descríbanla. Escriban cinco oraciones diferentes y usen los verbos **ser** y **tener** correctamente. Cuando terminen *(When finished)*, léanle *(read to)* las oraciones a la clase. ¿Sus compañeros pueden adivinar *(guess)* quién es?

1. ...   3. ...   5. ...
2. ...   4. ...

2-12 La familia de...

Paso 1: Entrevista a un(a) compañero(a) y completa el siguiente cuadro *(table)*.

PARIENTE(S)	NOMBRE(S)	EDAD(ES)	DESCRIPCIÓN(-ONES)	ACTIVIDADES FAVORITAS
padre				
madre				
hermano(a/os/as)				
abuelos				
tíos				
primos				

Paso 2: Preséntenle al resto de la clase la información sobre dos o tres de los miembros de la familia del (de la) compañero(a). ¿Quisieran conocer *(Would you like to know)* a estas personas?

■ Integración

2-13 Una familia de la televisión Túrnense *(Take turns)* para describir a los miembros de la familia de algún *(any)* programa de televisión. ¿Tu compañero(a) puede adivinar *(guess)* quiénes son?

MODELO   E1: *Es una familia muy interesante. El padre es gordo, alto y calvo. La madre tiene mucho pelo y es alta. Ellos tienen tres hijos: un hijo y dos hijas. El hijo es bajo y...*
         E2: *¡Los Simpson!*

2-14 Mi familia Usa la descripción de tu familia de la actividad 2-7 e *(and)* incluye *(include)* una descripción física de tus parientes inmediatos. Recuerda que algunos de tus compañeros van a leer *(will read)* tu trabajo.

III. Funciones y estructuras: Expressing possession

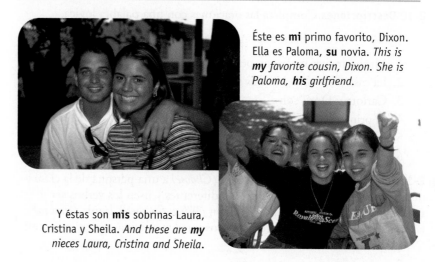

Éste es **mi** primo favorito, Dixon. Ella es Paloma, **su** novia. *This is **my** favorite cousin, Dixon. She is Paloma, **his** girlfriend.*

Y éstas son **mis** sobrinas Laura, Cristina y Sheila. *And these are **my** nieces Laura, Cristina and Sheila.*

To express possession you may use the following adjectives.

ONE OWNER OR POSSESSOR	MORE THAN ONE OWNER OR POSSESSOR
mi(s) *my*	**nuestro(a/os/as)** *our*
tu(s) *your* (informal)	**vuestro(a/os/as)** *your* (informal in Spain)
su(s) *his/her/your* (formal)	**su(s)** *their/your* (Latin America)

Possessive adjectives have more than one form because, like other adjectives, they agree in gender and number with the noun they describe. Notice though that possessive adjectives do not reflect the gender of the possessor or owner. Thus, when we say **nuestras clases**, **nuestras** is feminine plural because **clases** is a feminine plural noun, regardless of the gender of the people whose classes we are talking about.

¡Son **mis cosas**, no **nuestras cosas**!

*These are **my things**, not **our things**!*

Sus hijos son amigos de **vuestros hijos**.

***Their children** are friends with **your** (pl.) **children**.*

Although context provides clarity, using the adjectives **su** and **sus** may lead to ambiguity because they have multiple meanings (i.e., *his/her/your* [sing, formal], *their,* and *your* [pl.]). In these cases you may use the following structure with the preposition **de**:

> (noun) + **de** + (possessor or owner)

Lobo es el perro **de** ella.
Ésa es la esposa **de** él.

*Lobo is **her** dog.*
*That is **his** wife.*

The same structure is used in cases in which we would use an apostrophe to indicate possession in English. Apostrophes are not used in Spanish.

Charo es la nieta **de** Teresa.
Mota es la gata **del** Sr. Vizcaíno.

Charo is Teresa's granddaughter.
Mota is Mr. Vizcaíno's cat.

When the preposition **de** is followed by the article **el**, they contract to **del**. The use of this contraction is obligatory in Spanish.

■ Asimilación

2-15 Parientes Mira los dibujos *(Look at the illustrations)* y escoge el adjetivo posesivo más apropiado.

Marcela es (nuestra / sus / mi) esposa.

Juan Pablo y Reina son (su / mis / nuestro) hijos.

Juana es (mi / nuestra / sus) madre.

¿Es (nuestras / sus / tu) familia?

2-16 ¿Cierto o falso? Indica si las siguientes oraciones son **ciertas (C)** o **falsas (F)**. Al terminar, compara tus respuestas con las de un(a) compañero(a). ¿Qué tienen en común?

_____ 1. Mis parientes son altos.

_____ 2. Las familias de mis amigos son pequeñas.

_____ 3. Los padres de mi madre viven en la Florida.

_____ 4. Mi casa es grande.

_____ 5. Muchos de mis primos son morenos.

_____ 6. El padre de mi mejor amigo(a) es flaco.

■ Aplicaciones

2-17 En una reunión familiar Lean las preguntas que Waldemar les hace a varias personas en una reunión familiar y escojan la respuesta más lógica.

1. ¿Quién es ella?
   a. Es nuestro sobrino.
   b. Son los nietos de Tila.
   c. Es mi abuela.

2. ¿Son sus hermanos?
   a. No, son nuestros tíos.
   b. No, son tus hermanos.
   c. Sí, es mi cuñada.

3. ¿Son los padres de Ricardo?
   a. No, son sus abuelos.
   b. Sí, son mis hermanastros.
   c. Sí, es mi yerno.

4. ¿Es tu amiga Patricia?
   a. Sí, es tu cuñado.
   b. Sí, es mi amiga.
   c. Sí, es la amiga de Patricia.

5. ¿Quiénes son?
   a. Son nuestras primas.
   b. Es su nieta.
   c. Es el padre de ellos.

2-18 ¿Y la familia del (de la) profesor(a)? Escriban cinco preguntas para el (la) profesor(a) sobre su familia.

> MODELO   *¿Su hermano tiene pelo castaño?*
>
> 1. ...   2. ...   3. ...   4. ...   5. ...

2-19 Una encuesta *(survey)*

Paso 1: Para cada pariente o grupo de parientes, marca la alternativa que se aplique a ti *(that applies to you).*

PARIENTE(S)	ALTERNATIVAS	
madre	_____ trabaja	_____ no trabaja
hermanos	_____ son alegres	_____ son aburridos
tía	_____ nunca cocina	_____ siempre cocina
abuelos	_____ asisten a bingos	_____ no asisten a bingos
suegros	_____ son simpáticos	_____ son antipáticos
padre	_____ tiene menos *(less)* de 50 años	_____ tiene más de 50 años
novio(a) o esposo(a)	_____ practica deportes	_____ no practica ningún deporte
hijos	_____ desayunan en casa	_____ no desayunan en casa

Paso 2: Ahora, en grupos de tres o cuatro estudiantes, háganse preguntas *(ask one another questions)* para determinar las semejanzas *(similarities)* y diferencias entre sus familias. Tomen notas. Cuando terminen, preparen un informe escrito.

You may use the phrase **No tengo...** if necessary.

> MODELO   E1: *Mi madre trabaja. ¿Tu madre trabaja, Stephanie?*
> E2: *Sí, mi madre trabaja. ¿Y tu madre, Jonathan?*
> E3: *No, mi madre no trabaja.*

■ Integración

2-20 ¡Los reto! *(I challenge you!)* In groups of three or four, take turns providing details about the places and things listed. Do not move on to the next item until nobody has anything else to say. The student who provides the most details wins!

> MODELO   (en) nuestra ciudad
> E1: *Nuestra ciudad es bonita.*
> E2: *En nuestra ciudad viven muchas personas.*
> E3: *Nuestra ciudad tiene muchos lugares interesantes.*
> ...

If you do not have anything to say, say **yo paso** *(I pass).*

1. (en) nuestra universidad
2. nuestro(a) profesor(a)
3. (en) nuestra clase de español
4. (en) nuestro estado
5. (en) la familia de nuestro(a) profesor(a)
6. nuestros compañeros de clase

2-21 Las familias mexicanas Since you want to learn more Spanish, you decided to spend next summer in Oaxaca, Mexico, with the Zapata Robles family. Before going, you want to learn more about typical Mexican families and about the Zapatas. Make a list of questions for Octavio, the Zapata's teenage son, and provide him with some information about your own family.

REMEMBER

The verb **hay** means *there is* and *there are.*

> MODELO   *¿Cuántos hijos hay en tu familia? En mi familia hay dos hijos y una hija.*
> *¿Cómo es tu madre? Mi madre es baja y tiene pelo rojo.*

IV. Perspectivas: La familia de José Miguel

▨ Antes de leer

Información ¿Qué información encuentran *(do you find)* en el Internet acerca de las familias? Marquen las opciones más lógicas.

____ nombres de los familiares   ____ lugar donde viven   ____ religión

____ profesiones   ____ fotografías   ____ ideas políticas

____ problemas médicos   ____ historia de la familia   ____ edades

▨ A leer

Ésta es mi familia

La foto muestra a mi familia. De izquierda a derecha, Uds. pueden ver a mi hermana Luisa Fernanda. Ella tiene dieciséis años, estudia en el Liceo Camilo Daza y cursa el sexto año de bachillerato. Después estoy yo, José Miguel, mi mamá Angélica (lo más lindo del mundo *[the most beautiful thing in the world]*), mi papá Miguel Hernando, que es ingeniero electrónico, y finalmente mi hermana mayor, Teresa, que tiene veintitrés años y es enfermera. Yo tengo veinte años y estudio arquitectura en la Universidad Javeriana. En mi tiempo libre, toco la guitarra y navego por el Internet.

▨ ¿Entendiste bien?

1. ¿Cuántas personas hay en la familia?
2. ¿Cuántas hermanas tiene este joven?
3. ¿Cuántos años tiene la hermana menor de José Miguel?
4. ¿Cuál es la profesión de su padre?
5. ¿Cuál es la profesión de su hermana mayor?
6. ¿Qué hace José Miguel en su tiempo libre?
7. ¿Esta familia es semejante o diferente a tu familia? Explica tu respuesta.

La personalidad

I. Vocabulario: Los rasgos personales

Mi hermana Mercedes es **simpática.**

Mi abuelo Juan es **gracioso.**

Mi hermano Joaquín es un poco *(somewhat)* **serio.**

tonto

inteligente

malo

bueno

perezoso

diligente

tímido

extrovertido

Vocabulario práctico

alegre *cheerful*	honrado *honest*
amable *kind*	ingenioso *resourceful*
antipático *unfriendly*	responsable *responsible*
egoísta *selfish*	sincero *sincere*
generoso *generous*	talentoso *talented*
grosero *rude*	voluble *fickle*

Asimilación

2-22 ¿Quién es? Indica el número de la oración *(sentence)* que describe cada dibujo *(each drawing)*.

a. Elsa

b. Marcela

c. Laura

1. _____ es simpática.
2. _____ es graciosa.
3. _____ es inteligente.

2-23 Tu familia Completa las oraciones con el nombre de la persona de tu familia que corresponda a la descripción.

1. Mi _____ es cómico(a).
2. Mis _____ son simpáticos.
3. Mi _____ es un poco perezoso(a).
4. Mis _____ son muy inteligentes.
5. Mi _____ es muy generoso(a).

Aplicaciones

2-24 ¿Cómo son? Expresa tu opinión según las opciones. Luego, compara tus respuestas con las de un(a) compañero(a). ¿Están de acuerdo? *(Do you agree?)*

1. Tom Hanks es...
   - a. simpático.
   - b. tímido.
   - c. tonto.
   - d. otra descripción

2. Jay Leno y Conan O'Brien son...
   - a. graciosos.
   - b. serios.
   - c. materialistas.
   - d. otra descripción

3. Gloria Estefan y Shakira son...
   - a. diligentes.
   - b. pesimistas.
   - c. graciosas.
   - d. otra descripción

4. El presidente de los Estados Unidos es...
   - a. materialista.
   - b. inteligente.
   - c. tímido.
   - d. otra descripción

5. _____ *(tu personaje favorito)* es...
   - a. idealista.
   - b. generoso(a).
   - c. sincero(a).
   - d. otra descripción

> **REMEMBER**
>
> Most adjective endings indicate the gender of the person being described.

2-25 Opuestos Completen la descripción de los miembros de la familia Jiménez.

OPCIONES: diligente, sincero, optimista, tímido, seria, generoso

Los Jiménez son muy diferentes entre sí *(among themselves)*. El señor Jiménez es un abogado _____. Por el contrario, la señora Jiménez es una pintora alegre y extrovertida. Guillermo, el hijo mayor, es _____, pero su hermanito Pedro es perezoso. Las niñas también son distintas: Cristina es graciosa; en cambio *(however),* Marcela es _____. A pesar de sus diferencias, todos se llevan bien.

2-26 ¿Quién es? Pick one of the following pictures and have your classmate guess your selection by describing in Spanish the personality traits you would associate with such an individual.

Foto 1

Foto 2

Foto 3

■ **Integración**

2-27 Entrevista Túrnense para hacer y responder a las preguntas. Al terminar, preséntenle un informe al resto de la clase.

1. ¿Cómo son tus padres? ¿Cuál es su profesión? ¿Qué hacen en su tiempo libre?
2. ¿Cuántos hermanos(as) tienes? ¿Cómo son? ¿Dónde trabajan o estudian tus hermanos(as)?
3. ¿Tienes novio(a) o esposo(a)? ¿Cómo es?
4. ¿Tienes sobrinos? ¿Cómo son?
5. Y tú, ¿cómo eres? ¿Qué haces los fines de semana o durante tu tiempo libre?

2-28 Mi familia Añádele *(Add)* información sobre la personalidad de los miembros de tu familia a la descripción que empezaste *(you began)* en el **Tema 1.**

II. Funciones y estructuras: Talking about location, conditions, and emotional states with the verbs *estar* and *tener*

Nelda y Cuca **están** en el parque. Ellas **están** contentas. *Nelda and Cuca are at the park. They are happy.*

El Sr. Delgado **tiene sueño. Está** muy cansado. *Mr. Delgado is sleepy. He is very tired.*

There are two ways of saying *to be* in Spanish: **ser** and **estar**. The verb **estar**, like **ser**, is irregular.

> **REMEMBER**
>
> **Ser** is used to talk about professions and occupations, place of origin, physical description and personality description.

yo **estoy**	nosotros(as) **estamos**
tú **estás**	vosotros(as) **estáis**
él/ella/usted **está**	ellos(as)/ustedes **están**

Estar is used to talk about:

- location

 ¡Mis hermanos **están** en el aeropuerto y yo todavía **estoy** aquí!   *My siblings **are** at the airport and I **am** still here!*

- conditions and emotional states

 Nora, ¿**estás** enojada? ¡Yo **estoy** feliz!   *Nora, **are you** angry? I **am** happy!*

The following are common adjectives of condition and emotion used with **estar**.

> These adjectives must also agree in gender and number with the noun described.

aburrido *bored*	enojado *angry*
alegre/contento/feliz *happy*	listo *ready*
cansado *tired*	nervioso *nervous*
deprimido *depressed*	ocupado *busy*
emocionado *excited*	preocupado *worried*
enfermo *sick*	triste *sad*

The verb **tener** *(to have)* can also be used to talk about certain states and conditions. Here are some expressions that require using this verb.

tener calor *to be hot*	tener prisa *to be in a hurry*
tener éxito *to be successful*	tener rabia *to be mad*
tener frío *to be cold*	tener sed *to be thirsty*
tener hambre *to be hungry*	tener sueño *to be sleepy*
tener miedo *to be afraid*	

To express degree of intensity, say **mucho(a)** *(very, much)* or **un poco de** *(a little bit [of])* after **tener**. Keep in mind that **hambre**, **prisa,** and **sed** are feminine nouns and are used with **mucha**.

Tengo (**mucha** / **un poco de**) hambre.
*I am (**very** / **a little bit**) hungry.*

Jaime, ¿tienes (**mucho** / **un poco de**) calor?
*James, are you (**very** / **a little bit**) hot?*

■ Asimilación

CD1–18 **2-29 ¿Dónde está Ignacio?** Escucha las oraciones sobre Ignacio e indica a qué dibujo se refieren.

a. _____   b. _____   c. _____   d. _____   e. _____

2-30 Reacciones Lean las siguientes situaciones y escojan el adjetivo más lógico.

1. Tengo un examen de economía esta tarde. El material es muy difícil y debo estudiar mucho. Estoy (alegre / preocupado / cansado).

2. Los amigos de Estela están de vacaciones. Ella está en su casa y no hay programas buenos en la televisión. Ella está (aburrida / lista / enferma).

3. Nina y tú tienen una fiesta esta noche. Deben ir al supermercado, limpiar la casa y preparar la comida. Tienen muchas cosas que hacer *(to do)* y poco tiempo. Ustedes están (contentas / deprimidas / ocupadas).

4. Mi novia y yo estamos en la Pirámide del Sol en México. Es un lugar espectacular y muy impresionante. Nosotros estamos (emocionados / listos / tristes).

5. Verónica no puede ir *(cannot go)* a Acapulco con su familia porque está muy ocupada. Ella trabaja para una compañía internacional y debe escribir varios informes. Ella está (feliz / cansada / enojada).

■ **Aplicaciones**

2-31 Conocimientos *(knowledge)* **geográficos** Túrnense para hacer preguntas sobre la localización de los siguientes lugares de interés *(landmarks)* del mundo.

> MODELO   la Estatua de la Libertad
> E1: *¿Dónde está la Estatua de la Libertad?*
> E2: *Está en Nueva York.*

1. el Coliseo Romano
2. Cancún y Cozumel
3. el Partenón
4. Hollywood
5. la Torre Eiffel y el Arco del Triunfo
6. las ciudades de Sydney y Melbourne

2-32 ¿Dónde? ¿Cómo? Describan los siguiente dibujos. Indiquen dónde están las personas y cómo están.

Here are some useful words: **aeropuerto** *(airport)*, **habitación** *(bedroom)*, and **restaurante** *(restaurant)*.

> MODELO   Francisco *está en su oficina y está cansado.*

Dolores y yo...

Aníbal...

Yo...

Ellas...

2-33 ¿Cómo te sientes *(you feel)* **cuando... ?** Túrnense para hacer preguntas con la siguiente información. Usen expresiones con **estar** y **tener** en las respuestas.

> MODELO caminar por el desierto
> E1: *¿Cómo te sientes cuando caminas por el desierto?*
> E2: *Cuando camino por el desierto, tengo sed y estoy cansado(a).*

Pay attention to the conjugation of the underlined verbs included in these phrases.

1. no <u>tener</u> tiempo para almorzar en la cafetería
2. <u>recibir</u> una nota mala en una clase
3. la temperatura es de 110º F en el verano
4. <u>tener</u> un examen en dos minutos y no <u>estar</u> listo(a)
5. <u>mirar</u> una película *(movie)* de horror
6. la temperatura es de 20° F en el invierno
7. son las 3:00 P.M. y no has comido *(have not eaten)* nada
8. <u>tener</u> tarea de todas las clases

■ Integración

2-34 Terapia grupal ¿Cómo estás? ¿Por qué? En grupos de tres o cuatro, túrnense para contestar estas preguntas. ¡Usen la imaginación! Además, reaccionen *(react)* a los comentarios de sus compañeros con sugerencias.

> MODELO E1: *Hoy estoy... porque... También estoy... porque...*
> E2: *Pues debes... porque...*

2-35 La historia más original Escribe un resumen *(summary)* de las respuestas y reacciones más originales de la actividad 2-34.

> MODELO *Deborah está... hoy porque... Charlie opina que ella debe...,*
> *pero Lisa opina que ella...*

III. Funciones y estructuras: Talking about likes and dislikes with *gustar*

A nosotras **nos gusta** hablar por teléfono. *We like to talk on the phone.*

A Romualdo **le gusta** leer en su tiempo libre. *Romualdo likes to read in his spare time.*

Spanish does not have a verb that is used exactly like the English verb *to like*. The verb used to talk about likes and dislikes is **gustar**, which works very much like the English *to be pleasing*.

Me gusta estudiar español.

To study Spanish is pleasing to me.

(= *I like to study Spanish.*)

In this example, **estudiar español** is the subject of the sentence (what is pleasing) and **me** is an indirect object pronoun that indicates the person to whom the subject is pleasing.

Sentences with **gustar** follow this pattern:

INDIRECT OBJECT PRONOUN	gustar	SUBJECT
me (*to me*) **te** (*to you,* informal) **le** (*to him/her/you,* formal)	gusta	+ { singular noun verb(s) (in the infinitive)
nos (*to us*) **os** (*to you,* informal, pl.) **les** (*to them/you,* formal and informal, pl.)	gustan	+ { plural noun

Notice that in the table above **gusta** is used when what is pleasing is a singular noun or an action (or series of actions) expressed in the infinitive form while **gustan** is used when what is pleasing is a plural noun.

A ella le **gusta la biología**, pero no le **gustan las matemáticas**.	*She likes **biology**, but she does not like **mathematics**.*
¿Te **gusta navegar** por el Internet en tu casa o en la biblioteca?	*Do you like **to surf** the Internet at home or at the library?*

If you want to clarify or emphasize the person(s) to whom something is pleasing, you may add a phrase introduced by the preposition **a** at the beginning of the sentence, especially if the indirect object pronoun may refer to several people as **le** and **les** do.

A Carolina le gustan las artes, pero **a Iván** le gustan los idiomas.	*Carolina likes the arts, but Iván likes languages.*
A ellos les gusta visitar a la familia, pero **a ustedes** no les gusta.	*They like to visit their family, but you do not like to do that.*

To specify to what degree you like something, say **mucho** *(a lot)* or **un poco** *(a little bit)* after **gusta(n)**. On the other hand, to express that you do not like something at all, say **nada** after **gusta(n)**.

Me gusta **mucho** la música clásica.	*I like classical music **a lot**.*
No me gusta **nada** la música rock.	*I do not like rock music **at all**.*

■ Asimilación

2-36 ¿Cuánto te gusta(n)? Indica cuánto te gustan las siguientes cosas y actividades. Al terminar, compara tus respuestas con las de un(a) compañero(a). ¿Tienen gustos *(likes)* semejantes o diferentes?

	ME GUSTA(N) MUCHO	ME GUSTA(N)	ME GUSTA(N) UN POCO	NO ME GUSTA(N)	NO ME GUSTA(N) NADA
1. el color amarillo	_____	_____	_____	_____	_____
2. el otoño	_____	_____	_____	_____	_____
3. mi hermano(a)	_____	_____	_____	_____	_____
4. tomar clases de noche	_____	_____	_____	_____	_____
5. los lunes	_____	_____	_____	_____	_____
6. el español	_____	_____	_____	_____	_____
7. mis profesores	_____	_____	_____	_____	_____
8. usar el Internet	_____	_____	_____	_____	_____

CD1-19 🎧 **2-37 Los gustos de Tere y los de sus padres** Escucha a Tere hablar de sus gustos y de los gustos de sus padres, y completa la tabla que sigue.

	le gusta(an)	no le gusta(n)
A Tere...		
	les gusta(n)	no les gusta(n)
A sus padres...		

■ Aplicaciones

2-38 ¡Qué difícil de complacer *(to please)*! Lean la conversación entre Daniel, Paca y Silvia, y llenen los espacios en blanco con el pronombre de objeto indirecto (**me**, **te**, **le**, etc.) y la forma correcta de **gustar.**

Silvia: ¿Quieren ir al Museo de Arte Moderno esta tarde?

Daniel: No, Silvia. A nosotros no _____ _____ el arte. Personalmente, a mí no _____ _____ nada las pinturas ni las esculturas modernas.

Paca: ¡No es cierto, Daniel! ¡A ti _____ _____ las pinturas de Frida Kahlo! Además, a mí _____ _____ mucho Picasso.

Daniel: ¿Qué dices? A Camilo y a Rosa sí que _____ _____ otras cosas, como Frida Kahlo, pero a mí no. A mí _____ _____ las actividades al aire libre *(outdoors)*.

Paca: Silvia, en realidad, a Daniel no _____ _____ hacer *(to do)* nada. En cambio, a mí _____ _____ tu idea. Vamos al museo.

Silvia: ¡Ay, Daniel! ¡Qué difícil de complacer eres!

2-39 Los gustos del (de la) profesor(a) De acuerdo con *(according to)* lo que saben *(you know)* sobre su profesor(a), escriban cinco oraciones sobre sus gustos. Incluyan oraciones afirmativas y negativas. Cuando terminen, lean las oraciones. El (La) profesor(a) debe decir si son **ciertas** o **falsas.**

MODELO   Profesor(a), a usted..., ¿verdad?

1. ...   4. ...
2. ...   5. ...
3. ...

2-40 Entre *(Between)* **tú y yo**

Paso 1: Escoge dos elementos de cada columna e indica si te gustan o no te gustan, en oraciones diferentes.

> MODELO   el azul
> *No me gusta el azul.*

A	**B**	**C**
la química	los viernes	tener prisa
el básquetbol	los cantantes hispanos	estudiar en esta universidad
la primavera	las personas perezosas	vivir en este estado
la música rap	las hamburguesas	beber cerveza

Paso 2: Túrnense para averiguar *(find out)* si al otro le gustan o no le gustan las cosas que escogieron. Tomen notas. Cuando terminen, preparen un informe escrito y preséntenlo a la clase.

> MODELO   E1: *Betsy, ¿te gusta el azul?*
> E2: *Sí, me gusta mucho el azul.*

In your written report you may use connectors such as **y** *(and)*, **pero** *(but)*, **sin embargo** *(however)*, and **por otro lado** *(on the other hand)*.

EN TU COMUNIDAD

Interview at least ten members of the community to find out how they feel about a particular person (a politician, a local leader, a person who has been in the news a lot, etc.) or thing (a product, a new plan, a new measure, etc.) and present your findings to the class.

■ Integración

 2-41 El (La) nuevo(a) empleado(a) *(employee)* Representa la siguiente situación con un(a) compañero(a).

You may talk about different topics you are familiar with such as leisure time activities, family, and routines.

El (La) nuevo(a) empleado(a)	**El (La) empleado(a) con experiencia**
This is your first day of work at a big company in a big city and you do not know anybody yet. A co-worker approaches you and strikes up a conversation. ■ Greet him/her. ■ Say your name and where you come from. ■ Find out about his/her likes and dislikes.	There is a new employee who does not know anybody in the company. Start a conversation with him/her and try to make a very good impression. ■ Greet him/her and introduce yourself. ■ Find out his/her name and where he/she comes from. ■ Find out about his/her likes and dislikes.

Review the list of adjectives used with **estar** and the expressions with **tener** you learned in the previous **Funciones y estructuras** section.

2-42 Reflexionando sobre tu comportamiento *(behavior)* ¿Qué te gusta hacer cuando te sientes de cierta manera *(you feel a certain way)*? ¿Y qué no te gusta hacer? Escribe una auto-reflexión sobre tu comportamiento.

> MODELO   *Cuando estoy enojado(a), me gusta... , pero no me gusta... Sin embargo, cuando tengo hambre me gusta..., pero no me gusta...*

IV. Vídeo: Los compañeros se conocen mejor

■ Preparación

A. Las imágenes Practice using contextual clues by answering the questions below about the brief portion of the video segment that you are about to see without audio.

1. Who is talking?
2. Where are they?
3. What are they doing?
4. What do you think they are talking about?

Now watch again, this time with audio. Were you correct?

B. ¿Qué compañero(a)? In this video segment the roommates reveal information about themselves and their first impressions of their new housemates.

Paso 1: As you watch the video, indicate who provides the following information about himself/herself: Alejandra (A), Antonio (T), Javier (J), Sofía (S) or Valeria (V).

_____ a. «Me gusta escuchar música y salir con amigas... ¡y con amigos!»

_____ b. «Me gusta leer y escribir. Quiero ser escritora.»

_____ c. «Tengo un hermano mayor. Tiene 29 años y es médico.»

_____ d. «A mí me gusta la naturaleza, las actividades al aire libre.»

_____ e. «Mi mamá es una modelo jubilada. Y mis dos hermanas practican el modelaje, como yo.»

Paso 2: Watch the video again and this time pay attention to what the roommates have to say about each other. Indicate WHO says the following about WHOM.

	¿QUIÉN?	¿SOBRE QUIÉN?
a. «...tu madre es blanca de pelo negro, y bajita como tú. Te pareces mucho a ella.»	_____	_____
b. «Él cree que es muy gracioso, pero a mí me parece muy pesado.»	_____	_____
c. «...ya somos amigos y compartimos el mismo cuarto.»	_____	_____
d. «Creo que a nadie le gusta —aunque a mí no me disgusta del todo.»	_____	_____
e. «Es una muchacha inteligente. Además, le gustan mis fotos.»	_____	_____
f. «...es una chica muy guapa... pero es insoportable.»	_____	_____
g. «Yo creo que a él no le gusta su carrera para nada.»	_____	_____

C. Un retrato más detallado de los compañeros After watching this video segment, you have learned more about each roommate. Now describe each one of them in detail, starting with his/her physical appearance and continuing with his/her personal traits. Do not forget to review the use of adjectives with **ser** and **tener**. When you finish, share your descriptions with a classmate.

D. Enfoque comunitario Get in touch with the office of international students in your school and interview one of their Spanish-speaking students. Ask him/her to describe his/her family and prepare for your instructor a brief summary of your findings in Spanish. If possible, invite the student to visit your class.

Nuestro hogar *(Our home)*

I. Vocabulario: Los espacios y los muebles de una casa *(house)*

Los espacios de una casa

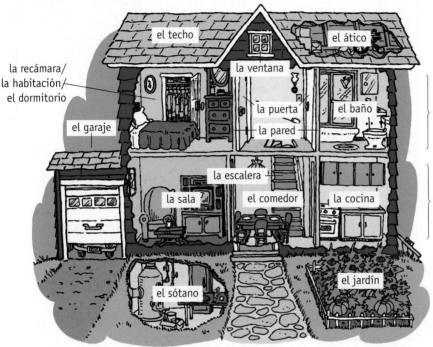

el techo
el ático
la recámara/ la habitación/ el dormitorio
la ventana
la puerta
el baño
la pared
el garaje
el primer piso
la escalera
la sala
el comedor
la cocina
la planta baja
el sótano
el jardín

SABOR REGIONAL

In some Spanish-speaking countries, **la planta baja** is called **el primer piso** and **el primer piso** is called **el segundo piso.**

SABOR REGIONAL

In Cuban, Dominican, and Puerto Rican Spanish, *armchair* is **butaca**. On the other hand, a closet is called **ropero** in Bolivia, Chile, Costa Rica, Ecuador, and Uruguay, while the word **cocina** also refers to *stove* in Argentina, Bolivia, Chile, Peru, Spain, and Uruguay.

Los muebles de una casa

las cortinas
la estufa
el refrigerador/ la nevera
el horno microondas
la lámpara
el espejo
el clóset / el armario
el estéreo
el cuadro
la mesa
el despertador
la silla
la cama
el estante/ el librero
la mesita/ mesa de noche/ mesa de luz
la mesita/ mesa de centro
la computadora/ el ordenador
el sofá
el sillón
la alfombra
el escritorio
el teléfono
la silla
el televisor

■ Asimilación

2-43 ¿Qué casa les conviene? Lee los anuncios *(ads)* y escoge la mejor opción para cada familia. Compara luego tus respuestas con las de un(a) compañero(a). ¿Están de acuerdo?

CASAS EN VENTA
1. ABASTOS UNA RECÁMARA, 2 BAÑOS, FACILIDADES 349.000 TEL. 684 5889

2. BOSQUES LOMAS, EXCELENTE, 3 RECÁMARAS, OPCIÓN 4, PISCINA, 4 BAÑOS, SALÓN JUEGOS, 1,900,000.00, OTRA EN LOMAS 1.600.000 TEL. 905 412 6818 Y 359 1333 CLAVE 19024

3. RESIDENCIA EN ZONA SUR, LAS ÁGUILAS, TORRENTES 127, ACABA-DOS DE LUJO, TODOS LOS SERVICIOS, CON PUERTA AUTOMÁTICA, COCINA EQUIPADA, ESTACIONAMIENTO PARA TRES AUTOS, TEL. 601 0494

4. ÁGUILAS AXOMIATLA, PRECIOSA RESIDENCIA, VIGILANCIA, VISTA PANORÁMICA, $ 2.200.000 TEL. 635 1952

5. BOSQUES LOMAS «LISTA PARA HABITARSE» TRES RECÁMARAS, ESTUDIO, 3 BAÑOS, $ 2.850.000 TEL. 540 3501 «DATO»]

---

1. Marcela tiene muchos amigos y necesita espacio para sus fiestas. Busca la casa más grande posible. Debe considerar el anuncio número ____.
2. El señor Gómez, su esposa y su hijo Fernando trabajan fuera de casa y tienen tres coches. Deben considerar el anuncio número ____.
3. Doña Mercedes recibe solamente una pensión y necesita comprar una casa económica. Debe considerar el anuncio número ____.

CD1-20 **2-44 La sala del (de la) profesor(a)** Tu profesor(a) va a describir lo que hay en su sala. Identifica los artículos que escuches.

____ sofá   ____ lámparas   ____ alfombras

____ sillas   ____ mesas   ____ cuadros

____ sillones   ____ espejos   ____ estantes

■ Aplicaciones

2-45 ¿Qué parte es? Túrnense para describir y adivinar los nombres de los diferentes espacios de una casa. **¡OJO!** ¡Tienen sólo dos oportunidades!

The following are some of the verbs you can use in this activity: **cocinar, charlar, estudiar, descansar, guardar** *(to keep, put away)* **el auto, comer, escuchar música, ver televisión, hablar por teléfono.**

MODELO   E1: *Es el lugar* (place) *donde come la familia.*
            E2: *¿La cocina?*
            E1: *No exactamente. La familia come, pero **no** prepara la comida ahí* (there).
            E2: *Entonces* (Then, what about), *¿el comedor?*
            E1: *¡Exactamente!*

2-46 Una casa a todo dar *(A really neat home)* Tu profesor(a) ha terminado de decorar su casa. Completa la descripción.

OPCIONES: sillas   sillones   cuadros   lámparas   estante

Su sala-comedor es muy bonita. En las paredes hay varios
_____ grandes. El comedor es moderno, con una mesa grande
y varias _____ de color negro. Hay dos _____, una
sobre una mesa y otra colgada *(hung)* del techo. Tiene también un par
de plantas y un _____ grande. Los _____ en la sala
son grandes y cómodos.

2-47 ¿Cómo es tu casa? Averigua *(Find out)* cómo es la casa (o el
apartamento) de tu compañero(a). Al terminar, preséntale un pequeño
informe al resto de la clase.

Remember to use questions such
as: **¿Cuántos pisos tiene? ¿Cuántas
habitaciones tiene? ¿Tiene
garaje?** etc.

■ Integración

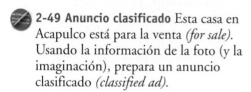
2-48 Mi casa ideal Representa la siguiente situación con un(a)
compañero(a).

Agente de bienes raíces	**Cliente**
(Real estate agent)	You and your spouse are looking for your first home. At this point you would like to buy a house with enough room for the children you expect to have in the near future. Find out what this agent has to offer. Don't rush into anything!
A customer is looking for a new home. Describe for him/her the house in the next activity and convince him/her that it is the best house on the market.	
Vocabulario opcional	**Vocabulario opcional**
To express admiration you may use expressions such as: **¡Es fantástico(a)! ¡Es perfecto(a)! ¡Es ideal! ¡Es maravilloso(a)!** *(It's wonderful!)*	To express what you are interested in, use **Quisiera** *(I would like)* or **Necesito** *(I need)*. To express doubt you may use expressions such as: **No sé** *(I don't know);* **Necesito consultarlo con mi esposo(a).** *(I have to consult with my husband/ wife.);* **Tengo que pensarlo.** *(I have to think about it.)*
To urge your client to buy the house you may say: **Cómprala ahora mismo.** *(Buy it right now.)* or **No deje pasar esta oportunidad.** *(Don't let this opportunity pass you by.)*	

SABOR REGIONAL

Padrísimo(a) is a colloquial term
used in Mexico to describe
something exceptionally nice or
convenient (like the word *cool* in
American English). In other countries, you can expect to find
different words to refer to the
same concept, for instance, **ché-
vere** in Venezuela, Colombia,
and Puerto Rico, **bárbaro** in Argentina, and **guay** in Spain.

EN TU COMUNIDAD

Find out about housing in your
community. You can consider issues such as cost, affordability,
availability, construction, and
public versus private. Visit real
estate agencies as well as government offices and then share
your findings with the class.

2-49 Anuncio clasificado Esta casa en
Acapulco está para la venta *(for sale)*.
Usando la información de la foto (y la
imaginación), prepara un anuncio
clasificado *(classified ad)*.

II. Funciones y estructuras: Talking about location with prepositions

La lámpara está **sobre** el escritorio. *The lamp is on the desk.*
La ventana está **detrás de** la cama. *The window is behind the bed.*
El libro está **al lado de** la silla. *The book is next to the chair.*

To talk about the specific location of things, people, or places, you may use the verb **estar** and the following prepositions.

Vocabulario práctico

al lado de *next to*	en *at, in, on*
arriba de *above*	enfrente de *in front of*
cerca de *close to*	entre *between*
debajo de *under*	fuera de *outside of*
dentro de *inside of*	lejos de *far from*
detrás de *behind*	sobre/encima de *on, over, above*

As you have seen before, when one of the prepositions that end in **de** is followed by the masculine singular definite article **el**, it contracts to **del**. Remember that this contraction is obligatory in Spanish.

La cocina está cerca **del** comedor.	*The kitchen is close **to the** dining room.*
La estufa está enfrente **del** refrigerador.	*The stove is in front **of the** refrigerator.*

■ Asimilación

CD1–21 **2-50 ¿Cuál de los dos dormitorios?** Escucha las oraciones e indica si se refieren al dormitorio A, al dormitorio B, o a los dos.

dormitorio A

dormitorio B

1. ... _____
2. ... _____
3. ... _____
4. ... _____
5. ... _____
6. ... _____
7. ... _____
8. ... _____

2-51 ¿Qué está... ? Miren el segundo dibujo *(Look at the second drawing)* de la página 83 y completen las siguientes oraciones.

Pay attention to the use of **de la** and **del**.

MODELO   La lámpara está al lado *del sillón*.

1. La mesa de centro está entre _____ y _____.
2. La computadora está encima _____.
3. Los libros están en _____.
4. En la cocina, la mesa está enfrente _____.
5. El teléfono está al lado _____.
6. El despertador está lejos _____.
7. La lámpara está detrás _____.
8. En el dormitorio, el cuadro está encima _____.

■ Aplicaciones

2-52 En la clase de español Escriban seis oraciones sobre la localización de algunos compañeros con relación a otros compañeros o a los muebles del salón de clase. Escriban oraciones ciertas y oraciones falsas. Luego, lean las oraciones y pídanle *(ask)* a un(a) compañero(a) que diga si son ciertas o falsas.

MODELO   E1: *Michael está detrás de JoAnne.*
          E2: *Falso.*

2-53 ¡Ésta es mi universidad! Usen la siguiente información para hacer preguntas sobre los diferentes edificios de su universidad y sobre su localización. Túrnense para hacer las preguntas.

MODELO   Administración de Empresas
        E1: *¿Cuál es el edificio de Administración de Empresas?*
        E2: *Es Partridge Hall.*
        E1: *¿Dónde está Partridge Hall?*
        E2: *Está al lado de Calcia Hall.*

1. Artes
2. Ciencias Naturales
3. Humanidades
4. Ingeniería
5. Matemáticas
6. Ciencias Sociales
7. Comunicaciones
8. Educación
9. Derecho
10. Educación Física

2-54 La habitación de mi compañero(a)

The following expressions may help you talk about the specific location of your room furniture: **a la izquierda de** *(to the left of)* y **a la derecha de** *(to the right of)*.

Paso 1: Averigua qué muebles tiene tu compañero(a) en su habitación y dónde están localizados. Toma notas.

MODELO   E1: *¿Tienes una computadora en tu habitación?*
        E2: *Sí, tengo una computadora.*
        E1: *¿Dónde está?*
        E2: *Está al lado de mi cama, sobre el escritorio.*

Paso 2: Ahora, trata de dibujar un plano de la habitación de tu compañero(a). ¿Qué opina él/ella de tu representación artística?

■ Integración

2-55 La universidad Túrnense para hacer preguntas sobre la localización de algunos edificios en su universidad. Sean *(Be)* lo más específicos que puedan.

MODELO   E1: *¿Dónde está el edificio... ?*
        E2: *Está entre... y... , detrás de...*

2-56 Mi ciudad o pueblo ¿Recuerdas a Octavio, el hijo de la familia Zapata Robles de Oaxaca, México, con la cual *(with which)* vas a vivir este verano? Él quiere saber más sobre tu ciudad o pueblo porque le interesa visitarte en el futuro. Escribe una breve descripción siguiendo el modelo.

MODELO   *Octavio, yo vivo en... , en el estado de... Mi pueblo está al lado de la ciudad de...*

III. Funciones y estructuras: Expressing obligation with *tener que...* and *hay que...*

Este fin de semana...

Arminda **tiene que** lavar la ropa...
*Arminda **has to** do laundry...*

y **hay que** limpiar la casa.
*and my house **has to be** cleaned.*

The verb **tener** can also be used to talk about obligations and things people have to do. To express this, use the following structure: a form of **tener** + **que** + a verb in the infinitive.

Celia **tiene que** cocinar y nosotras **tenemos que** aspirar.

*Celia **has to** cook and we **have to** vacuum.*

Mi padre **tiene que** cortar el césped y yo **tengo que** lavar el carro.

*My father **has to** cut the grass and I **have to** wash the car.*

Here are some household chores you can use to talk about obligations.

Vocabulario práctico

arreglar la casa *to tidy up the house*

aspirar *to vacuum*

cocinar *to cook*

cortar el césped *to cut the grass*

hacer la cama *to make the bed*

lavar el carro/coche *to wash the car*

lavar los platos *to do the dishes*

lavar la ropa *to do laundry*

limpiar la casa *to clean the house*

sacar la basura *to take out the garbage*

Another verb that can be used to talk about obligations is **hay**. It is used in the following structure: **hay que** + verb in the infinitive. Unlike the structure **tener** + **que** + infinitive, this structure is used when the speaker does not want to or cannot specify who is in charge of doing the action. It is equivalent to the English expressions *has/have to be* + past participle and *it is necessary to.*

¡Chicos, **hay que** limpiar el apartamento antes de la fiesta!

Hay que cortar el césped hoy.

*Guys, the apartment **has to be** cleaned before the party!*

It is necessary to cut the grass today.

When you use this structure, only the verb **tener** changes endings. The other verb remains in the infinitive form. You have learned other structures that work similarly: **deber** *(should, must)* + infinitive and **gustar** *(to be pleasing)* + infinitive.

SABOR REGIONAL

Other words for *grass* are **pasto** (Argentina, Chile, Colombia, Mexico, and Peru), **yerba** (Cuba), and **grama** (El Salvador, Guatemala, Honduras, Puerto Rico, and Venezuela).

REMEMBER

In **Capítulo preparatorio** you learned that **hay** *(there is, there are)* is an impersonal form of the verb **haber** that is invariable when used to express existence and to talk about quantities: **En mi casa *hay* dos televisores.** *In my house **there are** two television sets.*

SABOR REGIONAL

The word **carro** is more commonly used in Latin America whereas **coche** is more commonly used in Spain.

■ Asimilación

CD1–22 **2-57 Recomendaciones** Escucha lo que dicen varios de tus amigos y escoge la recomendación más lógica que les puedes dar. Luego compara tus respuestas con las de un(a) compañero(a).

_____ a. Tienes que cortar el césped.

_____ b. Tienes que cocinar.

_____ c. Tienes que limpiar la casa.

_____ d. Tienes que arreglar la casa.

_____ e. Tienes que lavar los platos.

_____ f. Tienes que lavar la ropa.

2-58 Un estudiante universitario exitoso (_successful_) ¿Qué hay que hacer para ser un estudiante universitario exitoso? Indica si las siguientes sugerencias son lógicas o no. Escribe **sí** o **no.**

Para ser un estudiante universitario exitoso, hay que...

_____ estudiar regularmente.

_____ tener mucho dinero.

_____ saber usar una computadora.

_____ ser disciplinado.

_____ tomar buenas notas en clase.

_____ comprar un buen carro.

■ Aplicaciones

2-59 La agenda de Josefina Túrnense para hacer y responder a preguntas sobre la agenda de Josefina para esta semana. También traten de mencionar otras cosas relacionadas que ella tiene que hacer.

lunes	a.m.	ir a la cita con el doctor
	p.m.	cenar con los Vélez Fernández
martes	a.m.	
	p.m.	limpiar la casa
miércoles	a.m.	confirmar la reservación en el hotel en Cozumel
	p.m.	asistir a la clase de administración y supervisión
jueves	a.m.	desayunar con Adalberto
	p.m.	
viernes	a.m.	escribir el informe para la clase
	p.m.	lavar la ropa
sábado	a.m.	visitar a mis padres
	p.m.	comprar el sillón
domingo	a.m.	llamar a la hermana de Adalberto
	p.m.	¡descansar!

As in English, the verb **hacer** _(to do)_ is not used in most answers to questions that include this verb: **¿Qué tienes que** _hacer_**? Tengo que estudiar para un examen.** _What do you have to do? I have to study for a test._

REMEMBER

To indicate on what day an action takes place, use the definite article **el** before the day of the week: **el lunes, el martes, el miércoles**, etc.

MODELO   E1: _¿Qué tiene que hacer Josefina el lunes por la mañana?_
           E2: _Ella tiene que ir a la cita con el doctor. Ella está enferma._

2-60 Las responsabilidades profesionales Piensen en las cosas que hacen las personas que tienen las siguientes profesiones y completen las oraciones. Luego, indiquen qué cosas son necesarias para tener estas profesiones. Al terminar, preséntenle sus respuestas al resto de la clase.

MODELO   Los profesores *tienen que enseñar varias clases, corregir exámenes y preparar lecciones.* Para ser profesor *hay que comprender a los estudiantes.*

1. Los actores...
   Para ser actor o actriz...
2. Los médicos...
   Para ser médico...
3. Los cocineros...
   Para ser cocinero...
4. Los vendedores...
   Para ser vendedor(a)...
5. Los enfermeros...
   Para ser enfermero(a)...
6. Los periodistas...
   Para ser periodista...

2-61 Este fin de semana

Paso 1: Haz una lista de seis cosas que tienes que hacer este fin de semana.

MODELO   *Tengo que ir a la biblioteca.*

1. ...   3. ...   5. ...
2. ...   4. ...   6. ...

Paso 2: Ahora, averigua si tu compañero(a) tiene que hacer las mismas *(same)* cosas. Toma notas. Cuando termines, prepara un informe y preséntalo a la clase. ¿Los estudiantes tienen obligaciones semejantes o diferentes?

MODELO: E1: *Zach, ¿tienes que ir a la biblioteca este fin de semana?*
           E2: *Sí, tengo que ir a la biblioteca este fin de semana.*
           o   *No, no tengo que ir a la biblioteca.*

■ Integración

2-62 Consejos prácticos *(Practical pieces of advice)*

Paso 1: Individualmente, inventa *(make up)* una situación un poco trágica. ¡Incluye muchos detalles!

MODELO   *Soy una persona muy tímida. No me gusta hablar con las personas y soy introvertido. Nunca voy a lugares públicos.*

Paso 2: En grupos de tres o cuatro estudiantes, túrnense para leer las situaciones y reaccionar con consejos prácticos.

MODELO   E1: ...
           E2: *Tienes que hablar con más personas e ir a muchos lugares. También tienes que ver a un sicólogo.*
           E3: *Pues yo creo que tienes que...*

2-63 Las obligaciones de mi familia Escribe un párrafo sobre las obligaciones que tienen algunos miembros de tu familia la próxima semana.

Use connectors such as **por otro lado** *(on the other hand)*, **en contraste** *(in contrast)*, **por el contrario** *(on the contrary)*, and **sin embargo** *(however)*.

MODELO   *El lunes por la mañana tengo que asistir a mi clase de economía. Por la tarde tengo que... Por otro lado, el lunes por la mañana mi padre tiene que...*

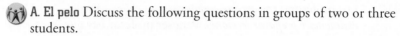

IV. Lectura: *La casa en Mango Street*—Inmigrantes mexicanos en los Estados Unidos

Antes de leer

A. El pelo Discuss the following questions in groups of two or three students.

1. Do you think one's type of hair has anything to do with one's personality? Explain.

You have already learned the words **corto** *(short)* and **largo** *(long)*. The following words are also used to describe hair type: **liso/lacio** *(straight)*, **rizado** *(curly)*, **teñido** *(color treated)*, **calvo** *(bald)*.

2. Complete the following chart with information about the members of your group.

Nombre del (de la) compañero(a)	Tipo (o estilo) de pelo	Personalidad (dos adjetivos)

CRITICAL THINKING SKILLS

Analyzing Use cognates to anticipate the content of the reading.

READING STRATEGY

Skimming and Scanning You do not have to understand every word. Concentrate on identifying the main points of the story and answering the comprehension questions that follow.

B. Cognados With a partner, make a list of all the cognates you can find in the reading. Based on your findings, what do you expect this story to be about?

A leer

Sandra Cisneros

Las familias hispanas en los Estados Unidos tratan de mantener *(try to maintain)* su cultura y sus tradiciones, al mismo tiempo que *(while)* se integran a su nueva vida *(new life)* en Norteamérica. Sandra Cisneros es una autora chicana que nació en Chicago en 1954. El siguiente es un fragmento de su libro *La casa en Mango Street*.

La casa en Mango Street (fragmento)

Pelos

Cada uno en mi familia tiene pelo diferente. El de mi papá **se para** en el aire como escoba. Y yo, el mío es **flojo.** Nunca **hace caso de** broches o diademas. El pelo de Carlos es grueso y derechito, no necesita **peinárselo.** El de Nenny es **resbaloso,** se escurre de tu mano, y Kiki, que es el menor, tiene pelo de **peluche.** Pero el pelo de mi madre, el pelo de mi madre, es de rositas en botón, como **rueditas** de caramelo todo rizado y bonito porque **se hizo anchoas todo el día,** fragante para meter en él la nariz cuando ella está **abrazándote** y te sientes **segura,** es el **olor** cálido del pan antes de **hornearlo,** es el olor de cuando ella te **hace un campito** en su cama aún tibia de su piel, y una duerme a su lado, cae la lluvia afuera y papá **ronca.** El ronquido, la lluvia y el pelo de mamá oloroso a pan.

sticks up
loose / pays attention to

to comb it / slippery
plush
little wheels
made anchovies the whole day
hugging you
safe / smell / baking it
makes some space
snores

■ ¿Entendiste bien?

C. Ideas principales Complete the following chart with the information found in the text.

Personajes *(Characters)*	Tipo de pelo
Papá	*se para en el aire*
Narradora *(Narrator)*	
Carlos	
Nenny	
Kiki	*de peluche*
Mamá	

D. Inferencias In groups of three or four students, complete the following chart describing the personalities of the different characters introduced in the previous novel fragment.

Personajes	Personalidad
Papá	*serio*
Narradora	
Carlos	
Nenny	
Kiki	*simpática*
Mamá	

E. Actividad de extensión Following Sandra Cisneros' model, write a description of the personalities of different members of your family based on the type of hair they have.

CRITICAL THINKING SKILLS

Making Associations and Creating Use the author's idea by applying it in an imaginative way.

La familia

el (la) abuelo(a)	*grandfather/ grandmother*
el (la) cuñado(a)	*brother-in-law/ sister-in-law*
el (la) esposo(a)	*husband/wife*
el (la) hermanastro(a)	*stepbrother/stepsister*
el (la) hermano(a) (mayor/menor)	*(older/younger) brother/sister*
el (la) hijo(a) (mayor/menor)	*(older/younger) son/ daughter*
la madrastra	*stepmother*
la madre/mamá	*mother*
el (la) nieto(a)	*grandson/granddaughter*
el padrastro	*stepfather*
el padre/papá	*father*
el (la) pariente	*relative*
el (la) primo(a)	*cousin*
el (la) sobrino(a)	*nephew/niece*
el (la) suegro(a)	*father-in-law/ mother-in-law*
el (la) tío(a)	*uncle/aunt*

Descripciones

alto	*tall*
bajo	*short* (height)
bonito	*pretty, beautiful*
corto	*short* (length)
delgado	*thin*
difícil	*difficult*
fácil	*easy*
feo	*ugly*
flaco(a)	*skinny*
gordo	*fat*
grande	*big*
guapo	*handsome*
largo	*long*
moreno	*dark-haired*
nuevo	*new*
pequeño	*small*
rubio	*blond(e)*
el pelo blanco	*gray hair*
el pelo castaño	*brown hair*
el pelo negro	*black hair*
el pelo rojo	*red hair*
el pelo rubio	*blond hair*

Rasgos personales / *Personal traits*

bueno	*good*
diligente	*diligent*
cómico/gracioso/de buen humor	*funny*
extrovertido	*extroverted*
inteligente	*intelligent*
listo	*smart*
malo	*bad, mean*
perezoso	*lazy*
tímido	*shy*
tonto/estúpido	*foolish, stupid*
trabajador(a)	*hardworking*
serio	*serious*
simpático	*nice*

¿Cómo estás? / *How are you?*

aburrido	*bored*
alegre/contento/feliz	*happy*
cansado	*tired*
deprimido	*depressed*
emocionado	*excited*
enfermo	*sick*
enojado	*angry*
listo	*ready*
nervioso	*nervous*
ocupado	*busy*
preocupado	*worried*
triste	*sad*

Más conectores

en cambio	*instead*
mientras que	*while, whereas*

La casa / *House*

el ático	*attic*
el baño	*bathroom*
la cocina	*kitchen*
el comedor	*dining room*
la escalera	*stairs*
el garaje	*garage*
el jardín	*garden*
la pared	*wall*
la planta baja	*first floor*
el primer piso	*second floor*
la puerta	*door*
la recámara / la habitación / el dormitorio	*bedroom*
la sala	*living room*
el sótano	*basement*
el techo	*roof*
la ventana	*window*

Los muebles / *Furniture*

la alfombra	*carpet*
el armario / clóset	*closet*
la cama	*bed*
la computadora / el ordenador	*computer*

las cortinas	*curtains*
el cuadro	*painting*
el despertador	*alarm clock*
el escritorio	*desk*
el espejo	*mirror*
el estante	*bookcase*
el estéreo	*stereo*
la estufa	*stove*
el horno microondas	*microwave oven*
la lámpara	*lamp*
la mesa	*table*
la mesa de centro	*coffee table*
la mesa de noche / mesa de luz	*bedside table*
el refrigerador / la nevera	*refrigerator*
la silla	*chair*
el sillón	*armchair*
el sofá	*sofa*
el teléfono	*telephone*
el televisor	*TV*

Exclamaciones

¡Es fantástico!
¡Es ideal!
¡Es maravilloso!
¡Es perfecto!
 It's wonderful!

Los quehaceres del hogar | *Household chores*

arreglar la casa	*to tidy up the house*
aspirar	*to vacuum*
cocinar	*to cook*
cortar el césped	*to cut the grass*
hacer la cama	*to make the bed*
lavar el carro/coche	*to wash the car*
lavar los platos	*to do the dishes*
lavar la ropa	*to do laundry*
limpiar la casa	*to clean the house*
sacar la basura	*to take out the garbage*

Funciones y estructuras

Expresiones con **tener**, p. 73
Preposiciones de lugar, p. 86

Puesta en acción

SITUACIÓN:	You have decided to host a Mexican exchange student in your home.
MISIÓN:	To establish contact with this student, find out about his background, learn about his culture, and exchange information about each other's family and life.
DESTREZAS *(SKILLS):*	Reading and responding to electronic communications, providing personal information, and researching information.

A. Un mensaje electrónico. José Francisco Reyes Galindo, el estudiante de intercambio mexicano, te envía el siguiente mensaje.

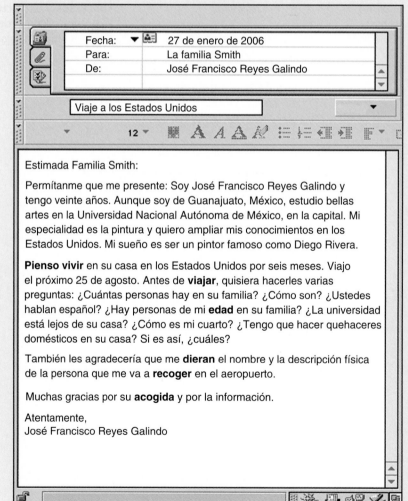

Fecha:	27 de enero de 2006
Para:	La familia Smith
De:	José Francisco Reyes Galindo

Viaje a los Estados Unidos

12

Estimada Familia Smith:

Permítanme que me presente: Soy José Francisco Reyes Galindo y tengo veinte años. Aunque soy de Guanajuato, México, estudio bellas artes en la Universidad Nacional Autónoma de México, en la capital. Mi especialidad es la pintura y quiero ampliar mis conocimientos en los Estados Unidos. Mi sueño es ser un pintor famoso como Diego Rivera.

I am planning on living
travel

Pienso vivir en su casa en los Estados Unidos por seis meses. Viajo el próximo 25 de agosto. Antes de **viajar**, quisiera hacerles varias preguntas: ¿Cuántas personas hay en su familia? ¿Cómo son? ¿Ustedes

age

hablan español? ¿Hay personas de mi **edad** en su familia? ¿La universidad está lejos de su casa? ¿Cómo es mi cuarto? ¿Tengo que hacer quehaceres domésticos en su casa? Si es así, ¿cuáles?

give me
pick up

También les agradecería que me **dieran** el nombre y la descripción física de la persona que me va a **recoger** en el aeropuerto.

welcome

Muchas gracias por su **acogida** y por la información.

Atentamente,
José Francisco Reyes Galindo

B. ¿Dónde está Guanajuato? Busquen *(Find)* en el mapa en la página vi la ciudad de origen de José Francisco (Guanajuato). Expliquen dónde está, usando las preposiciones de lugar **cerca de**, **lejos de**, **al lado de**, etc.

También pueden usar las frases **al norte de** *(north of)*, **al sur de** *(south of)*, **al este de** *(east of)* y **al oeste de** *(west of)*.

C. El Estado de Guanajuato. Busca información en la biblioteca o en el Internet acerca del Estado de Guanajuato.

CRITICAL THINKING SKILLS

Researching Find other opportunities to learn about Mexico.

Guanajuato	
Población	
Industrias	
Atracciones turísticas	
Fiestas *(Holidays)*	
Ciudades importantes	
Otros datos importantes	

D. Un artista famoso Diego Rivera, the artist that José Francisco mentioned in his message, is one of the most famous Mexican painters of the twentieth century. To understand better why José Francisco wishes to be like him one day, find out about Diego Rivera's life and works. Complete the chart below with the information you find.

Biografía de Diego Rivera	
Fecha y lugar de su nacimiento	
Fecha y lugar de su muerte *(death)*	
Tipo de pintura	
Lugar donde están sus pinturas hoy	
Temas principales de sus pinturas	
Nombre de su esposa	
Profesión de su esposa	

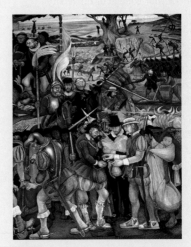

You may want to visit one of the many Diego Rivera sites on the web to find the information requested.

E. La respuesta Write a letter to José Francisco and provide the information he requested in his electronic message. Follow these steps.

Paso 1: Greet him **(Estimado José Francisco:),** identify yourself, and say how you are today.

Paso 2: Answer the questions José Francisco posed:

1. ¿Cuántas personas hay en su familia?
2. ¿Cómo son?
3. ¿Ustedes hablan español?
4. ¿Hay personas de mi edad *(age)* en su familia?
5. ¿La universidad está lejos de su casa?
6. ¿Cómo es mi cuarto?
7. ¿Tengo que hacer quehaceres domésticos en su casa? Si es así, ¿cuáles?

The person who is going to pick you up at the airport = **la persona que te va a recoger en el aeropuerto**

Paso 3: Now describe the person who is going to pick him up at the airport: yourself. Give as many details as possible. Then, finish the letter with the appropriate expressions (**Esperamos conocerte pronto. Atentamente** [your name]).

Paso 4: Reread the letter and make sure you use connectors such as **y** *(and)*, **también** *(also)*, **pero** *(but)*, **sin embargo** *(however)*, **por otro lado** *(on the other hand)*, and **finalmente** *(finally)*. When you have your first draft ready, exchange drafts with a classmate. Use the following checklist as a guide to correct his or her work.

- Did your partner answer all of José Francisco's questions?
- Is the letter clear and well organized?
- Underline all the adjectives. Do they agree in number and gender with the noun they describe? Then, circle all the verbs. Are they properly conjugated?

When you get the first draft back from your classmate, make all the necessary revisions and give the second draft to your instructor for additional feedback.

F. El árbol genealógico *(family tree)* **de José Francisco.** You just opened the attachment with José Francisco's family tree. You printed it out and, unfortunately, ended up with half of the tree on one sheet and the other half on another. Have one of your classmates describe one of the halves to you and complete the illustration. Then do the same so your classmate can complete his/her part of the illustration. Look at the model to know how to ask for and provide clues. One of you must turn the book upside-down. Do not let your classmate see your part of the family tree!

MODELO
E1: *¿Cómo se llama el abuelo paterno de José Francisco?*
E2: *Se llama Alberto Reyes Gómez.*
E1: *¿Cuántos años tiene?*
E2: *Él tiene setenta y ocho años.*

Estudiante 1

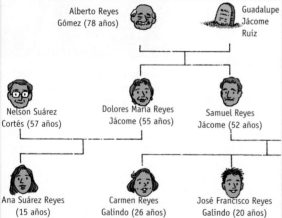

Estudiante 2

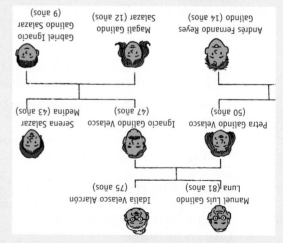

Unidad 2

Puerto Rico y España

In this unit you will learn how to plan a vacation in Spanish, to find your way around a Spanish-speaking city, and to get access to goods and services. Also, you will talk about daily routines and express your preferences with regard to clothing, food, and leisure activities. The readings will give you a taste of everyday life in Puerto Rico and Spain, and the videos will show you people giving directions and shopping for clothing in these countries. At the end of the unit you will plan the logistics of a business meeting in Puerto Rico. You will also be able to connect with your community by researching services available to Spanish speakers at local businesses and government agencies.

La vida diaria

Capítulo 3

Para comenzar

- Observa las fotografías de Puerto Rico y completa la siguiente oración.
- Puerto Rico es un lugar ideal para..., ... y...

¿Dónde y cuándo?

In this chapter you will learn . . .

- how to talk about location and destination
- how to tell time and express frequency
- how to shop
- how to talk about food and order in a restaurant
- how to talk about future plans
- about tourism opportunities in Puerto Rico

	TEMA 1 Orientándonos en la ciudad	**TEMA 2** De compras	**TEMA 3** La comida
Vocabulario	Lugares de interés	Las compras y las formas de pago	Vamos a comer
Funciones y estructuras	Talking about location and destination with the verbs **estar** and **ir** Telling time	Talking about daily activities with irregular **yo** form verbs Adverbs of frequency	Talking about daily activities with e→i stem-changing verbs Talking about future plans
Lecturas y vídeo	Perspectivas: Turismo en Puerto Rico	Vídeo: El día de la primera excursión en Puerto Rico	Lectura: La dieta mediterránea

Las playas de Isla Verde

Las tiendas de artesanías

El Viejo San Juan

Enfoque

A. ¿Qué sabes ya de Puerto Rico? Antes de ver el vídeo, empareja los siguientes lugares con sus descripciones. Cuando termines *(When you finish)*, compara tus respuestas con las de otro(a) estudiante(a).

Lugar	**¿Qué es?**
1. Puerto Rico	la capital del país
2. El Yunque	una ciudad
3. Ponce	una fortaleza
4. San Felipe del Morro	un bosque tropical
5. San Juan	una isla

B. Puerto Rico con más detalle Lee las siguientes frases sobre los lugares de la actividad anterior. Luego, mira el vídeo y escribe el número del lugar (1–5) que corresponde a cada frase. **¡OJO!** Tienes que usar uno de los números dos veces *(twice)*.

_____ a. un refugio de muchas especies de animales raros

_____ b. Isla del Encanto

_____ c. un importante destino turístico debido a sus monumentos históricos y atractivas playas

_____ d. La Perla del Sur

_____ e. una de las ciudades españolas más antiguas de las Américas

_____ f. construida en el siglo XVI por los españoles

C. Mis preferencias y las de la clase Sigue los siguientes pasos para determinar tus preferencias y las de tus compañeros de clase sobre lugares de interés en Puerto Rico.

Paso 1: Pon en orden los lugares mencionados en el vídeo según el interés que tienes en visitarlos. (1 = de mayor interés; 5 = de menor interés)

_____ San Juan   _____ El Yunque

_____ Ponce   _____ las playas puertorriqueñas

_____ San Felipe del Morro

Paso 2: En grupos de cuatro o cinco estudiantes, comparen sus preferencias. Determinen cuál es el lugar favorito de su grupo y escojan a un(a) representante.

For more info, you may want to check the **Temas** site: http://temas.heinle.com

Orientándonos en la ciudad

I. Vocabulario: Lugares de interés

SABOR REGIONAL

Other Spanish words for *parking lot* are **el aparcamiento** (Spain) and **el parqueadero** (Colombia and Panama).

Vocabulario práctico

**Puntos de referencia
(Reference points)**

el bar / la barra *bar*

el cajero automático *automatic teller machine*

el centro *downtown*

la cuadra/manzana *city block*

el edificio *building*

la esquina *corner*

la estación de (trenes/autobús/ metro) *(train/bus/subway) station*

la lavandería *laundromat*

la librería *bookstore*

la parada de (autobús/tren/ metro) *(bus/train/subway) stop*

la peluquería / el salón de belleza *barber shop, beauty parlor*

el semáforo *traffic light*

la tienda / el almacén *store*

la tintorería *dry cleaners*

■ Asimilación

3-1 ¿Dónde? Indiquen dónde ustedes pueden *(where you can)* obtener los siguientes servicios.

_____ 1. Como platos deliciosos en...	a. el gimnasio
_____ 2. Recibo atención médica en...	b. la biblioteca
_____ 3. Hago ejercicios aeróbicos en...	c. la iglesia
_____ 4. Leo libros y estudio en...	d. el centro comercial
_____ 5. Reservo una habitación en...	e. el cine
_____ 6. Asisto a un servicio religioso en...	f. el hotel
_____ 7. Miro una película de acción en...	g. el hospital
_____ 8. Compro ropa *(clothes)* en...	h. el restaurante

CD1–24 **3-2 ¿Adónde tiene que ir** *(to go)*? Tu profesor(a) tiene mucho que hacer hoy. Indica los lugares adonde tiene que ir.

_____ cajero automático	__✓__ restaurante
_____ hotel	__✓__ supermercado
_____ lavandería	_____ hospital
_____ cine	__✓__ peluquería
_____ iglesia	

■ Aplicaciones

3-3 ¿Dónde...? Túrnense para hacer y para responder a las preguntas.

MODELO   nadar
            E1: *¿Dónde nadas?*
            E2: *Nado en el gimnasio High Energy.*

1. ver películas
2. buscar un libro
3. estudiar
4. hacer compras
5. recibir servicios médicos
6. rezar *(to pray)*

3-4 Puntos de referencia Completen las oraciones con el punto de refe-rencia más apropiado. **¡OJO!** En algunos casos deben usar la forma plural de la palabra.

OPCIONES: centro   edificio   iglesia   cuadra   parque   esquina
               plaza   estacionamiento

Hola, me llamo Martín Díaz. Vivo más o menos a diez _____ de la escuela, en un _____ de diez pisos, y trabajo en el supermercado que está en la _____ de la avenida San Mateo y la calle Toribio. Me gusta mi barrio porque tiene muchos _____ y porque está cerca del _____.

3-5 En San Juan Observen el mapa del Viejo San Juan (zona histórica) y contesten las preguntas.

MODELO   E1: *¿Dónde puedo* (Where can I) *comer platos típicos de Puerto Rico?*
E2: *En el restaurante El Patio de Sam.*

1. ¿Dónde puedo ver *(to see)* una exposición de arte?
2. ¿Dónde puedo hacer unas compras?
3. ¿Dónde puedo comprar unas aspirinas?
4. ¿Dónde puedo cambiar un cheque?
5. ¿Dónde puedo obtener información acerca de Puerto Rico?

Ahora, observen el mapa otra vez y completen la siguiente tarjeta postal *(postcard)*.

¡Hola a todos!

Estamos felices en Puerto Rico. Todo aquí es muy bonito. Hay muchos lugares históricos como ____ y ____. También hay muchas tiendas como ____ y, desde luego, excelentes restaurantes como ____, donde sirven la deliciosa comida de este país.

Un abrazo,

Juan Carlos

■ Integración

3-6 ¿Qué lugares de interés hay en esta ciudad? En parejas, discutan y decidan cuáles son los **cinco** lugares más importantes de su ciudad.

MODELO   E1: *El museo de arte moderno es un lugar de interés para los turistas, ¿no?*
E2: *Sí, estoy de acuerdo.*

EN TU COMUNIDAD

Prepare a brief report on the services available for Spanish speakers at prominent historical landmarks in your town or region.

3-7 Lugares de interés Preparen un folleto *(pamphlet)* para los turistas hispanos de su ciudad con las siguientes recomendaciones e información general. ¡El diseño *(design)* del folleto debe ser atractivo! Incluyan un título, un mapa del centro de la ciudad y una lista de los lugares de interés con indicaciones *(directions)* generales.

MODELO   *Lugares de interés en Boston*
Algunos lugares de interés en esta ciudad son:
■ *La iglesia Old North. Está en la calle Salem cerca del puerto.*
■ *El Museo de Arte de Boston está en la calle Huntington cerca de la Universidad Northeastern.*

II. Funciones y estructuras: Talking about location and destination with the verbs *estar* and *ir*

¿Dónde **está** Inés? Ella **está** en el salón de belleza?
*Where **is** Ines? She **is** at the beauty parlor.*

As you learned in **Capítulo 2, Tema 2**, one of the uses of the verb **estar** is to talk about the location of people and things.

Mis primas **están** en la iglesia.
La pintura **está** en el Museo de Arte de Ponce.

*My cousins **are** at church.*
*The painting **is** at the Museum of Art of Ponce.*

REMEMBER

Do you recall how to conjugate the irregular verb **estar**? Its six forms are: (yo) **estoy**, (tú) **estás**, (él/ella/usted) **está**, (nosotros[as]) **estamos**, (vosotros[as]) **estáis**, and (ellos[as]/ustedes) **están**.

Ellos **van** al parque por la tarde.
*They **go** to the park in the afternoon.*

The verb **ir** *(to go)*, on the other hand, is used to express movement and destination. Like **estar**, this verb has an irregular conjugation.

Note that the irregular **yo** form of **ir** (**voy**) ends in **-oy**, like the **yo** forms of **ser** (**soy**) and **estar** (**estoy**).

yo **voy**	nosotros(as) **vamos**
tú **vas**	vosotros(as) **vais**
él/ella/usted **va**	ellos(as)/ustedes **van**

¿Adónde **vas** los sábados, Milagros?
Siempre **voy** al centro con mi madre.

*Where do you **go** on Saturdays, Milagros?*
*I always **go** downtown with my mother.*

When making a statement, the verb **ir** is used in the following structure.

ir + **a** + article + name of place

Hoy **vamos a la biblioteca** y mañana **vamos al cine**.

*Today we **go to the library** and tomorrow we **go to the movie theater**.*

Note that when the preposition **a** is followed by the masculine singular article **el**, it is necessary to form the contraction **al**. As you may remember, the same applies to **de** + **el** (= **del**).

■ Asimilación

3-8 En el Viejo San Juan Mira el mapa del Viejo San Juan de la página 104 y determina si las siguientes oraciones son ciertas (**C**) o falsas (**F**).

_____ 1. La Tienda el Artesano está en la calle Tetuán.

_____ 2. La Iglesia de San Francisco está en la esquina de la calle San Francisco y la calle Tanca.

_____ 3. La Fortaleza está cerca del Hard Rock Café.

_____ 4. La Catedral de San Juan está entre las calles Cristo y San José.

_____ 5. El Paseo de la Princesa no está lejos de los muelles de barcos de crucero.

_____ 6. El Patio de Sam está al este _(east)_ del Museo Pablo Casals.

CD1–25

3-9 Un día normal Escucha la descripción que da Noel sobre un día normal en la vida de su familia. Luego, indica si las siguientes acciones se refieren a Noel, a su madre, a su padre o a su hermana.

_____ 1. Va al gimnasio.

_____ 2. Va al hospital por la tarde.

_____ 3. Va a la escuela.

_____ 4. Va a la casa de una amiga.

_____ 5. Va a la universidad.

_____ 6. Va a la escuela de baile.

_____ 7. Va a la oficina.

_____ 8. Va al supermercado

■ Aplicaciones

3-10 ¿Dónde estamos? Túrnense para leer las claves y decir dónde están las personas indicadas. Usen el verbo **estar** correctamente.

MODELO   E1: _Ramiro tiene hambre y desea comer._
                   E2: _Ramiro está en el restaurante._

1. Sara y Penélope tienen que enviarle un paquete a su amigo de Puerto Rico.

2. Nosotros tenemos que depositar dinero en nuestra cuenta de ahorros.

3. Argelio está de vacaciones en San Juan de Puerto Rico y tiene sueño.

4. Yo estoy enfermo y necesito comprar una medicina.

5. Ellas necesitan lavar la ropa lo antes posible.

6. Tú tienes que tomar el autobús para llegar a tu trabajo.

3-11 Los fines de semana

Paso 1: Escribe por lo menos seis oraciones sobre los lugares a los que generalmente vas durante los fines de semana.

1. …	4. …
2. …	5. …
3. …	6. …

Paso 2: Ahora, entrevista a tu compañero(a) para saber si él/ella va a los mismos lugares. Tomen notas. Cuando terminen, preparen un informe y preséntenlo a la clase.

MODELO   E1: *Martín, ¿vas a las tiendas los fines de semana?*
          E2: *Sí, voy a las tiendas los fines de semana.*
          o   *No, no voy a las tiendas los fines de semana.*

3-12 ¿Dónde están o adónde van? Túrnense para decir en dónde están ustedes o adónde van en los momentos que se mencionan a continuación.

MODELO   E1: *Los lunes a las ocho de la mañana estoy en la clase de biología.*
          E2: *Y yo voy al trabajo los lunes por la mañana.*

1. el Día de Año Nuevo
2. los viernes a las nueve de la noche
3. el 4 de julio
4. el día de mi cumpleaños
5. en julio y en agosto
6. el Día de San Valentín
7. los miércoles a las tres de la tarde
8. en el receso *(break)* de primavera

■ Integración

3-13 Un día perfecto Imagínate que estás viviendo *(you are living)* un día perfecto y descríbeles a tus compañeros de grupo dónde estás y adónde vas. Da *(Give)* todos los detalles que puedas. **¡OJO!** Debes estar preparado(a) para responder a las preguntas de tus compañeros.

You may use some of the connectors (**primero, después, luego, finalmente**, etc.) and time expressions (**por la mañana, por la tarde, por la noche**).

3-14 El día perfecto de... Ahora, escribe dónde está y adónde va en su día perfecto uno de tus compañeros de grupo de la actividad 3–13. Incluye todos los detalles *(details)* que recuerdes. Al terminar, entrégale *(turn in)* el trabajo a tu profesor(a) para que lo corrija.

III. Funciones y estructuras: Telling time

To ask for the time in Spanish, say **¿Qué hora es?** When the time is between the hour and the half hour, use the following expression.

ser + article + hour (+ **y** + minutes)

You may want to review the list of numbers presented in **Capítulo preparatorio**.

Son las doce y media.

Son las cuatro en punto.

Son las nueve y veinticinco.

Es la una y cuarto.

Note that **es la** is used when the hour is one while **son las** is used for all other hours. Also, note the use of **en punto** (o'clock), **cuarto** (quarter of an hour = 15 minutes) and **media** (half an hour = 30 minutes).

■ Use **Es mediodía** for *It's noon* and **Es medianoche** for *It's midnight*.

When the time is between the half hour and the hour, use the following expression.

ser + article + next hour + **menos** + minutes to the hour

Es la una menos cuarto.

Son las siete menos veinte.

As a general rule, use **de la tarde** until 6:30 p.m.

■ To specify the time of the day, add the expression **de la mañana** *(in the morning)*, **de la tarde** *(in the afternoon)*, or **de la noche** *(in the evening / at night)*.

To find out at what time an action takes place, say **¿A qué hora... ?** To answer this question, use the preposition **a** instead of **es** or **son**.

—**¿A qué hora** vas a la universidad?   *At what time do you go to school?*

—Voy **a** las siete y media de la mañana.   *I go at 7:30 a.m.*

▪ Asimilación

3-15 La hora Empareja *(Match)* las horas de la izquierda con las oraciones de la derecha. Cuando termines, compara tus respuestas con las de un(a) compañero(a).

____ 1. 6:00 p.m.	a. Son las cinco y doce de la mañana.
____ 2. 4:15 a.m.	b. Son las cuatro y cuarto de la mañana.
____ 3. 6:54 p.m.	c. Son las cuatro menos cuarto de la tarde.
____ 4. 6:30 a.m.	d. Son las seis en punto de la tarde.
____ 5. 1:00 p.m.	e. Es la una menos veinte de la mañana.
____ 6. 3:45 p.m.	f. Son las siete menos seis de la noche.
____ 7. 5:12 a.m.	g. Es la una en punto de la tarde.
____ 8. 12:40 a.m.	h. Son las seis y media de la mañana.

CD1–26 **3-16 La agenda de Elsa** Escucha la descripción que da Elsa de sus actividades para el día de hoy. Luego, completa la agenda a continuación, escribiendo la acción correcta al lado de la hora correspondiente.

OPCIONES: cenar con Betty   estudiar para el examen de historia
almorzar con Pedro   ir a la clase de física   trabajar
buscar a Andrés   ir al laboratorio de química

```
                                          miércoles, 8 de febrero

 8:00 a.m. –  _____

10:30 a.m. –  _____

12:00 p.m. –  _____

 1:30 p.m. –  _____

 4:45 p.m. –  _____

 7:00 p.m. –  _____

 9:00 p.m. –  _____
```

▪ Aplicaciones

3-17 ¿Qué hora es? Túrnense para decir qué hora es (en oraciones completas). Especifiquen el momento del día.

MODELO   10:00 p.m.
          E1: *¿Qué hora es?*
          E2: *Son las diez en punto de la noche.*

1. 3:05 p.m.	3. 8:00 p.m.	5. 10:50 p.m.	7. 9:00 a.m.
2. 12:35 a.m.	4. 2:15 p.m.	6. 4:30 p.m.	8. 9:45 a.m.

3-18 Programas de televisión Túrnense para hacer y responder a preguntas sobre varios programas de televisión.

MODELO   E1: *¿A qué hora es el programa 20/20?*
          E2: *Es a las diez en punto de la noche los viernes.*

3-19 Preferencias diferentes Formen oraciones diferentes usando elementos de cada columna. Conjuguen los verbos correctamente *(correctly)* y terminen cada oración con una hora lógica. Pueden añadir información adicional.

MODELO: nosotros(as)   desayunar
Nosotros desayunamos en casa a las siete en punto de la mañana.

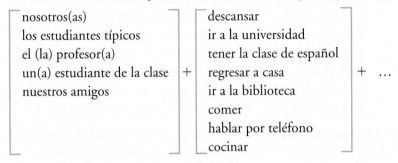

nosotros(as)		descansar	
los estudiantes típicos		ir a la universidad	
el (la) profesor(a)	+	tener la clase de español	+ ...
un(a) estudiante de la clase		regresar a casa	
nuestros amigos		ir a la biblioteca	
		comer	
		hablar por teléfono	
		cocinar	

▇ Integración

3-20 Mis compañeros de clase y yo

Paso 1: Toma unos minutos para completar la primera columna de la tabla que sigue con cinco actividades cotidianas *(daily)* diferentes. Puedes usar verbos en el infinitivo. Luego, escribe la hora a la que generalmente haces *(you do)* esa actividad en la segunda columna.

Actividades	Yo	Nombre: _____	Nombre: _____

Paso 2: Ahora, entrevista a dos compañeros de clase para saber a qué hora generalmente hacen esas actividades. Tomen notas.

MODELO   E1: *Laura, ¿a qué hora estudias para la clase de español?*
E2: *Generalmente estudio a las dos en punto de la tarde.*
E1: *Y tú, Brandon, ¿a qué hora... ?*
E3: ...

Use connectors such as **por ejemplo** *(for example)*, **por otro lado** *(on the other hand)*, **en cambio** *(in contrast)*, **por el contrario** *(on the contrary)*, and **sin embargo** *(however)*.

3-21 ¿Diferentes o semejantes? De acuerdo con la información de la actividad 3-20, ¿tus compañeros de clase y tú son diferentes o semejantes? Escribe un breve informe y entrégaselo a tu profesor(a).

IV. Perspectivas: Turismo en Puerto Rico

■ Antes de leer

A. ¿Qué sabes de Puerto Rico? La lectura siguiente es sobre Puerto Rico. Escribe una lista de palabras que asocias con esta isla.

B. Expectativas Ahora, lee el artículo. ¿Cuáles de las palabras de tu lista aparecen en la lectura?

■ A leer

Turismo en Puerto Rico

Si lo que busca es descansar... esta isla es pura tranquilidad... Si lo que desea es acción... las noches no duermen en esta isla de música y color. Puerto Rico le ofrece todo un continente de variedad del que nunca se cansará y que querrá visitar una y otra vez. Si lo que busca es hoteles, los hay de todos los precios y para todos los gustos... cerca de la playa... con hermosas vistas y fascinantes posibilidades... o arriba en la montaña o cerca de los **campos**... con diferentes estilos y *fields* entretenimientos diversos... o si desea, rodeados de campos de golf, canchas de tenis, caminos para **pasear a caballo** o simplemente... espacios amplios donde olvidar *ride horseback* todo... Las zonas turísticas del Viejo San Juan, Condado e Isla Verde le ofrecen toda una serie de hoteles, donde encuentra desde el mejor servicio hasta las mejores tiendas con excelentes precios... Por la noche, los casinos están **dispuestos** para que Ud. pruebe su suerte... los *ready* restaurantes están listos para sorprender el gusto más exigente... y las mejores orquestas y artistas están preparados para hacerle pasar una noche **inolvidable**... *unforgettable*

Si desea, puede escaparse en excursiones que lo lleven a visitar el Yunque, el único **bosque tropical** bajo el cuidado del Servicio *rain forest* Nacional de Parques de los Estados Unidos... o las **cuevas** de Camuy, *caves* extraordinarias cavernas naturales con formas caprichosas que tomaron cientos de años en formarse... o visitar una vieja hacienda de café... o de **caña**... y si desea, puede pasar la noche en una casa hacienda del *sugar cane* **siglo** pasado... o puede pasear de noche en una de nuestras bahías *century* **fosforescentes**, donde la luna y la naturaleza le juegan una **broma** *fluorescent / joke* curiosa a su imaginación... o puede visitar el futuro... en el radio-observatorio de Arecibo, el más grande del mundo... Si lo que quiere es ver algo substancialmente distinto... pruebe las villas al este de la isla... o los hoteles espectaculares que incluyen hasta una isla propia... Por la noche, el tiempo parece detenerse en los **adoquines** del Viejo *cobblestones* San Juan... mientras jóvenes y adultos disfrutan de las múltiples actividades en los alrededores de la ciudad capital... Si la historia le llama la atención, una visita a las fortificaciones que dejaron los conquistadores españoles lo hará comprender por qué San Juan es la capital más antigua bajo la bandera estrellada.

■ **¿Entendiste bien?**

C. Temas Indica si se mencionan los siguientes aspectos de la vida en Puerto Rico.

_____ el descanso

_____ la historia

_____ los deportes

_____ la gente

_____ las montañas

_____ la política

_____ la comida

_____ la diversión

_____ las compras

_____ las playas

D. Aspectos lingüísticos Identifica en el texto los verbos de acción y completa el cuadro.

Verbos -*ar*	Verbos -*er*	Verbos -*ir*

E. Para conversar en grupos ¿Qué aspecto de la isla les parece más interesante? Expliquen por qué.

F. Actividad de extensión Imagínense que trabajan para la corporación de turismo de su región. Preparen un artículo semejante al artículo «Turismo en Puerto Rico» de la página 111 acerca de su ciudad, su región o su estado.

De compras

I. Vocabulario: Las compras y las formas de pago

D1–27

DEPENDIENTE:	¿En qué puedo servirle, señor?
CLIENTE:	Busco un libro de García Márquez que se titula *Crónica de un secuestro*.
DEPENDIENTE:	Sí, señor, tenemos ese libro. Lo puede encontrar en la sección de autores colombianos.
CLIENTE:	De acuerdo, muchas gracias.

Más tarde...

DEPENDIENTE:	El siguiente, por favor... Son 20 dólares, señor.
CLIENTE:	¿Aceptan tarjetas de crédito?
DEPENDIENTE:	Sí, todas, excepto American Express.
CLIENTE:	Aquí tiene mi tarjeta. Muchas gracias.
DEPENDIENTE:	De nada. Vuelva pronto.

la tarjeta de crédito

el cheque

el efectivo

el cambio

Asimilación

3-22 ¿El cliente o el dependiente? Indica quién dice cada frase.

1. De nada.
2. ¿Aceptan tarjetas de crédito?
3. Busco un libro.
4. ¿En qué puedo servirle, señor?
5. Son 20 dólares.

CD1–28 **3-23 ¿Cómo prefieres pagar?** Escucha la descripción de cómo paga usualmente sus cuentas esta persona. Selecciona la opción (o las opciones) que corresponda(n).

	Lleva efectivo	Usa una tarjeta de crédito	Paga con cheque
cuando *(when)* va de compras al supermercado			
cuando va de compras al centro comercial			
cuando sale a almorzar			
cuando sale a cenar con amigos			
cuando sale de vacaciones			
cuando paga los servicios públicos (agua, electricidad, teléfono)			

Aplicaciones

 3-24 De compras Ordenen la siguiente conversación.

_____ Azul o negro, por favor.

_____ Buenos días, ¿en qué puedo servirle?

_____ No, señor. Solamente aceptamos pagos en efectivo.

_____ Aquí tiene. Son 18 dólares.

_____ ¿Qué color prefiere?

_____ ¿Aceptan tarjetas de crédito?

_____ Busco una camiseta.

_____ Bueno, entonces tengo que pasar por un cajero automático primero.

3-25 Normalmente... Indica la forma de pago más común de los siguientes artículos. Compara tus respuestas con las de otros compañeros.

1. el alquiler de un apartamento
2. un boleto de avión
3. una camiseta *(T-shirt)*
4. chicle *(chewing gum)*
5. tus libros
6. el almuerzo
7. el estacionamiento
8. un taxi
9. tu cuenta de teléfono
10. tu matrícula *(tuition)*

3-26 Necesito enviar un fax Escojan la oración más apropiada para completar el diálogo.

1. DEPENDIENTE: ____
   a. ¿Qué desea comer esta noche?
   b. ¿Cuántos quiere?
   c. ¿En qué puedo servirle?

2. DEPENDIENTE: ____
   a. ¿Cuántas personas?
   b. ¿Qué color prefiere?
   c. ¿Cuál es el número?

   TÚ: Es el 212-555-1234.

3. DEPENDIENTE: ____
   a. Aquí tiene.
   b. ¿Algo más?
   c. Éste es el número.

   TÚ: No, gracias. Nada más.

4. TÚ: Quiero este cuaderno. ¿Cuánto es?
   DEPENDIENTE: ____
   a. Son 3 dólares.
   b. Necesita otra talla.
   c. Sí, de nada.

5. TÚ: ¿Aceptan tarjetas de crédito?
   DEPENDIENTE: ____
   a. No, sólo efectivo.
   b. Vuelva pronto.
   c. Hasta mañana.

6. TÚ: Muy bien. Aquí tiene.
   DEPENDIENTE: ____
   a. Gracias y vuelva pronto.
   b. Está al fondo a la derecha.
   c. Sí, voy a llamar un taxi.

■ Integración

3-27 De compras Representa la siguiente situación con un(a) compañero(a).

Turista	Dependiente
During your trip to Puerto Rico you discovered a great salsa group and you want to buy one of their CDs. Make sure to a) tell the clerk what you are looking for; b) indicate the type of music you want; c) ask any pertinent questions (price, accepted forms of payment, etc.); and d) pay for your CD.	You are the clerk in a store in San Juan. A tourist wants to make a purchase. Wait on him/her appropriately. Make sure to a) greet your client; b) inquire about his/her needs; c) tell him/her what section (type of music) to look for; d) answer any questions he/she may have; and e) ring up the purchase.

3-28 Devoluciones *(Refunds)* Representa la siguiente situación con un(a) compañero(a).

Turista	Dependiente
Your CD does not have the songs you wanted. Ask for a refund. You may want to use some of the following expressions in this conversation: **Quiero otro** *(I want another one)*, **Me gustaría cambiarlo** *(I would like to exchange it)*, and **Quiero mi dinero** *(I want my money back)*.	This customer has changed his/her mind and wants a refund. Explain that you usually do not accept exchanges or returns. You may want to use some of the following expressions in this conversation: **Imposible** *(Impossible)*, **No puedo** *(I can't)*, **Lo siento** *(I'm sorry)*, **No me está permitido** *(I'm not allowed)*, and **¿Tiene el recibo?** *(Do you have your receipt?)*.

EN TU COMUNIDAD

Interview a local Spanish-speaking store owner to find out: 1) if his/her business has a significant immigrant clientele (and if so, from what countries or continents); 2) if he/she can speak a foreign language; and 3) if he/she thinks that speaking a foreign language helps (or would help) his/her business. Then, discuss your findings in small groups and present a general conclusion.

II. Funciones y estructuras: Talking about daily activities with irregular *yo* form verbs

Todas las mañanas, cuando **salgo** para el trabajo, le **doy** un abrazo a mi esposo.

So far you have learned how to use several irregular verbs like **ser, estar, tener,** and **ir.** Spanish also has a number of verbs that are irregular only in the **yo** form (much like **estar**). The following is a list of some of these verbs.

VERB	MEANING	CONJUGATION
dar	to give	**doy**, das, da, damos, dais, dan
conocer	to know (to be acquainted or familiar with somebody or something)	**conozco**, conoces, conoce, conocemos, conocéis, conocen
hacer	to do, to make	**hago**, haces, hace, hacemos, hacéis, hacen
poner	to put	**pongo**, pones, pone, ponemos, ponéis, ponen
saber	to know (information or how to do something)	**sé**, sabes, sabe, sabemos, sabéis, saben
salir	to go out, to leave	**salgo**, sales, sale, salimos, salís, salen
traer	to bring	**traigo**, traes, trae, traemos, traéis, traen

Most questions that include the verb **hacer** are answered with sentences that have a different verb.

¿Qué **haces** los domingos por la mañana?
*What do **you do** on Sunday mornings?*

Voy a la iglesia con mis hijos.
*I **go** to church with my children.*

These are some common idioms with the verb **hacer.**

hacer cola/fila *to stand in line*	hacer mandados/diligencias *to run errands*
hacer la comida *to cook*	hacer una pregunta *to ask a question*
hacer compras *to shop*	hacer tareas *to do homework*
hacer ejercicio *to work out*	hacer un viaje *to go on a trip*

Asimilación

3-29 Acciones rutinarias Lee las siguientes oraciones e indica si son ciertas (**C**) o falsas (**F**). Al terminar, compara las respuestas con las de un(a) compañero(a). ¿Son diferentes o semejantes?

_____ 1. Doy fiestas en mi casa los fines de semana.

_____ 2. Hago ejercicio por lo menos tres veces por semana.

_____ 3. Conozco bien a todos mis profesores.

_____ 4. Siempre salgo de mi casa con una tarjeta de crédito.

_____ 5. Sé hablar más de una lengua.

_____ 6. Traigo muchos libros a la universidad.

_____ 7. Cuando llego a casa, pongo mis libros sobre el escritorio.

_____ 8. Hago por lo menos un viaje todos los años.

CD1–29 **3-30 De compras** Escucha la rutina de compras de Alisa y escoge las oraciones correctas.

_____ Conoce bien las tiendas del centro comercial.

_____ Lleva _(Takes)_ cheques para hacer sus compras.

_____ Sale de compras los viernes por la tarde.

_____ Sabe que puede encontrar buenas ofertas _(sales)_.

_____ Les da regalos a sus padres.

_____ Su madre hace la comida.

_____ No va a las tiendas del centro.

_____ Sale de su casa muy temprano.

Aplicaciones

3-31 Causa y consecuencia Para cada situación, escojan una consecuencia lógica de la lista. Cambien los verbos a la forma **yo**.

MODELO Quiero estar en buena condición física. → _Hago ejercicio regularmente._

OPCIONES: traer una fruta de casa   dar dinero a la Cruz _(Cross)_ Roja
poner todo en su lugar   saber que debo estudiar todos los días
hacer muchas preguntas   salir con mis amigos

1. No me gusta estar solo en casa. →

2. Soy una persona muy organizada. →

3. No quiero gastar dinero para comer. →

4. Me gusta ayudar a otras personas. →

5. Necesito sacar buenas notas este semestre. →

6. Me gusta participar en las clases. →

3-32 ¡Adivina, adivinador! Túrnense para darse _(give each other)_ claves _(clues)_ relacionadas con las expresiones con el verbo **hacer.**

MODELO E1: _Los sábados, hacer compras, ir al banco, ir a la tintorería._
E2: _Hacer mandados o diligencias._
E1: _¡Sí!_

3-33 Firma aquí *(Sign here)*, **por favor** Usa las siguientes frases para hacerles preguntas a tus compañeros de clase. Si alguien responde negativamente, di *(say)* **Gracias** y pregúntale a otra persona. Si alguien responde afirmativamente, di **Firma aquí, por favor.** Debes obtener una firma para cada frase. Cuando termines, prepara un informe para la clase.

> MODELO   salir todos los viernes por la noche
> E1: *¿Sales todos los viernes por la noche?*
> E2: *No, no salgo los viernes.*
> E1: *Gracias.*
> o
> E2: *Sí, salgo todos los viernes por la noche.*
> E1: *Firma aquí, por favor.*

                                                       Firma

1. conocer a alguien de España   _____
2. dar regalos *(gifts)* a tus amigos   _____
3. hacer tareas en la biblioteca   _____
4. saber cuál es la capital de
   Puerto Rico   _____
5. traer lápices a clase   _____
6. poner los libros en una mochila   _____

■ Integración

 3-34 La Oficina de Asuntos Estudiantiles *(Student Affairs)* Representa la siguiente situación con un(a) compañero(a). Al terminar, cambien de papel *(exchange roles)*.

Here are some questions the Office of Student Affairs employee may ask:
¿Qué haces después de clase? Regularmente, ¿haces tareas? ¿Traes una computadora portátil a la universidad? ¿Conoces a tu consejero *(advisor)***? ¿Pones la radio para estudiar? ¿Con quién sales?** etc.

Empleado(a) de la Oficina de Asuntos Estudiantiles	Estudiante
You work for the Office of Student Affairs of your university and are conducting an informal survey about some of the things students do, bring to school, and know. You also want to know what they do when they go out. Be prepared to ask as many follow-up questions as you can.	An employee of the Office of Student Affairs of your university is calling you as part of a survey. He/She wants general information about what you do, bring to school and know, as well as information about what you do when you go out. Provide as many details as possible.

3-35 Cuestionario El empleado de la Oficina de Asuntos Estudiantiles de la actividad 3-34 te ha pedido que hagas *(has asked you to create)* un cuestionario de veinte preguntas para dárselo a los estudiantes de tu universidad. Este funcionario *(official)* desea obtener más información sobre las acciones rutinarias de los estudiantes. ¡Sé creativo(a) *(Be creative)* y original! Usa los verbos en la forma **yo** e incluye todos los verbos que aprendiste en esta sección. Al terminar, dale el cuestionario a un(a) compañero(a) para que lo conteste indicando **sí** o **no.**

III. Funciones y estructuras: Adverbs of frequency

Nunca llego a la oficina a las siete de la mañana.

A menudo almuerzo con clientes.

Siempre tengo que escribir informes hasta después de las ocho de la noche.

In this section you will review some adverbs of frequency you already know and will learn some new ones. Here is a complete list.

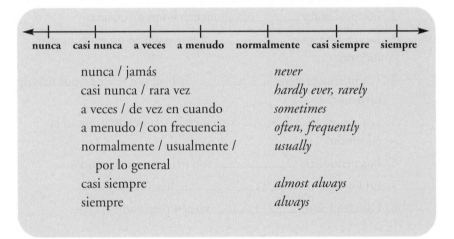

nunca	casi nunca	a veces	a menudo	normalmente	casi siempre	siempre

nunca / jamás	*never*
casi nunca / rara vez	*hardly ever, rarely*
a veces / de vez en cuando	*sometimes*
a menudo / con frecuencia	*often, frequently*
normalmente / usualmente / por lo general	*usually*
casi siempre	*almost always*
siempre	*always*

■ Asimilación

3-36 ¿Con qué frecuencia...? Indica con qué frecuencia haces las siguientes cosas. Al terminar, compara tus respuestas con las de un(a) compañero(a). ¿Qué cosas tienen en común?

ACTIVIDAD	jamás	rara vez	de vez en cuando	usualmente	casi siempre	siempre
Hago la comida.						
Pago con cheque.						
Leo el correo electrónico.						
Voy a un museo.						
Trabajo los fines de semana.						
Hablo español en clase.						
Salgo a un bar.						
No tengo que hacer tareas.						

CD1-30 **3-37 Los cumpleaños de Mauricio** Mauricio va a decir cómo pasa el día de su cumpleaños. Escucha su descripción y luego determina si las siguientes oraciones son ciertas (**C**) o falsas (**F**).

_____ 1. La esposa de Mauricio rara vez le prepara desayuno.

_____ 2. Sus hijos nunca le cantan «Feliz cumpleaños».

_____ 3. Mauricio a veces va a un parque con su familia.

_____ 4. Sus padres siempre lo visitan.

_____ 5. De vez en cuando, él sale con sus amigos por la noche.

_____ 6. Los cumpleaños de Mauricio nunca son aburridos.

■ **Aplicaciones**

3-38 Situaciones diversas Completen las siguientes oraciones con un adverbio de frecuencia lógico.

1. _____ compramos una Coca-Cola con tarjeta de crédito.

2. Los profesores _____ tienen horas de oficina.

3. La gente *(people)*_____ come pasta en un restaurante italiano.

4. Los buenos amigos _____ hablan por teléfono por más de media hora.

5. Los niños _____ comen en la sala mientras miran la televisión.

6. Los periodistas _____ son personas introvertidas.

7. En los supermercados _____ hay mucha gente.

8. Los estudiantes _____ vienen preparados a clase.

3-39 Los famosos Formen oraciones sobre las siguientes personas famosas. Escojan un adverbio de la segunda columna y completen las oraciones con actividades diferentes.

MODELO   Regis Philbin   nunca
Regis Philbin nunca usa ropa de The Gap.

Las gemelas Olson
Tiger Woods
La familia Simpson
Julia Roberts   +
El presidente
…

nunca
casi nunca
de vez en cuando
con frecuencia   +   …
usualmente
casi siempre
siempre

3-40 Preguntas para el (la) profesor(a) Escriban por lo menos seis preguntas para su profesor(a) sobre la frecuencia con que él/ella hace ciertas actividades.

MODELO   *¿Usted enseña clases de noche normalmente?*

Integración

3-41 El (La) estudiante ejemplar

Paso 1: Primero, piensen en las características de un(a) estudiante ejemplar. ¿Qué cosas hace siempre o usualmente? ¿Y qué cosas no hace nunca? Luego, en grupos de tres o cuatro estudiantes, háganse preguntas para determinar quién es el (la) estudiante ejemplar del grupo. Tomen notas.

Paso 2: Compartan su opinión con el resto de la clase. ¿Quién es el (la) estudiante ejemplar? ¿Por qué?

3-42 ¿Y el (la) profesor(a) ejemplar? ¡Ahora tienes la oportunidad de describir las características de un(a) profesor(a) ejemplar! Explica qué cosas hace siempre, casi siempre, por lo general, a menudo y de vez en cuando. También, explica qué cosas no hace nunca o casi nunca. Al terminar, comparte lo que escribiste con un(a) compañero(a) para que te dé su opinión.

You may ask your professor about the following actions: **manejar a la universidad, beber café por la mañana, asistir a conciertos de rock, cortar el césped, ser diligente, estar cansado(a), tener que corregir algún trabajo, gustarle sus clases, ir al laboratorio de lenguas.**

These are some of the questions you may ask: **¿Con frecuencia estudias mucho antes de un examen? ¿De vez en cuando hablas con los profesores después de clase? ¿Siempre haces muchas preguntas? ¿Casi siempre llegas temprano a tus clases?**

IV. Vídeo: El día de la primera excursión en Puerto Rico

iLrn

■ Preparación

A. ¿Qué hacen los compañeros hoy? Antes de ver el vídeo, emparejen las horas con las actividades de los compañeros.

_____ A las ocho y treinta y cinco de la mañana.

_____ A las nueve en punto de la mañana.

_____ A la una en punto de la tarde.

_____ A las cuatro en punto de la tarde.

_____ A las cinco en punto de la tarde.

1. Los compañeros tienen que salir de la casa.
2. Todos los compañeros tienen que volver a La Plaza de la Rogativa para luego ir todos juntos a casa.
3. Los compañeros hacen cola para usar el baño.
4. Sofía y Javier tienen que regresar al centro.
5. Como los compañeros no quieren hacer las mismas cosas, deciden separarse.

COMPREHENSION STRATEGY

Listening for Details As you watch the video and do the following listening comprehension activities, keep in mind that you are listening for recognition of specific pieces of information about what the roommates do during their first full day together in Puerto Rico.

■ ¿Entendiste bien?

B. Un día lleno de actividades Mientras miras el vídeo, comprueba tus respuestas para la actividad A. Luego, indica la respuesta correcta para las siguientes preguntas.

1. ¿Cuánto tiempo lleva Valeria en el baño?
   a. unos quince minutos
   b. una media hora
   c. una hora
2. ¿Qué compañero(a) dice que le gusta levantarse temprano por la mañana, tomar un café y luego tomar una ducha?
   a. Javier
   b. Alejandra
   c. Sofía
3. ¿Adónde van Sofía y Javier?
   a. de compras a tiendas
   b. a un mercado
   c. al Castillo de San Felipe del Morro
4. ¿Qué hacen Antonio y Alejandra?
   a. van al Paseo de la Princesa
   b. almuerzan comida típica
   c. se pierden en las calles del Viejo San Juan
5. Completa las direcciones sobre cómo llegar a la Plaza de la Rogativa que le da la mujer a Valeria: «De esta _____, caminas
   _____ cuadras. Tomas la izquierda *(left)*, tres
   _____ más y la tienes justo frente a ti».

C. Su rutina diaria Describe un día típico de los compañeros de la Hacienda Vista Alegre. Enlaza tus ideas con palabras como **primero, después, luego, finalmente,** etc., y usa expresiones de tiempo como **por la mañana** y **por la tarde.** Usa la información del vídeo y también la imaginación.

D. Enfoque comunitario Preparen un panfleto en español para la oficina de estudiantes internacionales de su escuela con una descripción detallada sobre la localización de los siguientes lugares:

1. de interés histórico: un monumento, una plaza, etc.
2. de interés comercial: una zona de compras, un centro comercial, una zona de negocios, etc.
3. de interés turístico: un parque, un museo, un restaurante famoso, etc.

La comida

I. Vocabulario: Vamos a comer

el pan tostado

el cereal

el jugo/
el zumo de
naranja

el panqueque

el café

Desayuno

la hamburguesa

las patatas/
las papas fritas

el emparedado/
el sándwich/
el bocadillo

el refresco

la ensalada

la pizza

la sopa

Almuerzo/Comida

la carne   el pescado

las legumbres/
las verduras

el vino

las papas/
las patatas

el agua/
el agua
mineral

el pollo

la pasta

el arroz

Cena

las galletas

la torta

el helado

el flan

Postres

CD1–31

RECEPCIONISTA:	Buenas noches, ¿en qué puedo servirle?
CLIENTE:	Tengo una reservación a nombre de José Luis García.
RECEPCIONISTA:	Sí, señor. Sígame, por favor.

Más tarde...

MESERO:	¿Desea ordenar algo de tomar?
CLIENTE:	Sí. Tráigame una botella de vino tinto de la casa, por favor.
MESERO:	Con mucho gusto.
MESERO:	¿Está listo para pedir?
CLIENTE:	Sí. De entrada, una sopa de ajo.
MESERO:	¿Y de plato principal?
CLIENTE:	Un filete de ternera con patatas.

Más tarde...

MESERO: ¿Desea algún postre? ¿O quizás un café?

CLIENTE: No, gracias. La cuenta, por favor.

MESERO: Aquí tiene, señor.

CLIENTE: Muchas gracias.

la lechuga   el tomate   la banana/el plátano

la manzana

la cebolla   el ajo   la uva   la naranja

Verduras   Frutas

el bistec

el tocino

la chuleta (de cerdo)

la salchicha

Carnes

la langosta

los camarones/ las gambas

el filete de salmón

el cangrejo

Pescado y mariscos

Vocabulario práctico

Condimentos (Seasonings)

el aceite *oil*

el aderezo *dressing*

el azúcar *sugar*

la mayonesa *mayonnaise*

la miel *honey*

la mostaza *mustard*

la pimienta *pepper*

la sal *salt*

la salsa de tomate *catsup*

el vinagre *vinegar*

Platos y cubiertos (China and silverware)

la copa *wine glass*

la cuchara *spoon*

la cucharita *teaspoon*

el cuchillo *knife*

el mantel *tablecloth*

el plato *plate (dish)*

la servilleta *napkin*

la taza *cup*

el tenedor *fork*

el vaso *glass*

En el restaurante

el aperitivo *before-dinner drink*

la carta *menu*

la cuenta *check*

la entrada / el entremés *appetizer*

el plato principal *entrée, main course*

la propina *tip*

la sección de no fumar *nonsmoking section*

■ Asimilación

3-43 ¿Cuál no corresponde? Identifiquen el alimento *(food item)* que no pertenece *(belongs)* al grupo. Expliquen por qué.

1. el café, el vino, el ajo
2. el bistec, el tocino, el café
3. la uva, el cereal, la manzana
4. las galletas, las tortas, las carnes
5. las gambas, la langosta, la cebolla
6. la sal, el aderezo, el agua mineral
7. el tenedor, el azúcar, el cuchillo
8. la servilleta, la cuenta, la propina

CD1–32 **3-44 ¿Qué va a comer?** Escucha la siguiente conversación e indica los alimentos que pide el cliente.

_____ un agua mineral   _____ una naranja

_____ un bocadillo   _____ unas legumbres

_____ pollo   _____ un helado

_____ un jugo   _____ un café

_____ una ensalada   _____ pescado

_____ una sopa

■ Aplicaciones

CD1–33 **3-45 En la cafetería** Escuchen y practiquen la siguiente conversación entre dos amigos.

A: ¿Qué vas a comer?

B: Yo quisiera <u>un emparedado</u>, ¿y tú? (**otras opciones:** ensalada, sopa, pizza)

A: ¿Qué me sugieres?

B: Pues aquí venden <u>unas ensaladas</u> deliciosas. (**otras opciones:** pastas, patatas fritas, hamburguesas)

A: Bueno, entonces, para mí, <u>una ensalada</u>.

B: ¿Y qué vas a tomar?

A: <u>Un refresco</u>. (**otras opciones:** café, agua mineral, jugo de naranja)

B: Y yo voy a tomar <u>un café</u>. (**otras opciones:** leche, limonada, té)

3-46 ¿Qué falta? Completa las siguientes comidas de una manera lógica. Al terminar, compara tus respuestas con las de un(a) compañero(a). ¿En qué están de acuerdo?

OPCIONES: cereal   café   pan tostado   hamburguesa   ensalada
sopa   agua mineral   legumbres   helado   huevos
jugo de naranja

1. ensalada, pasta y _____
2. café, jugo de naranja y _____
3. patatas, carne y _____
4. pan tostado, café y _____
5. pollo, arroz y _____

3-47 Costumbres Entrevista a tu compañero(a) para saber más acerca de sus hábitos alimenticios *(eating habits)*. Luego, preséntale un resumen de sus respuestas al resto de la clase.

You may use questions like:
1. ¿Desayunas? ¿Normalmente dónde desayunas? ¿A qué hora? ¿Qué (no) comes? (¿Por qué sí o por qué no?)
2. ¿Almuerzas? ¿Usualmente dónde almuerzas? ¿A qué hora? ¿Qué (no) comes? (¿Por qué sí o por qué no?)
3. ¿Cenas? ¿Por lo general dónde cenas? ¿A qué hora? ¿Qué (no) comes? (¿Por qué sí o por qué no?)

Integración

3-48 En el restaurante Representa la siguiente situación con un(a) compañero(a).

Cliente(a) vegetariano(a)

Imagine that you are in a restaurant and want to order a vegetarian meal. (Refer to the list of foods on pages 124 and 125.) Make sure to: a) greet the waiter; b) tell him/her about your diet restrictions; c) ask for recommendations (**¿Qué me recomienda?**); d) place your order; and e) ask for the check.

Mesero(a)

Help this vegetarian client order his/her meal. Make sure to: a) greet the client; b) offer him/her a drink before ordering; c) suggest some vegetarian alternatives (**Le recomiendo...**); d) offer him/her dessert; and e) give him/her the check.

3-49 Nutricionistas Imagínense que tienen invitados en su casa este fin de semana. Preparen el menú de cada día *(each day)*. **¡OJO!** ¡No olviden planear una dieta bien balanceada!

II. Funciones y estructuras: Talking about daily activities with *e→i* stem-changing verbs

FERNANDA:	Darío, este restaurante es muy bonito. ¿Qué tipo de comida **sirven** aquí?
DARÍO:	**Sirven** platos caribeños. Su especialidad es la cocina puertorriqueña.
FERNANDA:	¿Y qué **pides** cuando vienes?
DARÍO:	Generalmente **pido** algún plato con arroz y frijoles.
FERNANDA:	¡Mmm! ¡Me suena bien! *(It sounds good to me!)*

You have already learned how to use verbs that undergo stem changes in their conjugation, like the verb **tener**. You will now learn about a group of verbs whose stem vowel **e** changes to **i** in the present tense. One of these verbs is **pedir** *(to order* [in a restaurant], *to ask for, to request).*

yo p**i**do	nosotros(as) **pedimos**
tú p**i**des	vosotros(as) **pedís**
él/ella/usted p**i**de	ellos(as)/ustedes p**i**den

Notice that the stem vowel **e** does not change to **i** in the **nosotros(as)** and **vosotros(as)** forms.

The **yo** form of **seguir** is **sigo** (similar to **hago, salgo, traigo,** etc.).

From now on, when you learn new **e→i** stem-changing verbs, they will have the letter **i** in parentheses next to the infinitive: **servir (i).**

The following is a list of other **e→i** stem-changing verbs.

competir *to compete*	seguir *to continue, to follow*
conseguir *to get, to find*	servir *to serve*
repetir *to repeat, to have seconds*	vestir *to dress, to wear*

■ Asimilación

 3-50 ¿Siempre, a veces o nunca? Indica si haces las siguientes actividades **siempre**, **a veces** o **nunca**. Cuando termines, compara tus respuestas con las de un(a) compañero(a). ¿Son semejantes o diferentes?

_____ 1. Aunque no tengo hambre, sigo comiendo.

_____ 2. Me visto con ropa elegante para ir a los restaurantes.

_____ 3. Pido el mismo plato en mi restaurante favorito.

_____ 4. Compito con mis amigos para ver quién come más.

_____ 5. Consigo frutas frescas en mi supermercado favorito.

_____ 6. Si me gusta mucho la comida, repito.

_____ 7. Sirvo frutas y verduras en mis fiestas.

_____ 8. Sigo las instrucciones de las recetas _(recipes)_ cuando cocino.

01-34 **3-51 Tomás, Blanca y Herminio** Escucha las descripciones que hacen Tomás, Blanca y Herminio de sus restaurantes favoritos. Luego, completa la tabla que sigue con la información correcta. **¡OJO!** Escribe una **X** si no se provee la información.

	Tomás	Blanca	Herminio
Restaurante favorito	Del Mar	Planeta Verde	La Parrillada
¿Qué sirven?			
¿Qué piden?			
¿Y de postre?			

■ Aplicaciones

3-52 Categorías

Paso 1: Escribe por lo menos dos palabras o frases que se relacionen con cada uno de los verbos de la tabla.

repetir	servir	conseguir
una materia	_comida internacional_	_un buen restaurante_
competir	**vestir**	**pedir**
partido de fútbol	_informal_	_la cuenta_

Paso 2: Ahora, escribe por lo menos cuatro oraciones sobre ti mismo(a) _(yourself)_ usando cuatro de estos verbos y frases de la tabla.

MODELO   _Generalmente no voy a restaurantes que sirven comida internacional._

3-53 En los restaurantes de mi ciudad Comenten los platos que sirven y que ustedes piden en algunos de los restaurantes de su ciudad.

MODELO   E1: *¿Qué sirven en China Garden?*
E2: *En China Garden sirven comida china, como* (like)
arroz, carnes, pollo y fideos (noodles).
E1: *¿Qué pides en China Garden?*
E2: *Pido sopa de huevo y pollo con verduras.*

3-54 Entrevista

Paso 1: Escoge la alternativa que, en tu opinión, mejor complete cada oración. Puedes incluir una alternativa diferente.

1. Nunca pido (ensalada/pasta/carne/_____) en mi restaurante favorito.
2. En mis fiestas, casi siempre sirvo (papas y salsa/galletas/queso/_____).
3. Casi siempre visto ropa (ligera/formal/festiva/_____) para ir a un restaurante.
4. La comida del día en la que posiblemente repito es (el desayuno/el almuerzo/la cena/_____).
5. A veces compito con (mi hermano[a]/mi primo[a]/mi amigo[a]/_____).
6. Por lo general, consigo buenos precios en (el supermercado/la tienda de ropa/la librería de la universidad/_____).

Paso 2: Convierte las oraciones del **Paso 1** en preguntas para tu compañero(a). Haz los cambios necesarios y toma notas. Cuando termines, prepara un informe para la clase.

MODELO   E1: *Marisa, ¿nunca pides ensalada en tu restaurante favorito?*
E2: *No, nunca pido ensalada.*
o   *Sí, pido ensalada, pero nunca pido postre.*

■ Integración

3-55 Una cena especial Averigua qué hacen tres de tus compañeros de clase para tener una cena especial con uno de sus seres queridos *(loved ones)*. Primero, piensa en las preguntas que tienes que hacer para obtener la siguiente información. Toma notas durante las entrevistas.

With whom they go, What restaurant they go to and why, What they serve at this restaurant, What they order and why, How they dress and why

3-56 ¡El (La) ganador(a) *(winner)* **es... !** Decide cuál de las descripciones de tus compañeros de clase en la actividad 3-55 te parece más original y escribe un resumen. Además, compara algunas de las cosas que hace esta persona para tener una cena especial con algunas de las cosas que tú haces.

III. Funciones y estructuras: Talking about future plans

En Puerto Rico, **voy a visitar** las playas de Cabo Rojo. **Espero tomar** muchas fotos.

When you want to talk about actions that will take place in the immediate future, use the following Spanish structure.

> **ir** + **a** + verb in the infinitive

Voy a desayunar con Ana.	*I am going to have breakfast with Ana.*
Vamos a pedir cuentas separadas.	*We are going to ask for separate checks.*

In this structure, **ir** is the auxiliary verb, while the infinitive is the main verb. The auxiliary verb is the one that agrees with the subject, not the main verb.

You can use other verbs and phrases to imply general intention, wish or desire, and obligation. They are also followed by infinitives.

GENERAL INTENTION	WISH OR DESIRE	OBLIGATION
pensar *(to think)*	querer *(to want)*	tener que *(to have to)*
planear *(to plan)*	desear *(to wish, to desire)*	deber *(should)*
	esperar *(to hope)*	

Carmelo **planea abrir** un restaurante.	*Carmelo **is planning to open** a restaurant.*
¿**Deseas tomar** algo?	*Do **you wish to drink** anything?*
Ustedes **deben comer** comida más saludable.	*You **should eat** healthier food.*

Here is a list of time expressions you can use to talk about the future:

esta tarde	*this afternoon*
esta noche	*tonight*
mañana	*tomorrow*
este lunes (martes/etc.)	*this Monday (Tuesday/etc.)*
el lunes (martes/etc.)	*on Monday (Tuesday/etc.)*
la próxima semana	*next week*
el próximo mes (año)	*next month (year)*

■ Asimilación

3-57 ¿Posible o imposible? ¿Qué piensas que tu profesor(a) va a hacer mañana? Lee las siguientes oraciones e indica si esas acciones son probables (**P**) o improbables (**I**). Luego, compara tus respuestas con las de un(a) compañero(a). ¿Están de acuerdo?

_____ 1. Va a hacer ejercicio.

_____ 2. Tiene que trabajar todo el día.

_____ 3. Planea corregir exámenes.

_____ 4. Debe ir al médico.

_____ 5. Va a tomar una clase de yoga.

_____ 6. Debe dormir muchas horas mañana.

_____ 7. Desea ir a una discoteca.

_____ 8. Va a ir al cine.

_____ 9. Espera salir por la noche.

_____ 10. Va a hacer un viaje.

CD1–35 **3-58 Preguntas personales** Piensa en lo que vas a hacer esta noche. Luego, contesta las preguntas personales que vas a escuchar con **sí** o **no**.

1. sí / no	3. sí / no	5. sí / no	7. sí / no
2. sí / no	4. sí / no	6. sí / no	8. sí / no

■ Aplicaciones

3-59 La próxima semana ¿Qué van a hacer las siguientes personas la próxima semana? En parejas, completen las oraciones con por lo menos una actividad lógica.

MODELO   Jennifer López
Jennifer López va a dar un concierto y va a salir a bailar.

1. Lance Armstrong
2. muchos estudiantes <u>no</u>
3. Goldie Hawn y Kurt Russell
4. mi compañero(a) y yo <u>no</u>
5. (compañero[a] de clase)
6. Bill Gates y su esposa <u>no</u>
7. el/la rector(a) *(president)* de la universidad
8. nuestra familia y nosotros

3-60 Reacciones Escriban una reacción lógica para cada situación.

> MODELO ¡Tengo mucha hambre! Yo _voy a comer_.

1. Estamos muy aburridos. No tenemos nada que hacer. Nosotros
   _____.

2. Hay elecciones este año. El presidente de los Estados Unidos
   _____.

3. Leonor planea perder peso, pero no le gustan las verduras. Ella
   _____.

4. Tú eres muy buena para las matemáticas. (Tú) _____.

5. Mis padres trabajan mucho y finalmente tienen vacaciones. Ellos
   _____.

6. Estoy muy enferma desde esta mañana. Yo _____.

7. A mi familia y a mí nos gusta el arte contemporáneo. Nosotros
   _____.

8. Froilán y tú son amantes de los deportes acuáticos. Ustedes
   _____.

3-61 Este fin de semana

Paso 1: Haz una lista de por lo menos seis actividades que deseas hacer este fin de semana.

1. …	3. …	5. …
2. …	4. …	6. …

Paso 2: Ahora, averigua si tu compañero(a) va a hacer las mismas cosas. Al terminar, compartan la información con el resto de la clase.

> MODELO _Este fin de semana, mi compañero y yo vamos a trabajar. Además, yo espero ir a una fiesta, pero mi compañero espera visitar a sus tíos en…_

■ Integración

3-62 ¡Unas vacaciones! Tu compañero(a) y tú ya son tan buenos(as) amigos(as) que desean ir de vacaciones juntos(as). Hagan planes y preparen un itinerario de actividades. Incluyan los siguientes temas en su conversación.

- lugar de vacaciones
- actividades
- lugares para visitar
- comidas típicas
- regalos para sus familiares
- preparativos para el viaje

3-63 El itinerario de las vacaciones Ahora, prepara el itinerario del viaje que planeaste (_you planned_) con tu compañero(a). Cuando termines, dale una copia a él/ella para ver si olvidaste (_you forgot_) algún detalle importante. Finalmente, dale una copia a tu profesor(a).

> You may use these connectors to help the reader create a better picture of what you want to do during this vacation: **primero** (first), **segundo** (second), **tercero** (third), **luego** (then), **después** (afterwards), **más tarde** (later), **además** (also), and **finalmente** (finally). In addition, make sure you are using the verb structure **auxiliary verb** + **a** + **infinitive** correctly.

IV. Lectura: La dieta mediterránea

■ Antes de leer

A. Para conversar En grupos, contesten las siguientes preguntas.

1. ¿Cuáles son las dietas más populares en este momento?
2. ¿Cuáles son los ingredientes básicos de una de esas dietas?
3. ¿Es fácil o difícil para un estudiante universitario seguir una dieta? ¿Por qué?

B. Vocabulario y conceptos Empareja cada palabra con la definición correspondiente.

____ 1. dieta	a. bueno
____ 2. saludable	b. hacer menor una cantidad
____ 3. seguir	c. la comida de todos los días
____ 4. reducir	d. cantidad (su símbolo es % [por ciento])
____ 5. porcentaje	e. adherirse, llevar hasta el fin

■ A leer

READING STRATEGY

Let us practice the reading strategies that you have learned so far.

1. **Using format clues and cognates** By looking at the titles and subtitles, what do you think this text is about?

2. **Skimming** Now, skim the text. Which of the following summarizes best the article? The Mediterranean diet . . . a) is delicious, b) is good for you, c) helps you lose weight.

3. **Scanning** Read the questions at the end of the reading and concentrate on locating only the information that will help you answer them.

La dieta mediterránea también reduce el cáncer y la mortalidad en general

Un nuevo estudio indica que la dieta mediterránea no solamente beneficia el sistema cardiovascular, sino que también reduce el número de casos de cáncer y la mortalidad en general.

La dieta mediterránea, a base de frutas, verduras, pescado, legumbres y aceite de oliva, es en realidad la forma de alimentación tradicional de los países del sur de Europa y norte de África.

risks → La mayor investigación realizada hasta ahora sobre los efectos beneficiosos de esa forma de alimentación señala que esta dieta reduce en un 33 por ciento los **riesgos** de mortalidad por problemas cardio-vasculares y en un 24 por ciento los de cáncer.

Greece → El estudio, publicado en la revista *New England Journal of Medicine,* fue realizado en **Grecia** por científicos de la Facultad de Medicina de las universidades de Atenas y Harvard (Massachusetts) en un total de 22.043 adultos sanos de entre 20 y 86 años de edad.

underwent / exhausting interview → Cada persona **fue sometida** a una **entrevista agotadora** para determinar sus hábitos de alimentación, y se le asignaron puntos en función de cuánto seguía la dieta mediterránea.

Este régimen alimenticio incluye también el consumo casi a diario de yogur, cereales integrales y frutos secos, así como de vino en dosis moderadas, con una reducida cantidad de carnes rojas.

Los sujetos que participaron en el estudio fueron sometidos a un **seguimiento** medio de 44 meses, durante los cuales se determinó que aquéllos **que siguieron** la dieta mediterránea presentaron una menor mortalidad por cáncer y problemas cardiovasculares.

follow up
who followed

Diversos estudios científicos **realizados** en los últimos años habían confirmado las virtudes de esta dieta en el sistema cardiovascular, pero los efectos tan favorables en la prevención del cáncer son una auténtica **novedad.**

carried out

novelty/news

«**Cuanto más se sigue la dieta mediterránea,** menor es la mortalidad por enfermedades cardiovasculares y cáncer», dice Frank Hu, profesor de nutrición de la Escuela de Salud Pública de la Universidad de Harvard, quien admite que las nuevas **ventajas** sobre el cáncer «son muy intrigantes».

The more the Mediterranean diet is followed

advantages

Un factor interesante es que los beneficios de la dieta se producen cuando esta forma de alimentación se sigue en su totalidad, sin excluir ninguno de sus elementos, y los científicos se preguntan por qué.

Hu indica que ello puede deberse a dos posibilidades: que los efectos de cada grupo alimentario **sean demasiado pequeños** como para tener un impacto considerable de forma individual o que hay efectos sinérgicos entre los componentes de la dieta.

may be / too small

En los hábitos de alimentación mediterráneos, aproximadamente el 40 por ciento de las calorías **procede de** grasas consideradas «saludables», como el aceite de oliva y el pescado, y el restante 50 por ciento de carbohidratos **complejos,** procedentes de cereales integrales, frutas y legumbres.

come from

complex

Otro factor muy importante es el ejercicio físico. La investigación también determinó que la realización de una hora de ejercicio intenso diario —fuera en el trabajo o por diversión— contribuye a aumentar aún más los beneficios de la dieta mediterránea, ya que el riesgo de mortalidad que presentaron los participantes **fue** un 28 por ciento menor.

was

■ ¿Entendiste bien?

C. Ingredientes Indiquen cuáles de los siguientes ingredientes forman parte de la dieta mediterránea:

___ pescado	___ vino	___ arroz
___ bananas	___ carnes	___ tomates
___ refrescos	___ manzanas	___ helado
___ pollo	___ lechuga	
___ pizza	___ aceite de oliva	

D. ¿Cierto o falso? Indiquen si las oraciones son ciertas (**C**) o falsas (**F**).

_____ 1. El artículo presenta los resultados de investigaciones de científicos españoles.

_____ 2. La dieta mediterránea reduce la incidencia de problemas cardiovasculares.

_____ 3. La dieta mediterránea no reduce la incidencia de cáncer.

_____ 4. La dieta mediterránea es efectiva solamente cuando se sigue en su totalidad.

_____ 5. El ejercicio físico incrementa la efectividad de la dieta mediterránea.

E. Datos y resultados Completen las frases con la información del artículo.

1. Número total de participantes en el estudio:

2. Duración del estudio:

3. Edad de los participantes en el estudio:

4. Porcentaje de reducción de problemas cardiovasculares:

5. Porcentaje de reducción del cáncer:

6. Porcentaje de calorías que proceden de grasas saludables en la dieta mediterránea:

7. Porcentaje de calorías que proceden de carbohidratos complejos en la dieta mediterránea:

8. Cantidad de ejercicio diario recomendado:

EN TU COMUNIDAD

Prepare a brief report or share with the class information about the types of services that are available in your community to assist Spanish-speaking immigrants dealing with weight concerns.

F. Para conversar ¿Qué es mejor, la dieta mediterránea o la dieta de Atkins (mucha proteína y muy pocos carbohidratos)? ¿Por qué?

G. Enfoque comunitario ¿Dónde puedes encontrar _(can you find)_ la dieta mediterránea? Prepara una lista de lugares en (o cerca de) tu universidad que ofrecen comidas de la dieta mediterránea.

	Lugar	Menú
Desayuno		
Almuerzo		
Cena		

Vocabulario

Lugares de interés	**Landmarks**
el aeropuerto	*airport*
el banco	*bank*
el bar / la barra	*bar*
la biblioteca	*library*
el cajero automático	*ATM*
la calle	*street*
el centro comercial	*shopping mall*
el cine	*movie theater*
la cuadra/manzana	*city block*
el edificio	*building*
la esquina	*street corner*
la estación de policía	*police station*
la estación de (trenes/ autobús/metro)	*(train/bus/subway) station*
el estacionamiento/ parqueadero/ aparcamiento	*parking lot*
la farmacia	*pharmacy*
el gimnasio	*gym*
el hospital	*hospital*
el hotel	*hotel*
la iglesia	*church*
la lavandería	*laundromat*
la librería	*bookstore*
el museo	*museum*
la oficina de correos	*post office*
la oficina de turismo	*tourist office*
la parada de (autobús/ tren/metro)	*(bus/train/ subway) stop*
el parque	*park*
la peluquería / el salón de belleza	*barber shop, beauty parlor*
la plaza	*town square*
el restaurante	*restaurant*
el semáforo	*traffic light*
el supermercado	*supermarket*
la tienda / el almacén	*store*
la tienda de ropa	*clothing store*
la tintorería	*dry cleaners*

Formas de pago

el cambio	*change*
el cheque	*check*
el efectivo	*cash*
la tarjeta de crédito	*credit card*

Expresiones para ir de compras

¿En qué puedo servirle, señor?	*How can I help you, sir?*
Busco...	*I am looking for . . .*
Aquí tiene.	*Here you are.*
¿Aceptan tarjetas de crédito?	*Do you take credit cards?*
De nada. / A sus órdenes. / A su servicio. / Con mucho gusto.	*You are welcome.*
Vuelva pronto.	*Come back soon.*

Desayuno	**Breakfast**
el café	*coffee*
el cereal	*cereal*
los huevos	*eggs*
revueltos	*scrambled*
fritos	*fried*
el jugo/el zumo de naranja	*orange juice*
la leche	*milk*
la mantequilla	*butter*
la mermelada	*marmalade, jam, jelly*
el pan tostado	*toast*
el té	*tea*

Almuerzo/Comida	**Lunch**
el emparedado/sándwich/ bocadillo	*sandwich*
de jamón	*ham*
de atún	*tuna*
de queso	*cheese*
de pavo	*turkey*
la ensalada	*salad*
la hamburguesa	*hamburger*
la limonada	*lemonade*
las patatas/las papas fritas	*French fries*
la pizza	*pizza*
el refresco	*soda*
la sopa	*soup*

Cena	**Dinner**	**Pescado y mariscos**	**Fish and seafood**
el agua mineral	mineral water	las almejas	clams
el arroz	rice	los camarones / las	shrimp
la carne	meat	gambas	
las legumbres / los	vegetables	el cangrejo	crab
vegetales		el filete de salmón	salmon filet
la pasta	pasta	la langosta	lobster
las patatas/las papas	potatoes	los mejillones	mussels
el pescado	fish	el róbalo	bass
el pollo	chicken	la trucha	trout
el vino	wine		

Postres	**Desserts**	**Condimentos**	
las galletas	cookies	el aceite	oil
el helado	ice cream	el aderezo	dressing
la torta / el pastel	cake, pie	el azúcar	sugar
		la mostaza	mustard

Verduras	**Vegetables**	la miel	honey
el ajo	garlic	la pimienta	pepper
las arvejas / los chícharos	peas	la sal	salt
el brócoli	broccoli	la salsa de tomate	tomato sauce
la cebolla	onion	el vinagre	vinegar
el champiñón	mushroom		
los espárragos	asparagus	**Los cubiertos**	**Tableware**
los frijoles / las judías	string beans	la copa	wine glass
verdes		la cuchara	spoon
la lechuga	lettuce	la cucharita	teaspoon
el maíz	corn	el cuchillo	knife
el plátano	plantain	el individual	placemat
el tomate	tomato	el mantel	tablecloth
la zanahoria	carrot	el platillo	saucer
		el plato	plate (dish)
Frutas	**Fruits**	la servilleta	napkin
la banana / el plátano	banana	la taza	cup
la fresa	strawberry	el tenedor	fork
el mango	mango	el vaso	glass
la manzana	apple		
el melón	melon	**En el restaurante**	
la naranja	orange	el aperitivo	before-dinner drink
la pera	pear	la carta	menu
la piña	pineapple	la cuenta	check
la sandía	watermelon	la entrada / el entremés	appetizer
la uva	grape	el mesero	waiter
		el plato principal	entrée (main course)
Carnes	**Meats**	la propina	tip
el bistec	beef steak	la sección de no fumar	nonsmoking section
la chuleta (de cerdo)	(pork) chop		
el filete de res	beef filet		
la salchicha	sausage (hot dog)		
la ternera	veal		
el tocino	bacon		

Expresiones en el restaurante

¿Algo más?	*Anything else?*
Bienvenidos.	*Welcome.*
¿Desean ordenar algo de tomar?	*Anything to drink?*
Están/Son como para chuparse los dedos.	*They are finger licking good.*
¿Están listos para pedir?	*Are you ready to order?*
¿Me podría traer... ?	*Could you bring me . . . ?*
Tenemos una reservación a nombre de...	*We have a reservation. The name is . . .*

Funciones y estructuras

Capítulo 4

Preferencias y prioridades

Para comenzar

Para cada foto de España, escoge la descripción que le corresponde.

- España es un país rico en historia y tradiciones.
- Tiene industrias modernas.
- También es famosa por sus ciudades cosmopolitas.

In this chapter you will learn . . .

- how to describe weather conditions
- how to talk about clothing preferences
- how to make comparisons
- how to express what is happening at the moment
- how to talk about sports and one's daily routine
- about vacation customs in Spain

	TEMA 1 El tiempo	**TEMA 2** La ropa	**TEMA 3** La diversión
Vocabulario	El estado del tiempo y las estaciones	Ropa de diario y accesorios	Los deportes
Funciones y estructuras	Talking about ongoing actions and events with the present progressive Comparing and contrasting with comparatives and superlatives	Talking about daily activities with e→ie and o→ue stem-changing verbs Talking about daily routines with reflexive verbs	Talking about daily activities with irregular present tense verbs Describing people and objects with the verbs **ser** and **estar**
Lecturas y vídeo	Perspectivas: Las variaciones climáticas en el mundo hispano	Vídeo: Una charla sobre la ropa	Lectura: De vacaciones

Foto 1

Foto 2

Foto 3

Enfoque

A. ¿Qué sabes ya de España? Antes de ver el vídeo, decide si las siguientes oraciones son ciertas (C) o falsas (F) y después compara tus respuestas con las de un(a) compañero(a).

_____ 1. España se encuentra en el suroeste de Europa, en la Península Ibérica, al oeste de Portugal.

_____ 2. La capital de España es Barcelona, una de las grandes ciudades europeas.

_____ 3. España está formada por 17 comunidades autónomas.

B. La diversidad dentro de España El vídeo te va a presentar con más detalle **seis** comunidades autónomas. Indica con qué comunidad autónoma se relaciona cada ciudad, lengua o característica.

OPCIONES: Andalucía (A)   Cataluña (C)
la Comunidad Valenciana (V)   Galicia (G)
El País Vasco (PV)   Castilla-La Mancha (CM)

A 1. Sevilla   C 5. un centro financiero   A 9. el flamenco
PV 2. Vitoria   CM 6. Toledo   V 10. un antiguo reino moro
CM 3. un terreno llano C 7. el catalán   G 11. Santiago de Compostela
G 4. el gallego   PV 8. el euskera   V 12. el valenciano

C. Nuestra comunidad autónoma Ahora, divídanse en seis grupos (un grupo para cada comunidad autónoma descrita en el vídeo) y hagan las siguientes actividades:

1. Mientras ven el vídeo por segunda vez, presten atención a la información (**hablada y visual**) sobre **su** comunidad autónoma: la geografía (¿dónde se encuentra? ¿es una zona montañosa, llana, costera? etc.); la capital; ciudades importantes; idiomas (¿se habla otro idioma además del castellano, o sea, el español?) y otras características.

2. Compartan su información y escriban juntos una descripción de su comunidad autónoma para presentarla a la clase.

3. Después de escuchar las presentaciones de las seis comunidades autónomas, infórmenles a sus compañeros de grupo a qué comunidad irían (*you would go*) durante un viaje a España y explíquenles por qué.

For more info, you may want to check the **Temas** site: http://temas.heinle.com

El tiempo

iLrn

I. Vocabulario: El estado del tiempo y las estaciones

invierno (diciembre, enero, febrero)

Nos gusta el **invierno** porque **nieva** y **hace** mucho **frío**.

primavera (marzo, abril, mayo)

Yo prefiero la **primavera** porque **llueve** y **hace fresco**.

verano (junio, julio, agosto)

Nos gusta el **verano** porque **hace sol** y mucho **calor**.

otoño (septiembre, octubre, noviembre)

Bueno, a mí me gusta mucho el **otoño** porque casi siempre **está nublado** y **hace viento**.

The verb **hacer** *(to do, to make)* is used to talk about several weather conditions.

¿Qué tiempo **hace**?	*What is the weather like?*
Hace viento.	*It's windy.*
Hace (buen/mal) tiempo.	*The weather is (good/bad).*

The words **un poco de** *(a bit, somewhat)* and **mucho** *(very, quite a bit)* can be used to indicate the degree of a given weather condition.

Hace **mucho** frío hoy.	*It's **very** cold today.*
Hace **un poco de** viento esta mañana.	*It's **a bit** windy this morning.*
Llueve **mucho** en esta ciudad.	*It rains **a lot** in this city.*

■ Asimilación

4-1 En los Estados Unidos... Completa la oración con la información más apropiada, de acuerdo con el contexto.

1. En los Estados Unidos hace calor durante los meses de ___.
   a. junio, julio y agosto   c. marzo, abril y mayo
   b. diciembre, enero y febrero
2. Por lo general, en este país hace fresco durante los meses de ___.
   a. diciembre y enero   c. abril y octubre
   b. junio y julio
3. Aquí siempre hace frío en ___.
   a. diciembre y enero   c. abril y octubre
   b. junio y julio
4. Llueve mucho en ___.
   a. diciembre y enero   c. abril y octubre
   b. junio y julio
5. Casi siempre nieva durante los meses de ___.
   a. diciembre y enero   c. abril y octubre
   b. junio y julio

01-37 **4-2 Informe meteorológico** Escucha el siguiente informe del tiempo y escoge la respuesta apropiada para cada ciudad.

_____ 1. En Madrid...
     a. hace sol.   b. hace frío.   c. hace viento.

_____ 2. En Bilbao...
     a. está nublado.   b. nieva.   c. llueve.

_____ 3. En Valencia...
     a. hace sol.   b. está nublado.   c. hace viento.

_____ 4. En Málaga...
     a. está nublado.   b. nieva.   c. hace sol.

_____ 5. En Barcelona...
     a. hace sol.   b. llueve.   c. hace calor.

■ **Aplicaciones**

4-3 ¿Qué tiempo hace? Describan el tiempo en cada una de las siguientes imágenes.

MODELO   *Hace frío. Parece que* (it seems like) *hace un poco de viento y no hace sol,...*

Imagen 1

Imagen 2

Imagen 3

4-4 El tiempo hoy Con un(a) compañero(a), describan el estado del tiempo el día de hoy.

MODELO   *Hoy hace sol y hace un poco de calor. También...*

4-5 El estado del tiempo en España Completen el pronóstico del tiempo *(weather forecast)* para España, de acuerdo con el siguiente mapa.

En el norte, en las regiones de Galicia, la Cordillera Cantábrica, Castilla y León, Navarra, La Rioja, Aragón y el norte de Cataluña, _____. En el sur de Cataluña y en el norte de La Mancha, de Extremadura y de Valencia _____. En el sur, en Extremadura, Andalucía y las Islas Canarias, _____. Finalmente, en Galicia, Asturias y el Estrecho de Gibraltar _____.

■ Integración

4-6 ¿Cuál es tu estación favorita? Prepara varias preguntas para determinar cuál es la estación favorita de uno(a) de tus compañeros y por qué. Luego, preséntale un breve informe de sus respuestas al resto de la clase.

4-7 El tiempo en los Estados Unidos Completen la siguiente tabla con el estado del tiempo y las actividades más recomendables para el día de hoy en las diferentes regiones de los Estados Unidos.

	Previsión del tiempo	Actividades recomendadas
El noreste		
El sureste		
El centro		
Las montañas		
El noroeste		
El suroeste		

II. Funciones y estructuras: Talking about ongoing actions and events with the present progressive

Hoy hace muy buen tiempo. Por eso **estamos nadando** en la piscina.

When you want to emphasize that an action is taking place right at this moment, you may use the present progressive tense, the equivalent of the English structure *to be + -ing*. This tense is formed with the verb **estar** followed by the present participle form (**gerundio** in Spanish) of the main verb.

Como **está lloviendo, estamos mirando** una película en casa. Raquel y David **están estudiando** en Madrid.	*Since **it is raining, we are watching** a movie at home. Raquel and David **are studying** in Madrid.*

The present participle of **-ar** verbs is formed by attaching the **-ando** ending to the stem of the verb while the present participle of **-er** and **-ir** verbs is formed by attaching the **-iendo** ending to the stem.

VERB	STEM	PRESENT PARTICIPLE
-ar: tomar	tom-	tom**ando**
-er: comer	com-	com**iendo**
-ir: escribir	escrib-	escrib**iendo**

When the stem of an **-er** or **-ir** verb ends in a vowel, the ending **-iendo** is changed to **-yendo**.

VERB	STEM	PRESENT PARTICIPLE
leer	le-	le**yendo**
oír	o-	o**yendo**
ir	X	**yendo**

-ir verbs that undergo stem changes in the present tense also have stem changes in the present participle.

pedir (i, **i**)	p**i**diendo
preferir (ie, **i**)	pref**i**riendo
dormir (ue, **u**)	d**u**rmiendo

As you learned in **Capítulo 3, Tema 3**, stem changes are indicated in parentheses. For example, the verb **pedir** has a change e→i in both the present tense and the present participle.

■ Asimilación

4-8 El tiempo, las estaciones y nuestras acciones Para cada situación, indica si la actividad es lógica (**L**) o ilógica (**I**).

_____ 1. Es invierno. Nosotros estamos nadando en la playa.

_____ 2. Está lloviendo mucho. Yo estoy caminando por el parque.

_____ 3. Es verano. Estás mirando un partido de béisbol en la televisión.

_____ 4. Hace calor. Ricardo y José Luis están esquiando en las montañas.

_____ 5. Es otoño. Dora está celebrando el Día de San Valentín con su novio.

_____ 6. Hace buen tiempo. Tú estás jugando en el patio de tu casa.

CD1–38 **4-9 ¿Quién?** Escucha el mensaje que Tere le deja a su madre en el contestador (*answering machine*). Luego, contesta las preguntas que siguen.

OPCIONES: Tere Miguelito Consuelo el bebé el padre Marta

1. ¿Quién está lavando el carro? _____ Papa _____
2. ¿Quién está escuchando música? _____ Miguelito _____
3. ¿Quién está preparando el almuerzo? _____ Marta _____
4. ¿Quién está leyendo un libro? _____ C. _____
5. ¿Quién está durmiendo? _____ el bebe _____
6. ¿Quién está haciendo tareas? _____ Tere _____

■ Aplicaciones

4-10 ¿Qué hacen aquí? Indiquen qué están haciendo las siguientes personas en estos lugares.

Since the cultural focus of this chapter is Spain, you will get the chance to use and practice the **vosotros(as)** form of the verb. Remember that this pronoun, which means *all of you* (informal), is used in the northern and central part of Spain.

MODELO Ellos están en el supermercado. Ellos *están comprando alimentos*.

1. Yo estoy en la lavandería. Yo...
2. Gladis está en el museo. Ella...
3. Nosotros estamos en la parada de metro. Nosotros...
4. Vosotros estáis en el centro. Vosotros...
5. El Sr. Nogueras y la Sra. Guzmán están en la oficina. Ellos...
6. Tú estás en el aeropuerto. Tú...

4-11 Un día en el Parque del Retiro Digan qué está haciendo la gente que está en el Parque del Retiro en este momento.

4-12 Tu ambiente y tú Tu compañero(a) quiere saber cómo reaccionas a ciertos estímulos relacionados con el ambiente, particularmente con el tiempo y las estaciones. Escucha la clave e indica dónde estás y qué estás haciendo. ¡Usa la imaginación! Al terminar, cambien de papel.

MODELO   E1: *Es verano y hace mucho sol.*
               E2: *Estoy en una playa de Málaga, España. Estoy tomando el*
                    sol, nadando en el mar y bebiendo zumo.

■ Integración

4-13 Un miércoles como cualquier otro *(as any other)* Averigua qué hace tu compañero(a) a diferentes horas los miércoles. Hagan preguntas específicas y reaccionen a lo que el otro dice.

MODELO   E1: *Lorraine, generalmente, ¿qué estás haciendo los miércoles*
                    a las diez en punto de la mañana?
               E2: *Generalmente estoy estudiando en la biblioteca.*
               E1: *¿Con qué frecuencia estudias en la biblioteca?*
                    ¡No me gusta estudiar ahí!
               E2: *Pues yo usualmente estudio en la biblioteca.*
               E1: *¿Y qué estás haciendo los miércoles al mediodía?*
               E2: …

4-14 Una tarjeta postal Imagínate que estás de vacaciones viajando por diferentes partes de España y escríbele una tarjeta postal a tu mejor amigo(a). Dile qué cosas estás haciendo. ¡Usa la imaginación! Al terminar, intercambia *(exchange)* tu tarjeta con la de un(a) compañero(a) de clase. Háganse preguntas y digan qué cosas están haciendo diariamente en sus vacaciones.

III. Funciones y estructuras: Comparing and contrasting with comparatives and superlatives

—En España, ¿la primavera es **más lluviosa que** el invierno?
—No, el invierno es **la estación más lluviosa**. El invierno es **tan lluvioso como** la primavera en los Estados Unidos.

■ To make comparisons of equality, use the following structures.

> **tan** + (adjective/adverb) + **como**

Julio es **tan caluroso como** agosto.	*July is **as hot as** August.*
Hoy llueve **tan intensamente como** ayer.	*Today it is raining **as intensely as** yesterday.*

Notice that the adjective **(caluroso)** must agree in gender and number with the noun it describes **(julio).**

> **tanto/a/os/as** + noun + **como**

To express equality among nouns you may also use the expression **el/la/los/las** + **mismo/a/os/as** + noun + **que**: *Esta semana tenemos **la misma temperatura que** la semana pasada.*

En Seattle no hay **tantos días soleados como** en Miami.	*In Seattle there are not **as many sunny days as** in Miami.*

Notice that the form of **tanto (tantos)** must agree in number and gender with the noun **(días).**

> verb + **tanto como**

En Boston **llueve tanto como** en Nueva York.	*In Boston **it rains as much as** in New York.*

■ To make comparisons of inequality, use the following structures.

> **más/menos** + (adjective/adverb/noun) + **que**

La primavera es **menos fría que** el invierno.	*Spring is **less cold than** winter.*
Enero tiene **más días que** febrero.	*January has **more days than** February.*

■ The Spanish superlative is formed using the following structure.

> **el/la/los/las** + noun + **más/menos** + adjective + **de...**

El otoño es **la estación más aburrida.**	*Fall is **the most boring season.***
Julio y agosto son **los meses menos agradables del año.**	*July and August are **the least pleasant months of the year.***

The ending **de...** is only used when the speaker wants to mention the group to which the noun belongs. The preposition **de** must be followed by a definite article (**el/la/los/las**). Keep in mind that **de** + **el** = **del**.

The following adjectives have irregular comparative and superlative forms.

ADJECTIVE	COMPARATIVE	SUPERLATIVE
bueno (good)	**mejor(es)** (better) El verano es **mejor** que el invierno.	(el/la/los/las) **mejor(es)** (the best) El verano es **la mejor** estación.
malo (bad)	**peor(es)** (worse) El calor es **peor** que el frío.	(el/la/los/las) **peor(es)** (the worst) El calor es **el peor** tipo de clima.
grande, viejo (big/old)	**mayor(es)** (bigger/older) Sara es **mayor** que ustedes.	(el/la/los/las) **mayor(es)** (the biggest/oldest) Sara es **la mayor** de su familia.
pequeño, joven (small/young)	**menor(es)** (smaller/younger) Nosotros somos **menores** que Lucas.	(el/la/los/las) **menor(es)** (the smallest/youngest) Somos **los menores** de todos los hijos.

■ Asimilación

4-15 El tiempo Completen las oraciones que siguen con las alternativas más lógicas.

1. Quebec es tan fría como _____.
   - a. Madrid
   - b. Montreal
   - c. California
2. En _____ hace más calor que en el otoño.
   - a. la primavera
   - b. el invierno
   - c. el verano
3. En Albuquerque llueve menos frecuentemente que en _____.
   - a. Phoenix
   - b. Las Vegas
   - c. Seattle
4. _____ es uno de los lugares del mundo donde más nieva.
   - a. La selva del Amazonas
   - b. Siberia
   - c. El Caribe
5. En San Juan hace tanto calor como en _____.
   - a. Santo Domingo
   - b. París
   - c. Buenos Aires
6. _____ es una de las ciudades donde hace más viento.
   - a. Atlanta
   - b. San Luis
   - c. Chicago

CD1–39 **4-16 ¿Qué opinas de los alimentos?** Escucha las preguntas sobre los alimentos y selecciona la alternativa más lógica. Luego, compara tus respuestas con las de un(a) compañero(a). ¿Están de acuerdo?

1. los refrescos / el vino
2. la lechuga / el brócoli
3. los camarones / la pizza
4. el pan / el pollo
5. las papas / la langosta
6. el helado / el tomate

■ Aplicaciones

4-17 El mundo de las estrellas Completen las siguientes oraciones con los nombres de personas famosas. ¡Cuidado con la concordancia!

MODELO *Cindy Lauper* es menos popular que *Madonna*.

1. _____ es el mejor cantante del mundo.
2. _____ y _____ tienen menos talento que _____.
3. _____ es la peor actriz de los Estados Unidos.
4. _____ es tan presumido *(conceited)* como _____.
5. _____ y _____ son más simpáticas que _____.
6. _____ es el/la animador(a) *(host/hostess)* más cómico(a) de la televisión.

4-18 Las personas de la clase Formen oraciones para comparar a las personas de la clase.

MODELO *Warren es más estudioso que Mike.*
Kate y Joseph son los estudiantes menos altos de la clase.

You may use some of these options:

ADJETIVOS: **alto, bueno, interesante, guapo, atractivo, responsable, simpático**

SUSTANTIVOS: **interés en la clase, cuadernos, libros**

VERBOS: **hablar español, llegar tarde a clase, salir al baño**

4-19 Guía turística de Barcelona Completen el siguiente párrafo con las frases de la lista.

OPCIONES: los museos más importantes   la zona más antigua
la mejor vista *(view)*   los mejores restaurantes
el almacén más popular   la temporada más turística

Barcelona es una ciudad fascinante. _____ se llama Barrio Gótico y tiene muchas iglesias y monumentos medievales. _____ están en La Ribera y ofrecen gran variedad de comidas y precios. _____ es El Corte Inglés y está en la Plaza Catalunya. _____ son los de Picasso y Miró, los cuales están abiertos de martes a domingo. _____ es desde Montjuïc, al suroeste de la ciudad. Desde allí se puede ver el puerto y toda Barcelona. El verano es _____ de esta ciudad; por eso es preciso hacer reservaciones con tiempo.

EN TU COMUNIDAD

Compile a list of restaurants in the community that specialize in Spanish or Latin American food. Besides providing their names and location, you should investigate their schedules, prices, and most popular dishes to create a basic restaurant directory to be posted at the Office of International Students.

■ Integración

4-20 Así es la familia Túrnense para hacer y responder a preguntas sobre su familia. Cubran temas diversos y den *(provide)* detalles.

You may ask questions such as the following: **¿Eres tan alto(a) como tus hermanos? ¿Tu madre es más estricta que tu padre? ¿Cuál es tu tío más hablador? ¿Eres mayor que tus primos? ¿Tus parientes saben tanto como tú?**

4-21 Apreciación culinaria Escribe tu propia crítica sobre los restaurantes de tu ciudad o tu región. ¡Debes tratar de convencer a tu profesor(a) con tus argumentos! Usa algunas de los siguientes frases.

...tiene los precios más económicos, ...es más/menos caro, en... sirven los mejores/peores..., ...es el más bonito, en... tienen el mejor/peor servicio, en... el menú es más/menos variado.

IV. Perspectivas: Las variaciones climáticas en el mundo hispano

■ **Antes de leer**

En grupos, contesten y expliquen su respuesta a la siguiente pregunta:

¿Es el clima en el mundo hispano similar o diferente al de los Estados Unidos?

■ **A leer**

Variaciones climáticas

La mayoría de los países hispanos están en la zona tropical y no tienen fluctuaciones térmicas significativas durante el año. En estos países se habla, en cambio, de períodos secos y períodos lluviosos. Un factor muy importante en el clima de algunos de los países de habla hispana es la altura *(elevation);* siempre hace frío o fresco en las regiones altas y calor en las bajas, o sea, al nivel del mar *(sea level)*. Las estaciones en países como Argentina y Chile son opuestas a las de España (o los Estados Unidos) debido a su ubicación en el hemisferio sur.

Diferencias en las escalas de temperatura

En España y Latinoamérica se usa la escala Celsius para medir la temperatura. Para la conversión de temperaturas entre el sistema centígrado y el Fahrenheit, usa la siguiente fórmula:

$$°C = 0.55 \times (°F - 32).$$

■ **¿Entendiste bien?**

A. ¡Qué variación! Clasifica los siguientes países de acuerdo con la información dada en la nota anterior.

OPCIONES: No tiene estaciones.
   En enero es verano.
   En enero es invierno.

1. Argentina
2. Chile
3. Colombia
4. España
5. Costa Rica
6. Estados Unidos

B. Conversiones Convierte las siguientes temperaturas de la escala Celsius a la escala Fahrenheit.

Las temperaturas en Madrid		
Mes	**Escala Celsius**	**Escala Fahrenheit**
diciembre y enero	Entre 2 y 11 °C	Entre ____ y ____ °F
marzo y octubre	Entre 5 y 18 °C	Entre ____ y ____ °F
julio y agosto	Entre 17 y 31 °C	Entre ____ y ____ °F

C. ¿Cierto o falso? Indica si las siguientes oraciones acerca de la temperatura en Madrid corresponden o no con la información de la tabla.

____ 1. En enero hace mucho calor en Madrid.

____ 2. Julio es un mes fresco.

____ 3. En octubre la temperatura es de más o menos 15 grados centígrados.

____ 4. Las temperaturas durante el mes de abril en Madrid oscilan entre los 50 y los 70 grados Fahrenheit.

El invierno en Madrid

La ropa

I. Vocabulario: Ropa de diario y accesorios

los lentes de sol · la camiseta · la corbata · la blusa · la camisa · el impermeable · Damas · el abrigo · el vestido · la ropa interior · la falda · los guantes · la chaqueta (americana) · los pantalones · el reloj · los aretes/pendientes · las botas · los tacones · el collar · los calcetines/las medias · los zapatos · la gorra · Caballeros · el traje · el chaleco · el suéter · el cinturón

Vocabulario práctico

Materiales

el algodón *cotton*
el cuero *leather*
de fantasía *costume jewelry*
la lana *wool*
el material sintético (acrílico,
     poliéster) *synthetic material*
     (acrylic, polyester)
el metal *metal*
el oro *gold*
la pana *corduroy*
la plata *silver*
la seda *silk*
la tela *fabric*

Diseños *(Designs)*

a cuadros *checked*
a rayas *striped*
de puntos/lunares *polka-dots*
estampado *print*
liso / de un solo tono *solid color*

Otras prendas *(Other garments)*

las sandalias *sandals*
los tejanos / los vaqueros *jeans*
el traje de baño / el bañador
     bathing suit
las zapatillas *slippers*
los zapatos de tenis / las zapatillas
     tennis shoes / sneakers

SABOR REGIONAL

Sneakers are called **zapatillas** in Argentina, Chile, Panama, Peru, and Uruguay.

To describe what something is made of, use the expression **ser + de** followed by the material.

El chaleco **es de cuero.** *The vest **is made of leather.***
Estos abrigos **son de lana.** *These coats **are made of wool.***

You may describe articles of clothing with colors or by using the expression **de color** followed by the masculine singular form of the color.

Mis medias son **amarillas.** *My socks are **yellow.***
Tus pantalones son **verdes/negros.** *Your pants are **green/black.***
El cinturón es **de color** blanco. *The belt is **white (in color).***

■ Asimilación

4-22 ¿Qué prenda es? Empareja las prendas con sus descripciones.

_____ 1. la falda   a. Es una prenda que usas cuando hace frío.

_____ 2. los pantalones   b. Los llevas en los pies para caminar.

_____ 3. el abrigo   c. Generalmente son cortos en el verano.

_____ 4. los zapatos   d. Los hombres de negocios las prefieren blancas.

_____ 5. la camisa   e. La llevan solamente las mujeres.

CD1–40 **4-23 ¿Quién es?** Identifica la persona que se describe a continuación.

Foto 1

Foto 2

■ Aplicaciones

4-24 Recomendaciones Un(a) amigo(a) está preparándose para ir a esquiar a las montañas. ¿Qué ropa creen que debe (o no debe) llevar? Preparen una lista.

4-25 Los materiales Normalmente, ¿de qué material son las siguientes prendas? Indica tus respuestas y, al terminar, compáralas con las de un(a) compañero(a).

OPCIONES: seda   oro   lana   algodón   cuero   material sintético

1. los cinturones: _____   3. las blusas: _____
2. los impermeables: _____   4. los aretes: _____
                                      5. los tejanos: _____

4-26 Variaciones de acuerdo con la estación Clasifica los siguientes artículos según la estación. **¡OJO!** Algunas prendas y accesorios se pueden usar en más de una época del año.

chaqueta	lentes de sol	abrigo	tejanos
gorra	camiseta	aretes	bermudas
zapatillas	corbata	sandalias	guantes
blusa	impermeable	bañador/traje de baño	cinturón
botas	vestido		

primavera	
verano	
otoño	
invierno	

■ Integración

 4-27 De compras Representa la siguiente conversación con un(a) compañero(a).

Comprador(a)

Imagine that you are in Spain and are buying clothes for a special occasion. Tell the clerk what you are looking for, explore your options (different colors, materials, designs, etc.), and complete the transaction. Remember: This is not a shopping spree! You are traveling on a budget.

You may want to use expressions such as: **Busco...** *(I'm looking for . . .)* **¿Dónde está el vestidor?** *(Where is your fitting room?)* **¿Tiene otros colores/materiales/diseños?** *(Do you have any other colors/materials/designs?)* **¿Tiene una talla más grande/chica?** *(Do you carry bigger/smaller sizes?)* **¿Cuánto cuesta?** *(How much is it?)* **¿Aceptan tarjetas de crédito?** *(Do you take credit cards?)*

Vendedor(a)

Imagine that you are a clerk at a department store in Spain. Help this customer with his/her purchase. Remember: You work on commission, so you want to encourage this client to buy as many items of clothing and accessories as possible!

You may want to use expressions such as: **¿Le puedo ayudar en algo?** *(How may I help you?)* **Le queda muy bien.** *(It looks great on you.)* **Está en rebaja.** *(It is on sale.)* **Le recomiendo también este cinturón que va muy bien con esos pantalones.** *(I also recommend this belt that goes well with those pants.)*

4-28 Desfile de modas *(Fashion show)* Formen grupos de cuatro estudiantes. Su misión es presentar las modas de los estudiantes universitarios de los Estados Unidos. Dos estudiantes van a actuar como modelos y los otros dos van a describir los colores, materiales y diseños de sus prendas de vestir.

1. Decidan qué prendas van a llevar los modelos.
2. Escriban lo que van a decir los anfitriones *(presenters)* y cómo van a presentar a los modelos.

EN TU COMUNIDAD

Visit a local department store and locate garments made in Spain or Latin America. In your reports, you should compare the price, quality, and style of these garments with those made in Asia and/or the United States.

II. Funciones y estructuras: Talking about daily activities with *e→ie* and *o→ue* stem-changing verbs

NELLY: ¿Qué **piensas** de estos zapatos?
PALOMA: ¡Son preciosos! ¿Cuánto **cuestan**?
NELLY: Sólo veinticinco dólares.
PALOMA: ¡**Quiero** unos para mí también! ¿**Puedo** verlos?

As you learned in **Capítulo 3, Tema 3**, the stem of some Spanish verbs changes when the verb is conjugated (**pedir: pi**do, **pi**des, **pi**de, etc.). In this section you will learn about two more stem changes: **e → ie** and **o → ue**. Look at the conjugations of the verbs **pensar** *(to think)* and **poder** *(to be able to)*.

*Notice that the stem in the **nosotros(as)** and **vosotros(as)** forms does not change, as with the **e→i** stem-changing verbs.

pensar (e→ie)	poder (o→ue)
yo **pienso**	yo **puedo**
tú **piensas**	tú **puedes**
él/ella/usted **piensa**	él/ella/usted **puede**
nosotros(as) **pensamos**	nosotros(as) **podemos**
vosotros(as) **pensáis**	vosotros(as) **podéis**
ellos(as)/ustedes **piensan**	ellos(as)/ustedes **pueden**

Here is a list of some common **e→ie** and **o→ue** stem-changing verbs.

e→ie	o→ue
cerrar *to close*	acostar *to put to bed*
comenzar *to begin*	almorzar *to have lunch*
despertar *to wake*	contar (con) *to count (on)*
empezar *to begin*	costar *to cost*
mentir *to lie*	demostrar *to demonstrate*
pensar *to think*	devolver *to return*
perder *to lose*	dormir *to sleep*
preferir *to prefer*	encontrar *to find*
querer *to want*	llover *to rain*
sentir *to feel*	morir *to die*
	mostrar *to show*
	mover *to move*
	poder *to be able to*
	probar *to taste, to try*
	recordar *to remember*
	soñar *to dream*
	volar *to fly*
	volver *to return*

Even though the verb **jugar** *(to play a sport or game)* does not have an **o** in its stem, it behaves like any **o→ue** stem-changing verb: **juego, juegas, juega, jugamos, jugáis, juegan.**

The stem of those **-ir** verbs that have the **e→ie** change uses an **i** in the present participle: **mentir → mintiendo**. On the other hand, the stem of those **-ir** verbs that have the **o → ue** change uses a **u: dormir → durmiendo**.

■ Asimilación

4-29 ¿Con qué frecuencia? Indica con qué frecuencia haces las siguientes actividades. Cuando termines, compara tus respuestas con las de un(a) compañero(a). ¿Qué cosas tienen en común?

ACTIVIDAD	FRECUENCIA
1. Sueño con monstruos y fantasmas.	
2. Pierdo prendas de vestir.	
3. Almuerzo en la cafetería de la universidad.	
4. Comienzo a celebrar mi cumpleaños el día anterior.	
5. No recuerdo fechas importantes.	
6. Prefiero vestir con tejanos y camiseta.	
7. Me pruebo la ropa antes de comprarla.	
8. Devuelvo las cosas que les pido a mis amigos.	

CD1–41 **4-30 Los estudiantes de tu universidad** Escucha las oraciones e indica si se aplican o no se aplican a los estudiantes de tu universidad.

1. se aplica / no se aplica
2. se aplica / no se aplica
3. se aplica / no se aplica
4. se aplica / no se aplica
5. se aplica / no se aplica
6. se aplica / no se aplica

■ Aplicaciones

4-31 Categorías Escriban cada palabra o frase de la lista al lado del verbo con el que se relaciona.

OPCIONES: una identificación   un aniversario   mucho dinero
el aeropuerto   la billetera   el cementerio   la puerta
la ventana   una bebida   una oportunidad   la licencia
una blusa   un viaje   la tarea   la funeraria   un diploma

querer: _____   morir: _____

recordar: _____   mostrar: _____

perder: _____   probar: _____

cerrar: _____   volar: _____

4-32 Dependiendo del tiempo... Escribe las palabras y frases de la lista al lado de la expresión de tiempo (en el cuadro en la página 158) con la que más las relaciones para formar oraciones. Puedes usar algunas frases más de una vez *(more than once)*. Cuando termines, comparte la información con el resto de la clase.

The expression **empezar + a** *(to begin to)* is always followed by a verb in the infinitive, much like **ir + a: Ella empieza a trabajar el lunes.** *She begins to work on Monday.*

OPCIONES: preferir...   (no) querer...   (no) poder...   dormir...
(no) pensar que...   preferir llevar...   (no) querer llevar...
recordar...   sentir que...   empezar a...

Cuando...	ACTIVIDADES
hace calor	*No quiero trabajar.*
hace mucho frío	
llueve	
hace mucho viento	

4-33 Mi hija la distraída *(absent-minded)* Completen el siguiente párrafo con los verbos de la lista. Conjúguenlos correctamente.

> volver   tener   querer   perder   poder   encontrar   despertar
> recordar

> Mi hija es muy distraída. Por las mañanas, ella nunca *encuentra* la ropa que (ella) *quiere* llevar para el colegio. Por eso, siempre llego tarde al trabajo, a pesar de que (yo) me *despierto* dos horas antes que ella. Por otro lado, ella nunca *recuerda* dónde están sus libros o sus cuadernos. Yo le pido que busque con cuidado, pero (ella) siempre _____ y me dice: «¡Mamá, no sé dónde están!» Para colmo *(on top of that)*, (ella) siempre _____ el dinero que le doy para el almuerzo. ¡(Yo) No _____ tolerar más esta situación! ¡Mi hija _____ que cambiar!

■ Integración

4-34 Una invitación Representa la siguiente situación con un(a) compañero(a).

Here are some expressions student B may use to refuse student A's invitation: **Lo siento, No puedo porque tengo que..., No quiero...,** and **Prefiero...**

Estudiante A	Estudiante B
The weather is perfect and you would like to spend the day with your friend. Tell him/her all the details of what you prefer, want, and/or are able to do today. Try to convince him/her!	Although the weather is perfect today, you do not feel like doing the things your friend wants to do today. Try to convince him/her to do the activities you prefer, want, and/or are able to do today.

4-35 La ropa apropiada Describe la ropa que prefieres llevar y qué cosas no quieres llevar a por lo menos tres eventos o lugares de la lista. Además, explica por qué. Cuando termines, entrégale una copia a tu profesor(a).

OPCIONES: a la iglesia
a un picnic en el parque   al cine   a la universidad
a una cena formal en un hotel lujoso

MODELO   *Para ir a..., yo PREFERIR llevar..., ... y ... porque...*
Por otro lado, no QUERER llevar... porque... Si llevo...,
yo (no) PODER...

III. Funciones y estructuras: Talking about daily routines with reflexive verbs

Julia **se despierta** a las seis y media de la mañana, ...

se cepilla los dientes, ...

se viste rápidamente ...

y **se va** para el trabajo.

In the previous examples, **Julia** is doing something to or for herself. These actions in which the doer (subject) and recipient (object) are the same require the use of reflexive pronouns. Here is the list of Spanish reflexive pronouns.

*Notice that, for a reflexive structure to be constructed correctly, the subject, the reflexive pronoun, and the verb must refer to the same person. For example, in the sentence **Mirna se maquilla mucho**, **Mirna** (subject), **se** (pronoun), and **maquilla** (verb) are all in the third person singular.

REFLEXIVE PRONOUNS			
me	*myself*	**nos**	*ourselves*
te	*yourself* (informal)	**os**	*yourselves* (Spain)
se	*himself, herself, yourself* (formal)	**se**	*themselves, yourselves*

Reflexive pronouns are placed before the conjugated verb. When they are used in a verb phrase that includes an infinitive or a past participle, they may be placed before the auxiliary verb or attached to the main verb.

Nosotras no **nos** maquillamos.
Me voy a vestir / Voy a vestir**me** de negro.
Carlos **se** está afeitando / está afeitándo**se**.

*We do not **wear make-up**.*
I am going to dress in black.
*Carlos **is shaving**.*

Past participles with a pronoun attached to them take a written accent mark in the third-to-the-last syllable as in **afeitándose**.

The following is a list of some common Spanish reflexive verbs.

*Notice that the infinitive form of reflexive verbs ends in **-se.**

The meaning of many of these reflexive verbs varies significantly from their nonreflexive form: **dormir** *(to sleep)* – **dormirse** *(to fall asleep)*, **ir** *(to go)* – **irse** *(to leave)*, **poner** *(to put)* – **ponerse** *(to put on [clothing])*, etc.

acostarse (ue)	*to go to bed*	levantarse	*to get up*
afeitarse	*to shave*	llamarse	*to be called*
arreglarse	*to fix up, get ready*	llevarse	*to take away, to get along*
arrepentirse	*to regret*	maquillarse	*to put on make-up*
bañarse	*to bathe*	peinarse	*to comb (one's hair)*
cepillarse	*to brush*	perfumarse	*to put on perfume*
despertarse (ie)	*to wake up*	ponerse	*to put on (clothing)*
divertirse (ie)	*to have fun*	prepararse	*to get ready*
dormirse (ue)	*to fall asleep*	probarse (ue)	*to try on (clothing)*
ducharse	*to shower*	quedarse	*to stay*
graduarse	*to graduate*	quitarse	*to take off (clothing)*
irse	*to leave*	sentarse (ie)	*to sit down*
lavarse	*to wash up*	vestirse (i)	*to get dressed*

■ Asimilación

4-36 Con frecuencia... Indica cuáles de estas acciones haces con frecuencia. Luego, compara tus respuestas con las de un(a) compañero(a). ¿Qué actividades tienen en común?

_____ Me maquillo para ir a la universidad.

_____ Me pruebo la ropa antes de comprarla.

_____ Me ducho antes de desayunar.

_____ Me voy a casa después de la clase de español.

_____ Me levanto tan pronto *(as soon as)* suena *(goes off)* el despertador.

_____ Me quedo en casa los viernes por la noche.

_____ Me lavo el pelo todos los días.

CD1-42 **4-37 La rutina matutina de Pilar** Escucha la descripción de la rutina matutina de Pilar y selecciona las oraciones que sean ciertas.

_____ Se maquilla en casa.

_____ Se despierta temprano.

_____ Se queda en la cama un rato.

_____ No desayuna.

_____ Se cepilla los dientes después de mirar las noticias.

_____ Se baña por la mañana.

■ Aplicaciones

4-38 En orden lógico Pongan las siguientes actividades en orden.

MODELO   irse para el trabajo   levantarse temprano   prepararse
Primero nos levantamos temprano, luego nos preparamos y finalmente nos vamos para el trabajo.

1. divertirse en la fiesta, ponerse la ropa, quitarse la ropa
2. bañarse, peinarse, vestirse elegantemente
3. dormirse temprano, despertarse por la mañana, acostarse tarde
4. afeitarse, ducharse rápidamente, probarse diferentes camisas
5. prepararse para tomar el examen, sentarse en la sala de clase, irse para la universidad

4-39 Los Padilla Completen el siguiente párrafo con los verbos de la lista. Conjúguenlos correctamente.

OPCIONES: acostarse   levantarse   arrepentirse   llamarse   afeitarse
llevarse   bañarse   sentarse

Las mañanas en mi casa son un poco locas. Yo _____ temprano, pero mi esposo y mis hijos no. Mi esposo siempre usa el baño primero. Él _____ y _____, y después me ayuda a preparar el desayuno. Mi hija mayor, que _____ Mónica, es la más problemática. Ella _____ muy tarde mirando la televisión y por la mañana no quiere ir a la escuela. Mónica y mi hija menor, Lily, no _____ bien y discuten *(argue)* constantemente, hasta cuando (nosotros) _____ a la mesa a desayunar. Mi casa puede ser un caos por las mañanas, pero (yo) no _____ de tener una familia tan particular.

4-40 Gustos *(likes and dislikes)* **diferentes**

Paso 1: Completa las siguientes frases de manera lógica y de acuerdo con tus propios gustos.

MODELO   PERFUMARSE para ir a *una cita*

1. PONERSE _____ para ir a un baile
2. DESPERTARSE tarde los _____ (día[s])
3. ACOSTARSE a la(s) _____ los lunes por la noche
4. VESTIRSE con ropa _____ para venir a la universidad
5. LLEVARSE mal con _____
6. GRADUARSE de la universidad en el año _____

Paso 2: Ahora, usa la información del **Paso 1** para hacerle preguntas a un(a) compañero(a). Toma notas. Cuando termines, prepara un informe para el resto de la clase.

MODELO   E1: *Mary, ¿te perfumas para ir a una cita?*
E2: *Sí, me perfumo para ir a una cita y también me perfumo para ir a mi trabajo.*

■ **Integración**

4-41 Una entrevista de trabajo (I) Imagínate que tienes una entrevista de trabajo muy importante mañana por la mañana. Explícale a tu compañero(a) las cosas que vas a hacer antes de ir a la entrevista. ¡Debes estar preparado(a) para las preguntas de tu compañero(a)! Toma notas cuando tu compañero(a) explique lo que él/ella va a hacer.

4-42 Una entrevista de trabajo (II) Ahora, haz un resumen de las cosas que tu compañero(a) va a hacer antes de ir a su entrevista de trabajo. Cuando termines, dale una copia a él/ella para ver si tienes todos los detalles necesarios.

REMEMBER

In this activity you have to use the structure **ir + a +** infinitive and other expressions you learned in **Capítulo 3, Tema 3**. Remember that in these structures the reflexive pronoun may be placed before the auxiliary (conjugated) verb or attached to the infinitive.

You can use the following connectors for activities 4-41 and 4-42: **primero** *(first)*, **antes de...** *(before . . .)*, **después** *(afterward)*, **luego** *(then)*, **entonces** *(then)*, and **finalmente** *(finally)*.

IV. Vídeo: Una charla sobre la ropa

▓ Preparación

A. La ropa de Sofía En el vídeo, Sofía le va a enseñar a Alejandra su ropa. Antes de ver el vídeo, indica cuáles de las siguientes prendas crees que Sofía tiene en su armario. **¡OJO!** No olvides *(Do not forget)* que ella está en Puerto Rico y hace buen tiempo.

_____ abrigo	_____ guantes	_____ vestido de playa
_____ blusa	_____ impermeable	_____ vaqueros
_____ calcetines	_____ pantalones	_____ zapatos
_____ camisetas	_____ sandalias	_____ chaqueta
_____ falda	_____ traje de baño	_____ corbata

 Ahora, mira el vídeo y revisa tus respuestas de la actividad A. Luego, compara tus respuestas con las de un(a) compañero(a).

▓ ¿Entendiste bien?

B. Gustos diferentes Mira el vídeo por segunda vez. Como ves, Sofía y Alejandra tienen gustos y opiniones muy diferentes sobre la ropa. Completa cada oración con el nombre de la chica correspondiente.

1. A _____ le gusta tener mucha ropa y accesorios como bolsos y aretes. Le gusta comprar cosas nuevas y siempre estar a la moda.

2. _____ no tiene mucha ropa y piensa que la moda no es tan importante. No le gusta la ropa muy colorida ni demasiado atrevida *(daring, risqué)*.

 C. ¿Mejor o peor? Miren las fotos de Sofía (la «de antes» y la «de después») y contesten las siguientes preguntas.

■ ¿Prefieren las prendas originales de Sofía o las que Alejandra le prestó *(loaned)*? ¿Por qué?

■ ¿Creen que Alejandra está realmente a la moda? Comparen su estilo con la moda actual de los estudiantes universitarios de los Estados Unidos.

D. Enfoque comunitario Imaginen que son dependientes en una tienda local. Preparen una lista de expresiones que deben usar para atender a clientes hispanos que no hablen bien inglés. Incluyan expresiones para averiguar *(to ascertain)* sus preferencias (color, material, precio, etc.) y también para responder a sus dudas o sus quejas *(complaints)*.

La diversión

I. Vocabulario: Los deportes

Margarita **hace aeróbicos** tres veces por semana.

Lucho y sus amigos **juegan baloncesto** en la cancha de su barrio.

Doña Gabriela lleva a sus hijas a la práctica de **fútbol** los jueves por la tarde.

Esteban **patina sobre hielo** durante el invierno.

Vocabulario práctico

el árbitro *referee*
el equipo *team*
el jugador *player*

Otros deportes (Other sports)
el atletismo *track and field*
el béisbol *baseball*
el esquí *ski*
el fútbol americano *football*
la gimnasia *gymnastics*
el levantamiento de pesas
   weight lifting
la lucha libre *wrestling*
la natación *swimming*
el tenis *tennis*
el vóleibol *volleyball*

Verbos
hacer (ejercicio/deporte) *to work
   out, to exercise*
hacer (aeróbicos/gimnasia) *to do
   (aerobics/gymnastics)*
levantar pesas *to lift weights*
patinar (sobre hielo) *to (ice) skate*
practicar (baloncesto/béisbol/
   fútbol/vóleibol/tenis) *to play
   (basketball/baseball/soccer/
   volleyball/tennis)*
practicar (atletismo/natación/lucha
   libre) *to do track and field/
   to swim/to wrestle*

■ Asimilación

4-43 ¿Se necesita un balón? *(Do you need a ball?)* Indica si los siguientes deportes requieren el uso de un balón (o pelota). Al terminar, compara tus respuestas con las de otros compañeros.

¿Sí o no?

1. baloncesto _____
2. fútbol _____
3. natación _____
4. gimnasia _____
5. lucha libre _____

6. esquí _____
7. vóleibol _____
8. ciclismo _____
9. patinaje _____

CD1-43 **4-44 Medallas de oro** *(Gold medals)* Escucha el siguiente informe deportivo y completa el cuadro con el número de medallas obtenidas por el Equipo Olímpico *(Olympic Team)* de los Estados Unidos.

Deporte	Número de medallas de oro
El atletismo	3
La gimnasia	0
La lucha libre	7
La natación	9
El levantamiento de pesas	0

■ Aplicaciones

4-45 ¿Cuándo se practican estos deportes? Escriban algunos de los deportes típicos de cada estación (primavera, verano, otoño, invierno) en los Estados Unidos.

4-46 Comparaciones Formen oraciones para comparar los deportes que se mencionan.

> MODELO   el béisbol – la natación
> *El béisbol es más popular que la natación en los Estados Unidos.*

REMEMBER

To complete this activity, you can use a variety of expressions: **más... que, menos... que, tan... como, el más..., el menos...**, etc.

1. el fútbol – el fútbol americano
2. la lucha libre – el atletismo
3. el ciclismo – el vóleibol – la natación
4. el baloncesto – el béisbol – el fútbol americano
5. la gimnasia – los aeróbicos

4-47 ¡A dibujar y a adivinar! *(Let's draw and guess!)* Túrnense para seleccionar un deporte y luego dibujar en un papel algo relacionado con ese deporte (una persona que practica el deporte, el equipo necesario, dónde se practica el deporte, etc.). El otro (La otra) estudiante debe adivinar de qué deporte se trata. **¡OJO!** Sólo tienen 20 segundos.

■ Integración

4-48 Entrevista Túrnense para hacer y responder a las siguientes preguntas. **Importante:** Tomen notas de las respuestas de su compañero(a).

1. ¿Te interesa algún deporte en particular? ¿Cuál?
2. ¿Practicas ese deporte?
3. ¿Cuál es tu equipo (o jugador) favorito? ¿Por qué?
4. ¿Qué opinión tienes de los equipos de tu universidad? (¿Son buenos, mediocres, malos... ?)
5. ¿Cuál consideras que es el deporte más representativo de los Estados Unidos? ¿Por qué?

4-49 Los intereses deportivos de mi compañero(a) Usa las notas de la conversación anterior para escribir un informe acerca de los intereses deportivos de tu compañero(a).

> MODELO   *A mi compañero(a) le gusta mucho el fútbol americano. Él (Ella) practica fútbol todos los fines de semana con sus amigos. Su equipo favorito es los Eagles. A mi compañero(a) no le gusta el golf ni la natación. Con respecto a los deportes en la universidad, mi compañero(a) prefiere...*

II. Funciones y estructuras: Talking about daily activities with irregular present tense verbs

Pertenezco al equipo de fútbol de mi universidad. **Vengo** a práctica tres veces por semana. Me gusta mucho porque me **mantengo** en excelente condición física y me **río** mucho con mis compañeros.

You have already learned how to use many irregular verbs, including the verbs **ser**, **estar**, and **ir** and other verbs with stem changes. In this section you will learn how to use verbs with orthographic changes and other irregularities.

To maintain the sound of certain letters included in their stems, some **-er** and **-ir** Spanish verbs suffer changes in the first person singular (**yo**) conjugation. Here is a list of those changes.

CHANGES	EXAMPLES	OTHER VERBS
c→z	vencer (to win) (yo) **venzo**, (tú) **vences**, ...	cocer (ue) (to cook) convencer (to convince) torcer (ue) (to twist)
c→zc	conocer (to know) (yo) **conozco**, (tú) **conoces**, ...	conducir (to drive) introducir (to introduce) merecer (to deserve) parecer (to seem) pertenecer a (to belong to) producir (to produce) reconocer (to recognize)
g→j	proteger (to protect) (yo) **protejo**, (tú) **proteges**, ...	coger (to grab) corregir (i) (to correct) dirigir (to direct) escoger (to select) recoger (to pick up)

✱ Notice that some of these verbs have other stem changes (**cocer**, **torcer**, and **corregir**). Remember that these changes do not affect the **nosotros(as)** and **vosotros(as)** forms.

Voy al médico cuando me **tuerzo** un tobillo.
*I go to the doctor when **I twist** my ankle.*

Creo que **merezco** la medalla de oro este año.
*I think **I deserve** the gold medal this year.*

Muchachos, yo **recojo** el equipo.
*Guys, **I will pick up** the equipment.*

The following are other verbs with irregular present tense conjugations. Irregularities are highlighted in bold.

VERBS	CONJUGATIONS
decir *(to say)*	**dig**o, **dic**es, **dic**e, decimos, decís, **dic**en
mantener *(to maintain)*	manten**go**, mant**ie**nes, mant**ie**ne, mantenemos, mantenéis, mant**ie**nen
oír *(to hear)*	**oig**o, o**y**es, o**y**e, oímos, oís, o**y**en
reír *(to laugh)*	**rí**o, **rí**es, **rí**e, reímos, reís, **rí**en
venir *(to come)*	ven**go**, v**ie**nes, v**ie**ne, venimos, venís, v**ie**nen
ver *(to see)*	**ve**o, ves, ve, vemos, veis, ven

Other derived verbs that end in **-tener** (e.g., **mantener**) are also irregular and are conjugated like **tener**: **contener** *(to contain)*, **detener** *(to detain)*, **entretener** *(to entertain)*, and **obtener** *(to obtain)*.

Cuando **oigo** o **veo** a mi jugador favorito, me **río**.

*When **I hear** or **see** my favorite player, **I laugh**.*

■ Asimilación

4-50 ¿Sí o no? Indica si las siguientes oraciones se aplican a tu vida diaria o no. Al terminar, compara tus respuestas con las de un(a) compañero(a). ¿Qué tienen en común?

_____ 1. Oigo música *country*.

_____ 2. Veo partidos de béisbol por televisión.

_____ 3. Escojo las mejores clases todos los semestres.

_____ 4. Cuezo bien las carnes cuando cocino.

_____ 5. Merezco una A en la clase de español.

_____ 6. Me río con personas que no conozco.

CD1-44

4-51 ¿Qué hace el (la) profesor(a)? El (La) profesor(a) va a decirte qué hace normalmente en la universidad. Marca con **X** las actividades que menciona.

_____ Dirige varios clubes.

_____ Recoge la oficina.

_____ Se ríe con las historias de sus colegas.

_____ Escoge libros en la biblioteca.

_____ Conoce a sus colegas en la universidad.

_____ Ayuda al estudiante que lo merece.

_____ Corrige trabajos.

_____ Oye las cintas que hacen sus estudiantes.

■ Aplicaciones

4-52 Asociaciones Escriban las frases de la lista bajo el verbo con el que más se relacionen.

OPCIONES: el equipo opuesto   una orquesta   una fiesta
lugares de interés   exámenes   música   los invitados
un partido de vóleibol   una persona famosa
una compañía   tareas   la radio

conocer	dirigir	entretener
vencer	oír	corregir

4-53 Las cualidades *(qualities)* ¿Cuál es tu mejor cualidad? Las siguientes personas están dando su respuesta para esta pregunta. Para saber qué responden, combinen las palabras y conjuguen los verbos correctamente.

1. SELENA: Yo / reconocer / mis errores.
2. JUAN: Yo / proteger / a mi familia y a mis amigos.
3. GABY: Yo / contener / mis emociones negativas.
4. BERTO: Yo siempre / decir / la verdad.
5. KARINA: Yo / mantener / buenas relaciones con los demás.
6. FRANK: Yo / escoger / buenas amistades.

4-54 Tú y yo

Paso 1: Lee otra vez las oraciones que escribiste en la actividad 4-53 e indica si tú también tienes esas cualidades o no.

1. ...   3. ...   5. ...
2. ...   4. ...   6. ...

Paso 2: Ahora, averigua si tu compañero(a) tiene las mismas cualidades. Al terminar, prepara un resumen y preséntalo al resto de la clase.

MODELO   E1: *Desirée, ¿reconoces tus errores?*
          E2: *Sí, reconozco mis errores.*
          o   *No, no reconozco mis errores.*

▧ Integración

4-55 Entrevista Túrnense para hacer y responder a las siguientes preguntas. Tomen notas.

1. ¿Oyes la radio? ¿Qué tipo de programa (musical, de noticias, de comentarios, de deportes) oyes? ¿Y qué música oyes regularmente?

2. ¿Ves programas de deportes en la televisión? ¿Qué otros programas ves?

3. ¿Conduces a la universidad? Si no, ¿cómo vienes (en autobús, en tren, en metro o a pie)?

4. ¿Perteneces a alguna organización estudiantil? ¿A cuál?

5. Generalmente, ¿obtienes las cosas que deseas en la vida? ¿Puedes dar ejemplos?

4-56 Mi compañero(a) Ahora, usa la información de la actividad 4-55 para escribir una breve descripción de tu compañero(a) de clase.

EN TU COMUNIDAD

Interview a student from Spain or Latin America about his/her daily routine here in the United States. You must include in your reports information about the most significant adjustments that your interviewee had to make to his/her daily routine upon arriving in America.

III. Funciones y estructuras: Describing people and objects with the verbs *ser* and *estar*

Aníbal **es** muy buen ciclista. Él **es** de Valencia. **Está** practicando para una competencia.

Kim y Rosita **son** jugadoras de vóleibol de playa. **Están** en perfecta condición física. **Son** muy simpáticas.

As you know, the verbs **ser** and **estar** mean *to be*. Although they have the same meaning, they are used in different contexts.

Other expressions with **estar** are **¡Está bien!** *(All right!)* and **¡Está de más!** *(It is not necessary!)*.

ser is used . . .	estar is used . . .
• to describe inherent characteristics: *Sammy Sosa* **es** *muy talentoso.*	• to talk about location: *El estadio* **está** *en la ciudad de Chicago.*
• to talk about origin and nationality: *Él no* **es** *de España.* **Es** *dominicano.*	• to talk about condition: *Mi hermano* **está** *enfermo hoy y no puede venir.*
• to talk about professions and occupations: *Sammy* **es** *jugador de béisbol.*	• to talk about emotional state: **Está** *muy enojado por eso.*
• to tell the time: **Son** *las dos de la tarde. El partido* **es** *en una hora.*	• as part of the progressive tense: **Estoy** *esperando a mi amigo Sancho para salir.*
• to express possession: *Los boletos para el partido* **son** *de mi hermano.*	• as part of certain expressions: **¡Estoy** *de acuerdo! ¡El partido va a estar estupendo!*

A number of adjectives change in meaning when used with either **ser** or **estar.**

ADJECTIVE	ser	estar
aburrido	*to be boring*	*to be bored*
listo	*to be smart*	*to be ready*
rico	*to be rich*	*to be delicious*
verde	*to be green*	*to be unripe*

Eres aburrida. / Estás aburrida.
Estas manzanas **son verdes.** /
Estas manzanas **están verdes.**

*You **are boring.** / You **are bored.***
*These apples **are green.** / These apples **are unripe.***

Some adjectives, including **bonito** *(pretty),* **guapo** *(handsome),* **callado** *(quiet),* and **frío** *(cold),* can be used with either **ser** or **estar**. Although the verb choice depends on what the speaker wants to emphasize, in general, the use of **estar** implies that the characteristic is not permanent (the equivalent of the English verbs *to feel, to look,* or *to seem*).

Nela **es** bonita.	*Nela **is** pretty.*
Lupe **está** bonita (hoy).	*Lupe **looks** pretty (today).*
Daniel **es** callado.	*Daniel **is** a quiet person.*
Chucho **está** callado (ahora).	*Chucho **seems** quiet (now).*

■ Asimilación

4-57 Yo estoy... Selecciona las frases que se apliquen a ti en este momento. Al terminar, compara tus respuestas con las de un(a) compañero(a). ¿Qué tienen en común?

En este momento, yo estoy...

____ enfermo(a).   ____ nervioso(a).   ____ tomando café.

____ en la biblioteca.   ____ en mi habitación.   ____ cansado(a).

____ muy contento(a).   ____ relajado(a).   ____ en el salón de clase.

____ estudiando.   ____ aburrido(a).   ____ triste.

____ en mi casa.   ____ mascando chicle   ____ listo para trabajar.
                              (chewing gum).

D1-45 **4-58 ¿Cómo soy?** Escucha cómo las siguientes personas se describen a sí mismas. Luego, selecciona la alternativa que mejor conteste la pregunta **¿Cómo soy?**

1. a. Eres antipático.   b. Eres diligente.   c. Eres alto.
2. a. Eres pesimista.   b. Eres paciente.   c. Eres optimista.
3. a. Eres bajo.   b. Eres mayor.   c. Eres joven.
4. a. Eres alegre.   b. Eres activa.   c. Eres sincera.
5. a. Eres rico.   b. Eres inteligente. c. Eres entusiasta.
6. a. Eres morena.   b. Eres pelirroja.   c. Eres rubia.

■ Aplicaciones

4-59 Mi amigo Nelson Completen las oraciones con la forma correcta del verbo **ser** o **estar**.

Éste _____ mi amigo Nelson. Él _____ de Sevilla, España. _____ estudiando computación en un instituto técnico. _____ muy contento con sus estudios. Él _____ extrovertido y muy alegre. Sus padres _____ madrileños. Ellos _____ de vacaciones en Almería, al sureste del país. (Ellos) _____ profesores de matemática en el mismo instituto técnico. Nelson también _____ un excelente jugador de tenis. Creo que (él) ya _____ listo para formar parte del equipo olímpico de tenis de España.

4-60 En el restaurante Describan la escena que ven en el dibujo. Usen los verbos **ser** y **estar** correctamente.

> MODELO *Las personas están en un restaurante. El señor de la camisa azul está...*

4-61 ¡Soy más preguntón(-ona) que tú! Primero, decidan quién va a hacer preguntas con **ser** y quién va a hacer preguntas con **estar**. Luego, túrnense para hacer y responder a sus preguntas sin parar. ¡Sean creativos! ¿Cuál de los dos puede hacer más preguntas?

> MODELO E1: *¿**Eres** simpático(a)?*
> E2: *Sí, **soy** simpático(a). ¿**Estás** en la librería?*
> E1: *No, no **estoy** en la librería. **Estoy** en la clase de español. ¿...?*
> E2: *...*

■ Integración

4-62 Con el consejero(a) *(advisor)* Representa la siguiente situación con un(a) compañero(a). Al terminar, cambien de papel.

El (La) consejero(a)	El (La) estudiante
You are meeting one of your advisees for the first time. Ask him/her as many questions as you can to get to know him/her better. Some of the questions may include the following: where the student is from, his/her major, his/her personal traits, how he/she feels at this institution.	You have been assigned a new advisor and decided to stop by his/her office to get to know him/her. Be prepared to answer his/her questions and to ask him/her questions of your own.

4-63 Una descripción personal El (La) consejero(a) de la actividad 4-62 quiere que escribas un breve resumen sobre tu origen, tu personalidad y tus metas *(goals)* académicas para ponerlo en tu expediente *(file)*. Piensa en los temas que discutieron *(you talked about)* en la conversación. Cuando termines, dale una copia a tu profesor(a) para que la corrija.

IV. Lectura: De vacaciones

■ Antes de leer

A. Las vacaciones de los norteamericanos Contesten las siguientes preguntas.

1. ¿Les gusta a ustedes salir de vacaciones con su familia?
2. ¿Cómo son las vacaciones de una familia típicamente norteamericana? Describe el comportamiento *(behavior)* típico de cada una de las siguientes personas:
   - el padre (la madre) planea el viaje/maneja el coche...
   - los hijos pelean/discuten/juegan...
   - los abuelos leen/duermen/caminan...

B. Vocabulario y conceptos Las siguientes palabras son importantes para la comprensión del texto. Lean sus definiciones y completen las oraciones.

amueblado: que tiene muebles (sillas, camas, mesas, etc.)

descolorido: que no tiene color, pálido

quemado: de color oscuro por el efecto del sol

triste: lo opuesto de alegre

Completa las oraciones con el adjetivo más apropiado.

1. Siempre me siento _____ cuando terminan las vacaciones.
2. Este pantalón está _____.
3. Después de tres días en el sol estoy _____.
4. Quiero pasar mis vacaciones en un apartamento bien _____.

«Las vacaciones»

Gomaespuma

Gomaespuma es un dúo español nuevo, formado por los periodistas Guillermo Fesser y Juan Luis Cano, que nació en 1982 en la estación de televisión Antena 3. Debido al éxito *(success)* de su trabajo en televisión, en 1986 fundaron *(founded)* Gomaespuma Producciones, una empresa dedicada a la creatividad en el mundo de los medios de comunicación. Desde entonces, Gomaespuma ha producido *(has produced)* varios libros humorísticos sobre la vida diaria de los españoles, entre ellos *Marchando una de mili, Navidad con orejas, Pasando olímpicamente* y *Familia no hay más que una.*

Suele ser el período de descanso en el verano.

Por fin se llega al apartamento. Es un **cuchitril** mal amueblado, porque los propietarios prefieren tener muebles viejos y feos ya que todos los veranos queda **destrozado**.

Se asignan las habitaciones y aquí siempre hay problemas. Al final la mejor es para la hija, mientras los chicos toman la pequeña. La abuela duerme con la chica en una **cama-mueble**.

dilapidated dwelling

destroyed

sofa-bed

skin	El primer día de la playa todo es estupendo, excepto el color de la **piel.** Mientras todo el mundo presenta un moreno maravilloso, la familia está más pálida que alguien que ha visto un **fantasma.** El hijo mayor lleva un bañador **ajustado,** el pequeño uno de dibujos hasta la **rodilla,** la chica un bikini **que trae al padre por la calle de la amargura** porque se transparenta todo, la madre un bañador estampado y un gorro de baño de flores que se pone en la cabeza cada vez que se mete en el agua, el padre lleva un bañador azul descolorido por el efecto del tiempo, y la abuela va vestida completamente, excepto los pies, que los lleva desnudos.

ghost — *fantasma*
tight / knee
that is driving the father crazy

pick up — El primer día...

A las dos, la madre, el padre y la abuela **recogen** sus sillitas y sus toallas y se suben al apartamento.

a short while
flunked / to cram
drowsiness

Después de comer todos duermen un **ratito** de siesta, excepto la chica que ha **cateado** latín y se tiene que quedar a **empollar** con todo el **sopor** de después de la comida.

to go hang out
board game
late
gets mad / reprimands

Por la noche los chicos piden permiso para **salir por ahí.** El pequeño se queda en casa jugando **al cinquillo** con la madre y la abuela y el chico mayor y la chica salen a tomar algo. Regresan **a las tantas.** El padre **se cabrea** y los **regaña** desde la cama y al día siguiente cuando desayunan, pero se vuelve a repetir la historia durante todo el mes.

madly
muy triste

La hija se enamora **perdidamente** de un chico de Valencia y cuando se acaba el verano se va **tristísima** porque deja a su amor, aunque han quedado en escribirse y en ir a visitarse.

■ ¿Entendiste bien?

C. Un día típico en la playa ¿Cómo es un día típico de vacaciones en España, según Gomaespuma? Organicen los siguientes eventos.

_____ Duermen la siesta.

_____ Todos se ponen sus bañadores y van a la playa.

_____ Los chicos salen por ahí.

_____ Los padres recogen las sillas y regresan al apartamento.

_____ Los chicos regresan tarde.

D. ¿Por qué? Respondan a las siguientes preguntas.

1. ¿Por qué está el apartamento mal amueblado?
2. ¿Por qué no duerme la siesta la hija?
3. ¿Por qué se disgusta el padre?

E. Enfoque lingüístico Identifiquen cinco verbos referentes a las actividades típicas de una familia española durante las vacaciones de verano.

F. Para conversar ¿Qué opinan Uds.? ¿Las vacaciones de las familias españolas son semejantes o diferentes a las vacaciones familiares de los norteamericanos? Presenten algunos puntos concretos.

G. Actividad de extensión Usa las notas de la actividad A en la página 171 para escribir una descripción cómica de unas vacaciones en familia, semejante a la de Gomaespuma.

Vocabulario

Las estaciones	Seasons
la primavera	spring
el verano	summer
el otoño	fall
el invierno	winter

El tiempo	The weather
estar (parcialmente) nublado	to be (partly) cloudy
hacer buen/mal tiempo	to be good/bad weather
hacer calor	to be hot
hacer fresco	to be cool
hacer frío	to be cold
hacer sol	to be sunny
hacer viento	to be windy
llover (ue)	to rain
nevar (ie)	to snow
¿Qué tiempo hace?	What is the weather like?

Las prendas de vestir	
el abrigo	coat
la blusa	blouse
las botas	boots
la camisa	shirt
la camiseta	T-shirt
el chaleco	vest
la chaqueta (americana)	jacket
la falda	skirt
la gorra	cap
el impermeable	raincoat
la minifalda	mini-skirt
los pantalones	pants
los pantalones cortos	shorts
la ropa	clothing items
la ropa interior	underwear
las sandalias	sandals
el sombrero de sol	sun hat
el suéter	sweater
los tejanos/vaqueros	blue jeans
el traje	suit
el traje de baño / el bañador	swimsuit
el vestido	dress
los zapatos	shoes
los zapatos altos/de tacones	high heel shoes
los zapatos de tenis	sneakers
las zapatillas	slippers
llevar/usar	to wear

Accesorios	
los aretes/pendientes	earrings
los calcetines / las medias	socks
el cinturón	belt
el collar	necklace
la corbata	tie
los guantes	gloves
los lentes de sol	sunglasses
las medias	stockings
la pulsera	bracelet
el reloj	watch

Materiales	
el algodón	cotton
el cuero	leather
de fantasía	costume (jewelry)
la lana	wool
el material sintético, acrílico, poliéster	synthetic material, acrylic, polyester
el metal	metal
el oro	gold
la pana	corduroy
la plata	silver
la seda	silk
la tela	fabric

Diseños	Designs
a cuadros	plaid, checked
a rayas	striped
de puntos/lunares	polka-dots
de un solo tono/liso	solid color
estampado	print

Los deportes	Sports
los aeróbicos	aerobics
el árbitro	referee
el atletismo	track and field
el baloncesto	basketball
el béisbol	baseball
el equipo	team
el esquí	ski
el fútbol	soccer
el fútbol americano	football
la gimnasia	gymnastics
el jugador	player
el levantamiento de pesas	weight lifting
la lucha libre	wrestling
la natación	swimming
el patinaje (sobre hielo)	(ice) skating
el tenis	tennis
el vóleibol	volleyball

Funciones y estructuras

Comparaciones de adjetivos, p. 148
Verbos con cambio del radical **e → ie**, p. 156
Verbos con cambio del radical **o → ue**, p. 156
Verbos reflexivos, p. 159
Ser y **estar**, p. 168
Otros verbos, p. 165

Puesta en acción

SITUACIÓN:	You are working for a company with business interests in Latin America. Between April 12 and 14, there will be a shareholders' meeting in Puerto Rico. About 100 people from Latin America, Spain, and the United States will meet in San Juan for this event. Since you know some Spanish, your company has asked you to participate in planning the logistics of this important meeting.
MISIÓN:	To make all the strategic plans for this meeting and to organize and communicate the meeting agenda to all the participants.
DESTREZAS:	Organizing a business meeting; organizing and communicating the agenda for a business meeting; and informing participants about meeting conditions, plans, and requirements.

Include as many verbs from the following list as possible: **cerrar, comenzar, conseguir, convencer, encontrar, escoger, ir, mover, obtener, oír, ver, volar, volver**.

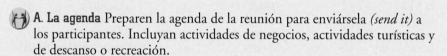 **A. La agenda** Preparen la agenda de la reunión para enviársela *(send it)* a los participantes. Incluyan actividades de negocios, actividades turísticas y de descanso o recreación.

HORA	12 de abril	13 de abril	14 de abril
8:00 a.m.	Desayunan en el hotel.		
10:00 a.m.	Comienza la reunión en la sala #3.		
12:00 a.m.		Almuerzan en el restaurante del hotel.	
2:00 p.m.			
4:00 p.m.			
6:00 p.m.			Vuelan a...
8:00 p.m.			

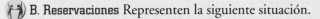

B. Reservaciones Representen la siguiente situación.

Organizador(a) de la reunión

As organizer of this important meeting, you have to make hotel reservations for the company's shareholders. Call the hotel in San Juan and find out if they have adequate facilities. If that is the case, make the necessary reservations for 100 people.

You may use some of the following expressions: **¿Me podría decir si su hotel tiene... ?** (Could you tell me if your hotel has . . . ?) **¿Hay buenos restaurantes cerca del hotel?** (Are there good restaurants near the hotel?) **¿Qué lugares de interés hay en el área?** (What places of interest are there in the area?) **Me gustaría hacer una reservación para...** (I would like to make a reservation for . . .)

Recepcionista del hotel

An important client is calling to find out about the services at your hotel. Provide this client with all the information he/she needs about the hotel amenities and services and use the chart below to write down the information you need to process the reservation.

You may use some of the following expressions: **Desde luego. / Por supuesto.** (Of course.) **Con mucho gusto.** (My pleasure.) **¿Cuántas habitaciones necesita?** (How many rooms do you need?) **Necesito algunos datos.** (I need some information.)

| Hotel El Convento |
| Reservas |

Nombre: Servicios requeridos:
Fecha de llegada: Número de teléfono:
Fecha de partida: Correo electrónico:
Tipo(s) de habitación(-ones):   Tarjeta de crédito:

C. Un memo Escríbele un memo a tu supervisor, el Sr. Tomasini, para describirle el hotel que reservaste para la reunión. Incluye detalles sobre la localización, el costo y los servicios.

D. El tiempo en San Juan, la ropa y las comidas Preparen un volante *(flyer)* para enviarles a los participantes de la reunión. Incluyan información sobre las condiciones del tiempo en San Juan en el mes de abril y recomendaciones acerca de la ropa y los accesorios que deben traer para asistir a las reuniones y para hacer turismo. Además, incluyan una lista de platos típicos puertorriqueños que desean sugerir para los desayunos, los almuerzos y las cenas. Incluyan algunos platos vegetarianos.

Estado del tiempo	Ropa y accesorios	Menú

To find out what the weather is like in Puerto Rico during the month of April, go to **www.weather.com.**

E. Información de interés general Tu asistente y tú desean preparar una lista de lugares de interés para los participantes de la reunión. Túrnense para hacer preguntas sobre los lugares donde pueden hacer las actividades de su lista y para responder usando la información de sus mapas.

MODELO   E1: *¿Adónde puede ir una persona que quiere comprar una medicina?*

                E2: *Puede ir a la Farmacia El Amal.*

Estudiante 1

Actividad	Nombre del lugar
comprar una medicina	*Farmacia El Amal*
ir a un concierto	
comer un sándwich criollo	
correr o caminar	
comprar algo para comer en el hotel	
leer un libro sobre historia de Puerto Rico	
sacar dinero	

San Juan, Puerto Rico

San Juan, Puerto Rico

Estudiante 2

Actividad	Nombre del lugar
hacer unas compras	
apreciar pinturas de artistas locales	
nadar o tomar un poco de sol	
hacerse un estudio médico	
comprar un libro de recetas puertorriqueñas	
ver arte religioso	

Perú, Ecuador, Bolivia, Nicaragua y Costa Rica

In this unit you will talk about past events and describe how things used to be. The readings will introduce you to life in the rural and urban areas of the Spanish-speaking world. In turn, the videos will introduce you to people from Central and South America who will talk about their backgrounds and their memories as they were growing up in their homelands. At the end of the unit you will create a newsletter in Spanish to be posted on the web. You will also be able to connect with your community by educating others about the importance of recycling and taking care of the environment, solving some of the problems that affect your area, and informing Spanish speakers about available health services.

Ayer y hoy

Capítulo 5

Para comenzar

¿A qué foto se refiere la siguiente información?

- Quito
- Las culturas indígenas
- Las Islas Galápagos

Mi pasado

In this chapter you will learn . . .

- how to talk about landmark events in your life
- how to describe how things used to be
- how to avoid redundancy
- about legends and traditions of the Spanish-speaking people

	TEMA 1 Eventos importantes	TEMA 2 Buenos recuerdos	TEMA 3 Incidentes
Vocabulario	Los eventos importantes y las fechas	Los preparativos para un viaje	El cuerpo humano
Funciones y estructuras	Talking about past activities with the preterite tense Referring to past events with **hace... que**	Talking about past activities with stem-changing verbs in the preterite and the verbs **dar, ir, ser,** and **ver** Avoiding repetition with direct object pronouns	Talking about past activities with other stem-changing verbs Talking about incidents and mishaps
Lecturas y vídeo	Perspectivas: En el periódico	Vídeo: Otra excursión en Puerto Rico	Lectura: Leyenda del origen de los Incas

Foto 1

Foto 2

Foto 3

Enfoque

A. ¿Qué sabes ya de Ecuador? Antes de ver el vídeo, completa las siguientes oraciones con la información que aparece en **Para comenzar** e indica a qué foto se refiere cada oración. Después, compara tus respuestas con las de otro(a) compañero(a).

1. _____, la capital de Ecuador, está situada al pie del volcán Pichicha.

2. Hoy en día _____ siguen manteniendo sus tradiciones.

3. _____ están situadas a unas 650 millas de distancia del continente y ofrecen una experiencia inolvidable para los visitantes interesados en la historia natural.

B. Ecuador, continente e islas Miren el vídeo y emparejen las siguientes frases sobre Ecuador. Luego, indiquen con qué foto se asocia la frase: las Islas Galápagos (I), Quito (Q) o las culturas indígenas (C).

____ 1. Los habitantes del pueblo de Otabal...

____ 2. Este archipiélago es de origen volcánico...

____ 3. Esta capital es una ciudad en donde...

a. la arquitectura colonial y las construcciones modernas se complementan.

b. son famosos por sus textiles y su música.

c. y está formado por trece islas grandes, seis islas pequeñas y cuarenta y dos islotes.

C. ¡Descubran las Islas Galápagos! Lean las siguientes descripciones de distintos tipos de excursiones que pueden hacer en las Islas Galápagos. Luego, en grupos, escojan **una** excursión y prepárense para explicarle a la clase por qué prefieren esa excursión.

Opción #1: *Trekking* Hagan *trekking* en el Parque Nacional. A las personas deportistas esta excursión les permite explorar el interior de las islas y ver sitios diferentes a los de los cruceros. Las caminatas van desde tres hasta seis horas, pero no son de mucha distancia, y les da tiempo suficiente para observar la riqueza de la flora y la fauna de las Galápagos.

Opción #2: Buceo Vengan a la Reserva Marina de Galápagos para un día de buceo. Descubran la belleza del fondo marino del archipiélago. Buceen rodeados de espectaculares arrecifes de coral e impactante fauna marina: tortugas, lobos marinos, pingüinos, peces espada, delfines e incluso ballenas. ¡Una experiencia inolvidable!

For more info, you may want to check the **Temas** site:
http://temas.heinle.com

Eventos importantes

I. Vocabulario: Los eventos importantes y las fechas

Nacimiento (1946)

Bautizo (1947)

Cumpleaños (1948)

Graduación (1968)

SABOR REGIONAL

In some Spanish-speaking countries, the words **la boda** and **el casamiento** are synonyms of **el matrimonio.** In other countries, they refer specifically to the wedding ceremony.

Matrimonio (1970)

Aniversario (1995)

Jubilación (2000)

■ Los números después de 100

cien	100	seiscientos(as)	600	diez mil dos	10.002
ciento uno(a)	101	setecientos(as)	700	cien mil	100.000
ciento dos	102	ochocientos(as)	800	cien mil uno(a)	100.001
ciento tres	103	novecientos(as)	900	cien mil dos	100.002
doscientos(as)	200	mil	1.000	novecientos mil	900.000
doscientos uno(a)	201	mil uno(a)	1.001	novecientos	999.000
doscientos dos	202	mil dos	1.002	noventa y nueve mil	
doscientos tres	203	dos mil	2.000	un millón	1.000.000
trescientos(as)	300	tres mil	3.000	dos millones	2.000.000
cuatrocientos(as)	400	diez mil	10.000		
quinientos(as)	500	diez mil uno(a)	10.001		

The word **cien** is used before nouns.

> Los padres del Sr. Jones llegaron a América hace más de **cien** años.
> *Mr. Jones's parents arrived in America more than **one hundred** years ago.*

> Su casa está a unas **cien** millas de Boston.
> *His house is about **one hundred** miles from Boston.*

Ciento is used to express quantities from 101 to 199. Notice that there is no **y** following the word **ciento.**

> El Sr. Jones vive en el número **ciento** quince de la calle Main.
> *Mr. Jones lives at 115 Main Street.*

> Su casa tiene más de **ciento** ochenta y cinco años.
> *His house is more than **one hundred** eighty-five years old.*

The ending **-cientos** changes to **-cientas** before feminine nouns.

> Su casa cuesta ahora unos ocho**cientos** mil dólares.
> *His house is worth now about eight **hundred** thousand dollars.*

> Su casa está a unas dos**cientas** millas de la playa.
> *His house is about two **hundred** miles from the beach.*

Dates after the year 2000 are expressed as follows:

> La graduación de su hijo fue en 2003 **(dos mil tres).**
> *His son's graduation was in **two thousand three.***

When expressing exact quantities, the word **mil** does not have a plural form, but **millón** does **(millones).**

> El Sr. Jones gana ochenta y cinco **mil** dólares al año.
> *Mr. Jones makes eighty-five **thousand** dollars a year.*

> El presupuesto de su compañía es de ocho **millones** de dólares.
> *His company's budget is eight **million** dollars.*

✳Notice that the word **millón(-ones)** is followed by **de** before nouns.

■ Asimilación

 5-1 ¿Cuándo ocurrió? *(When did it happen?)* Identifiquen el año de los siguientes eventos históricos.

____ 1. Los ingleses establecen su primera colonia en América (Jamestown)

____ 2. La Declaración de Independencia

____ 3. Lincoln pronuncia el discurso de Gettysburg

____ 4. Los hermanos Wright vuelan por primera vez

____ 5. Los autobuses son desegregados en Alabama gracias al boycot organizado por Martin Luther King, Jr.

____ 6. Los astronautas Armstrong y Aldrin caminan en la Luna

a. mil setecientos setenta y seis

b. mil novecientos cincuenta y seis

c. mil novecientos tres

d. mil novecientos sesenta y nueve

e. mil seiscientos siete

f. mil ochocientos sesenta y tres

CD1-47 **5-2 Eventos importantes en la vida del profesor Martínez** Escucha la información e indica cuál es la fecha correcta. Al terminar, compara tus respuestas con las de a un(a) compañero(a).

1. Fecha de su graduación:
   a. 1983
   b. 1993
   c. 1973

2. Fecha de su matrimonio:
   a. 1978
   b. 1968
   c. 1998

3. Fecha del nacimiento de su primer hijo:
   a. 2002
   b. 2001
   c. 2000

■ Aplicaciones

5-3 ¿De qué evento se trata? Identifiquen el evento según la descripción.

1. Es una celebración que tiene lugar todos los años. La gente usualmente recibe tarjetas o regalos en este día.

2. Es la celebración del fin de un curso de estudios. Los estudiantes por lo general reciben un diploma.

3. Es una ceremonia religiosa. Los padres usualmente llevan a sus hijos pequeños a la iglesia y les asignan un nombre.

4. Es la unión de dos personas que quieren formar una familia. Puede ser una ceremonia religiosa o civil.

5-4 ¿Cuánto es? Túrnense para leer y resolver los siguientes problemas:

1. $100 + 200 =$
2. $350 + 500 =$
3. $550 + 1 =$
4. $1.000 - 1 =$
5. $5.000 - 2.000 =$
6. $900.000 - 10.000 =$
7. $400 \times 10 =$
8. $30 \times 50 =$
9. $200 \times 200 =$
10. $10.000 \div 2 =$
11. $200.000 \div 5 =$
12. $700 \div 7 =$

REMEMBER

To ask the question use one of the following expressions.
¿Cuántos son *cien más trescientos*? $(100 + 300)$
¿Cuántos son *trescientos menos cien*? $(300 - 100)$
¿Cuántos son *trescientos por cien*? (300×100)
¿Cuántos son *trescientos dividido por cien*? $(300 \div 100)$

5-5 ¿Cuándo fue? *(When did it take place?)* Indica la fecha de los siguientes eventos y luego intercambia información con un(a) compañero(a). Al terminar, preséntenle un informe breve al resto de la clase.

MODELO   E1: *¿Cuándo fue tu graduación de la escuela secundaria?*
         E2: *Mi graduación fue en dos mil cinco.*

1. nacimiento
2. graduación de la escuela primaria
3. graduación de la escuela secundaria
4. cumpleaños número quince
5. inicio de los estudios universitarios

■ Integración

5-6 Investigacion Un amigo quiere estudiar *(wants to study)* en los Estados Unidos. Indica el costo de las siguientes cosas.

1. la matrícula *(tuition)* en tu universidad
2. los libros cada semestre
3. un coche nuevo
4. el alquiler *(rent)* de un apartmento
5. comida para un mes

5-7 El costo de vida *(cost of living)* Representa la siguiente situación con un(a) compañero(a).

Estudiante extranjero(a)	Estudiante estadounidense
Tú deseas estudiar en los Estados Unidos, pero necesitas más información acerca del costo de vida en ese país. Pregúntale a tu amigo(a) estadounidense el precio de algunas cosas básicas (como, por ejemplo, el hospedaje, la comida, los libros, etc.). También, pregúntale si hay trabajos para estudiantes dentro o fuera de la universidad. Averigua dónde pueden trabajar los estudiantes, qué tienen que hacer, cuánto les pagan, etc.	Responde a las preguntas de este(a) estudiante internacional acerca del costo de vida en los Estados Unidos. Háblale del costo del hospedaje, de la comida, de los libros, etc. También, dale información sobre las oportunidades de trabajo que existen dentro y fuera de la universidad.

EN TU COMUNIDAD

Interview an international student (preferably, but not necessarily, from a Spanish-speaking country) and prepare a brief report on the cost of living in his/her home country. To help you focus your interview, concentrate on investigating the cost of housing, food, transportation, and clothing. In groups, discuss your findings and present a summary.

II. Funciones y estructuras: Talking about past activities with the preterite tense

Mi sobrina Alanita **nació** en 2004.
*My niece Alanita **was born** in 2004.*

Sus padres **celebraron** su quinto aniversario en 2005. *Her parents **celebrated** their fifth anniversary in 2005.*

The preterite tense is used to talk about actions, states, or events that were completed in the past, regardless of how long it took to complete them.

Ayer por la noche **cené** con Meche, **estudié** y **me acosté** tarde.

*Last night **I had dinner** with Meche, **I studied,** and **I went to bed** late.*

The following is a list of the endings used to conjugate regular verbs in the preterite.

* Notice that the conjugation of regular **-er** and **-ir** verbs is the same in the preterite. Also, notice that the **nosotros(as)** forms of **-ar** and **-ir** verbs are identical in the present and preterite tenses. Context will generally allow you to figure out what tense is being used.

-ar verbs	**-er** verbs	**-ir** verbs
estudiar *(to study)*	**beber** *(to drink)*	**vivir** *(to live)*
estudié	bebí	viví
estudiaste	bebiste	viviste
estudió	bebió	vivió
estudiamos	bebimos	vivimos
estudiasteis	bebisteis	vivisteis
estudiaron	bebieron	vivieron

There is a group of verbs that suffer orthographic changes in the **yo** form in order to maintain the sound of the last letter in the verb stem. These changes affect verbs that end in **-car, -gar,** and **-zar** in the infinitive.

c→qu	g→gu	z→c
sacar *(to take out)*	**llegar** *(to arrive)*	**empezar** *(to begin)*
saqué	llegué	empecé
sacaste	llegaste	empezaste
sacó	llegó	empezó
...	...	...
Other verbs: **buscar** *(to look for)* and **tocar** *(to touch, to play [an instrument])*	Other verbs: **conjugar** *(to conjugate),* **entregar** *(to deliver, to hand [in/over]),* **jugar** *(to play [a sport or game]),* and **pagar** *(to pay)*	Other verbs: **almorzar** *(to have lunch),* **comenzar** *(to begin),* **organizar** *(to organize),* and **realizar** *(to do, to carry out)*

Here is a list of common expressions you can use to indicate when a past action, state, or event took place.

anoche	*last night*
ayer	*yesterday*
el (jueves/mes/verano/ año/...) pasado	*last (Thursday/month/summer/ year/ . . .)*
esta mañana/tarde	*this morning/afternoon*
hace (dos semanas/cuatro meses/un año/...)	*(two weeks/four months/ a year/. . .) ago*

■ Asimilación

5-8 Ayer Piensa en las cosas que hiciste *(you did)* ayer y escoge la alternativa que mejor complete cada oración. Luego, compara tus respuestas con las de un(a) compañero(a). ¿Qué tienen en común?

1. Me levanté...   a. temprano.   b. tarde.
2. Estudié... horas.   a. menos de dos   b. más de dos
3. Almorcé...   a. en la cafetería.   b. en otro lugar.
4. Bebí... en la cena.   a. un refresco   b. otra cosa
5. Asistí a... clases.   a. menos de cuatro   b. más de tres
6. Miré televisión...   a. por la tarde.   b. por la noche.

CD1–48 **5-9 ¿Cuándo?** Escucha la descripción del día que tuvo Pablo ayer e indica en qué momento hizo las siguientes actividades.

Actividad	Por la mañana	Por la tarde	Por la noche
Entregó una monografía de sociología.			
Bailó música de todo tipo.			
Limpió su habitación.			
Visitó a unos amigos.			
Compró un pastel para un cumpleaños.			
Se preparó para ir a una fiesta.			

■ Aplicaciones

5-10 La semana pasada Para saber qué hicieron *(they did)* estas personas la semana pasada, escojan el verbo lógico y conjúguenlo en el pretérito.

> MODELO Leticia (estudiar/comer/patinar) sobre hielo con su familia.
> *patinar → patinó*

1. Yo (levantarse/salir/organizar) una reunión en mi trabajo.
2. Fermín y Verónica (quedarse/perder/traer) en un hotel lujoso.
3. Mi jefe y yo (salir/hablar/anunciar) de viaje para Quito, Ecuador.
4. La Sra. Montalbán (tomar/jugar/vender) su apartamento.
5. Yo (cocinar/sacar/vencer) vídeos de películas extranjeras.
6. Yo (nadar/jugar/hacer) fútbol en el parque de mi pueblo.
7. Doña Fela (comprar/asistir/pasar) tiempo con su familia.

5-11 ¿Qué hizo el (la) profesor(a)? ¿Qué creen que hizo el (la) profesor(a) esta mañana? Escriban por lo menos seis preguntas para él/ella usando la forma **usted** de los verbos.

> MODELO *Profesor(a), ¿usted desayunó esta mañana?*

5-12 ¿Qué tenemos en común?

Paso 1: Completa la siguiente tabla con algunas actividades que hiciste en los momentos indicados. Escribe por lo menos una actividad en cada espacio.

anoche	el fin de semana pasado	hace dos meses	el verano pasado

Paso 2: Hazle preguntas a tu compañero(a) para saber si hizo *(he/she did)* las mismas actividades que tú. Toma notas. Cuando termines, prepara un resumen y compártelo con la clase.

> MODELO E1: *James, ¿trabajaste anoche?*
> E1: *Sí, trabajé anoche.* o *No, no trabajé anoche.*

■ Integración

5-13 Los eventos importantes Entrevista a tu compañero(a) para averiguar cuándo celebró los eventos importantes de la lista. Además, trata de averiguar todos los detalles que puedas.

nacer*	**casarse***	**celebrar su**
bautizarse*	**jubilarse***	**cumpleaños**
graduarse* **de la escuela**	**celebrar su aniversario**	**número...**
(primaria/intermedia/	**número...**	
secundaria)		

5-14 Una experiencia personal Cuéntale *(Tell)* a tu profesor(a) qué ocurrió en un evento importante o especial de tu vida. Puedes escribir sobre un evento trágico, cómico o interesante (¡o puedes usar la imaginación!). Cuando termines, entrégale una copia a tu profesor(a) para que te dé *(so that he/she gives you)* su opinión.

Here is a list of phrases you may use to form your questions: **levantarse temprano, manejar a la universidad, hablar con sus colegas, comer pan tostado, responder a los mensajes de correo electrónico, tomar té, escribir un informe, recibir buenas noticias, pagar algunas cuentas.**

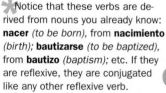

＊Notice that these verbs are derived from nouns you already know: **nacer** *(to be born),* from **nacimiento** *(birth);* **bautizarse** *(to be baptized),* from **bautizo** *(baptism);* etc. If they are reflexive, they are conjugated like any other reflexive verb.

REMEMBER

You will have to ask questions with interrogative words such as **¿cuándo? ¿dónde? ¿por qué? ¿quién? ¿cómo?**

You may connect your ideas by using expressions such as **entonces, después, de pronto** *(suddenly),* **inmediatamente, un poco más tarde,** and **finalmente.**

III. Funciones y estructuras: Referring to past events with *hace... que*

—¿**Cuánto tiempo hace que** te jubilaste, Olga?
—**Hace dos años que** me jubilé.

How long ago did you retire, Olga?
*I retired **two years ago**.*

To find out how long ago an action or event took place, use the following question.

> **¿Cuánto (tiempo) hace que** + verb in the preterite tense?

The use of the word **tiempo** in this question is optional.

And to answer these questions, use one of the following structures.

> **Hace** + length of time + **que** + verb in the preterite tense
> Verb in the preterite tense + **hace** + length of time

—¿**Cuánto hace que** te graduaste de la escuela secundaria?
—**Hace seis meses que** me gradué. / Me gradué **hace seis meses.**

How long ago did you graduate from high school?
*I graduated **six months ago**.*

If the action of the verb started in the past and continues in the present, the present tense is used instead of the preterite.

—¿Cuánto hace que Tito **vive** en Bolivia?
—Hace un año y medio que **vive** ahí. / **Vive** ahí hace un año y medio.

*How long **has** Tito **been living** in Bolivia?*
*He **has been living** there for a year and a half.*

When the action continues in the present, you can also use the question: **¿Desde cuándo** + verb in the present tense? **¿Desde cuándo estudian** en esta universidad? (**How long have you been studying** at this university?)

◼ Asimilación

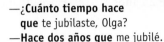 **5-15 El pasado** Escoge las oraciones que sean ciertas. Cuando termines, compara tus respuestas con las de un(a) compañero(a). Comenten las diferencias.

____ Comí una hamburguesa hace más de veinticuatro horas.

____ Hace más de un año que tomé una clase de matemáticas.

____ Hace menos de seis horas que me levanté.

____ Limpié mi habitación hace más de una semana.

____ Hace solamente unas horas que estudié en la biblioteca.

____ Nací hace más de veinticinco años.

____ Me afeité hace más de dos días.

____ Hace más de un año que me casé.

REMEMBER

Más de means *more than* and **menos de** means *less than*.

CD1–49 **5-16 Los Hernández** Escucha a la Sra. Hernández hablar de algunos de los eventos en la vida de su esposo y de ella. Luego, escoge las alternativas que mejor completen las siguientes oraciones. **¡OJO!** Imagínate que estamos en el año 2000.

1. Los Hernández se casaron...
   a. hace 45 años.   b. hace 40 años.   c. hace 50 años.

2. ...que el Sr. Hernández se graduó de la universidad.
   a. Hace 40 años   b. Hace 42 años   c. Hace 38 años

3. ...que ellos celebraron su vigésimo quinto *(twenty-fifth)* aniversario de boda.
   a. Hace 30 años   b. Hace 25 años   c. Hace 20 años

4. Ellos se jubilaron...
   a. hace 5 años.   b. hace 10 años.   c. hace 15 años.

5. Su primer bisnieto *(great-grandchild)* nació...
   a. hace 10 años.   b. hace 15 años.   c. hace 20 años.

■ Aplicaciones

 5-17 ¿Cuánto tiempo hace que... ? Túrnense para hacer y responder a preguntas usando los siguientes datos.

MODELO   Noelia / tomar unas vacaciones / cuatro años
              E1: *¿Cuánto hace que Noelia tomó unas vacaciones?*
              E2: *Hace cuatro años que Noelia tomó unas vacaciones.*
           o   *Noelia tomó unas vacaciones hace cuatro años.*

1. Andrés y Luis / conocerse / un año
2. doña Gabriela / preparar unas tortillas / seis horas
3. el Sr. Bonilla / salir del trabajo / unos minutos
4. los niños / enfermarse / dos semanas
5. Mariel y Anneris / empezar a estudiar / dos horas
6. tus amigos / reunirse / tres meses

5-18 ¿Cuánto saben de mí? Toma unos minutos para escribir por lo menos cinco preguntas sobre ti. Luego, hazles las preguntas a tus compañeros de clase para ver quién puede dar la respuesta correcta. Guíalos *(Guide them)* respondiendo **más** o **menos** si no te dan la respuesta correcta.

MODELO   E1: *¿Cuánto tiempo hace que cumplí cinco años?*
              E2: *Hace trece años que cumpliste cinco años.*
              E1: *Más.*
              E3: *Hace quince años que cumpliste cinco años.*
              E1: *¡Correcto!*

5-19 Tú y yo

Paso 1: Toma unos minutos para indicar cuánto tiempo hace que hiciste las siguientes actividades.

1. comenzar a aprender español
2. graduarse de la escuela secundaria
3. conocer a mi mejor amigo(a)
4. bañarse
5. recibir una visita inesperada *(unexpected)*
6. comprar unos tejanos nuevos

Paso 2: Ahora, usa la misma lista de actividades para entrevistar a tu compañero(a). Toma notas y, al terminar, prepara un resumen.

MODELO   E1: *¿Cuánto tiempo hace que comenzaste a aprender español?*
          E2: ...

■ Integración

 5-20 Buscando un(a) compañero(a) de apartamento Representa la siguiente situación con un(a) compañero(a).

Estudiante A

Imagínate que estás buscando a la persona apropiada para compartir un nuevo apartamento. Quieres que esta persona sea responsable, tranquila, que no tenga vicios *(addictions)* y que te ayude con la limpieza. Entrevista a tu compañero(a) y averigua cómo es, cuáles son algunos de sus hábitos y actividades favoritas y cuánto tiempo hace que hace esas actividades.

Estudiante B

Necesitas encontrar un lugar donde vivir y vas a una entrevista con una persona que está buscando un(a) compañero(a) de apartamento. Él/Ella quiere saber cómo eres, cuáles son algunos de tus hábitos y actividades favoritas y cuánto tiempo hace que haces esas actividades. Para ti la honestidad es muy importante y quieres que él/ella sepa que eres una persona de espíritu libre *(free spirit)* y aventurera.

Para que la interacción sea interesante y controvertida, pueden hablar de temas como **fumar** *(to smoke)*, **tomar bebidas alcohólicas, dar fiestas todos los fines de semana, escuchar música a todo volumen, limpiar (la cocina/el baño/...), lavar los platos, no graduarse de la escuela secundaria, no creer en el matrimonio**, etc.

REMEMBER

You must use the present tense in questions and answers with **hace... que** if the action began in the past and continues in the present. Otherwise, use the preterite.

 5-21 Una persona admirable ¿A qué persona admiras por sus logros *(achievements)*? Haz una lista de algunas de las cosas que esta persona ha logrado en su vida y compártela con tu profesor(a). Puedes escribir sobre algún pariente, amigo o persona famosa.

MODELO   *Mi madre nació hace cuarenta años, en el año 1966.*
          Ella se graduó de... hace... años... y trabaja en...
          hace... años.

IV. Perspectivas: En el periódico

▦ Antes de leer

 A. El periódico Observen el periódico local e identifiquen las siguientes secciones.

Noticias *(news)* internacionales   Cultura

Noticias nacionales   Eventos sociales

Noticias locales   Clasificados

Deportes

B. ¿Qué sección recibe más cobertura *(coverage)*? Identifiquen la sección que tiene más cobertura.

C. La sección social ¿Qué eventos se mencionan en esta sección? (Mencionen los tres más importantes.)

▦ A leer

Observa ahora esta sección de eventos sociales tomada del periódico peruano *El Comercio*.

Cóctel en el Marriott

corporate bonds

Con motivo de la presentación de la primera emisión de **bonos corporativos,** el Banco Financiero del Perú organizó un cóctel en el Salón San Martín del Hotel Marriott. Ramón Anaya, gerente general de esta **entidad,** fue el **encargado** de la presentación.

entity, corporation
person in charge

La despedida de Juan Diego

En San Isidro, Octavio y Teresa Fernández ofrecieron una cena en honor del tenor peruano Juan Diego Flórez. Después de la última función de *La Figlia del Regimento,* el sábado en el Teatro Segura, el invitado especial llegó para compartir un simpático momento junto a los invitados. Ellos y sus *hosts* **anfitriones** disfrutaron una noche de *lasted* baile que se **prolongó** por varias horas.

evening party

Velada musical en la embajada rusa

En el marco de las celebraciones por el trigésimo quinto (treinta y cinco) aniversario del restablecimiento de las relaciones diplomáticas ruso-peruanas, el embajador de dicho país, Anatoly Moltchanov, ofreció una velada musical con la participación de la maestra rusa Larissa Petrovski y el maestro peruano Fernando de Luna.

Salcedo - Asturias

En ceremonia llevada a cabo en su casa de Totoritas, al sur de Lima, Liliana Asturias Botero contrajo matrimonio con Luis Salcedo Triviño. La novia es hija de Luis Asturias Carmona y de Anita Botero de Asturias. El novio es hijo de Eduardo Salcedo Meléndez y de Maruja Triviño de Salcedo. La pareja partió en viaje de bodas al Brasil.

Benavides - Cárdenas

En ceremonia llevada a cabo en la iglesia Nuestra Señora del Carmen, de San Miguel, contrajeron matrimonio César Antonio Benavides Galindo y Claudia Patricia Cárdenas Medina. La novia es hija de Pedro Alfonso Cárdenas Valenzuela y de María Gabriela Medina de Cárdenas. El novio es hijo de César Antonio Benavides Oviedo y de Ana María Galindo de Benavides.

¿Entendiste bien?

D. Eventos importantes ¿Cuáles de los siguientes eventos se presentan en esta sección? Marca los que correspondan.

_____ nacimientos

_____ bautizos

_____ cumpleaños

_____ graduaciones

_____ matrimonios

_____ aniversarios

_____ otros: _____

E. ¿Cierto o falso? Indiquen si las siguientes oraciones son ciertas (**C**) o falsas (**F**) según el artículo.

_____ El padre de Claudia Patricia Cárdenas se llama Pedro.

_____ El suegro de Liliana Asturias se llama Alberto.

_____ Perú restableció relaciones diplomáticas con Rusia en 1995.

_____ Ramón Anaya es el gerente del hotel Marriott de Lima.

_____ Juan Diego Flórez es un famoso cantante peruano.

_____ César Benavides y su esposa Claudia viajaron a Francia después de su boda *(wedding)*.

F. Actividad de extensión Preparen una pequeña reseña en español para informar acerca de los eventos sociales más importantes de esta semana en su universidad.

Buenos recuerdos

I. Vocabulario: Los preparativos para un viaje

Los documentos de viaje

| el boleto/ billete | la tarjeta de embarque | el pasaporte | la visa | los cheques de viajero |

El equipaje

| el maletín | la maleta | la mochila | la cartera | la billetera |

SABOR REGIONAL

In Mexico the word for suitcase is **la valija,** and in Spain the word for visa is **el visado.**

Vocabulario práctico

el asiento *seat*
el equipaje de mano *carry on luggage*
el pasillo *aisle*
la sala de espera *boarding area*
el terminal internacional *international departures terminal*
la ventanilla *window*

Verbos

abordar *to board*
cambiar *to exchange*
empacar *to pack*
mostrar(ue) *to show*
sacar *to get, obtain*

■ Asimilación

5-22 ¿En qué orden? Organiza los siguientes eventos de una manera lógica.

____ Abordo el avión.

____ Saco el pasaporte.

____ Presento la tarjeta de embarque.

____ Empaco la maleta.

____ Compro el boleto.

____ Compro los cheques de viajero.

01–50 **5-23 ¿Qué es?** Identifica el objeto basándote en las descripciones que vas a escuchar.

1. a. los cheques de viajero
   b. el maletín de mano
   c. el pasaporte
2. a. la tarjeta de embarque
   b. la visa
   c. el pasaporte
3. a. el boleto
   b. la ventanilla
   c. la maleta
4. a. la tarjeta de embarque
   b. los cheques de viajero
   c. el boleto

■ Aplicaciones

5-24 Preparativos de viaje Completen las oraciones con la palabra o frase del vocabulario más apropiada.

OPCIONES: pasaporte   boleto   tarjeta de embarque
cheques de viajero   maletas

1. Necesito llamar a la agencia de viajes para comprar un _____ de ida y vuelta a La Paz, Bolivia.
2. Tengo que tomarme una fotografía para mi _____.
3. Me gustaría pasar por el banco esta tarde para comprar unos _____.
4. Sólo permiten dos _____ en vuelos internacionales.
5. Mi _____ indica que mi asiento es el 10L.

5-25 Prioridades Imagínense que están preparando un viaje a un país de habla hispana. ¿Adónde quieren ir? ¿Por qué? ¿Qué necesitan para el viaje? Preparen una lista.

CD1-51 **5-26 En el aeropuerto** Túrnense para hacer el papel de la empleada y el papel del viajero en la siguiente conversación.

EMPLEADA: Buenos días, señor. Su pasaporte y su boleto, por favor.
VIAJERO: Aquí los tiene.
EMPLEADA: ¿Cuántas maletas lleva?
VIAJERO: Dos y un maletín de mano.
EMPLEADA: ¿Prefiere pasillo o ventanilla?
VIAJERO: Ventanilla, por favor.
EMPLEADA: Muy bien. Su asiento es el 6A. Aquí tiene su tarjeta de embarque, su boleto y su pasaporte. Pase inmediatamente a la sala de espera 5.
VIAJERO: Muchas gracias.
EMPLEADA: Con gusto. Que tenga un buen viaje.

■ Integración

5-27 Quiero viajar al extranjero Representa la siguiente situación con un(a) compañero(a).

Ask your friend questions to make sure he/she has what is needed. Use the vocabulary list as a checklist and point of departure. Also suggest clothing depending on your partner's destination.

Use Internet resources to investigate the travel documents required for the different Spanish-speaking countries (they vary considerably), and also the baggage allowances and restrictions of an American carrier of your choice.

Estudiante A	**Estudiante B**
Tú eres un(a) viajero(a) muy experimentado(a) (has viajado por todo el mundo), pero tu amigo(a) nunca ha viajado fuera del país. Ayúdale a decidir adónde puede ir y explícale lo que tiene que hacer para preparar su viaje.	Tú quieres ir de viaje a un lugar diferente y exótico, pero no sabes adónde ir o cómo prepararte para el viaje. Pídele información a tu amigo(a); él/ella ha viajado mucho y sabe mucho sobre este tema.

EN TU COMUNIDAD

Visit a travel agency and obtain brochures on vacation packages to Spain and/or Latin America. In small groups, select and briefly describe the most attractive vacation package. Then, share with the class the reasons for your selection.

5-28 Antes de venir a los Estados Unidos... Imagínate que trabajas para la revista de una aerolínea estadounidense. Escribe un artículo breve para ayudar a los visitantes hispanos a prepararse para su viaje a los Estados Unidos.

II. Funciones y estructuras: Talking about past activities with stem-changing verbs in the preterite and the verbs *dar, ir, ser,* and *ver*

Nathan y Jenny **se fueron** para Perú esta mañana. Ellos **pidieron** asiento de ventanilla. Durante el vuelo, **leyeron** revistas sobre lugares de interés en el centro de Lima y **durmieron** un poco. **Fue** un vuelo muy bueno.

You are already familiarized with stem changes in the present tense. You will find it interesting that **-ar** and **-er** verbs that undergo stem changes in the present tense do not undergo such changes in the preterite tense.

Encontré la maleta en el ático.	***I found*** *the suitcase in the attic.*
La Sra. Estrada **perdió** el vuelo ayer.	*Mrs. Estrada **missed** her flight yesterday.*

On the other hand, many **-ir** verbs that suffer stem changes in the present tense also suffer stem changes in the preterite. These changes only affect the **él/ella/usted** and **ellos(as)/ustedes** forms.

e→i		o→u	
sentir *(to feel)*		**dormir** *(to sleep)*	
sentí	sentimos	dormí	dormimos
sentiste	sentisteis	dormiste	dormisteis
sintió	sintieron	durmió	durmieron

Other similar verbs:	Other similar verbs: **morir** *(to die)*
competir *(to compete)*, **conseguir** *(to find)*, **despedirse** *(to say good-bye)*, **divertirse** *(to have fun)*, **mentir** *(to lie)*, **preferir** *(to prefer)*, **reírse** *(to laugh)*, **repetir** *(to repeat)*, **seguir** *(to follow)*, **servir** *(to serve)*, **sonreír** *(to smile)*, **sugerir** *(to suggest)*, **vestirse** *(to get dressed)*	

REMEMBER

Stem changes are noted in parentheses next to the infinitive form of the verb in vocabulary lists. For example, the entry **mentir (ie, i)** tells you that the **e** in the stem of this verb changes to **ie** in the present tense (except in the **nosotros[as]** and **vosotros[as]** forms) while it changes to **i** in the present participle and the preterite tense (only in the **él/ella/usted** and **ellos[as]/ustedes** forms).

Mi madre **se vistió** cómoda para el viaje.	*My mother **dressed** comfortably for the trip.*
Ellos **prefirieron** llevar cheques de viajero, no efectivo.	*They **preferred** to take traveler's checks, not cash.*

Verbs whose stems end in a vowel also suffer changes in the **él/ella/usted** and **ellos(as)/ustedes** forms of the preterite tense. These verbs take a **y** in these forms.

leer *(to read)*	
leí	leímos
leíste	leísteis
leyó	leyeron
Other similar verbs: **caer(se)** *(to fall)*, **construir** *(to build)*, **creer** *(to believe)*, **distribuir** *(to distribute)*, **incluir** *(to include)*, **oír** *(to hear)*	

Notice that the forms that take a **y** also lose the **i** of the regular ending (**-ió→yó** and **-ieron→yeron**).

Samuel **oyó** el anuncio, salió corriendo y se **cayó**.

*Samuel **heard** the announcement, left running, and **fell**.*

The following is a group of verbs with different irregularities and changes.

dar *(to give)*	**ir** *(to go)* / **ser** *(to be)*	**ver** *(to see)*
di	fui	vi
diste	fuiste	viste
dio	fue	vio
dimos	fuimos	vimos
disteis	fuisteis	visteis
dieron	fueron	vieron

As you may have noticed, the preterite endings of **dar** and **ver** do not have accent marks. Also, the verbs **ir** and **ser** have exactly the same forms in the preterite tense. In this case, context will help you identify which verb is used.

Cuando **fuimos** a Guayaquil, **vimos** muchas artesanías indígenas.

*When **we went** to Guayaquil **we saw** a lot of indigenous crafts.*

■ Asimilación

5-29 De viaje ¿En qué orden hicieron Tatiana y Lázaro las siguientes cosas? Ponlas *(Put them)* en orden y compara tus respuestas con las de un(a) compañero(a).

_____ El empleado de la aerolínea les dio la tarjeta de embarque.

_____ Se vistieron.

_____ Prefirieron tomar un taxi para ir al aeropuerto.

_____ Durmieron hasta las seis en punto de la mañana.

_____ Pidieron asiento de pasillo.

_____ Oyeron el llamado *(call)* para abordar.

_____ Cuando llegaron al aeropuerto, fueron a la ventanilla de la aerolínea.

_____ Se despidieron del empleado de la aerolínea.

1–52 **5-30 ¿Qué hizo Lázaro?** Primero, empareja las frases de la izquierda con las frases de la derecha. Luego, escucha lo que dice Lázaro sobre las cosas que hizo ayer e indica si las oraciones que formaste son ciertas (**C**) o falsas (**F**).

_____ 1. Lázaro fue...   a. el periódico. _____

_____ 2. Él construyó...   b. a la playa. _____

　　　para su hija.   c. muy enojado. _____

_____ 3. Leyó...   d. a varios colegas del trabajo. _____

_____ 4. Allí vio...   e. un castillo de arena (*sand castle*). _____

_____ 5. Él se sintió...

■ Aplicaciones

5-31 Situaciones Completen las siguientes oraciones con los verbos que se proveen y conjúguenlos correctamente. **¡OJO!** Hay un verbo adicional en cada grupo.

reírse　　ir　　morir　　ver

En el cine: Jesús y yo _____ una película en el cine anoche. En esta película, una mujer _____ de amor porque su novio la abandonó. Jesús _____ muchísimo porque la historia le pareció ridícula.

oír　　vestirse　　servir　　despedirse

¡Tremenda fiesta!: Romualdo fue a una fiesta muy elegante el miércoles. Él _____ elegantemente con un traje negro muy fino. En la fiesta (ellos) _____ caviar, camarones y langosta. A la medianoche, Romualdo _____ de toda la gente porque tenía que trabajar el jueves por la mañana.

creer　　dormir　　preferir　　ser

Mis compañeras de cuarto: Ayer _____ un día muy raro para mis compañeras de cuarto. ¡El día empezó muy mal para ellas! (Ellas) _____ sólo hasta las cinco de la mañana porque (ellas) _____ que el examen de física era (*was*) ayer. ¡Pero ayer era domingo!

5-32 Preguntas indiscretas Usen la siguiente información para hacerle preguntas a su profesor(a) usando la forma **usted** del verbo. Añadan información adicional y expresiones de tiempo.

MODELO　　repetir un curso
　　　　　　¿Ud. repitió un curso en la universidad alguna vez?

1. leer el libro... de...   5. preferir estudiar...
2. caerse en...   6. pedir... cuando ir a...
3. ser...   7. dar dinero a...
4. vestirse... para ir a...   8. sentirse... en ...

5-33 Las mejores vacaciones Hazle las siguientes preguntas a tu compañero(a) para saber cómo fueron sus mejores vacaciones. Toma notas. Cuando terminen, cambien de papel.

1. ¿Adónde fuiste en tus últimas vacaciones? ¿Cuándo fuiste? ¿Con quién fuiste?

2. ¿Conseguiste un buen paquete vacacional? ¿Qué incluyó el paquete?

3. ¿Cómo fuiste (en avión/en carro/en tren/...)? ¿Cuántas maletas llevaste?

4. ¿Te divertiste? ¿Qué hiciste? ¿Dormiste mucho?

5. ¿Cómo te vestiste para viajar? ¿Por qué?

6. ¿Qué cosas viste? ¿Qué lugares visitaste?

7. ¿Compraste muchas cosas? ¿Conseguiste buenos precios?

8. ¿Cómo te sentiste cuando regresaste?

You can use questions like **¿Dónde fue la fiesta? ¿Cuántas personas fueron? ¿Qué sirvieron? ¿Cómo se sintieron los invitados? ¿Cómo se vistieron? ¿Algunas personas se durmieron? ¿Qué tipo de música oyeron?** Come up with other original questions and be creative in your answers!

■ Integración

5-34 La última fiesta Tu compañero(a) y tú van a describir cómo fue la última fiesta a la que fueron. Háganse preguntas y respondan de acuerdo con el dibujo que les corresponde. El estudiante B debe voltear su libro al revés *(turn his/her book upside down)*.

Estudiante A

Estudiante B

REMEMBER

You may use expressions you already know such as **en primer lugar, por otro lado, además, luego, después,** and **finalmente.**

5-35 Unas vacaciones inolvidables Usa la información que recopilaste en la actividad 5-33 y prepara un resumen sobre las mejores vacaciones de tu compañero(a). Cuando termines, dale una copia a él/ella para que te dé más información. Cuando añadas esta información, dale una copia del resumen a tu profesor(a).

III. Funciones y estructuras: Avoiding repetition with direct object pronouns

—Efraín, ¿tienes los billetes? *Efraín, do you have the tickets?*
—Sí, aquí **los** tengo. *Yes, I have **them** here.*
—¿Y mi cartera? *And my purse?*
—Gustavo **la** tiene. *Gustavo has **it**.*

The direct object is the part of the sentence that refers to the person or thing that receives or is directly affected by the action of the verb. For example, in the following examples, **una mochila** receives the action of the verb **comprar** (it is the thing that is bought) and **mi agente de viajes** is the person affected by the verb **llamar** (the person who is called).

Matilde compró **una mochila nueva.** *Matilde bought **a new backpack.***
Tengo que llamar a **mi agente de viajes.** *I have to call **my travel agent.***

> The preposition **a** is used before direct objects that are human beings or pets. It is known as the *personal a.*

When the direct object has already been mentioned in the conversation, we can use direct object pronouns instead. In the third person singular and the third person plural, Spanish direct object pronouns must agree in number (singular or plural) and gender (masculine or feminine) with the noun to which they refer.

DIRECT OBJECT PRONOUNS	
me *me*	**nos** *us*
te *you* (informal sing.)	**os** *you* (informal plural, in Spain)
lo *you* (formal sing., m.), *him, it* (m.)	**los** *you* (formal plural), *them* (m., m.+f.)
la *you* (formal sing., f.), *her, it* (f.)	**las** *you* (formal plural), *them* (f.)

—¿Conseguiste **los pasaportes**? *Did you get **the passport**?*
—Sí, **los** conseguí. *Yes, I got **them**.*
—¿Marcos **te** conoce? *Does Marcos know **you**?*
—No, él no **me** conoce. *No, he does not know **me**.*

As you may have noticed, direct object pronouns are placed before the conjugated verb and after **no.** When they are used in sentences with verb phrases (phrases that consist of an auxiliary verb and a main verb), these pronouns can be placed either before the auxiliary verb or attached to the main verb (which could be an infinitive or a present participle).

¿Los libros? Yo **los** voy a traer. / Yo voy a traer**los.**

The books. I am going to bring **them.**

¿Ricardo? **Lo** tengo que visitar. / Tengo que visitar**lo.**

Ricardo? I have to visit **him.**

Nina **me** está ayudando. / Nina está ayudándo**me.**

Nina is helping **me.**

Most of the verbs you have been using with reflexive pronouns can also be used with direct object pronouns. Notice how the meanings change in these two examples.

Mi madre **se despierta** temprano.   *My mother wakes (herself) up early.*
Mi madre **nos despierta** temprano.   *My mother wakes us up early.*

■ Asimilación

5-36 ¿Cierto o falso? Indica si las siguientes alternativas son ciertas (**C**) o falsas (**F**). Al terminar, compara tus respuestas con las de un(a) compañero(a). ¿Tienen mucho en común?

_____ 1. ¿La comida? Mi madre la prepara.

_____ 2. ¿El libro de español? Lo detesto.

_____ 3. ¿A mí? Mis amigos no me invitan a fiestas.

_____ 4. ¿Mis vacaciones? Las voy a tomar en el verano.

_____ 5. ¿El presidente de los Estados Unidos? No lo tolero.

_____ 6. ¿La clase de español? El (La) profesor(a) la hace muy interesante.

CD1-53 **5-37 ¿A qué se refieren?** Escucha las oraciones y selecciona a qué se refieren los pronombres de complemento directo.

1. a. el bolso   b. la maleta   c. los sombreros

2. a. las gafas   b. el vestido   c. los pantalones

3. a. a Delia   b. los anuncios   c. el programa

4. a. el sándwich   b. las pastas   c. la tortilla de huevos

5. a. a María y a Silvia b. a Silvia y a Berto   c. a María

Aplicaciones

5-38 ¡Ya hicimos todo! Imagínense que la clase va de viaje a Perú para visitar Machu Picchu. El (La) profesor(a) quiere estar seguro(a) de que ustedes están listos(as) y les hace las siguientes preguntas. Respóndanle afirmativamente.

> MODELO ¿Solicitaron la visa?
> *Sí, ya la solicitamos.*

1. ¿Recibieron sus pasaportes?
2. ¿Leyeron las regulaciones sobre el equipaje?
3. ¿Fueron a comprar las maletas?
4. ¿Llamaron al agente de viajes?
5. ¿Buscaron los cheques de viajero?
6. ¿Pidieron asiento de ventanilla?

5-39 Preguntas y más preguntas Túrnense para hacer y responder a preguntas con la información dada. Deben incluir un pronombre de objeto directo en cada pregunta y respuesta.

> MODELO las películas de Tom Cruise / ver (Uds. / no)
> E1: *¿Las ven?*
> E2: *No, no las vemos.*

1. a Clotilde y a Juan / tener que invitar al baile (nosotros / sí)
2. a mí / llamar con frecuencia (tú / no)
3. a mi amigo y a mí / comprender cuando hablamos español (el [la] profesor[a] / sí)
4. la lección / estudiar antes de la clase (Elín y Patricia / sí)
5. el periódico / ir a leer ahora (ella / no)
6. los músicos sudamericanos / conocer bien (tú / no)

5-40 ¡Firma aquí, por favor!

Paso 1: Busca compañeros de clase que respondan afirmativamente a las siguientes preguntas. Cuando encuentres a alguien, dile **Firma aquí, por favor.** Si alguien responde negativamente, dile **gracias** y pregúntale a otra persona.

Firma

_____ 1. ¿Tus amigos te invitan a salir todos los fines de semana?

_____ 2. ¿Tus compañeros te ayudan con la tarea de español?

_____ 3. ¿Tu familia te apoya en tus decisiones?

_____ 4. ¿Tus compañeros de clase te conocen bien?

_____ 5. ¿Tus parientes te ven regularmente?

_____ 6. ¿Tu consejero(a) académico(a) te escucha con atención?

Paso 2: Comparte la información con la clase y da tu opinión personal. Haz los cambios necesarios.

> MODELO *La madre de Angeline la despierta por la mañana y mi madre me despierta por la mañana también.*
> o ..., *pero mi madre no me despierta por la mañana.*

Some of the verbs you can use to talk about relatives with whom you do not have a good relationship are **detestar** *(to detest)*, **no querer** *(do/does not love)*, **no tolerar** *(cannot tolerate)*, and **no soportar** *(cannot stand)*.

■ Integración

5-41 En familia ¿Qué cosas hacen diferentes miembros de tu familia por ti? ¿Y qué sienten ellos verdaderamente hacia ti? Comenta estas cosas con tu compañero(a). Puedes hablar de temas como: **ayudar con (los problemas personales / los quehaceres del hogar / el cuidado de los niños / las cuentas / ...), apoyar en (mis decisiones / mis estudios / mi relación con... / ...), aconsejar con relación a (mis estudios / mis problemas personales / mis finanzas / ...), admirar por (mis logros / mi personalidad / mis notas / mi sentido de responsabilidad / ...)** y **mantener económicamente.**

5-42 Aviso a nuestros pasajeros *(passengers)* Lee el siguiente aviso que una aerolínea fijó *(posted)* para todos sus pasajeros y reescríbelo incluyendo pronombres de objeto directo cuando sea posible.

will be in effect

SUGERENCIAS

You may follow these steps:
Paso 1: Underline the nouns you find.
Paso 2: Determine which nouns are repeated in each section and may be replaced with direct object pronouns.
Paso 3: Determine what pronouns you have to use.
Paso 4: Rewrite the sign. Be careful where you place the pronouns!

AVISO A NUESTROS PASAJEROS

Queremos avisarle que las siguientes reglas van a entrar en vigor* el 1° de enero:

- Ud. sólo va a poder registrar dos maletas. Debe registrar las maletas en nuestra ventanilla y nuestros asistentes le van a dar un recibo. Ud. tiene que mostrar el recibo para recoger sus maletas.

- Ud. sólo podrá llevar una pieza de equipaje de mano. Debe poner el equipaje de mano debajo del asiento delantero. También puede poner el equipaje de mano en el compartimiento de arriba.

- Ud. puede obtener su tarjeta de embarque en una de nuestras estaciones de computadora. Debe obtener la tarjeta de embarque antes de abordar y tiene que mostrar la tarjeta de embarque a uno de nuestros asistentes.

- Ud. debe mostrar una tarjeta de identificación reciente en la ventanilla. También debe tener disponible la tarjeta de identificación para abordar y para recoger su equipaje.

IV. Vídeo: Otra excursión en Puerto Rico

■ Preparación

A. Hacer esnórkeling En su próxima excursión, los compañeros van a hacer esnórkeling. Antes de ver el vídeo, lean el resumen de lo que van a ver e intenten adivinar *(guess)* el significado de las palabras en negrita *(bold)*.

> Al llegar los compañeros, Edwin, su guía, ya está esperándolos a bordo del bote. Suben al bote y Edwin les pregunta si están listos para (1) **zarpar.** Todos menos Valeria responden: «¡Sí! ¡Vámonos! ¡Vamos!». Navegan en el bote y llegan al sitio donde van a hacer esnórkeling. Sofía, Alejandra, Javier y Antonio se ponen el equipo de esnórkeling: las (2) **aletas** para ayudarles a nadar, (3) la **máscara** para poder ver bajo el agua y el tubo para poder respirar. Luego, desde el lado del bote, ellos (4) **brincan** al agua. Valeria los mira desde el bote porque ella no quiere hacer esnórkeling. Sofía, Alejandra, Javier y Antonio se divierten mucho. Bajo el agua ven (5) **peces** de colores, corales preciosos y algas marinas.

1. a. anchor   b. change course   c. set sail
2. a. mask   b. fins   c. esnórkel
3. a. mask   b. fins   c. esnórkel
4. a. swim   b. sunbathe   c. jump
5. a. fish   b. reefs   c. algae

ESTRATEGIA DE COMPRENSIÓN: GUESSING

Although a judicious use of the glossary and dictionary is always helpful, an efficient reader often guesses the meaning of unfamiliar terms based on the information provided by contextual clues.

■ ¿Entendiste bien?

B. ¿Qué hicieron? Primero, lee los siguientes eventos del día de esnórkeling. Luego, mira el vídeo y ponlos en orden cronológico. Finalmente, compara tus respuestas con las de un(a) compañero(a).

_____ Sofía, Alejandra, Javier y Antonio se vistieron para hacer esnórkeling.

_____ Edwin, su guía, les dio la bienvenida a los compañeros a bordo del bote.

_____ Los cinco compañeros fueron en coche al puerto.

_____ Bajo el agua vieron peces de colores, corales preciosos y algas marinas.

_____ Como no sabe nadar, Valeria se sintió avergonzada *(embarrassed)* y les mintió a los compañeros. Dijo que le da miedo hacer esnórkeling.

_____ Los compañeros se fueron a casa.

C. ¿Hacerlo o no hacerlo? Piensa en **una** de las siguientes situaciones y cuéntales a los otros miembros del grupo qué ocurrió.

Situación #1: Algo que hice por primera vez en mi vida y me gustó mucho.
- ¿Qué fue? (practicar un deporte, tocar un instrumento, ir a un evento de un club, etc.)
- ¿Cuándo?
- ¿Por qué te gustó?
- ¿Sigues haciéndolo? ¿Por qué sí o por qué no?

Situación #2: Algo que no hice.
- ¿Qué fue?
- ¿Por qué no lo hiciste? (posibles razones: te dio miedo, te contaron algo negativo, etc.)
- ¿Cuándo?
- ¿Te arrepientes de *(regret)* tu decisión? ¿Por qué sí o por qué no?

D. Enfoque comunitario Preparen la descripción de algunos eventos o festividades importantes que tienen lugar en su escuela o comunidad todos los años para incluirlas en un panfleto informativo para estudiantes internacionales. Para cada evento, incluyan la fecha, el lugar, el precio de la entrada y las actividades que se realizan.

Incidentes

I. Vocabulario: El cuerpo humano

El cuerpo humano

el pelo — la cabeza
los ojos
las orejas — la nariz — la cara
la boca — los dientes
la garganta — el cuello

los pulmones — el brazo
el corazón — el codo
la espalda
el estómago
la mano

el oído — los dedos

las piernas
las rodillas

la piel — los tobillos
los pies
los dedos del pie

Vocabulario práctico

las cejas *eyebrows*   el hueso *bone*
la cintura *waist*   las uñas *fingernails*
el hombro *shoulder*

■ Asimilación

5-43 ¿Cómo es Ana María? Observa la foto de esta muchacha y escoge la
palabra más apropiada para completar la descripción. Al terminar,
compara tus respuestas con las de un(a) compañero(a).

Ana María es (gorda / joven / vieja). Tiene el pelo (castaño / bajo / negro),
las piernas (altas / cortas / largas) y los brazos son (delgados / bajos /
pequeños). A ella le gusta hacer ejercicio; por eso tiene un abdomen muy
(grande / firme / corto).

CD1-54 **5-44 En la sala de emergencias** Escucha la siguiente conversación entre un paciente y un médico y marca en los diagramas con una **X** las partes del cuerpo que menciona el paciente. (Observa el modelo.)

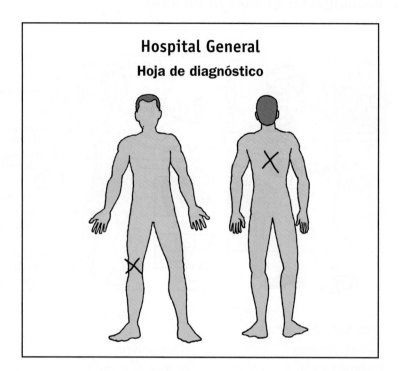

Hospital General
Hoja de diagnóstico

■ **Aplicaciones**

5-45 ¿Qué partes del cuerpo usas para...? Indica las partes del cuerpo que asocias con las siguientes actividades: **nadar, cantar, estudiar, bailar** y **escribir.**

5-46 Relaciones Indica la palabra que no se relaciona con las demás.

1. ojos, orejas, rodillas
2. rodillas, hombros, cuello
3. pecho, espalda, estómago
4. pelo, nariz, dedos
5. codo, pulmones, corazón

5-47 ¿Cómo es? Preparen una breve descripción de la apariencia física de este hombre. Incluyan por lo menos cinco de las siguientes palabras: **pelo, ojos, orejas, nariz, brazos, manos, cuello.**

■ Integración

5-48 ¿Dónde está? Un(a) estudiante debe describir la apariencia física de una de las personas en estas fotos. El (La) otro(a) estudiante debe adivinar en cuál de las tres fotos está esa persona.

You may use the description in activity 5-43 as a model.

Nota: Limiten las descripciones a la apariencia física de la persona. No incluyan información acerca de su ropa.

Foto 1

Foto 2

Foto 3

5-49 ¡Ayúdenme a encontrarlo! Mientras hacías compras con tu familia, tu primito de cuatro años se perdió *(got lost)*. Escribe una descripción detallada de su apariencia física para dársela al departamento de seguridad.

II. Funciones y estructuras: Talking about past activities with other stem-changing verbs

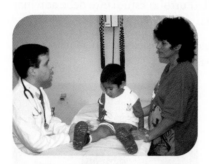

Luisito **estuvo** enfermo anoche y su mamá lo **trajo** al hospital. El doctor le **dijo** que tenía *(he had)* un virus estomacal.

Mi hija **vino** enferma de la escuela ayer y **tuve** que cuidarla. Le **hice** una sopa y se sintió mejor.

In **Tema 2** you learned about a group of verbs that have stem changes in the third person forms of the preterite. Now you will learn about verbs that have stem changes in all of their preterite forms. These verbs can be grouped into four categories: verbs that take an **i,** verbs that take a **u,** verbs that take **uv** and verbs that take a **j.**

i	u	uv	j
hacer *(to do/ make)*	**poder** *(to be able to)*	**estar** *(to be)*	**traer** *(to bring)*
hice	pude	estuve	traje
hiciste	pudiste	estuviste	trajiste
hizo*	pudo	estuvo	trajo
hicimos	pudimos	estuvimos	trajimos
hicisteis	pudisteis	estuvisteis	trajisteis
hicieron	pudieron	estuvieron	trajeron
Other similar verbs:	Other similar verbs:	Other similar verbs:	Other similar verbs:
decir→dij-	**haber**→hub-	**andar**→anduv-	**conducir**→conduj-
querer→quis-	**poner**→pus-	**tener**→tuv-	**introducir**→introduj-
venir→vin-	**saber**→sup-		**producir**→produj-
			traducir→traduj-

✳ Notice that the **él/ella/usted** preterite form of **hacer (hizo)** has a **c→z** change in order to maintain the sound of the letter **c** in the infinitive.

Verbs that take a **j** in the stem (including **decir,** which also takes an **i**) end in **-eron** (not **-ieron**) in the third person plural preterite form: **condujeron, dijeron, introdujeron,** etc.

As you may have noticed, these verbs are also irregular because they take a different set of endings, regardless of whether they are -**ar,** -**er,** or -**ir** verbs.

ENDINGS	
-e	-imos
-iste	-isteis
-o	-ieron

—Diana, ¿te **pusiste** la bolsa de hielo en la rodilla?

—**Quise** hacerlo, pero no **pude.**

—¡**Anduvimos** desde casa y nos duelen los pies!

—¿Por qué no **vinieron** en autobús?

*Diana, **did you put** the ice bag on your knee?*

*I **wanted** to do it, but **I was** not **able to.***

*We **walked** from home and our feet hurt!*

*Why **didn't you come** by bus?*

■ Asimilación

5-50 ¿Quién de la clase? Piensa en las cosas que pasaron en la clase la semana pasada y completa las oraciones con el nombre de la(s) persona(s) que hizo/hicieron estas cosas. Al terminar, compara tus respuestas con las de un(a) compañero(a). ¿Coincidieron en muchas cosas?

1. _____ estuvo enfermo(a).
2. _____ trajo comida a la clase.
3. _____ no dijo nada en clase.
4. _____ y _____ hicieron toda la tarea.
5. _____ y _____ vinieron tarde.
6. _____ tuvo que irse temprano un día.

CD1–55 **5-51 ¿Qué hizo ayer?** Escucha la información acerca de las actividades de tu profesor(a) el día de ayer y completa las oraciones.

1. Tuvo que ir a _____ .
2. Pudo hacer todo _____ porque llegó temprano.
3. Después hizo _____ en el supermercado.
4. Estuvo en el supermercado por _____ minutos.
5. Cuando llegó a casa, puso la comida en _____ .

■ Aplicaciones

5-52 En el consultorio del médico otra vez *(again)* Lee el diálogo entre Rómulo y su doctor, y complétalo con los verbos de la lista para saber qué ocurrió. Conjuga los verbos correctamente. **¡OJO!** Hay un verbo adicional.

OPCIONES: hacer venir traer decir poder ponerse tener

DOCTOR: ¡Rómulo, aquí otra vez! ¿Qué te ocurrió?

PACIENTE: Doctor, (yo) _____ a verlo otra vez porque el brazo me duele mucho todavía. (Yo) _____ que faltar al trabajo, pero fue necesario.

DOCTOR: ¿_____ (tú) las cosas que te (yo) _____ para mejorar la condición de tu brazo?

PACIENTE: Sí, doctor, todo.

DOCTOR: A ver. ¿Te tomaste las medicinas y (tú) _____ la crema para aliviar el dolor?

PACIENTE: Pues no, doctor. (Yo) No _____ comprar las medicinas ni la crema porque son muy caras.

DOCTOR: ¡Me lo imaginé! *(That's what I thought!)*

5-53 Causa y efecto Usen los verbos entre paréntesis para indicar una causa lógica para cada efecto.

> MODELO Carol *no trajo su libro.* → Carol tiene que usar el libro de su
> (no traer...) compañero.

1. Nosotros _____ → Nosotros ahora estamos en perfecto
   (hacer...). estado de salud.
2. Tú _____ → Tú tienes un horario de clases
   (poder...). perfecto.
3. Nelson _____ → Él vio a muchos actores y actrices
   (estar en...). famosos.
4. Yo _____ → Afortunadamente, ahora me siento
   (tener que...). muy bien.
5. Paulina y Leonardo _____ → Ahora tenemos los documen-
   (traducir...). tos en español y en inglés.
6. Tú _____ → Nosotros no podemos encontrar
   (poner...). los cubiertos.

5-54 El invierno pasado Combinen elementos de las dos columnas para formar oraciones sobre lo que estas personas hicieron durante el invierno pasado. ¡Sean creativos!

> MODELO mi familia y yo + (no) poder...
> *Mi familia y yo no pudimos ir a esquiar a Colorado el invierno pasado.*

mi familia y yo		(no) poder...
yo		(no) decir...
mi mejor amigo(a)		(no) hacer...
el (la) profesor(a)	+	(no) estar...
los estudiantes de la clase		(no) querer...
		(no) conducir a...
		(no) andar...
		(no) tener que...

■ **Integración**

5-55 ¿Qué hicieron? Cuéntales a tres de tus compañeros lo que hiciste para prepararte para tu vida de estudiante universitario(a). Trata de usar por lo menos ocho de los siguientes verbos: **decir, estar, hacer, poder, poner, querer, tener (que), traducir, traer** y **venir.** Toma notas sobre las cosas que ellos dicen.

REMEMBER

Some of the expressions you can use to organize your summary are **sin embargo, por otro lado, por ejemplo, en cambio,** and **finalmente.**

5-56 ¡No pensé en eso! Escribe un resumen de las cosas que tus compañeros mencionaron en la actividad 5-55 y que tú no hiciste para prepararte para tu vida de estudiante universitario(a). Cuando termines, dale una copia a tu profesor(a) para que te dé su opinión.

III. Funciones y estructuras: Talking about incidents and mishaps

El año pasado fue bastante trágico.

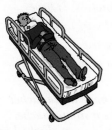

Simón tuvo un accidente de carro y **se rompió** el cuello,... *Simon had a car accident and **broke** his neck, . . .*

mi abuela **se cayó** y **se lastimó** un brazo y... *my grandmother **fell** and **hurt** her arm, and . . .*

Mario **se torció** un tobillo y se lo **enyesaron**. *Mario **twisted** an ankle and they **put it in a cast**.*

There are many reflexive verbs that can be used to talk about mishaps, incidents and accidents.

caerse *to fall*	hacerse daño *to hurt oneself*
contagiarse *to get infected*	hincharse *to swell*
cortarse *to get cut*	lastimarse *to injure oneself,*
darse (en/con)* *to hit (a body*	*to get hurt*
part), to bump into	quemarse *to burn oneself*
desmayarse *to faint*	resfriarse *to get a cold*
enfermarse *to get sick*	romperse *to break (a body part)*
fracturarse *to fracture (a body part)*	torcerse *to twist (a body part)*

* Use **darse en** before the body part that got hit and **darse con** before the object into which the person bumped.

Cuando **me caí, me fracturé** una rodilla.

Jacinta **se quemó** en la cocina de su casa.

Mi hermana **se dio con** la mesa y **se cortó**.

*When **I fell**, **I fractured** my knee.*

*Jacinta **got burned** in the kitchen of her house.*

*My sister **bumped into** the table and **got cut**.*

Note that body parts are generally used with definite articles, not with possessive adjectives. The reflexive pronoun indicates whose body part it is.

Here is a list of other verbs and expressions you can use to talk about negative events.

doler (ue) *to hurt*	tener dolor de garganta *to have*
enyesar *to put in a cast*	*a sore throat*
internar *to check into*	tener (fiebre/tos) *to have*
(a hospital)	*a (fever/cough)*
tener dolor de... *to have*	tropezar *to trip*
a . . . ache	vomitar *to vomit*

¿Tienes dolor de cabeza? Yo
   tengo dolor de estómago.
Internaron a don Juancho en
   el hospital.

Do you have a headache?
   I have a stomachache.
Don Juancho was checked into
   the hospital.

■ Asimilación

5-57 Una vez... *(One time . . .)* Lee las siguientes oraciones e indica si son ciertas (C) o falsas (F). Cuando termines, compara tus respuestas con las de un(a) compañero(a). ¿Qué cosas tienen en común?

Una vez...

_____ 1. me rompí una pierna.
_____ 2. me desmayé en el gimnasio.
_____ 3. me dio dolor de cabeza en clase.
_____ 4. me internaron en el hospital.
_____ 5. me quemé la mano cocinando.

_____ 6. me caí frente a muchas personas.
_____ 7. me enfermé el día de un examen.
_____ 8. me corté afeitándome.
_____ 9. me fracturé un dedo jugando.
_____ 10. me di con un espejo.

CD1–56 **5-58 Una llamada al 911** Escucha la llamada que una madre hizo al 911 y escoge las oraciones correctas.

_____ El niño se dio en la rodilla.
_____ Él se desmayó.
_____ Tiene dolor de estómago.
_____ Se rompió el brazo.

_____ Se cayó de la bicicleta.
_____ Se torció una muñeca.
_____ Un brazo se hinchó.
_____ Tiene un poco de fiebre.

■ Aplicaciones

5-59 Uno, dos y tres Organicen los eventos de cada grupo en orden lógico.

1. _____ La pierna se hinchó.
   _____ Me caí.
   _____ Me lastimé una pierna.

2. _____ Tropecé.
   _____ Me corté un dedo.
   _____ Me di con la puerta.

3. _____ Me desmayé y me caí.
   _____ Me di en la cabeza.
   _____ Me duele la cabeza.

4. _____ Me dolió mucho.
   _____ Lo enyesaron.
   _____ Me fracturé un brazo.

5-60 ¿Qué pasó? Completen las siguientes oraciones de forma lógica.

> MODELO   Comí mucho en la cena y ahora _tengo dolor de estómago_.

1. Santiago corrió diez millas esta tarde y _____ las piernas.
2. Nosotros estamos deshidratados; por eso _____.
3. Me di en una rodilla con el escritorio y la rodilla _____.
4. Ellas tropezaron con una silla y _____.
5. Tú no tuviste cuidado y _____ con el cuchillo.
6. Mara se dio con la cama y _____ un dedo del pie.

5-61 ¡A actuar! Adivinen cuál es la acción que otro(a) compañero(a) va a dramatizar. Túrnense para actuar y adivinar.

> MODELO   If your classmate acts as if he/she trips, falls, and hurts his/her foot, you say: _Tropezaste, te caíste y te lastimaste un pie._

■ Integración

5-62 Accidentes y enfermedades Representa la siguiente situación con un(a) compañero(a). Cuando terminen, cambien de papel.

Estudiante A	Estudiante B
Descríbele a tu compañero(a) qué te pasó y cómo te sentías *(how you felt)* la última vez que fuiste al doctor o a la sala de emergencias de un hospital. Debes mencionar todos los detalles pertinentes.	Tu compañero(a) va a narrar qué le pasó y cómo se sentía la última vez que fue al doctor o a la sala de emergencias. Como eres muy curioso(a), trata de averiguar todos los detalles pertinentes.

5-63 La peor experiencia Compara la experiencia que tu compañero(a) te narró en la actividad 5-62 con la experiencia que tú le narraste. ¿Cuál fue peor? ¿Quién recibió mejor atención médica? ¿Quién esperó más tiempo para ser atendido *(to be helped)*? Piensa en esto y escribe un párrafo breve. Al terminar, dale una copia a tu profesor(a) para que lo corrija.

ESTUDIANTE A

To talk about what the doctor(s) did, you may use these expressions: **me (recetó/recetaron) unas medicinas** *(prescribed some medicine for me)*, **me (puso/pusieron) una inyección** *(gave me a shot)*, **me (puso/pusieron) suero** *(gave me an IV)*, or **me (enyesó/enyesaron)** *(put me in a cast)*.

ESTUDIANTE B

Use the interrogative words that you already know: **cuándo, cómo, dónde, por qué, cuánto/os/as**, y **quién**.

REMEMBER

Some of the expressions you have to use to make comparisons are **tan... como, más/menos... que** and **tanto como**. Please refer to **Capítulo 4, Tema 1** to see a complete list.

IV. Lectura: Leyenda del origen de los Incas

■ Antes de leer

A. ¿Cuál es el origen del ser humano? ¿Cómo explican la ciencia y la religión el origen del ser humano? En dos o tres oraciones, presenten las ideas básicas de cada perspectiva.

- Explicación científica
- Explicación religiosa (identifiquen la religión correspondiente)

B. Vocabulario y conceptos Las siguientes palabras son importantes para comprender la leyenda. Emparéjalas con las definiciones de la derecha.

_____ crear	a. que no tiene luz o claridad
_____ vicio	b. mala costumbre o hábito
_____ castigar	c. lluvia muy fuerte y prolongada
_____ oscuridad	d. hacer algo nuevo
_____ diluvio	e. tener hijos
_____ procrear	f. imponer una penalidad física o moral a
_____ mandar	quien ha cometido una falta o delito
	g. ordenar, dar instrucciones o indicaciones

■ A leer

Leyenda del origen de los Incas

there was
sun / moon / stars

En el principio, **había** uno que llamaban Viracocha, el cual creó el mundo oscuro y sin **sol** ni **luna** ni **estrellas;** y por esta creación le llamaron Viracocha Pachayachachi, que quiere decir Creador de todas las cosas. Y después de creado el mundo formó unos gigantes deformes,

if it would be

para ver **si sería** bueno hacer los hombres de aquel tamaño. Y como le parecieron de muy mayor

his own
to be (subjunctive) / large / to be (future) / resemblance
to live (imperfect tense)

proporción que la **suya,** dijo: «No está bien que las gentes **sean** tan **crecidas;** mejor **será** que sean de mi tamaño». Y así creó a los hombres, a su **semejanza** como los que ahora son. Y **vivían** en oscuridad.

fights
under penalty
But / pride / greed

A éstos les mandó Viracocha vivir sin **desavenencias,** y conocerlo y servirlo; y les puso este precepto **so pena** de castigo. Guardaron este precepto algún tiempo. **Mas** como entre ellos nacieron vicios de **soberbia** y **codicia** y olvidaron el precepto de Viracocha Pachayachachi, éste se enojó y los

to curse (preterite)
to swallow (preterite)

maldijo. Unos fueron convertidos en piedras y otros en otras formas, a otros los **tragó** la tierra y a otros el mar, y sobre todos les mandó un diluvio general, al cual ellos llaman *uno pachacuti,* que quiere decir

to alter (preterite) / earth
to flood (preterite)

«agua que **trastornó** la **tierra**». Y dicen que llovió sesenta días y sesenta noches, y que **anegó** todo lo creado, y que sólo quedaron algunas señales de los que se convirtieron en piedras para memoria del hecho y para ejemplo de las futuras generaciones en los edificios de Pucara, que

league (measure)

está a sesenta **leguas** de Cuzco.

Viracocha guardó **consigo** tres hombres, el uno de los cuales se llamó Taguapacac, para servirle y ayudarle a crear las nuevas gentes que había de hacer en la segunda edad después del diluvio, lo cual hizo de esta manera: Pasado el diluvio y seca la tierra, determinó el Viracocha **poblar**la por segunda vez, y para hacerlo con más perfección determinó crear **luminarias** que diesen claridad. Y para **conseguir**lo se fue con sus criados a una gran laguna que está en el Collao, y en la laguna hay una isla llamada Titicaca, que quiere decir montes de **plomo.** Viracocha fue a esa isla y mandó salir el sol, la luna y las estrellas y que fueran al cielo para dar **luz** al mundo, y así fue hecho.

to himself

to populate
light sources
to achieve

lead

light

Viracocha les mandó algunas cosas a sus **criados,** pero el Taguapaca fue desobediente. El Viracocha, indignado, mandó a los otros dos criados que tomasen a Taguapaca, y **atado de pies y manos,** así lo echaron en una **balsa** a la laguna. El Taguapaca, ofendido, **amenazó** con volver a tomar **venganza.** Los criados lo llevaron entonces por el **desaguadero** de la laguna, y nadie volvió a ver al Taguapaca por mucho tiempo. Hecho esto, Viracocha fabricó en aquel lugar un altar en **señal** de lo que allí había hecho y creado.

servants

tied by hands and feet
raft / to threaten (preterite)
revenge
drain, outlet

sign

Viracocha dejó entonces la isla con sus dos criados y fue a un lugar que ahora llaman Tiaguanaco y en este lugar **esculpió** y **dibujó** en unas rocas grandes todas las naciones que **pensaba** crear. Entonces, les ordenó a sus dos criados memorizar los nombres que él les **decía** de aquellas **gentes** que allí **había pintado,** y de los valles y provincias y lugares de donde las tales **habían de salir,** que eran los de toda la **tierra.** Y a cada uno de ellos mandó ir por diferente **camino,** llamando las tales gentes, y mandándolas salir, procrear y **henchir** la tierra. Y los dichos criados suyos obedecieron el mandato de Viracocha, y el uno se fue por la sierra hacia el Mar del Sur, y el otro en dirección a las montañas que decimos de los Andes, al **levante** del dicho mar. Por estas sierras **iban caminando** y a altas voces diciendo: «¡Oh, gentes y naciones! ¡**Oíd y obedeced** el **mandato** del Tici Viracocha Pachayachachi, el cual **os manda** salir, multiplicar y henchir la tierra!» Y el mismo Viracocha **iba haciendo** lo mismo por las tierras intermedias de sus dos criados, nombrando todas las naciones y provincias por donde **pasaba.** Y a las **voces** que daban todo lugar obedeció y así salieron unos de lagos, otros de **fuentes,** valles, **cuevas,** árboles, cavernas, peñas y montes, e hinchieron las tierras y multiplicaron las naciones que son hoy el Perú.

to carve (preterite)
to draw (preterite)
to think, plan (imperfect tense)

decir (imperfect tense) / peoples /
had painted

were to emerge
earth / road
to populate

east
they were walking
listen and heed / command
commands you to
was doing

to pass by (imperfect tense) / loud
cries / springs / caves

Pedro Sarmiento de Gamboa. *Historia de los Incas.* 1572. (adaptado)

■ ¿Entendiste bien?

C. Orden de la creación Organicen los siguientes eventos de la creación del mundo, según las tradiciones de los Incas.

_____ Viracocha creó el sol, la luna y las estrellas.

_____ Viracocha creó unos gigantes.

_____ Viracocha creó los hombres a su imagen y semejanza.

_____ Viracocha ordenó un diluvio.

_____ Viracocha creó las diferentes naciones.

_____ Los primeros hombres desobedecieron los preceptos de Viracocha.

_____ Viracocha y sus criados ordenaron a las naciones multiplicarse y poblar la tierra.

D. Semejanzas Busque dos semejanzas entre la historia del origen del hombre en la tradición judeocristiana y la de los Incas.

E. Las diferentes caras del dios Viracocha Busquen en el texto referencias acerca de las diferentes manifestaciones del dios inca.

dios creador
dios destructor
dios administrador
dios artista

F. Enfoque lingüístico Identifiquen las formas del pretérito de los verbos en el primer párrafo y en el último párrafo. Luego, escriban las formas correspondientes del infinitivo.

G. Actividad de extensión: ¿Qué hizo después? Escribe un párrafo sobre lo que imaginas que el dios Viracocha realizó después de crear los pueblos y las naciones de la Tierra.

Eventos importantes

aniversario	*anniversary*
bautizo	*baptism*
cumpleaños	*birthday*
graduación	*graduation*
jubilación	*retirement*
matrimonio/boda/ casamiento	*wedding*
nacimiento	*birth*

Los números después de 100

cien	100
ciento uno/a	101
ciento dos	102
ciento tres	103
doscientos/as	200
doscientos uno/a	201
doscientos dos	202
doscientos tres	203
trescientos/as	300
cuatrocientos/as	400
quinientos/as	500
seiscientos/as	600
setecientos/as	700
ochocientos/as	800
novecientos/as	900
mil	1.000
mil uno/a	1.001
mil dos	1.002
diez mil	10.000
diez mil uno/a	10.001
diez mil dos	10.002
cien mil	100.000
cien mil uno/a	100.001
cien mil dos	100.002
novecientos mil	900.000
novecientos noventa y nueve mil	999.000
un millón	1.000.000
dos millones	2.000.000

Preparativos para un viaje

el asiento	*the seat*
la billetera	*wallet*
el boleto/billete	*airline ticket*
la cartera	*handbag*
los cheques de viajero	*traveler's checks*
el equipaje	*luggage*
el equipaje de mano	*carry on luggage*
la maleta	*suitcase*
el maletín	*briefcase*
la mochila	*backpack*

el terminal internacional	*international departures terminal*
el pasaporte	*passport*
el pasillo	*aisle*
la sala de espera	*boarding area*
la tarjeta de embarque	*boarding pass*
la ventanilla	*window*
abordar	*to board*
cambiar	*to exchange*
empacar	*to pack*
mostrar (ue)	*to show*
sacar	*to get, obtain*

El cuerpo humano

el abdomen	*abdomen*
la boca	*mouth*
los brazos	*arms*
la cabeza	*head*
la cara	*face*
las cejas	*eyebrows*
la cintura	*waist*
los codos	*elbows*
el corazón	*heart*
el cuello	*neck*
los dedos	*fingers*
los dedos del pie	*toes*
los dientes	*teeth*
la espalda	*back*
el estómago	*stomach*
la garganta	*throat*
el hombro	*shoulder*
el hueso	*bone*
las manos	*hands*
la nariz	*nose*
el oído	*inner ear*
los ojos	*eyes*
las orejas	*ears*
el pelo	*hair*
la piel	*skin*
las piernas	*legs*
los pies	*feet*
los pulmones	*lungs*
las rodillas	*knees*
los tobillos	*ankles*
las uñas	*fingernails*

Funciones y estructuras

Verbos con cambios ortográficos, p. 184
Verbos irregulares, pp. 195, 196
Verbos con terminaciones especiales, p. 208
Verbos para hablar de incidentes y accidentes, p. 211

Capítulo 6

Recuerdos

Para comenzar

- ¿Qué diferencias o semejanzas hay entre San José y tu localidad?
- ¿Cuáles son algunas de las ventajas de vivir en una ciudad como San José?
- ¿Hay algunas desventajas?
- ¿Qué prefieres tú?

In this chapter you will learn . . .

- how to talk about the differences between urban and rural life
- how to talk about the environment
- how to express generalizations
- how to describe in the past
- how to talk about one's life in the past
- about some of the environmental issues that affect Latin America today

	TEMA 1 La ciudad	**TEMA 2** La naturaleza	**TEMA 3** La conservación del medio ambiente
Vocabulario	El mundo urbano	La vida en el campo	La ecología
Funciones y estructuras	Expressing generalizations with indefinite words (and review of negative words) Describing the past with the imperfect tense	Describing the past with irregular verbs in the imperfect tense Expressing knowledge and familiarity with the verbs **saber** and **conocer**	Indicating location with demonstrative adjectives and pronouns Talking about the past with verbs that change meaning in the preterite
Lecturas y vídeo	Perspectivas: Saturación vehicular en Managua	Vídeo: Un baile folclórico puertorriqueño	Lectura: La leyenda del Zurquí

Vista aérea de la ciudad
de San José

El centro de la ciudad

Un barrio residencial

 # Enfoque

A. ¿Qué sabes ya de Costa Rica? Antes de ver el vídeo, completa las siguientes oraciones. Luego, compara tus respuestas con las de un(a) compañero(a).

1. Costa Rica comparte frontera con dos países: con _____ al norte y con _____ al sur.
   a. Honduras, Nicaragua   b. Nicaragua, Panamá   c. Panamá, Colombia

2. La divisa o moneda del país es el _____ costarricense.
   a. colón   b. peso   c. sol

3. Aunque *(Even though)* la cultura costarricense es el reflejo de la mezcla de razas que coexisten en el país, la influencia principal es la _____.
   a. europea   b. indígena   c. asiática

4. Desde 1948, Costa Rica no tiene _____. El dinero que se ahorra *(saves)* el país lo invierte en mejorar el nivel de vida de los costarricenses.
   a. iglesia oficial   b. ejército   c. gobierno central

B. Costa Rica – «Pura vida» Lee las siguientes oraciones sobre Costa Rica. Luego, marca con una **X** las que escuches en el vídeo. **¡OJO!** En el vídeo no se mencionan todas las oraciones.

____ 1. Costa Rica es un pequeño país centroamericano con más de tres millones de habitantes.

____ 2. En el Museo de Oro se puede ver artículos precolombinos, es decir, los artículos que los indígenas hicieron antes de la llegada de los españoles al continente americano.

____ 3. La economía de Costa Rica es principalmente agrícola; algunos productos importantes son las bananas y el café.

____ 4. Más o menos un 18% de Costa Rica está formado por reservas y parques nacionales, dos de los cuales fueron declarados Patrimonio de la Humanidad por la UNESCO.

____ 5. San José es la capital de Costa Rica; es el centro de la población, de la cultura y de la industria.

C. El ecoturismo Como vieron en el vídeo, los costarricenses son muy conscientes de la riqueza natural de su país y hacen esfuerzos para protegerla. ¿Cuánto saben del ecoturismo?

1. ¿Qué es y qué opinan del ecoturismo?
2. ¿Les gustaría *(would you like)* hacer ecoturismo? ¿Por qué sí o por qué no?
3. ¿Dónde se puede hacer ecoturismo en los Estados Unidos? ¿Hay un sitio en tu comunidad o cerca de ahí?

For more info, you may want to check the **Temas** site: http://temas.heinle.com

La ciudad

I. Vocabulario: El mundo urbano

Voy a mudarme a un nuevo apartamento,
así que necesito conectar varios servicios.

el agua
el alcantarillado
el cable
la conexión a Internet
el gas
la luz (la electricidad)
el teléfono

Los problemas de la vida urbana

la contaminación
el ruido
la congestión
el costo de vida
la delincuencia
la basura

Vocabulario práctico

el barrio *neighborhood*

el centro *downtown*

Los servicios sociales *(Social services)*

la educación *education*

la salud *health*

el transporte *transportation*

Los funcionarios públicos *(Public officials)*

el (la) alcalde (alcaldesa) *mayor*

los basureros *garbage haulers*

los bomberos *fire department (firefighters)*

los paramédicos *paramedics*

la policía *police*

la policía vial/de tránsito *traffic police*

▓ Asimilación

6-1 ¿Corresponde o no? En cada uno de los siguientes grupos hay un elemento que no corresponde. Determinen cuál es y expliquen por qué no es parte del grupo.

1. educación, transporte, salud, agua
2. hospital, gas, escuela, metro
3. transporte, cable, tráfico, ruido
4. agua, luz, museo, teléfono
5. camarero, alcalde, bombero, médico

CD1–58 **6-2 Su nuevo hogar en Managua** Un amigo tuyo viajó recientemente a Nicaragua para trabajar. Escucha su mensaje en el contestador.

1. Lo que más le gusta de Managua es...
   a. los museos.　　b. el centro.　　　　c. el parque.
2. Encontró en la ciudad...
   a. una casa.　　b. un apartamento.　　c. una oficina.
3. Ahora necesita instalar...
   a. el teléfono.　　b. la luz.　　　　　c. el agua.

▓ Aplicaciones

6-3 ¿Qué se requiere? Muchas de nuestras actividades cotidianas *(daily)* que parecen simples en realidad requieren la confluencia de muchos y complejos servicios. Indica cuáles se requieren para **tomar una ducha de agua caliente** *(to take a hot shower)*. Compara luego tus respuestas con las de otros compañeros.

____ gas
____ alcantarillado
____ teléfono
____ transporte

____ electricidad
____ salud
____ agua
____ educación

6-4 La vida en Managua Completa la siguiente carta de Marisa, tu *e-mail–pal* nicaragüense, sobre la vida en su ciudad.

Managua es una ciudad grande, con muchos lugares bonitos para visitar. El _____ es un poco congestionado, pero los _____ periféricos son tranquilos. El sistema de _____ es eficiente y económico. Hay autobuses y taxis, pero no hay metro. Como aumenta el número de automóviles particulares, el problema de la _____ y la congestión nos preocupa mucho ahora en la ciudad. Pero bueno, ¿y cómo es tu ciudad?

EN TU COMUNIDAD

Interview a real estate agent and write a report about recent trends in the housing market in your community (Are there more buyers or sellers at this time? What is the average sale price of a home? Are interest rates favorable?). Also, investigate the type of support available to non-English speakers in this agent's real estate firm.

SUGERENCIAS

Step 1: Make a list of the things that make your city or town unique and a list of some of its problems.
Step 2: Select the information that you will include in your composition and link related ideas with connectors such as **como** *(since)*, **además** *(in addition)*, **lo peor** *(the worst thing)*, **lo mejor** *(the best thing)*.
Step 3: Exchange compositions with a classmate and check the following aspects:
a. content (is the description of the town complete and fair?);
b. organization (is it easy to read? Are there any unclear segments?); **c. vocabulary** (did your classmate include a variety of words from this chapter?);
d. grammar (do you find any agreement problems?).

6-5 ¿Sabes? Describan la vida urbana.

1. Nombren tres cosas que debemos instalar en una casa nueva.
2. Nombren tres tipos de servicios sociales que se encuentran *(are found)* en una ciudad.
3. Nombren tres lugares donde trabaja la gente de la ciudad.
4. Nombren tres lugares donde la gente de la ciudad se divierte.
5. Nombren tres problemas que **no** tiene tu pueblo o tu ciudad.

■ Integración

6-6 Entrevista Trabajando en parejas, hagan y respondan a las siguientes preguntas. Al terminar, preparen un breve informe sobre las respuestas del (de la) compañero(a).

1. ¿Tienes suficiente luz natural en tu apartamento o en tu casa?
2. ¿Hay demasiado ruido en tu apartamento o en tu casa?
3. ¿Dónde tiras la basura?
4. ¿Quién saca la basura en tu casa?
5. ¿Hay mucha delincuencia en tu barrio?
6. ¿Hay mucho tráfico donde vives?
7. ¿Es alto el costo de vida en tu comunidad?

6-7 La vida en tu pueblo o en tu ciudad Escribe una breve descripción de tu ciudad para responder a la pregunta que Marisa hizo en el mensaje de la actividad 6-4.

II. Funciones y estructuras: Expressing generalizations with indefinite words (and review of negative words)

SERGIO: Hay **algo** que me preocupa: hay mucha basura en las calles. ¿Conoces a **alguna** persona que trabaje en la oficina del alcalde?

ANABEL: No, no conozco a **nadie**, pero podemos ir **algún día** para hablar con **alguien.**

In **Capítulo 1, Tema 3,** you learned how to use negative words such as **nada, nadie, ni... ni, ningún/ninguno(a), nunca,** and **tampoco.** As you may recall, these words are placed either before the verb or after a verb that is preceded by **no.**

No tenemos **ni** cable **ni** teléfono.
Nadie puede encontrar **ninguna** solución al problema de la delincuencia.

*We have **neither** cable **nor** phone.*
***Nobody** can find **any** solution for the delinquency problem.*

REMEMBER

Double negatives are correct in Spanish. See the examples provided.

The affirmative counterparts of these negative words are the indefinite words, which refer to people and objects in a generic and unspecified way. Here is a list of these words.

algo *something*
alguien *someone, somebody*
algún/alguno(a/os/as) *a/an, some, any*
algún día *some day*

alguna vez/una vez *sometime, ever/once*
o... o.../ y *either . . . or . . . / and*
siempre *always*
también *also*

To say *everybody*, use the expression **todo el mundo.**

The expressions **alguna vez** and **una vez** usually refer to actions in the past while **algún día** refers to actions in the future.

El ruido es **algo** que no tolero.
Alguien me dijo que los basureros están en huelga.

*Noise is **something** that I do not tolerate.*
***Somebody** told me that garbage haulers are on strike.*

The word **alguno** changes to **algún** when it is used before a masculine singular noun.

¿Hay **algún** funcionario en esta oficina?
¿Tienes **algún** problema con el transporte?

*Is there **any** public official in this office?*
*Do you have **any** transportation problem?*

■ Asimilación

 6-8 Los estudiantes de mi clase Escoge las oraciones que describan a los estudiantes de tu clase. Al terminar, compara tus respuestas con las de un(a) compañero(a). ¿Están de acuerdo?

____ Siempre quieren tomar clases por la mañana.

____ Toman algunas clases fáciles para mejorar el promedio *(grade point average)*.

____ Quieren ir a algún país de habla hispana algún día.

____ Alguna vez hicieron trampa *(cheated)* en un examen.

____ Cuando están enojados con el (la) profesor(a), dicen algo.

____ Buscan a alguien semejante a ellos para trabajar en grupos.

____ Todo el mundo llega a clase temprano.

____ Sacan A o sacan B en todos los trabajos.

CD1–59 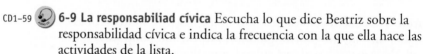 **6-9 La responsabiliad cívica** Escucha lo que dice Beatriz sobre la responsabilidad cívica e indica la frecuencia con la que ella hace las actividades de la lista.

Actividad	siempre	algunas veces	nunca
1. Evita el ruido excesivo.			
2. Participa en manifestaciones públicas.			
3. Camina al centro para ayudar con la congestión.			
4. Divide y recicla la basura.			
5. Habla con los jóvenes para prevenir la delincuencia.			

■ Aplicaciones

6-10 En este barrio Lean lo que dice Adolfo sobre su barrio y escojan las palabras correctas.

Me gusta mucho mi barrio porque (alguien / nadie) tira la basura a la calle y porque (siempre / nunca) hay mucho ruido. Además, es un barrio donde no hay delincuencia y (también / tampoco) hay contaminación (o / y / ni) congestión. Pero hay (algo / nada) que no es bueno: el costo de vida es muy alto. (Algunos / Ningún) funcionarios públicos prometen que esto va a mejorar, pero no lo creo. (También / Tampoco), desafortunadamente, hay (algunas / ningunas) personas que no se preocupan por la educación ni por los servicios públicos.

6-11 ¡Qué contradictorio(a)! Túrnense para leer y reaccionar a las siguientes oraciones en forma opuesta.

MODELO   E1: *Siempre me pongo ropa de colores oscuros.*
E2: *Pues yo nunca me pongo ropa de colores oscuros.*
      o *Pues yo no me pongo nunca ropa de colores oscuros.*

1. Creo que no hay ninguna película interesante en el cine.
2. Pienso que no hay nadie aburrido en esta clase.
3. Algún día espero tomar clases de acupuntura.
4. En mi casa cenamos juntos todos los días.
5. Una vez fui de vacaciones a Costa Rica.
6. Creo que alguien aquí se puso mucho perfume.

6-12 En nuestras familias

Paso 1: Piensa en las personas de tu familia y completa las siguientes oraciones.

1. En mi familia nadie _____.
2. Mis parientes siempre _____ y _____.
3. Ellos nunca _____ ni _____.
4. Algún día, nosotros vamos a _____.
5. Algo cómico en mi familia es que nosotros _____.
6. Ninguno de mis parientes es _____.

A simple way of turning these sentences into questions is by asking what is called an *echo question*, which consists of placing an interrogative word in the place where the answer would go, for example, **¿En tu familia nadie qué?**

Paso 2: Convierte las oraciones del **Paso 1** en preguntas para tu compañero(a). Escribe las respuestas que él/ella dé y prepara un breve informe.

■ Integración

6-13 ¿Qué opinan? En grupos de tres o cuatro estudiantes, describan cómo es la vida y cuáles son algunos aspectos positivos y negativos de alguna ciudad famosa de los Estados Unidos. Incorporen el vocabulario que se presentó al principio de este **Tema.**

You can use expressions such as **algo (interesante/aburrido/ridículo/que [no] me gusta) de esta ciudad es que...; aquí (siempre/nunca/nadie/todo el mundo)...; cuando alguien visita esta ciudad,...; en esta ciudad, (algunas personas/nadie)...; aquí hay (algún/os/as)...; aquí... y... también y aquí ni... ni... tampoco.**

6-14 La vida en tu pueblo o en tu ciudad Vuelve a leer *(Read again)* la descripción de tu ciudad que escribiste en la actividad 6-7 y añade más detalles. Usa las palabras y frases que aprendiste en esta sección. Cuando termines, dale una copia a tu profesor(a) para que la corrija.

You may want to use some of the expressions that were presented in activity 6-13.

III. Funciones y estructuras: Describing the past with the imperfect tense

En el barrio donde yo crecí **había** muchas casas y la playa **estaba** muy cerca.

Cuando era niño, yo **jugaba** con mis amigos todos los días. **Nos divertíamos** muchísimo.

As you may have noticed, the previous examples include verbs in a past tense that is not the preterite. This tense is called the imperfect. Here is a list of the basic uses of this tense.

- To talk about habitual actions in the past (the equivalent of *used to . . .*).

  Yo **visitaba** a mis abuelos todas las tardes.

  *I **used to visit** my grandparents every afternoon.*

- To provide descriptions.

  Su casa **tenía** un jardín muy grande.

  *Their house **had** a very big garden.*

- To talk about an event that was in progress while another action was taking place. The action that takes place while another action is in progress is reported in the preterite.

  Yo **estaba** en la escuela primaria cuando nos mudamos a otro barrio.

  *I **was** in elementary school when we moved to another neighborhood.*

- To provide descriptions of the participants who carry out the main events of a story, including age, physical appearance, conditions and emotions.

  Tenía diez años y **era** un chico muy bueno.

  *I **was** ten years old and **was** a very good boy.*

- To provide background information of past events, including time and weather conditions.

  Cuando salimos de la casa, **eran** como las tres de la tarde y **llovía**.

  *When we left the house, **it was** around three o'clock in the afternoon, and **it was raining**.*

You will learn more about the difference between the preterite and the imperfect tenses in **Capítulo 7, Tema 3.**

The endings of the imperfect tense are the following.

tomar *(to take, to drink)*	correr *(to run)*	vivir *(to live)*
tom**aba**	corr**ía**	viv**ía**
tom**abas**	corr**ías**	viv**ías**
tom**aba**	corr**ía**	viv**ía**
tom**ábamos**	corr**íamos**	viv**íamos**
tom**abais**	corr**íais**	viv**íais**
tom**aban**	corr**ían**	viv**ían**

*Notice that the endings for **-er** and **-ir** verbs are identical. Also, notice that only the endings for **-ar** verbs have the letter **b**.

Unlike in the preterite, there are not any stem-changing verbs in the imperfect tense.

Yo **pensaba** que **tenía** los mejores padres del mundo. Y **soñaba** con ser policía.

*I **used to think** that I **had** the best parents in in the world. And I **used to dream** about being a police officer.*

The imperfect tense form of the verb **haber** is **había** *(there used to be, there was/were)*.

En mi pueblo **había** muchas tiendas de antigüedades.

***There were** many antique shops in my town.*

■ Asimilación

6-15 Tu pueblo Escoge las oraciones que describan el pueblo en que creciste y sus habitantes. Luego, compara tus respuestas con las de un(a) compañero(a). ¿Eran pueblos semejantes o diferentes?

____ No tenía alcalde ni policía municipal.
____ Había muchos parques.
____ Tenía muchos habitantes.
____ Tenía muchas calles.
____ Estaba cerca de una ciudad.

____ Había mucha contaminación.
____ Mucha gente usaba transporte público.
____ No había un centro comercial.
____ Estaba lejos de esta universidad.
____ La gente se comunicaba bien.

6-16 ¿Cuándo? Abraham va a hablar de algunas de las cosas que hacía antes. Escucha lo que dice e indica si él hacía estas actividades cuando era niño o cuando estaba en la escuela secundaria. **¡OJO!** Hay actividades que Abraham no hacía.

Clave: a = cuando era niño   b = cuando estaba en la escuela secundaria

____ 1. Tomaba clases de karate.
____ 2. Miraba la televisión.
____ 3. Jugaba béisbol.
____ 4. Estaba en el club de teatro.
____ 5. Estudiaba más.
____ 6. Leía mucho.
____ 7. Patinaba.
____ 8. Trabajaba en el museo del pueblo.

■ Aplicaciones

 6-17 ¿Qué hacían? Mencionen por lo menos dos actividades que las siguientes personas posiblemente hacían cuando tenían diez años. ¡Sean originales!

MODELO   Donald Trump *tenía muchas novias y leía la revista* Forbes.

1. David Letterman
2. Venus y Serena Williams
3. el (la) gobernador(a) del estado
4. Madonna
5. Howard Stern
6. Halle Berry
7. el presidente de los Estados Unidos
8. otra persona: _____

 6-18 Mini-situaciones Completen las siguientes situaciones con detalles interesantes y cómicos.

MODELO   Cuando mi mejor amigo(a) llegó a su clase de español, *no había nadie en la sala de clase. El profesor lo esperaba con un examen y él/ella no estaba preparado(a).*

1. Cuando el (la) profesor(a) entró a su casa anoche,...
2. Cuando me mudé a la casa donde vivo ahora,...
3. Cuando nosotros comenzamos a estudiar español,...
4. Cuando tenía cinco años, yo...
5. Cuando los estudiantes de la clase de 1985 se graduaron,...

6-19 La niñez *(Childhood)*

Paso 1: Escribe seis oraciones sobre las cosas que hacías y que no hacías en tu niñez.

MODELO   *No regresaba a casa antes de las ocho de la noche.*

1. ...
2. ...
3. ...
4. ...
5. ...
6. ...

Paso 2: Usa las oraciones del **Paso 1** para formar preguntas para tus compañeros de clase. Debes buscar a seis personas diferentes que respondan afirmativamente a una de las preguntas. Cuando las encuentres, escribe los nombres. Al terminar, prepara un informe para la clase.

MODELO   *En tu niñez, ¿no regresabas a casa antes de las ocho de la noche?*

■ Integración

You may talk about clothing and colors, hair styles, the role of men and women in society, things children used to do, music, TV shows, food, etc.

You may use the following connectors to compare both decades: **primero** *(first)*, **segundo** *(second)*, **tercero** *(third)*, **en cambio** *(instead, on the other hand)*, **por el contrario** *(on the contrary)*, **sin embargo** *(however)*, **por ejemplo** *(for example)*, **además** *(in addition)*, and **finalmente** *(finally)*.

 6-20 ¡Cómo han cambiado las cosas! Descríbele a tu compañero(a) cómo era la vida en una década específica (los cincuenta, los sesenta, los setenta, los ochenta, los noventa, etc.). Luego, tu compañero(a) va a describir una década diferente. Si es necesario, busquen información sobre esto en el Internet.

6-21 La mejor década De acuerdo con la discusión que tuviste con tu compañero(a) en la actividad 6-20, ¿cuál fue la mejor década, la que tú describiste o la que él/ella describió? Escribe una composición corta para exponerle tu punto de vista *(point of view)* a tu profesor(a). Cuando termines, intercambia tu composición con un(a) compañero(a) para ver si te faltan *(if you are missing)* algunos detalles. Cuando hagas las correcciones, dale una copia a tu profesor(a). ¿Crees que lo/la vas a poder convencer?

IV. Perspectivas: Saturación vehicular en Managua

■ Antes de leer

A. ¿Qué opinan de esta declaración *(statement)*? Hay demasiados coches en este país.

B. ¿Eres un(a) conductor(a) responsable? Marca tus respuestas y compáralas con las de tu compañero(a).

Excedo el límite de velocidad.	Siempre / A veces / Nunca
Uso el cinturón de seguridad.	Siempre / A veces / Nunca
Respeto las leyes de tránsito.	Siempre / A veces / Nunca
Bebo antes de conducir.	Siempre / A veces / Nunca
Pongo a los niños en sillas especiales.	Siempre / A veces / Nunca

■ A leer

Sesenta y cuatro carros nuevos por día en las calles de Managua

Minsa y OPS expresan preocupación y piden endurecer sanciones a conductores irresponsables.

—**Lucía Navas**—

Cada día, la dirección de Tránsito de la Policía inscribe 64 nuevos vehículos para que circulen en Managua, lo cual está aumentando la saturación vehicular y potenciando más la accidentalidad.

Each day

Autoridades del **Minsa** y representantes de la Organización Panamericana de la Salud (OPS) dijeron que por ser los traumatismos causados por accidentes de tránsito «una epidemia», se debe aplicar mayores sanciones en contra de conductores que violenten las leyes.

Ministerio de Salud

Se insiste en que los conductores **ebrios,** la alta velocidad en las **carreteras,** el desuso de protectores (**cascos** y cinturones) y el irrespeto a las señales de tránsito por conductores y peatones provocan que las lesiones por accidentalidad en Nicaragua estén entre las primeras causas de muerte en grupos de 5 a 49 años.

drunk
highways/roads / helmets

«El sistema de vigilancia en hospitales en Nicaragua reporta que el 18 por ciento de las emergencias son por lesiones de tránsito y el 28 por ciento están relacionadas con el exceso de alcohol», dijo Montesano, de OPS.

rollovers / hit	Las muertes se dan por **volcones** de los carros, **atropellamiento** y por
falls	**caídas** de pasajeros del transporte público.
intoxication	Se planteó la suspensión de licencia de conducir por seis meses para quienes manejen en estado de **ebriedad,** y de por vida a quienes reincidan. La actual Ley de Tránsito permite que hasta la cuarta vez de
regulation	reincidencia se aplique la **medida.**

Más accidentes... más carros

El comisionado Gilberto Solís, de la Dirección de Tránsito Nacional,

número de autos indicó que el **parque vehicular** de Managua crece cada semana al darse 450 nuevas inscripciones de carros.

Dijo que los accidentes también ocurren por mala programación de los

weakness semáforos y la **debilidad** de la infraestructura de las carreteras.

«También hay mucha intolerancia e impaciencia en las carreteras, lo que provoca mayores niveles de estrés en los conductores, y ello genera más accidentes e infartos en los ciudadanos», explicó la comisionada Vilma Rosa Rosales, directora del Centro de Educación Vial.

Ministerio de Educación, Cultura y La Policía se coordina con el **MECD** para implementar la educación
Deportes / *pertaining to roads and* **vial** permanente en los centros escolares. Y con la creación del Consejo
highways de Seguridad Vial pretenden «formar, educar y corregir a los conductores y peatones». El obstáculo actual es que, físicamente, el centro como tal no existe, y que para subsanar la debilidad están aplicando mayores exigencias.

Entre lo recomendado por OPS está una campaña masiva de educación vial en el país, y que haya más **velocímetros** controlando las

speedometers carreteras. Además, que los carros particulares utilicen sillas especiales

para llevar niños en el **asiento trasero,** que se mejore la visibilidad de

back seat vehículos y peatones en la vía pública por las noches, y se insista en el

adherence to **cumplimiento de** las medidas de seguridad vial.

Source: *El nuevo diario.* Martes, 18 de mayo de 2004 (adaptado)
(http://www.elnuevodiario.com.ni/archivo/2004/mayo/18-mayo-
2004/nacional/nacional18.html)

■ ¿Entendiste bien?

C. Ideas principales Escoge la opción más apropiada según el texto.

1. ¿Cuántos nuevos autos inscribe la policía de Managua cada mes?
   a. más de 60
   b. más de 400
   c. más de 1900

2. Las autoridades nicaragüenses están preocupadas porque un aumento de autos resulta en...
   a. más contaminación.
   b. más accidentes.
   c. más tráfico.

3. En Managua, más de un cuarto de las emergencias por lesiones de tránsito están relacionadas con...
   a. la velocidad.
   b. el estrés.
   c. el alcohol.

4. Según el artículo, en Nicaragua **no** son causa principal de fatalidades de tránsito...
   a. los choques de autos.
   b. las caídas de pasajeros del transporte público.
   c. los atropellamientos.

5. La solución propuesta por el gobierno incluye...
   a. sanciones y nuevos semáforos.
   b. educación y una nueva infraestructura vial.
   c. sanciones y educación vial.

D. Detalles importantes Busquen la siguiente información.

1. Identifiquen los cuatro factores que provocan los accidentes de tránsito en Nicaragua.

2. Identifiquen las cinco propuestas presentadas por el gobierno nicaragüense para solucionar el problema de tránsito.

E. Para conversar ¿Qué otras soluciones debería considerar el gobierno nicaragüense para reducir la saturación vehicular y los accidentes en su país?

La naturaleza

I. Vocabulario: La vida en el campo

la isla

la montaña
el lago
el volcán

la playa

el mar
la arena

el valle

el árbol
la selva
el río

el ganado
el cultivo
el toro
la vaca
el pato
el agricultor
la gallina
el perro
la finca /
la hacienda
el caballo
el cerdo/
puerco
el gato
el pavo
la cosecha

El campo y los animales domésticos *(the countryside and farm animals)*

Vocabulario práctico

los campesinos/trabajadores
   workers
el campo *countryside (field)*
el suelo *soil*
Trabajo
alimentar *to feed*
cosechar *to harvest*
criar *to raise*
cultivar *to cultivate*
recoger *to pick*
sembrar (ie) *to sow*

Diversión
acampar *to camp*
bucear *to dive*
escalar *to climb, to hike*
esquiar *to ski*
esquiar en el agua *to waterski*
hacer surf *to surf*
montar a caballo *to horseback*
   ride
nadar *to swim*

■ **Asimilación**

6-22 El campo en los Estados Unidos Indiquen si las siguientes oraciones son ciertas (**C**) o falsas (**F**).

_____ 1. Crían mucho ganado en Texas.

_____ 2. Todas las fincas están en el centro del país.

_____ 3. Hay plantaciones de tabaco en Carolina del Sur.

_____ 4. Los cultivos de cereales en Kansas están muy tecnificados.

_____ 5. Las cosechas de naranjas son excelentes en Massachusetts.

_____ 6. Muchos inmigrantes hispanos recogen las cosechas en California.

CD1–61 **6-23 ¿Adónde fueron?** Escucha las descripciones de diferentes vacaciones que ha tomado el Sr. Espinoza e identifica el destino de sus viajes.

1. En 2001, los Espinoza fueron a...
   a. una finca.
   b. una ciudad.
   c. una playa.

2. En 2002 fueron a...
   a. un desierto.
   b. una selva.
   c. un río.

3. En 2004 fueron a...
   a. una finca.
   b. un desierto.
   c. una playa.

4. En 2005 fueron a...
   a. una finca.
   b. una selva.
   c. una ciudad.

■ **Aplicaciones**

6-24 Tres animales Mencionen tres animales con cada una de las siguientes características.

1. Tienen pelo.
2. Tienen plumas (*feathers*).
3. Son famosos por las películas.
4. Viven con los humanos en las ciudades.
5. Su nombre empieza con «p».

6-25 Adivina dónde Una persona tiene que pensar en un lugar y describir las actividades que se pueden hacer allí. La otra persona tiene que adivinar de qué lugar se trata.

MODELO   E1: *Puedes esquiar y escalar.*
                E2: *Las montañas.*

EN TU COMUNIDAD

Visit a farm and provide a report on property size, type of production (crops, animals, etc.), and number of employees required. Also, determine if this farm uses migrant workers in any aspect of production.

6-26 ¿Qué hicieron? Imaginen que Uds. pasaron sus vacaciones en Panamá. Mencionen por lo menos tres actividades que hicieron en cada uno de los siguientes lugares.

MODELO   *En la Ciudad de Panamá fuimos a varios museos, asistimos a un concierto y salimos a cenar en unos restaurantes muy buenos.*

1. Las islas de San Blas

2. La playa Río Mar

3. Parque Nacional de Darién

■ Integración

6-27 En la agencia de viajes Representa la siguiente situación con un(a) compañero(a).

Estudiante A	**Estudiante B**
Eres agente de viajes. Puedes ganar una comisión mayor si convences a tu cliente de tomar varias excursiones durante su visita a Panamá. Explícale qué puede ver en diferentes lugares de este país centroamericano. Sé *(Be)* persistente.	Vas a viajar a Panamá este invierno, pero no tienes mucho dinero. Te gustaría hacer alguna excursión, pero no sabes qué vale la pena visitar. Pide información sobre los destinos más interesantes en este país, pero no permitas que te vendan excursiones caras.

6-28 La belleza natural de mi país A Marisa, tu *e-mail-pal* nicaragüense, le fascina la naturaleza. Completa el siguiente mensaje electrónico con la descripción de tu sitio natural favorito en los Estados Unidos.

SUGERENCIAS

Mention the name of the place and its location, describe the landscape, list some of the activities you can carry out there, and indicate the approximate cost of food and lodging in the area.

De: _____ (your e-mail address)

Fecha: _____ (today's date)

Para: Marisa@sol.racsa.co.ni

Asunto: La naturaleza en mi país

Marisa:

En los Estados Unidos hay muchas oportunidades para disfrutar de unas vacaciones en medio de la naturaleza. Mi lugar favorito es...

Un abrazo,

_____ (tu nombre)

II. Funciones y estructuras: Describing the past with irregular verbs in the imperfect tense

Cuando niños, **íbamos** al campo a acampar. **Era** divertido porque siempre **veíamos** muchos animales diferentes.

There are only three irregular verbs in the imperfect tense: **ir, ser,** and **ver.**

ir	ser	ver
iba	era	veía
ibas	eras	veías
iba	era	veía
íbamos	éramos	veíamos
ibais	erais	veíais
iban	eran	veían

Notice that the **yo** and **él/ella/usted** forms of each of these verbs are identical.

▤ Asimilación

6-29 En el campo Piensa en las vacaciones que tomabas cuando eras niño(a) y escoge las alternativas que sean correctas. Cuando termines, compara tus respuestas con las de un(a) compañero(a). ¿Qué cosas eran diferentes?

____ Iba al campo todos los veranos.

____ Montar a caballo era mi actividad favorita.

____ Veía muchos animales salvajes.

____ Iba con toda mi familia.

____ Nosotros veíamos a las mismas personas todos los años.

____ Y también íbamos al mismo lugar todos los años.

____ Era un(a) niño(a) aventurero(a) y hacía muchas cosas como bucear y escalar montañas.

____ Nunca iba al campo de vacaciones.

CD1-62 **6-30 Las vacaciones de Iraida** Escucha lo que dice Iraida sobre las vacaciones que tomaba su familia cuando ella era niña y escoge la alternativa correcta para cada pregunta.

1. Iraida iba de vacaciones a...
   a. una selva.   b. un río.   c. un lago.

2. Este lugar estaba... de su casa.
   a. lejos   b. cerca   c. al lado

3. La cabaña *(cabin)* de madera era...
   a. pequeña.   b. cómoda.   c. grande.

4. Durante las vacaciones, Iraida veía a sus...
   a. abuelos.   b. tíos.   c. primos.

5. Ella... con ellos.
   a. hacía surf   b. escalaba   c. esquiaba

■ **Aplicaciones**

6-31 La casa de mi infancia Completen los espacios en blanco con las formas correctas de los verbos **ir**, **ser** y **ver.**

La casa de mi infancia _____ muy acogedora (cozy). Tenía sólo dos habitaciones, pero (las habitaciones) _____ bastante grandes. Desde el balcón de la casa, (nosotros) _____ las montañas y el río. Todos los sábados, mientras mi padre _____ a pescar, mis hermanos y yo _____ a jugar con los animales de la granja. A veces (nosotros) _____ a algunos turistas que estaban de vacaciones y jugábamos con los niños. ¡Vivir tan cerca de la naturaleza _____ magnífico!

6-32 ¿Cómo? ¿Adónde? ¿Qué?

Paso 1: Completa las siguientes oraciones para indicar cómo eras, adónde ibas en tu tiempo libre y qué programas de televisión veías cuando estabas en la escuela secundaria.

Yo era _____ y _____.

Yo iba a _____ y a _____.

Yo veía _____ y _____.

Paso 2: Usa la información del **Paso 1** para hacerle preguntas a tu compañero(a). Toma notas de sus respuestas.

MODELO   E1: *Leonard, ¿eras introvertido?*
          E2: *No, yo era extrovertido. También era...*
          E1: *¿Ibas al cine con tus amigos?*
          E2: ...

Paso 3: Usa la información que recopilaste en el **Paso 2** para escribir un breve informe.

MODELO   *Cuando estaba en la escuela secundaria, yo era introvertido;*
          pero Leonard era extrovertido y... Nosotros íbamos al cine y a...

6-33 Creemos que... Ahora, usen los modelos de la actividad 6-32 para describir los hábitos que dos personas de la clase tenían cuando estaban en la escuela secundaria. Escojan a dos personas que tengan personalidades similares. Al terminar, compartan la información con el resto de la clase. ¿Los demás estudiantes pueden adivinar de quiénes están hablando?

■ Integración

6-34 Una persona entrañable *(dear)* Descríbele a tu compañero(a) una persona que tuvo un efecto positivo en tu vida. ¿Cómo era esta persona? ¿Qué hacían juntos? ¿Adónde iban?

> You may talk about one of your elementary, middle or high school teachers, a relative who passed away, a childhood friend, etc.

6-35 Preguntas para un(a) compañero(a) de clase Prepara una serie de preguntas para saber un poco más de la vida en el pasado de un(a) compañero(a) de clase. Cuando termines, entrégale las preguntas a él/ella para que las conteste por escrito *(in writing)*. ¡Debes estar preparado(a) para que él/ella te haga preguntas también!

> You may write questions related to his/her personality, his/her favorite activities, his/her favorite TV shows, his/her relatives, places he/she used to visit, etc.

III. Funciones y estructuras: Expressing knowledge and familiarity with the verbs *saber* and *conocer*

—¿**Conoces** al agricultor que vende verduras en el mercado?
—Sí, lo **conozco**. Se llama Arturo.
—¿**Sabes** dónde está su finca?
—Creo que está en Villa Hermosa.

REMEMBER

The irregular **yo** forms of **saber** and **conocer** are **sé** and **conozco**.

As you already know, the verbs **saber** and **conocer** have the same meaning: *to know*. Nevertheless, these verbs are used in completely different contexts. Here is a list of their uses.

The verb **saber** is used to talk about knowing . . .	
■ facts and information.	
Yo **sé** dónde está Nicaragua.	*I know where Nicaragua is.*
¿**Sabías** que Panamá está al este de Costa Rica?	*Did you know that Panama is to the east of Costa Rica?*
■ how to do something.	
Mi abuela **sabe** cocinar muy bien.	*My grandmother knows how to cook very well.*
Ellas **saben** hablar inglés y francés.	*They know how to speak English and French.*
The verb **conocer** is used to talk about knowing . . .	
■ people and places (being familiar or acquainted).	
Conozco a los dueños de esta finca.	*I know the owners of this land.*
¿**Conoces** el Canal de Panamá?	*Do you know (are you familiar with) the Panama Canal?*

Notice that **conocer** requires the use of the personal **a** when the direct object is a person or pet.

■ Asimilación

6-36 ¿Cierto o falso? Indica si las siguientes oraciones son ciertas (**C**) o falsas (**F**) y compara tus respuestas con las de un(a) compañero(a). ¿Qué cosas tienen en común?

____　1.　No sé montar a caballo.

____　2.　Sé esquiar en el agua.

____　3.　No sé nadar.

____　4.　Sé los nombres científicos de muchos animales.

____　5.　Sé cultivar y cuidar plantas exóticas.

____　6.　Conozco a muchos campesinos.

____　7.　No conozco tiendas de productos agrícolas.

____　8.　Conozco las Montañas Apalaches.

____　9.　Conozco por lo menos uno de los grandes lagos.

___ 10.　No conozco al / a la secretario(a) de agricultura.

CD1–63 **6-37 Un mensaje telefónico** Escucha el mensaje que el Sr. Hidalgo dejó en el contestador de la Sra. Sánchez, que necesita un asistente para su agencia de turismo en Nicaragua. Escribe las cosas que él sabe y conoce bajo la columna correcta.

Sabe...	Conoce...

■ Aplicaciones

6-38 La respuesta La Sra. Sánchez escuchó el mensaje del Sr. Hidalgo, lo llamó y dejó este mensaje en su contestador. Lean la transcripción del mensaje y escojan el verbo correcto.

Buenas tardes, Sr. Hidalgo. Es la Sra. Sánchez, de la Agencia Turismo Centroamericano. Por lo que mencionó, (sé / conozco) que Ud. está muy bien cualificado para el puesto. Además, Ud. (sabe / conoce) los lugares turísticos de los que nosotros les hablamos a los turistas y (sabe / conoce) usar bien la computadora. Yo (sé / conozco) a su prima Deborah y ella le dio una excelente recomendación. (Sé / Conozco) que Ud. es el candidato perfecto. Llámeme mañana para hablar un poco más de las responsabilidades que el puesto exige. Gracias y hasta luego.

REMEMBER

The expression **¿cuánto tiempo hace que…?** is used with verbs in the present tense when the action began in the past and continues in the present.

6-39 ¿Cuánto tiempo hace que…? Averigüen cuánto tiempo hace que su compañero(a) sabe o conoce las siguientes cosas, personas y lugares.

> MODELO   manejar un carro
> E1: *¿Cuánto tiempo hace que sabes manejar un carro?*
> E2: *Hace cuatro años que sé manejar un carro. ¿Y tú?*
> E1: *Yo no sé manejar. Tomo el autobús.*

1. esta universidad
2. a tu mejor amigo(a)
3. usar el Internet
4. al / a la profesor(a)
5. tu restaurante favorito
6. tu lugar de vacaciones favorito
7. nadar
8. a tu novio(a) o esposo(a)

6-40 Talentos y conocimiento

Paso 1: Toma unos minutos para completar la siguiente tabla con información que los demás estudiantes no saben de ti. Escribe por lo menos tres oraciones en cada columna.

Yo sé…	Yo conozco…

Paso 2: Usa la información del **Paso 1** para hacerles preguntas a varios compañeros de clase. Toma notas de sus respuestas. Al terminar, prepara un resumen y preséntaselo a la clase.

> MODELO   E1: *Patricia, yo sé jugar tenis muy bien. Y tú, ¿sabes jugar tenis?*
> E2: *Sí, yo sé jugar tenis también.*
>   o *No, yo no sé jugar tenis.*

■ Integración

 6-41 Una entrevista de empleo Representa la siguiente situación con un(a) compañero(a). Al terminar, intercambien papeles.

El (La) entrevistador(a)	**El (La) entrevistado(a)**
Tú eres el (la) gerente de personal de Mundo Acción, una agencia que organiza excursiones turísticas para personas a quienes les gusta hacer actividades al aire libre *(outdoors)* en los Estados Unidos. Vas a entrevistar a una persona para un puesto y quieres que esta persona conozca lugares interesantes y atractivos y que sepa *(knows)* hacer las actividades que va a promocionar *(advertise)*. ¡Sé creativo(a) al hacer las preguntas!	Te interesa mucho trabajar para Mundo Acción, una agencia que organiza excursiones turísticas para personas a quienes les gusta hacer actividades al aire libre *(outdoors)* en los Estados Unidos. Crees que eres la persona ideal para este puesto porque conoces muchos lugares interesantes y atractivos y porque sabes hacer muchas actividades que generalmente se hacen al aire libre. ¡Impresiona al / a la entrevistador(a) con tu experiencia y conocimiento!

You may use vocabulary words that were presented in this **Tema** as well as expressions such as **saber jugar (béisbol/golf/...)**, **saber dónde es posible...**, **saber qué es necesario para...**, **conocer (el lago/el bosque/el río/la playa/las montañas)...**, and **saber qué se puede hacer en (el lago/el bosque/el río/la playa/las montañas)...**

6-42 Recomendado(a) o no recomendado(a) Imagínate que tu profesor(a) es el (la) dueño(a) de la agencia Mundo Acción y que tienes que enviarle un correo electrónico para recomendarle o no al / a la candidato(a) que entrevistaste en la actividad 6-41. De acuerdo con las respuestas que esta persona te dio, ¿le darías *(would you give him/her)* el puesto? Para justificar tu decisión, menciona las cosas que esta persona (no) sabe y (no) conoce.

De: _____ (your e-mail address)
Fecha: _____ (today's date)
Para: el (la) dueño(a)@mundoacción.com
Asunto: Entrevista a _____ (your partner's name)

Estimado(a) _____ (your professor's name):
Le escribo este mensaje para informarle que hoy entrevisté a _____
_____ y mi opinión es que (sí/no) debemos
contratarlo(la) por las siguientes razones:

Cordialmente,

_____ (your name)

IV. Vídeo: Un baile folclórico puertorriqueño

■ Preparación

A. Bailes típicos

1. Basándose en el título y en la foto de arriba, ¿qué creen que va a pasar en el vídeo?
2. ¿Conocen alguno de estos bailes puertorriqueños: la plena, la bomba, la danza? Descríbanlos si pueden.

■ ¿Entendiste bien?

ESTRATEGIA DE COMPRENSIÓN

Selective Listening You do not need to understand every word you hear. Concentrate on the specifc information required in order to complete the activity below.

B. La lección de baile folclórico Mira el vídeo y decide si las siguientes oraciones son ciertas (**C**) o falsas (**F**).

_____ 1. Valeria no quería bailar.

_____ 2. El baile que los compañeros estaban aprendiendo se llama la plena puertorriqueña.

_____ 3. Mientras bailaba, Alejandra se lastimó el tobillo.

_____ 4. Hace un año, Alejandra se rompió el pie y se lo enyesaron.

_____ 5. Sofía quería salir por la noche con Víctor, el instructor de baile.

Compara tus respuestas con las de un(a) compañero(a) y juntos corrijan las oraciones falsas.

C. ¡Bailar! Descríbele a un(a) compañero(a) la última vez que bailaste o viste a otras personas que estaban bailando.

- ¿Dónde estabas? (en la escuela, en una boda, en una discoteca, etc.)
- ¿Con quién estabas?
- ¿Qué tipo de música tocaban?
- Cuando tocaban la música, ¿bailabas, mirabas a la gente bailar o ambas cosas?
- Mientras los otros bailaban, ¿te divertías? Y las demás personas, ¿qué hacían?

D. Enfoque comunitario La música y los bailes son parte de nuestra cultura y evolucionan con los años (los estilos de música, los tipos de bailes, la manera de bailar, la ropa que lleva la gente, etc.). Entrevista a una persona mayor de tu comunidad sobre cómo eran la música y los bailes cuando él/ella tenía tu edad y presenta un informe oral en clase sobre sus respuestas.

La conservación del medio ambiente

I. Vocabulario

Rápidos del Río Reventazón
- Disfrute de naturaleza, belleza y aventura
- Ideal para principiantes y aventureros
- Excursión de rápidos más popular del país

Costa Rica
Su Mejor Destino

Volcán Arenal y aguas termales
- El volcán más activo del país
- Exuberante vegetación
- Aguas termales

Parque Nacional Tortuguero
- Sitio de la tortuga verde y tortuga baula
- Observación de aves y especies de fauna acuática
- Hospedaje en albergue rústico

Vocabulario práctico

El medio ambiente
(The environment)
la ecología *ecology*
el ecólogo *ecologist*
el ecosistema *ecosystem*
las especies *species*
la extinción *extinction*
la fauna *fauna, wildlife*
la flora *flora*
el guardaparques *park ranger*
la investigación *research*
el naturalista *naturalist*
los recursos naturales *natural resources*

el refugio natural/silvestre *wildlife reserve*
la reserva biológica *biological reserve*
la variedad *variety*

Verbos
conservar/preservar *to preserve*
extinguirse *to become extinct*
investigar *to research*
mantener (ie) *to maintain, to support*
proteger *to protect*
reciclar *to recycle*
reforestar *to reforest*

■ Asimilación

6-43 Asociaciones ¿Qué palabras asocian con los siguientes conceptos? En dos minutos, escriban todas las palabras posibles. El grupo con las listas más largas gana.

ecólogo	*parque nacional*	*ecoturismo*
investigación		
científico		
estudiar		
observar		
plantas		
etc.		

1–64 **6-44 Excursión al Volcán Poás y a Sarchí** Escucha el siguiente itinerario e indica las actividades principales de la excursión.

____ conocer una ciudad   ____ nadar en un río

____ bucear en el mar   ____ observar plantas y animales

____ observar el paisaje   ____ visitar dos cráteres de un volcán

____ comprar artesanías

■ Aplicaciones

6-45 Adivina Un(a) estudiante piensa en una palabra relacionada con la conservación del medio ambiente y da su definición. El (La) compañero(a) tiene que adivinar de qué palabra se trata.

MODELO   E1: *Es una persona que investiga los ecosistemas.*
               E2: *Un ecólogo.*

6-46 Una excursión ecológica Completa las oraciones con la palabra o frase más lógica.

OPCIONES: especies   ecosistema   reforestación   ecólogo
                  fauna   flora   reserva biológica

1. El siguiente es el itinerario de nuestra excursión a una

    _____.

2. Durante el recorrido, todos pueden admirar la _____

    y la _____ locales.

3. En el parque podemos estudiar un _____ fascinante.

4. Antes del almuerzo vamos a hacer una caminata por el bosque para apreciar las diversas _____ de plantas que existen en la reserva.

5. Después del almuerzo vamos a escuchar la charla de un famoso _____ y luego vamos a disfrutar una aventura de dos horas por el río.

6. Antes de regresar vamos a plantar un árbol para colaborar con los programas de _____ de este parque.

6-47 ¡Vamos a Costa Rica! Imagínense que se han ganado un viaje ecológico a Costa Rica con todos los gastos pagados. Completen el cuadro con los lugares que piensan visitar, las actividades que pueden hacer y las cosas que van a necesitar.

Lugares que quieren ver	Actividades que quieren realizar	Cosas que van a necesitar

■ Integración

6-48 Vacaciones ecológicas Representa la siguiente situación con un(a) compañero(a).

Useful expressions: **¿Me podría dar información acerca de...?** *(Could you give me information about . . .?)* **Me interesa...** *(I am interested in . . .)*

Useful expressions: **Tengo el plan perfecto para Ud.** *(I have the perfect plan for you.)* **No se preocupe.** *(Don't worry.)*

Turista hispano(a)	Guía
Eres un(a) turista hispano(a) que quiere disfrutar de la naturaleza durante tu visita a este país. Habla con este(a) guía para averiguar tus opciones.	Como guía turístico(a), tienes que ayudarle a la gente a organizar sus viajes. Ayúdale a este(a) viajero(a) hispano(a) a organizar una serie de actividades ecológicas en tu región. Usa la información de la actividad anterior como guía.

6-49 Ruta ecológica Imagínense que trabajan para la corporación de turismo de su estado. Preparen un itinerario en español para promover la conservación y la apreciación de la naturaleza en su región.

1. Preparen una lista de los sitios naturales en el área.
2. Piensen en las actividades ecológicas que pueden hacer allí.

II. Funciones y estructuras: Indicating location with demonstrative adjectives and pronouns

— Liana, ¿te gusta más **esta** excursión o **ésa**?
— Me gusta más **ésta** porque uno visita parques ecológicos. **Aquella** excursión sólo incluye visitas a lugares históricos.

Demonstratives are used to indicate the location (in space or in time) of people and things in relation to the speakers. They agree in number and gender with the noun they modify or refer to.

DEMONSTRATIVE ADJECTIVES	DEMONSTRATIVE PRONOUNS	MEANING	LOCATION
este, esta	éste, ésta	*this (one)*	**aquí** (*here*)
estos, estas	éstos, éstas	*these*	
ese, esa	ése, ésa	*that (one)*	**ahí** (*there*)
esos, esas	ésos, ésas	*those*	
aquel, aquella	aquél, aquélla	*that (over there)*	**allá/allí** (*over there*)
aquellos, aquellas	aquéllos, aquéllas	*those (over there)*	

In general, the forms of **este/éste** are used to refer to people or things that are close to the speaker while the forms of **ese/ése** are used to refer to people or things that are close to the listener. The forms of **aquel/aquél**, on the other hand, are used by both the speaker and the listener to refer to people or things that are far from both of them.

Demonstrative pronouns, which are used to refer to nouns that have already been mentioned in the discourse, are distinguished from their adjectival counterparts by accent marks.

¿Te gustan **estas** variedades de plantas o **éstas**?

*Do you like **these** varieties of plants or **these**?*

¿Vamos a reciclar **ese** recipiente o **ése**?

*Are we going to recycle **that** container or **that one**?*

Demonstrative pronouns also have a neuter form: **esto, eso,** and **aquello.** They are used when objects have not been identified yet or to refer to ideas, concepts, and situations.

¿Qué es **esto**? ¿Es una flor silvestre?
¿La extinción de animales? **¡Eso** es inaceptable!
Aquello no se podía creer.

*What is **this**? Is it a wild flower?*
*Animal extinction? **That's** unacceptable!*
***That** was hard to believe.*

■ **Asimilación**

6-50 En la sala de clase Imagínate que estás en la sala de clase, en el lugar donde normalmente te sientas. Luego, lee las oraciones que siguen e indica si podrías *(if you could)* decir estas cosas o no. Ten en cuenta *(keep in mind)* cuán *(how)* cerca o lejos estás de las personas y objetos que se mencionan.

_____ 1. Esta silla es muy cómoda.

_____ 2. Aquella ventana es grande.

_____ 3. Esta sala de clase tiene aire acondicionado.

_____ 4. Casi siempre trabajo con ese(a) compañero(a) de clase, no con éste(a).

_____ 5. Siempre pongo mis libros y cuadernos en esa silla.

_____ 6. El (La) mejor estudiante de la clase es aquél/aquélla.

CD1–65 **6-51 En mi antiguo** *(former)* **barrio** Escucha lo que Gabriel le dice a su amigo Rubén cuando le está mostrando su antiguo barrio. Escribe el número de la descripción debajo del dibujo correcto.

_____

_____

_____

■ Aplicaciones

6-52 De compras Hoy es sábado y tu compañero(a) y tú están de compras en un centro comercial. Escojan el demostrativo que usarían en las siguientes oraciones. **¡OJO!** Usen los adverbios **aquí, ahí** y **allá/allí** como claves *(clues)*.

1. Estas faldas están a buen precio, pero (éstas / ésas / aquéllas) que están ahí son un poco caras.
2. Aquellos vestidos son de seda y (estos / esos / aquellos) pantalones de aquí son de algodón.
3. Me gusta esta camiseta, pero (ésta / ésa / aquélla) que está allá me gusta más.
4. ¿Sabes cuánto cuestan (estos / esos / aquellos) sombreros que están ahí?
5. Esa tienda de artículos para el hogar no tiene mucha variedad. Vamos para (ésta / ésa / aquélla) de allí.
6. Aquellas lámparas son bonitas, pero (ésta / ésa / aquélla) que está aquí combina *(matches)* con los muebles de mi sala.
7. ¿Qué opinas de (estos / esos / aquellos) sillones que están ahí?
8. Creo que voy a comprar (estas / esas / aquellas) cortinas que están allá.

6-53 En el supermercado Luego de hacer compras en el centro comercial, Uds. deciden ir al supermercado para comprar los ingredientes que necesitan para preparar la cena. Completen las oraciones con el adjetivo o el pronombre demostrativo correcto.

1. Estos tomates están frescos, pero _____ *(these)* pimientos están aún más frescos.
2. Me gustan mucho las gambas, pero _____ *(those)* que están ahí son muy pequeñas, ¿no?
3. ¿Quieres comprar arroz de esa marca *(brand)* o de _____ *(this one)*?
4. ¡No hay frijoles negros! ¡_____ *(That)* es increíble!
5. Creo que debemos llevar jugo de naranja. _____ *(That one)* que está allá es el mejor.
6. ¿Quieres llevar de este pan o de _____ *(that one)*?
7. ¿Qué es _____ *(this)*? ¿No hay lechuga para la ensalada?
8. ¿Llevamos estas tortas o _____ *(those)* de allá?

6-54 La vida en este estado Túrnense para hacer y responder a las siguientes preguntas sobre el estado donde viven.

1. ¿Te gusta vivir en este estado?
2. ¿Qué cosas (no) hay en otros estados que (no) hay en éste?
3. ¿Qué piensan las personas de otros estados sobre éste? ¿Crees que tienen razón o no? ¿Algunas de esas cosas te molestan *(bother you)*?
4. ¿Tienes parientes en otros estados? ¿Visitas a esos parientes?
5. ¿Piensas vivir en otro estado cuando te gradúes? ¿Por qué te interesa hacer esto?

■ Integración

You may describe the following:
árboles, bosque, caballos, centro de visitantes, flores, hombre que está escalando la montaña, montañas, pájaros, pavos, plantas exóticas, recursos naturales, refugio natural, río, turistas, zona de acampar.

6-55 Guardaparques Tu compañero(a) y tú trabajan como guardaparques en un parque nacional y están con un grupo de visitantes. Túrnense para describir el paisaje del dibujo de abajo. **¡OJO!** Imaginen que los visitantes están al lado de Uds. ¡Sean creativos y traten de captar la atención y el interés de los visitantes con su descripción!

MODELO   *Estos pavos son nativos de esta región. Hay muchos en*
           este parque.

6-56 Visitantes Imagínate que estás visitando la reserva natural del dibujo de arriba. Como eres una persona muy curiosa y te interesa mucho la naturaleza, escribe una lista de preguntas que les quieres hacer a los guardaparques. Usa la lista de sugerencias de la actividad 6-55 e imagina que estás al lado de los guardaparques.

MODELO   *¿Qué comen estos pavos?*
           ¿De qué especie son aquellos pájaros?
           ¿Y ésos?...

III. Funciones y estructuras: Talking about the past with verbs that change meaning in the preterite

Ayer **conocí** algunas de las bellezas naturales de Costa Rica. Siempre **quise** venir aquí porque sabía que era un país espectacular. También **pude** probar la comida costarricense. ¡Es deliciosa!

The verbs **conocer** *(to know)*, **poder** *(to be able to)*, **querer** *(to want, to love)*, and **saber** *(to know)* change meanings when they are used in the preterite tense. Here is a summary of those changes.

*Notice that **poder** and **querer** have different meanings when they are used with the adverb **no**.

VERB	MEANING IN THE PRETERITE
conocer	*to meet; to visit, to get to see a place (for the first time)* ■ Ayer **conocí** a una ecóloga panameña. *Yesterday **I met** a Panamanian ecologist.* ■ Mi hermana **conoció** la ciudad de San José el mes pasado. *My sister **visited** the city of San José for the first time last month.*
poder	*to succeed* (**no poder** = *to fail*) ■ El Dr. Loveras **pudo** descubrir la causa de la epidemia. *Dr. Loveras **was able to** (**succeeded at**) discover the cause of the epidemic.* ■ Los científicos no **pudieron** prevenir la extinción de esas especies. *Scientists **could not** (**did not succeed at, were not able to, failed at**) prevent the extinction of those species.*
querer	*to try, to make an effort, to attempt* (**no querer** = *to refuse*) ■ Los funcionarios **quisieron** preservar el medio ambiente, pero la gente **no quiso** cooperar. *Public officials **tried** (**made an effort, attempted to**) preserve the environment, but people **refused** to cooperate.*
saber	*to find out, to hear* ■ **Supimos** que hay una cura naturalista para esta enfermedad. ***We found out** (**heard**) that there is a naturalistic cure for this illness.*

■ Asimilación

6-57 En los últimos meses ¿Qué cosas han pasado en los últimos meses? Empareja cada verbo de la izquierda con una frase lógica de la derecha e indica si cada oración que formas es cierta **(C)** o falsa **(F).** Cuando termines, compara tus respuestas con las de un(a) compañero(a). ¿Qué tienen en común?

_____ 1. Pude sacar...

_____ 2. No quise trabajar...

_____ 3. Supe que (yo)...

_____ 4. Conocí a...

_____ 5. Quise levantarme...

_____ 6. No pude ir...

a. mi novio(a). _____

b. de vacaciones a ningún lugar. _____

c. temprano todos los días para hacer ejercicio, pero no pude. _____

d. A en todos los exámenes que tomé. _____

e. mientras estudio. _____

f. no me puedo graduar este año. _____

CD1-66 **6-58 En el Parque Nacional Tortuguero** Sofía va a hablar de lo que Paco y ella hicieron en el Parque Nacional Tortuguero la semana pasada. Escúchala y completa el siguiente párrafo.

En el parque Nacional Tortuguero, Sofía y Paco pudieron _____ y _____. Ellos conocieron a _____. Quisieron _____, pero no pudieron. Supieron que no había _____.

■ Aplicaciones

6-59 Problemitas durante las vacaciones ¿Qué problemitas tuvieron los Vizcaíno durante sus vacaciones en el área del Río Reventazón? Para saber cómo responde esta pregunta el Sr. Vizcaíno, completen los siguientes párrafos con la forma correcta de los verbos de la lista.

OPCIONES: poder saber no querer no poder querer conocer

Éstas fueron unas vacaciones magníficas, pero tuvimos varios problemitas. Por ejemplo, yo _____ bañarme en el río, pero no pude porque el agua estaba muy turbulenta y casi me ahogo *(I almost drowned)*. Además, mis hijas se enojaron mucho cuando (ellas) _____ que eran demasiado pequeñas *(too young)* para ir a la excursión de los rápidos. Lo peor de todo fue que *(The worst thing of all was that)*, mi hijo Jaime _____ hacer nada porque el primer día se cayó y se lastimó una pierna.

A pesar de todo lo que pasó *(that happened)*, éstas fueron unas vacaciones magníficas. (Nosotros) _____ disfrutar de la naturaleza de Costa Rica. También (nosotros) _____ las bellezas naturales de este hermoso país. A mi esposa le gustó tanto que (ella) _____ regresar a casa el día que teníamos previsto *(that we had planned)* y extendimos la estadía una semana más.

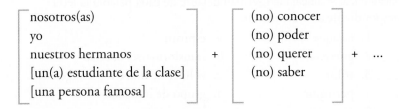

6-60 El año pasado... Formen oraciones lógicas sobre algunas de las cosas que pasaron en la vida de estas personas el año pasado. ¡Sean originales y añadan detalles interesantes!

MODELO   nosotros(as)   (no) poder
Nosotros no pudimos ir a la Florida en las vacaciones de primavera porque los profesores nos dieron mucha tarea.

$$\begin{bmatrix} \text{nosotros(as)} \\ \text{yo} \\ \text{nuestros hermanos} \\ \text{[un(a) estudiante de la clase]} \\ \text{[una persona famosa]} \end{bmatrix} + \begin{bmatrix} \text{(no) conocer} \\ \text{(no) poder} \\ \text{(no) querer} \\ \text{(no) saber} \end{bmatrix} + \ldots$$

6-61 La vida ajetreada *(busy)* **del / de la profesor(a)** Como Uds. saben, el (la) profesor(a) tiene una vida muy ajetreada. Escriban por lo menos cinco preguntas para saber cómo fue su día de ayer. Usen los verbos **conocer, (no) poder, (no) querer** y **saber.**

MODELO   *Profesor(a), ¿Ud. no quiso corregir nada ayer?*

■ Integración

6-62 Trabajo, estudio y diversión Los estudiantes típicos tienen un dilema todos los veranos: dedicarse a trabajar, a estudiar o a divertirse. Piensen en las cosas que hicieron el verano pasado para balancear estas tres cosas y explíquenle a su compañero(a) qué pudieron y no pudieron hacer, qué quisieron y no quisieron hacer, qué cosas supieron y a qué personas y lugares conocieron. ¿Fue un verano bueno o malo?

6-63 Un recuento de mis logros *(achievements)* Tu profesor(a) quiere saber un poco sobre algunas de las cosas que has logrado en tu vida. Haz un recuento de tus logros y entrégale una copia a él/ella.

Answer the following questions before you begin the writing process: **¿Qué cosas pudiste hacer? ¿Y qué cosas no pudiste hacer? ¿Conociste a alguien a quien querías conocer? ¿Qué piensan tus parientes y amigos sobre estos logros?**

IV. Lectura: La leyenda del Zurquí

A. El formato Observa el título y los dibujos que acompañan el cuento. De acuerdo con esto, identifica:

- los personajes principales
- los lugares donde sucede la acción

B. Vocabulario y conceptos Escriban delante de cada palabra la letra correspondiente a su definición.

_____ 1. cacique

_____ 2. guerrero

_____ 3. tribu

_____ 4. perseguir

_____ 5. convertirse

_____ 6. alma

a. espíritu

b. transformarse, hacerse

c. el líder de una tribu indígena

d. grupo de indígenas

e. buscar, acosar

f. soldado, luchador

A leer

Elías Zeledón (1953–)

Es un bibliotecólogo costarricense. Como investigador, se ha preocupado por recuperar los valores folclóricos de su país. Ha trabajado como editor de las revistas *El Rualdo*, *La Edad de Oro* y *Turí Guá* (las dos últimas dedicadas a los niños). Su libro *Leyendas costarricenses* es una compilación de cuentos e historias tradicionales escritas por diversos autores, muchas de las cuales pertenecen a la tradición oral.

La leyenda del Zurquí

Cerca de la ciudad de San José se encuentran los valles del volcán Barva.

Hace muchísimos años vivió allí una princesa térraba llamada Turi Uha.

Turi Uha vivía tranquila en el poblado en donde gobernaba su padre, el cacique. Pero un día, un guerrero fuerte y valiente cruzó los bosques del Zurquí para llegar a la tribu térraba.

——— ✳ ———

amar, imperfect tense

Él guerrero buscaba a Turi Uha, la mujer a quien **amaba**, la mujer más bella de la región. La princesa también amaba al guerrero, pero no podía casarse con él, ya que las tribus de sus padres eran enemigas y no permitirían su unión.

El amor no puede crecer en el territorio de guerra, y por eso Turi Uha huyó por la montaña con el guerrero. Sólo la acompañaron algunas amigas.

Cuando el cacique padre de Turi Uha **se dio cuenta** de que su hija había escapado con el guerrero de la tribu enemiga, se enfureció y salió con sus guerreros en busca de los fugitivos. El **retumbar** de los **pasos y** el **chasquido** de las **ramas rotas** al correr se oyeron por toda la montaña. Y el enamorado guerrero cayó **muerto** por sus perseguidores.

realized

echo / steps
snapping / broken twigs
dead

—— ❂ ——

El alma del valiente guerrero subió a la **cima del cerro**, allí donde, según la creencia de su gente, **habitaban** los muertos, en la **morada** del dios Sibú.

hilltop

vivían / casa

La princesa y sus amigas continuaron huyendo a través de la selva. Turi Uha **quería alcanzar** la cima, para habitar allí con el alma de su amado. Pero mientras la princesa y sus amigas huían de sus perseguidores, ocurrió algo maravilloso: poco a poco sus cuerpos se volvieron **ágiles**, su piel se transformó en **sedosas alas**…y convertidas en mariposas, alzaron vuelo para alcanzar el cielo.

wanted to reach

rápidos / silky wings

Es por eso que es común ver hermosas mariposas en grandes cantidades por las mágicas **cumbres** del Zurquí.

mountaintops

■ ¿Entendiste bien?

C. Primera aproximación a la lectura Sigue las instrucciones para entender mejor la lectura.

1. Lee rápidamente las primeras cuatro oraciones. Resume brevemente la idea principal.
2. Ahora, lee rápidamente el segundo segmento del texto. ¿Qué le pasó al guerrero? ¿Por qué?
3. Termina de leer el texto. ¿Qué les pasó a la princesa y a sus amigas?

D. A leer otra vez Lean el cuento una vez más y respondan a las siguientes preguntas:

1. **¿En qué orden?** Organicen los eventos de la historia.

____ El guerrero y la princesa huyeron de sus respectivas tribus.

____ Un guerrero se enamoró de la princesa.

____ El cacique persiguió y mató al guerrero.

____ La princesa Turi Uha vivía tranquila en su poblado.

____ La princesa y sus amigas se convirtieron en mariposas.

READING STRATEGY

Skimming Find out the general theme of the story.

READING STRATEGY

Scanning Keeping in mind the characters and context, look for facts about the story line.

2. **¿Qué pasó?** Respondan a las preguntas.

    a. ¿Por qué quería matar el cacique al guerrero?

    b. ¿Por qué quería alcanzar la cima del cerro la princesa?

    c. ¿Qué fenómenos naturales representa y explica esta leyenda?

E. Enfoque lingüístico Busquen ejemplos de usos del imperfecto en la lectura.

Para hablar de acciones habituales en el pasado	
Para hacer descripciones físicas, emocionales o psicológicas	

F. Actividad de extensión ¿Conocen alguna leyenda de su cultura o de otra cultura? ¿Qué fenómeno de la naturaleza explica o qué lección enseña? Comenten estas leyendas.

Los servicios públicos — Utilities

el agua	water
el alcantarillado	sewage system
el cable	cable
la conexión a Internet	Internet connection
el gas	natural gas
la luz/la electricidad	electricity
el teléfono	telephone

Los servicios sociales

la educación	education
la salud	health
el transporte	transportation

Los problemas urbanos

la basura	garbage
la congestión	traffic congestion
la contaminación	pollution
el costo de la vida	cost of living
la delincuencia (juvenil)	(youth) crime
el ruido	noise

Los funcionarios públicos — Public officials

el alcalde	mayor
los basureros	garbage haulers
los bomberos	firefighters
los paramédicos	paramedics
la policía	police
la policía vial/de tránsito	traffic police

La vida en el campo — Life in the countryside

el árbol	tree
la arena	sand
la isla	island
el lago	lake
el mar	sea
la montaña	mountain
la playa	beach
el río	river
la selva	jungle
el valle	valley
el volcán	volcano

La finca y los animales domésticos — The farm and farm animals

el agricultor	farmer
el caballo	horse
el cerdo/puerco	pig
la cosecha	harvest
el cultivo	crop
la gallina	hen
el ganado	livestock
el gato	cat
el pato	duck
el pavo	turkey
el perro	dog
el toro	bull
la vaca	cow

La producción agrícola

el campo	countryside (field)
el suelo	soil
los trabajadores/campesinos	workers

Trabajo

alimentar	to feed
cosechar	to harvest
criar	to raise
cultivar	to cultivate
recoger	to pick
sembrar (ie)	to sow

Diversión

acampar	to camp
bucear	to dive
escalar	to climb
esquiar	to ski
esquiar en el agua	to waterski
hacer surf	to surf
montar a caballo	to horseback ride
nadar	to swim

El medio ambiente — The environment

la ecología	ecology
el ecólogo	ecologist
el ecosistema	ecosystem
las especies	species
la extinción	extinction
la fauna	fauna, wildlife
la flora	flora
el guardaparques	park ranger
la investigación	research
el naturalista	naturalist
los recursos naturales	natural resources
el refugio natural/silvestre	wildlife reserve
la reserva biológica	biological reserve
la variedad	variety

Acciones relacionadas con el medio ambiente

conservar/preservar	to preserve
extinguirse	to become extinct
investigar	to research
mantener (ie)	to maintain, to support
proteger	to protect
reciclar	to recycle
reforestar	to reforest

Funciones y estructuras

Palabras negativas e indefinidas, p. 223
Adjetivos y pronombres demostrativos, p. 247

Puesta en acción

SITUACIÓN:	Tu universidad está interesada en tener una versión en español de su periódico para publicarla electrónicamente a través del Internet y de esta manera atraer a más estudiantes de habla hispana.
MISIÓN:	Publicar una edición completa del periódico universitario, incluyendo las secciones de eventos sociales, de turismo, de medio ambiente y de la vida diaria.
DESTREZAS:	Coordinar la publicación de un periódico, escoger temas de interés para los lectores, resumir y comunicar efectivamente la información relacionada con esos temas y publicar el periódico.

A. Noticias sobre el medio ambiente Antes de preparar tu artículo, sería bueno *(it would be good)* hacer un repaso del vocabulario y las estructuras gramaticales que vas a usar. Completa el siguiente párrafo con las palabras de la lista.

Opciones: fauna   fincas   reservas naturales
                 contaminación   medio ambiente

El gobierno nacional acaba de anunciar un plan para la conservación del _____ en la zona oriental del país. Debido al *(Due to)* aumento de las _____ ganaderas en la zona, el nivel de deforestación y de _____ de las aguas de los ríos locales, se ha puesto en peligro *(danger)* el futuro del frágil ecosistema de la región. Para evitar la desaparición de las especies nativas y para rescatar *(rescue)* el equilibrio ecológico de la región, se van a crear varias _____ . De esta manera, la _____ y la flora locales van a tener la oportunidad de regenerarse y prosperar como siempre lo han hecho en esta hermosa zona del país.

B. Noticias económicas Completa el siguiente artículo con la forma correcta del pretérito de los verbos entre paréntesis.

En una reunión auspiciada por la Cámara de Comercio local, el alcalde de la ciudad _____ (hablar) de su nuevo programa económico. El líder _____ (decir) que el problema principal de la ciudad era el desempleo y _____ (prometer) crear nuevos puestos en las áreas de manufactura y construcción. Por otro lado, su asistente _____ (concentrase) en probar que se ha superado la crisis de la inflación e _____ (indicar) que la presente administración va a reducir los impuestos. Tanto *(Both)* el alcalde como su asistente _____ (mencionar) que, de acuerdo con sus proyecciones, el déficit bajará un 10% en el próximo año fiscal y _____ (referirse) a la situación precaria que se vive en otras ciudades del país. Finalmente, cuando los periodistas _____ (preguntar) sobre el problema de salud pública, el alcalde _____ (preferir) no hacer ningún comentario.

C. Noticias internacionales Organicen las siguientes oraciones para formar un artículo con un orden lógico.

____ Varios científicos nicaragüenses lo esperaban.

____ Sus compañeros del Frente de Oposición a la minería se quedaron en Costa Rica. Están trabajando en otros proyectos.

____ Habló con los periodistas en el Aeropuerto Internacional de Managua.

____ Hoy se preparó todo el día para su participación en el Congreso sobre el medio ambiente.

____ Sale en dos días para Honduras.

____ Llegó ayer a Nicaragua Marco Tulio Araya Barboza, periodista y ambientalista costarricense.

____ Manifestó que se sentía muy contento de estar en la capital nicaragüense.

____ Estaba un poco cansado por el viaje.

____ Piensa pasar sólo unos días allí.

____ Su discurso fue muy positivo. Sirvió de inspiración para los que asistieron.

> To write a coherent article, you may use the following connectors: **así que** *(therefore)*, **aunque** *(even though)*, **como** *(since)*, **después** *(afterward)*, **luego** *(then, later)*, **más tarde** *(later)*, **porque** *(because)*, **y** *(and)*, **sin embargo** *(however)*.

D. Eventos sociales Usen la información que se provee para escribir las notas sobre eventos sociales en su comunidad. Añadan *(Add)* los detalles necesarios (tipo de evento, lugar, personas que celebraron el acontecimiento, etc.).

15 de febrero

Lorena Suárez Nogueras y David Escobar Negrón

20 de diciembre

Nidia María Agosto Toledo

6 de enero

Maximino Calderón Acevedo

Paso 1: Busquen información sobre la isla hondureña de Roatán y completen el cuadro que sigue. Luego, usen la información para escribir un artículo de interés turístico sobre este lugar.

Localización	
Tamaño	
Población	
Atractivos	
Actividades	
Otra información importante	

Paso 2: Tu compañero(a) y tú entrevistaron por separado a una persona que fue de vacaciones a la isla de Roatán recientemente. Imaginen que él/ella y tú tienen una conversación telefónica para obtener todos los datos sobre las vacaciones de esta persona. Túrnense para hacerse preguntas y para responderlas. Cuando terminen, usen la información para ampliar el artículo que escribieron en el **Paso 1.**

Estudiante 1

Fecha de llegada: 5 de junio
Fecha de salida: _____
Aerolínea: KAGY
Hotel: Mango Creek Lodge
Comidas favoritas: _____
Bebidas favoritas: _____
Artesanías favoritas: cerámicas, joyería de plata, pinturas
Actividades favoritas: _____
Información adicional: la gente de Roatán es muy simpática y hospitalaria,
_____

Estudiante 2

Fecha de llegada: _____

Fecha de salida: 11 de junio

Aerolínea: _____

Hotel: _____

Comidas favoritas: camarones, mariscos, ensaladas frescas

Bebidas favoritas: jugos de frutas

Artesanías favoritas: _____

Actividades favoritas: nadar, tomar el sol y hablar con la gente de la isla

Información adicional: es posible ir a Roatán en barco crucero.

 F. Proyecto final Traigan a clase un periódico reciente y sigan los siguientes pasos.

Paso 1: Decisión y discusión Escojan la sección sobre la cual quieren escribir (política, economía, vida social, salud pública, turismo, etc.) y reúnanse *(get together)* con los demás estudiantes que escogieron la misma sección. (Es preferible trabajar en grupos pequeños.) Comenten los posibles temas que van a incluir en su sección. (Decidan qué noticias van a cubrir.)

Paso 2: Investigación Consulten el periódico local y busquen noticias relacionadas con la sección que escogieron en el **Paso 1.** (También pueden consultar otras fuentes de información.)

Paso 3: Vocabulario y gramática Hagan una lista de las palabras del vocabulario que van a necesitar. Luego, hagan una lista de los eventos principales usando el pretérito. Finalmente, hagan una lista de frases descriptivas y de trasfondo *(background information)* sobre estos eventos usando el imperfecto.

CRITICAL THINKING SKILLS

Researching Find information on the topics you have selected. Use all the sources at your disposal (local newspapers, the Internet, TV, personal interviews, etc.).

Servicio comunitario

Contact someone from the university or from the local government and offer to provide one of the following services:

- Educate others about the importance of recycling and taking care of the environment.
- Organize groups to help solve problems that affect your community.
- Inform Spanish-speaking students (or members of the community) about available health services.

Para hacer en casa

Paso 4: Primer borrador *(draft)* Preparen una versión inicial de su informe. Incluyan fotos o dibujos para que el artículo tenga más interés visual.

- Seleccionen una noticia que tenga mucha cobertura *(coverage)*.
- Identifiquen a las personas y entidades involucradas *(involved)*.
- Capten la idea principal *(gist)* de la noticia y preparen un resumen.
- Parafraseen la noticia usando el vocabulario y las estructuras que saben. Presenten los hechos *(facts)* lo más claramente posible.
- Incluyan fotos o dibujos apropiados.

Para hacer en clase

Paso 5: Correcciones Intercambien este primer borrador con el de otro grupo y corrijan el borrador que ellos prepararon. Usen la siguiente guía.

- **Tema.** ¿Les parece que vale la pena incluir este tema en el periódico? Si la respuesta es negativa, expliquen brevemente por qué.
- **Contenido.** ¿Está toda la información necesaria? Si no es así, ¿qué otros aspectos importantes de la noticia se deben incluir?
- **Organización.** ¿Está claro de qué se trata el artículo? ¿Cuántos párrafos hay? ¿Cuál es la idea principal de cada párrafo? ¿Está clara la presentación?
- **Gramática.** ¿Se usó bien el pretérito (para hablar de los eventos importantes) y el imperfecto (para las descripciones y para la información de trasfondo)?
- **Formato y presentación.** ¿Hay elementos visuales y de diseño (fotos, diagramas, dibujos, etc.) interesantes y atractivos?

Para hacer en casa

Paso 6: Versión final y publicación Hagan las correcciones y cambios pertinentes. ¿Está listo el artículo para publicar en el Internet? Denle una copia al / a la profesor(a).

Cambios y transiciones

Cuba, la República Dominicana, Venezuela y Colombia

In this unit you will discuss issues pertaining to moving and relocating, such as finding a home, conducting financial and real estate transactions, and finding a new job. Also, you will discuss job-related topics such as experience, qualifications, and aspirations. The readings will give you insights into the experience of Cuban immigrants in the United States, while the videos will introduce you to the life of Cuban and Venezuelan professionals. At the end of the unit you will make all the necessary arrangements for an international job transfer.

Para comenzar

Compara las fotos de La Habana, Cuba, con las fotos de La Pequeña Habana de Miami.

■ ¿Qué aspectos comunes existen entre las dos ciudades?

■ ¿Encuentras algunas diferencias?

Cambios

In this chapter you will learn . . .

- how to talk about moving and relocating
- how to talk about financial and real estate transactions
- how to talk about past events
- how to talk about the immediate past
- how to express likes and dislikes
- how to refer to abstract notions
- about Cuban immigration to the U.S.

	TEMA 1 Mi tierra querida	TEMA 2 Es hora de partir	TEMA 3 A establecerse en una nueva casa
Vocabulario	Nostalgia	Preparativos para una mudanza	Los bienes raíces
Funciones y estructuras	Discussing memories with verbs like **gustar** Expressing generalizations with the neuter article **lo**	Expressing purpose or reason with **por** and **para** Referring to the beneficiary of an action using indirect object pronouns	Talking about the past with the preterite and the imperfect tenses Talking about the immediate past with **acabar de**
Lecturas y vídeo	Perspectivas: Dirección: El sur de la Florida	Vídeo: Un día triste para Valeria	Lectura: Soñar en cubano

La ciudad de La Habana, Cuba

La Pequeña Habana en Miami

Enfoque

A. ¿Qué sabes ya de Cuba? Antes de ver el vídeo, empareja las siguientes frases para formar oraciones verdaderas sobre Cuba. Luego, escribe en el espacio en blanco la letra de la categoría correspondiente.

OPCIONES: A = la agricultura   C = la capital   P = la política

____ 1. Como la República de Cuba es un estado socialista,...

____ 2. Por su clima tropical, Cuba es un país rico de una exuberante vegetación...

____ 3. Con más de 2.000.000 de personas,...

____ 4. El Partido Comunista de Cuba (el PCC)...

...todo el poder pertenece al pueblo trabajador.

...es la fuerza superior que gobierna la sociedad.

...es la ciudad más populosa del país y es el centro del gobierno.

...donde abundan el tabaco y el azúcar, y las frutas tropicales como la piña, el mango y el coco.

Compara tus respuestas con las de un(a) compañero(a).

B. Un recorrido El vídeo te lleva a recorrer varias áreas y atracciones turísticas de La Habana incluyendo los pequeños comercios (C), el Vedado (V), el Malecón (M), La Rampa (R) y La Plaza de la Revolución (P). Mientras ves el vídeo, indica dónde se encuentran las cosas que se mencionan a continuación. Escribe la letra correspondiente en el espacio en blanco.

____ 1. cintas de música afrocaribeña

____ 2. la mayoría de las organizaciones políticas y sociales

____ 3. el barrio más popular de La Habana

____ 4. un popular mercado de artesanías

Compara tus respuestas con las de un(a) compañero(a).

C. Nuestro recorrido por La Habana Según el vídeo: «Recorrer La Habana es volver a tiempos antiguos y a la vez volver a los años cincuenta y sesenta.» Si tuvieran sólo un día para recorrer La Habana y ver esta mezcla de lo antiguo y lo moderno, ¿adónde irían *(would you go)* y qué verían *(would you see)*? Planeen juntos su recorrido y contesten las siguientes preguntas. ¡Recuerden que no es posible hacerlo y verlo todo en un día!

■ ¿Qué sitios mencionados en el vídeo van a visitar, cuándo (por la mañana, tarde o noche) y por qué?

■ Si deciden ir de compras a los pequeños comercios, ¿qué recuerdos les gustaría comprar, para quién(es) y por qué?

For more info, you may want to check the **Temas** site: http://temas.heinle.com

Mi tierra querida

I. Vocabulario: Nostalgia

 CD2-2

MARTA: Amalia, supe que tu hermana te visitó el pasado fin de semana. ¿Lo pasaron bien?

AMALIA: Sí. Las dos somos muy unidas *(close)* y nos gusta reunirnos para hablar de los viejos tiempos.

MARTA: ¿Extrañan mucho Cuba?

AMALIA: Claro. Ya hace bastante tiempo que salimos de nuestra isla, pero todavía la recordamos con mucha nostalgia.

MARTA: Pero, pueden ir a Miami. Allí encuentran de todo lo cubano... ¡hasta una pequeña Habana!

AMALIA: Ay, chica, pero no es lo mismo...

MARTA: ¿Y qué es lo que más extrañas de tu tierra?

AMALIA: Pues todo, su clima tropical, su mar, sus montañas, la alegría de la gente, la comida...

MARTA: Me gustaría regresar a Cuba. ¿Y a ti?

AMALIA: Sí. La verdad es que yo no pierdo la esperanza de volver algún día.

Vocabulario práctico

Los recuerdos *(Memories)*
la tierra/patria *homeland*

Verbos
añorar *to long for*
extrañar/echar de menos *to miss*
irse *to leave*
mudarse *to move*
olvidar *to forget*
olvidarse de *to forget about*
regresar *to return*

■ Asimilación

7-1 ¿Entendiste bien? Indica si las siguientes oraciones son ciertas (**C**) o falsas (**F**) según la conversación anterior. Al terminar, compara tus respuestas con las de un(a) compañero(a).

_____ 1. Amalia y Marta son cubanas.

_____ 2. La hermana de Amalia vive en Miami.

_____ 3. Amalia recuerda y extraña Cuba.

_____ 4. Amalia quiere regresar algún día a Cuba.

CD2–3 **7-2 Mi primer trabajo** Escoge la opción más apropiada según la narración de un profesor acerca de su primer trabajo.

1. Su primer trabajo fue en...

   a. una escuela primaria.

   b. una escuela secundaria.

   c. una universidad.

   d. otro: _____

2. El profesor recuerda especialmente...

   a. el nombre del libro que usó.

   b. el nombre de todos sus estudiantes.

   c. el nombre de su supervisor.

   d. otra cosa: _____

3. El profesor...

   a. nunca regresó a esa escuela.

   b. recuerda y visita con regularidad esa escuela.

   c. aún trabaja en esa escuela.

■ Aplicaciones

7-3 Recuerdos ¿Qué extrañas de la escuela secundaria? Después de indicar tus respuestas, compáralas con las de otros estudiantes. Presenten un informe acerca de lo que tienen en común.

_____ los profesores

_____ los amigos

_____ las clases

_____ la comida de la cafetería

_____ las actividades extra-curriculares

_____ tu novio(a)

_____ otro: _____

Informe: _En nuestro grupo, todos extrañamos..., algunos extrañan... y otros extrañan... Nadie extraña..._

> **ESTRATEGIA DE COMPRENSIÓN**
>
> **_Anticipating_** Read the questions before you listen to the passage.

CD2–4 **7-4 Un cubano en Nueva York** Escucha el diálogo y completa las oraciones con las palabras más apropiadas.

OPCIONES: salgo   echo de menos   tierra   se mudó

ANA: ¿A quién le escribes?

BETO: A **Manuel.** _____ a **Nueva York** hace **dos meses** y lo _____ .

ANA: ¿Cuándo va a regresar a su _____ ?

BETO: No sé. Creo que se va a quedar a vivir allá.

ANA: Bueno, entonces vas a tener que ir a visitar**lo**...

BETO: Sí. _____ para **Nueva York a fin de mes.**

7-5 Su primer amor Hazle las siguientes preguntas a un(a) compañero(a) y prepara un breve resumen de sus respuestas.

1. ¿Cuántos años tenías cuando tuviste tu primer(a) novio(a)?
2. ¿Qué recuerdas de esa persona? Menciona por lo menos tres características.
3. ¿Lo/La extrañas?
4. ¿Son amigos todavía?

■ Integración

7-6 Entrevista Hazle las siguientes preguntas a un(a) compañero(a) y prepara un breve resumen de sus respuestas.

1. ¿Se ha mudado alguno de tus familiares de una región de los Estados Unidos a otra (o quizás de un país a otro)?
2. ¿De dónde se mudó? ¿Adónde fue?
3. ¿Cuándo se mudó a esa región o a ese país?
4. ¿Le gusta?
5. ¿Qué extraña de su antigua región o de su país?
6. ¿Crees que va a regresar algún día?

7-7 La vida de Ana Ana es una mujer cubana que vive ahora en Tampa. Haz las actividades con un(a) compañero(a) y, al terminar, usen sus respuestas para escribir una composición sobre la vida de Ana.

Paso 1: Escriban oraciones con las palabras indicadas. No se olviden de usar la forma correcta de los verbos y de añadir las palabras necesarias.

1. Ana / mudarse / 1999
2. Ana / encontrar / trabajo / Tampa
3. Ana / casarse / 2003
4. esposo / ser / español
5. Ana / echar de menos / familia
6. Ana y su esposo / extrañar / tierra

Paso 2: Respondan a las siguientes preguntas. ¡Usen la imaginación!

1. ¿Cómo era la vida de Ana en Cuba?
2. ¿Cómo era su familia?
3. ¿Qué extraña ella de su vida en Cuba?

Paso 3: Combinen sus respuestas para formar una composición coherente.

II. Funciones y estructuras: Discussing memories with verbs like *gustar*

En una cafetería cubana en La Pequeña Habana...

MAURICIO: ¡**Me encanta** esta cafetería! Preparan unos sándwiches cubanos que **me fascinan.**

DÉBORA: ¿Y qué más **te gusta**?

MAURICIO: ¡La carne frita! A mis padres **les parece** que es el mejor plato de este lugar.

DÉBORA: Pues la voy a probar.

As you may have noticed, the verbs in bold in the previous dialogue are accompanied by pronouns. These verbs work like the verb **gustar,** which you learned in **Capítulo 2, Tema 2,** in that they are used in the following structure.

INDIRECT OBJECT PRONOUN	VERB (IN THE THIRD PERSON)	SUBJECT
me *(to me)* te *(to you)* le *(to him/her/you)* nos *(to us)* os *(to you)* les *(to them/you)*	gusta/encanta/... + gustan/encantan/... +	esta tierra (noun in singular) recordar (infinitive) los cubanos (noun in plural)

Notice that, according to this structure, the subject in the Spanish sentence is the direct object in its English equivalent. On the contrary, the person(s) to whom the indirect object pronoun refers in the Spanish sentence is the subject in its English equivalent.

The third person singular form of these verbs is used when the subject is a noun in the singular form or an infinitive. The third person plural form, on the other hand, is used when the subject is a noun in the plural form.

Nos **importa la familia.**   *Family is important* to us.
¿Te **hace falta ir** a tu patria?   *Do you need to go* to your homeland?
Le **molestan los recuerdos**   *Unpleasant **memories bother***
   desagradables.   *him/her/you.*

The indirect object may be further specified by adding a phrase introduced by the preposition **a.** Although this would be redundant in English, it adds clarity in Spanish, especially when the speaker uses the pronouns **le** and **les.**

A María le preocupan las   *Bills worry her (María) = She*
   cuentas.   *(María) is worried about bills.*
A Paco y a Sila les falta dinero.   *Paco and Sila lack (need) money.*

Here is a list of verbs that work just like **gustar.**

convenir (ie, i) *to suit, to be suitable*	importar *to matter, to be important*
disgustar *to displease*	interesar *to interest, to be interested*
doler (ue) *to hurt, to ache*	molestar *to bother*
encantar *to love, to like very much*	parecer *to seem (like), to appear*
faltar *to lack, to need, to be missing*	preocupar *to worry, to be worried about*
fascinar *to love, to be fascinated*	quedar *to remain, to be left*
hacer falta *to lack, to need, to be missing*	tocar *to be one's turn, to be obligated*

The verb **tocar** does not work like **gustar** when it means *to touch* or *to play (an instrument).*

■ Asimilación

 7-8 De vacaciones Completa las actividades relacionadas con las siguientes ofertas vacacionales.

Paso 1: Busca los verbos como **gustar** en los siguientes anuncios.

¿Le encantan las aventuras bajo el sol?

¡Venga a Varadero!

Sol Club Las Sirenas
Avenida de las Américas y Calle K
Reparto La Torre,
Varadero, Matanzas, Cuba
Tel. (53-5) 667080
Fax (53-3) 667085

¿Le preocupa el dinero? Tranquilo, porque todo está incluido.

Tenemos programas para toda la familia y a los mejores precios del Caribe.

SUPERCLUBS – CUBA
¡Un resort con sabor latino para cada estilo de vida!
Club Varadero – Sierra Mar – Los Galeones

Si le hace falta un descanso...

Disfrute de unas vacaciones tranquilas en nuestros hoteles de cinco estrellas frente a las playas más bellas del mundo.

PLAYA ESMERALDA RESORT
Playa Esmeralda
Carretera de Guardalavaca,
Apartado Postal 007
Holguín, Cuba
Tel. (53-24) 30300
Fax (53-24) 30305

Paso 2: Completa las siguientes oraciones. Cuando termines, compara tus respuestas con las de un(a) compañero(a). ¿Están de acuerdo?

> *Me encanta la oferta... porque...*
> *No me gusta para nada la oferta... porque...*

CD2-5 **7-9 Una nueva vida** Escucha lo que dice Armando sobre su nueva vida en los Estados Unidos y escoge la palabra o frase que mejor complete cada una de las siguientes oraciones.

1. A Armando le encanta la vida en...
   a. los Estados Unidos. b. Cuba.

2. Le fascinan...
   a. las oportunidades de trabajo. b. las diferentes personas.

3. No le gusta...
   a. ir de vacaciones. b. el ritmo de vida acelerado.

4. A él le molesta...
   a. el frío. b. el verano.

5. A Armando le parece que es cuestión de...
   a. acostumbrarse. b. resignarse.

■ Aplicaciones

7-10 ¿Qué piensan? Digan qué piensan sobre los siguientes temas. Usen verbos como **gustar** y presten atención al uso de la forma singular y la forma plural de los verbos.

1. las ciencias naturales
2. la drogadicción
3. los chismosos (gossipers)
4. manejar con precaución
5. el (la) profesor(a) de español
6. tomar clases por la noche
7. tiempo para dormir
8. los meses de invierno

7-11 Situaciones Completen las siguientes situaciones con la forma correcta del presente de los verbos de cada lista. **¡OJO!** Hay un verbo adicional en cada grupo.

parecer   fascinar   convenir   quedar

1. A mi consejero _____ que no voy a poder graduarme este año. Yo creo que sí porque (a mí) sólo _____ cuatro cursos y los voy a tomar el próximo semestre. (A mí) _____ mucho graduarme pronto porque necesito empezar a ganar dinero.

hacer falta   importar   doler   gustar

2. Jaime está en el hospital porque _____ mucho el estómago. Creo que comió muchas cosas fritas en la fiesta de Nelia. Le dije que tuviera cuidado, pero ya sabes que a él no _____ su salud. ¡Y ahora está en el hospital, un lugar que no _____ nada!

molestar   preocupar   tocar   encantar

3. Señora, queremos decirle que a nosotras _____ los ruidos en su apartamento. Somos estudiantes universitarias y _____ no poder estudiar en silencio en nuestro propio apartamento. A Ud. _____ hacer algo al respecto (about it) o vamos a llamar al administrador del edificio.

Puedes repasar el vocabulario sobre este tema en **Capítulo 6, Tema 1.**

7-12 La vida en sociedad

Paso 1: Piensa en los problemas de la vida urbana y completa la siguiente tabla.

Me importa(n) mucho...	Me preocupa(n)...	Creo que me toca...
Me conviene(n)...	**Me molesta(n)...**	**Me hace(n) falta...**

Paso 2: Comparte la información del **Paso 1** con dos compañeros y averigua qué piensan. Al terminar, preparen un informe breve.

MODELO *A nosotros nos importa(n)... y nos preocupa(n)... Creemos que nos toca... y que nos conviene...*

▦ Integración

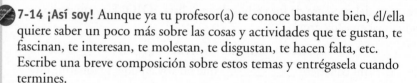

7-13 Los inmigrantes ¿Alguna vez Uds. se han puesto en la situación *(have put yourself in the situation)* de un(a) inmigrante en los Estados Unidos? Piensen en esto y traten de explicar su situación.

7-14 ¡Así soy! Aunque ya tu profesor(a) te conoce bastante bien, él/ella quiere saber un poco más sobre las cosas y actividades que te gustan, te fascinan, te interesan, te molestan, te disgustan, te hacen falta, etc. Escribe una breve composición sobre estos temas y entrégasela cuando termines.

III. Funciones y estructuras: Expressing generalizations with the neuter article *lo*

Lo hermoso de Cuba es el paisaje,...

¡pero **lo que más me gusta** es su gente!

In the previous sentences, the neuter article **lo** was used to refer to specific characteristics of things and to express an opinion. This article can be used:

The English translation of phrases with **lo** and an adjective include words such as *thing, part, aspect,* and *nature.*

- followed by an adjective in the masculine singular form.

Para mí, **lo difícil** fue dejar a mi familia.	*For me, **the difficult thing (part)** was to leave my family behind.*
Me encanta **lo tranquilo** de esta ciudad.	*I love the **tranquil nature** of this city.*

- followed by a clause introduced by **que.**

Esto es **lo que** menos me interesa del curso.	*This is **what** interests me the least about the course.*
Lo que queremos es regresar a nuestra patria.	***What** we want is to go back to our homeland.*

Asimilación

7-15 Lo mejor y lo peor de ti Escoge las frases de la lista para indicar qué es lo mejor y lo peor de ti. Luego, compara tus respuestas con las de un(a) compañero(a). ¿Son parecidos?

Lo mejor de mí es/son...	Lo peor de mí es/son...
_____ mi personalidad	_____ mi temperamento
_____ mi simpatía	_____ mi hábito de fumar
_____ mis hábitos de estudio	_____ mis cualidades físicas
_____ mi compasión	_____ mis hábitos de estudio
_____ mi sentido del humor	_____ mi personalidad
_____ mis sentimientos	_____ mis valores
_____ mis cualidades físicas	_____ mi falta de metas
_____ mi ética	_____ mi forma de gastar dinero
_____ mis valores religiosos	_____ mi falta de carácter
_____ otro aspecto	_____ otro aspecto

CD2-6 **7-16 Lo importante en la vida** Escucha lo que dice Matilde sobre lo que es importante en la vida y escribe por lo menos cuatro de las cosas que ella menciona.

1. ...

2. ...

3. ...

4. ...

Aplicaciones

7-17 Esta universidad Describan algunos aspectos de esta universidad. Pueden escribir sobre **lo más interesante, lo más aburrido, lo mejor, lo peor,** etc.

MODELO   *Lo más difícil de esta universidad es conseguir todas las clases que uno quiere. Por otro lado, lo más interesante es...*

7-18 La vida pasada de tu profesor(a) Preparen una lista de por lo menos ocho preguntas para saber un poco sobre el pasado del / de la profesor(a). ¡Usen adjetivos que sirvan para formar preguntas interesantes (**raro, desagradable, vergonzoso, tonto,** etc.)!

MODELO   *¿Qué fue lo más absurdo que le pasó en la escuela secundaria? ¿Qué fue lo más inesperado que le pasó en la universidad?*

7-19 Los estudiantes universitarios

Paso 1: Piensen en el (la) estudiante universitario(a) típico(a) y completen las siguientes oraciones con dos cosas o actividades.

1. Lo que menos le gusta(n) es/son _____.
2. Lo que prefiere hacer es _____.
3. Lo que nunca hace es _____.
4. Lo que le preocupa(n) es/son _____.
5. Lo que come regularmente es _____.
6. Lo que siempre trae a la universidad es _____.

Paso 2: Comparen sus respuestas con las de dos grupos más y tomen notas. Luego, preparen un resumen de todas las respuestas y preséntenlo en clase.

> MODELO   *Nosotros pensamos que lo que menos le gusta al estudiante universitario típico es/son... Por otro lado, lo que el estudiante típico prefiere hacer es...*

SUGERENCIAS

Usen palabras y frases como **por otro lado** *(on the other hand)*, **sin embargo** *(however)*, **además/ también** *(also)* y **finalmente** *(finally)* para conectar sus ideas de forma coherente.

■ Integración

7-20 Vivir en este pueblo o en esta ciudad En parejas, comenten qué piensan sobre el pueblo o sobre la ciudad donde viven. Por ejemplo, pueden dar su opinión sobre lo mejor, lo peor, lo más gracioso, lo más curioso, lo que más les gusta y lo que más les disgusta de vivir ahí. Tomen notas.

7-21 Un *e-mail pal* cubano Imagínate que tu *e-mail pal* cubano quiere saber qué opinas de tu pueblo o de tu ciudad. Escríbele un mensaje e incorpora la información que intercambiaste con tu compañero(a) en la actividad 7-20. Como quieres impresionar a tu amigo(a) con tu dominio del español, dale una copia del mensaje a tu compañero(a) para que lo corrija antes de que lo envíes *(send it)*.

SUGERENCIAS

Éstos son algunos de los temas que pueden comentar: la localización, los lugares de interés (las tiendas, las bibliotecas, los parques, etc.), la diversión (cafés, restaurantes, clubes, bares, museos, etc.), los servicios públicos (la electricidad, el agua, el cable, etc.), el sistema educativo, el sistema de salud pública, la diversidad étnica, los centros deportivos, los problemas urbanos, el clima y el costo de vida.

IV. Perspectivas: Dirección: El sur de la Florida

■ Antes de leer

A. Para conversar Respondan a las siguientes preguntas.

1. ¿Hay vecindades o barrios bien definidos en su ciudad? Si es así, ¿cuál es su vecindad favorita? (Expliquen por qué.)

2. ¿Cuáles son las características de una vecindad ideal? Preparen una lista (por ejemplo: seguridad, accesibilidad, servicios, etc.). Usen el diccionario si es necesario.

B. Vocabulario y conceptos Escriban junto a cada palabra la letra que corresponde a su definición.

____ 1. bienes raíces   a. barato

____ 2. segunda vivienda   b. una casa para pasar las
      familiar   vacaciones

____ 3. precio asequible   c. mucho tiempo para pagar

____ 4. financiamiento   d. costumbres, actividades, preferencias

____ 5. largo plazo   e. propiedades como casas y edificios

____ 6. estilo de vida   f. crédito, pago diferido con intereses

■ A leer

Dirección: El sur de la Florida
Los compradores internacionales alimentan la bonanza en bienes raíces de la Costa de Oro de la Florida

por Phyllis Apple

¿Por qué tanta gente quiere vivir en el sur de la Florida?

county

monopolize

En la zona metropolitana de Miami, en el **Condado** de Dade, aproximadamente el 25% de todas las compras de bienes raíces las realizan personas de otros países, quienes **acaparan** casi el 55% de todas las ventas de condominios destinados a usarse como segunda vivienda familiar. Los latinoamericanos representan un 60% de estas ventas.

Los precios asequibles del sur de la Florida, especialmente cuando se comparan con los de propiedades situadas frente al mar en América del Sur y Europa, así como la disponibilidad de un financiamiento a largo plazo y a bajo interés, son algunas de las razones principales de la fiebre de compras. Otros factores que influyen en este mercado son la seguridad, la accesibilidad y la gama de servicios modernos que los estadounidenses **dan por sentados.**

take for granted

«Llegar acá es fácil», observa Alicia Cervera, una de las principales agentes de bienes raíces de Miami, «pero vivir acá es más fácil todavía. Es preciso viajar al país latinoamericano más refinado para apreciar todo lo que tenemos aquí en términos de comodidad, seguridad, carreteras, así como servicios confiables. Estas cosas hacen que el clima y las playas del sur de Florida sean aún más llamativos para los latinoamericanos».

Con el objeto de satisfacer la demanda, los urbanistas entregan nuevos productos para satisfacer toda una gama de **presupuestos** y de estilos de vida. Desde las comunidades country club, donde la vida **gira alrededor** del tenis y del golf, hasta las propiedades frente al mar, diseñadas para los **amantes** de la playa y el **yatismo,** las opciones y los destinos son tan amplios como los compradores mismos. En virtud de la diversidad de opciones y la fuerte demanda, invertir en una residencia de lujo en la Costa de Oro del sur de la Florida representa hoy en día una decisión sólida y **provechosa.**

budgets
revolves around

lovers / yachting

advantageous

■ ¿Entendiste bien?

C. En resumen... En dos o tres oraciones, sintetiza la idea principal de este texto.

D. ¿Cierto o falso? Indica si las siguientes oraciones son ciertas **(C)** o falsas **(F).**

____ 1. Un 55% de todos los latinoamericanos tienen una segunda vivienda en la Florida.

____ 2. Un 60% de los compradores de bienes raíces en la Florida son extranjeros.

____ 3. Las propiedades frente al mar en Latinoamérica son más costosas que en la Florida.

____ 4. Según la autora, los términos de crédito son muy favorables en los Estados Unidos.

____ 5. Alicia Cervera sugiere que la vida en Estados Unidos es más fácil que en Latinoamérica.

E. Aspectos lingüísticos Adivina, según el contexto, el significado de las palabras en negrilla *(boldface).*

1. «Apreciar todo lo que tenemos aquí en términos de comodidad, seguridad, carreteras, así como servicios **confiables.**»
   a. feeble   b. funny   c. reliable

2. «Estas cosas hacen que el clima y las playas del sur de Florida sean aún más **llamativos** para los latinoamericanos.»
   a. expensive   b. appealing   c. modern

3. «Los urbanistas entregan nuevos productos para satisfacer toda una **gama** de presupuestos y de estilos de vida.»
   a. game   b. range   c. gold

ESTRATEGIA DE LECTURA

Scanning You do not have to understand every word. Concentrate on identifying the main points of the story and completing the following comprehension activity.

F. ¿Lo recuerdan?

1. Mencionen cuatro razones por las cuales los latinoamericanos están invirtiendo en el sur de la Florida.
2. Mencionen dos ejemplos del tipo de vivienda que les ofrecen los urbanistas a los compradores latinoamericanos.

G. Para conversar ¿Creen Uds. que la autora tiene una visión positiva o negativa acerca de la inversión en bienes raíces en el sur de la Florida por parte de los latinoamericanos? Justifiquen su respuesta.

H. Enfoque comunitario Imagínate que tienes que promover la inversión *(promote the investment)* de los latinoamericanos en casas de vacaciones en tu área. Escribe un folleto sobre las ventajas de hacer este tipo de inversión.

En el sur de la Florida

Es hora de partir

I. Vocabulario: Preparativos para una mudanza

Primero llamaron a la **compañía de mudanzas** para obtener una **cotización.**

Luego **empacaron** todo cuidadosamente en **cajas de cartón.**

Envolvieron los objetos delicados en **plástico de burbujas.**

El día de la **mudanza,** los **empacadores** llegaron temprano y **cargaron** todo el **embalaje** en el **camión** en menos de dos horas.

Ahora los González ya están en su nueva casa y sólo tienen que **desempacar** y **acomodar** su **menaje.**

Vocabulario práctico

la caja (de cartón) *(cardboard) box*

el camión de mudanzas *moving truck*

la cinta *tape*

la cotización / el estimado *price estimation*

el embalaje *packing*

los empacadores *packing staff*

el guardamuebles *storage*

la manta *blanket*

el marcador *marker*

el menaje *household goods, belongings*

la mudanza *move*

el plástico de burbujas *bubblewrap*

las tijeras *scissors*

el transporte *transportation*

el traslado *relocation, transfer*

Verbos

acomodar *to accommodate, to arrange*

alquilar *to rent*

cargar *to load*

desempacar *to unpack*

envolver (ue) *to wrap*

guardar *to store*

marcar *to label*

trasladarse *to relocate*

■ Asimilación

7-22 Preparativos Pon *(Put)* los siguientes preparativos en orden lógico. Al terminar, compara tus respuestas con las de un(a) compañero(a). ¿Están de acuerdo?

_____ acomodar el menaje en las diferentes habitaciones

_____ alquilar un camión de mudanzas

_____ envolver los objetos delicados en mantas o plástico de burbujas

_____ llamar a la compañía de mudanzas para pedir una cotización

_____ desempacar las cajas

_____ empacar todo cuidadosamente

_____ marcar las cajas con el nombre de la habitación correspondiente

_____ cargar el menaje en el camión

CD2–7　**7-23 ¿Qué le falta?** Escucha la siguiente narración y marca con una **X** los preparativos que faltan.

_____ conseguir más cajas de cartón

_____ reservar un camión

_____ comprar cinta

_____ comprar unos marcadores

_____ recoger unas mantas

_____ comprar plástico de burbujas

■ Aplicaciones

7-24 Adivina Túrnense para describir y adivinar objetos o actividades relacionados con las mudanzas.

MODELO　E1: *Es un objeto que usas para guardar o transportar la ropa o las cosas de la casa.*
E2: *¿Una caja?*
E1: *¡Eso es!*

7-25 Preguntas Un(a) amigo(a) hispano(a) está ayudándote con tu mudanza. Prepara varias preguntas para asegurarte de que todo está listo.

MODELO　las cajas de cartón / comprar
¿Compraste las cajas de cartón en la compañía de mudanzas?

1. la cinta y las tijeras / traer
2. las cajas / marcar
3. los objetos delicados / envolver
4. la cotización / pedir
5. la nueva dirección / dejar en el correo
6. el embalaje / cargar
7. la reservación del camión / hacer
8. los empacadores / llamar

EN TU COMUNIDAD

You may want to visit several companies that provide moving services and prepare a brief report on some of the things their clients do and do not do (purchase bubble wrap, tape, etc., through them; make reservations far in advance; get more than one estimate; have someone else do the packing and loading and unloading of the truck; etc.). Then, work in groups and present your findings in class. You may need to review the vocabulary related to numbers if you decide to present the results in percentages.

7-26 Entrevista Túrnense para hacerse y para responder a las siguientes preguntas. Al terminar, preparen un breve informe.

1. ¿Cuándo fue la última vez que te mudaste?
2. ¿Contrataste una compañía de mudanzas o hiciste la mudanza tú mismo(a) *(by yourself)*?
3. ¿Qué fue lo mejor de esa mudanza?
4. ¿Qué fue lo más difícil?

MODELO   *Mi compañero(a) se mudó el año pasado. Sus amigos lo ayudaron a mudarse...*

▓ Integración

7-27 Un traslado Representa la siguiente situación con un(a) compañero(a).

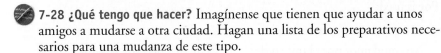

Estudiante A	Estudiante B
La empresa donde trabajas te va a trasladar a otra ciudad. Llama a una compañía de mudanzas para hacer los arreglos pertinentes.	Tú trabajas para una compañía de mudanzas. Un(a) cliente está preparando su traslado a otra ciudad. Ayúdalo(la) a hacer los preparativos pertinentes.

SUGERENCIAS

Recuerden que tienen que decidir los siguientes aspectos:
- materiales para la mudanza (cajas, cinta, marcadores, etc.)
- reservaciones (del camión, de avión, de hotel, etc.)
- empacar y desempacar
- cargar el menaje en el camión
- notificar del cambio de dirección

7-28 ¿Qué tengo que hacer? Imagínense que tienen que ayudar a unos amigos a mudarse a otra ciudad. Hagan una lista de los preparativos necesarios para una mudanza de este tipo.

II. Funciones y estructuras: Expressing purpose or reason with the prepositions *por* and *para*

CARMEN:	Ligia, ¿**para** dónde te mudas?
LIGIA:	**Para** los suburbios. Son más tranquilos.
CARMEN:	¿Y cuánto pagaste **por** la casa?
LIGIA:	Menos de trescientos mil dólares.

The most common use of the prepositions **por** and **para** is to convey the meaning of *for*. However, they have other very important uses. Here is a summary.

Por is used:

- to express reason or cause *(because of, due to)*.

Nos mudamos **por** el tráfico de la ciudad.	*We moved **because of (due to)** the traffic in the city.*

- to express *by means of (by, on)*.

Voy a Miami **por** avión.	*I am going to Miami **by** plane.*
Hablé **por** teléfono con los empacadores.	*I talked **on** the phone with the packing staff.*

- to express movement in space *(along, through, throughout, by)*.

El camion de mudanzas cruzó **por** tu pueblo.	*The moving truck crossed **through** your town.*
Voy a pasar **por** la bodega hoy.	*I am stopping **by** the warehouse today.*

- to express duration of time *(for, in, during)*.

Vamos a estar desempacando **por** muchas horas.	*We will be unpacking **for** many hours.*

- to express *on behalf of*.

¿Puedes velar el menaje **por** mí?	*Can you watch the household goods **on my behalf (for me)**?*

- to express general location *(around)*.

¿Viste la cinta **por** aquí?	*Did you see the tape **around** here?*

- to express that there was an exchange or purchase *(in exchange for)*.

No tuve que pagar nada **por** la cotización.	*I did not have to pay anything **(in exchange) for** the price estimation.*

■ in some fixed expressions.

por ciento *percent*	por fin *finally*
por cierto *by the way*	por la mañana *in the morning*
por ejemplo *for example*	por lo menos *at least*
por (ello/eso) *because of that*	por si acaso *just in case*
por esto *because of this*	por supuesto *of course*
por favor *please*	por todas partes *everywhere*

Para is used:

■ to express purpose or motive *(in order to)*.

Se mudaron **para** criar a sus hijos en otro ambiente.   *They moved **(in order) to** raise their kids in a different environment.*

■ to express who the recipient of something is *(for)*.

Este cheque es **para** su empleado.   *This check is **for** your employee.*

■ to express destination *(for)*.

¿Ya salieron **para** California?   *Did they leave **for** California already?*

■ to express the time or day by which an action must be completed *(for, by)*.

Esperamos estar allá **para** el sábado.   *We hope to be there **by** Saturday.*

■ **Asimilación**

7-29 Un lunes como cualquier otro *(like any other)* Piensa en las actividades que normalmente haces los lunes y escoge las oraciones correctas. Al terminar, compara tus respuestas con las de un(a) compañero(a). ¿Tienen rutinas semejantes o diferentes?

____ Voy a la universidad por la mañana.
____ Llego temprano para estudiar en la biblioteca.
____ Salgo para casa a eso de las seis de la tarde.
____ Tomo por lo menos cuatro clases.
____ Casi nunca paso por el centro de estudiantes.
____ No almuerzo por falta de tiempo.
____ Trabajo por más de cinco horas.
____ Por fin, me acuesto como a las once de la noche.

CD2-8 **7-30 ¡A completar!** Completa las oraciones que vas a escuchar con la frase más apropiada.

1. ____   3. ____   5. ____   7. ____
2. ____   4. ____   6. ____   8. ____

a. para mi esposo.
b. para terminar de empacar.
c. por eso no pudo venir a clase.
d. por tren.
e. por esta silla?

f. por la tarde.
g. por el supermercado?
h. para conseguir un mejor empleo

■ **Aplicaciones**

7-31 Planificando un viaje Completen el diálogo con las palabras y frases de la lista. Préstenle atención al uso de las preposiciones **por** y **para.**

OPCIONES: estudiar italiano   Venezuela   cierto   mañana
quinientos dólares   avión   mi hermano   la noche

ELENA: ¿Adónde vas este verano?

OMAR: Quisiera salir para _____ en junio.

ELENA: ¿Vas en barco crucero?

OMAR: No, en _____. Conseguí una oferta buenísima
por sólo _____. ¿Quieres venir conmigo?

ELENA: Mmm... Me encantaría, pero no puedo. Tengo que trabajar
por _____ en la tienda de mis padres.
Él quiere ir a Roma para _____.

OMAR: ¿Por qué no lo piensas y me das una respuesta definitiva
mañana por _____?

ELENA: Está bien. Voy a hablar con mis padres y ya tendré la respuesta
para _____. Por _____, ¿se
necesita pasaporte?

OMAR: Creo que no, pero luego hablamos de eso.

7-32 ¡Lista! Completen el siguiente mensaje telefónico con **por** o **para.**

¡Hola, Héctor! ¡Soy Norma! ¡Creo que estoy lista _____ la mudanza!
Ya tengo las cajas de cartón y la cinta que necesito _____ empacar.
Mi familia viene _____ ayudarme hoy _____ la tarde. Aunque
(Even though) mi padre no puede venir, mi cuñado viene _____ él.
También me comuniqué con el gerente de la compañía de mudanzas
_____ correo electrónico _____ pedirle que los empacadores
estén aquí _____ las siete de la mañana el viernes. _____
supuesto, también le pedí que trajeran algunas mantas. Si puedes y
tienes tiempo, ven _____ aquí y charlamos. Chao. Un beso.

SUGERENCIAS

La historia puede ser sobre una cena en un restaurante, una reunión familiar, un evento deportivo o unas vacaciones. Pueden consultar la lista de temas que ya han estudiado en el índice *(table of contents)*.

7-33 Una historia interesante Inventen una historia interesante relacionada con un tema que escojan entre los dos. Incorporen las preposiciones **por** y **para** y las expresiones **por cierto, por ejemplo, por (eso/ello/esto), por la (mañana/tarde/noche), por si acaso, por supuesto, por todas partes** y **por fin.** ¡Sean creativos!

Integración

7-34 El proceso de mudarse Imagínate que vas a mudarte en las próximas semanas y explícale a tu compañero(a) en qué consiste este proceso. Considera las siguientes preguntas antes de empezar.

- Where are you moving?
- When are you moving?
- How are you getting there?
- What towns or cities do you have to drive through to get there?
- What steps did you have to take to get ready to move and why?
- Who is going to help you and do things for you?

7-35 Tu comportamiento *(behavior)* ¿Sabes por qué y para qué haces algunas de las cosas que haces en tu vida? Piensa en esto y escribe un breve resumen. Cuando termines, entrégaselo a tu profesor(a) para que te dé su opinión.

III. Funciones y estructuras: Referring to the beneficiary of an action by using indirect object pronouns

LARA: ¿**Le** enviaste los documentos al gerente de la compañía de mudanzas?

NORBERTO: Sí, ya lo hice. ¿Y él **te** envió la cotización?

LARA: **Me** la envió por fax esta mañana.

Notice that some of these pronouns also function as direct object pronouns, which you studied in **Capítulo 5, Tema 2.** Context, as well as the meaning of the verb, will always help you figure out the specific function of these pronouns.

The pronouns in bold in the preceding dialogue are indirect object pronouns. The indirect object is the person or thing that benefits from the action of the verb. For example, the pronoun **le** refers to the manager of the moving company, the person who benefited from the action of the verb *to send* and received the documents. To identify the indirect object you may ask **¿a quién?** *(to whom?)* or **¿para quién?** *(for whom?)* to the verb.

Here is a list of the indirect object pronouns in Spanish.

REMEMBER

These pronouns are also used with verbs like **gustar** (**encantar, fascinar, faltar,** etc.).

INDIRECT OBJECT PRONOUNS	
me *(to or for me)*	**nos** *(to or for us)*
te *(to or for you,* familiar singular)	**os** *(to or for you,* familiar plural in Spain)
le *(to or for him/her/it/you,* formal singular)	**les** *(to or for them/you,* formal plural)

The verbs **aconsejar** *(to give advice),* **dar, decir (i), doler, enviar, escribir, explicar, hablar de, llevar, ofrecer** *(irreg.),* **pedir (i), preguntar, prestar** *(to lend),* **prometer que, recomendar (ie), regalar** *(to give a gift),* **responder,** and **sugerir (ie)** *(to suggest)* are often used with indirect object pronouns because they imply doing something to or for a beneficiary.

Estela **me** dijo que necesitaba más plástico de burbujas.

¿**Les** preguntaste si venían a las ocho?

*Estela told **me** that she needed more bubblewrap.*

*Did you ask **them** if they were coming at eight?*

As you may have noticed, indirect object pronouns are placed before the conjugated verb. When you use a verb phrase, they can be placed before the auxiliary verb or attached to the main verb (an infinitive or a present participle).

Te van a traer / Van a traer**te** un buen marcador.

¿**Me** estás empacando / Estás empacando**me** la vajilla?

*They are going to bring **you** a good marker.*

*Are you packing the china **for me**?*

Besides using an indirect object pronoun, you may also use a phrase introduced by the preposition **a** to add clarity and emphasis. This is particularly helpful in the case of **le** and **les,** which may refer to different people. Although this would be redundant in English, it is perfectly correct in Spanish.

Les di las gracias **a los empacadores.**	*I thanked **them (the packing staff)**.*
Le prometí **a mi madre** que iba a ayudar.	*I promised **her (my mother)** that I was going to help.*

▥ Asimilación

7-36 ¿Cierto o falso? Lee cada oración e indica si es cierta **(C)** o falsa **(F)**. Luego, compara tus respuestas con las de un(a) compañero(a). ¿Qué tienen en común?

_____ 1. Mis padres me dan dinero.

_____ 2. Mi profesor(a) de español me hace muchas preguntas en clase.

_____ 3. Mis amigos me dicen siempre la verdad.

_____ 4. Mi novio(a) o esposo(a) me da regalos caros.

_____ 5. Mis hermanos me piden que los ayude con la tarea.

_____ 6. Mi mejor amigo(a) me habla por teléfono diariamente.

_____ 7. Mis compañeros me dicen «hola» cuando entro al salón de clase.

_____ 8. Mi madre me prepara mi plato favorito todos los fines de semana.

CD2–9 **7-37 Anuncios** Escucha los tres anuncios e indica a qué se refiere el pronombre **le** o **les** en cada caso.

1. _____ los clientes   _____ las tiendas   _____ las compras

2. _____ la película   _____ las bebidas   _____ al público

3. _____ la aerolínea   _____ el tiempo   _____ los pasajeros

■ Aplicaciones

7-38 Un correo electrónico Completen el siguiente mensaje de correo electrónico con los pronombres de complemento indirecto correctos.

```
De:      Marta
Fecha:   16 de septiembre
Para:    Mateo
Asunto:  ¡Estamos en nuestra nueva casa!

Querido Mateo:

_____ escribo para decirte que todo salió bien en la mudanza. ¡Ya estamos
en nuestra nueva casa! La compañía _____ entregó todo en muy buenas
condiciones (a nosotros) y no _____ tuvimos que pagar más de lo que decía
la cotización (a ellos). Estamos muy contentos, pero tenemos mucho que hacer.

Los nuevos vecinos son magníficos. Tan pronto llegamos, _____ dieron la
bienvenida y _____ ofrecieron algo de comer (a nosotros).

Necesito un favor: ¿_____ puedes enviar la dirección de Ligia (a mí)? Tengo
que enviar_____ una tarjeta de agradecimiento (a ella) por ayudarnos tanto.

Un abrazo,

Marta
```

7-39 A ti y a mí

Paso 1: Usa la siguiente información para formar oraciones sobre las cosas que otras personas te hacían cuando eras niño(a).

> MODELO   amigos / prestar dinero
> *Mis amigos (no) me prestaban dinero.*

1. padres / dar sermones *(lectures)* con frecuencia
2. abuelos / comprar dulces
3. compañeros de clase / hacer preguntas en los exámenes
4. madre / llevar la comida a la cama cuando estaba enfermo(a)
5. profesores / dar muchas tareas
6. hermanos / leer libros

Paso 2: Ahora, convierte las oraciones del **Paso 1** en preguntas para tu compañero(a). Toma notas y, al terminar, prepara un breve informe comparando tus respuestas y las respuestas de él/ella.

> MODELO   *¿Tus amigos te prestaban dinero?*

7-40 ¿Y a otras personas? Formen oraciones con elementos de cada columna. Reemplacen los puntos suspensivos (...) por información original. Usen los pronombres **le** y **les** correctamente. ¡Sean creativos!

> MODELO   nosotros   causar...   a...
> *Nosotros les causamos problemas a nuestros padres.*

nosotros
el (la) profesor(a)
el presidente
nuestros hermanos
los estudiantes de la clase
...

causar...
dar...
escribir...
decir...
ofrecer...
recomendar...
pedir...
preguntar...
prestar...
regalar...

a...

▨ Integración

7-41 Reciprocidad

Paso 1: Escriban los nombres de cinco personas importantes en sus vidas y su relación con ellas. Luego, intercambien sus notas.

Paso 2: Averigüen qué hace su compañero(a) para expresar su afecto por esas personas y ellas por él/ella.

> MODELO   E1: *Chris, ¿le regalas perfumes caros a Nancy, tu novia?*
> E2: *Sí, le regalo perfumes caros.*
> E1: *¿Qué perfumes le regalas?*
> E2: *...*
> E1: *¿Y ella te regala perfumes caros a ti?*
> E2: *...*

SUGERENCIAS

Pueden usar los verbos que se mencionan en la anotación de la página 286.

7-42 Una compañía de mudanzas internacionales Escribe un anuncio comercial para una compañía de mudanzas internacionales. Menciona los servicios que ofrece y los países en los que tiene oficinas.

IV. Vídeo: Un día triste para Valeria

iLrn

ESTRATEGIA DE
COMPRENSIÓN

Anticipating Consider the context of a birthday party and the similarities and differences between how we celebrate our birthdays as children and as adults.

A. Los cumpleaños de antes y los de ahora Antes de ver el vídeo, piensen en cómo son las fiestas de cumpleaños y completen el siguiente cuadro.

	Los cumpleaños de niños	Los cumpleaños de adultos
¿Dónde se celebran?		
¿Quiénes asisten?		
¿Qué se come y se bebe?		
¿Qué se hace durante la celebración? (por ejemplo, jugar, bailar, etc.)		
¿Cómo se siente la persona que cumple años? ¿Por qué?		

¿Entendiste bien?

B. Valeria y Alejandra se ponen nostálgicas

1. Lee las siguientes preguntas y luego mira el vídeo para poder contestarlas.

   ■ ¿Cuántos años cumple Valeria hoy?

   ■ ¿Por qué está triste?

   ■ ¿Quiénes se olvidaron del cumpleaños de Valeria?

2. Completa lo que le dice Alejandra a Valeria para intentar animarla *(cheer her up):*

   «*Ay, bueno, pero no lo tomes tan a pecho. Quizás tus _____ piensan que estás muy _____ aquí en Puerto Rico y no tienes tiempo para revisar tu _____. Es cierto, ¿no? Casi nunca estamos en _____ desde que llegamos a Puerto Rico.*»

3. ¿Se asocian las siguientes cosas con los cumpleaños de Valeria **(V)** o los de Alejandra **(A)**?

____ a. una fiesta de cumpleaños con los compañeros de escuela

____ b. su comida favorita

____ c. un pastel de cumpleaños, refrescos y helados

____ d. la piñata

____ e. fiestas de cumpleaños muy grandes

____ f. un ramo de flores

____ g. bolsitas con confites

Compara tus respuestas con las de un(a) compañero(a).

C. ¿Es mejor ser niño(a) o adulto(a)? Entrevista a un(a) compañero(a) sobre los cambios en su vida al crecer *(grow up)* y si le parece mejor ser niño(a) o adulto(a).

1. ¿Cuáles de estas cosas extrañas de tu niñez? ¿Por qué?

____ los amigos

____ vivir en la casa de tus padres

____ la escuela (primaria y secundaria)

____ las celebraciones (cumpleaños, días festivos, etc.)

____ las actividades, juegos, deportes, etc.

____ la falta de preocupaciones

____ otra: _____

2. ¿Cuáles de las siguientes cosas son ventajas de ser adulto(a)?

____ la independencia

____ los amigos

____ el poder tener hijos

____ el poder casarse

____ tener una casa propia

____ otra: _____

3. ¿Te hace falta algo que tenías de niño(a)?

4. ¿Qué te tocaba hacer cuando eras niño(a) que no haces ahora y viceversa?

5. ¿Puedes pensar en algunas cosas que ahora te importan, pero que no te importaban cuando eras niño(a) y viceversa?

6. Si tuvieras *(you had)* la posibilidad, ¿te interesaría revivir tu niñez? ¿Por qué sí o no?

Ahora, basándote en las respuestas de tu compañero(a), ¿crees que a él/ella le gusta más ser niño(a) o adulto(a)? ¿Por qué? Explícale a tu compañero(a) tu opinión y averigua si él/ella está de acuerdo contigo o no.

D. Enfoque comunitario ¿Hay muchos estudiantes cubanos en tu universidad? Investiga y trata de localizar a algún estudiante que sea de origen cubano. Invítalo(la) a la clase para que hable de su país, sus tradiciones o costumbres familiares (cumpleaños, bodas, etc.) y sobre sus experiencias en los Estados Unidos.

A establecerse en una nueva casa

I. Vocabulario: Los bienes raíces

¿Cuánto es la cuota inicial?   Queremos una hipoteca a 20 años.

Vocabulario práctico

los bienes raíces *real estate*
el contrato *contract*
la cuota inicial / el anticipo
    down payment
la hipoteca *mortgage*
la inmobiliaria / agencia de
    bienes raíces *real estate agency*

los planos *blueprints*
el préstamo *loan*
la propiedad *property*
los términos de financiamiento
    credit terms
la ubicación *location*

■ Asimilación

7-43 Atractivos Indica cuáles son los principales atractivos de estos condominios.

____ la cuota inicial   ____ los términos de la hipoteca
____ la ubicación   ____ las facilidades para obtener préstamos

---

Key Biscayne

**Una comunidad exclusiva y segura en la Isla de Key Biscayne, Florida.
Con excelentes términos de financiamiento disponibles.
Perfecto para un ambiente familiar.**

THE OCEAN CLUB
Key Biscayne

The Ocean Club, en la Isla de Key Biscayne, en la Florida, a minutos de Miami, le ofrece lujosos condominios en una comunidad privada. Con vistas al Océano Atlántico, la Bahía de Biscayne, los rascacielos de Miami y un lago privado. 300 metros de playa; Un club de tenis con canchas de arcilla; Un Club de Playa donde se puede cenar formalmente o al aire libre; Gimnasio y spa; Cabañas privadas en la playa; Piscinas; Parques para los niños; Y mucho más.

Todo esto a sólo un puente de Miami y a 20 minutos del Aeropuerto Internacional de Miami.

The Ocean Club puede recomendarle a excelentes entidades bancarias para facilitarle el financiamiento, el cual tiene una cuota inicial del 30% e hipotecas de 15 a 30 años.

Si usted busca una residencia a orillas del mar en la Florida, no tiene que ir más allá de Key Biscayne y The Ocean Club.

Apresúrese. Las residencias se están vendiendo muy rápido.

Con precios desde los $300.000 a los $2.100.000.

Para recibir un folleto y vídeo gratis, llame a nuestra oficina en Key Biscayne.

D2–10 **7-44 ¿Sí o no?** Indica si las oraciones que vas a escuchar corresponden o no a la información del anuncio.

1. ...   4. ...
2. ...   5. ...
3. ...

■ Aplicaciones

7-45 Busco un condominio Completa la carta con el vocabulario más apropiado.

OPCIONES: hipoteca   bienes raíces   ubicación   financiamiento

Inmobiliaria Punto Norte

Estimados señores:

Me dirijo a Uds. para solicitar los servicios de uno de sus agentes de _____. Estoy buscando un condominio de dos o tres habitaciones, preferiblemente en el sur de la ciudad, con buena _____ (tal vez cerca de un supermercado o de una línea del metro). Les agradecería también información acerca de oportunidades de _____ a través de bancos locales. (Necesito una _____ a 30 años.)

Les agradecería que me enviaran la información a la siguiente dirección: 2315 S.W. 8th Street. Miami, FL 33135. Tel: 305-642-1788.

Atentamente,

Juanita Martínez

 7-46 Tengo algo para Ud. Organicen las siguientes frases y luego reconstruyan el texto de la carta que le envió el agente de bienes raíces a Juanita.

- Alberto Jaramillo
- Atentamente,
- nuestros / sólo / ofrecen / Desgraciadamente / financiamiento /entre / 15 y 25 años / bancos
- condominio / un / encontré / ideal / para / Ud.
- recuerdo / le / que / la / del 20% / es / cuota inicial
- si es posible, / esta semana / hablar / con Ud. / me gustaría
- Srta. Martínez / Estimada
- Tiene / estación del metro / a dos cuadras / tres habitaciones y dos baños / y / está / tres cuadras /de / una

7-47 Preguntas Preparen cuatro preguntas que Juanita debería hacerle al agente de bienes raíces acerca del condominio.

■ Integración

7-48 Necesito... Representa la siguiente situación con un(a) compañero(a).

Comprador(a)

Deseas mudarte a una nueva casa o a un nuevo apartamento. Llama al / a la agente de bienes raíces para averiguar qué tiene disponible *(available)*. Pregúntale también acerca de sus planes de financiamiento.

Agente de bienes raíces

Tú eres agente de bienes raíces. Recibe la llamada de este(a) cliente y escribe toda la información que necesitas para empezar tu búsqueda *(search)*. Infórmale también acerca de los planes de financiamiento que puedes ofrecerle.

7-49 Condominios en Miami Imagina que trabajas como agente de bienes raíces en el sur de la Florida. Escribe una carta para un cliente latinoamericano y descríbele un condominio en Miami.

II. Funciones y estructuras: Talking about the past with the preterite and the imperfect tenses

Llamé a la inmobiliaria y el agente me **dijo** que el contrato **estaba** listo y que **tenía** que pasar por allá para discutir algunos términos de financiamiento. **Fui** inmediatamente.

The previous caption includes verbs conjugated in the preterite tense and verbs conjugated in the imperfect tense. Can you identify them? If you said that **llamé, dijo,** and **fui** are in the preterite and **estaba** and **tenía** are in the imperfect, you were right! Now, can you explain why these verbs are used in these tenses? This may be somewhat more difficult. To help you, here is a summary of the uses of these two past tenses.

REMEMBER

The verbs **conocer, poder, querer,** and **saber** have different meanings in the preterite and in the imperfect. You may review this in **Capítulo 6, Tema 3.**

The **preterite** tense is used to talk about:

- the beginning or the end of an action that took place in the past.

  La reunión **empezó** a las diez y **terminó** al mediodía.

  *The meeting **began** at ten and **ended** at noon.*

- actions that took place at specific moments in the past (usually accompanied by expressions such as **ayer, anoche, una vez** *[once]*, **el** [day/**mes/año**] **pasado, la semana pasada,** and **a la[s]** [time]).

  El martes pasado me **aprobaron** el préstamo.

  *Last Tuesday they **approved** my loan.*

  Ayer **firmamos** el contrato.

  *Yesterday we **signed** the contract.*

- actions that are perceived as completed.

  El cierre **fue** en noviembre.

  *The closing **was** in November.*

- a series of actions thet were completed in the past.

  Ella **vio** la casa, le **gustó** e **hizo** una oferta, todo el mismo día.

  *She **saw** the house, **liked** it and **made** an offer, all in the same day.*

The **imperfect** tense is used to talk about:

- habitual actions in the past (usually accompanied by the expressions **todos los días/años** *[every day/year]* **todas las semanas** *[every week]*, **siempre,** or **frecuentemente**).

  Cuando niña, siempre **jugaba** en el patio de mi casa.

  *When I was a child, I always **used to play** in my house's yard.*

- descriptions.

| El patio **era** grande y **tenía** una piscina. | *The yard **was** big and it **had** a pool.* |

- events that were in progress while other actions were taking place (usually introduced by the word **mientras** [*while*]).

| Cuando emigramos a los Estados Unidos, yo **estaba** en la escuela primaria. | *When we emigrated to the United States, I **was** in elementary school.* |
| Mientras mis padres **buscaban** casa, **vivíamos** con mi tío Luis. | *While my parents **looked for** a house, we **were living** with my uncle Luis.* |

The action that takes place while another action is in progress is reported in the preterite and is usually introduced by the word **cuando.**

- descriptions of the participants who carry out the main events of a story (including age, physical appearance, conditions, and emotions).

| Luna, la primera persona que conocí, **tenía** diez años y **era** muy graciosa. | *Luna, the first person I met, **was** ten years old and **was** very funny.* |

- background information of past events (including time and weather conditions).

| Recuerdo que, cuando la conocí, **hacía** mucho sol y **eran** como las dos. | *I remember that, when I met her, it **was** sunny and it **was** about two.* |

▦ Asimilación

7-50 Acciones y reacciones Empareja las acciones de la izquierda con las reacciones de la derecha. Luego, organiza las oraciones que formes en orden lógico usando números. Cuando termines, compara tus respuestas con las de un(a) compañero(a). ¿Están de acuerdo?

___ ___ El agente de la inmobiliaria quería ayudarla...	a. se mudó en sólo dos meses.
___ ___ A Delia no le gustaba su vecindario...	b. pero escogió una casa cerca de sus padres
___ ___ Aunque no le parecía que iba a ser tan fácil,...	c. y le mostró fotos de diferentes casas
___ ___ Ella quería buscar información...	d. y fue a una inmobiliaria
___ ___ Delia estaba indecisa,...	e. y decidió hacer algo para mudarse

CD2–11 **7-51 Carlos Acosta** Escucha la historia de Carlos Acosta, un bailarín cubano, y clasifica los verbos que escuches usando la siguiente tabla.

PRETÉRITO	IMPERFECTO	
	Descripción	
	Acciones o estados habituales	

Carlos Acosta

■ Aplicaciones

7-52 ¡Qué vergüenza! *(How embarrassing!)* Seleccionen la forma verbal correcta para completar la siguiente narración.

Anoche, mientras (miré / miraba) la televisión, (escuché / escuchaba) un ruido en la cocina. (Salí / Salía) corriendo y (fui / iba) a la casa de mi vecino. Aunque (fueron / eran) más de las once de la noche y él (estuvo / estaba) durmiendo, lo (desperté / despertaba). Le (pedí / pedía) que viniera a ver qué (hubo / había) en la cocina y (entramos / entrábamos) juntos. Cuando él (encendió / encendía) la luz, (vimos / veíamos) que mi gato (estuvo / estaba) comiéndose tranquilamente el pastel que yo había dejado *(I had left)* sobre la mesa. ¡Qué vergüenza! ¡No (supe / sabía) qué decir! ¡Tanta conmoción por un triste gato!

7-53 Una historia aburrida La siguiente historia sólo incluye las acciones principales. Vuelvan a escribirla y añadan los detalles que consideren necesarios (descripciones [edad, apariencia física, estados y emociones], acciones simultáneas, trasfondo [tiempo y hora], etc.). ¡El resultado debe ser una historia interesante y original! Tengan en cuenta las reglas de uso del pretérito y del imperfecto.

Mario se levantó temprano. Se afeitó y después tomó café. Se vistió y se fue para el trabajo. En el autobús conoció a una chica preciosa. Hablaron un rato y le pidió su número de teléfono. Él pensó en ella todo el día. Cuando llegó a su casa por la tarde, la llamó. La invitó a cenar y ella aceptó. Fueron a un restaurante francés. Mario regresó a casa muy contento e ilusionado.

7-54 La vida pasada del / de la profesor(a) Escriban por lo menos seis preguntas que quieran hacerle al / a la profesor(a) para saber un poco más sobre su vida pasada. Usen el pretérito y el imperfecto correctamente.

■ Integración

7-55 ¡Invéntala! En grupos de cuatro o cinco estudiantes, túrnense para añadirle algo a una historia curiosa que van a inventar. Cada estudiante debe prestar atención a lo que dicen los demás para poder decir algo pertinente e interesante. El (La) estudiante que tarde más de cinco segundos en hablar, queda eliminado(a). ¿Quién gana al final?

7-56 Un cuento *(story)* **infantil** ¿Recuerdas algunos de los cuentos infantiles que te gustaban cuando eras niño(a) (como «La Cenicienta» [*Cinderella*] o «Hansel y Gretel»)? Escribe un resumen del cuento que más te gustaba y dale una copia a un(a) compañero(a) para que lo corrija usando los criterios de la lista de sugerencias. Haz las correcciones y dale una copia a tu profesor(a). Repasa los usos del pretérito y del imperfecto antes de comenzar.

SUGERENCIAS

Usen conectores como **érase una vez** *(once upon a time)*, **de pronto** *(suddenly)*, **además** *(also)*, **por otro lado** *(on the other hand)*, **sin embargo** *(however)*, **por el contrario** *(on the contrary)*, **por ejemplo** *(for example)*, y **finalmente** *(finally)*.

SUGERENCIAS

Para corregir el resumen de tu compañero(a), presta atención a los siguientes elementos:
Contenido: ¿La información del cuento infantil es correcta? ¿Falta algún detalle importante?
Organización: ¿El resumen sigue una secuencia lógica? ¿Es necesario usar frases conectoras?
Vocabulario: ¿La selección de vocabulario es apropiada? ¿Hay algún término usado de forma incorrecta?
Lenguaje: ¿El uso del pretérito y del imperfecto sigue las reglas? ¿Los verbos están bien conjugados?

III. Funciones y estructuras: Talking about the immediate past with *acabar de*

CELIA: ¡Leo, **acabo de comprar** la casa de mis sueños!
LEO: ¡Felicidades! ¡Pues vamos a celebrar!

The expression **acabar de** + infinitive is used to talk about actions that took place in the immediate past.

Maite **acaba de regresar** de Cuba.	Maite **just came back** from Cuba.
Nosotros **acabamos de firmar** el contrato.	We **just signed** the contract.

When you have to use a direct object, indirect object, or reflexive pronoun, it may be placed either before the form of **acabar** or attached to the main verb.

Lo acabo de llamar. / Acabo de llamar**lo**.	I just called **him.**
Le acabo de decir que no. / Acabo de decir**le** que no.	I just told **him/her** no.
Me acabo de bañar. / Acabo de bañar**me**.	I just took a bath (bathed **myself**).

Here is a list of other verbs that require the use of the preposition **de** followed by a verb in the infinitive form.

> acordarse (ue) de *to remember*
> asegurarse de *to make sure*
> dejar de *to stop doing something*
> ocuparse de *to take care of*
> olvidarse de *to forget*
> tener ganas de *to feel like doing something*
> tratar de *to try*

■ Asimilación

7-57 Acaba de... ¿Conoces bien a tus compañeros de clase? Completa las siguientes oraciones con el nombre de un(a) compañero(a) que, en tu opinión, acaba de hacer estas actividades. Luego, compara tus respuestas con las de un(a) compañero(a). ¿En qué coincidieron?

1. _____ acaba de tomar café.
2. _____ acaba de despertarse.
3. _____ acaba de comer algo.
4. _____ acaba de salir de una clase.
5. _____ acaba de venir de la biblioteca.
6. _____ acaba de abrir el libro.
7. _____ acaba de decirle algo al / a la profesor(a).
8. _____ acaba de entrar al salón de clase.

7-58 Buenas y malas noticias Escucha la conversación entre Moisés y Daniel e indica qué actividades acaban de hacer. Escribe algunos de los detalles que recuerdes.

02-12

Moisés acaba de...
DETALLES:
Daniel acaba de...
DETALLES:

■ Aplicaciones

7-59 Actividades Escriban por lo menos dos cosas que las personas con las siguientes profesiones posiblemente acaban de hacer: **un cocinero, una secretaria, un agente de bienes raíces, una enfermera, un arquitecto.**

MODELO   *Una periodista posiblemente acaba de entrevistar a un político y de escribir un artículo para un periódico.*

7-60 Comparaciones

Paso 1: Haz una lista de cinco cosas que acabas de hacer.

1. ...   4. ...
2. ...   5. ...
3. ...

Paso 2. Busca a otros compañeros que acaban de hacer las mismas cosas que tú. Apunta sus nombres.

7-61 Pues estabas en... Túrnense para describir cosas que acaban de hacer y para adivinar dónde estaban haciendo esas cosas.

MODELO   E1: *Acabo de enviarle un paquete a mi mejor amiga, de comprar sellos y de buscar mis cartas. ¿Dónde estaba?*
                 E2: *Pues estabas en la oficina de correos.*
                 E1: *¡Correcto!*

■ Integración

7-62 ¿Y ahora qué? Representa la siguiente situación con un(a) compañero(a).

Estudiante A	Estudiante B
Imagínate que acabas de graduarte de la universidad y, de pronto *(suddenly)*, no sabes qué hacer para preparente para tu vida profesional. Llama a tu mejor amigo(a), háblale de tu preocupación y pídele un consejo *(advice)*.	Tu mejor amigo(a) acaba de graduarse de la universidad y necesita tu consejo sobre qué debe hacer para prepararse para su vida profesional. Cuando te llame, escúchalo(a) y dale tu consejo *(advice)*.

7-63 En la clase de hoy Imagínate que uno de tus compañeros no pudo venir a clase hoy. Mándale un correo electrónico para informarle lo que pasó en la clase. Puedes usar oraciones con **acabar de** y las expresiones **acuérdate de..., asegúrate de..., deja de..., olvídate de..., ocúpate de...** y **trata de...**

IV. Lectura: Soñar en cubano

■ Antes de leer

 A. Para conversar En grupos de cuatro o cinco estudiantes, intercambien opiniones sobre las siguientes preguntas.

1. ¿Qué aspectos de la vida en los Estados Unidos creen que pueden sorprender a un inmigrante hispanoamericano que viene de la zona del Caribe?

2. En general, ¿quién creen que se va a adaptar más rápidamente a este nuevo país: un niño o un adulto? Expliquen por qué.

B. Vocabulario y conceptos Las siguientes palabras son importantes para la comprensión del texto que vas a leer a continuación. Para cada una, escribe la letra de su definición. (Consulta el diccionario si es necesario.)

____ 1. el fracaso   a. bajar mucho la temperatura, formar hielo

____ 2. la intervención   b. hacer sonidos semejantes a algo que se

____ 3. helar   quiebra o se fragmenta

____ 4. crujir   c. la ruina, la destrucción, el fin

                           d. intromisión, participación arbitraria en

                           un asunto ajeno

■ A leer

Cristina García

Nació en La Habana, Cuba, en 1958, y creció en Nueva York. Asistió a Barnard College y a la Escuela de Estudios Internacionales Avanzados de la Universidad Johns Hopkins. Cristina García ha trabajado como corresponsal para la revista *Time* en San Francisco, Miami y Los Ángeles, donde vive con su esposo. *Soñar en cubano* es su primera novela.

Soñar en cubano (fragmento)

Recuerdo cuando llegamos a Nueva York. Vivimos durante cinco meses en un hotel de Manhattan, mientras mis padres esperaban el fracaso de la revolución o la intervención de los norteamericanos en Cuba. Mi madre me sacaba a pasear por Central Park.

Una vez, uno de los agentes del **espectáculo** de Art Linkletter nos **detuvo** en el zoo infantil y le preguntó a mi madre si yo podía formar parte en el show. Pero yo todavía no sabía hablar inglés, y mi madre **siguió** caminando. Mamá me vestía con un abriguito de lana rojo oscuro con el cuello y los **puños** de **terciopelo** negro. El aire era distinto al de Cuba. Tenía un olor a frío, a **humo,** que helaba mis **pulmones.** El cielo y los árboles

*Note that the word **abriguito** is derived from the word **abrigo.** The colloquial endings **-ito** and **-cito** are used to indicate small size or affection.*
Examples: Ana: Anita   casa: casita
papá: papito
Pepe: Pepito   libros: libritos
hijos: hijitos
carro: carrito   mamá: mamita
corazón: corazoncito

show
to stop (preterite)

to continue (preterite)

cuffs / velvet
smoke / lungs

dry leaves piled up
palm trees
naked branches

también eran diferentes. Yo me ponía a correr sobre las **hojas secas amontonadas** para escucharlas crujir como las **palmeras** de Cuba durante los huracanes. Pero luego me sentía triste al ver las **ramas desnudas** y pensaba en abuela Celia. Me pregunto cómo sería mi vida con ella en Cuba.

¿Entendiste bien?

C. Preguntas y respuestas Respondan a las siguientes preguntas.

1. ¿Adónde se mudó la familia de la narradora después de salir de Cuba?
2. ¿Por qué vivían en un hotel? (¿No tenían dinero para alquilar *[rent]* o comprar una casa?)
3. ¿Qué recuerda especialmente la narradora acerca de esa época?
4. ¿Sus recuerdos son alegres o tristes? Explica por qué.
5. Dibuja la escena de la narradora en el Central Park.

D. Conjeturas Al final del fragmento, la niña dice: «Me pregunto cómo sería mi vida con ella en Cuba». Usando la imaginación, describan la vida de esta niña en la isla. (¿Cómo es su casa y su vecindad? ¿A qué se dedica? ¿Es feliz?, etc.)

E. Enfoque lingüístico Clasifiquen los verbos en pretérito o imperfecto que encuentren en la lectura usando la siguiente tabla.

PRETÉRITO	IMPERFECTO	
	Descripción	
	Acciones habituales	

F. Enfoque comunitario Entrevisten a un(a) estudiante extranjero(a) de cualquier nacionalidad y averigüen qué le gusta de los Estados Unidos, qué extraña de su país natal y qué ajustes ha tenido que hacer para vivir en este país. Presenten un informe oral sobre sus respuestas.

Vocabulario

Los recuerdos — *Memories*
la tierra/patria — *homeland*

Verbos para hablar de los recuerdos
añorar — *to long for*
extrañar/echar de menos — *to miss*
irse — *to leave*
mudarse — *to move*
olvidar — *to forget*
olvidarse de — *to forget about*
regresar — *to return*

Preparativos para una mudanza — *Preparations for a move*
la caja (de cartón) — *(cardboard) box*
el camión de mudanzas — *moving truck*
la cinta — *tape*
la cotización / el estimado — *price estimation*
el embalaje — *packing*
los empacadores — *packing staff*
el guardamuebles — *storage*
la manta — *blanket*
el marcador — *marker*
el menaje — *household goods, belongings*
la mudanza — *move*
el plástico de burbujas — *bubblewrap*
las tijeras — *scissors*
el transporte — *transportation*
el traslado — *relocation, transfer*

Verbos para hablar de mudanzas
acomodar — *to accommodate, to arrange*
alquilar — *to rent*
cargar — *to load*
desempacar — *to unpack*
envolver (ue) — *to wrap*
guardar — *to store*
marcar — *to label*
trasladarse — *to relocate*

Los bienes raíces — *Real estate*
el contrato — *contract*
la cuota inicial / el anticipo — *down payment*
la hipoteca — *mortgage*
la inmobiliaria/agencia de bienes raíces — *real estate agency*
los planos — *blueprints*
el préstamo — *loan*
la propiedad — *property*
los términos de financiamiento — *credit terms*
la ubicación — *location*

Funciones y estructuras
Verbos como **gustar,** p. 269
Expresiones con **por,** p. 282
Verbos que requieren **de,** p. 298

Capítulo 8

¡A trabajar!

Para comenzar

- Túrnense para describir estas fotografías y adivinar de qué lugar se trata. **¡OJO!** ¡Sólo tienen **dos** oportunidades para adivinar!
- ¿Conocen algunos lugares similares a éstos en los Estados Unidos? ¿Dónde están?

In this chapter you will learn . . .

- how to talk about jobs, salary, and benefits
- how to express work experience and qualifications
- how to make a business call
- how to give instructions
- about job opportunities and conditions in Latin America and Spain today

Venezuela es uno de los principales productores mundiales de petróleo.

La ciudad de Caracas tiene una población aproximada de 4 millones de habitantes.

Cartagena, Colombia, es un importante puerto caribeño desde la época colonial.

Enfoque

A. **¿Qué sabes ya de Venezuela?** Antes de ver el vídeo, intenta contestar las siguientes preguntas.

1. ¿Quién es Simón Bolívar y dónde nació?
2. ¿Qué porcentaje de gente vive en los centros urbanos de Venezuela?
   a. el 40%   b. el 60%   c. el 90%
3. En Venezuela, ¿hasta qué edad es gratuita y obligatoria la educación?
   a. los 14 años b. los 16 años c. los 18 años

4. ¿Qué porcentaje de la población sabe leer y escribir?
   a. el 65%   b. el 77%   c. el 91%

Compara tus respuestas con las de un(a) compañero(a).

B. **Vivir y trabajar en Venezuela** Imagínense que tienen la oportunidad de vivir y trabajar en Venezuela. Busquen en el Internet información acerca de estas ciudades: Maracaibo, Caracas y Maturín. Decidan qué ciudad escogerían *(you would choose)* para vivir y trabajar. Comenten con la clase su elección y las razones por las que escogieron esa ciudad.

C. **Venezuela, un país encantador** Mientras ves el vídeo, indica si las siguientes oraciones son ciertas **(C)** o falsas **(F)**.

____ 1. Caracas, la capital, tiene un buen sistema de metro que la gente usa con frecuencia por su gran eficiencia.

____ 2. Los centros comerciales de Caracas también son centros sociales donde los jóvenes se reúnen para divertirse y para ir de compras.

____ 3. En Caracas se pueden ver varios ejemplos de la arquitectura modernista, como la hermosa catedral y el impresionante Panteón Nacional.

____ 4. Entre semana, después del trabajo, la gente sale mucho.

For more info, you may want to check the **Temas** site:
http://temas.heinle.com

Compara tus respuestas con las de un(a) compañero(a) y corrijan las frases falsas.

En busca de trabajo

I. Vocabulario: Los anuncios clasificados

Un buen abogado debe tener mucha **experiencia** para **defender** apropiadamente a sus clientes.

Esta ingeniera tiene excelentes **referencias** y una gran **facilidad de expresión.**

Los técnicos **se encargan de manejar** y **reparar** los equipos.

Vocabulario práctico

la buena presencia *good personal appearance*
la facilidad de expresión *ease of expression, ability to speak*
la hoja de vida / el currículum *résumé*
el técnico *technician*
el trabajador no calificado *unqualified worker*

Verbos

arreglar/reparar *to fix*
colaborar *to collaborate*
cuidar *to care for, to watch over*
defender (ie) *to defend*
encargarse de + infinitive *to be responsible for doing something*
entretener (ie) *to entertain*
manejar *to operate, to handle*
presentarse *to present oneself, to appear*
solicitar *to request*

■ Asimilación

8-1 Clasificados

Paso 1: Lean los siguientes anuncios clasificados.

(1)
Solicitamos varios técnicos en fotocopiadoras, fax, máquinas de escribir, sumadoras, microondas, televisores, equipos electrónicos, impresoras, CPU, fuentes de energía. 541.5946, 541.6809.

(2)
Se solicita secretaria recepcionista, mínimo 5 años experiencia, excelentes referencias, manejo de Word y Excel, para oficina de ingeniería en Chacaíto. Telf. 261.3559, 261.3549, fax 263.7827, Sra. Elena.

(3)
Importante empresa solicita vendedores con buena presencia. Facilidad de expresión y trato con el público. Traer hoja de vida a la Avenida Libertador. Centro Comercial Sambil nivel Feria, local FR-20. Telf. 0149-233697, 0149-233916.

(4)
Seguridad Berna requiere para vinculación inmediata veinte supervisores de vigilancia, experiencia, libreta militar, de primera, 30–45 años. Presentarse lunes a viernes horas de oficina en la Avenida Urdaneta, entre Veroes y Santa Capilla, edificio Cipriano Morales, piso 1, oficina B.

(5)
Solicitamos mensajeros a pie, motorizados, bachilleres, experiencia Caracas, ciudades vecinas, dirección: Av. Las Palmas, Boleíta Sur, Centro Inoesa, piso dos.

(6)
Solicitamos asistente técnico en reparaciones, mantenimientos computadoras, impresoras, monitores. Empresa Celedatos 763.2115, 763.0841. Entrevista lunes a viernes.

Paso 2: ¿Qué tipo de trabajo es? Clasifiquen las ofertas de empleo según las siguientes categorías. Escriban los números de los anuncios correspondientes.

Trabajo técnico	Relaciones públicas	Seguridad	Trabajo no calificado

Paso 3: A mí (no) me gusta... ¿Te interesa alguno de esos trabajos? Conversa con tu compañero(a) sobre el trabajo (o los trabajos) de la lista que más (o menos) te gustaría desempeñar. Explica tus razones.

CD2–14 **8-2 ¿Reconoces estas profesiones?** Identifica la profesión que corresponde a cada descripción que vas a escuchar.

____ médico   ____ policía

____ ingeniero de sistemas   ____ cantante

____ periodista

■ **Aplicaciones**

8-3 ¿Qué hacen y dónde trabajan? Describe las actividades de una de estas personas para que tu compañero(a) adivine de qué ocupación se trata. **¡OJO!** Tienen sólo cinco segundos para contestar.

ingeniero   enfermera   gerente   científico
artista   programador de computadoras

MODELO   E1: *Atiende a pacientes como un médico, pero sólo les examina los dientes.*
E2: *¿El dentista?*
E1: *¡Sí!*

8-4 Buscamos... Imaginen que están en Venezuela y que necesitan algunos colaboradores *(helpers).* Preparen los anuncios clasificados para enviarlos al periódico *El Universal.* (Usen como guía los anuncios de la actividad 8-1 de la sección **Asimilación.**)

1. un(a) enfermero(a)
2. una nana (niñera)
3. una criada
4. un chofer

8-5 Superación personal *(Self-improvement)* Lean la siguiente descripción de un curso por Internet que se ofrece en Caracas.

Instituto Tecnológico, Universidad Central de Venezuela, Aplicaciones instrumentales de Internet en Humanidades, Ciencias Sociales y afines

Qué ofrece: Dirigido más hacia el «¿cómo se hace?» que al «¿por qué ocurre?», este curso busca entrenar a usuarios calificados en el manejo de Internet y no formar expertos en el área técnica.

Dirigido a: Profesionales de las áreas de Humanidades, Ciencias Sociales y afines, quienes por formación y experiencia suelen desconocer los recursos adecuados para el manejo de Internet.

Duración: 20 horas.

Costo: 70 mil bolívares. Incluye material de apoyo, refrigerios y certificado de asistencia.

Los técnicos **se encargan de manejar** y **reparar** los equipos.

Inicio: Comienzan cursos mensualmente, en horario vespertino, jueves y viernes.

Información: Instituto Tecnológico, segundo piso, edificio del Decanato, Facultad de Ingeniería, Universidad Central de Venezuela.
E-mail: mendezn@fiucv.ing.ucv.ve

---

1. Este curso es para profesionales especializados en _____.
2. Los participantes aprenden a usar _____.
3. Los cursos comienzan cada _____.

■ Integración

 8-6 ¿Qué debo estudiar? Representa la siguiente situación con un(a) compañero(a).

Consejero(a)	Estudiante
Imagina que eres consejero(a) estudiantil y que a tu oficina llega un(a) estudiante que no sabe en qué especializarse.	Tú eres un(a) estudiante indeciso(a). Tu consejero(a) quiere ayudarte a escoger una buena carrera para el futuro. Pídele toda la información posible acerca de la carrera que te va a recomendar.
■ Averigua sus intereses y recomiéndale una carrera apropiada. ■ Indícale dónde puede estudiar esa carrera. ■ Indica qué requisitos se necesitan. ■ Recomiéndale dónde puede trabajar al terminar sus estudios.	■ ¿Dónde puedes estudiarla? ■ ¿Qué requisitos se necesitan? ■ ¿Dónde puedes trabajar al terminar tus estudios?

 8-7 ¿Qué hace mi compañero(a)? Descríbele tu carrera o tu especialización al / a la compañero(a). (Mientras una persona habla, la otra toma notas.) Después, presenta un informe al resto de la clase acerca de las respuestas del / de la compañero(a).

Asegúrense de incluir la siguiente información:

- ¿Cuál es la carrera del / de la compañero(a)? ¿Qué áreas o materias incluye?
- ¿Por qué escogió esa carrera?
- ¿Cuáles son sus objetivos en la vida?
- ¿Cuál es la importancia de esa carrera para el futuro del país?
- ¿Qué contribución piensa hacer tu compañero(a) en beneficio de la sociedad?

II. Funciones y estructuras: Referring to people and things with the relative pronouns *que* and *quien(es)*

(1)	(2)
Prestigiosa universidad privada solicita tutores **que** puedan trabajar durante los fines de semana. Los candidatos a **quienes** vamos a considerar deben tener una maestría en su área de especialización. Llamar a la Dra. Bermúdez. 248.9953.	Empresa **que** presta servicios a hospitales solicita técnicos de computadoras con experiencia. **Quien** esté interesado debe enviar su hoja de vida. Fax: 249.0611.

Relative pronouns are pronouns that refer to an entity that has already been mentioned in the discourse. This entity is called *the antecedent.* For example, in the first ad, **que** refers to **tutores** (its antecedent) and **quienes** refers to **candidatos** (its antecedent).

Quienes is used when the antecedent is plural.

While English has four main relative pronouns *(who, whom, that,* and *which),* Spanish has two (**que** and **quien[es]**).

The pronoun **que** is used to refer to:

- people *(who)*

El gerente **que** contrató a mi hermana renunció.	The manager **who** hired my sister resigned.

- things *(that, which)*

¿Ya recibió el currículum **que** le envié?	Did you receive the résumé **that** I sent you?
Estos trabajos, **que** no me gustan, pagan muy poco.	These jobs, **which** I do not like, pay very little.

The pronoun **quien(es)** is used to refer to:

- people *(who, whom)*—when **quien** comes after a preposition or when it is the first word in a nonrestrictive clause (a phrase that is enclosed in commas)

The speaker has the choice of using either **quien(es)** or **que** in nonrestrictive clauses. However, only **que** can be used in restrictive clauses.

Los hombres con **quienes** hablé tenían buena presencia.	The men with **whom** I spoke had good personal appearance.
La Sra. Mercado, **quien** se encarga de los archivos, es muy simpática.	Mrs. Mercado, **who** is responsible for filing, is very pleasant.

▓ Asimilación

8-8 ¿Qué o quién? Escribe el nombre de la cosa o de la(s) persona(s) que cumple(n) con cada descripción.

1. El (La) profesor(a) con quien mejor me llevo. _____
2. La clase que más me gusta. _____
3. Los compañeros de clase a quienes casi no les hablo. _____
4. La prenda de vestir que menos me gusta. _____
5. La persona a quien menos tolero. _____
6. Las cosas que siempre traigo a la universidad. _____

D2-15 **8-9 Después de una entrevista de empleo** Escucha lo que dice Blanca y selecciona las frases que mejor completen las siguientes oraciones.

1. Blanca cree que... en la entrevista.
   a. le fue mal
   b. le fue bien
   c. no actuó bien

2. La mujer con quien se entrevistó...
   a. era muy paciente.
   b. era antipática.
   c. no tenía interés.

3. Habló con otras personas, quienes se impresionaron con...
   a. su facilidad de expresión.
   b. su presencia.
   c. su experiencia.

4. El trabajo que más le interesa...
   a. es con computadoras.
   b. no está disponible.
   c. está cerca de la casa.

■ Aplicaciones

8-10 El mundo del trabajo Completen las oraciones con **que, quien** o **quienes.**

1. El jefe o la jefa, _____ toma las decisiones en una empresa, debe tener buena comunicación con sus empleados.

2. La característica de un administrador _____ más admiran sus compañeros de trabajo es la honestidad.

3. La persona _____ se encarga de contabilizar el dinero de una empresa tiene una responsabilidad muy grande.

4. Los supervisores con _____ uno trabaja deben dar el ejemplo de puntualidad y buena presencia.

5. El currículum _____ uno le entrega a un posible empleador *(employer)* cuando solicita un trabajo es un documento confidencial.

6. Un técnico _____ no repara bien las cosas no debe permanecer en un trabajo.

8-11 Opiniones personales Primero, seleccionen el pronombre correcto. Luego, escriban los datos necesarios para completar las oraciones.

1. Las personas con (que / quien / quienes) quiero trabajar deben ser _____ y _____.

2. La hoja de vida (que / quien / quienes) voy a preparar para solicitar mi trabajo ideal va a ser _____ y _____.

3. Una persona (que / quien / quienes) busca trabajo debe estar preparada para _____ y para _____.

4. Antes de contratar a un trabajador (que / quien / quienes) no está calificado, un empleador debe pensar en _____ y en _____.

5. Alguien con experiencia, (que / quien / quienes) tiene ventaja sobre otras personas, sólo tiene que preocuparse de _____ y de _____.

EN TU COMUNIDAD

You may wish to go to an employment agency or a career training agency and find out about the interview techniques their clients have considered most successful. Afterward, discuss your findings in groups and present an oral report on the most common techniques.

8-12 Preguntas

Paso 1: Completa las preguntas que le vas a hacer a un(a) compañero(a) con frases que empiecen con **que, quien** o **quienes.**

> MODELO   ¿Cuál es la persona con _quien más hablas de tu familia_?
> ¿Dónde está el restaurante _que visitas con más frecuencia_?

1. ¿Cómo se llama el (la) amigo(a) para _____?
2. ¿Cuál es la comida _____?
3. ¿Dónde compras los libros _____?
4. ¿Cómo es tu madre, _____?
5. ¿Te gusta estudiar en esta universidad, _____?

Paso 2: Hazle las preguntas a tu compañero(a) y toma notas. Después, informa al resto de la clase sobre sus respuestas.

■ Integración

8-13 Problemas Representa la siguiente situación con un(a) compañero(a). Cuando terminen, intercambien papeles.

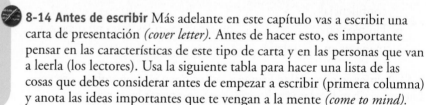

Estudiante A	**Estudiante B**
Toma unos minutos para inventar tres problemas. Luego, cuéntale a tu compañero(a) estos problemas y pídele que te dé su opinión. Como eres una persona testaruda *(stubborn)*, no aceptes sus consejos tan fácilmente.	Tu compañero(a) tiene varios problemas. Como buen(a) amigo(a), escúchalo(a) y dale tu opinión. ¡Debes estar listo(a) para defender tu punto de vista!

8-14 Antes de escribir Más adelante en este capítulo vas a escribir una carta de presentación *(cover letter)*. Antes de hacer esto, es importante pensar en las características de este tipo de carta y en las personas que van a leerla (los lectores). Usa la siguiente tabla para hacer una lista de las cosas que debes considerar antes de empezar a escribir (primera columna) y anota las ideas importantes que te vengan a la mente *(come to mind)*.

Cosas que debo considerar	Ideas importantes
1.	
2.	
3.	
4.	
5.	

III. Funciones y estructuras: Referring to past events that continue into the present with the present perfect tense

—¿Usted **ha trabajado** en una tienda de ropa antes?

—Sí, **he trabajado** en varias tiendas de ropa.

The present perfect (known as **pretérito perfecto** in Spanish) is used to talk about actions that began in the past and continue in the present. In English, it is formed with the auxiliary verb *has* or *have* followed by the past participle of the main verb (*I have studied, Anne has visited*, etc.).

To form the present perfect in Spanish, use the present tense of the auxiliary verb **haber** and the past participle of the main verb. The past participle ending of **-ar** verbs is **-ado** while the past participle ending of **-er** and **-ir** verbs is **-ido.**

PRESENT PERFECT		
AUXILIARY VERB **haber**	PAST PARTICIPLE OF THE MAIN VERB	
	-ar verbs	**-er/-ir** verbs
he has ha	estudiar → estudi**ado**	beber → beb**ido**
hemos habéis han	cantar → cant**ado**	salir → sal**ido**

Susana **ha completado** todos los formularios.	*Susan **has filled in** all the forms.*
Ellos **han defendido** a muchos criminales.	*They **have defended** many criminals.*

Several verbs have irregular past participle forms.

abrir → abierto	*opened*		morir → muerto	*died*	
cubrir → cubierto	*covered*		poner → puesto	*put, set*	
decir → dicho	*said*		resolver → resuelto	*solved*	
describir → descrito	*described*		romper → roto	*broken*	
escribir → escrito	*written*		satisfacer → satisfecho	*satisfied*	
freír → frito	*fried*		ver → visto	*seen*	
hacer → hecho	*done, made*		volver → vuelto	*returned*	

In Spanish, the unity of the auxiliary verb **haber** and the past participle may not be broken by negative words or pronouns: **Él nunca <u>ha colaborado</u> en ningún proyecto.** (He <u>has</u> never <u>collaborated</u> in any project.) **¿<u>Has</u> <u>visto</u> al Dr. Pérez?** (<u>Have</u> you <u>seen</u> Dr. Pérez?)

He hecho varios cambios en la empresa.

Nosotros hemos resuelto ese problema.

*I **have made*** *several changes in the company.*

*We **have solved*** *that problem.*

Here is a list of time expressions normally used with verbs conjugated in the present perfect.

To find out if something has *ever* happened, use the expression **alguna vez: ¿Alguna vez han trabajado Uds. en California?** (Have you ever worked in California?)

desde el lunes / el mes pasado / la semana pasada /...	*since Monday / last month / last week / . . .*
hasta ahora / el momento	*up until now*
por una semana / un mes / un año /...	*for a week / a month / a year / . . .*
todavía/aún	*yet*

■ **Asimilación**

8-15 ¿Qué has hecho hasta ahora? Piensa en las cosas que has hecho hasta ahora en el día de hoy y selecciona las oraciones que se apliquen a ti. Al terminar, compara tus respuestas con las de un(a) compañero(a). ¿Han hecho las mismas cosas?

_____ He visto televisión.

_____ He almorzado.

_____ He asistido a más de dos clases.

_____ He escrito una monografía.

_____ He ido al trabajo.

_____ He hablado por teléfono.

_____ He leído el periódico.

_____ Me he afeitado/ maquillado.

_____ He comprado una bebida.

_____ He roto algo.

CD2–16 **8-16 Empleados muy eficientes** Son sólo las once de la mañana y los empleados de la firma legal Ramírez y Asociados ya han hecho muchas cosas. Escucha al Lic. Ramírez y escribe por lo menos cinco de las actividades que han hecho. Escribe la forma del infinitivo de los verbos.

1. ...

2. ...

3. ...

4. ...

5. ...

■ Aplicaciones

8-17 ¿Qué han hecho? Den un ejemplo de algo que seguramente han hecho esta semana los siguientes profesionales. Pueden seleccionar verbos de la lista o usar otros.

MODELO   un cocinero
Un cocinero ha preparado una cena espectacular para un cliente importante.

OPCIONES: descubrir   completar   romper   describir   defender
resolver   preparar   decir

1. un juez
2. un científico
3. un policía

4. un periodista
5. un atleta
6. un ingeniero

8-18 Mini-situaciones Completen las siguientes mini-situaciones con la forma correcta del pretérito perfecto de los verbos de cada lista. **¡OJO!** Hay verbos adicionales.

decidir   escribir   poner   tener   salir   decir

1. Yo no _____ la monografía para la clase de historia porque no _____ tiempo. Pero el profesor nos _____ que podemos entregarla tarde. Un amigo de la clase y yo _____ que vamos a trabajar juntos hoy, pero él no _____ del trabajo todavía.

poner   presentarse   tomar   satisfacer   hacer   ofrecer

2. El Sr. Nieves y yo _____ una decisión: vamos a despedir *(fire)* a la Sra. Jiménez. Desafortunadamente, ella no _____ su trabajo como es debido. Por otro lado, (ella) no _____ a ninguno de los talleres *(training sessions)* que la compañía _____. Lamentablemente, su desempeño *(performance)* no nos _____.

8-19 Desde que empecé a estudiar en esta universidad...

Paso 1: Escribe por lo menos cinco cosas que has hecho o logrado *(accomplished)* desde que empezaste a estudiar en esta universidad.

MODELO   *He aprendido a hablar español.*

1. ...
2. ...
3. ...

4. ...
5. ...

Paso 2: Convierte las oraciones del **Paso 1** en preguntas, y entrevista a tres o cuatro de tus compañeros de clase. Toma notas y, cuando termines, prepara un informe y preséntalo al resto de la clase.

MODELO   *¿Has aprendido a hablar español?*

TEMA 1

■ Integración

8-20 Presidente(a) de la Asociación de Estudiantes Representa la siguiente situación con un(a) compañero(a).

SUGERENCIAS

Para convencer a alguien de que tienes las cualidades y la experiencia necesarias, y de que estás de acuerdo con sus ideas, puedes reaccionar a sus preguntas y comentarios usando las siguientes expresiones: **¡Desde luego!** / **¡Por supuesto!** *(Of course!)* **¡Sin lugar a dudas!** *(Without a doubt!)* **¡Efectivamente!** *(Indeed!)*

SUGERENCIAS

Puedes hacerle preguntas sobre los siguientes temas: **años en la universidad; cursos; experiencia trabajando con estudiantes, profesores y la administración; necesidades de los estudiantes; ideas sobre cómo mejorar las condiciones físicas y académicas de la universidad;** etc.

Aspirante a Presidente(a) de la Asociación de Estudiantes

Tú eres uno(a) de los candidatos a la presidencia de la Asociación de Estudiantes de tu universidad. Estás reunido(a) con uno(a) de los delegados de esta asociación, quien quiere saber más sobre tu experiencia en diversas áreas importantes para este puesto. Habla con este(a) estudiante y convéncelo(a) de que eres el (la) mejor candidato(a).

Delegado(a) de la Asociación de Estudiantes

Tú eres el (la) delegado(a) de tu facultad *(college)* en la Asociación de Estudiantes de tu universidad. Estás reunido(a) con uno(a) de los candidatos a la presidencia de esta organización estudiantil. Quieres conocerlo(la) mejor y saber qué tipo de experiencia tiene en diferentes áreas importantes. También debes darle tu opinión sobre estos temas. Entrevista a esta persona para determinar si le vas a dar tu voto o no.

8-21 Mi carta de presentación En la actividad 8-14 tuviste la oportunidad de pensar en las cosas que debes tomar en cuenta antes de escribir tu carta de presentación. Ahora vas a comenzar a escribir la carta. Sigue estos pasos:

1. Haz una lista de actividades recientes relacionadas con tu trabajo y con tu preparación académica y personal («He asistido a dos congresos sobre...», «He participado en un proyecto de investigación con el Dr. / la Dra...», etc.).

2. Organiza estas actividades en dos o tres categorías: experiencia académica, experiencia laboral, experiencia de investigación, etc.

3. Prepara un bosquejo *(outline)* usando las categorías que creaste.

IV. Perspectivas: Trabajos vía Internet

■ Antes de leer

A. Para conversar ¿Cómo puede uno encontrar un empleo? Hagan una lista de las maneras en las que una persona puede informarse acerca de oportunidades laborales. De la lista que prepararon, ¿cuál creen que es la manera más efectiva? Expliquen por qué.

> MODELO   La radio, la televisión...
> *Creemos que la radio es más efectiva porque...*

B. Vocabulario y conceptos Escribe junto a cada palabra la letra de la definición más apropiada. (Usa el diccionario si es necesario.)

_____ 1. la búsqueda	a.	que molesta, que no es agradable
_____ 2. la solicitud	b.	encontrar, descubrir
_____ 3. odioso(a)	c.	proceso para encontrar algo
_____ 4. hallar	d.	muy atractivo(a)
_____ 5. tentador(a)	e.	espacio cibernético que contiene mucha información
_____ 6. la Red	f.	un documento con información personal que enviamos cuando queremos un empleo

■ A leer

Dale una lectura rápida al texto y contesta las preguntas.

Encontrar trabajo vía cibernética, una alternativa poco explorada

Jay Dougherty DPA / *El Universal*

Caracas ¿Busca usted un nuevo empleo o quiere cambiar de carrera?

Para la generación cibernética de hoy, el **hurgar** en los **avisos** de la prensa y enviar solicitudes de trabajo por correo es una odiosa tarea que **pertenece** al pasado.

to dig
ads

belongs

Quien quiera tener hoy éxito en la búsqueda de un cambio en la vida **no tiene más que encender** su computadora y consultar el Internet. «Internet es la mejor forma de hallar un empleo, especialmente para aquellos que posean una cierta habilidad técnica. Hay allí buenos consejos para todos los campos de trabajo», dice Joel Oleson, especialista en Internet en Utah.

only has to turn on

realize
to get the ball rolling

screen

marketing / will be expanded

Quienes buscan trabajo **se dan cuenta** rápidamente de que el usar el Internet es sólo el primer paso para **echar la bola a rodar.** Si tiene usted estudios y experiencia, su nombre y su currículum pasarán, sin que usted lo sepa, de mano en mano por el Internet. Y más pronto de lo que usted se imagina, tendrá más de una tentadora oferta de trabajo bajo la forma de email en su **pantalla.** En el Internet abundan las ofertas en ciertas categorías de empleos, en especial en alta tecnología, informática y computación, además de servicios, educación y **mercadeo.** Pero eso se **ampliará** tan rápido como evoluciona la «red». Aparte de los grupos de noticias Usenet, otra fuente de búsqueda de trabajo son los llamados «motores de búsqueda» de la Red, como Yahoo o InfoSeek.

■ ¿Entendiste bien?

C. Ideas principales Responde a las siguientes preguntas.

1. **¿Sí o no?**

   ____ Es relativamente fácil encontrar trabajos en el Internet.

   ____ La práctica tradicional de enviar solicitudes de trabajo por correo está desapareciendo.

   ____ En la red hay muchas oportunidades de trabajo en diferentes campos.

   ____ Se puede usar un motor de búsqueda como Yahoo para encontrar un trabajo.

   ____ Los materiales que se envían por Internet son siempre privados y secretos.

2. ¿En qué campos abundan las ofertas de trabajo en el Internet?

3. Según el autor, ¿quiénes se benefician más de las ofertas de trabajo en el Internet? ¿Por qué?

D. Actividad de extensión Consulta el Internet para investigar cuáles son las oportunidades de trabajo que hay en tu campo en este momento. Presenta en clase ejemplos de los trabajos que ofrecen (dónde, cuánto dinero ofrecen, qué requisitos tienen, etc.).

Mis antecedentes y expectativas laborales

I. Vocabulario: La hoja de vida

Un arquitecto Busca la siguiente información en la hoja de vida de Juan Fernando.

1. ¿Cuál es su profesión?
2. ¿De dónde es él?
3. ¿Cuántos años tiene?
4. ¿Dónde estudió?

5. ¿Cuántos años de experiencia tiene?
6. Además de la arquitectura, ¿qué otras aptitudes tiene Juan Fernando?

JUAN FERNANDO LENIS TAMAYO
arquitecto

DATOS PERSONALES

Nombre: Juan Fernando Lenis Tamayo
Lugar y fecha de nacimiento: Caracas, 29 de enero de 1968
Dirección: Edificio Torre Las Mercedes, Avenida la Estancia, Chuao
Teléfonos: 993.4156 - 993.3880 Fax: 993.6289
Correo electrónico: jflenis@latino.net.ve
Matrícula profesional: 257670-2423 Caracas, Venezuela

ESTUDIOS REALIZADOS

Primarios: Colegio San Francisco de Asís, Caracas, Venezuela
Secundarios: Lycée Claude Bernard, París, Francia
Universitarios: Universidad Central de Venezuela, Caracas Facultad de Arquitectura y Urbanismo
Fecha de grado: 12 de septiembre de 2000

EXPERIENCIA LABORAL

R.B.M. ARQUITECTOS (Jorge Rueda Borda y Esteban Morales Díaz)
Octubre a diciembre de 2000: Participación en el concurso para el diseño de la Policlínica Metropolitana

MELÉNDEZ-MELÉNDEZ ARQUITECTOS LTDA. (Isaías Meléndez e hijos) Enero a diciembre de 2001: Diseño de edificio multifamiliar de 53 apartamentos en Sabana Grande, Caracas (6000 m2)

L.T.S. ARQUITECTOS LTDA. (Felipe Serpa-Gutiérrez y Juan Fernando Lenis Tamayo) Febrero de 2002 a la actualidad: Diseño, dirección arquitectónica y promoción de 17 proyectos en las ciudades de Valencia y Caracas

IDIOMAS Y OTROS

Idiomas: español, inglés, francés
Programas de computación: Autocard 13, Office 98, Windows, Corel Draw

Marzo de 2006

Vocabulario práctico

la carta de presentación *cover letter*

los datos personales *personal information*

la entrevista *interview*

los estudios realizados *studies completed*

la experiencia laboral *work experience*

la fecha de grado *graduation date*

la matrícula/licencia profesional *professional license*

solicitar trabajo *to apply for a job*

la solicitud *application*

■ Asimilación

8-22 Todo en orden Ana está preparando su hoja de vida. ¿Dónde debe escribir la siguiente información? Para cada punto, indica la letra de la categoría a la que corresponde.

_____ 1. inglés e italiano

_____ 2. Valencia, 2 de mayo de 1978

_____ 3. Orquesta Filarmónica Nacional

_____ 4. Universidad Central de Venezuela, Escuela de Artes

_____ 5. Ana Mercedes López Vallejo

a. datos personales

b. estudios realizados

c. experiencia laboral

d. idiomas y otros

CD2–17 **8-23 Efraín Meneses Gómez** Completa las oraciones con la información que vas a escuchar.

1. Datos personales: Nació el _____ en _____.
2. Estudios realizados:
3. Experiencia laboral:
4. Idiomas y otros:

ESTRATEGIAS PARA LA COMPRENSIÓN

Note-taking If you are unable to understand a word, write it down the way it sounds and continue listening. Later you can compare notes with a classmate.

■ Aplicaciones

8-24 Preguntas y respuestas Preparen las preguntas que hay que hacer para averiguar los siguientes datos.

DATOS PERSONALES

Nombre: *¿Cómo se llama Ud.?*
Lugar y fecha de nacimiento: _____
Domicilio: _____
Teléfonos: _____
Correo electrónico: _____

ESTUDIOS

Primarios: _____
Secundarios: _____
Universitarios: _____
Fecha de grado: _____

OTROS ANTECEDENTES

Experiencia laboral: _____
Idiomas: _____
Programas de computación: _____

8-25 Entrevista Completa la hoja de vida de tu compañero(a) usando las preguntas que preparaste en el ejercicio anterior.

DATOS PERSONALES

Nombre: _____
Lugar y fecha de nacimiento: _____
Domicilio: _____
Teléfonos: _____
Correo electrónico: _____

ESTUDIOS REALIZADOS

Primarios: _____
Secundarios: _____
Universitarios: _____
Fecha de grado: _____

EXPERIENCIA LABORAL

_____

_____

IDIOMAS Y OTROS

Idiomas: _____
Programas de computación: _____

8-26 Una carta de presentación Pongan en orden las siguientes oraciones para formar la carta de presentación.

_____ Me dirijo a Uds. para solicitar un puesto como abogado en su firma.

_____ Terminé mis estudios de leyes en 1995 y me gradué con honores.

_____ Atentamente,

_____ Como pueden comprobar por mis referencias, me caracterizo por ser dedicado y creativo.

_____ Puedo hacer una contribución importante a su compañía.

_____ Estimados señores:

_____ Desde entonces, he trabajado en dos de las principales oficinas de abogados de esta ciudad.

_____ Sírvanse comunicarse conmigo en caso de que deseen más información.

_____ Me adapto muy bien a cualquier situación y trabajo bien en equipo.

■ Integración

8-27 Una entrevista de trabajo Representa la siguiente situación con un(a) compañero(a).

Jefe(a) de personal
(Human Resources Manager / Personnel Director)

Tu compañía está buscando un(a) candidato(a) para ocupar un puesto muy importante. Entrevista al / a la siguiente candidato(a) para saber si es la persona adecuada.

- Averigua sus datos personales.
- Averigua sus antecedentes académicos y laborales.
- Trata de determinar algunas de sus cualidades personales.

Aspirante

Tú deseas un trabajo en esta compañía. Responde a las preguntas del / de la jefe(a) de personal acerca de tus datos personales, así como tus antecedentes académicos y laborales. Recuerda que sus preguntas también van dirigidas a *(are intended to)* determinar tus cualidades personales. ¡Trata de dar una buena impresión!

8-28 Mi solicitud de empleo Prepara tu hoja de vida y una carta de presentación para solicitar un empleo.

1. Saca la hoja de vida que preparaste con tu compañero(a) al principio de este tema (página 321).
2. Repasa la lista de cualidades laborales y elabora un poco más la sección de «experiencia laboral».
3. Saca el bosquejo de la carta que preparaste en el **Tema 1.**
4. Elabora el bosquejo para escribir un primer borrador *(draft)*.

II. Funciones y estructuras: Influencing others with formal commands

—Imprenta Robles, buenos días.
—Quisiera solicitar trabajo en la imprenta. ¿Qué debo hacer?
—**Venga** a nuestras oficinas y **llene** una solicitud. Si lo desea,
  envíe su currículum por fax.
—Muchas gracias. Voy a ir en persona.

One of the ways to get others to do what we want them to do is by using direct commands like *Come in, Don't call again!,* and *Please, sit down.* When giving direct commands to others in Spanish you must keep in mind the distinction between formal and informal commands. Formal commands are those you would give to people you would refer to as **usted** whereas informal commands are those you would give to people you would refer to as **tú.** The plural form of the **usted** command, however, may be used in both formal and informal contexts.

To give an *affirmative* command, (1) drop the -**o** from the **yo** form of the present tense and (2) add -**e/-en** if the verb is an -**ar** verb and -**a/-an** if it is an -**er** or -**ir** verb.

> **REMEMBER**
>
> Use **tú** with relatives, friends and people your age or younger. Use **usted** with people who are older than you or whom you do not know.

VERB	llen**ar**	le**er**	ven**ir**
yo present tense form	llen**o**	le**o**	veng**o**
(1)	llen-	le-	veng-
(2)	llen**e** (Ud.)	le**a** (Ud.)	veng**a** (Ud.)
	llen**en** (Uds.)	le**an** (Uds.)	veng**an** (Uds.)

Sra. Asencio, **traiga** su licencia profesional, por favor.

Señores, **esperen** su turno.

*Mrs. Asencio, please **bring** your professional license.*

*Gentlemen, **wait** for your turn.*

To make a *negative* command simply place **no** before the verb.

Por favor, **no entren** todavía.

Doña Luisa, **no firme** ese formulario.

*Please, **do not enter** yet.*

*Mrs. Luisa, **do not sign** that form.*

In some contexts, using these command forms may be considered rude by the interlocutor, especially if this person is an authority figure with more status than the speaker. To soften the imperative, make sure to add the expression **por favor.**

Verbs that end in **-car, -gar,** and **-zar** in their infinitive form have a spelling change in order to maintain the pronunciation of the letters **c, g,** and **z.**

-car: c → qu	-gar: g → gu	-zar: z → c
bus**car**	pa**gar**	empe**zar** (ie)
bus**que** (Ud.)	pa**gue** (Ud.)	empie**ce** (Ud.)
bus**quen** (Uds.)	pa**guen** (Uds.)	empie**cen** (Uds.)

The verbs **dar, ir, saber,** and **ser** have irregular formal command forms.

dar	ir	saber	ser
dé (Ud.)	vaya (Ud.)	sepa (Ud.)	sea (Ud.)
den (Uds.)	vayan (Uds.)	sepan (Uds.)	sean (Uds.)

■ Asimilación

8-29 ¿Apropiado o inapropiado? Indica si consideras apropiado o inapropiado decirle las siguientes cosas a tu profesor(a). Escribe los números de las oraciones en la categoría correcta. Cuando termines, compara las respuestas con las de un(a) compañero(a). ¿Piensan de la misma forma?

Por favor,...

1. explique eso otra vez.
2. venga a clase en bañador.
3. no dé clase hoy.
4. salga del salón durante el examen.
5. repita esta palabra.
6. lea nuestro periódico en Internet.
7. devuelva las tareas a tiempo.
8. diga qué significa esa frase.
9. no hable español.
10. acepte los trabajos dos semanas después.

Mandatos apropiados:
_____

Mandatos inapropiados:
_____

02–18 **8-30 Dos anuncios** Primero, familiarízate con los siguientes anuncios. Luego, escucha las oraciones e indica si se asocian con el anuncio A o con el anuncio B.

Anuncio A   **Anuncio B**

1. ____   2. ____   3. ____   4. ____   5. ____   6. ____

■ Aplicaciones

8-31 En una agencia de empleo Imaginen que trabajan en una agencia de empleo y que les dan consejos a las personas que se presentan. Seleccionen un verbo lógico para formar una oración que le podrían decir a un cliente. Escríbanlo en la forma de mandato formal singular.

> **MODELO**   (presentar / mover / comprar) su matrícula profesional
> *Presente su matrícula profesional.*

1. (leer / incluir / llamar) la fecha de grado en la solicitud
2. (salir / poner / llegar) temprano a la entrevista
3. (escuchar / dirigir / escribir) sus datos personales aquí
4. (mostrar / sacar / saber) evidencia de su experiencia laboral
5. (dar / tener / comenzar) paciencia y va a conseguir trabajo
6. (ir / solicitar / contribuir) a la oficina número tres, por favor
7. (practicar / viajar / entretener) antes de la entrevista
8. (alcanzar / buscar / contra) una solicitud en la próxima ventanilla

8-32 Consejos y reacciones Escriban un mandato afirmativo lógico y un mandato negativo lógico para cada situación. Usen verbos diferentes. ¡Sean creativos!

SITUACIÓN	MANDATO AFIRMATIVO	MANDATO NEGATIVO
1		
2		
3		

1. La Sra. Echevarría siempre gasta mucho dinero cuando va de compras y nunca paga las cuentas a tiempo. Si continúa, su crédito se va a afectar.

2. Daniel y Berta no son muy dedicados. Salen todas las noches y no hacen las tareas de sus clases. Es posible que fracasen en todas sus clases este semestre.

3. Los Beltrán no son muy buenos vecinos. Llegan muy tarde a la casa y hacen demasiado ruido. Además, tiran la basura frente a la casa, tienen un perro muy agresivo y no mantienen su propiedad en buenas condiciones.

8-33 Entre compañeros Escriban una lista de cinco mandatos para el (la) profesor(a) y cinco mandatos para dos estudiantes de la clase. Cuando les toque su turno, léanlos. ¡El (La) profesor(a) y sus dos compañeros de clase tienen que hacer lo que Uds. les digan!

MODELOS   *Profesor(a), diga la fecha de su cumpleaños.*
            Joe y Kate, corran por el salón de clase.

■ Integración

8-34 Falta de comunicación Imaginen que Uds. son los padres o hermanos mayores de cinco niños muy activos. Esta noche van a salir al teatro y los van a dejar con un(a) niñero(a). Díganles a los niños las cosas que quieren que hagan y que no hagan. **¡OJO!** Uds. tienen opiniones diferentes sobre cómo criar a sus hijos o hermanos y se contradicen constantemente.

8-35 Con el (la) Rector(a) *(president)* **de la universidad** Imagina que el (la) rector(a) de tu universidad te ha pedido que trabajes como su asesor(a) personal. Él/Ella quiere saber qué cosas te gustan y no te gustan de su administración. Prepara una lista de las cosas que le vas a decir en una reunión la próxima semana. Incluye mandatos formales afirmativos y negativos. Dale una copia a tu profesor(a) para que te dé su opinión.

III. Funciones y estructuras: Using pronouns and formal commands

Do you notice anything different in the command forms of the verbs at
the top of these ads? If you said that they have pronouns attached to
them, you are correct! In fact, reflexive, direct object, and indirect object
pronouns are attached to the affirmative command form of the verb.

REFLEXIVE:	Cálme**se**, Sra. Vega. *(Calm down, Mrs. Vega.)* Páren**se**, señores. *(Stand up, gentlemen.)*
DIRECT OBJECT:	Tráiga**la**, por favor. *(Bring **it**, please.)* Póngan**los** ahí. *(Put **them** there.)*
INDIRECT OBJECT:	Díga**le** que no puedo. *(Tell **him** that I can't.)* Den**me** las cartas. *(Give **me** the letters.)*

✱ Notice that you must place an
accent mark on the vowel with the
stress when you use affirmative
commands with pronouns and there
are more than two syllables.

In the case of negative commands, the pronouns are placed between **no**
and the verb.

REFLEXIVE:	No **se** preocupe. *(Do not worry.)* No **se** pongan ansiosos. *(Do not get anxious.)*
DIRECT OBJECT:	No **las** entregue. *(Do not hand **them** in.)* No **lo** compren. *(Do not buy **it**.)*
INDIRECT OBJECT:	¡No **me** diga! *(You're kidding [me]!)* ¡No **me** mientan! *(Don't lie to **me**!)*

Asimilación

8-36 ¿Qué dice... ? Para contestar las siguientes preguntas, selecciona la alternativa más lógica. Al terminar, compara tus respuestas con las de un(a) compañero(a). ¿Están de acuerdo?

¿Qué dice...

____ 1. un profesor?   ____ 4. una abogada?

____ 2. un mesero?   ____ 5. un arquitecto?

____ 3. una recepcionista?   ____ 6. una ama de casa?

a. Siéntense, por favor. El doctor los va a atender enseguida *(soon)*.
b. Consígame los planos del edificio de la avenida Bolívar.
c. ¿Las composiciones? Escríbanlas en la computadora.
d. ¡Váyase de mi oficina! ¡Yo no defiendo a criminales!
e. ¿Los paquetes? Pónganlos sobre la mesa del comedor. Gracias.
f. Llévales las bebidas a los señores de la mesa diez.

CD2-19 **8-37 ¿Sí o no?** Es un día como todos en la agencia de empleos donde trabajas. A ésta vienen personas muy simpáticas, pero también personas muy imprudentes. Responde de manera lógica a las preguntas que vas a escuchar.

1. a. Sí, escríbalo.   b. No, no lo escriba.
2. a. Sí, tráigame flores.   b. No, no me traiga flores.
3. a. Sí, invíteme.   b. No, no me invite.
4. a. Sí, mándelas.   b. No, no las mande.
5. a. Sí, vístase bien.   b. No, no se vista bien.
6. a. Sí, inclúyala.   b. No, no la incluya.

Aplicaciones

8-38 Recomendaciones Usen la siguiente información para escribir una serie de recomendaciones para una persona que está buscando trabajo. Si dicen que **no** a algo, den una alternativa. Usen pronombres en sus respuestas.

MODELO   no escribir la fecha de nacimiento en la carta de presentación
No la escriba en la carta de presentación. Escríbala en la hoja de vida.

1. no sentarse en el escritorio del entrevistador
2. incluir una carta de recomendación con la solicitud
3. vestirse bien para la entrevista
4. no dar datos falsos sobre la experiencia laboral
5. no decir mentiras al entrevistador
6. no sacar el maquillaje durante la entrevista
7. no poner los datos personales en la carta de presentación
8. no irse sin decir «gracias» luego de la entrevista

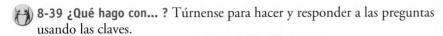

8-39 ¿Qué hago con... ? Túrnense para hacer y responder a las preguntas usando las claves.

> MODELO   las cartas / no mandar / corregir
> E1: *¿Qué hago con las cartas?*
> E2: *No las mande. Corríjalas.*

1. estos documentos / organizar
2. los papeles / poner en el escritorio
3. esta hoja de vida / no archivar / dejar en la mesa
4. las computadoras / apagar
5. mis correcciones / no escribir en el margen / escribir en otro papel
6. estos libros / llevar a la sala de reuniones
7. las fotocopias / no distribuir / contar
8. mi almuerzo / meter en el refrigerador

8-40 Antes de una entrevista Escriban una lista de recomendaciones sobre lo que las personas deben hacer y no deben hacer antes y durante una entrevista de trabajo. Usen los verbos de la lista.

> MODELO   levantarse: *No se levanten tarde. / Levántense temprano.*

OPCIONES: bañarse   ponerse perfume   desayunarse   peinarse
maquillarse   llegar...   saludar   despedirse   conversar
estar...   ponerse ropa...   irse...   ponerse (adjetivo)

■ Integración

8-41 Conseguir un buen empleo Representa la siguiente situación con dos compañeros(as).

Consejero(a) estudiantil	Estudiantes preocupados(as)
Tú eres consejero(a) estudiantil y estás hablando con dos estudiantes que quieren saber qué deben hacer y qué no deben hacer para asegurarse de conseguir un buen empleo cuando se gradúen. Escúchalos(las) y dales las recomendaciones pertinentes.	Tu amigo(a) y tú están preocupados(as) y están hablando con un(a) consejero(a) estudiantil. Uds. quieren saber qué deben hacer y qué no deben hacer para conseguir un buen empleo cuando se gradúen de la universidad. Explíquenle su preocupación y pídanle un consejo.

8-42 Un volante *(flier)* Como quedaste tan satisfecho(a) después de hablar con el (la) consejero(a) de la actividad 8-41, decidiste preparar un volante informativo para los estudiantes de tu universidad. Incluye las cosas que los estudiantes deben hacer y no deben hacer para conseguir un buen trabajo después de graduarse. Cuando termines, dale una copia a un(a) compañero(a) para que te dé su opinión.

SUGERENCIAS

Puedes usar expresiones de apoyo *(support)* como: **No se preocupen.** *(Don't worry.)* **Sigan adelante.** *(Keep going.)* **Tengan paciencia.** *(Be patient.)* **Sean optimistas.** *(Be optimistic.)* **Confíen en Uds. mismos(as).** *(Have faith in yourselves.)*

SUGERENCIAS

Para reflejar preocupación, pueden usar las siguientes expresiones: **¿Qué hacemos?** *(What do we do?)* **No sabemos qué hacer.** *(We do not know what to do.)* **Estamos preocupados(as).** *(We are worried.)* **Aconséjenos, por favor.** *(Advise us, please.)*

IV. Vídeo: El secreto de Sofía

■ Preparación

 A. ¡Secretos, secretos! Sofía tiene un secreto que está a punto de ser revelado. Antes de ver el vídeo, piensen en lo que ya saben de Sofía (qué tipo de persona es, qué le interesa, etc.) y completen las oraciones.

- Creemos que el secreto de Sofía es que ella...
- Es posible que ése sea su secreto porque...

Ahora, presenten su opinión a la clase. Un(a) voluntario(a) debe escribir las ideas de cada grupo en la pizarra. ¡Veamos si algún grupo adivinó correctamente el secreto de Sofía!

■ ¿Entendiste bien?

ESTRATEGIA DE COMPRENSIÓN

Scanning Concentrate on identifying the information requested in **Paso 1** of activity B.

B. Sofía revela su secreto Esta actividad se divide en dos pasos. Primero vas a contestar algunas preguntas específicas sobre lo que pasa en el segmento. Luego vas a adivinar y a seguir viendo el segmento para averiguar si tenías razón o no.

Paso 1: Lee las siguientes preguntas y luego mira el vídeo para poder contestarlas.

1. Al principio Sofía le mintió a Javier sobre lo que leía en el periódico. Le dijo que...
   a. leía su horóscopo.
   b. leía los resultados de la lotería.
   c. leía los anuncios.
2. ¿Qué hacía Sofía *de verdad* cuando Javier la asustó?
   a. Leía su horóscopo.
   b. Leía los resultados de la lotería.
   c. Leía los anuncios.

3. Completa la siguiente información sobre el plan de Sofía:

Sofía le confesó a Javier que leía el periódico porque buscaba un
_____. Le contó su plan de quedarse a vivir en
_____ después de que termine el mes del proyecto.
También le dijo que fue algo que pensó antes de venir, desde que
estaba en _____. Luego, Sofía reveló la razón principal
de su decisión: quiere _____.

4. ¿Dónde ha pensado Sofía buscar trabajo? ¿Haciendo qué?

Paso 2: Compara tus respuestas al **Paso 1** con las de un(a) compañero(a).
Luego, contesten las siguientes preguntas sobre el trabajo de Sofía
antes de ver la conclusión del segmento.

1. ¿Creen que Sofía ha conseguido el tipo de trabajo que quería?
   ¿Por qué sí o no?
2. ¿Dónde creen que trabaja Sofía? ¿Por qué?
3. Basándose en su respuesta a la pregunta 2, den ejemplos de por lo
   menos cinco actividades que creen que Sofía ha hecho en su trabajo.

C. Nuestros sueños en la vida Todos tenemos aspiraciones y sueños personales y profesionales que queremos realizar *(fulfill)*. Pueden ser cosas
fáciles o difíciles de conseguir; por ejemplo, vivir en otro país, aprender
un idioma, practicar un deporte, graduarse, conseguir un trabajo, tener
un carro y una casa propios, etc. En esta actividad vas a pensar en un
sueño tuyo y luego vas a compartirlo con tus compañeros(as) de clase.

Paso 1: Mi sueño ¿Cuál es tu sueño? Puede ser algo que ahora mismo
estás intentado realizar o algo que ya has realizado. Contesta las preguntas
correspondientes.

OPCIÓN A: Un sueño que estás tratando de realizar

- ¿Le has revelado tu sueño a alguien, por ejemplo, a un(a) amigo(a)
  o a un miembro de tu familia? ¿Por qué sí o por qué no? Si has
  respondido que sí, ¿cómo reaccionó esa persona? ¿Te ha apoyado
  (supported)? ¿Te ha ofrecido ayuda para alcanzar tu sueño?

- ¿Qué has hecho para realizar tu sueño? Sé específico(a). Piensa en tus
  acciones y en el tiempo que ha sido necesario para realizar cada acción.

OPCIÓN B: Un sueño que ya has realizado

- ¿Fue un secreto tu sueño o lo compartiste con un(a) amigo(a) o
  miembro de tu familia? ¿Por qué?

- ¿Qué hiciste para realizar tu sueño? Sé específico(a). Piensa en cada
  acción que hiciste y en el tiempo que te llevó hacer cada acción.

- ¿Cómo te sentiste al realizar tu sueño?

Paso 2: Nuestros sueños Trabajando en grupos, túrnense para hacerle
preguntas a cada miembro del grupo sobre su sueño.

D. Enfoque comunitario Un sueño común que casi todos los inmigrantes
tienen es conseguir un empleo en el país al que se han mudado. Entrevista a un(a) inmigrante que viva en tu comunidad. Pregúntale cómo
consiguió su empleo, si está contento(a) con su trabajo y con su forma de
vida, y qué actividades hace cada día. Presenta un informe oral en clase.

El nuevo empleo

I. Vocabulario: Las tareas de oficina

atender (ie) al público

asistir a reuniones

preparar informes

imprimir expedientes

(enviar/recibir) un fax

(hacer/recibir) llamadas telefónicas

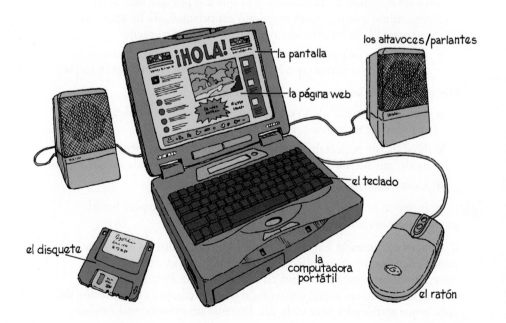

la pantalla

la página web

los altavoces/parlantes

el teclado

el disquete

la computadora portátil

el ratón

Vocabulario práctico

el archivo *file*
el correo electrónico *e-mail*

Verbos

abrir un programa *to open a program*
cerrar [ie] / abandonar un programa *to close / to quit a program*
consultar un motor de búsqueda *to use a search engine*
encender [ie] / apagar la computadora *to turn on / to turn off the computer*
enviar un mensaje electrónico *to send an e-mail*

guardar un documento *to save a document*
hacer clic / oprimir / cliquear *to click*
imprimir un documento *to print a document*
insertar el disco *to insert the CD*
instalar un programa *to install a program*
navegar el (la) Internet *to surf the net*
revisar el buzón/correo *to check the mailbox*

▦ Asimilación

8-43 ¿En qué orden? Indica el orden lógico de las siguientes actividades. Al terminar, compara tus respuestas con las de un(a) compañero(a). ¿Están de acuerdo?

_____ apagar la computadora
_____ encender la computadora
_____ abrir el programa de navegación

_____ imprimir el documento deseado
_____ consultar un motor de búsqueda
_____ cerrar el programa de navegación

CD2–20 **8-44 Instrucciones** Tu jefe ha tenido problemas con su vuelo y te ha dejado un mensaje en el contestador. Indica qué cosas debes hacer, según sus indicaciones.

_____ Atender a unos clientes
_____ Asistir a una reunión
_____ Buscar unos documentos

_____ Preparar un informe
_____ Imprimir un informe
_____ Enviar un fax

▦ Aplicaciones

8-45 Tareas Completa el párrafo con la palabra más apropiada.

OPCIONES: hacer unas llamadas   imprimir   preparar un informe
asistir

Tengo mucho que hacer hoy. Primero tengo que _____ para presentarlo esta tarde en la reunión de inversionistas y luego tengo que _____ quince copias para todos los asistentes. Al mediodía tengo que _____ a un almuerzo de negocios con mi jefe y en la tarde debo _____ a varios clientes en la capital. Va a ser un día muy largo.

8-46 Experiencia Ustedes trabajan en una compañía multinacional y necesitan un(a) nuevo(a) secretario(a). Preparen por lo menos cinco preguntas para evaluar la experiencia de los aspirantes.

> MODELO   *¿Ha preparado Ud. un informe alguna vez? ¿Ha enviado un fax?*

8-47 Entrevista Hazle las siguientes preguntas a un(a) compañero(a) y prepara un breve informe sobre sus respuestas.

1. ¿Te interesan las computadoras?
2. ¿Qué tipo de computadora tienes?
3. ¿Con qué frecuencia la usas? ¿Para qué la usas?
4. ¿Cuáles son tus programas favoritos? (¿Procesador de textos? ¿Procesador de datos? ¿Navegador? ¿Otros?)
5. En tu opinión, ¿qué es lo mejor de las computadoras? ¿Y lo peor?

■ Integración

 8-48 Entrevista de trabajo Representa la siguiente situación con un(a) compañero(a).

Entrevistador(a)	Aspirante
Usted trabaja para una compañía multinacional y tiene que contratar a un(a) asistente de oficina. Esta persona debe poder hablar español y tiene que ser capaz de desempeñar diferentes tareas de oficina (como hacer y recibir llamadas, preparar informes, usar la computadora, etc.). Entreviste a este(a) aspirante y determine si debe ser contratado(a) para ese puesto.	Usted necesita un trabajo y sabe que esta compañía multinacional busca un(a) asistente de oficina. Convenza al / a la entrevistador(a) de que Ud. puede desempeñar muy bien las diferentes tareas que se requieren (hacer y recibir llamadas, preparar informes, usar la computadora, etc.).

8-49 Carta de presentación Amplía la carta de presentación que preparaste en el **Tema 2** de este capítulo para incluir tus habilidades con respecto a tareas de oficina y computación.

II. Funciones y estructuras: Avoiding stating who or what is performing an action with the passive *se*

Para buscar información en el Internet, **se enciende** la computadora, **se consulta** un motor de búsqueda y **se escriben** las palabras clave.

In Spanish, when you do not want to (or cannot) specify who or what is performing an action, you may use a passive **se** construction. This construction consists of the pronoun **se** followed by the third-person form of the verb. It translates as *is/are + -ed* or as a generic *they* in English.

> This *they* is considered generic because it does not refer to anybody or anything in particular, as in the sentence: *On TV* **they** *said that it is going to rain tomorrow.*

Aquí **se contesta** el teléfono rápidamente.	*Here the phone **is answered** quickly. (**they** answer the phone quickly)*
Y **se preparan** informes diariamente.	*And reports **are prepared** daily. (**they** prepare reports daily)*

As you may have noticed, the number of the verb (singular or plural) is determined by the number of the noun that follows, which is actually the subject of the sentence.

se +	{ verb in the third person singular +	singular noun }
	{ verb in the third person plural +	plural noun }

The passive **se** is often used to talk about activities that are performed on a regular basis and activities that are associated with specific places.

En Japón **se** fabrican muchas computadoras.	*In Japan **they** make a lot of computers.*
En esta tienda **se** vende lo mejor en tecnología.	*In this store **they** sell the best in technology.*

Here is a list of expressions with **se.**

se incluye(n)...	*. . . is/are included*
se necesita(n)...	*. . . is/are necessary*
se recomienda(n)...	*. . . is/are recommended*
se require(n)...	*. . . is/are required*
se vende(n)...	*. . . is/are sold*

> The verbs in these expressions are used in the third-person singular when they are followed by an infinitive: **Se recomienda leer las instrucciones.** *(Reading the instructions is recommended.)*

■ **Asimilación**

8-50 ¿Qué se hace? Usa números para poner en orden las oraciones de cada grupo. Cuando termines, compara tus respuestas con las de un(a) compañero(a). ¿Están de acuerdo?

1. Para guardar un documento...

_____ se selecciona «guardar» del menú

_____ se oprime «guardar»

_____ se da un nombre al documento

2. Para enviar un mensaje electrónico...

_____ se oprime «enviar»

_____ se escribe el mensaje

_____ se entra al buzón personal

3. Para imprimir un documento...

_____ se especifican las páginas que se van a imprimir

_____ se selecciona «imprimir» del menú

_____ se oprime «imprimir»

CD2-21 **8-51 En el nuevo empleo** Escucha la descripción que da Pablo de su nuevo empleo y escribe cada actividad en la categoría correcta.

OPCIONES: imprimir los documentos   enviar las cartas
archivar la información   organizar las oficinas
asistir a reuniones   atender al público   recibir las llamadas
hacer el mantenimiento de las computadoras

Temprano en la mañana	Antes del mediodía	Por la tarde

■ **Aplicaciones**

8-52 En diferentes lugares Digan qué se hace en los siguientes lugares.

MODELO   En una biblioteca *se leen libros y revistas, y se estudia.*

1. En un restaurante...
2. En una iglesia...
3. En una oficina de correos...
4. En una plaza...
5. En la clase de español...
6. En una tienda de ropa...
7. En un museo...
8. En un aeropuerto...

8-53 Productos internacionales Indiquen qué se produce o se fabrica en los siguientes países.

MODELO   Alemania: *En Alemania se fabrican carros de muy buena calidad.*

1. Venezuela
2. Rusia
3. Italia
4. Holanda
5. Francia
6. Sudáfrica
7. Chile
8. Estados Unidos

8-54 En casa

Paso 1: Escribe por lo menos tres actividades que se hacen en tu casa en los siguientes días.

Los sábados	Los domingos	Los miércoles

Paso 2: Compara tu información con la de dos compañeros y prepara un informe breve.

MODELO   *En nuestras casas se... y se... los sábados. En la casa de... también se..., pero en mi casa se... los... y en la casa de... se... los...*

■ Integración

8-55 ¡Por fin! ¡Tu compañero(a) y tú ya saben todo lo que hay que saber para obtener un buen empleo! Hagan un recuento *(summary)* de todos los pasos que se deben seguir. Incorporen el vocabulario de este capítulo e indiquen qué se recomienda, qué se necesita y qué se requiere.

8-56 Ahora, ¡por escrito! Haz un repaso escrito de la información que tu compañero(a) y tú mencionaron en la actividad 8-55. Al terminar, dale una copia a tu compañero(a) para que te dé ideas. Organiza tu repaso siguiendo el siguiente esquema:

- En una carta de presentación se incluye(n):
- En una hoja de vida se incluye(n):
- Para obtener un buen empleo se requiere(n):
- Para obtener un buen empleo se recomienda(n):

III. Funciones y estructuras: Avoiding repetition using double object pronouns

MANOLO:	¡Coral, felicidades por el nuevo empleo!
CORAL:	¡Gracias! **Me lo** ofrecieron el lunes.
MANOLO:	Me alegro. Voy a decír**selo** a Felipe.

REMEMBER

Think of the mnemonic **I-D**
(**I** = indirect, **D** = direct).

When both direct and indirect object pronouns are used in a sentence, the indirect object pronoun always precedes the direct object pronoun. No other word may break the unity of these two pronouns.

¿La computadora? **Te la** voy a encender ahora mismo.

¿El documento? Guárda**melo**, por favor.

*The computer? I am going to turn **it** on **for you** right now.*

*The document? Save **it for me**, please.*

When the indirect object pronouns **le** and **les** are used before the direct object pronouns **lo, la, los** or **las,** the indirect object pronoun changes to **se.** Remember that a phrase introduced by the preposition **a** can be used to specify the referent of **se.**

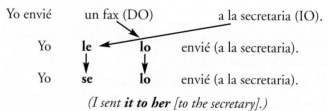

Yo envié   un fax (DO)   a la secretaria (IO).

Yo   **le** ← **lo**   envié (a la secretaria).

Yo   **se**   **lo**   envié (a la secretaria).

*(I sent **it to her** [to the secretary].)*

Indirect and direct object pronouns are placed:

- before conjugated verbs (but after negative words like **no** and **nunca**):

Me lo <u>contaron</u> ayer.   *They told (**it to**) **me** yesterday.*
Se las <u>quiero</u> comprar a ella.   *I want to buy **them for her.***
¿Ellos nunca **te la** <u>entregaron</u>?   *They never delivered **it to you**?*

REMEMBER

Pronouns may also be placed before the auxiliary verb: ***Se lo vamos a dar hoy.***

- attached to infinitives and past participles in verb phrases:

Vamos a <u>arreglár**telo**</u>   *We are going to fix **it for you***
    mañana.   *tomorrow.*
Están <u>preparándo**melas**</u>   *They are preparing **them for***
    ahora.   ***me** now.*

- attached to affirmative commands:

Sra. López, <u>dé</u>**melos,** por   *Mrs. López, give **them to me**,*
    favor.   *please.*
Chicos, <u>póngan</u>**selo** ahí.   *Guys, put **it** there **for him**.*

- between **no** and the verb in negative commands:

<u>No</u> **me la** <u>expliques</u> todavía.   *Do not explain **it to me** yet.*
Señores, <u>no</u> **se lo** <u>instalen</u>   *Gentlemen, do not install **it for***
    hoy.   ***him** today.*

■ Asimilación

8-57 Publicidad ¿Puedes encontrar el verbo con pronombre de objeto indirecto y objeto directo en el anuncio? ¿A qué se refieren estos pronombres? Contesta estas preguntas y compara tus respuestas con las de un(a) compañero(a). ¿Han respondido lo mismo?

EL FUEGO DE LA ACIDEZ SE LO QUITA EL BUEN SABOR DE MAALOX

Rápido alivio

El más usado en el mundo

Agradables sabores de Menta y Cereza

Maalox Plus

CD2–22 **8-58 Preguntas y respuestas** Escucha las preguntas y selecciona las respuestas más lógicas.

1. a. Te los va a archivar. b. Me la va a archivar.
2. a. Voy a traértela hoy. b. Voy a traérsela hoy.
3. a. Quiero devolvérsela. b. Quiero devolvérselo.
4. a. Estamos organizándotelas. b. Estamos organizándoselo.
5. a. No se los envíes todavía. b. No me los envíes todavía.

■ Aplicaciones

8-59 Ayer en la oficina Ayer ocurrieron cosas que normalmente no ocurren en la oficina. Uno(a) de Uds. faltó al trabajo *(took the day off)* y el (la) otro(a) lo está poniendo al día *(giving you an update)*. Túrnense para ser la persona que faltó.

MODELO   E1: *Gabriela nos trajo el desayuno a todos los empleados.*
E2: *¿Qué?*
E1: *Sí, Gabriela nos lo trajo.*

1. La Sra. Padró les devolvió las evaluaciones a las secretarias.
2. El contable me dio los informes.
3. Lola le entregó su renuncia al director.
4. Le instalé el monitor nuevo a mi compañero.
5. Pedro te guardó los documentos en la computadora.
6. Rosa y yo le enviamos los faxes a Esteban.
7. Saúl le atendió los clientes al Sr. García.
8. El mensajero me llevó las cartas a la oficina de correos.

8-60 Hoy en la oficina Ahora, túrnense para hacer y responder preguntas sobre las personas que se están encargando de hacer diferentes actividades en este momento en la oficina. Miren el dibujo y usen los verbos de la lista.

MODELO   E1: *¿Y las copias del Sr. Feliciano?*
                E2: *José se las está haciendo. / José está sacándoselas.*

OPCIONES: preparar hacer dar instalar buscar enviar

1. ¿Y el informe de la Sra. Salazar?
2. ¿Y el monitor de Leonor y Beatriz?
3. ¿Y la computadora de Eulalia?
4. ¿Y los expedientes del Lic. Balboa?
5. ¿Y el fax del Lic. Guzmán y del Lic. Rubio?

8-61 Mañana en la oficina Tu compañero(a) y tú son muy organizados y quieren saber exactamente qué deben hacer mañana en la oficina. Túrnense para hacer y responder a preguntas usando las claves.

> MODELO E1: *¿Qué hago con estos sobres?* (mandar / a Héctor)
> E2: *Mándeselos a Héctor.*

1. ¿Qué hago con esta impresora? (dejar / a mí / ahí)
2. ¿Y con estas solicitudes? (<u>no</u> llevar / al Sr. Rodríguez – llevar / a la Srta. Ochoteco)
3. ¿Qué hago con el informe del personal? (<u>no</u> imprimir / a mí – guardar en la computadora / a mí)
4. ¿Y qué hago con los mensajes del Sr. Torres? (revisar / a él)
5. ¿Y el programa nuevo? (instalar / a nosostros)
6. ¿Qué hago con los discos? (<u>no</u> sacar de aquí / a mí – poner en el escritorio / a Ángel)

■ **Integración**

8-62 Pertenencias *(Belongings)* Individualmente, hagan una lista de los cinco objetos más preciados *(most valued)* que tienen y otra lista de cinco cosas que tienen y de las que quieren deshacerse *(want to give away)*. Cuando terminen, intercambien papeles. Luego, túrnense para hacer y responder a preguntas sobre quién les dio las cosas más preciadas y a quién les van a dar las cosas de las que se quieren deshacer.

> MODELOS E1: *Los aretes de oro, ¿te los dio/regaló tu madre?*
> E2: *No, me los dio/regaló mi abuelo.*
> E1: *La mesa de noche, ¿se la vas a dar a tu hermana menor?*
> E2: *No, voy a dársela a mi prima.*

8-63 Carta de presentación En parejas, revisen las cartas de presentación que han venido preparando en este capítulo. ¿Necesitan usar pronombres para evitar repeticiones innecesarias? Identifiquen las frases que se pueden mejorar y hagan las debidas correcciones en casa. Entréguenle una copia al / a la profesor(a) en la próxima clase.

IV. Lectura: «Mi amigo»

■ Antes de leer

A. Para conversar Contesten las siguientes preguntas.

1. ¿Qué es una «disculpa» o una «excusa»?
2. ¿En qué circunstancias se usan las disculpas? Indiquen las más apropiadas.

   ____ cuando no se quiere hacer algo

   ____ cuando no se puede hacer algo

   ____ cuando se tienen otros compromisos (obligaciones)

   ____ otras circunstancias:

3. ¿Consideran que las excusas o disculpas son buenas o malas? Expliquen por qué.

B. Vocabulario y conceptos Las siguientes palabras son importantes para la comprensión de la lectura. Para cada palabra, indiquen la letra de la definición apropiada.

____ 1. obstáculo	a. cosas útiles o indispensables
____ 2. interferencias	b. pagar, sostener
____ 3. faltar	c. no tener, necesitar
____ 4. necesidades	d. problemas, intromisiones
____ 5. mantener	e. impedimento, dificultad

■ A leer

Germán Cuervo

Germán Cuervo es un pintor y cuentista nacido en Cali, Colombia, en 1950. Es autor de varios libros de cuentos y novelas, entre ellos *Los indios que mató John Wayne* (1985), *Historias de amor, salsa y dolor* (1990) y *El mar* (1994).

«Mi amigo»

Mi amigo quería ser escritor, pero no podía hacerlo porque no tenía máquina de escribir. Al fin consiguió una. Aún así, no pudo comenzar, pues le hacía falta una habitación privada. **Al cabo de** dos días pudo saltar ese obstáculo, pero en aquella nueva habitación había mucho ruido e interferencias. Fue **preciso,** entonces, **conseguir** una casa. **Tomando prestado** de aquí y allá, con ayuda de su familia, mi amigo pudo conseguir una casa solitaria y **retirada** para poder comenzar su trabajo de escritura.

after

necesario / to find
Borrowing

distant

Said and done
endeavor / at the end of, after

Al cabo de un tiempo me lo encontré en la calle muy deprimido y le pregunté qué le pasaba. «Ya tengo máquina de escribir, un cuarto y una casa —me dijo— sin embargo, no puedo hacerlo. Algo muy importante me hace falta para poder escribir; me hace falta una mujer. Necesito compañía». **Dicho y hecho,** mi amigo se puso en aquel **empeño** y **a la vuelta** de los días tenía una mujer cálida y buena que lo acompañaba en su difícil trabajo de la escritura. Ahora solamente le faltaba ponerse a hacerlo; sin embargo, no lo hizo, pues si ya tenía máquina, cuarto, casa retirada y mujer, le hacía falta, **por añadidura lógica,** un auto. Se puso entonces en ese empeño consiguiendo un trabajo que le **devengaba** el dinero suficiente para mantener esa cadena de necesidades. La última vez que lo encontré le pregunté si estaba escribiendo.

after all
daba

«No —me contestó—. Si ya tengo máquina de escribir, cuarto, casa, mujer, carro y trabajo, para qué me voy a poner a escribir. Ahora estoy viendo cómo conseguir un betamax».

■ ¿Entendiste bien?

C. ¿En qué orden sucedieron los hechos? Ordenen los siguientes eventos de la historia.

_____ Su amigo consiguió un auto.

_____ Su amigo consiguió un trabajo.

_____ Su amigo consiguió una esposa.

_____ Su amigo consiguió una casa tranquila.

_____ Su amigo consiguió una máquina de escribir.

_____ Su amigo consiguió una habitación privada.

D. Para conversar ¿Por qué creen Uds. que este hombre nunca pudo ser escritor?

E. Enfoque lingüístico Clasifiquen los verbos que se usan en la lectura.

REMEMBER

- The preterite tense is used to narrate completed past events.
- The imperfect tense is used to provide background descriptions and to talk about habitual or ongoing actions in the past.

Pretérito (narración de eventos pasados)	Imperfecto (descripciones, acciones habituales en el pasado)

F. Enfoque comunitario Entrevisten a algún (alguna) artista o profesional de habla hispana acerca de qué obstáculos encontró mientras estaba comenzando a practicar su arte o profesión. Pregúntenle cómo superó *(overcame)* esos obstáculos. Después, presenten una breve biografía de esa persona a la clase.

Los anuncios clasificados | *Classified ads*

la buena presencia	*good personal appearance*
la facilidad de expresión	*ease of expression, ability to speak*
la hoja de vida / el currículum	*résumé*
el técnico	*technician*
el trabajador no calificado	*unqualified worker*

Verbos para hablar de buscar trabajo

arreglar/reparar	*to fix*
colaborar	*to collaborate*
cuidar	*to care for, to watch over*
defender (ie)	*to defend*
encargarse de + *verb*	*to be responsible for doing something*
entretener (ie)	*to entertain*
manejar	*to operate, to handle*
presentarse	*to present oneself, to appear*
solicitar	*to request*

La hoja de vida | *Résumé*

la carta de presentación	*cover letter*
los datos personales	*personal information*
la entrevista	*interview*
los estudios realizados	*studies completed*
la experiencia laboral	*work experience*
la fecha de grado	*graduation date*
la matrícula/licencia profesional	*professional license*
solicitar trabajo	*to apply for a job*
la solicitud	*application*

Las tareas de oficina | *Office duties*

atender (ie) al público	*to deal with customers*
asistir a reuniones	*to attend meetings*
preparar informes	*to prepare reports*
imprimir expedientes	*to print files*
enviar/recibir un fax	*to send/receive a fax*
hacer/recibir llamadas telefónicas	*to make/receive phone calls*

Las computadoras/ los ordenadores | *Computers*

el archivo	*file*
el CD	*CD-ROM*
la computadora portátil	*laptop computer*
el correo electrónico	*e-mail*
la impresora	*printer*
la pantalla	*screen*
los parlantes/altavoces	*speakers*
el ratón	*mouse*
el teclado	*keyboard*

Verbos para hablar de las computadoras

abrir un programa	*to open a program*
cerrar (ie) / abandonar un programa	*to close / to quit a program*
consultar un motor de búsqueda	*to use a search engine*
encender (ie) / apagar la computadora	*to turn on / to turn off the computer*
enviar un mensaje electrónico	*to send an e-mail*
guardar un documento	*to save a document*
hacer clic/oprimir/ cliquear	*to click*
imprimir un documento	*to print a document*
insertar el disco	*to insert the CD*
instalar un programa	*to install a program*
navegar el (la) Internet	*to surf the net*
revisar el buzón	*to check the mailbox*

Funciones y estructuras

Expresiones de tiempo que se usan con el pretérito perfecto, pp. 313

Expresiones con **se,** p. 327

Puesta en acción

SITUACIÓN:	La empresa multinacional para la que trabajas te ha anunciado que tiene planes de trasladarte a Caracas, Venezuela, para abrir una nueva oficina regional.
MISIÓN:	Coordinar la mudanza, organizar tu nueva casa y establecer la nueva oficina regional de tu compañía en Venezuela.
DESTREZAS:	Planificar un viaje internacional de negocios, ir a una entrevista y escribir una carta y un mensaje electrónico de negocios.

1. La mudanza

A. La mudanza a Venezuela Lee el siguiente mensaje electrónico y luego contesta las preguntas.

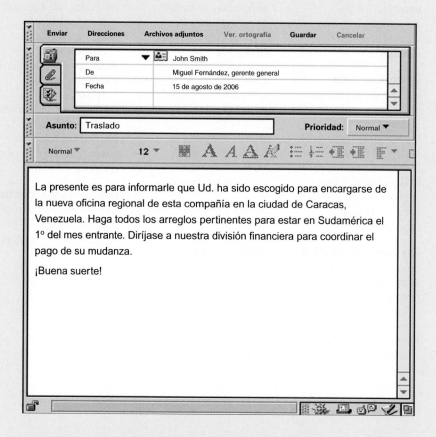

Enviar	Direcciones	Archivos adjuntos	Ver. ortografía	Guardar	Cancelar

Para	▼	John Smith
De		Miguel Fernández, gerente general
Fecha		15 de agosto de 2006

Asunto: Traslado   **Prioridad:** Normal ▼

Normal ▼   12 ▼

La presente es para informarle que Ud. ha sido escogido para encargarse de la nueva oficina regional de esta compañía en la ciudad de Caracas, Venezuela. Haga todos los arreglos pertinentes para estar en Sudamérica el 1º del mes entrante. Diríjase a nuestra división financiera para coordinar el pago de su mudanza.

¡Buena suerte!

- ¿Qué te dice el gerente general de la compañía?
- ¿Cuándo comienza la nueva asignación?
- ¿Quién va a pagar la mudanza?

B. ¿Qué tengo que hacer? Preparen una lista de los preparativos que necesitan hacer para el viaje.

Llamar a...	Ir a...	Obtener...

CRITICAL THINKING
SKILLS

Prioritizing Determine essential
elements for successful planning.

C. En la agencia de viajes Representa la siguiente situación con un(a) compañero(a).

Empleado(a) trasladado(a)	Agente de viajes
Tu compañía te va a trasladar a Caracas, Venezuela, y necesitas hacer los preparativos para el viaje. Habla con tu agente de viajes para hacer los arreglos necesarios.	Uno(a) de tus clientes ha sido trasladado(a) a Caracas, Venezuela, por su compañía. Ayúdale a hacer los arreglos correspondientes. Tu cliente necesita:

Empleado(a) trasladado(a):
- compra los boletos de avión,
- haz las reservaciones en un buen hotel de Caracas y
- pide información general sobre Venezuela, tal como: lugares para visitar, cosas que hay que saber, el clima, la ropa que se debe llevar, etc.

Agente de viajes:
- boletos de avión,
- reservaciones en un buen hotel e
- información general sobre Venezuela.

D. Dinero Ahora, completa esta carta para concretar los aspectos financieros de tu traslado. Escribe **por** o **para.**

Miami, 20 de agosto de 2006

Señores:
Banco Central de Venezuela

Me mudo _____ Venezuela el mes entrante y necesito saber qué debo hacer _____ transferir mi dinero electrónicamente desde mi banco en los Estados Unidos. _____ mí es muy importante tener acceso fácil e inmediato a mi dinero. Además, _____ favor, díganme qué documentos exigen _____ abrir una cuenta corriente y qué servicios especiales tienen _____ sus clientes.

Muchísimas gracias _____ su gentil ayuda.

Atentamente,

_____

E. En busca de una casa Ahora, escribe una carta a la inmobiliaria Sabana Grande en Caracas con una descripción de tu casa ideal. (Usa la carta anterior como guía.) Asegúrate de incluir la siguiente información:

- ubicación
- número de habitaciones
- tipo de vecindario
- precio

2. La organización de la nueva oficina regional

F. Prioridades Lo primero que necesitas es un(a) asistente. Escribe el anuncio clasificado correspondiente. (Usa los anuncios clasificados de la actividad de **Asimilación 8.1,** pág. 307, como modelo.)

G. Datos sobre los aspirantes Túrnense para hacer y responder a preguntas sobre la información de los aspirantes al puesto de asistente.

Estudiante 1

Nombre	Especialidad	Años de experiencia	Datos sobresalientes	Lo que le gusta del puesto
Celia Mercado		8		
	finanzas			el prestigio de la compañía
		12	ha trabajado para la compañía	
Sonia Useche	ciencias secretariales		ha terminado sus estudios de postgrado	la oportunidad de ascender
Julio Beltrán		3		

Estudiante 2

Nombre	Especialidad	Años de experiencia	Datos sobresalientes	Lo que le gusta del puesto
	administración de empresas		ha vivido en el extranjero	la flexibilidad del horario
Arturo Mejías		10	ha estudiado tres lenguas	
Demetrio Salas	economía			la oportunidad de quedarse en Venezuela
		2		
	relaciones públicas		ha recibido premios por su trabajo	trabajar para esta compañía

Estudiante 2 must turn the book upside down.

 H. Entrevista de trabajo Representa la siguiente situación con un(a) compañero(a).

Jefe(a)	Aspirante
Vas a entrevistar a uno(a) de los aspirantes al puesto de asistente. Por medio de preguntas, determina si ésta es la persona con quien quieres trabajar. Averigua: ■ sus antecedentes académicos ■ sus antecedentes laborales ■ algunas de sus características personales	Tienes la gran oportunidad de trabajar en una compañía multinacional. Asegúrate de dar una buena impresión durante la entrevista. Habla de: ■ los estudios que has hecho ■ las experiencias laborales que has tenido ■ tus cualidades personales más sobresalientes

 I. Instrucciones Completen el siguiente mensaje electrónico con las tareas que debe hacer el (la) asistente el día de hoy.

a. Conversa con un(a) compañero(a) sobre las tareas más importantes que debe realizar este(a) asistente el primer día de trabajo.
b. Organiza las actividades en orden de prioridad.
c. Escribe los mandatos correspondientes.
d. Prepara un saludo y una despedida apropiados para este tipo de comunicación electrónica.

CRITICAL THINKING SKILLS

Prioritizing List the most important tasks a manager's new assistant might have to do.

Intercambia este primer borrador con otro(a) estudiante y respondan a las siguientes preguntas:

Paso 1: Contenido. ¿La carta incluye toda la información necesaria? Si no es así, ¿qué falta?

Paso 2: Organización. ¿Están claras las tareas y las prioridades? ¿El mensaje tiene un saludo y una despedida?

Paso 3: Gramática. ¿Los mandatos formales están bien formados?

Para hacer en casa:

Paso 4: Revisión. Revisa tu carta y entrégasela a tu profesor(a) el día de la próxima clase.

| Enviar | Direcciones | Archivos adjuntos | Ver. ortografía | Guardar | Cancelar |

Para
De
Fecha

Asunto: | Prioridad: Normal ▼

Normal ▼   12 ▼

_____:
Las siguientes son sus tareas para el día de hoy:
1.
2.
3.
4.
...
_____

Servicio comunitario

Contact your local school district and offer to provide one of the following services:

- Buddy system for students who recently moved to your area.
- Basic computer courses for students and their parents.
- Workshops on how to prepare a résumé and a cover letter for youngsters who wish to get a part-time or summer job.

Guatemala, Honduras, El Salvador, Argentina y Uruguay

In this unit you will talk about relationships (friendship, love, and conflict), fitness, health, and leisure. Also, you will learn to make suggestions, express emotions, and talk about hypothetical situations. The readings will explore issues pertaining to relationships and leisure time activities. In turn, the videos will show you how South American people spend their free time. At the end of the unit, you will design a personal enrichment program for workers in a Spanish-speaking corporate setting. You will also be able to connect with your community by providing services at a local community center.

Interacciones

Capítulo

9

Acuerdos y desacuerdos

Para comenzar

Escoge la descripción más apropriada para cada fotografía:

- El futuro de El Salvador
- La tradición indígena de Guatemala
- La producción agrícola de Honduras

In this chapter you will learn . . .

- how to describe different types of personal relationships (with friends, with coworkers, with spouses, etc.)
- how to make suggestions
- how to express emotions
- how to express doubt
- how to talk about hypothetical situations
- about interpersonal relationships in the Spanish-speaking world

	TEMA 1 Las amistades	**TEMA 2** Relaciones laborales	**TEMA 3** Relaciones de pareja
Vocabulario	Un buen amigo	Los compañeros y los jefes	Amor, noviazgo y matrimonio
Funciones y estructuras	Giving advice with the subjunctive (regular verbs) Giving advice with the subjunctive (irregular verbs)	Expressing wishes and requests Expressing emotions and feelings	Expressing doubt and denial Talking about hypothetical situations with the subjunctive
Lecturas y vídeo	Perspectivas: La timidez	Vídeo: ¿Algo más que una amistad?	Lectura: La hija del caníbal

Foto 1

Foto 2

Foto 3

Enfoque

For more info, you may want to check the **Temas** site: http://temas.heinle.com

A. ¿Qué sabes ya de Guatemala? Antes de ver el vídeo, decide si las siguientes oraciones son ciertas **(C)** o falsas **(F).** Después, compara tus respuestas con las de un(a) compañero(a) y corrijan las oraciones falsas.

_____ 1. Guatemala es el país más al sur de Centroamérica.

_____ 2. La mayoría de los guatemaltecos son mestizos, una combinación de lo indígena y lo europeo.

_____ 3. El 40% de la población vive en la pobreza.

_____ 4. En Guatemala hubo una guerra que duró 36 años. Terminó formalmente en 1996, cuando el gobierno firmó un tratado *(treaty).*

_____ 5. La base de la economía guatemalteca es el petróleo.

B. La ciudad de Antigua Lee las oraciones que aparecen a continuación sobre la ciudad de Antigua. Mientras ves el vídeo, marca con una **X** las oraciones que escuches. Después, compara tus respuestas con tres de un(a) compañero(a).

_____ 1. Antigua se encuentra en el Valle de Pancho, a sólo 45 minutos de la actual capital.

_____ 2. Fundada en 1543, Antigua es la capital colonial más antigua de Centroamérica.

_____ 3. Por los frecuentes terremotos, no hay edificios altos en la ciudad.

_____ 4. La Casa Popenoe es un buen ejemplo de las elegantes casas coloniales construidas en el siglo XVIII.

_____ 5. En las discotecas y en los bares, los guatemaltecos y los visitantes de Antigua disfrutan de un ambiente cosmopolita.

C. Tiempo libre en Antigua A continuación hay una lista de actividades y excursiones que se pueden hacer en la ciudad de Antigua. Cada miembro del grupo debe escoger **una** de las opciones y explicarles a los otros miembros por qué le parece interesante.

1. **Pasear en bicicleta** Recorran en bicicleta los sitios más destacados de Antigua y de sus alrededores.

2. **Conocer la arquitectura de estilo barroco** Visiten el Palacio de los Capitanes Generales, el ayuntamiento, la catedral, las iglesias y monasterios de las Capuchinas, Santa Clara y La Merced, y vean la arquitectura de la época colonial.

3. **Ver una plantación de café** Hagan un recorrido por una plantación de café, infórmense sobre el proceso de cultivo del café y vean aves, lagartijas e insectos nativos de la región.

4. **Ir de compras** Descubran las tiendas especializadas en artesanía, muñecos de cerámica de Sacatepéquez, vajillas (platos, tazas y vasos) decoradas con palabras en lengua maya, artículos de jade y trajes típicos de los pueblos indígenas.

Las amistades

(iLrn)

I. Vocabulario: Un(a) buen(a) amigo(a)...

Se preocupa por ti. Te **escucha** cuando tienes algún problema y te **da consejos** cuando los necesitas.

Es **leal.** Sabes que puedes contar con él porque siempre está dispuesto a **apoyarte.**

Es **honesta.** Siempre te dice la verdad y hasta te **corrige** si estás errada.

Comparte contigo los buenos y los malos momentos.

Te **acepta** tal y como eres y te **quiere** incondicionalmente.

Vocabulario práctico

Adjetivos

confiable *trustworthy*
generoso *generous*
honesto *honest*
leal *loyal*
paciente *patient*

Verbos

aceptar *to accept*
apoyar *to support*
compartir *to share*

contar (ue) con *to count on*
corregir (i, i) *to correct*
dar consejos *to give advice*
estar dispuesto a... *to be ready (eager) to . . .*
fallar *to fail (not be there)*
juzgar *to judge*
preocuparse por *to worry about*
querer/amar *to love*

■ Asimilación

9-1 ¿Eres un(a) buen(a) amigo(a)? Toma la prueba y determina si cumples con los criterios para ser un(a) buen(a) amigo(a). Compara tus respuestas con las de algunos de tus compañeros. ¿Quién obtuvo el mayor puntaje?

____ ¿Te preocupas mucho por tus amigos?

____ ¿Eres leal?

____ ¿Estás siempre dispuesto(a) a escuchar sus problemas?

____ ¿Los corriges si están cometiendo algún error?

____ ¿Los apoyas siempre en sus proyectos?

____ ¿Compartes con ellos los buenos y los malos momentos?

____ ¿Les das consejos cuando los necesitan?

____ ¿Tratas de no fallarles nunca?

____ ¿Eres paciente con ellos?

____ ¿Los quieres incondicionalmente?

Tabulación

Entre 8 y 10 respuestas afirmativas

¡Felicitaciones! Eres un(a) amigo(a) ideal.

Entre 5 y 7 respuestas afirmativas

Aunque a veces fallas, eres un(a) buen(a) amigo(a). Trata de corregir tus áreas débiles.

Entre 0 y 4 respuestas afirmativas

Tienes que hacer un gran esfuerzo por mejorar. Un(a) buen(a) amigo(a) es un tesoro que debemos apreciar y cultivar.

D2–24

9-2 Su mejor amiga Vas a escuchar un párrafo acerca de una persona importante en la vida de la narradora. Anota su nombre y por lo menos **cuatro** razones por las que la narradora la considera su mejor amiga.

Nombre de su mejor amiga:

Razones por las que la considera su mejor amiga:

1. ...
2. ...
3. ...
4. ...

ESTRATEGIAS PARA LA COMPRENSIÓN

Selective Listening Do not try to understand every word. Concentrate on recognizing familiar words and expressions related to the topic of conversation (in this case, friendship).

■ Aplicaciones

9-3 ¿Cómo es? Cada uno(a) debe describir una de las siguientes características. El (La) compañero(a) debe escuchar con atención y adivinar de qué característica se trata. **¡OJO!** Sólo tienen dos oportunidades para adivinar.

OPCIONES: confiable   generoso   honesto   leal   paciente   simpático

MODELO   E1: *Una persona que no se enoja fácilmente, que es tolerante...*
E2: *¿Paciente?*
E1: *¡Correcto!*

9-4 ¿Quién es tu mejor amigo(a)? Prepara preguntas para averiguar quién es el (la) mejor amigo(a) de uno(a) de tus compañeros y por qué. Haz la entrevista, toma notas y, al terminar, cuéntale a la clase lo que averiguaste.

9-5 Todos podemos mejorar Acabas de encontrar este artículo en una revista española. ¿Cuál de sus consejos te gustaría aplicar a tu vida?

MODELO   *De ahora en adelante* (From now on), *voy a tratar de **sonreír** un poco más.*

CÓMO HACER AMIGOS

1. Hable con las personas que lo rodean. No hay nada más agradable que un saludo entusiasta.

2. Sonría. Se necesita mover 65 músculos para hacer mala cara y sólo 15 para sonreír.

3. Llame a las personas por su nombre. No hay música más dulce a los oídos que escuchar el propio nombre.

4. Sea amigable y cooperador. Para tener amigos hay que ser un buen amigo.

5. Sea cordial. Hable y actúe como si cada cosa que hiciera le causara un gran placer.

6. Interésese genuinamente por los demás. Todos le pueden llegar a **caer bien,** si se esfuerza.

7. Sea generoso en elogiar y **parco** en criticar.

8. **Tome muy en cuenta** los sentimientos de los demás. Le será grandemente reconocido.

9. Tome en cuenta las opiniones de los demás. Hay tres puntos de vista en cada controversia: el suyo, el del otro y... el correcto.

10. Esté atento a prestar un servicio. Lo que más cuenta en esta vida es lo que hacemos por los demás.

to like (a person)

moderate

take into account

■ **Integración**

9-6 Cómo hacer amigos Representa la siguiente situación con un(a) compañero(a).

Una persona muy popular	**El (La) solitario(a)**
Tú eres una persona muy popular en esta universidad y tienes muchos amigos. Tu compañero(a), sin embargo, es nuevo(a) y no conoce a nadie. Contesta sus preguntas y ofrécele algunos consejos prácticos *(tips)*.	Eres nuevo(a) en esta universidad y todavía no tienes muchos amigos. Tu compañero(a), por el contrario, es una persona muy popular y quiere darte algunos consejos para hacer amigos aquí. Pregúntale... ■ qué debes y qué no debes hacer para hacer nuevos amigos en esta universidad ■ a qué lugares debes ir y ■ en qué actividades debes participar para conocer a más personas.

REMEMBER

To give formal commands, you drop the **-o** from the **yo** form of the present tense and add **-e/-en** for **-ar** verbs and **-a/-an** for **-er** and **-ir** verbs.

MODELO estudiar
   Estudie sus lecciones con tiempo.
   No **estudie** a último momento.

9-7 ¿Cómo hacer amigos en los Estados Unidos? Imagínense que son consejeros de estudiantes extranjeros. En parejas, preparen un documento con sugerencias prácticas sobre cómo hacer amigos en este país.

1. Intercambien ideas (¿Qué hacer? ¿Qué no hacer? ¿Adónde ir para hacer amigos en este país? etc.).
2. Preparen una lista de actividades y luego decidan en qué orden van a presentar la información.
3. Preparen el primer borrador de su lista de sugerencias. (Recuerden usar los mandatos formales.)
4. Traigan el primer borrador de su composición a la próxima clase para hacer las revisiones necesarias.
5. Revisen su composición y entréguensela a su profesor(a) para que les sugiera más correcciones.

Correcciones

Intercambien composiciones y comenten los siguientes aspectos.

Paso 1: Contenido. ¿Tiene toda la información necesaria? ¿Qué falta? ¿Qué sobra? *(What is not necessary?)*

Paso 2: Organización. ¿La presentación está organizada de una manera lógica? ¿Qué cambios son necesarios?

Paso 3: Gramática. Subraya los mandatos formales y asegúrate de que estén correctamente conjugados.

II. Funciones y estructuras: Giving advice with the subjunctive (regular verbs)

ESTELA: Hola, doña Tere. Soy Estela.

DOÑA TERE: ¿Qué te pasa, Estela? ¿Por qué estás llorando?

ESTELA: Tuve una discusión muy fuerte con mi amiga Penélope y...

DOÑA TERE: Mira, es importante que **tomes** las cosas con calma. Todas las relaciones tienen sus altibajos *(ups and downs)*. Te recomiendo que la **invites** a un café y que **hables** con ella. Ya verás que todo se resuelve. ¡Anímate, mujer!

ESTELA: Bueno... No sé si vaya a resultar bien, pero lo voy a intentar.

Up until now, all the verb tenses you have studied belong to the indicative mode. Generally speaking, the indicative mode is associated with objectivity. However, there is another mode that is associated with subjectivity: the subjunctive mode. For instance, in the above conversation, the verbs in bold refer to doña Tere's personal opinion about what Estela should do to solve the problem she has with her friend Penélope. These verbs are used in the subjunctive mode because doña Tere has a subjective perspective about what should be done.

The subjunctive is used in sentences with a main clause and a subordinate clause (with more than one subject). Consider the following examples (the subjects are underlined):

> When there is only one subject or when the statement applies to the speaker, the verb in the subordinate clause is used in the infinitive.

MAIN CLAUSE	SUBORDINATE CLAUSE
<u>Jorge</u> recomienda	que (<u>nosotros</u>) **apoyemos** a Lila.
Jorge recommends	*(that) we **support** Lila.*
Es necesario	que (<u>tú</u>) **estés** dispuesta a cambiar.
It is necessary	*for <u>you</u> **to be** willing to change.*

> Although the use of *that* is optional in English, the use of **que** is obligatory in Spanish.

One of the uses of the subjunctive mode is to give advice. Here is a list of verbs and impersonal expressions used for this purpose.

VERBS		IMPERSONAL EXPRESSIONS	
aconsejar	*to advise*	es aconsejable que...	*it is advisable that . . .*
recomendar (ie)	*to recommend*	es bueno que...	*it is good that . . .*
sugerir (ie, i)	*to suggest*	es importante que...	*it is important that . . .*
		es justo que...	*it is fitting that . . .*
		es mejor que...	*it is better that . . .*
		es necesario que...	*it is necessary that . . .*
		es preferible que...	*it is preferable that . . .*
		es urgente que...	*it is urgent that . . .*

The present subjunctive of regular verbs is formed by dropping the **-ar,** **-er,** or **-ir** from the infinitive and adding the following endings. Notice that **-er** and **-ir** verbs share the same set of endings and that the **yo** and **él/ella/Ud.** forms are the same.

You are already familiarized with the **él/ella/Ud.** and **ellos(as)/Uds.** forms because they are just like the command forms you learned in **Capítulo 8, Tema 2.**

-ar VERBS		-er/-ir VERBS		
ENDINGS	hablar	ENDINGS	comer	vivir
e	hable	a	coma	viva
es	hables	as	comas	vivas
e	hable	a	coma	viva
emos	hablemos	amos	comamos	vivamos
éis	habléis	áis	comáis	viváis
en	hablen	an	coman	vivan

■ Asimilación

9-8 Relaciones amistosas sanas *(healthy)* ¿Qué le recomendarías a una persona para mantener relaciones amistosas sanas? Escoge las alternativas más lógicas y, al terminar, compara tus respuestas con las de un(a) compañero(a). ¿Están de acuerdo acerca de cómo se debe tratar a los amigos?

1. Le recomiendo que...
   a. respete sus opiniones.
   b. los visite todos los días.
   c. no los llame por teléfono.

2. Es preferible que nunca...
   a. coman juntos en restaurantes.
   b. hablen de sus preferencias personales.
   c. compartan secretos de otras personas.

3. Le sugiero que...
   a. no esté dispuesto(a) a ayudar.
   b. no escuche a sus amigos.
   c. no les falle cuando lo/la necesiten.

4. Es importante que...
   a. confíe en sus amigos.
   b. dude de la integridad de sus amigos.
   c. trabaje con estas personas.

CD2–25 **9-9 ¿Típico o atípico?** Escucha los consejos que los padres le dan a un adolescente e indica si son consejos típicos **(T)** o atípicos **(A).**

1. __
2. __
3. __
4. __

5. __
6. __
7. __
8. __

Aplicaciones

 9-10 Una situación delicada El siguiente diálogo es la continuación de la conversación de doña Tere y Estela. Completen las oraciones con la forma correcta de los verbos de la lista para saber qué ocurrió. **¡OJO!** Hay un verbo adicional.

OPCIONES: comprender insistir arreglar aceptar participar tratar

DOÑA TERE: ¡No digas eso, Estela! Si quieres mantener la amistad con Penélope, es muy importante que _____ en verla. Te aconsejo que _____ esta situación antes de que sea tarde.

ESTELA: Eso es lo que quiero, ¡pero ella es tan terca!

DOÑA TERE: Pues es necesario que cada una _____ el punto de vista de la otra y que las dos _____ de buscar una solución. ¡Son muchos años de amistad!

ESTELA: Es cierto... ¿Y Ud. cree que es posible que ella _____ mi invitación para hablar?

DOÑA TERE: No sé, pero sólo hay una forma de saberlo. ¡Llámala ahora mismo!

ESTELA: Está bien. La voy a llamar. Hasta luego y gracias, doña Tere.

DOÑA TERE: Buena suerte. Hablamos luego.

— end —

■ Integración

9-13 Una persona tímida Representa la siguiente situación con un(a) compañero(a).

Persona tímida	**Consejero(a)**
Imagínate que eres una persona muy tímida a la que se le hace muy difícil hacer amistades. Quieres ser un poco más sociable y decides visitar a tu consejero(a) para que te ayude a modificar este rasgo de tu personalidad. Descríbele tu problema y escucha su opinión profesional.	Imagínate que eres consejero(a) en esta universidad. Un(a) estudiante tiene un problema serio de timidez que le impide hacer amistades y ha decidido venir a tu oficina a buscar tu ayuda profesional. Escucha la descripción de su problema y dale tu opinión.

SUGERENCIAS

Para dar consejos, puedes usar estas expresiones y preguntas:

¿Me puede ayudar?	*Can you help me?*
Necesito su ayuda.	*I need your help.*
¿Qué piensa de...?	*What do you think about . . .?*
Quisiera saber su opinión con respecto a...	*I would like to know your opinion about . . .*

9-14 Consejo electrónico Lee el siguiente mensaje de correo electrónico y luego escribe una respuesta con tus consejos.

SUGERENCIAS

Aquí tienes expresiones útiles para alentar:

¡Anímate!	*Cheer up!*
¡No te preocupes!	*Don't worry!*
¡Todo va a salir bien!	*Everything's going to be fine!*

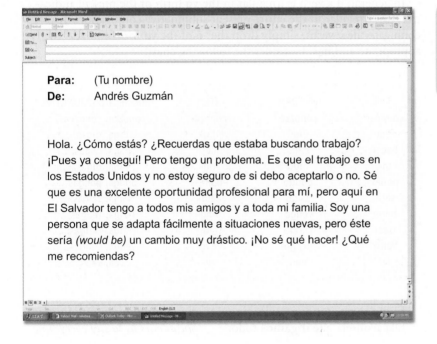

Para: (Tu nombre)
De: Andrés Guzmán

Hola. ¿Cómo estás? ¿Recuerdas que estaba buscando trabajo? ¡Pues ya conseguí! Pero tengo un problema. Es que el trabajo es en los Estados Unidos y no estoy seguro de si debo aceptarlo o no. Sé que es una excelente oportunidad profesional para mí, pero aquí en El Salvador tengo a todos mis amigos y a toda mi familia. Soy una persona que se adapta fácilmente a situaciones nuevas, pero éste sería *(would be)* un cambio muy drástico. ¡No sé qué hacer! ¿Qué me recomiendas?

III. Funciones y estructuras: Giving advice with the subjunctive (irregular verbs)

ROLANDO: Beatriz, mi hijo es un chico muy solitario. No tiene amigos en la escuela y siempre está solo. ¿Qué me recomiendas?

BEATRIZ: Bueno, pues te recomiendo que le **busques** ayuda profesional. Es importante que él **conozca** a chicos de su edad y que se **sienta** cómodo con ellos. Es mejor que **resuelvas** este pequeño problema ahora, ¿no crees?

In the previous grammar section you learned how to form the present subjunctive tense and used it to give advice. You will now learn about irregular verbs in this tense.

In general, if a verb is irregular in the **yo** form of the present indicative, it is irregular in the entire present subjunctive conjugation. To conjugate these verbs, simply drop the **-o** of the **yo** form and add the appropriate endings. Consider the following chart.

VERB	**yo** FORM	STEM	PRESENT SUBJUNCTIVE
conocer	conozco	conozc-	conozca, conozcas, ...
decir	digo	dig-	diga, digas, ...
hacer	hago	hag-	haga, hagas, ...
oír	oigo	oig-	oiga, oigas, ...
poner	pongo	pong-	ponga, pongas, ...
salir	salgo	salg-	salga, salgas, ...
tener	tengo	teng-	tenga, tengas, ...
traer	traigo	traig-	traiga, traigas, ...
venir	vengo	veng-	venga, vengas, ...
ver	veo	ve-	vea, veas, ...

Es mejor que **tengan** paciencia.   *It is better that you **have** patience.*
Ella aconseja que **digamos** todo.   *She advises us **to say** everything.*

There are two exceptions to this rule:

- **-ar** and **-er** verbs with e→ie and o→ue stem changes: the changes do not affect the **nosotros** and **vosotros** forms.

  pensar (ie): p**ie**nse, p**ie**nses, p**ie**nse, pensemos, penséis, p**ie**nsen
  poder (ue): p**ue**da, p**ue**das, p**ue**da, podamos, podáis, p**ue**dan

■ -ir verbs with **e→i, e→ie,** and **o→ue** stem changes: they also show a change in the **nosotros** and **vosotros** forms (the same change that appears in the present participle).

pedir (i, i): p**i**da, p**i**das, p**i**da, p**i**damos, p**i**dáis, p**i**dan
sentir (ie, i): s**ie**nta, s**ie**ntas, s**ie**nta, s**i**ntamos, s**i**ntáis, s**ie**ntan
dormir (ue, u): d**ue**rma, d**ue**rmas, d**ue**rma, d**u**rmamos, d**u**rmáis, d**ue**rman

Verbs that end in **-car, -gar, -guar,** and **-zar** are irregular in the present subjunctive. They undergo orthographic changes in order to maintain the sound of the letters **c, g, g + u,** and **z.** These changes affect all the forms of the verb.

-car: c → qu	tocar	to**que**, to**qu**es, ...
-gar: g → gu	pagar	pa**gu**e, pa**gu**es, ...
-ger/-gir: g → j	corregir	corri**j**a, corri**j**as, ...
-guar: gu → gü*	averiguar	averi**gü**e, averi**gü**es, ...
-zar: z → c	empezar	empie**c**e, empie**c**es, ...

The two dots over the letter **u** are called **diéresis.** They are used to indicate that this letter *does* sound, unlike in **pag̲u̲e, pag̲u̲es,** etc.

Finally, there is a small group of verbs that show various irregularities.

dar	dé, des, dé,...	**ir**	vaya, vayas, vaya,...
estar	esté, estés, esté,...	**saber**	sepa, sepas, sepa,...
haber	haya, hayas, haya,...	**ser**	sea, seas, sea,...

■ Asimilación

9-15 A tu mejor amigo(a) Indica si le recomiendas a una persona hacer las siguientes cosas para mantener una buena relación con su mejor amigo(a). Escribe **sí** o **no.** Al terminar, compara las respuestas con las de un(a) compañero(a). ¿Piensan igual?

____ Le recomiendo que le diga mentiras.

____ Le aconsejo que sea honesto con él/ella.

____ No es bueno que piense en sus sentimientos antes de hablar.

____ Es importante que le dé dinero siempre.

____ Le sugiero que conozca sus gustos.

____ Pienso que es necesario que su amigo sepa todo sobre Ud.

____ Es preferible que le pida favores con frecuencia.

____ No le recomiendo que escuchen el mismo tipo de música.

CD2–26 **9-16 En la oficina** Escucha las instrucciones que les da el Lic. Viera a sus empleados. Marca con una **X** las frases que escuches.

____ volver a redactar una carta

____ hacer llamadas telefónicas temprano

____ buscar los documentos

____ analizar el caso de los Roldán

____ tener la agenda al día

____ no ser agresivos con el Lic. Ortiz

____ entender la propuesta del Sr. Hernández

____ entregar corregidos unos documentos

■ **Aplicaciones**

9-17 Situaciones Completen las oraciones con los verbos de la lista. **¡OJO!** Cada grupo tiene un verbo adicional.

dar   haber   hacer   ir

1. Para estar en forma, te recomiendo que _____ ejercicios tres veces por semana. Además, te sugiero que _____ a la oficina de un experto en nutrición para que él/ella te _____ ideas sobre cómo puedes balancear tu dieta.

empezar   pagar   utilizar   tener

2. Si quieren tener un buen crédito, les aconsejamos (a Uds.) que _____ sus cuentas a tiempo. Es muy importante que _____ cuidado cuando usan sus tarjetas de crédito. Es mejor que las _____ sólo en caso de emergencia.

comenzar   ver   estar   morir

3. Para sacar buenas notas en la clase de español, la profesora nos recomienda que (nosotros) _____ a estudiar varios días antes de las pruebas y que _____ programas de televisión en español. Ella también nos dice que es bueno que _____ atentos en clase.

9-18 Le aconsejamos que... ¿Qué les aconsejan Uds. a las siguientes personas? Den dos consejos por persona. ¡Sean creativos!

MODELO   al / a la profesor(a)
Le aconsejamos que duerma más y que empiece la clase media hora más tarde.

1. al presidente de los Estados Unidos
2. a un(a) cantante famoso(a)
3. a un(a) deportista famoso(a)
4. a un(a) estudiante de la clase
5. a los estudiantes de esta universidad
6. a nadie

9-19 Lo que debes y no debes hacer Imagínense que todo el mundo viene para pedirles consejos porque Uds. saben de todo. Túrnense para dar un consejo afirmativo y uno negativo para cada caso. Usen diferentes expresiones como: (**Te sugiero que...**, **Te recomiendo que...**, **Es necesario que...**, **Es mejor que...**, etc.).

MODELO E1: *No tengo muchos amigos.*
E2: *Te aconsejo que hables con los estudiantes de la universidad y que no te quedes en la residencia estudiantil en tu tiempo libre.*

1. Siempre estoy cansado(a).
2. No me gusta la comida de la cafetería.
3. Soy un poco tímido(a).
4. Nunca termino los trabajos a tiempo.
5. Llego tarde a mis clases todos los días.
6. Necesito ganar más dinero.
7. No sé hablar español muy bien.
8. Me encantan los países centroamericanos.

■ Integración

9-20 La 1ª (primera) opinión de los expertos Representa la siguiente situación con un(a) compañero(a).

Estudiante A	Estudiante B
Escoge uno de los siguientes temas y pídele sugerencias a tu compañero(a):	Escoge uno de los siguientes temas y pídele sugerencias a tu compañero(a):
■ Cómo preparar un plato que nunca has preparado. ■ Cómo conseguir un buen trabajo. Tu compañero(a) también te va a pedir sugerencias sobre un tema específico. Debes estar preparado(a) para dar tu opinión de experto(a).	■ Cómo perder peso y mejorar la salud. ■ Cómo tener una vida estudiantil exitosa *(successful)* y fructífera. Tu compañero(a) también te va a pedir sugerencias sobre un tema específico. Debes estar preparado(a) para dar tu opinión de experto(a).

SUGERENCIAS

Para organizar tus ideas, puedes usar las siguientes expresiones: **en primer lugar** *(first of all)*, **en segundo lugar** *(second of all)*, **además** *(also)*, **por otro lado** *(on the other hand)*, **por el contrario** *(on the contrary)*, **sin embargo** *(however)*, and **por fin** *(finally)*.

9-21 La 2ª (segunda) opinión de los expertos Ahora, haz un resumen de lo que sugieres para hacer las cosas que ni tu compañero(a) ni tú escogieron en la actividad 9-20. Sigue las sugerencias que se dieron para esa actividad. Cuando termines, dale una copia de tu resumen a tu profesor(a) para que te dé su opinión.

IV. Perspectivas: La timidez

■ Antes de leer

A. Para conversar Responde a las preguntas y luego comparte tus respuestas con otros compañeros.

1. ¿En qué situaciones te pones nervioso(a)? (Indica todas las que correspondan.)

____ cuando estoy con gente que no conozco

____ cuando tengo que hablar en público

____ en una cita

____ en una entrevista de trabajo

____ en otra(s) situación (situaciones): _____

2. ¿Qué haces cuando te pones nervioso(a)?

____ Me pongo rojo(a) y a veces sudo *(sweat)*.

____ Trato de salir de la situación rápidamente.

____ Otra(s) estrategia(s): _____

B. Vocabulario y conceptos Para cada palabra de la izquierda, escriban la letra de su definición. Consulten el diccionario si es necesario.

____ 1. superar
____ 2. huir
____ 3. perder el control
____ 4. seguridad en sí mismo
____ 5. afrontar
____ 6. truco

a. no tener el dominio de una situación
b. hacer frente, manejar directamente
c. escapar, evitar
d. estrategia, procedimiento ingenioso
e. confianza, no dudar de las capacidades
f. vencer, terminar

■ A leer

Lee el siguiente artículo sobre estrategias para superar la timidez.

Cómo superar el miedo

Para superar cualquier tipo de ansiedad social debemos aprender lo que los expertos denominan «estrategias de exposición», que básicamente consisten en no huir a la primera ocurrencia de cambio de las situaciones que nos provocan **temor**. Los sicólogos recomiendan elaborar un plan de ataque para poner en práctica en cada una de las situaciones que nos hacen perder el control.

fear

Miedo a llamar la atención. Aprende a ser espontáneo. Para perder la rigidez, acostúmbrate a **transgredir** tus propias normas una vez a la semana. Por ejemplo, ponte ropa más **llamativa,** cambia el corte de pelo o ve al trabajo en bicicleta. Hacer pequeñas **locuras** te ayudará a sentir más seguridad en ti mismo y a perder el miedo a llamar la atención.

to break
attractive
silly things

Miedo al ridículo. Cuando la timidez **esconde** un grave problema de autoestima, conviene dejar a un lado los pensamientos negativos acerca de tus **supuestos** defectos físicos o psíquicos. Aprende a **reírte** de ti mismo.

hides

assumed / to laugh

Temor a sentir la soledad en lugares públicos. Acostúmbrate a salir solo una o dos veces por semana, así te obligarás a afrontar tú mismo cualquier situación que **surja,** sin **escudarte ni esconderte en acompañantes.** Actividades como ir al cine o a ver una exposición son una forma de entrenamiento para superar el miedo a enfrentarte a la gente. Una vez que hayas superado esto, puedes realizar otra serie de actividades como ir de compras, tomar café o ir a comer a un restaurante, en las que tendrás que hablar con **desconocidos,** y que te ayudarán a ver las relaciones con **extraños** con más naturalidad.

surfaces, appears / to hide behind companions

strangers
strangers

Quedarse en blanco. Piensa que la mayoría de las conversaciones empiezan con temas más bien superficiales y que puedes iniciar la charla con una simple pregunta. De esta forma, llamarás la atención de la otra persona y le demostrarás que también tienes interés por hablar y dar tu opinión.

Miedo a hablar en público. Se denomina «miedo escénico» y un truco efectivo para **vencerlo** es ser el primero en empezar una conversación.

to overcome it

Incomodidad con grupos. Lo ideal para recuperar la simpatía de tus colegas o para introducirte en un grupo del que estás excluido es empezar centrándote en una sola persona, que te ayudará a que los demás te vean con mejores ojos.

*Eludir a los vecinos **por miedo.*** Simplemente empieza mostrándoles una sonrisa amable o sosteniéndoles la puerta del ascensor en lugar de **cerrársela en las narices.** Después, limítate a responder a lo que ellos te pregunten.

out of fear

to shut it in their faces

■ ¿Entendiste bien?

ESTRATEGIA DE LECTURA

Scanning Look for terms that refer to social behavior and social context.

C. Resumen Completen el siguiente cuadro con sus propias palabras.

Miedo a...	Estrategia para superarlo
Los grupos	
Los vecinos	
La soledad en sitios públicos	
Hablar en público	
Llamar la atención	

D. Enfoque lingüístico Según el contexto, ¿qué creen que significan las siguientes declaraciones?

1. «Debemos aprender lo que los expertos denominan... "estrategias de exposición", que básicamente consisten en no huir **a la primera ocurrencia de cambio** de las situaciones que nos provocan temor».
   a. con dinero local
   b. rápidamente
   c. lo ideal, lo mejor

2. «Cuando la timidez esconde un grave problema de autoestima, conviene **dejar a un lado** los pensamientos negativos».
   a. abandonar, olvidar
   b. decir, explicar
   c. recordar, repetir

3. «Lo ideal... es empezar centrándote en una sola persona, que te ayudará a que los demás **te vean con mejores ojos**».
   a. poder ver bien
   b. aceptar, apreciar
   c. observar con atención

E. Actividad de extensión: Más estrategias para superar la timidez ¿Qué otras estrategias se pueden usar para superar estas situaciones de timidez? Preséntenle sus recomendaciones al resto de la clase.

Relaciones laborales

I. Vocabulario: Los compañeros y los jefes

Vocabulario práctico

Adjetivos

accesible *accessible*

agresivo *aggressive*

buen(a) compañero(a) *good colleague*

competente *competent*

creativo *creative*

cumplidor *reliable, trustworthy*

eficiente *efficient*

firme *firm*

honesto *honest*

leal *loyal*

puntual *punctual*

respetuoso *respectful*

responsable *responsible*

seguro de sí mismo *confident*

trabajador *hard working*

Sustantivos

el buen sentido del humor *good sense of humor*

Verbos

amar el trabajo *to love one's work*

delegar parte del poder *to delegate power*

promover (ue) un ambiente positivo de trabajo *to promote a positive working environment*

respetar a los empleados *to respect the employees*

saber escuchar *to know how to listen*

tener metas *to have goals*

tomar riesgos/arriesgarse *to take risks*

Marta es una mujer **segura de sí misma.**

González tiene un gran **sentido del humor.**

■ Asimilación

9-22 Comportamientos Indica qué término describe mejor los siguientes comportamientos. Al terminar, compara tus respuestas con las de un(a) compañero(a).

1. Un compañero que habla fuerte y que no tiene miedo de expresar sus ideas.
   a. tímido   b. trabajador   c. seguro de sí mismo

2. Un compañero que va a la oficina todos los días, aún los fines de semana.
   a. puntual   b. trabajador   c. seguro de sí mismo

3. Un compañero que siempre está de buen ánimo y se ofrece a ayudar a los demás.
   a. agresivo   b. puntual   c. buen compañero

4. Un compañero que siempre quiere ser el número uno y que hace todo lo posible para lograrlo.
   a. que tiene metas   b. honesto   c. respetuoso

5. Un compañero que nunca llega tarde a una reunión y que siempre entrega sus informes a tiempo.
   a. agresivo   b. tímido   c. cumplidor/puntual

Nuestro jefe es muy **accesible.** Sabe escuchar.

Alicia es la mujer más **competente** que conozco.

CD2-27 **9-23 La nueva asistente de la profesora** Vas a escuchar la descripción de una asistente. Anota las **dos** características por las que obtuvo el puesto y las **tres** cualidades que reveló en los primeros tres meses de trabajo.

Nombre de la asistente:

Características que reveló en la entrevista:

Cualidades en los primeros tres meses:

■ Aplicaciones

 9-24 Necesitamos... Imagínense que tienen que entrevistar a varios candidatos para diferentes trabajos. Indiquen las características que desean en cada caso. **¡OJO!** ¡Sólo pueden escoger **dos** características para cada ocupación!

EN TU COMUNIDAD

Start a research about openings in your university. Try to find out what types of jobs are available (teaching, administrative, etc.) and make a list of the qualifications listed in some of the ads. Afterwards, discuss your findings in groups and present a summary in class.

Para...	Necesitamos un candidato...
cuidar a unos niños	
manejar una empresa	
vender productos por teléfono	
diseñar materiales de multimedia	
organizar recepciones y fiestas	
hacer investigaciones científicas	

9-25 ¿Qué es más importante? Clasifica las siguientes características de un buen jefe o una buena jefa en orden de importancia (1 = más importante, 6 = menos importante). Luego, compara tus respuestas con las de un(a) compañero(a). ¿Están de acuerdo?

____ saber escuchar ____ respetar a los empleados

____ ser creativo(a) ____ ser firme

____ saber delegar poder ____ amar el trabajo

9-26 ¿Buen(a) o mal(a) compañero(a)? Preparen cinco preguntas para determinar si alguien tiene las cualidades indicadas. Después, hagan y respondan a las preguntas que han preparado.

MODELO ser cumplidor(a)
E1: *¿Entrega Ud. sus trabajos a tiempo?*
E2: *Desde luego. Yo soy muy cumplidor(a).*

1. tener buen sentido del humor
2. ser responsable
3. ser agresivo(a)
4. ser seguro(a) de sí mismo(a)
5. ser honesto

▪ Integración

 9-27 En busca del candidato ideal Representa la siguiente situación con un(a) compañero(a).

Entrevistador(a)	**Candidato(a)**
Estás buscando un(a) nuevo(a) asistente para tu oficina. Es fundamental que esta persona se lleve bien con los jefes y los otros empleados.	Necesitas un trabajo y esta compañía te ha dado una entrevista. Presenta tus antecedentes personales y demuestra que eres el (la) mejor candidato(a). **¡OJO!** Esta empresa busca una persona que se lleve muy bien con sus jefes y compañeros.
Entrevista a este(a) aspirante y decide si es un(a) buen(a) candidato(a) para el puesto.	▪ Saluda al / a la entrevistador(a).
▪ Salúdalo(la).	▪ Presenta tus antecedentes.
▪ Averigua sus antecedentes.	▪ Demuestra que te relacionas muy bien con otras personas.
▪ Hazle preguntas para saber cómo se relaciona con otras personas.	▪ Averigua cuándo puedes saber cuál fue la decisión.
▪ Termina la conversación indicando cuándo vas a tomar una decisión.	

 9-28 Consejos Tu amiga Alejandra tiene problemas en su trabajo y te ha mandado el siguiente mensaje electrónico. Respóndele con algunos consejos prácticos.

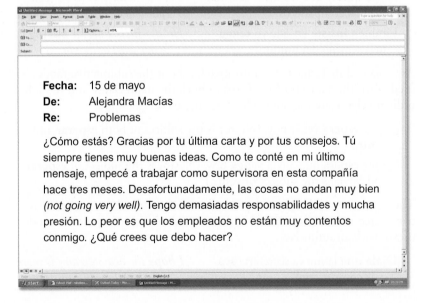

Fecha: 15 de mayo
De: Alejandra Macías
Re: Problemas

¿Cómo estás? Gracias por tu última carta y por tus consejos. Tú siempre tienes muy buenas ideas. Como te conté en mi último mensaje, empecé a trabajar como supervisora en esta compañía hace tres meses. Desafortunadamente, las cosas no andan muy bien *(not going very well)*. Tengo demasiadas responsabilidades y mucha presión. Lo peor es que los empleados no están muy contentos conmigo. ¿Qué crees que debo hacer?

II. Funciones y estructuras: Expressing wishes and requests

Espero que el nuevo empleado **llegue** temprano hoy.
Quiero que Sonia y Elías **escuchen** bien a la Sra. Ferrer.
Prohíbo que Velázquez y Bazán **discutan** el nuevo proyecto.

Some of these verbs would be considered stronger than others. For example, the use of **insistir (en), exigir, mandar,** and **prohibir** would be considered less polite and courteous and more of an expression of power.

The subjunctive mode is also used when the verb of the main clause expresses a wish or a request. Here is a list of verbs that trigger this use of the subjunctive.

desear *to wish, to want*	pedir (i, i) *to ask for, to request*
esperar *to hope, to expect*	permitir *to allow, to permit*
exigir *to demand*	preferir (ie, i) *to prefer*
insistir (en) *to insist (on)*	prohibir *to forbid, to prohibit*
mandar *to order*	querer *to want*
necesitar *to need*	rogar (ue) *to beg*

El jefe **quiere** que nosotros **seamos** buenos compañeros.

*The boss **wants** us **to be** good colleagues.*

También **insiste en** que yo **tenga** más sentido del humor.

*He also **insists on** me **having** a better sense of humor.*

As explained in **Tema 1,** the infinitive (and not the subjunctive mode) is used when the subjects of the verbs in both the main clause and the subordinate clause are the same. Consider these two examples.

Néstor **espera venir** hoy. (Néstor is the subject of both **esperar** and **venir.**)

Néstor **espera** que Silvia **venga** hoy. (Néstor is the subject of **esperar** and Silvia is the subject of **venir.**)

The expression **ojalá que** *(I hope)* is also used to talk about wishes. It is considered more informal and is always used with the subjunctive mode (never with an infinitive).

¡**Ojalá que** la nueva secretaria **sea** más competente!

I hope the new secretary is more competent!

■ Asimilación

9-29 ¿Quién lo dice? Lee las siguientes oraciones e indica si las dice un(a) jefe(a) **(J)** o un(a) empleado(a) **(E).** Cuando termines, compara tus respuestas con las de un(a) compañero(a). ¿Cuántas respuestas tienen en común?

____ 1. Espero que nos aumenten el sueldo.

____ 2. No permito que las secretarias trabajen menos de ocho horas diarias.

____ 3. Quiero que Rivera sea más puntual.

____ 4. Insisto en que la gente asuma riesgos en mi compañía.

____ 5. Ojalá que los supervisores sean respetuosos.

____ 6. Deseo que mis colegas sepan escuchar.

____ 7. Espero que el nuevo mensajero sea cumplidor.

____ 8. Exijo que en la oficina haya un ambiente de respeto mutuo.

9-30 ¿Qué se va a hacer hoy? La Sra. Martínez no va a trabajar hoy y dejó un mensaje en el contestador de su secretaria. Escucha el mensaje y empareja las siguientes oraciones.

La Sra. Martínez...

____ 1. desea que Carlos...   a. termine el informe de gastos.

____ 2. quiere que Eleonora...   b. dirija la discusión sobre un proyecto.

____ 3. prefiere que Vidal...   c. le informe si hay problemas.

____ 4. pide que Claudia...   d. llame al técnico de computadoras.

____ 5. espera que Luis...   e. no asista a la reunión.

■ Aplicaciones

9-31 ¡Todavía no! Imagínense que Uds. son supervisores(as) en una compañía y están preocupados(as) porque algunos empleados todavía no han hecho ciertas cosas o no han demostrado tener ciertas cualidades. Lean las claves y escriban una reacción. Usen diferentes expresiones como: **Esperamos que..., Insistimos en que..., Preferimos que...,** etc.

> MODELO   Estefanía no ha archivado los contratos.
> *Esperamos que Estefanía archive los contratos.*

1. Marcos y Rebeca no han atendido bien al público últimamente.
2. Don Ángel no ha enviado el fax todavía.
3. Zelma no ha instalado el programa nuevo en nuestra computadora.
4. Juan y Rigoberto no han puesto los monitores en el sótano.
5. La Sra. López no ha sabido responder apropiadamente a las preguntas de Miguel.
6. Gustavo no es una persona segura de sí misma.
7. Los empleados de limpieza no han recogido las cajas todavía.
8. Mirna y Santiago no les han dicho todo a los auditores.

CD2-28

9-32 Profesores(as) por un día Imagínense que su profesor(a) no puede venir a clase hoy y les pide que lo/la substituyan. Escriban por lo menos seis cosas que **esperan, quieren, prefieren,** etc. que la clase haga. ¡Sean creativos(as)!

> MODELO *Queremos que Uds. hablen solamente en español.*
> *Esperamos que Cindy no se duerma en clase hoy.*

9-33 Padres e hijos

Paso 1: ¿Cuáles son algunas de las cosas que tus padres esperan de ti y de tus hermanos? Haz una lista de cinco cosas.

> MODELO *Mis padres esperan que nosotros saquemos buenas notas.*

Paso 2: Compara tu lista con las de dos compañeros(as). ¿Qué tienen en común? Prepara un informe y compártelo con la clase.

■ Integración

9-34 El mundo del futuro ¿Qué esperan del mundo del futuro? ¿Qué cosas deben cambiar? ¿Qué cosas les preocupan? Saquen unos minutos para pensar en estas preguntas y respóndanlas usando diferentes expresiones como: **Ruego que..., Deseo que..., No quiero que...,** etc.

9-35 En el trabajo En el **Capítulo 8** tuviste la oportunidad de preparar tu hoja de vida y tu carta de presentación. ¿Has tenido la oportunidad de pensar en lo que realmente esperas de tu futuro empleo, de tu futuro jefe y de tus futuros compañeros de trabajo? Piensa en esto y escribe un breve informe. Cuando termines, dale una copia a tu profesor(a) para que te dé su opinión.

III. Funciones y estructuras: Expressing emotion and feelings

DIEGO: **Me alegra mucho** que **quieras** continuar tus estudios, Nuria.

NURIA: Ay, gracias. Yo también **estoy muy contenta de** que en esta empresa nos **permitan** combinar el trabajo y los estudios.

ANTONIO: Así es. Pero **es una lástima** que no **haya** más personas que **aprovechen** esta oportunidad, ¿no?

CÉSAR: Sí, **siento** que **sea** así, ¡pero las cosas van a cambiar! ¡Yo también voy a continuar mis estudios!

So far you have learned how to use the subjunctive mode to give advice and to talk about wishes and requests. Another use of this verb mode is to talk about emotions and feelings. Here is a list of useful verbs and impersonal expressions you can use with this purpose.

Verbs	Impersonal expressions
agradar* *to like*	es un abuso que... *it is an abuse that . . .*
alegrarse (de) *to be glad*	
doler (ue)* *to be hurt*	es bueno que... *it is good that . . .*
estar contento(a) (de) *to be happy*	es curioso que... *it is odd that . . .*
	es extraño que... *it is strange that . . .*
estar furioso (de) *to be angry*	es impresionante que... *it is impressive that . . .*
gustar* *to be pleased*	es increíble que... *it is incredible that . . .*
molestar* *to be bothered*	
parecer fantástico* *to consider great*	es una lástima que... *it is a shame that . . .*
parecer terrible* *to consider terrible*	es malo que... *it is bad that . . .*
	es una pena que... *it is a pity that . . .*
parecer triste* *to consider sad*	es raro que... *it is unusual that . . .*
sentir *to feel, to lament*	es ridículo que... *it is ridiculous that . . .*
temer *to fear*	
tener miedo *to be afraid*	es terrible que... *it is terrible that . . .*

* These verbs are used with indirect object pronouns (**me, te, le, nos, os, les**).

Nos **molesta** que Álvarez **sea** tan descortés.
Es ridículo que no nos **den** un aumento.

*The fact that Álvarez **is** so impolite **bothers** us.*
*__It is ridiculous__ that they are not **giving** us a raise.*

The adjectives and nouns in the impersonal expressions can also be used in exclamations with **qué.**

¡Qué pena que la Sra. Díaz no **promueva** un ambiente positivo!	*What a pity* that Mrs. Díaz does *not* **promote** *a positive environment!*
¡Qué terrible que no se **respeten** nuestros derechos!	*How terrible* that they do not **respect** *our rights!*

Just as with the verbs used to give advice and to express wishes and requests, when the subject of the verbs in the main clause and in the subordinate clause are the same, the verb form used is the infinitive. The same applies to cases in which an impersonal expression is used in a generic sense (which would apply to the speaker as well).

<u>Estoy</u> **contento** de **trabajar** aquí.	*I am* **glad to work** *here.*
<u>Ella</u> **dice** que **es magnífico poder** aprender tanto de Ud.	<u>*She*</u> **says** *(that)* **it is great to be able** *to learn so much from you.*

■ Asimilación

9-36 En esta universidad Escoge los comentarios que puede hacer un(a) estudiante típico(a) de esta universidad. Al terminar, compara tus respuesas con las de un(a) compañero(a). ¿Están de acuerdo en todo?

_____ Es una lástima que haya tan pocas computadoras en el laboratorio de lengua.

_____ Estoy contento(a) de que mis profesores sean tan accesibles.

_____ Me parece terrible que no ofrezcan más clases de español.

_____ Temo que el estudiante típico no se gradúe en cuatro años.

_____ Es impresionante que construyan tantos edificios modernos.

_____ Es curioso que la comida de la cafetería sea buena.

_____ Es bueno que en la biblioteca haya muchas colecciones interesantes y útiles.

_____ Me parece fantástico que los estudiantes siempre encuentren estacionamiento enseguida.

CD2–29 **9-37 Un profesor muy chapado a la antigua** *(old-fashioned)* Escucha al profesor Olmedo hablar de las cosas que le agradan y las cosas que le molestan. Luego, completa las siguientes oraciones.

Al Prof. Olmedo le agrada que sus estudiantes...

■ lleguen a clase...

■ lo traten con el pronombre...

■ sepan...

Pero le molesta que sus estudiantes...

■ lo interrumpan...

■ traigan...

■ no se interesen en...

Aplicaciones

9-38 Tu nuevo empleo Acabas de conseguir un nuevo empleo y tu nuevo jefe te ha enviado una lista de detalles sobre las condiciones de trabajo. Túrnense para leer los distintos puntos y para reaccionar usando las expresiones que estudiaron para reflejar emoción y sentimientos.

MODELO   E1: *Luis y tú van a compartir la oficina.*
             E2: *Me parece terrible que Luis y yo tengamos que compartir la oficina.*

1. Todo el mundo debe escribir varios informes semanales.
2. El sueldo es bastante alto.
3. Ningún empleado puede almorzar fuera de la oficina.
4. Nosotros pagamos por todos los viajes de negocio.
5. Todos los supervisores deben obtener un doctorado en su área.
6. Hay un mes completo de vacaciones durante el verano.
7. Te daremos un bono por cada nuevo cliente que consigas.
8. Yo decido cómo te debes vestir.

9-39 Cinco minutos antes de la fiesta Imagínense que Uds. van a dar una fiesta en su apartamento y faltan cinco minutos para que lleguen los primeros invitados. Algunas cosas están saliendo bien, pero otras no. Lean las claves y escriban una reacción apropiada.

MODELO   Lisa / saber preparar bebidas muy buenas
           Me parece fantástico que Lisa sepa preparar bebidas muy buenas.

1. el apartamento / estar completamente limpio
2. haber mucho espacio para entretener a los invitados
3. Sara y Josefa / no tener buena música
4. los entremeses / ser variados
5. Bernardo / querer ver a Elisa para reclamarle varias cosas
6. Leo y Diana / no venir porque tenían otro compromiso
7. tener permiso de los dueños del edificio para festejar hasta muy tarde
8. Ernesto / traer a quince personas que no conocemos

9-40 En la clase de español Hagan una lista de las cosas positivas y negativas de la clase de español. Luego, compártanla con la clase. ¿Saben cómo va a reaccionar el (la) profesor(a)?

MODELO   *Nos alegra que el libro explique bien las estructuras.*
           ¡Es bueno que tengamos que hablar sólo en español!

■ Integración

 9-41 Diferencia de opiniones Representa la siguiente situación con un(a) compañero(a).

Estudiante preocupado(a)

Imagínate que acabas de cuestionarle a un profesor la nota que recibiste en un examen. Es obvio que él y tú tienen diferentes opiniones en cuanto a tu desempeño *(performance)* en este examen y quieres resolver la situación. Como estás muy preocupado(a), decides hablar con uno(a) de tus mejores amigos(as). Cuéntale qué pasó, dile cómo te sientes y pídele su consejo.

Un(a) buen(a) amigo(a)

Uno(a) de tus mejores amigos(as) está pasando por un momento difícil y necesita tu ayuda y tu apoyo. Él/Ella acaba de cuestionarle a un profesor la nota que sacó en un examen, pero no logró resolver la situación. Pregúntale qué le pasa, ofrécele tu ayuda y dale algunos consejos prácticos.

9-42 Andrés Guzmán Termina la carta que le escribiste a Andrés Guzmán en la actividad 9-14 del **Tema 1** (pág. 361). Incorpora expresiones que reflejen tus sentimientos y tu opinión sobre la oferta de trabajo que él recibió y expresiones que reflejen tus deseos.

MODELO   *Me alegra mucho que puedas venir a los Estados Unidos, pero... Espero que tu familia y tus amigos te apoyen...*

El Salvador

Los Estados Unidos

IV. Vídeo: ¿Algo más que una amistad?

■ Preparación

A. Haciendo amigos Hasta ahora han visto la llegada de los compañeros a Puerto Rico, algunas de las excursiones que han hecho juntos y muchas conversaciones que han tenido sobre varios temas. Basándose en lo que ya han visto y lo que ahora conocen sobre cada persona, contesten las siguientes preguntas.

ESTRATEGIA DE COMPRENSIÓN

Global comprehension and contextual clues Listen to get an overall understanding of each person in this context. In addition, use all the visual contextual clues (facial expressions and gestures) available to better understand the different emotions that each person feels during the conversation.

1. Ya Uds. leyeron el artículo titulado «Cómo hacer amigos» (pág. 356). ¿Creen que los compañeros han seguido los diez consejos? ¿Por qué sí o por qué no?

2. ¿Hay alguien en particular que Uds. creen que no se ha hecho amigo(a) de los demás compañeros? ¿Qué le recomendarían a esa persona para cultivar una relación más amistosa con sus compañeros? Usen expresiones como **Le recomendamos que..., Es preferible que..., Le aconsejamos que..., Es mejor que...,** etc.

3. A veces, la amistad puede convertirse en algo más. ¿Creen que existe la posibilidad de una relación romántica entre algunos de los compañeros? ¿Entre quiénes? ¿Por qué?

■ ¿Entendiste bien?

B. Las relaciones son complicadas Mira el vídeo y trata simplemente de identificar el tema general de la conversación y cómo se sienten las personas que hablan.

1. Valeria y Antonio están hablando de...

   a. sus relaciones amorosas actuales.

   b. sus relaciones amorosas ya terminadas.

2. Indica cuáles de las siguientes emociones experimentan Valeria y Antonio en el segmento del vídeo. Escribe **V** para Valeria, **A** para Antonio y **AM** para ambos.

   ____ aburrido(a)   ____ enojado(a)

   ____ cansado(a)   ____ feliz

   ____ celoso(a) *(jealous)*   ____ nervioso(a)

   ____ enfermo(a)   ____ curioso(a)

Compara tus respuestas con las de un(a) compañero(a).

3. Ahora vas a ver el vídeo por segunda vez. Lee las siguientes oraciones y ponlas en orden según lo que sucede en el vídeo.

____ Antonio le preguntó a Valeria si estaba bien.

____ Valeria acusó a Antonio de estar espiándola y se enfadó con él.

____ Antonio le contó a Valeria lo que pasó entre Raquel, su ex-novia, y Rubén, su mejor amigo.

____ Antonio le preguntó a Valeria si quería hacer algo con él por la noche.

____ Valeria insistió en que nunca engañó a César y en que por eso no tenía por qué estar tan celoso.

____ Mientras hablaba por teléfono con César, Valeria se enfadó con él.

____ Valeria le explicó a Antonio por qué ella y César habían terminado *(had broken up)* su relación.

C. En nuestra opinión... Todos tenemos opiniones y experiencias personales que podemos usar para darles consejos a otras personas. ¿Qué opinan de lo que acaban de ver en el vídeo y qué consejos les darían a Valeria y a Antonio? Usen las siguientes preguntas para iniciar su conversación, pero no se limiten a ellas solamente. Compartan sus opiniones y experiencias y prepárense para presentarle sus conclusiones a la clase.

1. Valeria y Antonio quedaron en salir por la noche, pero no hicieron planes específicos sobre qué iban a hacer. ¿Qué les sugieren que hagan (ir a un café, cenar juntos, dar un paseo, ver una película, etc.)?

2. ¿Creen que ellos deben empezar una relación amorosa mientras están en Puerto Rico? ¿Por qué sí o por qué no?

3. ¿Es bueno o malo que las amistades se conviertan en relaciones amorosas?

4. ¿Qué creen que va a pasar entre Valeria y Antonio al final del mes, cuando tengan que volver a sus respectivos países?

D. Enfoque comunitario Visita tu tienda de vídeos favorita e investiga qué películas de España y Latinoamérica tienen disponibles. Escoge una que te parezca interesante y, mientras la ves, concéntrate en las relaciones entre los personajes (amistad, amor, conflicto, etc.). Escribe un breve resumen de la película en el que expliques qué tipos de relaciones había y finalmente tu opinión sobre la película diciendo si te gustó, si se la recomendarías a tus compañeros de clase, etc. Debes estar preparado(a) para presentarle tu resumen y tu opinión a la clase.

Relaciones de pareja

I. Vocabulario: amor, noviazgo y matrimonio

El señor y la señora González llevan 25 años de **casados.**

Juan y Marta se acaban de **separar,** pero todavía son buenos amigos.

Carmín y Augusto son **novios.**

El estado civil *Marital Status*

Adjetivos

casado *married*

comprometido *engaged*

divorciado *divorced*

soltero *single*

viudo *widower*

Verbos

casarse (por la Iglesia / por lo civil) *to get married (religious/civil ceremony)*

divorciarse *to get divorced*

enamorarse *to fall in love*

estar comprometido *to be engaged*

salir juntos *to go out, to date*

separarse *to get separated*

ser fiel/infiel *to be faithful/ unfaithful*

ser novios *to be dating, going out*

vivir juntos *to live together*

Juan y Ángela **son novios** desde hace más de un año.
*Juan and Ángela **have been dating** for over a year.*

La hermana de Juan **está comprometida** con un muchacho hondureño.
*Juan's sister **is engaged** to a guy from Honduras.*

El sacerdote los **declaró** marido y mujer.
*The priest **declared** them husband and wife.*

Doña Matilde es **viuda** y su hermano David es **divorciado.**
*Doña Matilde is **a widow** and her brother David is **divorced.***

TEMA 3

■ Asimilación

9-43 Primero... Organicen las siguientes etapas de las relaciones de pareja en un orden lógico.

____ comprometidos   ____ divorciados

____ novios   ____ amigos

____ separados   ____ casados

CD2-30 **9-44 Estado civil** Escucha la descripción de la familia de Ana María y anota el estado civil de las siguientes personas.

Pedro y Alicia: _____   Sus padres: _____

Patricia y Fernando: _____   Tía Estela: _____

Juan: _____

■ Aplicaciones

9-45 Opiniones Completa las oraciones con la palabra más apropiada. Al terminar, compara tus respuestas con las de un(a) compañero(a). Puedes usar las palabras más de una vez.

OPCIONES: enamorarse   ser fiel   vivir juntos   se casan por lo civil   marido   amantes   matrimonio   separados   divorciarse   novios

1. Es imposible _____ a primera vista. El amor requiere tiempo.
2. Es mejor ser _____ por varios años antes de casarse.
3. Las parejas que sólo _____ usualmente se separan muy pronto.
4. El _____ debe tener la última palabra en la casa.
5. Las parejas que no se comprenden deben _____.
6. Las mujeres no deben tolerar que sus esposos tengan _____.
7. _____ sin estar casados es inmoral e inaceptable. Las parejas deben contraer matrimonio antes de cohabitar.
8. Los _____ deben pensarlo muy bien antes de formalizar su relación.
9. El _____ es lo más importante en la vida de una persona.
10. Los hijos de padres _____ siempre tienen muchos problemas psicológicos.

CRITICAL THINKING SKILLS

Making Personal Value Judgments Determine whether or not the statements in activity 9-45 agree with your own value system.

9-46 ¿Qué opinas tú? Reacciona de una manera crítica a las oraciones de la actividad 9-45. Si no estás de acuerdo con algunas, vuelve a escribirlas para que reflejen mejor tu modo de pensar *(way of thinking)*.

MODELO   *No creo que las parejas que sólo se casan por lo civil se separen pronto. Todo depende de las personas y de su compromiso.*

382   trescientos ochenta y dos | Unidad 5 | Capítulo 9

9-47 Entrevista Hazle las siguientes preguntas a un(a) compañero(a) y presenta a la clase un resumen de sus respuestas.

1. ¿Estás saliendo con alguien en especial? Si no es así, ¿por qué? ¿Qué tipo de persona te gustaría tener como pareja *(as a partner)*?
2. Si tienes pareja, ¿qué es lo que más te gusta de esa persona?
3. ¿Qué crees que se necesita para tener éxito en una relación de pareja?

■ **Integración**

9-48 ¿Matrimonio? Representa la siguiente situación con un(a) compañero(a).

¡Quiero casarme ya!	¡Piénsalo!
Tú estás muy enamorado(a) y quieres casarte de inmediato. Tu amigo(a) es muy inteligente y quiere darte buenos consejos.	Tu amigo(a) parece estar muy enamorado(a) y quiere casarse de inmediato.
	Tú sabes de los problemas que se pueden presentar cuando se toma este tipo de decisión a la ligera *(lightly)*.
1. Describe tu noviazgo, contestando preguntas como: ¿Quién es el (la) afortunado(a)? ¿Por qué estás tan enamorado(a)? etc.	1. Averigua más acerca de su noviazgo: ¿Quién es el (la) afortunado(a)? ¿Por qué están tan enamorados? etc.
2. Habla de tus planes de matrimonio, indicando cuándo, cómo, dónde, etc. va a tener lugar *(going to take place)*.	2. Pregúntale acerca de sus planes de matrimonio para saber cuándo, cómo, dónde, etc. va a tener lugar.
3. Pídele su opinión.	3. Dale tu opinión al respecto. ¿Piensas tú que es una buena idea? ¿Qué crees que deben tener en cuenta antes de tomar esa decisión? etc.

9-49 Problemas de pareja

 Paso 1: En los Estados Unidos hay una tasa *(rate)* de divorcio de aproximadamente el 50%. ¿A qué creen que se debe esto? En grupos, preparen una lista de factores que ponen en peligro los matrimonios en este país.

Paso 2: Ahora, lee el siguiente artículo y escribe tu reacción personal. Usa las siguientes preguntas como guía.

1. ¿Estás de acuerdo con las ideas presentadas en el artículo?
2. ¿Qué factores de riesgo tienes, o cuáles te preocupan más?
3. ¿Qué pueden hacer las parejas para evitar la influencia negativa de cada uno de estos factores?

Parejas en alto riesgo

Aunque en muchas ocasiones las parejas se rompen por **hechos puntuales,** algunos factores te pueden **poner en riesgo** más fácilmente:

specific reasons
put at risk

- *Vivir en una ciudad.* En la ciudad existe un mayor riesgo de separación que en las zonas rurales, ya que hay más oportunidades de conocer gente —especialmente cuando los dos trabajan. Además, la presión familiar y social es mayor.

- *La juventud.* Los jóvenes tienen mayor predisposición a la ruptura porque la mayoría de ellos no considera difícil volver a encontrar una nueva pareja.

- *Antecedentes familiares.* Los hijos de padres divorciados pueden tener más tendencia a la separación porque la ven como un acontecimiento más normal.

to take on
to face
will entail

- *Las personas arriesgadas.* Quienes están acostumbrados a **asumir** riesgos en su vida sienten menos miedo a **afrontar** lo que **acarreará** la ruptura.

- *La promiscuidad.* Cuando los miembros de la pareja han tenido muchas relaciones amorosas gratificantes antes de casarse, existe más posibilidad de que haya ruptura porque ven como una liberación el poner fin a una relación infeliz.

- *Mujeres de mayor nivel cultural y profesional.* Aceptan con más facilidad el divorcio, mientras que las que no trabajan o no tienen ingresos suficientes tienden a **temerle.** En cambio, algunos hombres que tienen estatus profesional alto **rehúsan** el divorcio por temor a las consecuencias negativas que pueda tener en su imagen profesional.

to be afraid of it
refuse

- *Las parejas con hijos.* En contra de la creencia popular de que los hijos unen al matrimonio, la mayoría de los expertos, así como las estadísticas, confirman que los niños contribuyen a menudo a romper el equilibrio del hogar y la **convivencia.**

life together

II. Funciones y estructuras: Expressing doubt and denial

SOL: ¿Supiste que Raúl y Lucía están saliendo juntos?

CHARO: ¡No! **Dudo** que **sean** novios... ¡Raúl sale con Tatiana!

SOL: ¡Pues créelo!

CHARO: Mmm... **Es posible** que sólo **sean** muy buenos amigos, ¿no?

SOL: ¡Charo, no lo creo! A otro con ese cuento.

The use of the subjunctive mode is also triggered by the use of verbs and impersonal expressions that convey the idea of doubt or denial. Here is a list of some of those verbs and expressions.

Verbs	Impersonal expressions
dudar *to doubt*	es dudoso que... *it is doubtful that . . .*
negar (ie) *to deny*	es imposible que... *it is impossible that . . .*
no creer *to disbelieve*	es improbable que... *it is not likely that . . .*
no estar seguro(a) (de) *to be unsure (of)*	es posible que... *it is possible that . . .*
no pensar *to not think*	es probable que... *it is likely that . . .*
	no es cierto que... *it is not certain that . . .*
	no es seguro que... *it is not sure that . . .*
	no es verdad que... *it is not true that . . .*

The affirmative counterpart of some of these verbs and expressions **(creer, estar seguro[a], pensar, es cierto que..., es seguro que...,** and **es verdad que...)** are usually followed by verbs in the indicative mode because they do not express doubt or denial.

Mi hermana **niega** que su novio y ella **estén** comprometidos.

*My sister **denies** that her boyfriend and she **are** engaged.*

¡**Es imposible** que **vivamos** juntos antes de casarnos!

*It is not possible for us to **live** together before getting married!*

Once again, if the subject of the verb in the main and subordinate clauses is the same, use the infinitive form of verb. The same applies when the impersonal expression is used to refer to people in general.

Paco **no cree poder** asistir a la boda.

*Paco **does not think** he **can** attend the wedding.*

¿**Es posible enamorarse** a primera vista?

*Is it possible to **fall in love** at first sight?*

■ Asimilación

9-50 ¿Duda o certeza? Escoge la forma verbal correcta. Al terminar, compara tus respuestas con las de un(a) compañero(a). ¿Están de acuerdo?

1. Es verdad que mis padres (van a divorciarse / vayan a divorciarse) pronto.
2. No estamos seguros de que el Sr. Juárez (es / sea) viudo.
3. Es improbable que mi hermano y mi cuñada se (separan / separen).
4. ¿Piensas que esa chica (está / esté) comprometida?
5. Celia duda que Lalo y ella se (casan / casen) sólo por lo civil.
6. Estoy seguro de que ellos (viven / vivan) juntos.
7. ¿Es cierto que Betty y el Sr. Pérez (son / sean) novios?
8. La Sra. Cruz niega que su hija (está / esté) separada.

CD2-31 **9-51 Preguntas personales** Escucha las preguntas y contéstalas en oraciones completas. En algunos casos es posible usar diferentes expresiones como: (**Creo que..., Pienso..., Estoy seguro[a] ...,** etc.).

1. ...
2. ...
3. ...
4. ...
5. ...

■ Aplicaciones

9-52 ¡Mentiras y más mentiras! Túrnense para leer y reaccionar a las siguientes oraciones. Usen diferentes expresiones.

MODELO   E1: *Me caso la próxima semana.*
           E2: *Dudo que te cases la próxima semana.*

1. Soy una persona divorciada.
2. Mi novio(a) tiene sesenta años.
3. Mi hermana y un atleta famoso salen juntos.
4. No creo en el matrimonio.
5. El (La) profesor(a) es soltero(a).
6. El presidente y su esposa se van a separar en menos de un mes.
7. Me encuentro con mi novio(a) en el parque todas las tardes.
8. Las bodas están pasadas de moda *(out of style)*.

9-53 ¿Conocen bien al (a la) profesor(a)? De acuerdo con lo que saben de su profesor(a) y de sus hábitos, ¿qué cosas dudan y niegan que vayan a pasar en la próxima clase? Usen diferentes expresiones. Cuando terminen, compartan las oraciones con él/ella para ver si está de acuerdo.

MODELO   *No creemos que el (la) profesor(a) no dé tarea.*
           Es imposible que él/ella llegue tarde.

9-54 En los próximos días

Paso 1: Piensa en las cosas que tienes que hacer y las cosas que no vas a poder hacer en los próximos días. Luego, completa las siguientes oraciones.

No es seguro que... *Dudo que...* *No creo que...*

Es posible que... *Es increíble que...*

Paso 2: Compara tus oraciones con las de dos compañeros(as) y prepara un breve informe. Al terminar, léeselo al resto de la clase.

MODELO *No es seguro que yo visite a mi novio. Tampoco es seguro que Vicky vaya hoy a la biblioteca y que Richard lave toda su ropa. Por otro lado,...*

■ **Integración**

9-55 ¿Cierto o falso? Individualmente, preparen una lista de diez datos ciertos y diez datos falsos sobre su vida (no deben estar en orden). Luego, túrnense para leer esos datos y reaccionar según el caso. Si crees que el dato que ha leído tu compañero(a) es falso, debes explicar por qué. Al final, ¿quién conoce mejor al / a la otro(a)?

MODELO E1: *Mis padres viven en otro estado.*
E2: *Sí, creo que tus padres viven en otro estado.*
E1: *¡Correcto!*
E2: *Mi hermano tiene novia y esposa.*
E1: *¡Dudo que tu hermano tenga novia y esposa porque eso es ser infiel!*
E2: *Mmm...*

9-56 Inseguridades Escríbele una carta a tu profesor(a) sobre algunas de las inseguridades académicas y profesionales que tienes. Usa diferentes expresiones de duda y negación. Antes de entregarle la carta, dale una copia a un(a) compañero(a) para que la corrija según los siguientes criterios:

- **Contenido:** ¿Es convincente? ¿Las ideas son claras?

- **Organización:** ¿La secuencia de ideas es lógica? ¿Sigue la estructura de una carta?

- **Vocabulario:** ¿La selección de vocabulario es efectiva? ¿Usa diferentes expresiones de duda y negación?

- **Gramática:** ¿Usa el subjuntivo correctamente? ¿Hay errores de concordancia *(agreement)* entre sustantivos y adjetivos o entre sujetos y verbos?

> **SUGERENCIAS**
>
> Los datos pueden ser sobre: **las materias que toman, su familia** (personalidad, características físicas, etc.), **su casa, la comida, los gustos** (deportes, pasatiempos, etc.), **su pueblo o su ciudad, su trabajo, sus relaciones,** etc.

III. Funciones y estructuras: Talking about hypothetical situations with the subjunctive

CARLA: Elena, me acabo de enterar de que te casas. ¡Felicidades!

ELENA: Gracias, Carla. Estoy súper feliz. ¿Y cuándo te casas tú?

CARLA: No sé... ¡Primero tengo que encontrar un hombre que **sea** guapo y simpático como tu Alberto. Pero dime, ¿dónde va a ser la recepción?

ELENA: Todavía no sabemos. Estamos buscando un lugar que **tenga** cabida para muchas personas y que no **esté** lejos.

The subjunctive mode is used in adjectival clauses that describe a non-specific antecedent (a person, a place, or an object). For example, in the previous dialogue, Carla is looking for a man with certain qualities, but this person may or may not exist. Elena, on the other hand, is looking for a reception hall with certain characteristics, but she has not found it yet. Compare the following examples.

SPECIFIC AND DEFINITE ANTECEDENTS → indicative	NON-SPECIFIC AND INDEFINITE ANTECEDENTS → subjunctive
Hay una persona que me **atrae.**	No hay nadie que me **atraiga.**
Conozco un restaurante donde **sirven** comida guatemalteca.	Busco un restaurante donde **sirvan** comida guatemalteca.
Veo algo que me **llama** la atención.	No veo nada que me **llame** la atención.

When **nadie** and **nada** are followed by an adjectival clause, it must contain a verb in the subjunctive because these pronouns always refer to non-specific entities.

The subjunctive is also used in questions with **algo** or **alguien** and an adjectival clause. The answer has a verb in the indicative mode if the antecedent is specific.

¿Hay **(algo/alguien)** que te **interese**?

*Is there **(anything/anybody)** that **interests** you?*

Sí, (eso/esa persona) me **interesa** mucho.

*Yes, (that/that person) **interests** me a lot.*

BUT

No, no hay (nada/nadie) que me **interese.**

*No, (nothing/nobody) **interests** me.*

■ Asimilación

9-57 En mi familia... Escoge las alternativas que se apliquen a tu familia y luego compara tus respuestas con las de un(a) compañero(a). ¿Tienen familias semejantes o diferentes?

En mi familia hay alguien que...

____ está divorciado.
____ está comprometido.
____ es viudo.
____ está separado.
____ vive con su pareja sin casarse.
____ tiene novio(a).
____ se casa este año.
____ no cree en el matrimonio.

En mi familia no hay nadie que...

____ esté divorciado.
____ esté comprometido.
____ sea viudo.
____ esté separado.
____ viva con su pareja sin casarse.
____ tenga novio(a).
____ se case este año.
____ no crea en el matrimonio.

D2–32 **9-58 ¿Cuál es la mejor candidata?** Esteban Salcedo está buscando su media naranja *(his better half)*. Escucha la descripción que hace de la mujer de sus sueños. Luego, observa las fotos, lee las descripciones de las candidatas y escoge la que consideres más apropiada para él.

1.

2.

3.

Soy estudiante de ingeniería. Me gusta leer y jugar al tenis.

Soy abogada. Me encanta el deporte y hago ejercicios aeróbicos todos los días.

Soy estudiante de medicina. No tengo mucho tiempo libre, pero me gusta ir de vez en cuando a conciertos.

MODELO   *Pues pienso que la mejor candidata es la número... porque...*

■ Aplicaciones

9-59 Preferencias Completen las siguientes oraciones de forma lógica.

MODELO   Queremos un trabajo que *nos permita ganar mucho dinero.*

1. Necesitamos un carro que...
2. Buscamos un(a) profesor(a) que...
3. Queremos viajar a un país donde...
4. El sábado vamos a ir a un lugar que...
5. En esta universidad no hay nada que...
6. No nos gusta hablar con personas que...
7. Nos encanta llevar ropa que...
8. La pareja ideal es una persona que...
9. Entre nuestros amigos no hay nadie que...
10. No conocemos a nadie que...

EN TU COMUNIDAD

Interview at least five of your friends and family members about the personality traits they look for in a partner. In class, share your findings with other classmates and present brief oral reports.

9-60 En la clase de español Escribe por lo menos seis preguntas sobre tus compañeros de clase. Luego, hazle las preguntas a un(a) compañero(a). ¿Están de acuerdo?

> MODELO E1: *¿En la clase hay alguien que fume?*
> E2: *No, no hay nadie que fume.* or *Sí, hay alguien que fuma— Francine.*
> E1: *¡Claro que sí! ¡Francine fuma!* or *¡Estoy de acuerdo!*

1. ...   3. ...   5. ...
2. ...   4. ...   6. ...

9-61 Donde vivimos Túrnense para hacer y responder a preguntas sobre las ciudades o los pueblos donde viven. Pueden hacer preguntas adicionales para saber más detalles. Al final, ¿les gusta el lugar donde viven o prefieren el lugar donde vive el (la) otro(a) estudiante?

> MODELO E1: *¿Hay un restaurante donde sirvan buenas ensaladas?*
> E2: *Sí, se llama Demetrio's Café.*
> E1: *¿Tienen ensalada de mariscos?*
> E1: *Creo que sí. ¿Y en tu ciudad hay algún centro comercial que sea grande?*
> E2: ...

■ Integración

9-62 Aspiraciones para el futuro Explícale a tu compañero(a) algunas de tus aspiraciones para el futuro. ¡Debes estar preparado(a) para sus preguntas!

9-63 Clasificados Imagínate que eres el (la) gerente de personal de una empresa y que tienes que contratar una secretaria, un mensajero y un contable. Escribe las descripciones de las personas que buscas y dale una copia a tu profesor(a). Usa el siguiente anuncio como modelo.

SUGERENCIAS

Pueden hablar sobre **la pareja ideal, el trabajo ideal, la casa de sus sueños, la familia ideal,** y **el tipo de persona que quieren ser.**

> Distrito escolar con más de 20.000 estudiantes busca profesor(a) de matemáticas que tenga por lo menos cinco años de experiencia. Se prefiere un(a) candidato(a) al (a la) que le guste trabajar con niños de escuela primaria y que esté familiarizado(a) con las técnicas de enseñanza más innovadoras. Llame a la Dra. Talavera. (718) 555-1234.

IV. Lectura: El desamor

■ Antes de leer

A. Para conversar ¿Por qué se aburren algunas personas en su matrimonio? Preparen una lista de los factores que pueden acabar con el entusiasmo de una pareja con respecto a su matrimonio.

B. Vocabulario y conceptos Para cada palabra, indiquen la letra de la definición que corresponda.

____ 1. rutina	a.	tolerar, resistir, aceptar
____ 2. manera de ser	b.	costumbre, algo que hacemos de manera habitual
____ 3. ausencia		
____ 4. soportar	c.	que no tiene solución
____ 5. irritar	d.	personalidad
____ 6. irremediable	e.	enojar, molestar
	f.	no estar presente

■ A leer

Rosa Montero

Rosa Montero es una de las más sobresalientes *(outstanding)* escritoras españolas contemporáneas. Nació en Madrid, donde estudió periodismo y sicología. Desde 1976 trabaja en el diario *El País*. En 1980 ganó el Premio Nacional de Periodismo y en 1997 el Premio Primavera de Novela por su obra *La hija del caníbal*. Entre sus novelas más destacadas *(prominent)* se encuentran: *Crónicas del desamor, La función Delta, Te trataré como una reina* y *Bella oscura*.

La hija del caníbal (fragmento)

De manera que cogí un taxi y me fui a casa, y cuando comprobé lo que ya sabía, esto es, que Ramón tampoco estaba allí, me acerqué a la **comisaría** a presentar denuncia. Me hicieron multitud de preguntas, todas **desagradables:** que cómo nos llevábamos él y yo, que si Ramón tenía amantes, que si tenía enemigos, que si habíamos discutido, que si estaba nervioso, que si tomaba drogas, que si había cambiado últimamente de manera de ser. Y, aunque **fingí** una seguridad **ultrajada** al contestarles, el cuestionario me hizo advertir lo poco que me fijaba en mi marido, lo mal que conocía las respuestas, la inmensa ignorancia con que la rutina **cubre** al otro.

police station

unpleasant

pretended / insulted

covers

Pero esa noche, en la cama, aturdida por lo incomprensible de las cosas, me sorprendió sentir un dolor que hacía tiempo que no experimentaba: el dolor de la ausencia de Ramón. A fin de cuentas llevábamos diez años viviendo juntos, durmiendo juntos, soportando nuestros **ronquidos** y nuestras **toses,** los calores de agosto, los pies tan congelados en invierno.

snores

coughs

pondering

to rub (imperfect tense) / bald spot / daily routine / ties / love, affection

uneasy / empty

No le amaba, incluso me irritaba, llevaba mucho tiempo **planteándome** la posibilidad de separarme, pero él era el único que me esperaba cuando yo volvía de viaje y yo era la única que sabía que él se **frotaba** monoxidil todas las mañanas en la **calva.** La **cotidianeidad** tiene estos **lazos**, el **entrañamiento** del aire que se respira a dos, del sudor que se mezcla, la ternura animal de lo irremediable.

Así es que aquella noche, insomne y **desasosegada** en la cama **vacía,** comprendí que tenía que buscarlo y encontrarlo, que no podría descansar hasta saber qué le había ocurrido. Ramón era mi responsabilidad, no por ser mi hombre, sino mi costumbre.

¿Entendiste bien?

C. Ideas principales Respondan a las siguientes preguntas.

1. ¿Cómo se llama el esposo de la narradora?
   a. Juan   b. Ramón   c. Pedro
2. ¿Cuánto tiempo llevan de casados?
   a. un año   b. cinco años   c. diez años
3. ¿Adónde fue la narradora cuando descubrió que su esposo no estaba en casa?
   a. a su trabajo   b. a la comisaría   c. al aeropuerto
4. ¿Qué descubrió ella en este lugar?
   a. que no conocía muy   c. que necesitaba unas
      bien a su marido   vacaciones
   b. que amaba mucho a   d. que su marido tenía una
      su esposo   amante
5. ¿Ama la narradora a su esposo?
   a. sí   b. no   c. tal vez
6. Menciona por lo menos tres cosas que tiene la narradora en común con su marido en este momento.

D. Enfoque lingüístico Basándote en el contexto, ¿cuál es el significado de las siguientes palabras?

1. «De manera que cogí un taxi y me fui a casa, y cuando comprobé lo que ya sabía, esto es, que Ramón tampoco estaba allí, me acerqué a la comisaría a presentar **denuncia.**»
   a. denounce   b. denial   c. report
2. «El cuestionario me hizo advertir lo poco que me **fijaba** en mi marido, lo mal que conocía las respuestas, la inmensa ignorancia con que la rutina cubre al otro.»
   a. fight   b. notice   c. find
3. «Pero esa noche, en la cama, **aturdida** por lo incomprensible de las cosas, me sorprendió sentir un dolor que hacía tiempo que no experimentaba: el dolor de la ausencia de Ramón.»
   a. confused   b. helpless   c. ashamed

E. Actividad de extensión ¿Qué creen que debe hacer esta mujer para revitalizar su matrimonio? Comenten qué recomendaciones le darían *(you would give)* a la protagonista si tuvieran *(if you had)* la oportunidad de hablar con ella sobre este asunto *(matter)*.

ESTRATEGIA DE LECTURA

Scanning Keep in mind the context of marriage as you scan the text for the following information.

CRITICAL THINKING SKILLS

Analyzing and Inferring Consider the protagonist's statements in order to determine what her true feelings may be.

ESTRATEGIA DE LECTURA

Guessing from Context Consider the entire text as well as each sentence as you try to guess the meaning of the different sentences.

CRITICAL THINKING SKILLS

Making Associations and Creating Consider the protagonist's circumstances as you think of recommendations.

Buenos amigos
Good friends

Adjetivos
confiable	*trustworthy*
generoso	*generous*
honesto	*honest*
leal	*loyal*
paciente	*patient*

Verbos
aceptar	*to accept*
apoyar	*to support*
compartir	*to share*
contar (ue) con	*to count on*
corregir (i, i)	*to correct*
dar consejos	*to give advice*
estar dispuesto a...	*to be ready (eager) to . . .*
fallarle	*to fail (not be there)*
juzgar	*to judge*
preocuparse por	*to worry about*
querer/amar	*to love*

Los compañeros y los jefes
Co-workers and bosses

Adjetivos
accesible	*accessible*
agresivo	*aggressive*
buen compañero	*good colleague*
competente	*competent*
creativo	*creative*
cumplidor	*reliable*
eficiente	*efficient*
firme	*firm*
honesto	*honest*
leal	*loyal*
puntual	*punctual*
responsable	*responsible*
respetuoso	*respectful*
seguro de sí mismo	*confident*
tímido	*shy*
trabajador	*hard working*

Sustantivos
el buen sentido del humor	*good sense of humor*

Verbos
amar el trabajo	*to love one's work*
delegar parte del poder	*to delegate power*
promover (ue) un ambiente positivo de trabajo	*to promote a positive working environment*
respetar a los empleados	*to respect the employees*
saber escuchar	*to know how to listen*
ser creativo	*to be creative*
tener metas	*to have goals*
tomar riesgos/arriesgarse	*to take risks*

El estado civil
Marital Status

Adjetivos
casado	*married*
comprometido	*engaged*
divorciado	*divorced*
soltero	*single*
viudo	*widower*

Verbos
casarse por la iglesia/ por lo civil	*to get married in a religious/civil ceremony*
divorciarse	*to get divorced*
enamorarse	*to fall in love*
estar comprometido	*to be engaged*
salir juntos	*to go out, to date*
separarse	*to get separated*
ser fiel/infiel	*to be faithful/unfaithful*
ser novios	*to be dating, going out*
vivir juntos	*to live together*

Funciones y estructuras
Verbos y expresiones impersonales para dar consejos, pp. 358, 362
Verbos para expresar deseos y peticiones, p. 372
Verbos y expresiones impersonales para expresar emociones y sentimientos, p. 375
Verbos y expresiones impersonales para expresar duda, p. 385

Capítulo 10

¿Qué quieres hacer?

Para comenzar

Contesta las siguientes preguntas.

- ¿Qué actividades crees que se pueden hacer en estas regiones de Argentina y Uruguay?
- ¿Cuál de estas regiones te gustaría visitar?

In this chapter you will learn . . .

- how to talk about different leisure-time activities
- how to talk about health and fitness issues
- how to give informal commands
- how to talk about future events
- about outdoor activities and cultural events in Uruguay and Argentina

	TEMA 1 A mantenernos en forma	TEMA 2 La diversión en la ciudad	TEMA 3 Panorama cultural
Vocabulario	La buena salud y las enfermedades	Los deportes urbanos	Las bellas artes
Funciones y estructuras	Giving suggestions and instructions (review of formal commands and advice) Giving instructions with informal commands	Expressing opinion and emotion (review of the subjunctive) Expressing purpose, stipulation, or future time frame with the subjunctive in adverbial clauses	Giving directives and advice (review of formal and informal commands and introduction of **nosotros** commands) Talking about the future with the future tense
Lecturas y vídeo	Perspectivas: Una buena figura	Vídeo: Un desastre en la cocina	Lectura: El túnel

Las cataratas del Iguazú tienen una altura de más de 250 pies y son una maravilla natural que marca la frontera entre Argentina y Brasil.

La Avenida 9 de Julio y el Obelisco, en pleno centro de la ciudad de Buenos Aires.

Montevideo, capital y centro urbano más importante de Uruguay.

Enfoque

A. ¿Qué sabes ya de Argentina?

Antes de ver el vídeo, empareja cada frase de la columna A con una frase lógica de la columna B. Después, compara tus respuestas con las de un(a) compañero(a).

A	B
____ 1. el clima	a. altamente urbanizado
____ 2. los rioplatenses	b. de carácter abierto, generosos y amables
____ 3. las historias de gauchos	c. templado y agradable a lo largo del año
____ 4. una población	d. de inmigrantes provenientes de diversas partes del mundo
____ 5. un país	e. diversas e interesantes

B. Uruguay, urbano y rural

Lee las oraciones sobre Uruguay. Mientras ves el vídeo, marca con una **X** las oraciones que escuches. Luego, mientras compara tus respuestas con las de un(a) compañero(a).

1. Cerca de la mitad de la población vive en...
   a. la zona fronteriza con Argentina.
   b. la ciudad de Montevideo.
   c. los poblados de Durazno, Florida y Artigas.

2. Uruguay es conocido internacionalmente por...
   a. la calidad de las carnes que exporta.
   b. el desfile de Llamadas, el principal espectáculo del Carnaval.
   c. el mate, una infusión aromática.

3. ¿Con qué otro país comparte Uruguay el gran símbolo cultural del gaucho?
   a. Brasil
   b. Paraguay
   c. Argentina

4. ¿Cuál de las siguientes oraciones sobre la ciudad de Colonia del Sacramento *no* es verdad?
   a. Fue nombrada patrimonio cultural de la humanidad por la UNESCO.
   b. Es el lugar donde nació el escritor Eduardo Galeano.
   c. Fue una región disputada por España y Portugal.

C. ¿Qué quieren hacer en Uruguay?

Busquen en el Internet artículos sobre los tipos de turismo que pueden hacer en Uruguay. Luego, decidan qué tipo de turismo sería más adecuado para su grupo, según los intereses personales de los miembros. Prepárense para presentarle lo que decidieron a la clase y las razones por las cuales escogieron ese tipo de turismo para su grupo.

For more info, you may want to check the **Temas** site: http://temas.heinle.com

A mantenernos en forma

I. Vocabulario: La buena salud y las enfermedades

Además de **distraer,** el ejercicio sirve para **mantener un buen estado de salud** y para **combatir el estrés.**

Los ejercicios aeróbicos y de estiramiento son importantes para **mejorar** nuestra **elasticidad** y **resistencia.**

Para una buena **nutrición** es mejor evitar las **grasas animales** y los **productos refinados.**

Vocabulario práctico

Las ventajas del ejercicio físico

aumentar nuestra fuerza *to augment our strength*

bajar de/perder peso *to lose weight*

ganar/subir de peso *to gain weight*

mantenerse en forma/en buen estado de salud *to keep fit/in good health*

Es importante...

dejar de fumar *to quit/stop smoking*

hacer estiramiento *to stretch*

hacer un poco de calentamiento *to do some warm-up exercises*

Nutrición

la fibra *fiber*

los minerales *minerals*

la proteína *protein*

las vitaminas *vitamins*

Este niño tiene **fiebre** y un poco de **tos.** También **le duele la cabeza.** Él tiene un **resfriado.**

Su mamá piensa darle unas **pastillas** o un **jarabe.**

Este chico tuvo un accidente. El médico le tomó una **radiografía** y le puso un **yeso** en el brazo.

Vocabulario práctico

Problemas médicos (Medical problems)

la alergia *allergy*
la gripe/la influenza *flu*
los parásitos intestinales *intestinal parasites*

Verbos

doler (ue) *to ache, to hurt*
enfermarse *to get sick*
sentirse (ie, i) mal/mejor *to feel ill/better*
tener tos *to have a cough*

Síntomas (Symptoms)

la congestión *congestion*
el mareo *dizziness*

Ayudas terapéuticas y diagnósticas (Therapeutical and Diagnostic Aids)

el antibiótico *antibiotic*
el botiquín de primeros auxilios *first-aid kit*
la curita *Band-Aid*
el descanso *rest*
la inyección *shot, injection*
la receta *prescription*

■ Asimilación

 10-1 ¿Bueno o malo? Indica si las siguientes actividades son buenas o malas para la salud. Al terminar, compara tus respuestas con las de otros estudiantes. ¿Están todos de acuerdo?

1. hacer ejercicio aeróbico
2. llevar una vida sedentaria
3. consumir comidas ricas en grasas animales
4. escoger alimentos ricos en vitaminas y minerales
5. hacer ejercicios de calentamiento y estiramiento
6. dejar de fumar y de consumir alcohol
7. dormir cuatro horas o menos cada día

CD2-34 **10-2 Identifícalo** Vas a escuchar la descripción de varios tipos de ayudas terapéuticas y diagnósticas. ¿Puedes identificar los diferentes tipos? Indica el número de la descripción junto al tipo de ayuda que corresponda.

_____ unas pastillas   _____ un yeso

_____ una radiografía   _____ unos antibióticos

_____ un jarabe   _____ una inyección

■ Aplicaciones

10-3 ¿Qué haces? Completa el cuadro con tu información personal. (Menciona por lo menos dos cosas por cada categoría.) Al terminar, compara tus respuestas con las de otros estudiantes. ¿Tienen algo en común?

EN TU COMUNIDAD

Find out about home remedies different people use. Gather information about remedies associated with various cultures, countries, and ethnic groups. Then, discuss this information in groups of three and choose the most interesting or nontraditional remedy of the group.

¿Qué haces para...	
mantenerte en forma?	
combatir el estrés?	
mejorar tu nutrición?	
aumentar tu energía?	
distraerte?	

10-4 Síntomas Imagínense que están de vacaciones en un país de habla hispana y que necesitan atención médica. Preparen una descripción escrita de los síntomas asociados con cada una de las siguientes situaciones.

Parásitos intestinales	Una caída
Me duele el estómago.	*Me duele la espalda.*

10-5 ¿Qué debe hacer? Denle la recomendación más apropiada a cada individuo.

REMEMBER

When giving advice, remember that the verb in the subordinate clause goes in the subjunctive. **Te sugiero que** *estudies* **mucho. Te recomiendo que** *hagas* **deporte.**

MODELO   un joven turista que se cayó practicando esquí
Bueno, a este joven le recomendamos que se haga una radiografía. También es importante que tome unos analgésicos y que descanse lo más posible.

1. una chica que comió demasiado y tiene dolor de estómago
2. una señora a quien le duele mucho la cabeza
3. un señor que se encuentra muy tenso y preocupado
4. unos niños que están resfriados
5. una mujer que sufre de alergias

■ Integración

10-6 En la farmacia Representa la siguiente situación con un(a) compañero(a).

Turista

Estás de vacaciones en Argentina y desde hace dos días tienes problemas digestivos. (¡Parece que comiste demasiado asado [*grilled beef*]!) Ve a una farmacia y pídele ayuda a un(a) farmacéutico(a).

1. Salúdalo(la) formalmente.
2. Explícale tus síntomas.
3. Pídele un remedio.
4. Pregúntale cómo prevenir este tipo de problema en el futuro.

Farmacéutico(a)

Tú tienes una farmacia en el centro de Buenos Aires. Atiende a este(a) cliente(a) estadounidense. (¡Pobre! Se ve muy enfermo[a].)

1. Salúdalo(la) formalmente.
2. Pregúntale qué le pasa.
3. Dile qué remedios debe tomar.
4. Explícale las maneras de prevenir estos problemas en el futuro.

SUGERENCIAS

Para evitar (*To avoid*) los problemas digestivos, algunas sugerencias son:
- comer en lugares limpios (*clean*)
- tomar siempre agua embotellada (*bottled water*)
- no comer alimentos crudos (*raw*)
- evitar las frutas sin pelar (*not peeled*)
- pedir bebidas sin hielo (*without ice*)

 10-7 Para mantenerse en forma En grupos, preparen una campaña para motivar a otros estudiantes a mantenerse en forma. Denles recomendaciones y consejos específicos.

MODELO *Para mantenerse en forma es importante que Uds. le presten atención a su dieta. También es preciso que hagan más ejercicio y que no fumen...*

II. Funciones y estructuras: Giving suggestions and instructions (review of formal commands and advice)

SRA. NARVÁEZ:	¿Qué recomienda, doctor?
DOCTOR:	Bueno, **dele** comida sin grasa por unos días para controlar la irritación estomacal. También le **sugiero** que **compre** estas pastillas por si *(in case)* el dolor continúa.
SRA. NARVÁEZ:	Muchas gracias, doctor. ¿Algo más?
DOCTOR:	Sí. **Es necesario que** el niño **descanse** y que **tome** mucho líquido porque está un poco deshidratado.

In **Capítulo 8, Tema 2,** you learned how to give formal commands to people to whom you would refer as **usted** and **ustedes.** The verb forms of these commands are the same as the third-person singular and third-person plural forms of the present subjunctive.

Doña Graciela, **consuma** más fibra y proteína en su dieta.	*Mrs. Graciela, **eat** more fiber and protein in your diet.*
Sr. Alvarado, **no compre** tantos productos refinados.	*Mr. Alvarado, **do not buy** so many refined products.*

As you may remember, reflexive (**me, te, se, nos, os, se**), indirect object (**me, te, le, nos, os, les**), and direct object pronouns (**me, te, lo/la, nos, os, los/las**) are attached to the affirmative command and are placed between **no** and the verb in negative commands.

REMEMBER

Indirect object pronouns are placed before direct object pronouns. Also, remember that **le** and **les** change to **se** before the direct object pronouns **lo, la, los,** and **las.**

Por favor, **deme** un jarabe para la tos.	*Please **give me** a cough syrup.*
Demetrio, **no se ponga** nervioso. Va a mejorarse pronto.	*Demetrio, **do not get (become)** nervous. You are going to get better soon.*
¿Las pastillas? **No se las tomen** con el estómago vacío.	*The pills? **Do not take them** on an empty stomach.*

In **Capítulo 9, Tema 1,** you learned how to use verbs and impersonal expressions that allow you to give suggestions and instructions in a more polite and less direct manner. Here is a list of useful expressions.

REMEMBER

Using the formal command of the verb may be interpreted as rude and impolite in certain cases.

VERBS		IMPERSONAL EXPRESSIONS	
aconsejar *to advise*		es aconsejable que...	*it is advisable that . . .*
recomendar (ie) *to recommend*		es bueno que...	*it is good that . . .*
sugerir (ie, i) *to suggest*		es importante que...	*it is important that . . .*
		es justo que...	*it is fitting that . . .*
		es mejor que...	*it is better that . . .*
		es necesario que...	*it is necessary that . . .*
		es preferible que...	*it is preferable that . . .*
		es urgente que...	*it is urgent that . . .*

Les **sugiero** que **dejen** de fumar inmediatamente.	*I **suggest** that you **quit** smoking immediately.*
Es preferible que haga un poco de calentamiento primero.	***It is preferable that** you **do** some warm-up exercises first.*

■ Asimilación

10-8 Para mantenerse en buen estado de salud Indica si las siguientes recomendaciones para mantenerse en buen estado de salud son lógicas **(L)** o ilógicas **(I).** Cuando termines, compara tus respuestas con las de un(a) compañero(a). ¿Hay algo en lo que no están de acuerdo?

____ Aumenten su nivel de estrés.

____ Tomen una aspirina diaria.

____ Suban de peso.

____ Consuman muchas grasas animales.

____ Manténganse en forma.

____ No duerman más de cinco horas por día.

____ Eviten las vitaminas y los minerales.

____ Promuevan su bienestar emocional.

10-9 En la radio Imagínate que estás escuchando tu programa de consejos favorito. Escucha las sugerencias y escoge las alternativas que mejor completen las siguientes oraciones.

CD2-35

1. El especialista dice que uno no debe preocuparse por las presiones...

   a. de la familia.   b. de la vida moderna.   c. del dinero.

2. También piensa que hay que sacar tiempo para...

   a. cuidar de nuestro interior.   b. reducir el estrés.

   c. hacer cosas divertidas.

3. Él está en contra de *(against)*...

   a. no disfrutar de la vida.   b. tomar muchas medicinas.

   c. comer descontroladamente.

4. En general, uno de los problemas principales que el especialista menciona es...

   a. las emociones.   b. el trabajo.   c. nuestra voz interior.

■ Aplicaciones

10-10 ¡Las cosas cambian! La Sra. Martínez y el Sr. Pereira quieren que Uds. les den consejos prácticos para tener una buena salud. ¡Ahora son los adultos los que quieren que los más jóvenes les den consejos! Usen los verbos entre paréntesis.

Sra. Martínez,...

1. (tener) un botiquín de primeros auxilios para las emergencias.
2. (no sufrir) de gripe. (ponerse) una inyección contra la influenza todos los años.
3. (ganar) un poco de peso porque está muy delgada.
4. (no esperar) para ver al doctor si se siente mal.

Sr. Pereira,...

1. (incrementar) su actividad física.
2. si quiere sentirse mejor, (reducir) el estrés y (no comer) muchos productos con azúcar.
3. (mantenerse) en forma.
4. (sentirse) mejor haciendo cosas que le gusten.

10-11 Consejos prácticos Piensen en por lo menos ocho recomendaciones que les pueden dar a otros estudiantes de su universidad para salir bien en las clases.

> MODELO *Estudien todos los días. Les aconsejamos que no salgan si tienen un examen al día siguiente. Es importante que vayan preparados a clase.*

10-12 Una receta saludable Piensen en un plato saludable que le quieran recomendar al / a la profesor(a) y hagan una lista de los pasos que debe seguir para prepararlo. Asegúrense de incluir comentarios sobre cosas que no debe hacer y otras recomendaciones que debe seguir para que la receta quede bien.

SUGERENCIAS

Se usan los siguientes verbos en recetas: **añadir** *(to add)*, **batir** *(to shake)*, **calentar** *(to heat)*, **cortar** *(to cut)*, **echar** *(to put, to pour)*, **hervir** *(to boil)*, **mezclar** *(to mix)*, y **remover** *(to stir)*.

▓ Integración

10-13 Una consulta completa En grupos de tres estudiantes, imagínense que el Sr. Carmelo Feliciano está reunido con un(a) sicólogo(a), con un(a) nutricionista y con un(a) entrenador(a) porque quiere cambiar su estilo de vida y mejorar su salud. Lean lo que él les dice y aconséjenle de acuerdo con la profesión que escojan.

> SR. FELICIANO: «Tengo sesenta años y siento que no estoy en buen estado de salud. Tengo unas cuantas libras de sobrepeso, fumo y mi dieta es un desastre. No hago ningún tipo de ejercicio, como pueden ver. Además de esto, quiero mejorar mi actitud hacia la vida porque, aunque tengo todo el tiempo del mundo —soy jubilado—, no hago nada interesante. ¿Qué me aconsejan? ¡Quiero vivir muchos años más!»

SUGERENCIAS

Para dar consejos, puedes usar los verbos **aconsejar, recomendar,** y **sugerir** y las expresiones **es necesario/recomendable/ urgente que...**

El (La) sicólogo(a)	**El (La) nutricionista**	**El (La) entrenador(a)**
¿Qué le puedes aconsejar al Sr. Feliciano para tener una actitud más positiva hacia la vida? ¿Qué tipo de actividades le puedes recomendar? ¿Qué cosas debe modificar?	¿Qué le aconsejas al Sr. Feliciano para bajar de peso? ¿Qué cosas debe hacer para sentirse físicamente mejor? ¿Qué dieta le sugieres y qué pasos debe seguir para alcanzar esta meta?	¿Qué plan de actividad física le recomiendas a una persona de sesenta años que no es muy activa? ¿Qué cosas debe hacer para tener éxito y para lograr mejores resultados?

10-14 Un afiche *(poster)* Usen la información de la actividad 10-13 para hacer un afiche con una lista de las cosas que se deben y las que no se deben hacer para tener una vida saludable. Cuando esté listo, preséntenselo al resto de la clase.

III. Funciones y estructuras: Giving instructions with informal commands

¡Hombre! ¿Qué haces aquí? **¡No vayas** a clase hoy! **Visita** a tu médico o **toma** alguna medicina. **¡Anda, vete** a casa! **Llámame** si necesitas algo.

You are already familiar with the **usted** and **ustedes** (formal) command forms. You will now learn how to give commands in the **tú** (informal) form.

Affirmative **tú** verb commands have the same form as the **él, ella,** and **usted** present indicative form. Pronouns are attached to the end of the conjugated verb.

Elena, **descansa.** Te ves mal.	*Elena, **rest.** You look bad.*
Cheo, **dame** la medicina para la tos.	*Cheo, **give me** the cough medicine.*
Vístete. Vamos a hacer aeróbicos.	***Get dressed.** We are going to do aerobics.*

> Notice that, when adding a pronoun to a command form, a written accent mark is necessary if the stress is on the third-to-the-last syllable. Compare <u>**dame**</u> (the stress is in on the second-to-the-last syllable) and <u>**vístete**</u> (the stress is on the third-to-the-last syllable).

Some verbs have irregular **tú** affirmative command forms (that is, they do not coincide with the **él, ella,** and **usted** present indicative verb form). Here is a list of some of those verbs.

decir	**di**	salir	**sal**
hacer	**haz**	ser	**sé**
ir	**ve**	tener	**ten**
mantener	**mantén**	venir	**ven**
poner	**pon**		

Haz los ejercicios tres veces y después **ve** al cuarto de sauna.	***Do** three repetitions and then **go** to the sauna room.*
Ponte los tenis si quieres estar cómoda.	***Put on** your sneakers if you want to be comfortable.*

To give a negative **tú** command, use **no** or **nunca** and the **tú** present subjunctive verb form. As in the case of formal commands, pronouns are placed between **no** or **nunca** and the verb.

Nunca tomes riesgos innecesarios.	***Never take** unnecessary risks.*
Sofía, **no les des** tanta importancia a esas cosas.	*Sofía, **do not give** so much importance to those things.*
¡Por favor, **no te preocupes**!	*Please, **do not worry**!*

▨ Asimilación

 10-15 Antes de practicar un deporte Lee las siguientes recomendaciones para las personas que quieren practicar un deporte e identifica todos los mandatos en la forma **tú.**

1. Consulta a tu médico para asegurarte de que estás en buena condición física. Dile qué deporte quieres practicar y pregúntale si hay algún riesgo.

2. Busca toda la información posible sobre el deporte que escogiste. Decide qué equipo especial se necesita y cómpralo en una tienda especializada.

CD2-36 **10-16 Delegando responsabilidades** Escucha las instrucciones que les da la Sra. Lafuente a sus hijos e indica si las oraciones que siguen son ciertas **(C)** o falsas **(F).**

____ 1. La Sra. Lafuente quiere que Rosa haga el almuerzo.

____ 2. Antonio tiene que lavar el carro de su madre.

____ 3. A la Sra. Lafuente no le gusta que Pedrito traiga a sus amigos si ella no está en casa.

____ 4. Clarisa es responsable de hacer una sola tarea.

▨ Aplicaciones

10-17 ¿Qué debo hacer? Lean el siguiente diálogo entre Sandra y Perla sobre cómo mantenerse en forma. Completen las oraciones con la forma **tú** del mandato de los verbos de la lista. **¡OJO!** Deben usar pronombres de objeto directo y de objeto indirecto en algunos casos.

ir   tomar   hablar   ser   disminuir

SANDRA: Perla, quiero mantenerme en forma y no sé por dónde empezar.

PERLA: _____ a un gimnasio por lo menos tres veces por semana. El ejercicio cardiovascular es buenísimo y vas a ver que funciona.

SANDRA: Lo he pensado, ¡pero es que soy tan perezosa para eso!

PERLA: ¡Lo sé! Mira, conozco a un entrenador que trabaja en el gimnasio de la calle San Martín. _____ a él sobre tu problema y te va a ayudar. Es todo un profesional del ejercicio y del fisiculturismo.

SANDRA: Está bien. También voy a pedirle que me ayude a modificar mis hábitos alimenticios.

PERLA: Yo te puedo ayudar con eso. Para empezar, _____ la cantidad de calorías que consumes. Y los refrescos con azúcar, no _____. El agua es mucho mejor.

SANDRA: Bueno, no sé cómo comenzar. Ya vamos a ver cómo me va.

PERLA: ¡No _____ pesimista, mujer! Yo te voy a apoyar.

10-18 ¡A actuar! Escriban mandatos afirmativos y negativos para algunos compañeros de la clase. Cuando les toque el turno *(When your turn comes),* den los mandatos. Si la persona reacciona al recibir un mandato negativo, ésta pierde *(loses).* ¡Sean originales!

MODELO   *Cristina, corre por el salón. / Alberto, no le toques el pelo a Cinthia.*

10-19 ¿Qué hago para...? Túrnense y dense recomendaciones para lograr las siguientes cosas. Pueden usar los verbos sugeridos y otros verbos lógicos.

> MODELO   obtener una buena nota en la clase de español (estudiar, practicar, repasar, hablar inglés, prestar atención)
> E1: *¿Qué hago para obtener una buena nota en la clase de español?*
> E2: *Estudia todos los días, practica con tus compañeros, repasa los apuntes, no hables inglés en clase y préstale atención al / a la profesor(a).*

1. conseguir un buen trabajo (preparar, escribir, buscar, leer, considerar)
2. prepararme para una cita (bañarse, ponerse, comprar, maquillarse/ afeitarse)
3. mantenerme en forma (ir, practicar, hacer, comer, fumar)
4. preparar unos espaguetis (comprar, conseguir, hervir, servir)
5. tener la mente sana (ir, salir, evitar, distraerse, reducir)
6. prepararme para una mudanza (comprar, llamar, reservar, empacar, hacer)

■ Integración

10-20 Una nueva vida Representa la siguiente situación con un(a) compañero(a).

¡Me mudo!

Te vas a mudar para una ciudad grande de los Estados Unidos por motivos de trabajo y no sabes qué hacer ni qué esperar. Explícale tu situación a un(a) amigo(a) y pídele sugerencias. Pregúntale acerca de:

- los servicios básicos de tu nuevo apartamento
- cómo hacer nuevos amigos
- qué hacer para dar una buena impresión en tu trabajo
- las oportunidades de crecimiento profesional y personal

¡Mi amigo(a) se muda!

Uno(a) de tus mejores amigos(as) se muda para una ciudad grande de los Estados Unidos porque consiguió un trabajo excelente ahí. Ahora está muy abrumado(a) *(overwhelmed)* porque no sabe qué debe hacer para prepararse para este cambio tan importante. Escúchalo(la) y dale tus sugerencias acerca de las cosas que te pregunte.

SUGERENCIAS

Para responder negativamente a algo que diga tu compañero(a), puedes decir:

No sé.	*I don't know.*
Creo que no.	*I don't think so.*
No estoy seguro(a).	*I am not sure.*
No estoy de acuerdo.	*I don't agree.*

SUGERENCIAS

Para introducir una nueva idea, puedes decir:

¡Ya sé!	*I know!*
¡Ya lo entiendo!	*I got it!*
Tengo una idea.	*I have an idea.*

SUGERENCIAS

Los lugares de interés pueden ser **la biblioteca, la librería, el centro de estudiantes, la oficina de admisiones, la oficina del Registrador** *(Registrar's office)*, y **el edificio de la Facultad** *(School/Department)* **de Biología/ Humanidades/...**

10-21 Direcciones Uno de los usos más comunes de los mandatos es dar direcciones para ir de un lugar a otro. Imagínate que un estudiante de primer año que no conoce bien la universidad te pide direcciones para llegar a tres lugares diferentes. Escribe estas direcciones. Cuando termines, dale una copia a un(a) compañero(a) para que las revise. Usa las siguientes expresiones:

- **doblar a la derecha/izquierda**   *to turn right/left*
- **seguir derecho**   *to go straight*
- **bajar**   *to go down*
- **subir**   *to go up*
- **cruzar**   *to cross*

IV. Perspectivas: Una buena figura

■ Antes de leer

A. Para conversar Contesten las siguientes preguntas.

1. ¿Eres miembro de un gimnasio? Si es así, ¿cuánto cuesta tu membresía *(membership)* por mes?
2. ¿Te parece que el costo de las membresías de los gimnasios es alto o bajo? Explica por qué.
3. ¿Qué servicios ofrece tu gimnasio?
4. ¿Con qué frecuencia vas?
5. ¿Hay horas, días o meses en que hay demasiada gente en el gimnasio? Si es así, explica qué horas/días/meses son y por qué crees que va tanta gente.

■ A leer

La floreciente industria del cuerpo

arrival

Se cumple con exactitud matemática: con la **llegada** del buen tiempo, la gente comienza a hacer más ejercicio físico. Los clubes, las plazas de deportes y la **rambla** de Montevideo se llenan, en esta época del año, de nuevos aficionados que quieren ponerse **al día** con toda la actividad física que no hicieron durante los meses anteriores.

boardwalk

up-to-date

Como consecuencia de ello, aumenta en un promedio del 25% el número de **socios** en los gimnasios, en parte gracias a los planes que ofrecen estos centros. A causa de ello, las instituciones crean más grupos y se multiplican las horas de clases.

members

Pero la proliferación de gimnasios tiene su **contrapartida.** No hay controles oficiales sobre los nuevos centros y los más antiguos, incluso con varias décadas de funcionamiento, son los primeros en advertir este aspecto negativo.

counterpart

La cultura del cuerpo perfecto

En esta época del año es habitual que la gente se preocupe por realizar alguna actividad física. La proximidad del verano aparece **ligada** con el hecho de ir a la playa y con la exposición del cuerpo. En esta **estación,** todos empezamos a hacer una evaluación de nuestro cuerpo y tendemos a pensar que no estamos presentables para **descubrirnos** frente a los demás. Este sentimiento existió siempre; no se trata de un fenómeno reciente.

linked

season

to unveil, unrobe

De todas maneras, creo que hay dos factores vinculados con la **comunicación mediática** que influyen en gran forma en nuestros comportamientos.

mass media

El primero está asociado con el tipo de belleza física **que se venera** hoy en día. Esta belleza ha consistido en perder unos cuantos kilos, sobre todo en estos últimos años. Los medios nos imponen un modelo de mujer **escuálida.** Esto hace que la gente se compare y tienda a imitar a estas mujeres.

that is revered

emaciated

El segundo es que, en respuesta a esta tendencia, empiezan a aparecer una serie de servicios ligados al **afán** de conseguir una buena figura. Los mismos van desde gimnasios y dietas, hasta médicos especialistas.

urge

Los hombres y las mujeres no sienten la misma presión. Los estímulos **se han volcado** fundamentalmente sobre el mercado femenino. Nuestra cultura hace del cuerpo femenino un valor fundamental. Al varón se le permite ser un poco menos atractivo, mientras que la mujer debe cumplir con ciertos cánones de belleza.

have been focused

Estamos viviendo un redescubrimiento de la **corporalidad.** Antes la gente **se cubría** más que ahora. Tener un buen cuerpo genera **confianza,** prestigio y oportunidades. Hay un culto al cuerpo ágil, **liviano** y bien formado que se asocia, a la vez, con la **búsqueda** de la eterna juventud. Ésta constituye una preocupación que **desvela** a hombres y mujeres por igual.

related to the body
to cover oneself (imperfect tense) /
confidence, trust / light
search
keeps awake

Los uruguayos, en general, todavía nos permitimos ciertas libertades. Podemos presentarnos «**menos producidos**» ante los demás. De todas maneras, la preocupación por el cuerpo la estamos sintiendo cada vez más.

less worked, less developed

¿Entendiste bien?

B. Ideas principales Contesten las siguientes preguntas.

1. ¿Cuál es la época en que va más gente a los gimnasios en Uruguay? ¿Por qué?
2. ¿Cuál es el problema con la proliferación de gimnasios en este país sudamericano?
3. ¿Cuáles son los dos factores que explican el mayor interés que existe hoy en día en hacer ejercicio?
4. Según el artículo, ¿quiénes tienen más presión social por lucir un cuerpo «perfecto»?
5. ¿Cuál es el ideal físico de los uruguayos?

C. Detalles importantes Lean las siguientes oraciones e indiquen si son ciertas **(C)** o falsas **(F).**

_____ 1. El frío motiva a los uruguayos a ir al gimnasio.

_____ 2. Con el aumento de interés en el ejercicio, ha aumentado el número de gimnasios.

_____ 3. El gobierno tiene controles muy estrictos sobre estos negocios.

_____ 4. Los medios de comunicación son responsables de este interés en la industria del cuerpo.

_____ 5. Los uruguayos están obsesionados por alcanzar la perfección física.

D. Debate ¿Es la situación en Uruguay semejante o diferente a la de los Estados Unidos? Expliquen su respuesta.

E. Actividad de extensión Imagínense que están en Montevideo y que van a abrir un nuevo gimnasio. Preparen el anuncio comercial para atraer y motivar a más clientes.

La diversión en la ciudad

I. Vocabulario: Los deportes urbanos

Patinaje en línea: Los patines tienen tres o cuatro ruedas alineadas en una hilera única —cinco en las pruebas de velocidad. Es un deporte de moda tanto en Estados Unidos como en Europa. Equipo: patines, coderas, rodilleras y casco.

Ciclismo: Es una manera muy divertida de mantenerse en forma. Las modalidades más importantes practicables en la ciudad son: ciclismo en carretera, «citybike» y BMX acrobático. Equipo: una bicicleta de carreras, de «mountainbike» o de «citybike» y un casco.

Squash: Se practica en una cancha cerrada o un frontón, entre dos jugadores que usan raquetas para golpear una pelota antes de que toque dos veces el suelo. Equipo: una raqueta de squash, pelotas y unas gafas protectoras.

Los bolos: Se practica en una cancha especial, usualmente automatizada. Equipo: una bola, bolos y unas zapatillas livianas.

La escalada libre: Se practica en gimnasios provistos de paredes especiales. Equipo: arnés.

Vocabulario práctico

Equipo *Equipment*

al cubierto/bajo techo
  indoors
el arnés *harness*
la bicicleta *bicycle*
la cancha *court*
el casco *helmet*
la codera *elbow pad*
la cuerda *rope*
las gafas protectoras *goggles*
el juego/el set *set*

la pelota/la bola *ball*
la raqueta *racket*
la rodillera *knee pad*

Habilidades *Skills*

escalar *to climb*
golpear *to hit*
halar/jalar *to pull*
pedalear *to pedal*
tirar *to throw*

■ Asimilación

 10-22 Opiniones y preferencias Clasifica los deportes urbanos de acuerdo con las siguientes categorías. Luego, compara tus respuestas con las de otros compañeros. ¿En qué están todos de acuerdo?

OPCIONES: el squash   el patinaje en línea   la escalada libre
               los bolos   el ciclismo

Difícil	Peligroso (Dangerous)	Interesante	Costoso	Aburrido

CD2-37 **10-23 Identifícalo** Vas a escuchar la descripción de tres deportes urbanos. ¿Puedes identificarlos? Indica el número de la descripción que corresponda a cada deporte.

_____ el squash   _____ el ciclismo   _____ los bolos

_____ la escalada libre   _____ el patinaje en línea

■ Aplicaciones

 10-24 Adivina Menciona un lugar o un objeto relacionado con un deporte urbano. Tu compañero(a) debe adivinar de qué deporte se trata. Luego, intercambien papeles. **¡OJO!** ¡Sólo tienen dos oportunidades para adivinar!

MODELO   E1: *Casco.*
              E2: *Patinaje en línea.*
              E1: *Ése no, otro.*
              E2: *¿Ciclismo?*
              E1: *¡Correcto!*

10-25 ¿Qué deporte? Indiquen el deporte más apropiado para cada individuo y expliquen su elección.

MODELO   una joven que está en forma, pero que está aburrida con sus clases de aeróbicos
Bueno, creemos que esta joven debe practicar la escalada libre porque es un deporte ideal para personas en buena condición física.

1. una señora casada que tiene dos hijos pequeños
2. un joven a quien le encantan la velocidad y las emociones fuertes
3. una chica universitaria que quiere perder peso
4. un hombre de negocios muy competitivo
5. una pareja de recién casados

 10-26 Entrevista Hazle las siguientes preguntas a un(a) compañero(a) y comparte sus respuestas con el resto de la clase.

1. ¿Practicas algún deporte urbano?
2. ¿Cuáles de los deportes mencionados en este capítulo te gustaría aprender?
3. ¿Cuál(es) no te interesa(n)? ¿Por qué?
4. ¿Qué ventajas y qué inconvenientes tienen los deportes urbanos?

■ Integración

 10-27 Aburridos Representa la siguiente situación con un(a) compañero(a).

El (La) amante de la naturaleza	El (La) deportista urbano(a)
Hoy no tienes nada que hacer y te encuentras aburrido(a). Llama a tu amigo(a) para ver qué se le ocurre hacer. Importante: Trata de convencer a tu amigo(a) de hacer alguna actividad al aire libre. 1. Saluda a tu amigo(a). 2. Pregúntale qué está haciendo. 3. Si está libre, invítalo(la) a hacer alguna actividad al aire libre. 4. Explícale las ventajas de las actividades al aire libre y los inconvenientes de los deportes urbanos.	Hoy no tienes nada que hacer y te encuentras aburrido(a). Tu amigo(a) te llama para ver qué quieres hacer. Importante: Trata de convencer a tu amigo(a) de acompañarte a practicar tu deporte urbano favorito. 1. Saluda a tu amigo(a). 2. Dile que estás libre hoy. 3. Trata de convencerlo(la) de acompañarte a practicar tu deporte urbano favorito. 4. Explícale las ventajas de los deportes urbanos y los inconvenientes de las actividades al aire libre.

 10-28 El deporte ideal para Ud. es... En parejas, preparen un cuestionario para determinar el tipo de deporte que más le conviene *(is best for)* a una persona de acuerdo con sus preferencias y posibilidades. Por ejemplo: ¿Cuánto tiempo libre tiene? ¿Le gustan las actividades al aire libre? ¿Tiene Ud. bicicleta? etc. Al terminar, háganle esas preguntas a otra pareja, analicen sus respuestas y presenten sus recomendaciones.

MODELO   *A John le recomendamos que practique... porque... Por otra parte, a Jennifer le recomendamos... porque...*

SUGERENCIAS

Para persuadir a alguien de hacer algo diferente, puedes decir:

¿Sabes qué?	*You know what?*
En realidad no me gusta...	*I don't really like to . . .*
Mira, ¿por qué no...?	*Look, why don't we . . . ?*
¿Qué te parece si...?	*How about . . . ?*

SUGERENCIAS

Usa los siguientes conectores en tu informe:

por otra parte *on the other hand*
sin embargo *however*
en cambio *on the other hand*
también *also*
de la misma manera *by the same token*
igualmente *in the same way*

II. Funciones y estructuras: Expressing opinion and emotion (review of the subjunctive)

DIEGO: Pilar, **me alegra que hayas** decidido practicar ciclismo. Es un buen deporte para nosotros los que vivimos en la ciudad.

PILAR: Sí, hace tiempo que quería hacerlo, pero como no tenía bicicleta...

DIEGO: Claro. Y también **es bueno que tengas** un casco. Ya sabes: la seguridad ante todo.

PILAR: Así es. ¡Yo no montaría en bicicleta sin casco por estas avenidas ni loca!

As you learned in **Capítulo 9, Tema 2,** expressions of opinion and emotion like the ones Diego used in the conversation above trigger the use of the subjunctive mode. Here is a complete list of the verbs and impersonal expressions you learned in the previous chapter.

VERBS		IMPERSONAL EXPRESSIONS	
agradar*	to like	es un abuso que...	it is an abuse that . . .
alegrarse (de)	to be glad	es bueno que...	it is good that . . .
doler* (ue)	to be hurt	es curioso que...	it is odd that . . .
estar contento(a) (de)	to be happy	es extraño que...	it is strange that . . .
estar furioso (de)	to be angry	es impresionante que...	it is impressive that . . .
gustar*	to be pleased		
molestar*	to be bothered	es increíble que...	it is incredible that . . .
parecer fantástico*	to consider great	es una lástima que...	it is a shame that . . .
parecer terrible*	to consider terrible	es malo que...	it is bad that . . .
parecer triste*	to consider sad	es una pena que...	it is a pity that . . .
sentir	to feel, to lament	es raro que...	it is unusual that . . .
temer	to fear	es ridículo que...	it is ridiculous that . . .
tener miedo	to be afraid	es terrible que...	it is terrible that . . .

*Remember: These verbs are used with indirect object pronouns.

Es raro que Sergio y Leo, dos personas tan cuidadosas, no **usen** rodilleras.

*It is unusual that Sergio and Leo, two very careful people, do not **use** knee pads.*

A mi novio le **parece fantástico** que a mí me **guste** el patinaje en línea.

*My boyfriend **thinks it is great** that I **like** in-line skating.*

■ Asimilación

10-29 Opiniones Completa las siguientes oraciones de forma lógica. Al terminar, compara tus respuestas con las de un(a) compañero(a). ¿Tienen las mismas opiniones?

1. Es una pena que ustedes (lleven / no lleven) gafas protectoras.
2. ¡Estoy contenta de que nosotros (juguemos / no juguemos) a los bolos en familia los sábados!
3. Marla, es extraño que (traigas / no traigas) la raqueta si sabes que vamos a jugar.
4. Es ridículo que ellos (quieran / no quieran) jugar béisbol con una pelota de golf.
5. Temo que Fernando (pueda / no pueda) venir a la práctica hoy porque está enfermo.
6. Jaime, ¿te gusta que tu hijo (escale / no escale) esas paredes tan altas siendo tan pequeño?

10-30 La Casa del Deporte Escucha el anuncio de radio de La Casa del Deporte, una tienda de equipo deportivo, e indica si las oraciones que siguen son ciertas **(C)** o falsas **(F).**

CD2-38

____ 1. En esta ciudad hay muy pocas personas que practican deportes.

____ 2. En La Casa del Deporte hay una buena selección de cascos y rodilleras.

____ 3. También tienen una buena selección de cuerdas y gafas protectoras.

____ 4. Los empleados de esta tienda pueden ayudar al cliente a escoger una buena cancha para jugar.

____ 5. Parece que La Casa del Deporte es una tienda pequeña.

■ Aplicaciones

10-31 Es bueno que... Completen la tabla con dos cosas que recomiendan para practicar cada uno de los siguientes deportes.

el patinaje en línea	el ciclismo
Es bueno que...	Es bueno que...
los bolos	**la escalada libre**
Es bueno que...	Es bueno que...

EN TU COMUNIDAD

Find out if there are any laws related to safety while practicing certain sports in your community. Discuss your findings in groups and present an oral report in class.

10-32 ¿Qué piensan? Túrnense para leer las siguientes oraciones y reaccionar de forma lógica.

MODELO   E1: *Mis amigos piensan que jugar a los bolos es aburrido.*
E2: *Es una pena que tus amigos piensen que jugar a los bolos es aburrido. A mí me gusta mucho jugar a los bolos.*

1. La cancha de tenis de mi barrio es grande.
2. Quiero practicar algún deporte, pero no tengo tiempo.
3. Los hijos de mis vecinos no usan casco cuando montan en bicicleta.
4. Voy a comprar una nueva raqueta de squash.
5. Tengo que dejar de hacer escalada libre porque me duele mucho una rodilla.
6. No puedo ir al partido de béisbol esta noche porque tengo que estudiar.
7. Estas gafas protectoras sirven para practicar cualquier deporte.
8. Quiero ir con ustedes, pero mis patines están dañados *(broken: they don't work)*.

10-33 Eventos recientes *(current events)* ¿Qué cosas han pasado últimamente en el mundo de la política, el cine, el arte, la ciencia y la educación? ¿Qué piensan Uds. sobre estas cosas? Escriban por lo menos seis oraciones para expresar sus opiniones y sus sentimientos.

MODELO   *Nos alegra que... esté embarazada.*
Es terrible que el senador... diga que...

Integración

10-34 ¡Un momento! Representa la siguiente situación con un(a) compañero(a).

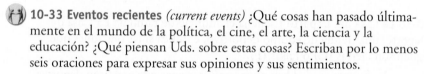

<table>
<tr><td>

Un(a) deportista que tiene demasiadas metas

Eres una persona que quiere poder practicar la mayor cantidad de deportes posible. Habla con un(a) entrenador(a) y trata de convencerlo(la) de que tienes las cualidades necesarias para lograr esta meta.

</td><td>

Un(a) entrenador(a) realista

Eres un(a) entrenador(a) y una de las personas con quien trabajas quiere practicar muchos deportes diferentes. Como eres muy realista, prefieres que esta persona aprenda deporte por deporte *(one sport at a time)*. Escucha lo que te dice y exprésale tu opinión y lo que sientes al respecto.

</td></tr>
</table>

SUGERENCIAS

Las siguientes expresiones pueden ayudarte a convencer a tu entrenador(a):

¡Estoy seguro(a)!	*I am sure!*
¡Tengo lo que se necesita!	*I have what it takes!*
¡Soy muy bueno(a) para...!	*I am very good at . . . !*
¡Estoy en excelente condición física para...!	*I am in excellent physical condition to . . . !*

SUGERENCIAS

Puedes usar las siguientes expresiones para convencer a tu cliente de que debe hacer las cosas de a poco:

Un momento!	*One moment!*
¡Con calma!	*Take it easy!*
¡Piénsalo bien!	*Think about it!*
¡No estoy de acuerdo!	*I don't agree!*

10-35 Una carta para tu supervisor(a) Imagínate que eres el (la) entrenador(a) de la actividad 10-34. Como esta persona no quedó completamente convencida de que debe tomar las cosas con calma y temes que se queje *(complains),* has decidido escribirle una carta a tu supervisor(a) para explicarle la situación. Usa los verbos y las frases para expresar emoción y opinión que ya sabes. Cuando termines, dale una copia a tu profesor(a) para que la corrija.

III. Funciones y estructuras: Expressing purpose, stipulation, or future time frame with the present subjunctive in adverbial clauses

> **¡Gran apertura!**
>
> GIMNASIO HÉRCULES
>
> Con el equipo más avanzado **para que pierda** peso y **desarrolle** un cuerpo espectacular en corto tiempo.
>
> Oferta introductoria de sólo $75 por mes.
>
> **¡Cuando vea** los resultados, va a quedar convencido(a)! **¡En caso de que no esté** satisfecho(a), le devolveremos su dinero!

The subjunctive mode is required in subordinate clauses that are introduced by certain conjunctions. These conjunctions can be grouped in three categories.

As with other expressions that trigger the use of the subjunctive mode, when the subject of the main clause and the subordinate clause is the same these expressions are followed by an infinitive (with some exceptions that you will learn about in **Capítulo 11, Tema 2**).

- conjunctions that express purpose or reason

> **a fin de que** *in order that, so that*　　**para que** *in order that, so that*

Voy a pasar por tu casa a las diez **para que vayamos** a patinar.
Decidí acompañarte **a fin de que** no **regreses** sola esta noche.

*I will stop by your house at ten **so that we can go** skating.*
*I decided to go with you **so that you** do not **come back** alone tonight.*

- conjunctions that express stipulation

> **a menos que** *unless*　　**en caso de que** *in case that,*
> **con tal de que** *provided that*　　　*in the event that*

Ella va a llegar al gimnasio a eso de las cinco **a menos que ocurra** algo en la oficina.
Llámame **en caso de que vayan** a jugar a los bolos esta tarde.

*She is going to get to the gym at around five **unless** something **happens** at the office.*
*Call me **in case that you go** bowling this afternoon.*

- adverbs and conjunctions that express future time frame

> **antes (de) que** *before*　　**en cuanto** *as soon as*
> **cuando** *when*　　**hasta que** *until*
> **después (de) que** *after*　　**mientras (que)** *while*

Cuando salgas de tu casa, trae los cascos y las coderas.
Vamos a construir una cancha bajo techo **en cuanto tengamos** el dinero.

***When you leave** home, bring the helmets and the elbow pads.*
*We are going to build an indoor court **as soon as we have** the money.*

■ Asimilación

10-36 ¿Cuándo? Empareja las frases de la izquierda con las de la derecha. Cuando termines, compara tus respuestas con las de un(a) compañero(a). ¿Crees que debes cambiar algo?

____ 1. No voy a poder estudiar...	a. antes de que yo la pague.
____ 2. Vamos a ver televisión...	b. en cuanto tenga la información.
____ 3. No puedes usar la bicicleta...	c. mientras estés escuchando música.
____ 4. Dice que va a leer...	d. hasta que lo entienda todo.
____ 5. Te aviso...	e. después de que tú limpies la sala.
____ 6. Vamos a jugar...	f. cuando abran la cancha.

CD2-39 **10-37 Preguntas** Escucha las preguntas y escoge la respuesta más lógica.

1. En caso de que...
   a. haya una emergencia. b. tenga que ir al doctor.
2. Para que...
   a. los músculos se relajen. b. no me dé alergia.
3. A fin de que nosotros...
   a. subamos un poco de peso. b. nos mantengamos en forma.
4. Cuando...
   a. me ponga un yeso. b. compre los parches *(patches)*
5. En cuanto...
   a. tome una pastilla. b. me duela el estómago.
6. Sí, a menos que...
   a. aumente mi elasticidad. b. me despierte tarde.

■ Aplicaciones

10-38 Propósitos y condiciones Unan los siguientes pares de oraciones y usen las conjunciones entre paréntesis. Hagan los cambios que sean necesarios.

MODELO   Ernesto lleva a sus hijos. Sus hijos juegan a los bolos también. (para que)
Ernesto lleva a sus hijos para que jueguen a los bolos también.

1. Patricia nunca trae el casco. Su madre se lo recuerda. (a menos que)
2. Andrés puede jugar. Su novia sale del trabajo. (después de que)
3. Quiero comprar la bicicleta. La oferta termina el jueves. (antes de que)
4. Vamos a traer el equipo. Ustedes lo pueden usar. (a fin de que)
5. Traje un cambio de ropa. Decidimos ir a un restaurante después de patinar. (en caso de que)
6. Te presto la raqueta. No quiero jugar más. (cuando)
7. Carmen y Tomás van a hacer aeróbicos. Cierran el gimnasio. (hasta que)
8. José motiva a su hermana. Ella pierde peso rápidamente. (para que)

10-39 Los estudios

Paso 1: Completa las siguientes oraciones de una manera lógica.

1. Mis padres quieren que termine mis estudios para que yo...
2. Voy a tener un buen promedio general este semestre a menos que...
3. Quiero graduarme antes de que...
4. Es posible que tome menos cursos el próximo semestre en caso de que...
5. Pienso tomar cursos de español hasta que...
6. Siempre saco buenas notas con tal de que...
7. Voy a seguir estudiando hasta que...
8. En cuanto..., espero comprar una casa grande y un carro nuevo.

Paso 2: Compara tus respuestas con las de un(a) compañero(a). Prepara un informe breve y preséntalo en clase.

> **MODELO** *Mis padres quieren que termine mis estudios para que yo pueda ganar mucho dinero, pero los padres de Danielle quieren que ella termine para que sea una abogada excelente.*

10-40 Causa y efecto Combinen elementos de las siguientes columnas para formar oraciones lógicas. Pueden usar otros verbos y expresiones.

> **MODELO** los padres   trabajar...   para que...
> *Los padres trabajan muchas horas para que sus hijos vivan bien.*

| los padres
el (la) profesor(a)
la gente
los niños
los atletas
los artistas
el gobierno | + | trabajar...
estudiar...
establecer...
decidir...
asignar...
comportarse...
respetar... | + | para que... |

■ Integración

10-41 Metas y perspectivas Túrnense para hacer y responder a las siguientes preguntas. Al terminar, preparen un informe breve y preséntenselo a la clase.

1. ¿Piensas hacer un postgrado? ¿Cuándo? ¿En qué disciplina?
2. ¿Esperas independizarte pronto? ¿Por qué o para qué? ¿Cuándo?
3. ¿Piensas abrir tu propia empresa? ¿Cuándo? ¿Para qué?
4. ¿Vas a perfeccionar tus conocimientos *(knowledge)* de español? ¿Por qué? ¿Cuándo? ¿Cómo?
5. ¿Piensas casarte? ¿Cuándo? ¿Con quién?
6. ¿Quieres tener hijos? ¿Cuándo? ¿Cuántos?

10-42 Analizando mi comportamiento Saca unos minutos para analizar tu comportamiento. ¿Siempre haces algunas cosas antes o después de que ocurren otras? ¿Haces ciertas cosas para obtener una reacción específica de los demás? ¿Y haces algo esperando otra cosa a cambio? Escribe un breve resumen sobre este tema y preséntaselo a tu profesor(a).

> **MODELO** *Creo que, desafortunadamente, les hago favores a mis amigos con tal de que ellos después me ayuden a mí. Pero también hago muchas cosas para que ellos se sientan bien, como...*

IV. Vídeo: Un desastre en la cocina

■ Preparación

A. La comida y la salud Todos sabemos que la buena nutrición es importantísima para la salud. Entrevista a un(a) compañero(a) sobre los siguientes aspectos de sus hábitos alimenticios:

- si se preocupa por comer saludablemente o no
- si sabe cocinar
    - ¿Le gusta cocinar? ¿Por qué sí o no?
    - ¿Sigue las instrucciones de las recetas o cocina más bien sin seguirlas?
- qué tipos de comida come diariamente
- si le gustaría cambiar algo respecto a su dieta

■ ¿Entendiste bien?

ESTRATEGIA DE COMPRENSIÓN

Selective listening Concentrate on the specific information required in order to complete the exercises below.

B. ¡Ay, qué complicado es cocinar! Mira a Valeria mientras se embarca en una aventura culinaria y completa la siguiente información que Alejandra le da para ayudarla a preparar la receta.

Cómo se preparan los chiles rellenos al horno...

Paso 1: Empecemos con los ingredientes y las cantidades. Valeria, vas a necesitar:

_____ chiles poblanos (asados, pelados y desvenados), una taza y media de _____ blanco guisado, una taza de _____, tres cebollitas de cambray, media cucharadita de _____, una taza de caldillo de jitomate, _____ añejo al gusto...

Paso 2: Ahora, hablemos de la preparación. Sigue los siguientes pasos con precisión.

- Rellena los _____ con el _____.
- Colócalos en un platón refractario *(heat-resistent)*.
- Licúa la _____, las cebollitas y la _____.
- Baña los chiles con el caldillo de jitomate.
- Échales *(Pour)* la crema por encima.
- Espolvorea *(Sprinkle)* el _____ añejo.
- Pon todo en el horno por _____ minutos a _____ grados centígrados.

Compara tus respuestas con las de un(a) compañero(a).

Paso 3: Ahora, miren el vídeo de nuevo y contesten las siguientes preguntas.

1. Valeria le admite a Alejandra que no le gusta cocinar para nada. Entonces ¿por qué quería preparar este plato?

2. Alejandra habla de la diferencia entre los nombres de alimentos en diferentes países hispanos.

   ■ ¿Qué ejemplo específico da? ¿Cómo se llama ese alimento en su país?
   ■ ¿Conocen más ejemplos? Hagan una lista.

3. ¿Cómo le queda la cena a Valeria? ¿Cómo reaccionan los demás compañeros?

C. Mi plato favorito Piensa en tu plato favorito y luego escoge <u>una</u> de las opciones siguientes (dependiendo de si sabes cocinar o no).

Opción 1: Los sabios de la cocina. Si sabes cocinar tu plato favorito, descríbele a tu compañero(a) cómo se prepara. Empieza con la lista de ingredientes y cantidades y luego los pasos específicos que hay que seguir. No te olvides de usar mandatos informales (**tú**) para darle a tu compañero(a) las instrucciones. Él/Ella debe apuntar toda la información que le des.

Opción 2: Los perdidos en la cocina. Si eres como Valeria (o sea, un desastre en la cocina), pídele ayuda a tu compañero(a). Dile cuál es tu plato favorito y deja que él/ella intente explicarte cómo se prepara. Pídele a tu compañero(a) que te diga todos los ingredientes y cantidades necesarios y apunta esa información. Luego, pregúntale acerca de cómo se prepara el plato paso por paso y apunta todo lo que te diga.

D. Enfoque comunitario Investiga acerca de qué servicios alimenticios ofrece tu universidad. ¿Hay una amplia oferta de diferentes tipos de comidas de países distintos? Y para una buena nutrición, ¿hay opciones que permitan seguir una dieta equilibrada y sana? Prepara un breve informe en español en el cual presentes tus conclusiones y recomendaciones para mejorar los servicios alimenticios. Debes estar preparado(a) para presentar tu informe en clase.

Panorama cultural

I. Vocabulario: Las bellas artes

Los artistas de la escuela **neoclásica** producen obras donde predomina el orden y **la proporción.**

Los impresionistas juegan con los efectos de la **luz y la perspectiva.**

Los cubistas usan **formas abstractas** para **representar** la realidad.

Los artistas de **la escuela Pop** utilizan imágenes de **la cultura masiva.**

Vocabulario práctico

El arte

el (la) artista *artist*
la cultura masiva *mass culture*
el dibujo *drawing*
la escena *scene*
el (la) escultor(a) *sculptor*
la escultura *sculpture*
la exposición *exposition*
la fotografía *photography*
la galería de arte *art gallery*
la imagen *image*
la luz *light*
el movimiento *movement/school*
la muestra *sample, show*
la obra *work*

la obra maestra *masterpiece*
el paisaje *landscape*
el pintor *painter*
la pintura/el cuadro *painting*
la proporción *proportion*
la sala *room*
la técnica *technique*

Verbos

presentar *to present*
producir *to produce*
representar *to represent*
usar *to use*
utilizar *to make use*

Asimilación

10-43 Unas exposiciones de arte Completa las frases con información de la guía cultural.

Guía cultural - Buenos Aires

En el **Museo Nacional de Buenos Aires (MNBA)** una muestra inolvidable, sin par, de un clásico atemporal: Henry Moore. Integrada por 53 esculturas y 72 dibujos. Organizó el British Council y la Fundación Henry Moore.

En el **Centro Cultural Recoleta (CCR)** expondrá **Manuel Cancel** sus típicos y apaisados paisajes ovales, expuestos anteriormente en la Galería Art House.

En el CCR una muestra que abarca desde el año 1983 a 1996 del gran artista **Miguel Barceló,** cuya vida transcurre entre París, Mallorca y Mali, expone hasta el 14 de diciembre 50 trabajos sobresalientes que despiertan enorme interés en el público asistente.

En el CCR expone **Joaquín Molina** «Paraísos custodiados», 20 trabajos con el laberinto como eje.

En la **Galería Benzacar** expuso sus recientes pinturas **Rogelio Polesello.** Después de la muestra «Brasil, nuevas propuestas».

En la **Art House** se realizó una muestra fuera de serie, «Calzar el arte», el zapato como un objeto de arte y como objeto de uso. Organización, selección de artistas, catálogo y montaje de Silvia de Ambrosini.

¿Entendiste bien?

1. Hay una exposición de escultura en _____.
2. _____ es un pintor argentino.
3. La muestra que se presenta en Art House se llama _____ y trata sobre _____.

EN TU COMUNIDAD

Visit a local museum and report on the art being exhibited in a particular section. You can do this in groups (invite your classmates!) or individually.

CD2-40 **10-44 ¿De qué pintura se trata?** Vas a escuchar la descripción de una pintura. Indica la imagen que corresponde a la descripción.

Pintura A _____   Pintura B _____   Pintura C _____

■ Aplicaciones

10-45 Las actividades del MNBA Completa la siguiente reseña con las palabras de la lista. Al terminar, compara tus respuestas con las de un(a) compañero(a).

OPCIONES: artista   exposición   pinturas   muestra   salas

En el Museo Nacional de Buenos Aires se acaba de inaugurar una _____ excepcional. Se trata de una _____ de la pintura del famoso pintor Pablo Picasso. En cinco _____ se presentan más de 50 de sus obras del período de 1930 a 1950. La mayoría de las _____ expuestas son de la escuela cubista. El museo está presentando también un documental sobre la vida del _____.

10-46 ¿A qué (o a quién) me refiero? Describe a un artista, una escuela de arte o una obra maestra. Tus compañeros deben adivinar de qué (o de quién) se trata.

MODELO   E1: *Fue un pintor y escultor italiano muy famoso. Pintó la cúpula de la Capilla Sixtina. Algunas de sus esculturas más conocidas son el David y La Piedad.*
          E2: *¿Miguel Ángel?*
          E1: *¡Así es!*

10-47 Entrevista Hazle las siguientes preguntas a un(a) compañero(a) y presenta un resumen de sus respuestas.

1. ¿Te gusta tener cuadros en las paredes de tu casa o de tu cuarto? ¿Por qué?
2. Sí es así, describe algunas de las pinturas que tienes. Específicamente, di qué tienen en común estas obras, tales como los temas, los colores, los estilos, los artistas, etc., y dónde están expuestas en tu casa.
3. ¿Te gusta el trabajo de algún artista en particular? Si es así, ¿quién es y qué tipo de obras hace?

SUGERENCIAS

Aquí tienes una lista de algunos de los movimientos y artistas más famosos de la historia.

Renacimiento: Leonardo da Vinci, Rafael, Miguel Ángel
Barroco: Diego Velázquez, Peter Paul Rubens
Impresionismo: Edouard Manet, Edgar Degas, Claude Monet, Pierre Renoir, Paul Cezanne, Vincent van Gogh
Cubismo: Pablo Picasso, Georges Bracques, Juan Gris
Surrealismo: Salvador Dalí, Joan Miró, René Magritte, Frida Kahlo, Remedios Varo
Arte Pop: Andy Warhol

▓ Integración

10-48 Amantes del arte Representa la siguiente situación con un(a) compañero(a).

Amante del arte	El arte no es mi punto fuerte
Estás en Buenos Aires y has convencido a un(a) amigo(a) de pasar por el Centro Cultural Recoleta. Desgraciadamente, a tu amigo(a) no le gusta mucho el arte y, evidentemente, está muy aburrido(a).	Estás de visita en Buenos Aires y tu amigo(a) te ha convencido de entrar a una exposición de arte en el Centro Cultural Recoleta. A ti no te interesa mucho la pintura y estás un poco aburrido(a).
1. Háblale acerca de estos dos cuadros y ayúdale a apreciar su mérito artístico. 2. Trata de convencerlo(a) de que se quede en la galería para ver el resto de la exposición.	1. Explícale que en realidad no te gusta mucho el arte y que estás aburrido(a). 2. Trata de convencer a tu amigo(a) de que vaya contigo a otra parte lo más pronto posible.

SUGERENCIAS

Para expresar que estás aburrido(a), y que quieres hacer algo diferente, di:

¿No crees que ya hemos visto suficientes cuadros? — *Don't you think we have seen enough paintings?*

¿Por qué no vamos a...? — *Why don't we go to . . . ?*

Quiero irme de esta galería ya. — *I want to leave this gallery right now.*

«Mundo», Alejandro Xul Solar

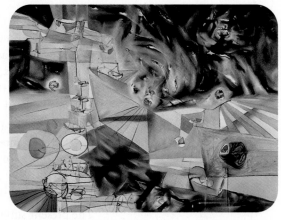

«Años de temor», Roberto Matta

10-49 Actividades culturales Investiga qué exposiciones hay en tu universidad o en tu ciudad en este momento. Visita la galería de arte que corresponda a tus intereses y lleva a clase una breve reseña de la exposición que tuviste la oportunidad de ver. Incluye la siguiente información:

- nombre del / de la artista
- número de pinturas (o esculturas)
- técnicas o estilos utilizados
- temas o escenas típicos
- opinión personal (si te gustó la exposición o no, y por qué)

II. Funciones y estructuras: Giving directives and advice (review of formal and informal commands and introduction of *nosotros* commands)

—Chicos, ya llegamos al Museo del Prado. **¡Disfrutemos** de las obras de Goya, Velázquez y El Greco! **No nos perdamos** porque el museo es grandísimo. ¡Ah! ¡Y **no comamos** nada ni **tomemos** fotos! ¡Por favor! ¿Estamos listos? Pues, **¡entremos!**

El Museo del Prado (Madrid)

You already know how to give affirmative and negative commands in the **usted, ustedes,** and **tú** forms. As you may recall, the form of these commands coincides with the verb forms of the present subjunctive, with the exception of affirmative **tú** commands, which coincide with the third-person singular present indicative verb forms.

USTED: **(No) Ponga** la escultura en el estante. — *(Don't) Put the sculpture on the shelf.*

USTEDES: **(No) Apliquen** esta técnica. — *(Don't) Apply this technique.*

TÚ: **(No hables) Habla** con el artista. — *(Don't) Speak with the artist.*

The present subjunctive **nosotros** form can also be used to give directives and advice that applies to the speaker. It is the equivalent of the *Let's . . .* English expression. Negative commands are formed by placing **no** before the verb.

¡Produzcamos una obra maestra, amigos! — *Let's produce a masterpiece, friends!*

Colegas, **no utilicemos** estas brochas. — *Colleagues, let's not use these brushes.*

Just like with **usted, ustedes,** and **tú** commands, indirect and direct object pronouns are attached to the verb in **nosotros** affirmative commands and are placed between **no** and the verb in **nosotros** negative commands.

Presentémosle esta pintura al dueño de la galería. — *Let's present this painting to the gallery owner (to him).*

No se la llevemos todavía. — *Let's not bring it to him yet.*

Busquémoselos ahora mismo. — *Let's find it for her right now.*

Notice that the verb takes a written accent mark when the pronoun is attached to it.

REMEMBER

The indirect object pronoun goes before the direct object pronoun and **le** and **les** change to **se** before **lo, la, los,** or **las.**

In the affirmative command form of reflexive verbs, the final **-s** of the present subjunctive **nosotros** form is dropped before attaching the reflexive pronoun **nos**.* This change does not affect the negative form.

Sentémonos (*not* **sentémosnos**) a admirar esta obra.

No nos vistamos formalmente para ir a la exposición.

Let's sit down *to admire this work.*

Let's not dress *formally to go to the exposition.*

*The same thing happens if the **nosotros** affirmative command has the pronouns **se + lo/la/los/las** attached to it: **Busquémoselos** ahora mismo. ***Let's find it for her*** *right now.*

▧ Asimilación

10-50 Una fotografía espectacular Imagínate que tu amigo(a) y tú son fotógrafos y quieren llegar a exponer una de sus fotografías en una galería famosa. Pon las siguientes oraciones en orden lógico. Cuando termines, compara el orden con el de un(a) compañero(a). ¿Crees que tienes que hacer cambios?

____ Hablemos con el (la) director(a) de una galería de arte.

____ No vayamos a la tienda de equipo fotográfico de la calle Viamonte.

____ Pensemos en una idea original para la fotografía.

____ No nos pongamos nerviosos cuando hablemos con él o ella.

____ Compremos el equipo que necesitamos.

____ Celebremos nuestro triunfo.

____ Trabajemos todos los días hasta tener la fotografía perfecta.

____ Expongámosla hasta que se venda.

10-51 ¿Para quién es la orden? Escucha a Cecilia Pereira, una profesora de arte, mientras les da indicaciones a ciertas personas. Luego, indica quién debe hacer las siguientes actividades. Presta atención a las formas verbales.

OPCIONES:　1 = su asistente (tú)
2 = un comprador *(buyer)* de alta sociedad (Ud.)
3 = dos estudiantes (Uds.)
4 = Cecilia Pereira y su secretaria (nosotras)

1. no preocuparse ____

2. no mover los dibujos de los estudiantes nocturnos ____

3. pasar a la oficina ____

4. buscar el catálogo de pinturas ____

5. irse a hablar con Esmeralda ____

6. comenzar a trabajar en el estudio ____

7. decirle a Serena que Cecilia Pereira va a llegar tarde a la reunión ____

CD2-41

Aplicaciones

10-52 ¡Sí! ¡No! Túrnense para leer y reaccionar a las siguientes oraciones. Deben decir lo opuesto y proveer detalles. **¡OJO!** Usen pronombres siempre que sea posible.

> MODELO   E1: *Estudiemos en la biblioteca.*
>   E2: *¡No! No estudiemos en la biblioteca. No me gusta estudiar ahí. Prefiero estudiar en un café.*

1. Digámosle al / a la profesor(a) que queremos un examen mañana.
2. No nos pongamos ropa cómoda para venir a la universidad.
3. No traduzcamos las instrucciones del español al inglés.
4. ¿Las clases? Tomémoslas los lunes, miércoles y viernes.
5. Empecemos a escribir la siguiente composición.
6. ¿El libro de español? No se lo prestemos a nadie.
7. Comámonos una ensalada en la cafetería de la universidad.

10-53 ¿Qué hacemos? Escriban un mandato afirmativo y un mandato negativo lógicos para cada situación. ¡Sean creativos!

> MODELO   Hoy es sábado. Son las ocho de la noche y estamos aburridos. *¡No abramos los libros por nada en el mundo! ¡Vayamos a algún lugar divertido en la ciudad!*

SUGERENCIAS

Para formar oraciones lógicas, puedes usar los siguientes verbos: **(no) ponerse, bañarse, (no) vestirse, afeitarse, peinarse, maquillarse, arreglarse, (no) comprar, (no) recoger, (no) sentirse, (no) llevar** y **(no) comer.**

1. Queremos conseguir un buen trabajo cuando nos graduemos.
2. Nuestro apartamento está muy sucio y tenemos visita esta noche.
3. Vamos a mudarnos en una semana y no tenemos nada listo.
4. Comimos demasiado y nos sentimos enfermos.
5. Nos preocupa la contaminación del medio ambiente.
6. Estamos en una tienda que tiene una oferta especial de una hora.
7. Nos interesa perder peso y mejorar nuestro estado de salud.

10-54 Una cita doble *(double date)* Imagínense que van a salir a una cita esta noche y quieren impresionar a sus respectivas parejas. ¿Qué cosas deben y no deben hacer? Escriban por lo menos ocho oraciones. (Importante: Traten de trabajar con una persona del mismo sexo.)

SUGERENCIAS

Puedes usar algunas de estas frases: **un hotel de (cuatro/cinco) estrellas, una habitación con vista al mar/a las montañas/a la ciudad, ropa deportiva/casual/formal, museos, galerías, parques, monumentos nacionales** y **playas.**

Integración

10-55 De vacaciones Representa la siguiente situación con un(a) compañero(a).

SUGERENCIAS

Para mostrarte en desacuerdo, puedes usar estas expresiones:
¡Estás loco(a)! *Are you crazy!*
¡No estoy de acuerdo! *I don't agree!*
¡No me parece una buena idea! *I don't think that's a good idea.*
¡Por supuesto que no! *Of course not!.)*

El (La) flexible
Tu amigo(a) y tú están planificando sus próximas vacaciones juntos(as). Sugiérele alternativas diferentes en cuanto al *(regarding)* destino turístico adonde van a ir, el hotel donde se van a quedar, la ropa que van a llevar y los lugares que van a visitar.

El (La) inflexible
Tu amigo(a) y tú están planificando sus próximas vacaciones juntos(as). Lamentablemente, no estás de acuerdo con ninguna de las cosas que él/ella sugiere. Reacciona a las cosas que dice y propón *(propose)* alternativas diferentes.

10-56 Una causa noble Prepara un afiche para animar *(encourage)* a tus compañeros de clase a involucrarse en una causa con la que te sientes identificado(a). Usa mandatos afirmativos y negativos con la forma de **nosotros.** Cuando lo tengas listo, muéstraselo a un(a) compañero(a) para que te dé su opinión y luego muéstraselo a la clase. ¿Qué reacción tienen tus compañeros?

III. Funciones y estructuras: Talking about the future with the future tense

> El Museo Nacional de Bellas Artes le extiende la más cordial invitación a una recepción que **se llevará** a cabo el sábado, 15 de mayo a las 18 horas, en la Sala Picasso del museo. Ud. y un invitado **podrán** admirar algunas de las pinturas del renombrado pintor argentino Fernando Cánovas, tales como *Pájaro de acero*, *Libertad* y *Final del viaje*. El aclamado pintor nos **honrará** con su presencia. ¡Los esperamos!

So far you have used expressions like **ir** + **a** + infinitive and **esperar** + infinitive to talk about actions that will take place in the future. Spanish also has a simple future tense form that is used primarily in written and formal speech. This tense is formed by attaching directly to the infinitive the same set of endings for **-ar, -er,** and **-ir** verbs.

ENDINGS	-ar VERBS	-er VERBS	-ir VERBS
é	tomar**é**	leer**é**	vivir**é**
ás	tomar**ás**	leer**ás**	vivir**ás**
á	tomar**á**	leer**á**	vivir**á**
emos	tomar**emos**	leer**emos**	vivir**emos**
éis	tomar**éis**	leer**éis**	vivir**éis**
án	tomar**án**	leer**án**	vivir**án**

Cuando revele las fotografías, **pasaré** por tu casa.

*When I get the pictures developed, I **will stop** by your house.*

¿Uds. **irán** a la exposición esta noche?

***Will you go** to the exposition tonight?*

Some verbs undergo changes in their infinitive form when conjugated in the future tense. They can be grouped in three categories:

■ the shortened-stem group

INFINITIVE	FUTURE TENSE STEM	CONJUGATION
decir	**dir-**	**dir**é, **dir**ás, **dir**á, **dir**emos, **dir**éis, **dir**án
hacer	**har-**	**har**é, **har**ás, **har**á, **har**emos, **har**éis, **har**án

La artista **hará** una presentación especial de su trabajo.

*The artist **will make** a special presentation of her work.*

¿Qué crees que **dirán** los críticos?

*What do you think the critics **will say**?*

■ the dropped **-e** group

INFINITIVE	FUTURE TENSE STEM	CONJUGATION
caber	**cabr-**	**cabré, cabrás, cabrá, cabremos, cabréis, cabrán**
haber	**habr-**	**habré, habrás, habrá, habremos, habréis, habrán**
poder	**podr-**	**podré, podrás, podrá, podremos, podréis, podrán**
querer	**querr-**	**querré, querrás, querrá, querremos, querréis, querrán**
saber	**sabr-**	**sabré, sabrás, sabrá, sabremos, sabréis, sabrán**

El domingo **habrá** una feria de pintores locales.	*There will be a fair of local painters on Sunday.*
¿Piensas que Vicente **querrá** ir conmigo?	*Do you think Vicente will want to go with me?*

■ the **-dr-** substitution group

INFINITIVE	FUTURE TENSE STEM	CONJUGATION
poner	**pondr-**	**pondré, pondrás, pondrá, pondremos, pondréis, pondrán**
salir	**saldr-**	**saldré, saldrás, saldrá, saldremos, saldréis, saldrán**
tener	**tendr-**	**tendré, tendrás, tendrá, tendremos, tendréis, tendrán**
valer	**valdr-**	**valdré, valdrás, valdrá, valdremos, valdréis, valdrán**
venir	**vendr-**	**vendré, vendrás, vendrá, vendremos, vendréis, vendrán**

Julia **tendrá** tiempo para terminar la obra esta noche.	*Julia will have time to finish her work tonight.*
Hernán y yo **vendremos** a verla mañana.	*Hernán and I will come to see it tomorrow.*

Asimilación

10-57 ¿Qué harás mañana? Piensa en las cosas que harás mañana y escoge las oraciones que sean ciertas. Al terminar, compara tus respuestas con las de un(a) compañero(a). ¿Van a hacer las mismas actividades?

____ Estudiaré.

____ Cenaré en mi restaurante favorito.

____ Practicaré algún deporte.

____ Iré al cine.

____ Vendré a la universidad.

____ Trabajaré.

____ No haré nada.

____ Me quedaré en casa.

____ Saldré con algunos amigos.

____ Tendré que limpiar mi habitación.

D2-42 **10-58 El futuro de un artista** Escucha los planes para el futuro que tiene este artista e indica si las siguientes oraciones son ciertas (**C**) o falsas (**F**).

____ 1. El artista expondrá sus pinturas en la galería de su colega.

____ 2. Según él, ganará mucho dinero.

____ 3. Expondrá sus obras en el museo de su pueblo.

____ 4. Se mudará a un país tropical.

____ 5. Desafortunadamente, nadie conocerá su nombre.

____ 6. En su opinión, él será famoso.

Aplicaciones

10-59 En la oficina Imagínense que Uds. trabajan en una oficina donde todo se sabe. Túrnense para hacer y responder a preguntas sobre lo que los siguientes empleados harán este fin de semana.

MODELO   Eleuterio – irse para el campo
E1: *¿Qué hará Eleuterio este fin de semana?*
E2: *Eleuterio se irá para el campo.*

1. Diego y Matilde – venir a la oficina a terminar el informe
2. doña Petra – poner cortinas nuevas en su casa
3. Dalia – tener una fiesta íntima en su apartamento
4. Nora y su familia – divertirse paseando por la ciudad
5. Norberto – cortarse el pelo
6. Igor y su esposa – salir a hacer compras
7. don Ricardo y Josué – ir a la cancha de tenis
8. Maribel – leer la nueva novela de García Márquez

10-60 Predicciones ¿Cómo será la vida en veinticinco años? Hagan predicciones sobre los siguientes temas.

MODELO   el transporte
Dentro de veinticinco años, todos los carros serán eléctricos.

1. la alimentación
2. la economía
3. el entretenimiento
4. las comunicaciones
5. la salud

6. la educación
7. la ecología
8. el arte
9. la política
10. el deporte

10-61 Nuestros planes para el futuro

Paso 1: Haz una lista de seis cosas que estás seguro(a) que harás en el futuro.

1. ...
2. ...
3. ...
4. ...
5. ...
6. ...

Paso 2: Convierte las oraciones del **Paso 1** en preguntas y entrevista a dos compañeros(as). Si responden negativamente, trata de hacer otras preguntas que se relacionen con el tema, tales como el trabajo, la vida personal, las aspiraciones académicas, etc. Apunta sus respuestas y prepara un resumen.

> MODELO   *Yo tendré mi propio negocio de bienes raíces. En cambio,*
> *Sasha tendrá su propio estudio de contabilidad y Johnny será*
> *médico. Por otro lado. Johnny y yo...*

■ Integración

10-62 Videntes *(Psychics)* Representa la siguiente situación con un(a) compañero(a).

El (La) preocupado(a)	El (La) vidente
Eres una persona que se preocupa mucho por el futuro. Un(a) amigo(a) te recomendó llamar a la línea directa de un(a) vidente y has decidido hacerlo. Responde a sus preguntas y prepárate para hacerle preguntas acerca de cosas que te interesen.	Tienes poderes síquicos y aceptas consultas telefónicas. Responde a la llamada de este(a) cliente(a) y predice su futuro. Además, responde a las preguntas que te haga.

10-63 Preguntas para mi profesor(a) Aunque conoces bastante bien a tu profesor(a), quieres saber un poco más sobre sus planes. Haz una lista de por lo menos diez preguntas que quieres que él/ella responda y entrégasela. ¿Cómo piensas que va a responder?

IV. Lectura: *El túnel*

■ Antes de leer

A. Para conversar Responde a las siguientes preguntas y luego comenta tus respuestas con otros compañeros.

1. ¿Crees que existe el amor a primera vista? ¿Por qué sí o por qué no?

2. ¿Cuál sería el lugar más apropiado para conocer a tu pareja ideal? Escoge un lugar y explica por qué.

____ en un estadio

____ por la calle

____ en una fiesta

____ en una galería de arte

____ en un teatro

____ en un salón de clase

____ en otro lugar

B. Vocabulario y conceptos Emparejen cada palabra con su definición. (Consulten el diccionario si es necesario.)

____ 1. la escena
____ 2. la soledad
____ 3. esencial
____ 4. la ansiedad
____ 5. vacilar

a. subdivisión de una obra dramática, evento o espectáculo digno de prestarle atención *(pay attention)*

b. lo más importante, algo indispensable

c. inquietud que se experimenta ante un peligro real o imaginario

d. se experimenta al sentirse alejado *(detached/alienated)* o separado del resto del mundo

e. dudar, no saber qué hacer

C. Aplicación Ahora, completen las oraciones con las palabras que acaban de identificar en la actividad anterior.

1. Para apreciar mejor esta exposición es _____ leer un poco sobre la historia del arte.

2. _____ en exponer mis pinturas porque tengo miedo de los críticos.

3. Muchos pintores prefieren la _____ para concentrarse más en sus creaciones.

4. La complejidad de esa obra se debe a que no contiene una, sino varias _____.

5. La _____ del personaje de esta pintura es evidente en la expresión de la cara.

■ **A leer**

Ernesto Sábato

Nació en la provincia de Buenos Aires en 1911. Hizo un doctorado en física y tomó cursos de filosofía en la Universidad de La Plata, pero abandonó las ciencias en 1945 para dedicarse a la literatura. Su producción tiene un tono existencialista y trata el tema de la angustia *(anguish)* del ser humano frente a la sociedad y la vida. Las novelas más famosas de este escritor son *El túnel* (1948), *Sobre héroes y tumbas* (1961) y *Abaddón, el exterminador* (1974). Su preocupación por la situación política y por los derechos humanos en su país lo llevó a presidir la Comisión Nacional sobre la Desaparición de Personas *(National Commission on Disappeared Persons)* y a escribir el libro *Nunca más* sobre los efectos de la guerra sucia durante la dictadura militar (1976–1983) en Argentina. En 1984, recibió el prestigioso Premio Cervantes de literatura.

El túnel (fragmento)

En el Salón de Primavera de 1946 presenté un cuadro llamado *Maternidad*. Era por el estilo de muchos otros anteriores: como dicen los críticos en su **insoportable** dialecto, era sólido, estaba bien arquitecturado. Tenía, en fin, los **atributos** que esos **charlatanes** encontraban siempre en mis **telas,** incluyendo «cierta cosa profundamente intelectual». Pero arriba, a la izquierda, a través de una ventanita, se veía una escena pequeña y remota: una playa solitaria y una mujer que miraba el mar. Era una mujer que miraba como esperando algo, quizá algún llamado **apagado** y distante. La escena **sugería,** en mi opinión, una soledad ansiosa y absoluta.

intolerable

qualities
charlatans
paintings

muffled / suggested

Nadie **se fijó en** esta escena: **pasaban la mirada por encima,** como por algo secundario, probablemente decorativo. Con excepción de una sola persona, nadie pareció comprender que esa escena constituía algo esencial. Fue el día de la inauguración. Una muchacha desconocida estuvo mucho tiempo **delante** de mi cuadro sin dar importancia, en apariencia, a la gran mujer **en primer plano,** la mujer que miraba jugar al niño. En cambio, miró **fijamente** la escena de la ventana y mientras lo hacía tuve la seguridad de que estaba **aislada** del mundo entero: no vio ni oyó a la gente que pasaba o se **detenía** frente a mi tela.

noticed / glanced over it

in front
foreground
attentively
isolated
stopped

La observé todo el tiempo con ansiedad. Después desapareció en la **multitud,** mientras yo **vacilaba** entre un miedo invencible y un angustioso deseo de llamarla.

crowd / hesitated

¿Miedo de qué? Quizá, algo así como miedo de jugar todo el dinero de que se dispone en la vida a un solo número. Sin embargo, cuando desapareció, me sentí irritado, infeliz, pensando que podría no verla más, perdida entre los millones de habitantes anónimos de Buenos Aires. Esa noche volví a casa nervioso, descontento, triste.

Hasta que **se clausuró** el salón, fui todos los días y **me colocaba** suficientemente cerca para reconocer a las personas que se detenían frente a mi cuadro. Pero no volvió a **aparecer.**

closed / found myself

to turn up, show up

Durante los meses que siguieron, sólo pensé en ella, en la posibilidad de volver a verla. Y en cierto modo, sólo pinté para ella. Fue como si la pequeña escena de la ventana empezara a crecer y a invadir toda la tela y toda mi obra.

■ **¿Entendiste bien?**

D. ¿Qué pasó? Organiza los siguientes eventos de acuerdo con la historia. Al terminar, compara tus respuestas con las de un(a) compañero(a).

____ El artista regresó a su casa nervioso y triste.

____ Una muchacha observó con interés la escena de la ventanita.

____ La exposición fue clausurada.

____ El artista fue a la exposición todos los días esperando el regreso de la muchacha.

____ Se abrió la exposición del artista en el Salón de Primavera.

____ El artista empezó a trabajar con la obsesión de ver a la muchacha.

____ La muchacha desapareció en la multitud.

E. Puntos clave Realicen las siguientes actividades.

1. Hagan un dibujo de la obra *Maternidad* basándose en la descripción que hace el narrador de la misma.
2. Expliquen por qué se obsesionó el artista con esa muchacha.

F. Los personajes Aunque el narrador no nos da muchos detalles acerca de los personajes, nos deja ver a través de sus acciones algunas de sus características más sobresalientes. Lean de nuevo el texto y traten de «leer entre líneas» *(read between the lines)* para concretar en palabras la imagen que nos quiere presentar el autor de estos personajes.

	Características
Narrador	
La muchacha	

G. Enfoque lingüístico Para narrar la historia, el autor usó las diferentes formas del pasado. Busquen ejemplos de cada una de estas formas.

H. Actividad de extensión Escriban el final de esta historia. (¿Creen Uds. que al fin se encontraron el artista y la muchacha? ¿Piensan que se hicieron amigos? ¿Que se casaron? O por el contrario, ¿piensan que ellos nunca más se volvieron a ver?)

CRITICAL THINKING SKILLS

Inferring and Classifying What do the characters' actions tell us about their personalities?

REMEMBER

1. The preterite tense is used to refer to completed past events.
2. The imperfect tense is used to refer to:
   ■ habitual past actions (things one used to do)
   ■ ongoing states or conditions in the past
   ■ the background of past events (time, weather, location, etc.)
   ■ physical or psychological characteristics of something or someone in the past
   ■ actions in progress at a given point in the past

Vocabulario

El ejercicio físico
bajar de/perder peso — to lose weight
distraer — to entertain, to amuse
evitar — to avoid
ganar/subir de peso — to gain weight
aumentar nuestra elasticidad y resistencia — to increase our flexibility and resistance
mantenerse en forma/en buen estado de salud — to keep fit/in good health
reducir/combatir el estrés — to reduce/combat stress

Es importante...
dejar de fumar — to quit, stop smoking
hacer estiramiento — to stretch
hacer un poco de calentamiento — to do some warm-up exercises

Nutrición
la fibra — fiber
las grasas animales — animal fat
los minerales — minerals
los productos refinados — refined products
la proteína — protein
las vitaminas — vitamins

Problemas médicos
la alergia — allergy
la gripe/la influenza — flu
los parásitos intestinales — intestinal parasites
el resfriado — cold

Verbos
doler (ue) — to ache, to hurt
enfermarse — to get sick
sentirse (ie, i) mal/mejor — to feel ill/better
tener tos — to have a cough

Síntomas
la congestión — congestion
el dolor de cabeza — headache
la fiebre — fever
el mareo — dizziness
la tos — cough

Ayudas terapéuticas y diagnósticas
el antibiótico — antibiotic
el botiquín de primeros auxilios — first-aid kit
la curita — Band-Aid

el descanso — rest
el jarabe — cough syrup
la pastilla — pill
la radiografía — x-ray
la receta — prescription
el yeso — cast

Deportes urbanos
los bolos — bowling
el ciclismo — bike riding
la escalada libre — rock climbing
el patinaje en línea — in-line skating

Equipo
al cubierto/bajo techo — indoors
el arnés — harness
la bicicleta — bicycle
la cancha — court
el casco — helmet
la codera — elbow pad
la cuerda — rope
las gafas protectoras — goggles
el juego/el set — set
la pelota/la bola — ball
la raqueta — racket
la rodillera — knee pad

Habilidades — **Skills**
escalar — to climb
golpear — to hit
halar/jalar — to pull
pedalear — to pedal
tirar — to throw

El arte
el artista — artist
la cultura masiva — mass culture
el dibujo — drawing
la escena — scene
el escultor — sculptor
la escultura — sculpture
la exposición — exposition
la fotografía — photography
la galería de arte — art gallery
la imagen — image
la luz — light
el movimiento — movement/school
la muestra — sample, show
la obra — work

la obra maestra	masterpiece
el paisaje	landscape
el pintor	painter
la pintura/el cuadro	painting
la proporción	proportion
la sala	room
la técnica	technique

Verbos

presentar	to present
producir	to produce
representar	to represent
usar	to use
utilizar	to make use

Funciones y estructuras

Expresiones adverbiales y conjunciones que se usan con verbos en el modo subjuntivo, pp. 400, 412

Puesta en acción

SITUACIÓN:	La empresa multinacional en la que trabajas requiere un nuevo programa de desarrollo personal para todos sus empleados.
MISIÓN:	Diseñar el programa de desarrollo personal para la empresa y desarrollar los mecanismos para diseminar la información entre los empleados de habla hispana.
DESTREZAS:	Diseñar un programa de desarrollo personal para los empleados de una empresa multinacional, diseñar una campaña de promoción e informar a los empleados sobre los servicios disponibles mediante este programa.

A. La campaña *(campaign)* Lee el siguiente mensaje electrónico.

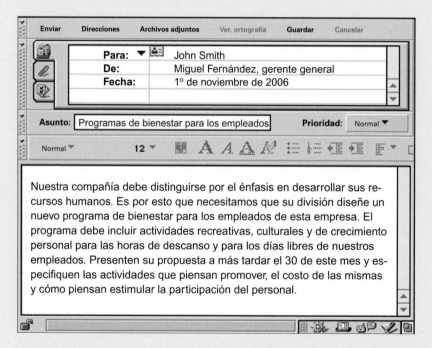

| Enviar | Direcciones | Archivos adjuntos | Ver. ortografía | Guardar | Cancelar |

Para: John Smith
De: Miguel Fernández, gerente general
Fecha: 1º de noviembre de 2006

Asunto: Programas de bienestar para los empleados   **Prioridad:** Normal ▼

Normal ▼   12 ▼

Nuestra compañía debe distinguirse por el énfasis en desarrollar sus recursos humanos. Es por esto que necesitamos que su división diseñe un nuevo programa de bienestar para los empleados de esta empresa. El programa debe incluir actividades recreativas, culturales y de crecimiento personal para las horas de descanso y para los días libres de nuestros empleados. Presenten su propuesta a más tardar el 30 de este mes y especifiquen las actividades que piensan promover, el costo de las mismas y cómo piensan estimular la participación del personal.

B. ¿Entendiste bien? Contesta las siguientes preguntas sobre el mensaje anterior.

    a. ¿Qué quiere el gerente general de la compañía?
    b. ¿Para cuándo debe estar lista la campaña?
    c. ¿Qué características debe tener esta campaña?

C. ¿Qué actividades podemos organizar? Preparen una lista de posibles actividades deportivas, culturales y de crecimiento personal para los empleados de la empresa.

Actividades deportivas (actividades físicas para mantenerse en forma o divertirse)	Actividades culturales (actividades de recreación, información o capacitación)	Actividades de crecimiento personal (actividades dirigidas al bienestar personal y familiar de los empleados)

D. La decisión Reúnanse con otra pareja de estudiantes y comenten las ideas que generaron en la actividad anterior. Los objetivos son:
- a. escoger la mejor actividad para cada una de las categorías y
- b. determinar los requisitos y materiales necesarios para cada actividad.

CRITICAL THINKING SKILLS

Prioritizing Choose the most effective and practical possibilities.

	Para las horas de descanso de los empleados	Para los fines de semana
Las mejores actividades deportivas	1.	1.
Requisitos y materiales		
Las mejores actividades culturales	2.	2.
Requisitos y materiales		
Las mejores actividades de crecimiento personal	3.	3.
Requisitos y materiales		

E. Justificaciones Completen el siguiente informe preliminar para comunicar sus ideas a la administración.

Actividades deportivas

- a. Para los descansos, recomendamos que los empleados _____ para que _____.
- b. Para los fines de semana, sugerimos que los empleados _____ a fin de que _____.

Actividades culturales

a. Durante los descansos, esperamos que los empleados _____ para que _____.

b. Para los fines de semana, recomendamos que los empleados _____ a fin de que _____.

Actividades de crecimiento personal

a. Para los descansos, recomendamos que los empleados _____ para que _____.

b. Para los fines de semana, sugerimos que los empleados _____ a fin de que _____.

F. Inscripciones Ahora, piensen en los pasos o procedimientos *(procedures)* que deben seguir los empleados de la compañía para participar en los diferentes programas que han diseñado. ¿Necesitan una evaluación médica? ¿Tienen que tomar exámenes de aptitud? ¿Deben llenar algún formulario? Escriban la lista de los pasos que se deben seguir.

MODELO   *Primero, hazte un examen médico.*
Segundo, toma un examen de aptitud.
Tercero, llena este formulario, etc.

G. Consejería Representa la siguiente situación con un(a) compañero(a).

Empleado(a)	Jefe(a) de personal
Has oído rumores acerca de los programas deportivos, culturales y de crecimiento personal que piensa ofrecer la empresa y te gustaría tener más información al respecto.	Los empleados ya se han enterado de los programas que va a ofrecer tu compañía. Ayuda a este(a) empleado(a) a escoger el programa que más le conviene.
■ Saluda al / a la jefe(a) de personal.	■ Dale la bienvenida.
■ Pregúntale acerca de estos programas de bienestar.	■ Explícale los programas y determina cuál es el tipo de actividad que más le conviene.
■ Averigua cuáles son los requisitos y materiales necesarios para cada uno de estos programas.	■ Infórmale acerca de los requisitos y materiales que necesita para participar en el programa que le recomendaste.

H. Campaña publicitaria Para informarles a todos los empleados de la compañía sobre los nuevos programas de bienestar, es necesario organizar una campaña publicitaria. Diseñen los volantes e incluyan lo siguiente:

- una lista de los datos de cada programa (actividades, fechas, horas, etc.)
- una breve explicación de la importancia de cada programa, con frases y oraciones motivadoras
- una lista de requisitos y materiales necesarios
- los pasos que deben seguir para inscribirse (instrucciones precisas de cómo se participa en los programas)

Sigan los siguientes pasos:

a. Decidan cómo está el diseño del volante y la manera como lo harán más interesante y atractivo.

b. Organicen y distribuyan en la página el contenido del volante (dónde van a ir los títulos, los datos, las frases descriptivas, los requisitos, los materiales, los gráficos, etc.).

c. Preparen cada una de las secciones (datos, instrucciones, motivación, etc.).

d. Incluyan el material visual necesario (imágenes, gráficos, etc.).

I. Dos empleados interesados Dos empleados de la compañía ya les enviaron una nota para informarles que están interesados en participar en los programas de bienestar. Primero, lean individualmente las notas que les corresponden. Luego, túrnense para hacer y responder a preguntas y completen la planilla.

CORRECCIONES

Intercambien el primer borrador de su volante con otro grupo y respondan a las siguientes preguntas.

Paso 1: Contenido. ¿El volante incluye toda la información necesaria? Si no es así, ¿qué falta?

Paso 2: Organización. ¿La información de los programas (fechas, requisitos, etc.) está clara? ¿La distribución de la información es clara, efectiva y visualmente atractiva?

Paso 3: Gramática. ¿Hay algún problema con el uso del subjuntivo en los mandatos y las recomendaciones?

Para hacer en casa:

Paso 4: Correcciones. Revisen su volante y entréguenselo al / a la profesor(a) el día de la próxima clase.

Estudiante 1

5 de diciembre de 2006

Estimado(a) jefe(a) de personal:

Le escribo esta nota para informarle que me interesa participar en los nuevos programas de bienestar de la compañía. En particular, mi esposa, mis dos hijos y yo quisiéramos participar en las actividades deportivas. Me parece que para nosotros sería más conveniente hacer esto los fines de semana. Para mí no es posible hacerlo en mis horas de descanso y quiero que mi familia participe. También les quisiera sugerir que inviten a los supervisores de la compañía para que podamos conocerlos mejor.

Cordialmente,
Nelson Estrada Millán

Nombre del / de la empleado(a)	
Programa que le interesa	
Participantes	
Razón por la que le interesa	
Sugerencias	

Estudiante 2 must turn the book upside down.

Estudiante 2

7 de diciembre de 2006

Estimado(a) jefe(a) de personal:

El propósito de esta comunicación es felicitarlo(a) por la implementación del programa de bienestar. Creo que es una estupenda idea. Personalmente me gustaría participar en el programa de crecimiento personal porque es importante que tengamos buena salud mental para poder hacer nuestro trabajo eficientemente. Quisiera participar en este programa durante las horas de descanso con mis compañeros de la oficina de contabilidad. Sería muy bueno que nos permitieran llevar nuestro almuerzo y así aprovechar el tiempo. ¿Qué opina Ud.?

Saludos,

Catalina Chacón Paz

Nombre del / de la empleado(a)	
Programa que le interesa	
Participantes	
Razón por la que le interesa	
Sugerencias	

Servicio comunitario

Visit a community service center in your area and offer to provide and/ or organize one of the following services:

- Workshops on how to cultivate healthy relationships.
- Workout sessions.
- Art classes.

Unidad 6

Chile, Paraguay y los Estados Unidos

In this unit you will talk about your hopes for and concerns about the future. Also, you will learn how to make hypotheses and conjectures. The readings will examine the impact of technological developments on the Spanish-speaking world and, more specifically, the current dynamics of social change in Paraguay and Chile. At the end of the unit you will explore the history, present situation, and future perspectives of Hispanics in the U.S. You will also have a chance to connect with your community by creating a program that will enhance and improve people's quality of life.

Expectativas

Capítulo 11

Mirando hacia el futuro

Para comenzar

Indica qué foto le corresponde a cada descripción.

- El Parque Vicente Pérez Rosales es el primer parque nacional de Chile.
- Vista aérea de la ciudad de Asunción, la capital de Paraguay.
- El árido desierto de Atacama se encuentra en el norte del país, entre la cordillera de los Andes y el Océano Pacífico.

In this chapter you will learn . . .

- how to make hypothetical statements
- how to express conjecture
- about the impact of technological development in the Spanish-speaking world
- about social change in the Spanish-speaking world

	TEMA 1 Proyectos personales	TEMA 2 Un futuro tecnificado	TEMA 3 Utopías
Vocabulario	Mis aspiraciones	Las comodidades de la era electrónica	Un mundo mejor
Funciones y estructuras	Talking about aspirations (review of the future tense) Expressing conjecture and probability with the conditional tense	Expressing opinion, emotion, wishes, doubt, stipulation, purpose and future time frame with the subjunctive and the infinitive Talking about the past using the imperfect subjunctive (regular verbs)	Talking about the past using the imperfect subjunctive (irregular verbs) Expressing condition (**si** clauses)
Lecturas y vídeo	Perspectivas: Las claves de la ilusión	Vídeo: Aspiraciones y planes para el futuro	Lectura: El albergue de las mujeres tristes

Foto 1

Foto 2

Foto 3

Enfoque

A. ¿Qué sabes ya de Chile? Antes de ver el vídeo, completa el siguiente párrafo sobre la economía de Chile.

El foco de la economía de Chile está en la explotación de _____, incluyendo el cobre, los nitratos y el hierro. Sólo el cobre, del que Chile es el mayor productor mundial, representa el 50% del total de las _____ a otros países. La economía de Chile es una de las más fuertes y estables de toda _____, con un ingreso per cápita de 12.500 dólares. La moneda del país es el _____.

Compara tus respuestas con las de otro(a) compañero(a).

B. La política de Chile Una categoría que no viste en la primera actividad es la política. Mientras ves el vídeo, pon en orden los siguientes eventos políticos de Chile.

____ el gobierno socialista de Salvador Allende

____ Patricio Alwyn lidera el país como presidente, pero no como jefe del ejército

____ la etapa reformista del presidente Eduardo Frey

____ la fundación de las ciudades de Santiago, Concepción y Valdivia por el español Pedro de Valdivia

____ Ricardo Lagos es electo presidente del país

____ la dictadura militar de Augusto Pinochet

For more info, you may want to check the **Temas** site: http://temas.heinle.com

C. Mirando hacia el futuro Reúnanse en grupos de tres o cuatro estudiantes. Luego, lean el siguiente dato demográfico de Chile y contesten la pregunta.

Los chilenos viven concentrados en grandes ciudades; siete de cada diez chilenos se hallan en las siguientes grandes urbes y sus alrededores: Santiago, Valparaíso y Concepción. En Santiago se concentra el 40% de la población total de Chile; es una de las áreas metropolitanas más pobladas de América Latina con cerca de 6 millones de personas. Las proyecciones demográficas indican que las futuras generaciones de chilenos vivirán en grandes ciudades. Actualmente hay más de 15.5 millones de habitantes y la población se duplicará en 50 años.

¿Qué opinan de esta proyección demográfica? ¿Es buena o mala?

Proyectos personales

I. Vocabulario: Mis aspiraciones

Mi **ilusión** es llegar a ser rico. Sé que voy a **hacer realidad** algún día mi **sueño** porque tengo mucha **constancia** y **disciplina.**

Lo que deseo es tener una familia unida y feliz. A pesar de los **retos,** sé que lo voy a **lograr.** Voy a **poner de mi parte** para **alcanzar** esta **meta.**

Vocabulario práctico

la ilusión *dream, illusion*
la meta *goal*
el reto / el desafío *challenge*
el sueño *dream*

alcanzar *to reach*
aspirar a *to aspire to*
enfrentar *to face; to confront*
hacer realidad *to make come true*

lograr *to achieve*
llegar a ser *to become*
tener constancia *to be constant,
    to persist*
tener disciplina *to be disciplined*
tener éxito *to be successful*
tener paciencia *to be patient*
tener suerte *to be lucky*

11-1 Mis metas personales Indica todas las metas que te correspondan. Luego, compara tus respuestas con las de un(a) compañero(a). ¿Tienen algunos sueños en común?

_____ Sueño con ser rico(a).

_____ Mi ilusión es vivir en otro país.

_____ Aspiro a ser famoso(a).

_____ Aspiro a conseguir un buen trabajo.

_____ Quiero viajar por todo el mundo.

_____ Mi sueño es tener un romance con...

_____ Deseo tener una familia.

_____ Otra(s) meta(s):

CD2-44 **11-2 Aspiraciones** Toma nota de la información que vas a escuchar para completar la siguiente tabla.

Cuando era pequeño(a)...	Ahora...

■ Aplicaciones

11-3 ¿Quién es? Túrnense para hablar de las metas y aspiraciones de personajes históricos.

MODELO   E1: *Quería ser un cantante original. Su sueño era la*
existencia de la paz y del amor en el mundo.
           E2: *¿John Lennon?*
           E1: *¡Correcto!*

11-4 ¿Qué tengo que hacer? Túrnense para indicar lo que tiene que hacer la otra persona para alcanzar sus metas. Usen por lo menos uno de los verbos de la lista en todas sus respuestas.

OPCIONES: tener constancia   tener disciplina   tener paciencia
               hacer realidad   tener éxito

MODELO   E1: *¡Quiero graduarme pronto!*
           E2: *Tienes que tener paciencia y aprobar todas tus asignaturas.*

1. ¡Quiero viajar por todo el mundo!
2. ¡Quiero ser millonario(a)!
3. ¡Quiero ser muy famoso(a)!
4. ¡Quiero ser feliz!
5. ¡Quiero hablar español fluidamente!
6. ¡Quiero tener éxito en mi carrera!

> **REMEMBER**
>
> The structure **tener** + **que** + *infinitive* is used to express obligation.
> **Tienes que trabajar.**
> *You have to work.*
> **Tenemos que salir pronto.**
> *We have to leave soon.*

11-5 Entrevista Túrnense para hacerse las siguientes preguntas con un(a) compañero(a). Tomen nota y preséntenle un informe de sus respuestas al resto de la clase.

1. ¿Qué tan importante es tu carrera para ti? (¿muy importante? ¿más o menos importante? ¿poco importante?)
2. ¿Qué metas concretas tienes con respecto a tu carrera? (¿Quieres prepararte mejor para encontrar un trabajo o quieres llegar a ser rico, famoso?)
3. ¿Cuáles son los mayores retos que enfrentas en este momento? (¿tiempo? ¿dinero? ¿paciencia?)

MODELO   *Para mi compañera, su carrera es muy importante. Su meta es...*

■ Integración

11-6 Las preocupaciones de los padres Representa la siguiente situación con un(a) compañero(a).

Padre/Madre preocupado(a)	**Hijo(a) desmotivado(a)**
Tu hijo(a) ha llegado a casa con calificaciones *(grades)* muy deficientes. 1. Averigua qué pasó. 2. Habla con tu hijo(a) sobre sus metas. 3. Háblale a tu hijo(a) acerca de la importancia de la educación para lograr esas metas.	Las cosas no van muy bien en la universidad. Es hora *(It's time)* de llevar a casa tus calificaciones y de seguro vas a recibir un regaño *(reprimand)*. 1. Explícale a tu padre/madre lo que pasó. 2. Habla de tus metas para el futuro. 3. Responde a sus consejos.

> **EN TU COMUNIDAD**
>
> Interview a Hispanic immigrant and find out about his/her goals and dreams. Inquire about what he/she wants to accomplish in life and about the reasons why he/she came to this country. In addition, ask him/her about challenges he has had to face and how he/she has overcome them.

11-7 ¿Cuáles son tus metas? Escribe un ensayo acerca de tus metas personales y lo que estás haciendo en este momento para alcanzarlas. También, menciona lo que tienes que hacer en el futuro inmediato para asegurar el éxito de tus planes.

II. Funciones y estructuras: Talking about aspirations (review of the future tense)

Para alcanzar mi sueño de ser la mejor abogada del mundo, **tendré** disciplina y paciencia, **estudiaré** mucho y **enfrentaré** todos los obstáculos que encuentre en mi camino. ¡Sé que lo **lograré**!

REMEMBER

The future tense endings are **-é, -ás, -á, -emos, -éis,** and **–án.**

In **Capítulo 10, Tema 3,** you learned how to use the future tense. This tense is formed by adding the same set of endings to the infinitive form of **-ar, -er,** and **-ir** verbs.

¿Crees que Lina y Josefa **llegarán** a ser ricas algún día?	*Do you think Lina and Josefa **will become** rich someday?*
Estoy seguro de que Alana y yo **seremos** muy buenas atletas.	*I am sure that Alana and I **will be** very good athletes.*

As you may remember, the infinitive form of a number of verbs undergoes changes in the future tense. These verbs were grouped in three categories:

1. the shortened stem group (**decir → dir-** and **hacer → har-**),

2. the dropped-**e**-group (**caber → cabr-, haber → habr-, poder → podr-, querer → querr-,** and **saber → sabr-**), and

3. the **-dr-** substitution group (**poner → pondr-, salir → saldr-, tener → tendr-, valer → valdr-,** and **venir → vendr-**).

Haré lo que sea necesario para alcanzar mi meta.	*I **will do** whatever is necessary to reach my goal.*
Ella **sabrá** enfrentar todos los retos.	*She **will know** how to face all the challenges.*
El éxito **vendrá** a su debido momento.	*Success **will come** at the right moment.*

■ Asimilación

11-8 Para tener éxito en mi carrera... Piensa en la carrera que has elegido y en las cosas que tendrás que hacer para ser una persona exitosa en ese campo. Luego, lee las siguientes oraciones e indica si se aplican o no a tu situación. Al terminar, compara tus respuestas con las de un(a) compañero(a). ¿Tienen retos semejantes o diferentes?

Tendré que...

_____ invertir mucho dinero.
_____ hacer estudios de postgrado.
_____ tener mi propia oficina.
_____ contratar a varios asistentes.
_____ sacrificar mi vida personal y familiar.

No tendré que...

_____ depender de nadie.
_____ viajar frecuentemente.
_____ estar disponible las veinticuatro horas del día.
_____ hacer trabajo en casa.
_____ tener un jefe o supervisor.

02-45

11-9 Actitudes Escucha lo que dicen Simón, Melinda y Beto sobre sus aspiraciones personales y profesionales y decide si tienen una buena actitud o no. Debes justificar tu opinión.

Simón: sí / no

Razones:

Melinda: sí / no

Razones:

Beto: sí / no

Razones:

■ Aplicaciones

11-10 De otra forma Vuelvan a escribir las siguientes oraciones usando verbos en el futuro.

MODELO   Minerva y yo vamos a salir del seminario de auto-mejoramiento a las dos.
Minerva y yo saldremos del seminario de auto-mejoramiento a las dos.

1. Voy a querer hacer estudios de postgrado cuando me gradúe.
2. A Andrés se le van a presentar muchas oportunidades en la vida profesional.
3. Sé que vas a triunfar porque tienes mucha constancia.
4. ¿Uds. van a asistir a la charla sobre disciplina personal?
5. Mauricio y yo vamos a ser grandes hombres de negocios.
6. Mi hermana va a poder ingresar en la universidad que quiera.
7. Voy a poner todo mi empeño para que mi sueño se haga realidad.
8. Nuestros consejeros nos van a decir cómo vencer estos problemas.

> **REMEMBER**
>
> The expression **ir** + **a** + *infinitive* is used to talk about actions that will take place in the future: **Yo *voy a estudiar* (= *estudiaré*) por tres horas.**

11-11 Planificando el futuro Hagan una lista de las cosas que harán para garantizar que Uds. tendrán éxito en los siguientes aspectos de la vida en el futuro. Usen la forma **nosotros(as)** de los verbos.

El aspecto sentimental	El aspecto familiar
El aspecto profesional	El aspecto social

11-12 Oye, fulano(a),... En parejas, escriban preguntas para hacerles a por lo menos seis compañeros de la clase para saber qué harán o qué esperan hacer en el futuro. Déjense llevar por lo que ya saben de estas personas. Luego, háganles las preguntas.

MODELO   *Nancy, ¿tendrás paciencia cuando seas profesora de un colegio? Robert y Sheila, ¿lograrán su sueño de ser biólogos?*

▣ Integración

SUGERENCIAS

Pueden hablar de un actor o actriz, de un(a) cantante, de un político o hasta de un(a) compañero(a) de clase.

11-13 Personas importantes del futuro ¿Qué personas jóvenes prometen ser aún más importantes e influyentes en el futuro? Individualmente, piensen en una de estas personas, describan las cosas que él/ella logrará y expliquen por qué piensan que será tan importante.

11-14 Una carta de agradecimiento Imagínate que quieres escribir una carta a una persona que siempre ha creído en ti y que te ha dado ánimo para seguir adelante en la vida. Sigue los pasos que se mencionan a continuación y, al terminar, intercambia cartas con un(a) compañero(a) de clase para que se hagan correcciones.

CORRECCIÓN

Al intercambiar cartas, usen las siguientes ideas para hacer sus correcciones:
Contenido: ¿Las ideas están bien presentadas? ¿Faltan detalles que apoyen alguna de las ideas?
Organización: ¿La carta sigue un orden lógico? ¿Incluye un saludo y una despedida?
Gramática: ¿Los verbos están bien conjugados? ¿Usó el futuro correctamente? ¿Hay concordancia de género y número entre los sustantivos y los adjetivos?

Paso 1: Planificación: Haz una lista de ejemplos que demuestre que la persona a quien le escribes la carta te ha apoyado, y otra lista de las cosas que harás para no defraudarla *(disappoint him/her)*.

Paso 2: La carta: Empieza la carta con un saludo cordial. Luego dale las gracias a esta persona y menciona las razones que apuntaste en el **Paso 1.** Además, incluye la lista de cosas que harás para no defraudarla y para demostrarle que has alcanzado tus metas. Finalmente, escribe una despedida cordial.

Paso 3: Revisión: Lee la carta y determina si está completa, si las ideas están bien organizadas y si necesitas usar palabras y frases conectoras (**por eso, por lo tanto, además, por el contrario, en conclusión,** etc.).

III. Funciones y estructuras: Expressing conjecture and probability with the conditional tense

ENTREVISTADORA: Señor, con su permiso. ¿Le puedo hacer algunas preguntas para una encuesta?

DIONISIO RUIZ: Claro, pero sea breve porque tengo poco tiempo.

ENTREVISTADORA: Muchas gracias. ¿Le **gustaría** tener más dinero o piensa que gana lo suficiente para ser feliz?

DIONISIO RUIZ: ¡Por supuesto que me **gustaría** tener más dinero! Así **podría** viajar más y mi familia **tendría** todo lo que necesita. ¡Y no **trabajaría** tanto, como ahora!

ENTREVISTADORA: ¿Y cree que ellos lo **querrían** más a Ud.?

DIONISIO RUIZ: Eso no. Ellos me quieren como soy. El tener más dinero no **cambiaría** nada... ¡Pero algunas cosas **serían** más fáciles!

The highlighted verbs in the previous conversation are conjugated in the conditional tense. This tense is the equivalent of the *would* + verb English expression used to talk about actions that *would* happen if certain conditions existed.

Si tuviera suerte, me **ganaría** la lotería.	*If I had luck, I **would win** the lottery.*
¿Te **sentirías** más satisfecha con tu vida si fueras más exitosa?	***Would you feel** more satisfied with your life if you were more successful?*

Just like the future tense, the conditional is formed by attaching identical sets of endings to the infinitive of the verb.

ENDINGS	-ar VERBS	-er VERBS	-ir VERBS
-ía	lograría	comería	viviría
-ías	lograrías	comerías	vivirías
-ía	lograría	comería	viviría
-íamos	lograríamos	comeríamos	viviríamos
-íais	lograríais	comeríais	viviríais
-ían	lograrían	comerían	vivirían

Notice that the **yo** and **él/ella/usted** forms are the same.

The verbs that show irregularities in the stem in the future tense (**decir, tener, salir,** etc.) show the same irregularities in the conditional tense.

En este trabajo **tendría** un mejor salario y **podría** ascender rápidamente.	*In this job **I would have** a better salary and **would be able** to get promoted quickly.*
¿Qué **harías** en esta situación? ¿Se lo **dirías** a tu jefe?	*What **would you do** in a situation like this? **Would you tell** your boss?*

REMEMBER

There are three types of irregularities. They were presented in the previous **Funciones y estructuras** section (p. 448).

The conditional is also used to express politeness when making requests or giving suggestions.

Sra. Peralta, Ud. **debería** ser más cuidadosa y astuta.

*Mrs. Peralta, you **should** be more careful and astute.*

¿**Podrías** ayudarme a escribir mi hoja de vida?

***Could** you help me write my résumé?*

The following expressions are often used with the conditional tense.

probablemente *probably*	**quizás** *maybe*	**tal vez** *maybe*

Si no estuviera casado, **tal vez volvería** a estudiar en la universidad

*If I were not married, **maybe I would go back** to college.*

Con más dinero en el banco, **quizás** me **jubilaría** ahora mismo.

*With more money in the bank, **maybe I would retire** right now.*

■ Asimilación

11-15 Si fuera *(If he/she were)* **presidente(a) de los Estados Unidos...** Lee las siguientes oraciones y complétalas con el nombre de una persona famosa que haría esa actividad si fuera presidente(a) de los Estados Unidos. Cuando termines, compara tus respuestas con las de un(a) compañero(a). ¿Quién formó las oraciones más originales?

...llevaría al país a la bancarrota *(bankrupcy)*.

...tendría fiestas en la Casa Blanca todos los días.

...no se preocuparía por nada.

...establecería la capital del país en Hollywood.

...le traería mucho prestigio al gobierno.

...sería el (la) mejor presidente(a) de la historia del país.

...nos obligaría a aceptar a más de una primera dama.

...no tendría una buena relación con los senadores y congresistas.

CD2-46 **11-16 Una vida diferente** Escucha la descripción que da el Sr. Miranda, administrador de una empresa de computación, sobre cómo sería su vida si pudiera empezar de nuevo. Luego, indica si las oraciones que siguen son ciertas (**C**) o falsas (**F**).

_____ 1. El Sr. Miranda no sería administrador de una empresa.

_____ 2. Él viviría en un área rural, no en un área urbana.

_____ 3. Podemos deducir que este señor no pasa mucho tiempo con su familia.

_____ 4. A él no le gusta viajar muy a menudo.

_____ 5. Si pudiera, él pintaría y esquiaría en su tiempo libre.

Aplicaciones

11-17 ¿Adónde vamos? Lee el diálogo entre David y Victoria y complétalo con la forma correcta del condicional de los verbos de la lista.

OPCIONES: tener gastar sugerir ser visitar divertirse
pasar gustar

DAVID: Victoria, ¿vamos a ir a Chile o a Paraguay durante las vacaciones de primavera?

VICTORIA: Si fuéramos a Chile, el precio _____ más bajo.

DAVID: No, creo que en Paraguay nosotros _____ menos dinero.

VICTORIA: Tienes razón, porque en Chile (nosotros) _____ que ir a Valparaíso.

DAVID: Pero, por otro lado, en Paraguay (nosotros) _____ otros lugares igualmente interesantes y bonitos.

VICTORIA: David, escúchame. Creo que yo lo _____ mejor en Chile. ¿Vas conmigo o no?

DAVID: ¡Tranquila!

VICTORIA: Me _____ que fueras conmigo porque (nosotros) _____ muchísimo, pero es obvio que tenemos gustos diferentes.

DAVID: Tienes razón. Te _____ que esperáramos unos días y que habláramos del asunto. ¿De acuerdo?

VICTORIA: ¡De acuerdo!

11-18 ¿Qué harías... ? Túrnense para hacer y responder a preguntas usando la información dada.

MODELO en el puesto *(position)* de rector(a) de la universidad
E1: *¿Qué harías en el puesto de rector(a) de la universidad?*
E2: *Yo mejoraría las instalaciones* (facilities) *de la universidad y cambiaría el menú de la cafetería.*

1. con cinco millones de dólares
2. con treinta años más de edad
3. en tu fiesta ideal
4. en las vacaciones ideales
5. en el puesto del / de la presidente(a) del país
6. para obtener un trabajo perfecto
7. para conseguir una casa perfecta
8. para perder peso

11-19 Profesores(as) por un mes Imagínense que tienen la oportunidad de ser profesores(as) de español por un mes. ¿Qué harían y qué no harían? Escriban por lo menos ocho oraciones originales.

MODELO   *Nosotros nunca daríamos exámenes y haríamos fiestas en clase.*

■ **Integración**

11-20 Hombres y mujeres ¿Alguna vez han pensado en qué harían si fueran personas del sexo opuesto?

- ¿Qué cosas cambiarían?
- ¿Y qué cosas harían de una manera diferente?

En parejas, intercambien opiniones sobre este asunto. ¡Aprovechen esta oportunidad para demostrarle a los (las) estudiantes del sexo opuesto que Uds. sí los/las conocen bien!

SUGERENCIAS

- Las mujeres pueden usar algunos de estos verbos y expresiones: **comprender, atender, apoyar, (no) trabajar, (no) mirar la televisión, (no) vestirse, escuchar, salir** y **(no) ponerse.**
- Los hombres pueden usar algunos de estos verbos y expresiones: **(no) maquillarse, (no) quejarse, (no) hablar, (no) vestirse, interesarse, compartir, (no) decir** y **(no) ponerse.**

11-21 Desde mi punto de vista Imagínate que uno(a) de tus mejores amigos(as) no tiene muchas aspiraciones para su futuro. ¿Qué le recomendarías? Escríbele una breve nota para motivarlo(la) a ser más positivo(a). Y para que no lo tome tan personalmente, usa la forma **yo** de los verbos. Cuando termines, dale una copia a tu profesor(a) para que te dé su opinión. ¿Tienes que cambiar algo? ¿Tienes que ser más persuasivo(a) y convincente?

IV. Perspectivas: Cómo convertir los sueños en una realidad

■ Antes de leer

A. Para conversar En grupos de tres o cuatro estudiantes, respondan a las siguientes preguntas.

1. ¿Es bueno o malo soñar despierto *(to daydream)*? Expliquen por qué.

2. ¿Pueden los sueños convertirse en realidad? ¿Cómo? Den ejemplos.

B. Vocabulario y conceptos Las siguientes palabras son importantes para comprender el texto. Para cada palabra, busca la letra que corresponda a su definición. (Consulten el diccionario si es necesario.)

____	1. la clave	a.	convertirse en una realidad
____	2. un fracaso	b.	objetivo, que no se basa en ilusiones
____	3. realista	c.	la suerte
____	4. cumplir	d.	la idea importante
____	5. el azar	e.	pronto, en un futuro cercano
____	6. a corto plazo	f.	algo que tuvo malos resultados, que no tuvo éxito

C. Aplicación Ahora, completen las oraciones con las palabras que acaban de aprender en la actividad anterior.

1. En un juego de lotería, el factor más importante es el _____.

2. Muchas personas le tienen miedo al _____, pero en realidad puede ser algo positivo.

3. Las fantasías son buenas, pero es mejor tener metas _____ para no tener desilusiones.

4. Mi abuelo dice que la _____ para tener éxito en la vida es ser honesto.

5. En el futuro quiero ser médico, pero por ahora, una de mis metas _____ es salir bien en el examen de esta tarde.

6. Sé que voy a _____ todas mis metas porque tengo mucha disciplina.

■ **A leer**

Lee rápidamente el siguiente artículo y responde a las preguntas que siguen.

Las claves de la ilusión [dreaming]

Aunque soñar despierto es muy positivo, lo cierto es que de la ilusión no se puede vivir. Por eso, todos los expertos **coinciden** en que si queremos convertir nuestros sueños en realidad, debemos **poner mucho de nuestra parte** y no olvidar una serie de puntos concretos.

agree

to make a big effort

Aceptar los fracasos. Muchos de los sueños que tenemos no se cumplen, pero esto no quiere decir que seamos unos fracasados. Es necesario aprender a mantener viva la ilusión, a aceptar que no hemos conseguido algo y a buscar siempre una salida positiva.

Planificar para conseguir los objetivos. Uno de los secretos para conseguir nuestras metas es planificar nuestra actuación. Y uno de los mejores **trucos,** según algunos sicólogos, es escribir estas metas.

tricks

Tener metas realistas. Es necesario soñar con cosas que no sean imposibles de conseguir. «Las personas que tienen expectativas demasiado desproporcionadas a la realidad terminan **cayendo** en una continua desilusión, porque es muy difícil que todos sus sueños se cumplan», explica el sociólogo Armando de Miguel.

falling

*Saber adaptarse a los **vaivenes**.* «La capacidad de adaptarse al **medio,** a lo que se tiene delante, es una **señal** de salud mental», comenta Héctor González. Es importante aceptar los **imprevistos** e ir variando los objetivos si la realidad nos dice que no podemos cumplirlos.

fluctuations / environment
sign
surprises

***Fijarse** objetivos a corto plazo.* Aunque está muy bien tener expectativas **a largo plazo,** si queremos que se cumplan es necesario que tengamos también objetivos a corto plazo, como **etapas** sucesivas hacia la **consecución** de esas metas finales. Por ejemplo, si lo que esperamos es aprobar una carrera, debemos **plantearnos** aprobar primero asignatura por asignatura, luego curso por curso...

Set
long term
stages
obtaining
to consider

Tener objetivos personales. «Es importante ilusionarse con cosas que realmente signifiquen algo para nosotros, que no nos llamen la atención sólo **por el simple hecho** de que están de moda o son populares en nuestro **entorno** inmediato», explica el sicólogo Pedro Rodríguez.

just because
social group

■ **¿Entendiste bien?**

D. Ideas generales Con un(a) compañero(a), respondan a las siguientes preguntas.

1. ¿Cuál es la idea principal del texto?
2. ¿Cuántos consejos presenta?
3. ¿Quiénes son los expertos citados como fuentes *(cited as sources)*?

E. ¿Sí o no? Ahora lee de nuevo el texto e indica si las siguientes oraciones corresponden a las ideas que presenta este artículo.

_____ 1. Debemos tener siempre una actitud positiva a pesar de *(in spite of)* los fracasos.

_____ 2. Para lograr nuestras metas no es necesario elaborar un plan de acción.

_____ 3. Para alcanzar nuestras metas, tenemos que ser flexibles.

_____ 4. Todas nuestras metas deben ser a largo plazo.

_____ 5. Nuestras metas deben ser originales.

F. Actividad de extensión Después de leer el artículo, ¿qué le dirían a una persona que quiere tener mucho éxito en su profesión y también tener una familia unida y feliz? Escriban por lo menos cinco recomendaciones.

MODELO   *Para lograr tus metas, es importante que...*

Un futuro tecnificado

I. Vocabulario: Las comodidades de la era electrónica

¿Qué es esto? Busquen en el dibujo cada uno de los artículos indicados.

la alarma	la videograbadora
el horno microondas	el calentador/la caldera de agua
la antena parabólica	el equipo de sonido / el estéreo
la lavaplatos / el lavavajillas	la lavadora
el sistema de riego automático	el contestador
la cafetera automática	la secadora
el aire acondicionado	el fax
el televisor	la nevera / el refrigerador
la puerta automática	la computadora / el ordenador

Instrucciones de uso

Conecte la unidad y **préndala** con el control remoto.
*Plug in the unit and **turn it on** with the remote control.*

Apague y **desconecte** el equipo después de cada uso.
*Turn off and **unplug** the equipment after each use.*

Presione el botón de encendido y use el teclado del control remoto para **programar** la máquina.
*Push the "on" button and use the keyboard on your remote control to **program** the machine.*

Inserte el disco compacto en la ranura.
Insert the compact disk in the slot.

Hale la perilla para activarla.
Pull the knob to activate it.

Vocabulario práctico

apagado *off*
encendido *on*
No funciona. *It doesn't work. / It's broken.*

digitar *to key in*
halar *to pull*
presionar/oprimir/pulsar *to push, to hit*

■ Asimilación

 11-22 ¿Lo tienes? Indica si tienes, quieres o no necesitas los siguientes aparatos. Luego, compara tus respuestas con las de un(a) compañero(a). ¿Tienen mucho o poco en común?

Aparato	Lo tengo	Me gustaría tenerlo	No lo necesito
una antena parabólica			
un sistema de aire acondicionado			
una lavadora			
una secadora			
un horno microondas			
una lavaplatos			
una cafetera automática			
una videograbadora			
un equipo de sonido			
un contestador			
una computadora			

02-47 **11-23 ¿Qué aparato es?** Escucha las siguientes instrucciones de uso. ¿A qué aparato se refiere cada una? Escoge la respuesta más apropiada.

1. lavadora, contestador, videograbadora
2. computadora, cafetera, alarma
3. calentador, aire acondicionado, antena parabólica
4. contestador, computadora, alarma
5. equipo de sonido, lavadora, aire acondicionado

■ Aplicaciones

 11-24 Manual de instrucciones

Paso 1: Ordenen las siguientes instrucciones para operar una máquina lavadora.

_____ Prepare los artículos para el lavado.

_____ Ponga la carga *(load)* de lavado en la lavadora.

_____ Añada el detergente.

_____ No sobrecargue *(overload)* la lavadora.

_____ Presione la perilla para iniciar el ciclo.

_____ Retire los artículos al terminar el ciclo.

Paso 2: Escojan otro aparato de uso doméstico y escriban las instrucciones de uso correspondientes.

 11-25 Publicidad Imagínense que tienen que vender los siguientes productos. Escriban los anuncios comerciales correspondientes.

a. videograbadora   b. lavadora   c. fax

 11-26 ¿Cómo van a ser las casas en el año 3000? Con un(a) compañero(a), piensen en las características de los hogares del futuro y diseñen su versión de la casa típica del año 3000.

■ Integración

11-27 ¿Qué es lo más importante? Formen grupos de tres estudiantes. Cada uno(a) va a leer una de las siguientes noticias sobre avances tecnológicos y va a informarle al resto del grupo acerca de sus ideas más importantes. Al terminar, decidan cuál es la información más importante y expliquen por qué.

Noticias tecnológicas

«Hoy el comercio electrónico es residual en la Red, sobre todo por las limitaciones en cuestión de seguridad, aunque en un futuro **se impondrá, ya que** se está avanzando en este terreno», **sostiene** Enrique García, de la UCE. Las ventajas pasan por la comodidad y por la reducción de precios, ya que tener una página «Web» es más barato que un **local.** Pero la principal desventaja es que no se ha conseguido que la seguridad en las transacciones económicas sea la adecuada, aunque se están desarrollando protocolos para encriptar los números de las tarjetas de crédito de los clientes.

will become dominant since
states

place of business

¿La energía del futuro?

La fusión nuclear es un proceso similar al que se produce en el núcleo del sol, el cual genera luz y calor. Ésta podría ser una de las principales **fuentes** de energía del futuro, ya que se trata de un proceso limpio que no produce gases contaminantes ni lluvia ácida. De hecho, todos los elementos químicos que se emplean son **inocuos** para el ser humano y el medio ambiente. Hay reservas para mil años de **litio,** metal necesario para producir el **tritio, a su vez** esencial para la fusión.

sources

harmless
lithium
trithium / in turn

¿Qué utilidad tendrá la estación «Alfa» para la humanidad?

La colaboración internacional ha sido la **pieza clave** para la construcción de la nueva estación. En ella se podrán investigar nuevos medicamentos, observar los cambios climáticos y saber si el hombre podrá viajar algún día a **Marte.** La estación internacional —la estructura más grande **jamás** construida en el espacio, con 110 metros de largo— **pesará** 405 **toneladas, se desplazará** a 29.000 km/h y dará una **vuelta** completa a la Tierra cada noventa minutos. Tendrá seis módulos que servirán de laboratorio, dos que **se destinarán** a viviendas —donde residirán hasta siete astronautas— y otros siete serán utilizados como almacén. **Se prevé** que esté en operación durante al menos diez años.

key piece

Mars

ever
will weigh
tons / will move
turn

will dedicate
It is foreseen

EN TU COMUNIDAD

Conduct an Internet search to find out if cellular phones, computers and wireless Internet connections are as readily available in Spanish-speaking countries such as Chile and Paraguay as in the United States. (You may choose other countries.) Also, find out how much these products and services cost. When you have all the necessary information, prepare a written report.

11-28 Opiniones Hazte las siguientes preguntas y presenta un informe escrito con tus conclusiones.

a. ¿Qué opinas de la tecnología? ¿Te parece algo positivo o negativo?
b. ¿Cuál de los siguientes avances del siglo XX consideras que fue el más importante? ¿Por qué?
   - el avión
   - la penicilina
   - la computadora
   - los satélites artificiales
   - los transbordadores espaciales *(space shuttles)*
   - la clonación genética
   - el Internet
c. Si pudieras diseñar un nuevo aparato para hacer la vida humana más cómoda, ¿qué aparato sería? (Describe las funciones y características que **tendría** este aparato.)

SUGERENCIAS

Para ponerle un nombre *(To give it a name)* a tu invento, puedes usar uno de los siguientes modelos: **para lavar platos: una lavaplatos, para contestar las llamadas: un contestador.** Algunos verbos útiles son **tener, poder, ser, resolver, ayudar, hacer, reemplazar, simplificar, preparar, decidir, curar.**

II. Funciones y estructuras: Expressing opinion, emotion, wishes, doubt, stipulation, purpose and future time frame with the subjunctive and the infinitive

DORIS: **Quiero conseguir** una casa con alarma, sistema de riego automático y un calentador de agua nuevo.

IRMA: Mmm... **Dudo que** la **consigas. Es imposible encontrar** una casa así en este vecindario.

DORIS: Te aseguro que la voy a conseguir **antes de casarme.**

IRMA: **Me parece fantástico que seas** tan optimista, pero recuerda que *yo* soy la agente de bienes raíces.

DORIS: Irma, **para lograr** algo **es aconsejable ser** positivo.

You have already studied the use of the subjunctive mode with verbs and impersonal expressions that convey:

- Opinion and advice

Es necesario que desenchufes los enseres antes de salir.

It is necessary for you to unplug the appliances before leaving.

- Wishes and requests

Prefiero que uses la secadora por la mañana.

I prefer for you to use the dryer in the morning.

- Emotions and feelings

Es increíble que este apartamento **tenga** tantas comodidades.

It is incredible that this apartment has so many comforts.

- Doubt

No estoy segura de que el horno microondas **funcione** bien.

I am not sure that the microwave oven works well.

The other use of the subjunctive (in adjectival clauses that refer to hypothetical antecedents) is not included in this discussion because the infinitive form of the verb is never used in this context. **Queremos una casa que** *tenga* **puertas automáticas.**

You have also studied the use of this mode with conjunctions of stipulation, purpose, and future time frame.

Compraré el aire acondicionado **para que durmamos** cómodamente.

*I will buy the air conditioner **so that we sleep** comfortably.*

When the subject of one of these verbs is the same as the subject of the verb in the subordinate clause, the verb in the latter is used in the infinitive form. Compare the following pairs of sentences. (The subjects are underlined.)

Notice that **que** is omitted when the main verb, the impersonal expression, or the conjunction is followed by an infinitive.

SUBJUNCTIVE: (<u>Yo</u>) Espero que <u>Ana</u> **compre** la videograbadora.
INFINITIVE: (<u>Yo</u>) Espero **comprar** la videograbadora.

Similarly, personal expressions are followed by an infinitive when the speaker is making a generic statement that applies to people in general, including himself or herself. This is also useful when the speaker wants to make a comment that affects the listener but in an indirect and polite manner. Compare these pairs of sentences.

SUBJUNCTIVE:	Es ridículo que ellos no **sepan** programar una computadora.
INFINITIVE:	Es ridículo no **saber** programar una computadora.

The only conjunctions that can be used with the infinitive form of the verb are **con tal de** and **en caso de** (stipulation); **a fin de** and **para** (purpose); and **antes de, después de,** and **hasta** (future time frame).

SUBJUNCTIVE:	Zelma limpia la casa a fin de que su madre **se sienta** bien.
INFINITIVE:	Zelma limpia la casa a fin de **sentirse** bien.

Although **cuando, en cuanto,** and **mientras** cannot be used with infinitives, they can be used with verbs in the indicative mode if the action of the subordinate clause does not refer to the future. The same applies to **antes de, después de,** and **hasta. Conecto la cafetera** *cuando* **mi madre desconecta el radio. Me iba de casa** *en cuanto* **terminaba de enviar los faxes. Elena me acompañaba** *hasta que yo* **estaba lista.**

■ Asimilación

11-29 Vivir bien hoy en día Lee las siguientes oraciones e indica si estás de acuerdo o no. Cuando termines, compara las respuestas con las de un(a) compañero(a). ¿Están de acuerdo? ¿Por qué?

Para vivir bien hoy día...

_____ es necesario tener un horno microondas.

_____ no es importante tener una secadora.

_____ no es aconsejable usar una lavaplatos.

_____ es recomendable comprar una antena parabólica.

_____ es mejor regar las plantas con un sistema de riego automático.

_____ es preciso pagar las cuentas por computadora.

_____ es imposible estar en ciertos *(certain)* lugares sin aire acondicionado.

_____ es posible informarnos solamente a través de la televisión.

CD2-48

11-30 Los recién casados Escucha el diálogo entre Estrella y Héctor, unos recién casados, y escoge las alternativas que mejor completen las siguientes oraciones.

1. Héctor piensa arreglar el calentador cuando...
   a. termine el partido.   b. Estrella se bañe.
   c. Estrella se vaya al trabajo.

2. Dadas las condiciones, Estrella dice que es imposible...
   a. descansar.   b. ir a trabajar.   c. bañarse.

3. Héctor duda que el agua...
   a. esté caliente.   b. esté fría.   c. no esté helada.

4. Estrella no puede creer que Héctor...
   a. duerma tanto.   b. no sea cooperador.
   c. no quiera trabajar.

5. Cuando Estrella se lleva el control remoto, Héctor dice que...
   a. no es imprescindible.   b. no es justo.
   c. no es importante.

■ Aplicaciones

11-31 En un almacén Lean el diálogo entre Marcos y el empleado de un almacén y decidan si el verbo debe usarse en el infinitivo o en el subjuntivo. Si debe usarse en el subjuntivo, conjúguenlo correctamente.

EMPLEADO: Buenas tardes, señor. ¿En qué puedo ayudarlo?

MARCOS: Hola. Estoy buscando un horno de microondas que no (costar) mucho y que (ser) de buena calidad.

EMPLEADO: Tenemos una amplia selección. Le recomiendo que (comprar) un modelo que (usar) poca electricidad, como éste.

MARCOS: Me parece bien. Creo que es importante (economizar) como sea, ¿no?

EMPLEADO: Estoy de acuerdo. ¿Y para Ud. es necesario (tener) un microondas con plato giratorio *(rotating)*?

MARCOS: Mmm... Sí. Quiero un horno que (distribuir) uniformemente el calor. ¿Tiene garantía?

EMPLEADO: De un año. Y, si lo desea, puede comprar un servicio de por vida que (cubrir) el arreglo de cualquier tipo de desperfecto.

MARCOS: Eso me interesa. Me lo llevo.

EMPLEADO: ¡Perfecto! Pues pase por aquella caja registradora para (pagar).

[Cinco minutos después.]

EMPLEADO: Hasta luego, señor. Espero que Ud. y su familia (disfrutar) del horno de microondas.

MARCOS: Gracias por todo. Hasta luego.

11-32 Planes futuros

Paso 1: Usa las claves para formar oraciones sobre tus planes para el futuro. Usa las conjunciones que se proveen. Puedes añadir la información que creas necesaria.

MODELO   trabajar / para (que) / mi familia
Trabajaré como dentista para sentirme productivo(a) y para que mi familia tenga lo que necesite.

1. casarme / después de (que) / mi futuro(a) esposo(a)

2. comprar / antes de (que) / mis futuros hijos

3. ahorrar / en caso de (que) / mis padres o mis hermanos

4. tener / con tal de (que) / alguien

5. ir / hasta (que) / mi mejor amigo(a)

6. ser / para (que) / todo el mundo

Paso 2: Compara las respuestas del **Paso 1** con las respuestas de un(a) compañero(a) de clase. ¿Cuáles de sus planes te parecen más interesantes, curiosos o extraños? Escoge tres de sus respuestas y escribe un breve informe.

> MODELO   *Me parece interesante que Nelson vaya a trabajar para ganar mucho dinero y para que su madre tenga la casa de sus sueños. Además, me parece curioso que él...*

11-33 Consejos Preparen una lista de ocho consejos que quieren darles a sus hijos cuando sean adolescentes.

> MODELO   *Les sugiero que estudien antes de pensar en el matrimonio. Es importante respetar a toda la gente.*

■ Integración

11-34 Las prioridades de la vida Representa la siguiente situación con un(a) compañero(a).

El (La) ambicioso(a) *(greedy)*

Eres una persona demasiado ambiciosa que sólo piensa en las cosas materiales que quieres conseguir. Háblale a tu amigo(a) de algunas de estas cosas y pídele su opinión. ¡Debes estar preparado(a) para su reacción y para defender tu punto de vista sobre las prioridades de la vida!

El (La) práctico(a)

Uno(a) de tus amigos(as) sólo habla de las cosas materiales que quiere en su vida. Ya estás cansado(a) de esto y vas a aprovechar la oportunidad para darle tu opinión. Explícale cuáles son las prioridades de la vida y defiende tu punto de vista.

SUGERENCIAS

Para expresar desacuerdo, puedes usar algunas de las siguientes expresiones:
No pienso de la misma manera.
I don't think the same way.
Tengo una opinión diferente.
I have a different opinion.
No estoy de acuerdo.
I don't agree.
Es tu opinión, no la mía.
That's your opinion, not mine.

11-35 Para alcanzar la felicidad De acuerdo con tu experiencia, ¿qué cosas son importantes, necesarias, imposibles, etc., para alcanzar la felicidad en la vida? Como a veces es mejor escribir las ideas, haz una lista de por lo menos diez cosas que no quieres olvidar en momentos difíciles.

SUGERENCIAS

Usa algunos de los verbos y expresiones impersonales que ya sabes para dar consejos, expresar emociones, duda y deseos, tales como: **aconsejar, recomendar, no creer, esperar, querer, es importante, es preciso, es increíble, es triste, es mejor**, etc.

III. Funciones y estructuras: Talking about the past using the imperfect subjunctive

¿Qué pasó ayer en la oficina?

El jefe me **dijo** que **enviara** este fax inmediatamente.

A los empleados no les **gustó** que la compañía les **pagara** menos este mes.

El jefe nos dijo que **era necesario** que **nos quedáramos** en la oficina **hasta** que **termináramos** de revisar todos los datos.

The subjunctive mode also has an imperfect tense. This tense is formed by dropping the **-ron** ending of the **ellos(as)/ustedes** preterite conjugation of the verb and adding the endings that follow to the remaining stem.

ENDINGS	-ar VERBS tomaron → toma-	-er VERBS comieron → comie-	-ir VERBS vivieron → vivie-
-ra	toma**ra**	comie**ra**	vivie**ra**
-ras	toma**ras**	comie**ras**	vivie**ras**
-ra	toma**ra**	comie**ra**	vivie**ra**
-ramos	tom**áramos**	comi**éramos**	vivi**éramos**
-rais	toma**rais**	comie**rais**	vivie**rais**
-ran	toma**ran**	comie**ran**	vivie**ran**

The **yo** and **él/ella/usted** endings are identical.

The **nosotros** form of the imperfect subjunctive takes a written accent mark on the third-to-last syllable.

The imperfect subjunctive is used in the same contexts in which the present subjunctive is used. The difference is that the imperfect subjunctive is used when the verb in the main clause is in the past tense (the preterite or the imperfect indicative).

■ advice and suggestions

| Mi colega me **sugirió** que **buscara** otro trabajo. | *My colleague **suggested looking for** another job.* |

■ wishes

| **Queríamos** que el jefe **escuchara** nuestras quejas. | *We **wanted** the boss **to listen** to our complaints.* |

■ emotion

| **Me alegré** mucho de que te **invitaran** a dar una charla. | *I **was** very **glad** to hear that they **invited** you to give a talk.* |

■ doubt and denial

| Ella nunca **dudó** que yo **terminara** el informe a tiempo. | *She never **doubted** that I **would finish** the report on time.* |

- hypothetical situations and antecedents

  La empresa **necesitaba** un abogado que nos **defendiera** en este caso.

  *The company **needed** a lawyer that **would defend** us in this case.*

- conjunctions of stipulation

  Nosotros **sabíamos** que la junta no aprobaría el proyecto <u>a menos que</u> **presentáramos** evidencia.

  *We **knew** that the board would not approve the project <u>unless</u> **we presented** evidence.*

- conjunctions of purpose

  Llamé a mi secretaria <u>para</u> pedirle que **sacara** las copias del documento.

  *I **called** my secretary to ask her **to make** copies of the document.*

- conjunctions that indicate future time frame

  Tuvimos que irnos <u>antes de que</u> **empezara** la reunión.

  *We **had** to leave <u>before</u> the meeting **started**.*

■ Asimilación

11-36 ¿Ocurrió o no? Primero, empareja cada frase de la izquierda con una frase lógica de la derecha. Después, indica si esas acciones ocurrieron o no en la clase de español la última vez que se reunieron los estudiantes. Al terminar, compara tus respuestas con las de un(a) compañero(a). ¿Quién tiene mejor memoria?

El (La) profesor(a) de español...

____ prohibió que habláramos...

____ nos pidió que empezáramos...

____ dijo que era importante que estudiáramos...

____ prometió que daría una fiesta cuando terminara...

____ dijo que era imposible que todos sacáramos...

____ confesó que no había estudiantes que trabajaran...

a. a estudiar para el examen.

b. inglés en clase.

c. más que nosotros.

d. una A en la clase.

e. todos los días.

f. el semestre.

11-37 La niñez Escucha lo que dice Emma de su niñez y escoge las alternativas que mejor completen las oraciones que siguen.

1. A ella le gustaba que su padres la llevaran a la casa de sus abuelos los...

   a. viernes.   b. sábados.   c. domingos.

2. Le gustaba que ellos la recibieran con...

   a. sorpresas.   b. regalos.   c. muchos besos.

3. Para los abuelos, era muy importante que la familia... lo más posible.

   a. compartiera   b. comiera   c. disfrutara

4. No volvían a casa hasta que todos hablaran...

   a. del amor familiar.   b. de la semana anterior.   c. de la niñez.

CD2-49

■ **Aplicaciones**

 11-38 Una encuesta A continuación se presenta un artículo sobre las expectativas de los estudiantes antes de ingresar en la universidad. Usa la información para saber si tu compañero(a) era un(a) estudiante típico(a) o no.

MODELO   E1: *¿Esperabas que los profesores incorporaran tecnología en sus cursos?*
                 E2: *Sí, esperaba que ellos incorporaran tecnología, pero no con tanta frecuencia.*

Los estudiantes universitarios del futuro

De acuerdo con una encuesta informal que se realizó en tres escuelas secundarias de esta ciudad, los estudiantes universitarios del futuro...

- esperan que los profesores incorporen tecnología en sus cursos

- están interesados en asistir a universidades que ofrezcan programas interdisciplinarios

- quieren tomar cursos que les permitan trabajar por la noche

- creen que es necesario hacer una práctica cuando completen la mayoría de los requisitos curriculares

- recomiendan que la administración responda a los reclamos de los estudiantes

- insisten en que el estacionamiento no les cueste nada

- no creen que sus padres acepten que vivan en una residencia estudiantil

- piensan que es dudoso que las computadoras reemplacen a los profesores

---

11-39 Compañeros(as) de apartamento Imagínense que Uds. son compañeros(as) de apartamento y quieren saber por qué o para qué compraron ciertas cosas. Túrnense para hacer y responder a las preguntas.

> MODELO   el horno de microondas
> E1: *¿Para qué compraste el horno de microondas?*
> E2: *Lo compré para que cocináramos más rápidamente.*

Verbos útiles: grabar   ver   secar   recibir   bañarse   vivir   proteger
ahorrar   divertirse   lavar

Expresiones útiles: más rápidamente   más efectivamente
más seguramente   más económicamente

1. la secadora
2. la antena parabólica
3. el lavavajillas
4. el aire acondicionado

5. el contestador
6. la alarma
7. la videograbadora
8. el calentador de agua

11-40 Cuando tenía como diez años... Piensen en su vida cuando tenían diez años y formen oraciones con elementos de las dos columnas. Terminen las oraciones de forma lógica y original.

> MODELO   nosotros + (no) querer que...
> *Nosotros no queríamos que nuestros amigos usaran nuestros juguetes.*

nosotros
nuestros padres
los profesores
nuestros amigos
nuestros hermanos
...

+

(no) querer que...
(no) insistir en que...
(no) pensar que era importante que...
(no) pedir que...
(no) esperar que...
(no) pensar que era posible que...
negar que...
desear que...
...

+   ...

■ Integración

11-41 Entrevista Individualmente, escriban diez preguntas para saber cómo era su compañero(a) cuando era niño(a). Luego, entrevístense y tomen notas.

11-42 Comparaciones Usa la información que recopilaste en la actividad 11-41 para compararte con tu compañero(a) cuando eran niños(as). Cuando termines, dale una copia a él/ella para que te dé su opinión.

> MODELO   *Creo que... y yo éramos semejantes/diferentes cuando éramos niños(as).*
> *En primer lugar, nosotros...*

SUGERENCIAS

Pueden usar las siguientes expresiones como modelo para hacer las preguntas:
¿Te molestaba que... ?
¿Te parecía (interesante/triste/curioso/...) que... ?
¿Le(s) decías a... que... ?
¿Siempre dudabas que... ?
¿Sentías que... ?
¿Creías que era (imposible/increíble/...) que... ?
¿Te alegrabas de que... ?
¿(Querían tus padres que estudiaras/jugaras...) hasta... ?

SUGERENCIAS

Usa los conectores que ya sabes para hacer esta comparación:
de igual forma *similarly*
por otro lado *on the other hand*
sin embargo *however*
además *in addition*
también *also*
por el contrario *on the contrary*
por ejemplo *for example*
en conclusión *in conclusion*

IV. Vídeo: Aspiraciones y planes para el futuro

■ Preparación

A. ¿Qué quieren hacer? En el vídeo, los compañeros van a hablar sobre sus aspiraciones y planes para el futuro. Basándose en lo que ya saben de cada compañero(a), adivinen qué quieren hacer Alejandra, Javier y Sofía. Escriban el nombre correcto al lado de cada descripción.

1. «Viajaré al extranjero y viviré en otro país. Tendré mi propia agencia de ecoturismo y deportes de aventura.» _____

2. «Cuando regrese a mi país, montaré una exposición de fotografía en el Museo de Arte.» _____

3. «Terminaré de escribir mi libro aquí en Puerto Rico y luego regresaré a mi país.» _____

En las oraciones anteriores no estaban incluidas ni las aspiraciones de Valeria ni las de Antonio. ¿Qué planes creen que tienen ellos?

Valeria:
Antonio:

■ ¿Entendiste bien?

B. El sueño de Javier Mientras ves el vídeo, completa el diagrama de la página 469 con las ideas y preguntas que tiene Javier sobre cómo hacer realidad su sueño.

¿QUÉ?

Mi sueño es _____

_____

_____

_____

DUDAS PARA RESOLVER

- ¿Cuánto cuesta un boleto de San Juan a Belice o Tegucigalpa?
- ¿Dónde compro los boletos?
- En _____, ¿qué es mejor, viajar por carretera o por _____?
  ¿Cuánto cuesta alquilar un _____?
- ¿Cuál es el medio de transporte más conveniente para unir los países de Centroamérica?

¿DÓNDE?

Aún no sé dónde me gustaría hacerlo, pero estoy considerando: las playas de _____ o _____ o las Islas Roatán en _____.

PASOS QUE HAY QUE SEGUIR

1. Tomar un avión a _____.
2. Visitar Belice, Honduras y Costa Rica.
3. En Costa Rica, recorrer la costa del _____ en bicicleta.
4. Tomar un avión a _____ y de allí un tren a Macchu Picchu.

Compara tus respuestas con las de un(a) compañero(a).

 C. Decisiones, decisiones Al final del episodio, Valeria le dijo a Antonio: «Déjame pensarlo...». Es una decisión difícil y seguramente le vendrían bien algunos consejos. En grupos, piensen qué pasaría si Valeria decidiera decirle a Antonio que sí. ¿Qué ventajas y desventajas tendría el dar una respuesta afirmativa? Luego, piensen qué pasaría si Valeria decidiera decirle que no. De nuevo, ¿qué ventajas y desventajas tendría esto? Finalmente, lleguen a una conclusión basada en sus razonamientos y completen la siguiente oración afirmativa o negativamente.

Si fuéramos Valeria, nosotros (no) aceptaríamos la propuesta de Antonio porque...

D. Enfoque comunitario Entrevista a algún (alguna) estudiante extranjero(a) de tu universidad para averiguar sus planes y sueños para el futuro. Graba *(Tape)* tu conversación y lleva la cinta a la clase. Asegúrate de incluir las siguientes preguntas en tu entrevista.

1. ¿Te gustaría quedarte a vivir en los Estados Unidos? ¿Por qué sí o por qué no?
2. En cualquiera de los casos *(In either case)*, ¿dónde te gustaría vivir y qué te gustaría hacer?

Utopías

I. Vocabulario: Un mundo mejor

—Me gustaría que hubiera menos violencia.

—Sí, deberíamos **respetar** más la vida y ser más tolerantes.

—Tenemos que hacer algo para **proteger** a las **especies en vías de extinción,** ¿no crees?

—De acuerdo. Es nuestra obligación **preservar** el **medio ambiente** para las próximas generaciones.

—¡Es terrible ver cuánta gente en el mundo sufre de **hambre** y vive en la más absoluta **miseria**!

—¿Qué te parece si **nos vinculamos** con algún grupo de **caridad** o **beneficencia**?

—Nadie debería conducir **embriagado.**

—Sí. El gobierno debería **invertir** más en campañas educativas para evitar estas tragedias.

Vocabulario práctico

la caridad / la beneficencia *charity*
los derechos humanos *human rights*
la discriminación *discrimination*
las especies en vías de extinción *endangered species*
la guerra *war*
el hambre *hunger*
la indiferencia *indifference*
la investigación *research*
el medio ambiente *the environment*
la miseria *extreme poverty*
el odio *hate*
el respeto *respect*

la solidaridad *solidarity*
la violencia *violence*

embriagado/borracho *drunk*
tolerante *tolerant*

consumir *to consume*
evitar *to avoid*
invertir (ie, i) *to invest*
pasar hambre *to go hungry*
preservar *to preserve*
proteger *to protect*
respetar *to respect*
salvar *to save*
vincularse *to get involved*

Asimilación

11-43 ¿Problema o solución? Usa la tabla para clasificar las siguientes palabras.

la contaminación   la investigación   la violencia   la solidaridad
la guerra   el hambre   la tolerancia   las enfermedades   el respeto
la justicia   la discriminación   la indiferencia

Problemas	Soluciones

11-44 Causa y efecto Vas a escuchar una serie de situaciones y problemas que nos afectan hoy en día. Para cada una, identifica su causa más probable.

_____ No existe una distribución justa de la riqueza.

_____ No somos tolerantes.

_____ No respetamos la vida.

_____ Alguna gente irresponsable conduce embriagada.

_____ Abusamos de los combustibles fósiles.

Aplicaciones

11-45 Adivina Túrnense para definir diferentes palabras del vocabulario. El (La) compañero(a) tiene sólo dos oportunidades para adivinar.

MODELO   E1: *Es un problema que existe en muchas partes del mundo.*
          Ocurre cuando la gente no tiene qué comer. La gente que
          tiene este problema se pone (becomes) *muy delgada*
          (skinny) *y enferma porque no tiene una nutrición*
          adecuada.
          E2: *¿El hambre?*
          E1: *¡Correcto!*

11-46 ¿Qué podemos hacer? Completa las oraciones de una manera lógica usando el presente del subjuntivo.

1. Para erradicar la violencia, es necesario que...
2. Para salvar las especies en vías de extinción, es importante que...
3. Para terminar con el narcotráfico, es urgente que...
4. Para evitar la proliferación del crimen, es mejor que...
5. Para reducir los efectos de la contaminación, es preciso que...

11-47 Preocupaciones Respondan a las siguientes preguntas y preparen un informe.

a. ¿Cuál de los siguientes problemas es el más grave en este momento?

____ el terrorismo

____ la corrupción

____ la guerra

____ la contaminación del medio ambiente

____ el hambre

____ otro:

b. ¿Qué podríamos hacer nosotros como estudiantes universitarios para ayudar a resolver ese problema? (Den algunos ejemplos concretos.)

■ Integración

 11-48 Las noticias Representa la siguiente situación con un(a) compañero(a).

Estudiante A	Estudiante B
Acabas de ver las noticias y estás muy preocupado(a) por la proliferación de actos de violencia y terrorismo en todo el mundo. Comenta tus preocupaciones con tu amigo(a) y traten juntos de ver si es posible hacer algo para cambiar esta situación.	Acabas de ver un informe del programa «60 Minutos» sobre la corrupción y estás muy preocupado(a) por la pérdida de valores morales en el mundo. Comenta tus preocupaciones con tu amigo(a) y traten juntos de ver si es posible hacer algo para cambiar esta situación.

11-49 Utopía ¿Cómo serían las noticias si viviéramos en un mundo perfecto? Tomen el periódico local y vuelvan a escribir los titulares de la primera página para que reflejen esa utopía.

II. Funciones y estructuras: Talking about the past using the imperfect subjunctive (irregular verbs)

«Esperábamos que el conflicto **estuviera** resuelto, pero las partes no han podido llegar a un acuerdo. No creíamos que el asunto **fuera** tan complicado. **Quisiéramos** que el pueblo **tuviera** un poco más de paciencia y que **hiciera** lo posible por comprender que esta situación es delicada.»

In **Tema 2** you learned how to use the imperfect subjunctive when the verb or the impersonal expression that conveys an opinion, a wish, an emotion or doubt is in the past tense. You also used verbs in this tense to describe hypothetical antecedents and to talk about stipulation, purpose and future time frame when the verb in the main clause is in the past tense.

A nosotros no nos gustó que el Sr. Rojas no **evitara** la violencia.	*We did not like that Mr. Rojas did not **avoid** violence.*
Íbamos a dictar una ley que **protegiera** el medio ambiente.	*We were going to issue a law that **would protect** the environment.*

Since the imperfect subjunctive is formed from the **ellos(as)/ustedes** preterite conjugation of the verb, all verbs that are irregular in the preterite are also irregular in the imperfect subjunctive. Here is a summary of the most common irregularities.

- verbs that take an **i**

INFINITIVE	PRETERITE	IMPERFECT SUBJUNCTIVE
decir	dijeron	**dijera, dijeras, dijera, dijéramos, dijerais, dijeran**
hacer	hicieron	**hiciera, hicieras, hiciera, hiciéramos, hicierais, hicieran**
pedir	pidieron	**pidiera, pidieras, pidiera, pidiéramos, pidierais, pidieran**
querer	quisieron	**quisiera, quisieras, quisiera, quisiéramos, quisierais, quisieran**
sentir	sintieron	**sintiera, sintieras, sintiera, sintiéramos, sintierais, sintieran**
venir	vinieron	**viniera, vinieras, viniera, viniéramos, vinierais, vinieran**

This summary only includes verbs that are used frequently. You may review the chapters and **Temas** that present irregular verbs in the preterite tense to find other verbs that are irregular in the imperfect subjunctive.

REMEMBER

To form the imperfect subjunctive, drop **-ron** from the **ellos(as)/ustedes** form of the preterite and add the endings **-ra, -ras, -ra, -ramos, -rais,** and **-ran: beber → bebieron → bebie- → bebiera, bebieras, bebiera, bebiéramos, bebierais, bebieran.**

■ verbs that take a **u**

INFINITIVE	PRETERITE	IMPERFECT SUBJUNCTIVE
dormir	durmieron	**durmiera, durmieras, durmiera, durmiéramos, durmierais, durmieran**
estar	estuvieron	**estuviera, estuvieras, estuviera, estuviéramos, estuvierais, estuvieran**
haber	hubieron	**hubiera, hubieras, hubiera, hubiéramos, hubierais, hubieran**
morir	murieron	**muriera, murieras, muriera, muriéramos, murierais, murieran**
poder	pudieron	**pudiera, pudieras, pudiera, pudiéramos, pudierais, pudieran**
poner	pusieron	**pusiera, pusieras, pusiera, pusiéramos, pusierais, pusieran**
saber	supieron	**supiera, supieras, supiera, supiéramos, supierais, supieran**
tener	tuvieron	**tuviera, tuvieras, tuviera, tuviéramos, tuvierais, tuvieran**

■ verbs that take a **y**

INFINITIVE	PRETERITE	IMPERFECT SUBJUNCTIVE
caer	cayeron	**cayera, cayeras, cayera, cayéramos, cayerais, cayeran**
creer	creyeron	**creyera, creyeras, creyera, creyéramos, creyerais, creyeran**
leer	leyeron	**leyera, leyeras, leyera, leyéramos, leyerais, leyeran**
oír	oyeron	**oyera, oyeras, oyera, oyéramos, oyerais, oyeran**

■ other irregular verbs

INFINITIVE	PRETERITE	IMPERFECT SUBJUNCTIVE
dar	dieron	**diera, dieras, diera, diéramos, dierais, dieran**
ir / ser	fueron	**fuera, fueras, fuera, fuéramos, fuerais, fueran**

The imperfect subjunctive conjugation of the verb **querer** is used to be polite when making requests.

Señor presidente, **quisiera** que Ud. hablara del problema de la discriminación en este país.

*Mr. President, **I would like** for you to talk about the discrimination problem in this country.*

■ Asimilación

11-50 La opinión y los deseos de los padres Lee las siguientes oraciones y escoge las alternativas que se apliquen a ti. Al terminar, compara tus respuestas con las respuestas de un(a) compañero(a). ¿Sus padres tenían las mismas opiniones y los mismos deseos?

Mi padres esperaban que yo fuera...

_____ doctor(a).

_____ ingeniero(a).

_____ profesor(a).

_____ abogado(a).

_____ sicólogo(a).

_____ otra profesión: _____

Ellos querían que yo tuviera...

_____ más paciencia.

_____ más responsabilidades.

_____ más dedicación a los estudios.

_____ más disciplina.

_____ más auto-estima.

_____ otra cualidad: _____

A ellos nunca les gustaba que yo les pidiera...

_____ dinero.

_____ más privacidad.

_____ permiso para regresar tarde.

_____ el carro.

_____ más libertad.

_____ otra cosa:_____

CD2-51

11-51 Un mensaje telefónico Marla faltó a la clase de francés hoy y su amigo César le dejó un mensaje en el contestador. Escucha el mensaje e indica si las siguientes oraciones son ciertas **(C)** o falsas **(F).**

_____ 1. César quería que Marla supiera qué hizo Martín en la clase hoy.

_____ 2. El profesor pidió que hicieran las actividades del cuaderno de ejercicios.

_____ 3. Él también dijo que esperaba que pudieran terminar el diálogo.

_____ 4. César quisiera que Marla fuera a su oficina para terminar el trabajo.

_____ 5. Él quisiera reunirse con Marla esta noche.

▪ Aplicaciones

11-52 Problemas mundiales Uds. trabajan para el periódico de la universidad y tienen que preparar un informe sobre las cosas que dijeron los panelistas de una charla sobre problemas mundiales.

Algunos de los verbos que se usan en artículos periodísticos para citar *(quote)* a otras personas son **decir, señalar, expresar, apuntar, afirmar** y **manifestar**.

> MODELO Dr. Fernández: «Es lamentable que todavía haya tanta miseria en el mundo.»
> *El Dr. Fernández dijo que era lamentable que todavía hubiera tanta miseria en el mundo.*

1. Dra. Zapata: «No podemos aceptar que tantos niños tengan hambre en el mundo.»
2. Sr. Palermo: «Quiero que la ONU y la UNESCO hagan algo con relación al problema de la violencia.»
3. Dr. Acosta: «Me parece muy triste que los oficiales gubernamentales no crean en los resultados de estos informes.»
4. Sra. Linares: «Los investigadores no piensan que la guerra sea la mejor alternativa.»
5. Dra. Jiménez: «Tenemos que hacer que las agencias pongan más recursos a disposición de los científicos.»
6. Dr. Bermúdez: «¡Voy a luchar hasta que podamos salvar las especies en vías de extinción!»

11-53 Mini-situaciones Completen las siguientes mini-situaciones con la forma correcta del imperfecto de subjuntivo de los verbos que se proveen. **¡OJO!** Hay un verbo adicional en cada grupo.

dormirse   ser   poner   oír

1. Me gustaría que mis nietos _____ más temprano y que no _____ esa música tan ruidosa. Así podría estar más tranquila cuando voy a visitar a mi hija y podríamos compartir más. ¡Es que son tan inquietos! Sería fantástico si los niños _____ como los niños de antes: respetuosos y obedientes.

leer   estar   poder   querer

2. Delia, (yo) _____ que (tú) _____ venir conmigo al concierto, pero entiendo que no tienes dinero para el boleto. Me da mucha pena que (tú) _____ tan ilusionada y que ahora no vayas. Bueno, ¿qué tal si te presto los cien dólares y me pagas cuando cobres?

dar   ir   sentir   pedir

3. Mis amigos Pablo y Margarita querían estudiar en una universidad que les _____ la oportunidad de tomar cursos nocturnos y sabatinos; por eso no quisieron estudiar en ésta. Yo les recomendé que se trasladaran *(transfer)* cuando (ellos) _____ que no tienen que trabajar tanto para pagar la matrícula. También les sugerí que _____ a la oficina de ayuda económica para ver si consiguen una beca.

11-54 Entrevista Túrnense para hacer y responder a las siguientes preguntas sobre la niñez. Cuando terminen, preparen un informe breve y preséntenselo al resto de la clase.

1. ¿Qué cosas querían tus padres que tú leyeras cuando eras niño(a)? ¿Y qué tipo de música querían que oyeras?
2. ¿Tus padres esperaban que tú fueras de cierta manera cuando eras niño(a)? Explica tu respuesta.
3. En cuanto a los quehaceres del hogar, ¿qué cosas se suponía que tú hicieras?
4. ¿Tus padres querían que compitieras en algún deporte? ¿En cuál(es)?
5. ¿Tus padres se alegraban de que supieras hacer ciertas cosas? ¿Cuáles?
6. ¿Alguna vez tus padres se enojaron porque tú dijeras una tontería o una grosería? Explica tu respuesta.

▪ Integración

11-55 Los críticos Escojan una película reciente y hablen de sus aspectos positivos y negativos. Pueden hablar del trabajo de los actores, de la trama, de la cinematografía y de los efectos especiales. Al final, ¿quién es más convincente?

MODELO   *Yo esperaba que la película... fuera más... y que la actuación de... tuviera más... en la trama. Sin embargo, me sorprendió que... pudiera...*

11-56 Una carta a un(a) funcionario(a) público(a) ¿Hay algún(a) funcionario(a) público(a) con cuyo *(whose)* trabajo no estés de acuerdo? Escríbele una carta y menciona las cosas que esperabas y que querías que él/ella hiciera durante su término como funcionario(a) público(a). Cuando termines, intercambia cartas con un(a) compañero(a) y corríjanlas siguiendo las siguientes pautas *(guidelines)*.

Contenido: ¿La carta es convincente? ¿Se proveen ejemplos que apoyen las ideas? ¿Hay algo más que se pueda incluir?

Organización: ¿La organización es efectiva? ¿La carta sigue un orden lógico? ¿Sigue la estructura tradicional de una carta (fecha, saludo, cuerpo y despedida)?

Gramática: ¿En la carta se usan las formas verbales de **usted** (formal)? ¿Se usan el modo indicativo y el modo subjuntivo correctamente? ¿Los verbos en el imperfecto de subjuntivo están conjugados correctamente?

SUGERENCIAS

Pueden usar las siguientes expresiones: **esperaba que..., quería que..., pienso que era (importante/necesario/preciso/...) que..., sería mejor si... (dijera/estuviera/fuera/pudiera/tuviera)...,** etc.

SUGERENCIAS

Recuerda usar los conectores que conoces:
por otro lado *on the other hand*
sin embargo *however*
además *in addition*
por el contrario *on the contrary*
por ejemplo *for example*
en conclusión *in conclusion*

III. Funciones y estructuras: Expressing condition (*si* clauses)

Escoge las frases que completen lógicamente la siguiente oración:

Si **protegiéramos** el medio ambiente,...

❏ el aire que respiramos **sería** más puro.
❏ **respetaríamos** los derechos humanos.
❏ los seres humanos no **pasarían** hambre.
❏ **habría** menos indiferencia.

❏ ciertas especies **tendrían** un lugar donde vivir.
❏ todo el mundo **se beneficiaría.**

In the previous exercise you were asked to indicate what *would* happen if we protected the environment. In the resulting sentences, the condition under which something else would happen (**protegiéramos**) is expressed in the imperfect subjunctive and is introduced by the conjunction **si** *(if)*. The actions that would occur given this condition (**el aire <u>sería</u> más puro, ciertas especies <u>tendrían</u> un lugar donde vivir,** and **todo el mundo <u>se beneficiaría</u>**) are expressed in the conditional tense. These sentences are called *contrary-to-fact sentences* because they refer to hypothetical situations.

Si **te vincularas** con una causa como la lucha contra el cáncer, **ayudarías** a mucha gente.	*If **you got involved** with a cause like the fight against cancer, **you would help** a lot of people.*
Si el gobierno **actuara** preventivamente, **evitaría** muchos problemas.	*If the government **acted** preventively, **it would avoid** many problems.*

When the condition under which something else would happen already exists or is likely to exist, use verbs in the indicative mode.

Si **tengo** tiempo, **llevo** comida a los albergues de mi ciudad.	*If **I have** time, **I bring** food to the shelters in my city.*
Si Ud. **ve** la miseria que existe en esos países, **querrá** hacer algo al respecto.	*If you **see** the extreme poverty that exists in those countries, **you will want** to do something about it.*

■ Asimilación

11-57 Acciones problables e hipótesis Indica si la persona que dice las siguientes oraciones piensa que las condiciones y los resultados de éstas son probables (**P**) o si sólo representan una hipótesis (**H**). Cuando termines, compara tus respuestas con las de un(a) compañero(a) y decide si están de acuerdo.

____ 1. «Si tuviera menos que hacer, me iría de vacaciones.»

____ 2. «Si me ganara la lotería, les compraría una casa nueva a mis padres.»

____ 3. «Si salgo temprano hoy, pasaré por la casa de Hilda.»

____ 4. «Si mejoro mi promedio general (*GPA*), hago estudios de postgrado.»

____ 5. «Si al profesor no le importaran sus estudiantes, les diría que no hicieran la tarea.»

____ 6. «Si como algún marisco, me enfermo inmediatamente.»

____ 7. «Si pudiera estar en otro lugar, estaría en Chile.»

____ 8. «Si hiciera mejor tiempo, podríamos ir a la playa.»

11-58 Deducciones Escucha lo que respondió Mariana cuando se le preguntó qué haría si tuviera más tiempo y escribe por lo menos cinco cosas que se pueden deducir sobre ella.

CD2-52

MODELO   *Ella no hace ejercicio con frecuencia.*

1. ...   4. ...
2. ...   5. ...
3. ...

■ Aplicaciones

11-59 Condiciones

Paso 1: Completa las siguientes oraciones de forma lógica.

MODELO   Si pudiera cambiar de especialización, *estudiaría teatro.*
            Si tuviera mucha hambre, me comería cuatro hamburguesas.

1. Si no fuera estudiante de esta universidad, _____.

2. _____, viviría en Europa.

3. Si tuviera millones de dólares en el banco, _____.

4. _____, sería el hombre / la mujer más feliz del mundo.

5. Si me dieran la oportunidad, _____.

6. _____, me daría mucho miedo.

Paso 2: Hazle preguntas a tu compañero(a) para averiguar cómo completó las oraciones del **Paso 1** y prepara un informe.

MODELO   *¿Qué harías si pudieras cambiar de especialización?*
            ¿Bajo qué circunstancias te comerías cuatro hamburguesas?

SUGERENCIAS

Empieza la pregunta con **¿Qué harías...** si se da la cláusula con **si** (#1, #3 y #5) y con **¿Bajo qué circunstancias...** *(Under what condition . . .)* si no se da (#2, #4 y #6).

11-60 Situaciones hipotéticas Indiquen bajo qué circunstancias harían las siguientes cosas.

> MODELO   dejar la universidad
> *Nosotros(as) dejaríamos la universidad si nuestras familias tuvieran problemas económicos.*

1. ser presidente(a) de los Estados Unidos
2. mentirle al / a la profesor(a)
3. trabajar gratis *(for free)*
4. olvidar nuestros principios morales
5. invertir en la bolsa de valores *(stock market)*
6. arriesgar *(to risk)* la vida
7. mudarse a otro país
8. aprender más español

11-61 Preguntas Escriban por lo menos seis preguntas hipotéticas para seis compañeros(as) diferentes.

> MODELO   *Jessica, si te enfermeras, ¿dejarías de fumar?*

1. ...
2. ...
3. ...
4. ...
5. ...
6. ...

■ **Integración**

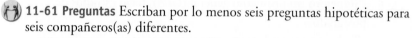

11-62 El (La) próximo(a) asesor(a) *(advisor)* **presidencial** Representa la siguiente situación con un(a) compañero(a).

El (La) candidato(a)	El (La) entrevistador(a)
Imagínate que tienes una entrevista para nada más y nada menos que el puesto de asesor(a) del / de la presidente(a) de los Estados Unidos sobre asuntos mundiales. Responde a las preguntas del / de la entrevistador(a) y demuéstrale que estás al tanto *(you are up-to-date)* de las cuestiones sobre los derechos humanos y sobre los problemas sociales en todo el mundo.	Tienes una responsabilidad muy grande. Tienes que entrevistar a un(a) candidato(a) para el puesto de asesor(a) del / de la presidente(a) de los Estados Unidos sobre asuntos mundiales. Hazle preguntas hipotéticas a esta persona para decidir si sería un(a) buen(a) asesor(a) o no. En tu opinión, esta persona debe ser inteligente y debe estar comprometida en la lucha por los derechos humanos y civiles, al igual en la lucha contra otros problemas del mundo de hoy.

11-63 Perfección Imagínate cómo sería tu vida si tuvieras la familia y el trabajo perfectos. Escribe un ensayo corto en el que describas tu vida y dale una copia a un(a) compañero(a) de clase para que lo revise. Cuando hagas las correcciones que tu compañero(a) te sugiera, entrégale el ensayo a tu profesor(a).

IV. Lectura: ¿Estamos listos para el cambio?

▪ Antes de leer

A. Para conversar Contesten las siguientes preguntas en grupo.

1. ¿Cómo han cambiado las relaciones entre los hombres y las mujeres en los últimos 50 años en este país? (Consideren temas como el poder, las oportunidades, la independencia, etc. Den algunos ejemplos concretos.)

   MODELO *Antes las mujeres no podían..., pero ahora sí pueden...*

2. ¿Cómo creen que serán las relaciones entre los hombres y las mujeres en el futuro?

B. Vocabulario y conceptos. Las siguientes son palabras y conceptos clave para la comprensión del texto. Escriban la letra de la definición de cada palabra.

____ 1. el albergue	a. enfermedad, dolencia, problema
____ 2. el mal	b. que se siente en peligro
____ 3. la autonomía	c. falta de afecto, alejamiento
____ 4. amenazado	d. despreciar, excluir
____ 5. rechazar	e. independencia
____ 6. el desamor	f. un tipo de hotel económico, un refugio

C. Aplicación Completen las oraciones con las palabras que aprendieron en la actividad anterior. **¡OJO!** ¡Asegúrense de conjugar los verbos cuando sea necesario!

1. La gripe es un _____ frecuente durante los meses de invierno.
2. No me gusta esa medicina y por eso siempre la _____.
3. Como no tengo mucho dinero, voy a pasar mis vacaciones en un

   _____.
4. La Sra. Díaz es muy independiente y defiende mucho su

   _____.
5. Siempre me siento un poco _____ cuando camino de noche por el centro.
6. El opuesto del amor es el _____.

■ A leer

Marcela Serrano

Es una de las escritoras más leídas en este momento en Latinoamérica. Nació en Santiago de Chile y es licenciada en grabado *(engraving)* de la Universidad Católica. En 1991 publicó su primera novela *(Nosotras que nos queremos tanto),* la cual recibió el Premio Sor Juana Inés de la Cruz, otorgado *(granted)* a la mejor novela latinoamericana escrita por una mujer en 1994. Otras de sus obras son *Para que no me olvides* (1993), *Antigua vida mía* (1995), *El albergue de las mujeres tristes* (1997), *Nuestra señora de la soledad* (1999) y *Un mundo raro* (2000).

El albergue de las mujeres tristes (fragmento)

—¿Y cómo se te ocurrió formar el Albergue? —pregunta Floreana mientras comienzan a escalar la **colina,** a la salida del pueblo.

—Mi padre era un hombre muy rico y construyó un hotel en esta isla por puro **capricho,** antes de que estuviera de moda, cuando no existía en este país un concepto del turismo como negocio. Lo recibí de **herencia** a su muerte. Mis hermanos decidieron que yo era la única **chiflada** de la familia que podía **sacarle algún provecho.**

—El lugar es estupendo y tiene una vista privilegiada. Si lo hubieras destinado a un hotel **común y corriente** habrías ganado mucha **plata.**

—No es tan cierto. Tendría clientes sólo en verano. ¿A quién se le ocurriría pasar aquí el invierno? Pero la verdad es que ni el **lucro** ni la hotelería me interesaban.

Floreana **constata** el buen estado físico de Elena a través de la fluidez con que habla, **a pesar del esfuerzo** que significa subir la colina.

—¿Cuándo te vino la idea del Albergue, entonces?

—Cuando detecté un nuevo mal: las mujeres ya no eran las mismas, pero no todos los resultados del cambio las **beneficiaban.**

—**¿O sea?**

—O sea que, alcanzada su autonomía, se quedaron a **medio camino** entre el amor romántico y la desprotección.

—¿Y eso es todo?

Glosses: hill / whim / inheritance / crazy / to get some benefit from it / average / money / profit / establishes / in spite of the effort / to benefit (imperfect tense) / In other words? / half way

—**No deja de ser.** Los hombres se sienten **amenazados** por nuestra independencia, y esto da lugar al rechazo, a la impotencia... y así empieza un círculo vicioso bastante dramático.

It is plenty / threatened

—A este rechazo masculino siguen el **desconcierto** y el miedo femeninos; ¿es ésa la idea?

confusion

—Es que las mujeres viven esta **lejanía** como agresión, lo que a su vez produce más distancia en ellos. ¿Te das cuenta del resultado? Las mujeres **se vuelcan** más hacia adentro, se afirman en **lo propio...**

distance

turn / one's own

—**Se quema la cara de la luna.**

The moon's face catches on fire.

Elena la mira interrogante.

—¡Olvídalo! Es parte de la mitología del pueblo **yagán.**

native group from Tierra del Fuego

—Bueno, el resultado es **lisa y llanamente** el desamor —dice Elena categórica.

plainly and simply

—Pero lo que no me has respondido es qué te trajo hasta aquí.

—A ver... Todo comenzó cuando partió Fernandina. Abandoné el trabajo político y fui desarrollando **a fondo** mi profesión. Al trabajar a fondo con los problemas sicológicos y culturales de mis pacientes, fui descubriendo que para poder **sanarlas,** en este mundo tan complejo, no basta la actividad siquiátrica que yo podía **ejercer** en la ciudad, era necesario darle un carácter más sistemático al proceso de recuperación de las mujeres.

thoroughly

to heal them
to practice one's profession

—¡**Menuda tarea!** ¿Cómo se puede lograr?

What a task!

—Mis objetivos son modestos. Algo se logra permitiéndoles «socializar» sus **penurias,** contarse sus dramas individuales, los que créeme, siempre terminan siendo colectivos, y generando así una atmósfera de compañerismo.

sadnesses

—¿A condición de estar a más de mil kilómetros de Santiago?

—Ironías aparte, sí. El silencio es vital, Floreana. **Concebí** un lugar lejos del **mundanal ruido,** donde las que necesitan recuperar la paz puedan hacerlo para luego **reinsertarse...**

came up with
mundane noise
reintegrate

—**A fin de cuentas**, Elena, ¿qué es el Albergue? ¿Una terapia, una **casa de reposo,** un hotel entretenido, un resort ecológico? ¿Puedes definírmelo?

At the end / sanatorium

—El Albergue es lo que tú quieras que sea.

■ ¿Entendiste bien?

D. **Aspectos literarios** Contesten las siguientes preguntas sobre la lectura.

1. **Personajes** Describan a cada uno de los personajes que participan en este diálogo. (¿Quiénes son? ¿Qué hacen? etc.)

Elena	
Floreana	

2. **Espacio** ¿Dónde está el albergue? ¿Cómo es?
3. **Temas centrales:**
   a. ¿Quiénes van al albergue? ¿Por qué?
   b. Completa el diagrama del círculo vicioso del desamor del que habla Elena.

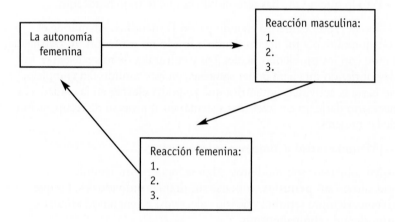

c. ¿Cómo es el tratamiento que les ofrece Elena a las mujeres en su albergue?

E. **Enfoque lingüístico** El condicional se usa para hacer hipótesis y conjeturas (**trabajaría, vendería, escribiría,** etc.). ¿Puedes encontrar algunos ejemplos del uso de este tiempo verbal en el fragmento de la obra de Serrano?

F. **Actividad de extensión: Debate** ¿Existe en los Estados Unidos una situación de desamor similar a la que describe Elena? ¿Cómo podrían las mujeres latinoamericanas superar *(to overcome)* ese círculo vicioso?

Las ilusiones — Dreams, illusions

la meta	goal
el reto / el desafío	challenge
el sueño	dream
alcanzar	to reach
aspirar a	to aspire to
enfrentar	to face; to confront
hacer realidad	to make come true
lograr	to achieve
llegar a ser	to become
tener constancia	to be constant, to persist
tener disciplina	to be disciplined
tener éxito	to be successful
tener paciencia	to be patient
tener suerte	to be lucky

Los aparatos electrónicos

apagado	off
encendido	on
No funciona.	It doesn't work. / It's broken.
apagar	to turn off
conectar/enchufar	to plug in
desconectar/desenchufar	to unplug
digitar	to key in
halar	to pull
insertar	to insert
prender	to turn on
presionar/oprimir/pulsar	to push, to hit
programar	to program

Un mundo mejor — A better world

la caridad / la beneficencia	charity
los derechos humanos	human rights
la discriminación	discrimination
las especies en vías de extinción	endangered species
la guerra	war
el hambre	hunger
la indiferencia	indifference
la investigación	research
el medio ambiente	the environment
la miseria	extreme poverty
el odio	hate
el respeto	respect
la solidaridad	solidarity
la violencia	violence
embriagado/borracho	drunk
tolerante	tolerant
consumir	to consume
evitar	to avoid
invertir (ie, i)	to invest
pasar hambre	to go hungry
preservar	to preserve
proteger	to protect
respetar	to respect
salvar	to save
vincularse	to get involved

Capítulo 12

La herencia hispana

Para comenzar

Para cada foto, indica la descripción que le corresponda.

- En Nueva York hay una comunidad hispana muy activa.
- Por su clima y su proximidad al Caribe, Miami atrae a hispanohablantes.
- En Los Ángeles hay grandes comunidades de origen hispano que expresan con sus murales su historia y sus costumbres.

In this chapter you will . . .

- review how to narrate and describe in the past
- review how to give advice and directions
- review how to make predictions and hypotheses
- explore the history of Spanish-speaking peoples in the U.S. and learn about their present concerns and aspirations

	TEMA 1 Historia de la presencia hispana en los Estados Unidos	TEMA 2 Abriendo caminos	TEMA 3 Desafíos
Funciones y estructuras	Talking about the past with the preterite, the imperfect, and the present perfect (review)	Giving commands, advice, and opinions (review)	Indicating probability with the future and conditional tenses (review)
Lecturas y vídeo	Lectura: Los antecedentes (Partes 1 y 2)	Vídeo: Se les fue volando el mes	Lectura: Entró y se sentó

Foto 1   Foto 2   Foto 3

Enfoque

A. ¿Qué sabes ya de los hispanos en los EE.UU.? Seguro que conoces a muchos hispanos influyentes que contribuyen a la vida cultural, social e intelectual de los Estados Unidos. Haz una lista de cinco hispanos (deportistas, actores, músicos, políticos, escritores, educadores, etc.) y una breve descripción de cada uno.

Léele los nombres de las personas de tu lista a un(a) compañero(a) y averigua si sabe quién es cada persona.

B. La presencia hispana en los EE.UU. Mientras ves el vídeo, indica si las siguientes oraciones son ciertas **(C)** o falsas **(F).** Compara tus respuestas con las de otro(a) estudiante y corrijan las oraciones falsas.

____ 1. Ya cerca de 36 millones de hispanohablantes viven en los Estados Unidos.

____ 2. Hoy en día, San Antonio es la segunda ciudad salvadoreña en extensión del mundo.

____ 3. En Los Ángeles, el 40% de la población es hispana, la mayoría de origen mexicano y centroamericano.

____ 4. La Pequeña Habana, situada cerca del centro de Miami, es un buen ejemplo de cómo los latinos han sabido mantener sus costumbres y su estilo de vida.

C. La herencia hispana en los EE.UU. Desde el año 1987, la Fundación de los Premios de la Herencia Hispana (HHAF) en los Estados Unidos ha rendido homenaje a hispanos por su contribución a la comunidad hispana y a la vida cultural, social e intelectual de los Estados Unidos. En 2004, algunas de las personas premiadas fueron **Juan D. González, Narciso Rodríguez, Sandra Benítez** y **Gloria G. Rodríguez.** Escriban el nombre de la persona junto a su descripción.

_____ 1. Este diseñador nacido en Nueva Jersey de padres de origen cubano ganó el premio de Visión.

_____ 2. Esta educadora de origen mexicano recibió el premio de Educación por su trabajo a favor de los niños y de la educación.

_____ 3. Este periodista puertorriqueño recibió el premio de Liderazgo por su activismo en asuntos laborales y de derechos civiles.

_____ 4. Esta escritora, de madre puertorriqueña y de padre de Missouri, ganó el premio de Literatura. Se inspira en las experiencias que tuvo durante su niñez en México, El Salvador y Missouri.

> For more info, you may want to check the **Temas** site:
> http://temas.heinle.com

Historia de la presencia hispana en los Estados Unidos

I. Funciones y estructuras: Talking about the past with the preterite, the imperfect and the present perfect (Review)

Los hispanos **se han convertido** en el grupo minoritario de mayor representación en los Estados Unidos. A pesar de la fuerza de su presencia y de que muchos de ellos ya **hicieron** realidad su «sueño norteamericano», hay muchos otros hispanos que todavía luchan por tener una vida mejor en suelo estadounidense. Éstos trabajan día a día para alcanzar las metas que **se propusieron** cuando **vivían** en sus respectivos países.

The **preterite** tense is used to talk about:

- the beginning or the end of an action that took place in the past (**El término «hispano» *empezó* a usarse hace más de treinta años.**)

- actions that took place at specific moments in the past (usually accompanied by expressions such as **ayer, anoche, una vez, el lunes/ mes/año pasado, la semana pasada,** etc.) (**Damaris *vivió* en Miami desde 1984 hasta 1990.**)

- actions that are perceived as completed (***Trabajamos* diez horas diarias en el campo.**)

- a series of actions that were completed in the past (***Llegamos, nos dedicamos* a luchar y *logramos* muchas cosas.**)

The endings for regular **-ar** verbs are **-é, -aste, -ó, -amos, -asteis,** and **-aron. (Mis padres *emigraron* de Cuba.)** For regular **-er** and **-ir** verbs, the endings are **-í, -iste, -ió, -imos, -isteis,** and **-ieron. (El Sr. Rivera *salió* de Honduras hace diez años.)**

Some of the most common irregular verbs in the preterite are **dar (di, diste, dio, ...), estar (estuve, estuviste, estuvo, ...), hacer (hice, hiciste, hizo, ...), ir/ser (fui, fuiste, fue, ...)** and **tener (tuve, tuviste, tuvo, ...). (Primero *estuve* en Houston y después *me fui* a Dallas.)**

The **imperfect** tense is used to talk about:

- habitual actions in the past (usually accompanied by the expressions **todos los lunes/días/años, siempre, frecuentemente,** etc.) (**Siempre *pensaba* en vivir aquí.**)

- descriptions (**Mi barrio *tenía* muchas calles estrechas.**)

- events that were in progress while other actions were taking place (**Mi esposa estudió en la universidad mientras yo *trabajaba*.**)

- descriptions of the participants who carry out the main events of a story (including age, physical appearance, conditions, and emotions) (*Éramos muy jóvenes* en aquel entonces.)
- background information of past events (including time and weather conditions) (**Cuando llegamos a Nueva York *hacía* un frío increíble.**)

The endings for regular **-ar** verbs in the imperfect are **-aba, -abas, -aba, -ábamos, -abais,** and **-aban.** (Leo *estudiaba* periodismo en su país.). For regular **-er** and **-ir** verbs, the endings are **-ía, -ías, -ía, -íamos, -íais,** and **-ían.** (Pero lo que *quería* era ser ingeniero.)

There are only three irregular verbs in the imperfect tense: **ir** (**iba, ibas, iba, ...**), **ser** (**era, eras, era, ...**), and **ver** (**veía, veías, veía, ...**). (**Cuando *era* más chico, *iba* al mercado con mi abuela.**)

The present perfect tense is used to talk about:

- actions that began in the past and have an effect in the present and perhaps in the immediate future (the equivalent of the English *has/have* + past participle). (**Todavía no *han podido* progresar.**)

The **present perfect** is formed with the present of **haber** (**he, has, ha, hemos, habéis,** and **han**) followed by the past participle of the main verb, which ends in **-ado** for **-ar** verbs and in **-ido** for **-er** and **-ir** verbs. (**Yo *he progresado*, Mirta *ha tenido* éxito y Ángel *ha vivido* muy bien desde que terminó los estudios.**)

Some of the most common verbs with irregular past participle forms are **decir (dicho), escribir (escrito), hacer (hecho),** and **poner (puesto).** (**¿Alguna vez le *has escrito* una carta a algún funcionario público?**)

> **REMEMBER**
>
> This tense is called **pretérito perfecto** in Spanish, not **presente perfecto.**

▪ Asimilación

12-1 Memorias Indica si los verbos en negritas *(bold)* están conjugados en el pretérito, el imperfecto o el pretérito perfecto y explica por qué. Cuando termines, compara tus respuestas con las de un(a) compañero(a). ¿Están de acuerdo?

> **MODELO**   vine: *pretérito – el verbo se refiere a una acción que se completó hace quince años*

Vine a los Estados Unidos hace quince años, cuando **tenía** apenas cinco años. Mi mamá y yo **llegamos** a la ciudad de Nueva York, donde **vivían** mi tío Gustavo, su esposa Victoria y mis primos Nino y Adriana. Al principio no me **gustaba** para nada vivir aquí, pero poco a poco me **fui** acostumbrando y **he aceptado** que éste es mi país. Mi mamá **empezó** a trabajar muy pronto y, aunque siempre **estaba** muy cansada, **sacaba** tiempo para compartir conmigo y para asegurarse de que yo me **sentía** a gusto. Todavía es así, y se lo **he agradecido** toda la vida.

CD2-54 **12-2 Preguntas personales** Escucha las preguntas y contéstalas en oraciones completas. Presta atención a la forma de los verbos.

1. ...   3. ...   5. ...
2. ...   4. ...   6. ...

■ Aplicaciones

12-3 Eventos negativos Escribe la fecha de tres eventos negativos que has tenido en tu vida y provee los detalles que se piden. Al terminar, intercambia la información con un(a) compañero(a).

Fecha	¿Qué pasó?	¿Dónde estabas?	¿Con quién estabas?	¿Cómo te ha afectado?
6 de enero de 1995	Me caí de una motocicleta y me rompí un brazo.	Estaba en un parque.	Estaba con mi hermano y con mi mejor amigo.	No he montado en motocicleta desde ese momento hasta ahora.

12-4 Cuentos (_Short stories_) Usen la información dada para inventar una historia relacionada con los dibujos que siguen. Pueden añadir detalles adicionales.

1. ser el día de la fiesta de graduación / Perla comprar un vestido / sentirse / entrar al salón / Diana tener el mismo vestido / preferir

2. Adalberto invitar a su novia / ir a un restaurante / pedir / pasarlo / llegar el mesero con la cuenta / darse cuenta / no tener / el restaurante no aceptar tarjetas de crédito / su novia estar

3. ser las tres / Doris estar tomando un examen / tener que salir bien / la profesora estar lista para irse / ella pedir más tiempo / la profesora ser muy estricta / Doris sentirse

12-5 Esta mañana Cuéntense qué hicieron esta mañana y cómo se sentían. Prepárense para hacerse preguntas mutuamente.

■ Integración

 12-6 La experiencia de un(a) inmigrante I En parejas, entrevisten a una persona de origen extranjero (preferiblemente de origen hispano) para averiguar cómo era su vida antes de venir a este país y cómo fue el proceso de llegada *(arrival)* a los Estados Unidos y de adaptación a su nueva vida aquí. Tomen notas.

 12-7 La experiencia de un(a) inmigrante II Usa la información que recopilaste en la actividad 12-6 para escribir las experiencias que has escuchado. Si tú fuiste el (la) entrevistado(a), escribe sobre tu propia experiencia. Cuando termines, intercambia composiciones con otro(a) estudiante y corríjanlas siguiendo los siguientes criterios.

Contenido:	¿Incluye toda la información que se menciona en la actividad 12-6 (la vida en su país de origen, el proceso de llegada a los Estados Unidos y el proceso de adaptación en este país)? ¿Se incluyen los detalles y ejemplos necesarios? ¿Se puede decir algo más?
Organización:	¿La composición tiene la introducción, el cuerpo y la conclusión bien definidos? ¿Los párrafos están bien estructurados? ¿Las ideas siguen un orden lógico?
Gramática:	¿Los verbos están bien conjugados en el pretérito y el imperfecto? ¿Se sigue la concordancia sustantivo-adjetivo y sujeto-verbo?

SUGERENCIAS

Pueden usar algunas de la siguientes expresiones: **levantarse temprano/tarde, (no) desayunar, hacer buen/mal tiempo, estar cansado(a)/contento(a)/triste porque..., salir de la casa** y **llegar a la universidad.**

EN TU COMUNIDAD

Note that you will need the information that will be gathered in activity 12-6 in order to do activity 12-7.

SUGERENCIAS

Pueden hacer preguntas sobre la familia, la casa, los amigos y la vida en general en el país de origen. Además, acuérdense de *(remember to)* usar los siguientes conectores cuando sea posible: **primero, después, más tarde, luego, también** y **finalmente.**

II. Lectura: La presencia hispana en los Estados Unidos

■ Antes de leer

A. Un poco de historia ¿Qué recuerdan de sus clases de historia? Traten de responder a las siguientes preguntas. (Más adelante van a tener la oportunidad de confirmar sus respuestas.)

1. ¿Cuándo llegaron los primeros hispanos a los Estados Unidos?
   a. en el Siglo XVI
   b. en el Siglo XIX
   c. en el Siglo XX

2. ¿Cuáles de las siguientes ciudades fueron fundadas por los españoles? Indica todas las que correspondan.
   a. Miami
   b. El Paso
   c. Santa Fe
   d. Los Ángeles
   e. Denver
   f. San Francisco

3. ¿Cómo se convirtió el estado de Texas en parte de los Estados Unidos?
   a. Fue comprado por los Estados Unidos después de la guerra con México.
   b. Fue ganado por los Estados Unidos a consecuencia de la guerra con México.
   c. Fue fundado por los Estados Unidos antes de la guerra con México.

4. ¿Qué otros territorios fueron anexados a los Estados Unidos después de 1836?
   a. California
   b. Nuevo México
   c. Colorado
   d. Arizona
   e. Utah
   f. Nevada

5. El fenómeno de la inmigración ilegal ha aumentado significativamente desde el año...
   a. 1902.
   b. 1929.
   c. 1965.
   d. 1975.

B. Vocabulario y conceptos Para cada palabra, indiquen la letra de la definición que corresponda. (Usen el diccionario si es necesario.)

___ 1. fundar
___ 2. despojar
___ 3. tratado
___ 4. la ciudadanía
___ 5. los braceros

a. crear, establecer, iniciar
b. convenio o acuerdo escrito entre dos gobiernos
c. condición especial (con derechos y deberes) que tienen las personas de un país o nación
d. quitar, robar, tomar sin permiso o sin derecho
e. jornaleros, trabajadores agrícolas no calificados que se emplean por días

C. Puesta en práctica Ahora, completen las oraciones con las palabras del ejercicio anterior. **¡OJO!** ¡Tienen que conjugar los verbos y adaptar las palabras según el contexto! Al terminar, comparen sus respuestas con las de otro grupo.

1. Los españoles _____ la misión de San Diego en 1769.
2. Los conquistadores _____ del oro a muchos indígenas.
3. Con el _____ Guadalupe-Hidalgo terminó la guerra entre México y los Estados Unidos.
4. En las granjas de California aún se emplean a muchos _____.
5. Los inmigrantes aspiran a obtener la _____ estadounidense.

■ A leer

Los antecedentes (primera parte)

Los primeros hispanos

La presencia hispana en Norteamérica no es un fenómeno reciente. **De hecho,** los primeros **asentamientos** europeos en lo que es hoy Estados Unidos **fueron establecidos** por los españoles. (El primero de ellos: San Agustín en la Florida, 1565.) De allí los conquistadores continuaron su labor de exploración y colonización hacia el oeste, fundando El Paso (Texas) en 1598, Santa Fe (Nuevo México) en 1609 y la misión de San Diego en 1769. Para el año de 1760, ya había más de 20.000 **colonos** españoles en Nuevo México y unos 25.000 en Texas.

«El Álamo, escenario de la guerra entre Estados Unidos y México en 1836»

In fact
settlements
were established

settlers

Los mexicanos

México declaró su independencia del control español en el año de 1821. Por esta fecha, muchos **pobladores** anglosajones empezaron a mudarse a lo que es hoy en día el estado de Texas. En 1836, los nuevos colonos

inhabitants

proclamaron la independencia de su territorio y le dieron el nombre de República de Texas. En vista de que encontraron una débil reacción mexicana, y de que se encontraban **bajo el amparo** de la doctrina del *Destino Manifiesto*,* los ejércitos norteamericanos invadieron México en 1846. La guerra entre los dos países **culminó** con la **firma** del Tratado Guadalupe-Hidalgo, según el cual México **se vio forzado a ceder** casi la mitad de su territorio a los Estados Unidos (incluyendo Texas, California, gran parte de Arizona y Nuevo México, partes de Colorado, Utah y Nevada). El tratado también **estipuló** que los habitantes de esos territorios tendrían **plazo** de un año para cambiar su nacionalidad. Así pues, en 1847, unos 75.000 mexicanos se convirtieron en ciudadanos de los Estados Unidos.

Aunque el Tratado Guadalupe-Hidalgo conservaba los derechos de **propiedad** de los mexicanos, no decía nada acerca de su lengua o su cultura. Entre 1850 y 1900 se aprobaron múltiples leyes de exclusión lingüística que limitaron sistemáticamente el acceso de los que **no eran angloparlantes** al voto, la justicia y la educación. Finalmente, en 1902 el Acta de Reclamación despojó a los hispanos de sus antiguas propiedades (excepto en Nuevo México). Ante condiciones tan adversas (y **a pesar de que** no existían todavía leyes de restricción migratoria), el flujo de mexicanos hacia los Estados Unidos durante la segunda mitad del siglo XIX fue muy limitado.

A principios del siglo XX en México, la dictadura de Porfirio Díaz (1877–1911) generó un gran descontento que terminó en una **revuelta** popular (La Revolución Mexicana, 1910–1917).

Muchos mexicanos decidieron entonces **huir** de la difícil situación en su país para establecerse en los Estados Unidos. (Aproximadamente un 30% de la población mexicana emigró hacia los Estados Unidos entre 1910 y 1930.)

Estos mexicanos fueron bienvenidos **debido a** la expansión económica y a las necesidades laborales de los Estados Unidos en ese momento. Aunque hubo un **descenso** migratorio durante los años de la depresión (1930–1940), la Segunda Guerra Mundial trajo consigo una segunda **oleada** de inmigración mexicana **compuesta** básicamente de trabajadores agrarios temporales o braceros (unos 350.000 mexicanos por año entre 1951 y 1964).

El constante y voluminoso flujo migratorio de mexicanos hacia los Estados Unidos durante el período de la posguerra llegó a su fin en 1965 cuando este país impuso por primera vez un límite a la inmigración de personas **provenientes** del hemisferio **occidental.** Tales restricciones se tradujeron eventualmente en el preocupante fenómeno de la inmigración ilegal que **abarca** en este momento a unos 5 millones de personas.

* Expansionist doctrine that dominated U.S. foreign policy during the nineteenth century.

¿Entendiste bien?

D. ¿Correcto o no? Revisen las respuestas que dieron a la actividad **Un poco de historia** de la sección **Antes de leer.**

E. Cronología de la presencia mexicana en los Estados Unidos Completen la gráfica con los eventos principales presentados en la sección «Los mexicanos».

Los mexicanos

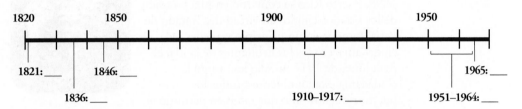

1820 1850 1900 1950

1821: ___ 1846: ___ 1965: ___

1836: ___ 1910–1917: ___ 1951–1964: ___

Los antecedentes (segunda parte)

Antes de leer

F. Para conversar ¿Saben Uds. de dónde son (o eran) las siguientes personalidades?

1. Desi Arnaz
2. Benicio Del Toro
3. Gloria Estefan
4. Andy García
5. Geraldo Rivera

G. Vocabulario y conceptos Para cada palabra, indiquen la letra de la definición que corresponda. (Usen el diccionario si es necesario.)

___ 1. la conquista
___ 2. otorgar
___ 3. refugiado
___ 4. un enclave
___ 5. la represión

a. cuando se detiene un movimiento colectivo
b. persona que busca (o encuentra) asilo en otro país, debido a una guerra o a un problema político
c. proceso por el cual se gana o toma posesión de un territorio por medio de las armas
d. una región o territorio especial
e. dar, entregar

H. Puesta en práctica Ahora, completen las oraciones con las palabras de la actividad anterior. Al terminar, comparen sus respuestas con las de otro grupo.

1. Muchos pobladores indígenas de América murieron durante el período de la _____.
2. En países donde no se respetan los derechos humanos hay mucha _____.
3. El barrio chino es un _____ de cultura asiática en la ciudad.
4. Los padres de mi amiga Liliana llegaron a este país como _____.
5. A este inmigrante le van a _____ un préstamo especial para que compre su primera casa.

■ A leer

El grupo puertorriqueño

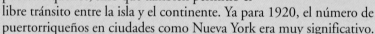

Los puertorriqueños, como los mexicanos, se convirtieron en ciudadanos americanos *by virtue of* **en virtud de** conquistas militares. Después de la guerra entre España y los Estados Unidos en 1898, Puerto Rico se convirtió en una posesión de los Estados Unidos en virtud del Tratado de París. Aunque en un principio no se les dio ciudadanía a todos los habitantes de la isla, el Acta Jones de 1917 no sólo les otorgó la ciudadanía estadounidense a todos los puertorriqueños, sino que también permitió el libre tránsito entre la isla y el continente. Ya para 1920, el número de puertorriqueños en ciudades como Nueva York era muy significativo.

Los cubanos

Al igual que Puerto Rico, Cuba se convirtió en posesión de los Estados Unidos (EE.UU.) en 1898 después del Tratado de París, dando fin a trescientos ochenta y siete años de control español. A diferencia de Puerto Rico, Cuba **se mantuvo** como territorio estadounidense sólo *remained* por un corto tiempo, logrando su independencia en 1902. El gran **flujo** migratorio de cubanos hacia los EE.UU. **tuvo lugar** con la *flow / took place* llegada de Fidel Castro al poder en 1959. Gran cantidad de profesionales y capitalistas buscaron refugio temporal en los Estados Unidos. La migración masiva fue detenida por Castro en 1973 y sólo hasta 1980 se les permitió la salida a 130.000 refugiados más hacia los EE.UU. (en la **controvertida** operación «Mariel», dada la inclusión en *controversial* este grupo de un cierto porcentaje de **presidiarios** y de enfermos *convicts* mentales). Hoy en día hay más de un millón de cubanos en los EE.UU., especialmente en la Florida, pero con enclaves importantes también en California, Illinois, Massachusetts, Nueva York y Nueva Jersey. Aunque muchos de los primeros refugiados pensaban volver a Cuba, la continuación del régimen socialista de Fidel Castro ha llevado a que muchos concluyan que no van a poder regresar y a que deben hacerse ciudadanos estadounidenses. Hoy en día, el grupo cubano es quizás el grupo hispano que mejor se ha integrado y que más éxito ha tenido en los Estados Unidos.

Otros grupos

En diferentes momentos de la historia, diferentes olas migratorias han llegado de otros países latinoamericanos como Nicaragua, Colombia, la República Dominicana, Guatemala, Honduras y El Salvador. Más de la mitad han llegado a los EE.UU. a partir de 1970 **debido a** la situación *due to* de violencia, guerra civil, pobreza o represión de su país de origen.

■ ¿Entendiste bien?

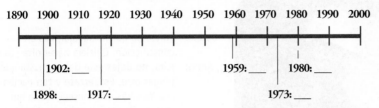

I. **Cronología de la presencia puertorriqueña y cubana en los Estados Unidos** Ahora, completen el cuadro con los eventos principales presentados en las secciones «El grupo puertorriqueño» y «Los cubanos».

Los puertorriqueños y los cubanos

1890 1900 1910 1920 1930 1940 1950 1960 1970 1980 1990 2000

1902: ___   1959: ___   1980: ___

1898: ___   1917: ___   1973: ___

J. **Actividad de extensión** Entrevista a una persona de origen hispano-americano y averigua cuándo y por qué su familia se mudó a este país. Prepara un breve informe para presentar en clase.

Abriendo caminos

iLrn

I. Funciones y estructuras: Giving commands, advice and opinions (review)

OBRERO: Chico, no quiero trabajar más en construcción. Quisiera hacer otra cosa.

AMIGO: Mira, **no dejes** este trabajo hasta que tengas otro. **Esfuérzate** y **ten** paciencia. Ya verás que conseguirás lo que quieres. **Te recomiendo que leas** los anuncios clasificados con frecuencia y que les **digas** a tus amigos que quieres cambiar de trabajo para que te avisen si se enteran de algo.

> Affirmative **tú** commands are formed with the third-person singular form of the present indicative: **Mi querida amiga,** *escribe* **la carta de presentación ahora mismo.**

Affirmative and negative commands in the **Ud., nosotros,** and **Uds.** forms are similar to the present subjunctive forms. The same applies to the negative commands in the **tú** form. (**Sr. Viera,** *firme* **aquí. Chicos,** *no entremos* **a la sala todavía. Carlos y Jimena,** *llamen* **a la Lic. Ortega. ¡Mario,** *no hables* **tanto!**)

The present subjunctive is formed by dropping the **-o** ending of the present indicative **yo** form of the verb and adding the endings **-e, -es, -e, -emos, -éis,** and **-en** for **-ar** verbs and the endings **-a, -as, -a, -amos, -áis,** and **-an** for **-er** and **-ir** verbs: **cantar → cante, cantes, cante, cantemos, cantéis, canten; beber → beba, bebas, beba, bebamos, bebáis, beban; vivir → viva, vivas, viva, vivamos, viváis, vivan.**

Some verbs have orthographic changes in the present subjunctive: **buscar → busque, busques, ...; llegar → llegue, llegues, ...; alcanzar → alcance, alcances, ...; producir → produzca, produzcas, ...,** etc.

Some of the most common irregular verbs in the present subjunctive are: **dar (dé, des, dé, ...), estar (esté, estés, esté, ...), ir (vaya, vayas, vaya, ...), saber (sepa, sepas, sepa, ...),** and **ser (sea, seas, sea, ...).**

The subjunctive is also used to give commands in a more indirect manner with verbs like **aconsejar, recomendar,** and **sugerir,** and with impersonal expressions like **es (mejor/peor/preferible/...) que...**

Les **recomiendo** que **piensen** en las consecuencias antes de actuar.
Es mejor que **hagas** un esfuerzo y **termines** los estudios.

Another use of the subjunctive is to give opinions with expressions of doubt, emotion, and wish; in adjectival clauses that describe hypothetical or non-existent antecendents; and in adverbial clauses with **a fin de que, para que, con tal de que, antes de que, después de que, hasta que** and **cuando.**

Siento que tengas que sacrificarte tanto para poder ayudar a tu familia.
¿Te gustaría conocer a **alguien** que **comparta** tus mismos valores?
Voy a insistir **hasta que me escuchen.**

■ Asimilación

12-8 Los futuros estudiantes de español ¿Cuáles de los siguientes consejos les darías a los futuros estudiantes de español? Compara tus respuestas con las de un(a) compañero(a) para saber si tienen opiniones semejantes.

____ Estudien la noche antes del examen.

____ Traten de hablar en español lo más que puedan.

____ Hagan los ejercicios del cuaderno de ejercicios con bastante anticipación.

____ No practiquen fuera del salón de clase.

____ No dejen el diccionario en la casa.

____ Escuchen con regularidad el disco compacto que acompaña el libro.

____ No tengan miedo de cometer errores en clase.

____ Estudien solamente el vocabulario, no la gramática.

____ No se preocupen por desarrollar las destrezas de escritura.

____ Si pueden, vayan a alguna comunidad donde se hable español para practicar.

CD2-55 **12-9 Propósitos y restricciones** Escucha las oraciones y complétalas de forma lógica desde tu punto de vista.

MODELO   ESCUCHAS: *Voy a estudiar en esta universidad hasta que...*
          ESCRIBES: *tome todos los cursos y me gradúe.*

1. ...   4. ...
2. ...   5. ...
3. ...

■ Aplicaciones

12-10 Consejos Mencionen por lo menos dos consejos que le darían a una persona que tiene los siguientes problemas. Usen mandatos formales.

1. No consigue trabajo.
2. Su hijo tiene problemas de salud
3. Extraña a sus familiares en su país.
4. Quiere encontrar a la persona de sus sueños.
5. Sufre de discriminación en su trabajo.
6. No sabe inglés.
7. Vive en un barrio donde hay mucha criminalidad.
8. Siente que su vida no tiene un propósito.

12-11 La vida en los Estados Unidos Imagínense que conocen a un(a) hispano(a) que llegó a los Estados Unidos hace poco tiempo y quiere informarse sobre diferentes aspectos de la vida en este país.

> MODELO la educación
> *Los padres quieren que sus hijos asistan a la universidad y se eduquen. En este país es importante tener un título universitario para poder vivir bien.*

1. los empleos
2. el papel de la mujer en la sociedad
3. el papel del hombre en la sociedad
4. los servicios médicos

5. la familia
6. las oportunidades económicas
7. la compra de una casa
8. las responsabilidades cívicas

12-12 ¿Qué recomiendan? Miren los siguientes dibujos y denles consejos a estas personas. Usen expresiones impersonales y verbos en la forma de mandato.

MODELO *No es aconsejable que maneje su auto. Llame a un amigo para que lo busque y espere. No tome más porque puede causarle problemas.*

Vocabulario útil: tener determinación, bajar de peso, hacer ejercicio, (no) comer...

Vocabulario útil: dejar de usar drogas, hablar con..., ser más responsables, buscar ayuda

Vocabulario útil: declarar tu amor, tener confianza en ti mismo, no esperar, ser arriesgado

■ Integración

12-13 Una carta Lean la siguiente carta que un hispano de California envió a un periódico local y comenten qué cosas debe hacer para mejorar su situación.

15 de noviembre de 2005

A todos los lectores del periódico El Latino:

Les escribe Miguel Talavera Pedraza para pedirles su consejo. Vivo en los Estados Unidos desde hace dos meses. Aunque tengo un buen trabajo —soy ingeniero químico— y me encanta vivir en esta ciudad, extraño mucho a mi familia. Desde aquí los puedo ayudar más y disfruto mucho de lo que este país tiene que ofrecer, pero me hace falta mi gente y estar en contacto directo con mi cultura. He conocido a muchas personas magníficas, pero no es lo mismo... Quisiera regresar a mi país, pero no quiero darme por vencido. ¿Qué debo hacer?

El confundido

EN TU COMUNIDAD

Find out about the resources available in your community to address the legal, medical, and psychological needs of immigrants. Get in touch with one of these agencies, inquire about their services, and prepare an oral report.

12-14 Una respuesta Ahora, escríbele una carta a Miguel Talavera Pedraza, «el confundido» de la actividad 12-13, para darle tu apoyo y tus recomendaciones. Cuando termines, dale una copia a tu profesor(a) para que te dé su opinión.

II. Vídeo: Se les fue volando el mes

■ Preparación

A. Una retrospectiva Ya que su estancia en Puerto Rico está casi por terminar, repasemos lo que les ha pasado a los compañeros. Ordenen cronológicamente los siguientes eventos en función de cuándo ocurrieron en el vídeo. Marquen el primer evento que ocurrió con el número **1** y el más reciente con el número **12.**

____ Valeria estaba triste porque nadie se había acordado de su cumpleaños.

____ Los compañeros expresaron sus aspiraciones y sus planes para el futuro.

____ Todos menos Valeria hicieron esnórkeling.

____ Cinco hispanos de distintos países viajaron a Puerto Rico para vivir juntos durante un mes.

____ Alejandra le prestó a Sofía algunas de sus prendas de vestir.

____ Antonio y Valeria hablaron sobre sus antiguas relaciones amorosas.

____ Javier, Sofía, Valeria, Antonio y Alejandra se conocieron por primera vez. Se presentaron y hablaron de sus países de origen y de sus estudios universitarios.

____ Los compañeros exploraron la ciudad de San Juan.

____ Los compañeros aprendieron a bailar la bomba.

____ Javier sugirió salir a cenar y los demás compañeros descubrieron que Sofía trabajaba de camarera.

____ Mientras todos deshacían sus maletas, Alejandra le enseñaba a Sofía unas fotos de su familia.

____ Valeria trató de preparar un plato mexicano: chiles rellenos al horno.

■ ¿Entendiste bien?

B. El momento de decir adiós Mientras ves el vídeo, indica con quién se asocian las siguientes oraciones. Usa la siguiente clave: **A** = Alejandra, **AN** = Antonio, **J** = Javier, **S** = Sofía.

____ 1. «Voy a extrañar a mis amigos y la casa y las montañas de Vista Alegre.»

____ 2. «Ellos cambiaron el destino de mi vida.»

____ 3. «He vivido una experiencia inolvidable... Un mes en Puerto Rico con cuatro personas maravillosas.»

____ 4. «Pensaba que mi aventura en Puerto Rico apenas estaba por comenzar.»

____ 5. «Es increíble todo lo que se aprende al convivir con cuatro extraños en una misma casa.»

____ 6. «La verdad es que al principio fue como un reto, pero luego se convirtió en una diversión muy especial.»

ESTRATEGIA DE COMPRENSIÓN

Scanning Concentrate on identifying the information requested in activity B.

Ahora, mira el vídeo de nuevo y concéntrate en lo que dice Valeria, la que tiene la última palabra. Completa lo que dice.

«Al principio, cuando llegué a esta casa me sentía muy _____. Todo era muy diferente para mí. Los muchachos me parecían _____. Javier era como raro, _____. Siempre andaba despeinado. Sofi, con su libro todo el tiempo. Era como muy _____. Alejandra, muy _____ para mi gusto, y Antonio siempre estaba _____. Pero ahora, ahora no podré vivir sin ninguno de ellos. Nunca los podré olvidar. Javier me enseñó que todo lo que se quiere en la vida se puede conseguir. Sofi me mostró el mundo desde su punto de vista, su cultura, sus libros. ¿Alejandra? Alejandra me enseñó a sonreír. Siempre está alegre. ¿Y Antonio? Antonio le puso ilusión a mi vida.»

Compara tus respuestas con las de un(a) compañero(a).

C. Las primeras impresiones Valeria habló de la primera impresión que tuvo de cada compañero y de cómo, al conocerlos mejor durante el mes, llegó a apreciar mucho a cada uno de ellos. En grupos, discutan lo siguiente: *¿Podemos confiar en la primera impresión que nos dan las personas?* Usen las siguientes preguntas para iniciar su conversación y preparen una respuesta con argumentos sólidos para presentárselos a la clase.

■ ¿En qué basamos nuestra primera impresión de una persona? ¿En sus características físicas, la ropa que lleva, el trabajo que tiene, lo que dice durante el primer encuentro, etc.?

■ ¿Pueden dar algún ejemplo de una situación en la que su primera impresión sobre una persona fue acertada *(right)*? ¿Y equivocada *(wrong)*?

D. Enfoque comunitario Entrevista a algún (alguna) estudiante extranjero(a) sobre su primera impresión de vivir en otro país. Averigua si esas primeras impresiones han cambiado o no. Puedes enfocar la entrevista en un tema específico o preguntarle sobre sus impresiones generales con relación a varios temas. Algunos de estos temas pueden ser:

■ la comunidad donde vive (la gente, las viviendas, los lugares de interés [parques, teatros, restaurantes, etc.], ...)

■ la vida universitaria (las asignaturas, los profesores, los otros alumnos, las actividades...)

Desafíos

I. Funciones y estructuras: Indicating probability with the future and conditional tenses (review)

Mmm... No salí bien en este examen. ¿**Estudiaría** lo suficiente? ¿**Me confundiría** con algunas de las preguntas? **Hablaré** con la profesora y le **preguntaré.**

The future tense is used to:

■ make predictions

En veinte años todos los carros **funcionarán** con electricidad.

> This is expressed in English with the verb *to wonder:* ¿**Quién *tocará* la puerta?** *I wonder who is knocking on the door.*

■ make conjectures about the present

¿Quién **será** ese hombre que está hablando con Federico? *I wonder who that man talking with Federico is?*

The future is formed by simply adding the following endings to the infinitive: **-é, -ás, -á, -emos, -éis,** and **-án.**

The conditional tense is used to:

■ express wishes in a polite manner

Me **gustaría** que me ayudaras a conseguir otro empleo.

> **REMEMBER**
>
> The verb that follows the conjunction **si** is conjugated in the imperfect subjunctive: **Si *fuéramos* más comprensivos, habría más tolerancia.**

■ hypothesize (usually in clauses with **si**)

En esa situación, yo no **me quedaría** con los brazos cruzados.

> This is also expressed in English with the verb *to wonder.*

■ make conjectures about the past

¿Quién me **llamaría** mientras estaba en la biblioteca? *I wonder who called me . . . ?*

These are some of the verbs with irregular stems in both the future and conditional tenses: **decir → dir-, hacer → har-, poder → podr-, poner → pondr-, salir → saldr-, tener → tendr-,** and **venir → vendr-.**

■ Asimilación

12-15 ¿Quién(es)? Piensa en las cosas que sabes de tus compañeros de clase. Luego, lee las siguientes oraciones y complétalas con los nombres de algunos(as) de ellos. Finalmente, compara tus respuestas con las de otro(a) estudiante. ¿Tienen opiniones semejantes o diferentes?

1. _____ será una excelente madre.
2. _____ y _____ tendrán su propio negocio.
3. _____ y _____ seguirán siendo muy buenos(as) amigos(as).
4. _____ se casará muy pronto.
5. _____ llegará a ser una persona famosa.
6. _____ y _____ se divertirán hasta el último momento de su vida.
7. _____ podrá viajar por todo el mundo.
8. _____ y _____ se postularán para puestos políticos.

CD2-56 **12-16 Hipótesis** Escucha las preguntas y contéstalas en oraciones completas.

1. ...
2. ...
3. ...
4. ...
5. ...

■ Aplicaciones

12-17 Monolingüismo y bilingüismo

Paso 1: ¿Qué pasaría si todos los estadounidenses fueran bilingües? Hagan una lista de por lo menos diez hipótesis.

> **MODELO** *Habría mejor comunicación entre la gente de diferentes culturas.*

Paso 2: ¿Y qué le pueden decir a una persona para convencerla de que el monolingüismo no es la mejor alternativa en un mundo global? Hagan una lista de por lo menos diez cosas que esta persona lograría si hablara más de un idioma.

> **MODELO** *Podrías comunicarte con personas de otros países.*

> **VERBOS ÚTILES**
>
> decir, comunicarse, hacer, llevarse, poder, tener, viajar

> **VERBOS ÚTILES**
>
> convivir *(to coexist)*, hacer, interactuar, salir, tener, comprender, hablar

12-18 Planes Túrnense para hacer y responder a las siguientes preguntas. Luego, preséntenle la información al resto de la clase. Usen el futuro y el condicional apropiadamente.

> **MODELO** E1: *Peter, ¿qué harás después de la clase?*
> E2: *Almorzaré en la cafetería.*
> E1: *Peter dijo que almorzaría en la cafetería después de la clase.*

1. ¿Qué harás al llegar a casa hoy?
2. ¿Qué harás después de cenar?
3. ¿Qué harás esta noche?
4. ¿Qué harás el próximo verano?
5. ¿Qué harás para alcanzar la felicidad en tu vida?
6. ¿Qué harás al graduarte de la universidad?
7. ¿Qué harás para combatir algún mal social?
8. ¿Qué harás para mejorar tus conocimientos de español?

12-19 Especulaciones

Paso 1: Imagínense que ayer Uds. vieron a las personas de los dibujos que siguen. Ahora están recordando lo que vieron y especulando sobre las características de esas personas y sobre lo que estaba ocurriendo. ¡Sean creativos!

MODELO *La señora tendría noventa años. Ella pensaría que era muy atractiva. Las demás personas estarían sorprendidas. Su perro se sentiría avergonzado.*

Paso 2: Ahora, imagínense que están caminando por la ciudad y ven a las siguientes personas. Como no las conocen ni saben lo que está ocurriendo, ¿qué preguntas de conjetura pueden hacer?

MODELO *¿Será un hippie? ¿Estará atrapado en el tiempo? ¿Pensará que es el año 1969? ¿Las demás personas creerán que está loco?*

▪ **Integración**

12-20 Tu comunidad ¿Qué cosas positivas creen que ocurrirán en su comunidad? ¿Y qué cosas negativas ocurrirán? Conversen en parejas.

12-21 Un tema de interés personal Escoge un tema que te interese (la educación bilingüe, el desempleo, la lucha contra el SIDA, etc.) y averigua qué harán y qué harían los funcionarios públicos y las personas de tu comunidad con respecto a esto. Luego, escribe un informe y preséntalo en clase.

SUGERENCIAS

Pueden hablar de la educación, la economía, el sistema de salud, los ancianos, los niños, los hispanos, el transporte, la criminalidad y los valores morales.

EN TU COMUNIDAD

Note that you will need the information that will be gathered in activity 12-20 in order to complete activity 12-21.

II. Lectura: «Entró y se sentó»

■ Antes de leer

A. Para conversar Contesten las siguientes preguntas.

1. ¿Qué puede hacer un universitario para ayudar a su comunidad? (Si es posible, den ejemplos de cómo los diferentes miembros del grupo colaboran con causas de beneficencia.)
2. ¿Cómo piensan servir a sus comunidades después de graduarse?

B. Vocabulario y conceptos Para cada palabra, indiquen la letra de la definición que corresponda. (Usen el diccionario si es necesario.)

_____ 1. ingrato	a.	conjunto de personas que tienen el mismo origen étnico
_____ 2. la raza	b.	dedicarse a algo
_____ 3. huelga	c.	persona que nunca dice «gracias»
_____ 4. comprometerse	d.	la manera como son las cosas, las instituciones, la sociedad
_____ 5. el sistema	e.	lo que hacen los trabajadores cuando paran de trabajar como protesta

C. Aplicaciones Ahora, completa las oraciones con las palabras del ejercicio anterior. Al terminar, compara tus respuestas con las de otro(a) compañero(a).

1. Si el _____ es injusto, hay que cambiarlo.

2. A nosotros nos preocupan mucho los problemas que enfrenta nuestra _____ en este momento.

3. Los empleados están en _____ porque quieren mejores salarios.

4. Si quieres tener éxito en tu proyecto, tienes que _____ a trabajar con paciencia y dedicación.

5. Tienes que venir a visitarnos, no seas _____.

In the following reading you will find many examples of Spanish slang (words and expressions used by people in informal situations). Although slang is widely used, keep in mind that it is considered to be outside standard polite use.

■ **A leer**

Rosaura Sánchez

Nació en San Ángelo, Texas, una población pequeña a 160 millas de la frontera con México. Cursó estudios de literatura en la Universidad de Texas en Austin y hoy en día es profesora en la Universidad de California, San Diego. Rosaura Sánchez escribe en español no sólo porque es su lengua nativa, sino también porque quiere dar voz a la vida y las contradicciones de los chicanos. Ha escrito y editado libros de cuentos en español como *Requisa treinta y dos* y ha publicado varios de sus estudios socio-lingüísticos, entre ellos *Telling Identities: The California Testimonios* y *Chicano Discourse: Socio-Historic Perspectives*.

Entró y se sentó

Entró y se sentó frente al enorme escritorio que le esperaba lleno de papeles y cartas.

behaved   Estaba furioso. Los estudiantes **se habían portado** como unos ingratos.

Wretched bunch (insult) / right in my face / Wretched bunch (insult)   —**Bola de infelices,** venir a gritarme a mí **en mis narices** que soy un «Poverty Pimp». **Bola de desgraciados.** Como si no lo hiciera todo por ellos, por la raza, pues.

cinnamon   Llamó a Mary Lou, la secretaria, y le pidió que le trajera un café y un pan dulce de **canela.**

nerve   —Y luego tienen el **descaro** de insultarme porque no me casé con una mexicana. Son bien cerrados, unos racistas de primera. Lo que pasa es que no se dan cuenta que yo acepté este puesto para ayudarlos, para animarlos a que continuaran su educación.

En ese momento sonó el teléfono. Era el Sr. White, el director universitario del departamento de educación. No, no habría más problemas. Él mismo hablaría con el principal Jones para resolver el

misunderstanding   problema. Era cosa de un **malentendido** que pronto se resolvería.

Mary Lou llegó con el café cuando terminó de hablar. Después de un

sip   **sorbo** de café, se puso a hacer el informe de gastos para el mes. Gasolina. Gastos de comida con visitantes importantes. Vuelo a Los Ángeles para la reunión de educadores en pro de la educación bilingüe. Motel.

—Para ellos yo sólo estoy aquí porque el sueldo es bueno. Si bien es verdad que pagan bien y que las oportunidades son muchas, también es verdad que los dolores de cabeza son diarios. Yo podría haberme dedicado a mi trabajo universitario y no haberme acordado de mi gente.

Se le permitía 22 dólares de gastos diarios y como había estado cinco días podía pedir 110 dólares. A eso **se agregaban** los gastos de taxi. Ahora querían que los **apoyara** en su huelga estudiantil. Pero eso ya era demasiado. Lo estaban comprometiendo.

they added
support

—Si supieran esos muchachos lo que he tenido que **sudar** yo para llegar aquí. Con esa **gritería** de que hay que cambiar el sistema no llegamos a ninguna parte. No se dan cuenta que lo que hay que hacer es estudiar para que el día de mañana puedan ser útiles a la sociedad.

to sweat
loud protest

De repente **se apagaron** las luces. Afuera comenzaba a **tronar** y la lluvia caía en torrentes. **Volteó** en su silla **rodante** y se acercó a la ventana. Primero vio los edificios grises universitarios que **se asemejaban** a los **recintos** de una prisión. Se oscureció más y más hasta que vio la **troca** perdida en la lluvia.

went out / to thunder
He turned / with wheels
resembled
compounds / truck (slang)

—Con este **aguacero** tendremos que parar un rato, hijo. Llegando a la **orilla** del **surco,** nos metemos debajo de la troca hasta que **escampe** un poco. **Pesó** el algodón pero no vació el **costal** arriba porque con la lluvia le estaba dando frío.

downpour
edge / furrow / stops raining
He weighed / sack

—Mira, hijo, si te vas a la escuela no sé cómo le vamos a hacer. Con lo que ganas de busboy y lo que hacemos los sábados **pizcando,** nos ayudamos bastante. Ya sabes que en mi trabajo no me pagan **gran cosa.**

hand picking
a lot

Sabía lo que era trabajar duro, de sol a sol, **sudando la gorda.** Entonces que **no me vengan a mí con cuentos,** señores. ¿Qué se han creído esos **babosos**? Después de tanto trabajo, tener que **lidiar** con estos **huevones.** Porque lo que pasa es que no quieren ponerse a trabajar, a estudiar como los **meros** hombres.

working very hard
don't come to me with stories
stupid (insult) / to deal with
idiots (insult)
real (slang)

—Mire, **apá,** le mandaré parte de mi préstamo federal cada mes. Verá que no me he de **desobligar** y ya estando en Austin, buscaré allá otro trabajito para poder ayudarles.

papá (slang)
to forget about an obligation

Éramos pocos los que estudiábamos entonces. Estos que tienen la **chiche** del gobierno no saben lo que es canela. Sólo sirven para quejarse de que no les dan más.

breast, source of nourishment (slang)

—Yo ya estoy muy viejo, hijo. Cuida a tu mami y a tus hermanos.

Seguía lloviendo y la electricidad no volvía. Afuera **relampagueó.**

there was lightning

El carro se les había parado en la esquina. El semáforo ya se había puesto verde pero el carro no **arrancaba.** Su papá salió, levantó el **capacete** y quitó el filtro. Mientras su papá ponía y quitaba la mano del carburador,

started / hood

to step on (imperfect tense) / to honk (imperfect tense) / to slide (imperfect tense) / upset / inconvenience / in the middle of / soaked / had cursed
to pull
to sink (imperfect tense) / plowed useless vehicles

effort / to auction off his hide / Supposedly (slang)

él **pisaba** el acelerador. Atrás los autos **pitaban** y pitaban. Por la izquierda y la derecha **se deslizaban** los Cadillacs y los Oldsmobiles de los rancheros **airados** con el **estorbo** en **plena** calle Chadbourne. Su papá estaba **empapado** por la lluvia cuando por fin arrancó el carro. Ese día los **había maldecido** a todos, a todos los gringos de la tierra que los hacían **arrastrar** los costales de algodón por los surcos mientras los zapatos se les **hundían** en la tierra **arada,** a los gringos que les pagaban tan poco que sólo podían comprar aquellas **garraletas** que nunca arrancaban. Años después se había casado con una gringa. Y ahora después de tanto **afán**, querían que **se rifara el pellejo. Qu'esque** por la causa. Como si fuera tan fácil cambiar el sistema. No señores, que no contaran con él.

Volvió la electricidad y se puso a ver la correspondencia.

—Gracias a Dios que tengo mi oficina aquí en la Universidad, en el sexto piso de esta monstruosidad donde no tengo que ver a nadie. No más le digo a la secretaria que diga que no estoy, así puedo dedicarme al **papeleo** que siempre hay que atender.

paperwork

Estos estudiantes del Cuerpo de Maestros van a tener que **sujetarse** a las reglas o si no, **pa'** fuera. Tiene uno que **ponerse duro**, porque si no, **se lo lleva la chingada.**

adhere to
para (slang) / to be tough
you are doomed

Alguna vez le contaré mi vida a esta gente... A ver... Bueno mañana no será. Tengo que ir a Washington a la reunión nacional de programas federales de educación para las minorías y luego... a ver... tengo que ir a San Antonio como consultante del programa bilingüe. Vale más llamar a Mary Lou para ver si me consiguió ya el pasaje de avión para mañana. Mary Lou... ah, si mmmhhhmmm, en el Hilton, del 8 al 10 de noviembre. Muy bien. Y ¿qué sabes del vuelo?... ¿Por Continental o American?...

Miró por la ventana y vio a su papá empapado en agua y lleno de grasa.

¿Entendiste bien?

D. La vida del profesor Organicen los siguientes eventos del cuento de manera cronológica. Piensen en el orden real de los sucesos (no el orden en que se presentan en el cuento).

ESTRATEGIA DE LECTURA

Skimming Skim the text to establish the actual sequence of events.

____ El carro de su padre tuvo problemas mecánicos en la carretera.

____ Su padre le pidió que no se fuera a estudiar a la universidad.

____ Se graduó de la facultad de educación.

____ Tuvo una discusión con los estudiantes latinos.

____ Preparó un informe de gastos para su jefe.

____ Fue a una convención de educación bilingüe.

E. Estudio de personajes Describan a los siguientes personajes de la historia. (Si es posible, indiquen cómo es su carácter, qué hacen y por qué son importantes en el cuento.)

Personaje	Descripción
el profesor	
los estudiantes	
el padre del profesor	
la secretaria	

F. Preguntas y respuestas Lean de nuevo la historia y contesten las siguientes preguntas.

1. ¿Qué esperaban los estudiantes del profesor? ¿Por qué lo insultan?
2. ¿Qué recuerdos le trae la lluvia al profesor? ¿Cómo fue su infancia?
3. ¿Cómo piensa el profesor que está ayudando a su comunidad?
4. ¿Por qué es tan importante para el profesor la imagen de su padre bajo la lluvia?
5. ¿Por qué crees que se llama este cuento «Entró y se sentó»?

G. Enfoque comunitario Averigua qué recursos hay en tu comunidad para ayudar y orientar a los inmigrantes. Si es posible, entrevista a una de las personas que trabaja allí para averiguar lo siguiente.

- ¿Por qué lo hace?

- ¿Qué es lo que más le gusta de su trabajo?

- ¿Cuáles son los problemas más graves que enfrenta?

- ¿Qué anécdotas o experiencias significativas ha tenido en su trabajo?

Puesta en acción

SITUACIÓN:	El Departamento de Relaciones Públicas de tu municipalidad, agencia gubernamental en la que trabajas, quiere saber qué opinan los ciudadanos sobre la calidad de vida y desea crear programas que ayuden a mejorarla.
MISIÓN:	Averiguar qué opinan los ciudadanos de tu municipalidad sobre diferentes temas de interés social, diseñar un programa que ayude a mejorar su calidad de vida y preparar una campaña publicitaria para diseminar la información relacionada con este programa.
DESTREZAS:	Recopilar datos mediante cuestionarios y entrevistas, diseñar un programa social que fomente el mejoramiento de la calidad de vida de los habitantes de tu municipalidad e informarles sobre este programa.

A. Un mensaje electrónico Lee el mensaje que te envió la directora del Departamento de Relaciones Públicas y contesta las preguntas que siguen.

> Enviar   Direcciones   Archivos adjuntos   Ver. ortografía   Guardar   Cancelar
>
> **Para:** ▼ John Smith
> **De:** Leonor Alarcón Rivas, directora
> **Fecha:** 20 de enero del 2007
>
> **Asunto:** La calidad de vida en nuestra municipalidad   **Prioridad:** Normal ▼
>
> Normal ▼   12 ▼
>
> Con el propósito de mejorar la calidad de vida de nuestros ciudadanos, el Departamento de Relaciones Públicas de esta municipalidad quisiera recopilar datos sobre lo que opinan los habitantes con relación a diferentes aspectos, como sus expectativas y aspiraciones, las comodidades del hogar y los problemas sociales. Por esta razón, quisiéramos que Ud. y sus asistentes se dieran a la tarea de preparar un cuestionario para distribuir entre todos los ciudadanos, y que entrevistaran a una muestra *(sample)* de la población. Además, nos gustaría que usaran la información que obtuvieran para diseñar un programa de mejoramiento comunitario. Sería ideal que éste incluyera seminarios y actividades culturales que integraran a todos los miembros de la comunidad. Esperamos que presente un informe sobre su investigación a finales del próximo mes y desearíamos que nos describiera el programa que piensa implementar a finales de marzo. Pueden contar con todos los recursos de nuestra oficina.

1. ¿Qué aspectos de la vida de los ciudadanos quiere la directora que investigues?
2. ¿Qué tipo de actividades debe incluir el programa de mejoramiento comunitario?
3. ¿Cuánto tiempo tienes disponible para recopilar los datos y diseñar el programa?

B. Aprendiendo sobre el tema Has decidido aprender un poco más sobre las cosas que le preocupan al ciudadano común antes de comenzar con tu proyecto, y encontraste información sobre dos estudios similares que se realizaron en comunidades vecinas *(neighboring)*. Primero, lean individualmente sus respectivos artículos. Luego, túrnense para hacer y responder a preguntas sobre estos estudios, y completen la planilla. Cuando terminen comenten en qué se diferencian estas dos comunidades y las personas que viven en ellas según los resultados de estos estudios.

Estudiante 1

Metas más importantes para los ciudadanos:

1. tener suerte para obtener un trabajo	46%
2. hacer realidad el sueño de tener una casa propia	32%
3. enfrentar sus problemas personales	20%

Importancia de tener los siguientes aparatos electrónicos en su casa:

1. lavadora y secadora	37%
2. televisor	25%
3. refrigerador	21%

Problemas sociales que más les preocupan:

1. la violencia	58%
2. la discriminación	39%
3. la miseria	27%

Metas	%	Aparatos electrónicos más importantes	%	Problemas sociales que más les preocupan	%
alcanzar bienestar económico			43		
			34	*la guerra*	
	20			*las especies en vías de extinción*	

Estudiante 2 must turn the book upside down.

Metas	%	Aparatos electrónicos más importantes	%	Problemas sociales que más les preocupan	%
		la violencia			45
		televisor			39
enfrentar sus problemas personales					

Estudiante 2

Metas más importantes para los ciudadanos:
1. alcanzar bienestar económico — 46%
2. tener éxito en el trabajo — 32%
3. enfrentar sus problemas personales — 20%

Importancia de tener los siguientes aparatos electrónicos en su casa:
1. computadora — 43%
2. puerta automática — 34%
3. cafetera automática — 30%

Problemas sociales que más les preocupan:
1. el hambre — 41%
2. la guerra — 35%
3. las especies en vías de extinción — 19%

C. El cuestionario

Paso 1: En parejas, preparen una lista de los posibles temas que pueden incluir en el cuestionario.

CRITICAL THINKING SKILLS

Prioritizing Choose the topics that would allow you to find out more vital information about the citizens of your town or city.

Expectativas y aspiraciones	Comodidades del hogar	Problemas sociales

Paso 2: Compartan con otro grupo las ideas que generaron en la actividad anterior.
  a. comenten la importancia de cada tema y
  b. escojan un mínimo de cinco temas para cada categoría

D. El diseño del cuestionario Diseñen el cuestionario que se va a distribuir entre todas las personas de la comunidad. Incluyan un ítem para cada uno de los temas que seleccionaron en la actividad anterior. Presten atención a la forma verbal que utilizarán en las preguntas.

E. Preguntas

Paso 1: Escriban por lo menos seis preguntas que quisieran hacerles a las personas de su comunidad para saber un poco sobre las cosas que han hecho durante el pasado año. Usen el pretérito, el imperfecto y el pretérito perfecto correctamente.

MODELO *¿Ha alcanzado Ud. todos sus sueños? ¿Compró una computadora o un teléfono celular durante el pasado año? ¿Sentía que el problema de la guerra era justificable?*

Paso 2: Ahora, escriban por lo menos seis preguntas hipotéticas con **si.**

MODELO *Si usted tuviera el tiempo, ¿sería más activo(a) en la comunidad? ¿Usted se sentiría más feliz si viviera en un lugar con menos problemas de intolerancia?*

F. Una entrevista Representa la siguiente situación con un(a) compañero(a).

El (La) entrevistador(a)	**El (La) entrevistado(a)**
Trabajas en el Departamento de Relaciones Públicas de tu comunidad. Como parte del proyecto de mejoramiento de la calidad de vida de los ciudadanos, vas a entrevistar a una de las personas que viven aquí. ■ Saluda a esta persona. ■ Explícale el propósito de este proyecto. ■ Hazle las preguntas que preparaste con un(a) compañero(a) en la actividad **E.** (Reacciona a las respuestas que te da esta persona con más preguntas pertinentes para obtener toda la información que puedas.)	Una de las personas que trabaja en el Departamento de Relaciones Públicas de tu comunidad quiere entrevistarte para obtener más información sobre la calidad de vida de los ciudadanos. ■ Saluda al / a la entrevistador(a). ■ Averigua cuál es el propósito de este proyecto. ■ Responde a sus preguntas. Provee todos los detalles que puedas.

G. La propuesta Preparen una lista de las actividades culturales y seminarios que coordinarán para mejorar la calidad de vida de las personas de su comunidad. Además, preparen una lista de otras cosas que harían si tuvieran los recursos necesarios. Asegúrense de incluir eventos para personas de diferentes edades y culturas y con diferentes preferencias. Usen el futuro y el condicional correctamente.

SUGERENCIAS

Pueden consultar un motor de búsqueda para encontrar ideas sobre cómo estructurar un buen cuestionario.

CRITICAL THINKING SKILLS

Evaluating Consider activities (seminars, meetings, orientation sessions, cultural events, etc.) that would help address some of the issues you included in the questionnaire and issues that personally interest you or affect you.

H. Campaña publicitaria Diseñen una página de Internet para informar a todas las personas de la municipalidad sobre los eventos que planificaron. Incluyan lo siguiente:

- un nombre original para el proyecto de mejoramiento de la calidad de vida,
- una descripción de todos los eventos y una explicación de cómo éstos ayudarán a la comunidad en general,
- la fecha, el lugar y la hora de cada evento y
- elementos visuales interesantes (gráficas, fotos, etc.)

Sigan los siguientes pasos.

a. Decidan cómo será el diseño de la página y cómo la van a hacer fácil de usar e informativa.

b. Organicen y distribuyan la información en diferentes ventanas. Pueden usar un papel diferente para representar cada ventana e incluir los enlaces *(links)*.

c. Decidan dónde van a ir los títulos, los datos, las descripciones, las gráficas, etc.

Servicio comunitario

Contact someone at the public relations office of your local government and offer to do what is included in activities G and H. You may even take this a step further and actually coordinate the activities that your group suggested.

Apéndices

Apendices

APÉNDICE A: Los verbos regulares

Infinitive	Present Indicative	Imperfect	Preterite	Future	Conditional	Present Subjunctive	Past Subjunctive	Commands
hablar *to speak*	hablo	hablaba	hablé	hablaré	hablaría	hable	hablara	habla (no hables)
	hablas	hablabas	hablaste	hablarás	hablarías	hables	hablaras	hable
	habla	hablaba	habló	hablará	hablaría	hable	hablara	hablad (no habléis)
	hablamos	hablábamos	hablamos	hablaremos	hablaríamos	hablemos	habláramos	hablen
	habláis	hablabais	hablasteis	hablaréis	hablaríais	habléis	hablarais	
	hablan	hablaban	hablaron	hablarán	hablarían	hablen	hablaran	
aprender *to learn*	aprendo	aprendía	aprendí	aprenderé	aprendería	aprenda	aprendiera	aprende (no aprendas)
	aprendes	aprendías	aprendiste	aprenderás	aprenderías	aprendas	aprendieras	aprenda
	aprende	aprendía	aprendió	aprenderá	aprendería	aprenda	aprendiera	aprended (no aprendáis)
	aprendemos	aprendíamos	aprendimos	aprenderemos	aprenderíamos	aprendamos	aprendiéramos	aprendan
	aprendéis	aprendíais	aprendisteis	aprenderéis	aprenderíais	aprendáis	aprendierais	
	aprenden	aprendían	aprendieron	aprenderán	aprenderían	aprendan	aprendieran	
vivir *to live*	vivo	vivía	viví	viviré	viviría	viva	viviera	vive (no vivas)
	vives	vivías	viviste	vivirás	vivirías	vivas	vivieras	viva
	vive	vivía	vivió	vivirá	viviría	viva	viviera	vivid (no viváis)
	vivimos	vivíamos	vivimos	viviremos	viviríamos	vivamos	viviéramos	vivan
	vivís	vivíais	vivisteis	viviréis	viviríais	viváis	vivierais	
	viven	vivían	vivieron	vivirán	vivirían	vivan	vivieran	

Compound tenses

Present progressive	estoy estás está estamos estáis están	hablando	aprendiendo	viviendo
Present perfect indicative	he has ha hemos habéis han	hablado	aprendido	vivido
Present perfect subjunctive	haya hayas haya hayamos hayáis hayan	hablado	aprendido	vivido
Past perfect indicative	había habías había habíamos habíais habían	hablado	aprendido	vivido

APÉNDICE B: Los verbos con cambios en la raíz

Infinitive / Present Participle / Past Participle	Present Indicative	Imperfect	Preterite	Future	Conditional	Present Subjunctive	Past Subjunctive	Commands
pensar *to think* *e → ie* pensando pensado	pienso piensas piensa pensamos pensáis piensan	pensaba pensabas pensaba pensábamos pensabais pensaban	pensé pensaste pensó pensamos pensasteis pensaron	pensaré pensarás pensará pensaremos pensaréis pensarán	pensaría pensarías pensaría pensaríamos pensaríais pensarían	piense pienses piense pensemos penséis piensen	pensara pensaras pensara pensáramos pensarais pensaran	piensa (no pienses) piense pensad (no penséis) piensen
acostarse *to go to bed* *o → ue* acostándose acostado	me acuesto te acuestas se acuesta nos acostamos os acostáis se acuestan	me acostaba te acostabas se acostaba nos acostábamos os acostabais se acostaban	me acosté te acostaste se acostó nos acostamos os acostasteis se acostaron	me acostaré te acostarás se acostará nos acostaremos os acostaréis se acostarán	me acostaría te acostarías se acostaría nos acostaríamos os acostaríais se acostarían	me acueste te acuestes se acueste nos acostemos os acostéis se acuesten	me acostara te acostaras se acostara nos acostáramos os acostarais se acostaran	acuéstate (no te acuestes) acuéstese acostaos (no os acostéis) acuéstense
sentir *to feel* *e → ie, i* sintiendo sentido	siento sientes siente sentimos sentís sienten	sentía sentías sentía sentíamos sentíais sentían	sentí sentiste sintió sentimos sentisteis sintieron	sentiré sentirás sentirá sentiremos sentiréis sentirán	sentiría sentirías sentiría sentiríamos sentiríais sentirían	sienta sientas sienta sintamos sintáis sientan	sintiera sintieras sintiera sintiéramos sintierais sintieran	siente (no sientas) sienta sentaos (no sintáis) sientan
pedir *to ask for* *e → i, i* pidiendo pedido	pido pides pide pedimos pedís piden	pedía pedías pedía pedíamos pedíais pedían	pedí pediste pidió pedimos pedisteis pidieron	pediré pedirás pedirá pediremos pediréis pedirán	pediría pedirías pediría pediríamos pediríais pedirían	pida pidas pida pidamos pidáis pidan	pidiera pidieras pidiera pidiéramos pidierais pidieran	pide (no pidas) pida pedid (no pidáis) pidan
dormir *to sleep* *o → ue, u* durmiendo dormido	duermo duermes duerme dormimos dormís duermen	dormía dormías dormía dormíamos dormíais dormían	dormí dormiste durmió dormimos dormisteis durmieron	dormiré dormirás dormirá dormiremos dormiréis dormirán	dormiría dormirías dormiría dormiríamos dormiríais dormirían	duerma duermas duerma durmamos durmáis duerman	durmiera durmieras durmiera durmiéramos durmierais durmieran	duerme (no duermas) duerma dormid (no durmáis) duerman

APÉNDICE C: Los verbos con cambios de ortografía

Infinitive / Present Participle / Past Participle	Present Indicative	Imperfect	Preterite	Future	Conditional	Present Subjunctive	Past Subjunctive	Commands
comenzar (e → ie) *to begin* z → c before e comenzando comenzado	comienzo comienzas comienza comenzamos comenzáis comienzan	comenzaba comenzabas comenzaba comenzábamos comenzabais comenzaban	**comencé** comenzaste comenzó comenzamos comenzasteis comenzaron	comenzaré comenzarás comenzará comenzaremos comenzaréis comenzarán	comenzaría comenzarías comenzaría comenzaríamos comenzaríais comenzarían	**comience** **comiences** **comience** **comencemos** **comencéis** **comiencen**	comenzara comenzaras comenzara comenzáramos comenzarais comenzaran	comienza (**no comiences**) **comience** comenzad (**no comencéis**) **comiencen**
conocer *to know* c → zc before a, o conociendo conocido	**conozco** conoces conoce conocemos conocéis conocen	conocía conocías conocía conocíamos conocíais conocían	conocí conociste conoció conocimos conocisteis conocieron	conoceré conocerás conocerá conoceremos conoceréis conocerán	conocería conocerías conocería conoceríamos conoceríais conocerían	**conozca** **conozcas** **conozca** **conozcamos** **conozcáis** **conozcan**	conociera conocieras conociera conociéramos conocierais conocieran	conoce (**no conozcas**) **conozca** conoced (**no conozcáis**) **conozcan**
construir *to build* i → y; y inserted before a, e, o construyendo construido	**construyo** **construyes** **construye** construimos construís **construyen**	construía construías construía construíamos construíais construían	construí construiste **construyó** construimos construisteis **construyeron**	construiré construirás construirá construiremos construiréis construirán	construiría construirías construiría construiríamos construiríais construirían	**construya** **construyas** **construya** **construyamos** **construyáis** **construyan**	**construyera** **construyeras** **construyera** **construyéramos** **construyerais** **construyeran**	**construye** (**no construyas**) **construya** construid (**no construyáis**) **construyan**
leer *to read* i → y; stressed i → í **leyendo** leído	leo lees lee leemos leéis leen	leía leías leía leíamos leíais leían	leí leíste **leyó** leímos leísteis **leyeron**	leeré leerás leerá leeremos leeréis **leyeron**	leería leerías leería leeríamos leeríais leerían	lea leas lea leamos leáis lean	**leyera** **leyeras** **leyera** **leyéramos** **leyerais** **leyeran**	lee (no leas) lea leed (no leáis) lean

APÉNDICE C: Los verbos con cambios de ortografía *(continued)*

Infinitive / Present Participle / Past Participle	Present Indicative	Imperfect	Preterite	Future	Conditional	Present Subjunctive	Past Subjunctive	Commands
pagar *to pay* **g → gu** **before e** pagando pagado	pago pagas paga pagamos pagáis pagan	pagaba pagabas pagaba pagábamos pagabais pagaban	**pagué** pagaste pagó pagamos pagasteis pagaron	pagaré pagarás pagará pagaremos pagaréis pagarán	pagaría pagarías pagaría pagaríamos pagaríais pagarían	**pague** **pagues** **pague** **paguemos** **paguéis** **paguen**	pagara pagaras pagara pagáramos pagarais pagaran	paga (**no pagues**) **pague** pagad (**no paguéis**) **paguen**
seguir (e → i; i) *to follow* **gu → g** **before a, o** siguiendo seguido	**sigo** sigues sigue seguimos seguís siguen	seguía seguías seguía seguíamos seguíais seguían	seguí seguiste siguió seguimos seguisteis siguieron	seguiré seguirás seguirá seguiremos seguiréis seguirán	seguiría seguirías seguiría seguiríamos seguiríais seguirían	**siga** **sigas** **siga** **sigamos** **sigáis** **sigan**	siguiera siguieras siguiera siguiéramos siguierais siguieran	sigue (**no sigas**) **siga** seguid (**no sigáis**) **sigan**
tocar *to play, to touch* **c → qu** **before e** tocando tocado	toco tocas toca tocamos tocáis tocan	tocaba tocabas tocaba tocábamos tocabais tocaban	**toqué** tocaste tocó tocamos tocasteis tocaron	tocaré tocará tocarás tocaremos tocaréis tocarán	tocaría tocarías tocaría tocaríamos tocaríais tocarían	**toque** **toques** **toque** **toquemos** **toquéis** **toquen**	tocara tocaras tocara tocáramos tocarais tocaran	toca (**no toques**) **toque** tocad (**no toquéis**) **toquen**

APÉNDICE D: Los verbos irregulares

Infinitive / Present Participle / Past Participle	Present Indicative	Imperfect	Preterite	Future	Conditional	Present Subjunctive	Past Subjunctive	Commands
andar *to walk* andando andado	ando andas anda andamos andáis andan	andaba andabas andaba andábamos andabais andaban	**anduve** **anduviste** **anduvo** **anduvimos** **anduvisteis** **anduvieron**	andaré andarás andará andaremos andaréis andarán	andaría andarías andaría andaríamos andaríais andarían	ande andes ande andemos andéis anden	**anduviera** **anduvieras** **anduviera** **anduviéramos** **anduvierais** **anduvieran**	anda (no andes) ande andad (no andéis) anden
*caer *to fall* **cayendo** caído	**caigo** caes cae caemos caéis caen	caía caías caía caíamos caíais caían	caí **caíste** **cayó** **caímos** **caísteis** **cayeron**	caeré caerás caerá caeremos caeréis caerán	caería caerías caería caeríamos caeríais caerían	**caiga** **caigas** **caiga** **caigamos** **caigáis** **caigan**	cayera cayeras cayera cayéramos cayerais cayeran	cae (no caigas) **caiga** caed (**no caigáis**) **caigan**
*dar *to give* dando dado	**doy** das da damos dais dan	daba dabas daba dábamos dabais daban	**di** diste dio dimos disteis dieron	daré darás dará daremos daréis darán	daría darías daría daríamos daríais darían	**dé** **des** **dé** **demos** **deis** **den**	diera dieras diera diéramos dierais dieran	da (no des) **dé** dad (**no deis**) den
*decir *to say, tell* **diciendo** **dicho**	**digo** **dices** **dice** decimos decís **dicen**	decía decías decía decíamos decíais decían	**dije** **dijiste** **dijo** **dijimos** **dijisteis** **dijeron**	**diré** **dirás** **dirá** **diremos** **diréis** **dirán**	**diría** **dirías** **diría** **diríamos** **diríais** **dirían**	**diga** **digas** **diga** **digamos** **digáis** **digan**	**dijera** **dijeras** **dijera** **dijéramos** **dijerais** **dijeran**	**di** (**no digas**) **diga** decid (**no digáis**) **digan**
*estar *to be* estando estado	**estoy** **estás** **está** estamos estáis **están**	estaba estabas estaba estábamos estabais estaban	**estuve** **estuviste** **estuvo** **estuvimos** **estuvisteis** **estuvieron**	estaré estarás estará estaremos estaréis estarán	estaría estarías estaría estaríamos estaríais estarían	**esté** **estés** **esté** **estemos** **estéis** **estén**	**estuviera** **estuvieras** **estuviera** **estuviéramos** **estuvierais** **estuvieran**	**está** (**no estés**) **esté** estad (**no estéis**) **estén**

Infinitive Present Participle Past Participle	Present Indicative	Imperfect	Preterite	Future	Conditional	Present Subjunctive	Past Subjunctive	Commands
haber *to have* habiendo habido	he has ha [hay] hemos habéis han	había habías había habíamos habíais habían	hube hubiste hubo hubimos hubisteis hubieron	habré habrás habrá habremos habréis habrán	habría habrías habría habríamos habríais habrían	haya hayas haya hayamos hayáis hayan	hubiera hubieras hubiera hubiéramos hubierais hubiéran	
★hacer *to make, do* haciendo **hecho**	**hago** haces hace hacemos hacéis hacen	hacía hacías hacía hacíamos hacíais hacían	hice hiciste hizo hicimos hicisteis hicieron	haré harás hará haremos haréis harán	haría harías haría haríamos haríais harían	haga hagas haga hagamos hagáis hagan	hiciera hicieras hiciera hiciéramos hiciérais hicieran	haz (no hagas) haga haced (no hagáis) hagan
ir *to go* **yendo** ido	**voy** vas va vamos vais van	iba ibas iba íbamos ibais iban	fui fuiste fue fuimos fuisteis fueron	iré irás irá iremos iréis irán	iría irías iría iríamos iríais irían	vaya vayas vaya vayamos vayáis vayan	fuara fueras fuera fuéramos fuerais fueran	ve (no vayas) vaya id (no vayáis) vayan
★oír *to hear* **oyendo** **oído**	**oigo** oyes oye oímos oías oyen	oía oías oía oíamos oíais oían	oí oíste oyó oímos oísteis oyeron	oiré oirás oirá oiremos oiréis oirán	oiría oirías oiría oiríamos oiríais oirían	oiga oigas oiga oigamos oigáis oigan	oyera oyeras oyera oyéramos oyerais oyeran	oye (no oigas) oiga oíd (no oigáis) oigan

APÉNDICE D: Los verbos irregulares *(continued)*

Infinitive / Present Participle / Past Participle	Present Indicative	Imperfect	Preterite	Future	Conditional	Present Subjunctive	Past Subjunctive	Commands
poder (o → ue) *can, to be able* **pudiendo** podido	**puedo** **puedes** **puede** podemos podéis **pueden**	podía podías podía podíamos podíais podían	**pude** **pudiste** **pudo** **pudimos** **pudisteis** **pudieron**	**podré** **podrás** **podrá** **podremos** **podréis** **podrán**	**podría** **podrías** **podría** **podríamos** **podríais** **podrían**	**pueda** **puedas** **pueda** podamos podáis **puedan**	**pudiera** **pudieras** **pudiera** **pudiéramos** **pudierais** **pudieran**	
*poner *to place, put* poniendo **puesto**	**pongo** pones pone ponemos ponéis ponen	ponía ponías ponía poníamos poníais ponían	**puse** **pusiste** **puso** **pusimos** **pusisteis** **pusieron**	**pondré** **pondrás** **pondrá** **pondremos** **pondréis** **pondrán**	**pondría** **pondrías** **pondría** **pondríamos** **pondríais** **pondrían**	**ponga** **pongas** **ponga** **pongamos** **pongáis** **pongan**	**pusiera** **pusieras** **pusiera** **pusiéramos** **pusierais** **pusieran**	**pon (no pongas)** **ponga** poned (no **pongáis)** **pongan**
querer (e → ie) *to want, wish* queriendo querido	**quiero** **quieres** **quiere** queremos queréis **quieren**	quería querías quería queríamos queríais querían	**quise** **quisiste** **quiso** **quisimos** **quisisteis** **quisieron**	**querré** **querrás** **querrá** **querremos** **querréis** **querrán**	**querría** **querrías** **querría** **querríamos** **querríais** **querrían**	**quiera** **quieras** **quiera** querramos querráis **quieran**	**quisiera** **quisieras** **quisiera** **quisiéramos** **quisierais** **quisieran**	**quiere (no quieras)** **quiera** quered (no querráis) **quieran**
reír *to laugh* **riendo** **reído**	**río** **ríes** **ríe** **reímos** reís **ríen**	reía reías reía reíamos reíais reían	reí **reíste** **rió** **reímos** **reísteis** **rieron**	reiré reirás reirá reiremos reiréis reirán	reiría reirías reiría reiríamos reiríais reirían	**ría** **rías** **ría** **riamos** **riáis** **rían**	riera rieras riera **riéramos** rierais rieran	**ríe (no rías)** **ría** **reíd (no riáis)** **rían**

*Verbs with irregular *yo*-forms in the present indicative

Infinitive Present Participle Past Participle	Present Indicative	Imperfect	Preterite	Future	Conditional	Present Subjunctive	Past Subjunctive	Commands
*saber to know sabiendo sabido	**sé** sabes sabe sabemos sabéis saben	sabía sabías sabía sabíamos sabíais sabían	**supe** **supiste** **supo** **supimos** **supisteis** **supieron**	**sabré** **sabrás** **sabrá** **sabremos** **sabréis** **sabrán**	**sabría** **sabrías** **sabría** **sabríamos** **sabríais** **sabrían**	**sepa** **sepas** **sepa** **sepamos** **sepáis** **sepan**	**supiera** **supieras** **supiera** **supiéramos** **supierais** **supieran**	sabe (**no sepas**) **sepa** sabed (**no sepáis**) **sepan**
*salir to go out saliendo salido	**salgo** sales sale salimos salís salen	salía salías salía salíamos salíais salían	salí saliste salió salimos salisteis salieron	**saldré** **saldrás** **saldrá** **saldremos** **saldréis** **saldrán**	**saldría** **saldrías** **saldría** **saldríamos** **saldríais** **saldrían**	**salga** **salgas** **salga** **salgamos** **salgáis** **salgan**	saliera salieras saliera saliéramos salierais salieran	**sal (no salgas)** **salga** salid (**no salgáis**) **salgan**
ser to be siendo sido	**soy** **eres** **es** **somos** **sois** **son**	**era** **eras** **era** **éramos** **erais** **eran**	**fui** **fuiste** **fue** **fuimos** **fuisteis** **fueron**	seré serás será seremos seréis serán	sería serías sería seríamos seríais serían	**sea** **seas** **sea** **seamos** **seáis** **sean**	**fuera** **fueras** **fuera** **fuéramos** **fuerais** **fueran**	**sé (no seas)** **sea** sed (**no seáis**) **sean**
*tener to have teniendo tenido	**tengo** **tienes** **tiene** tenemos tenéis **tienen**	tenía tenías tenía teníamos teníais tenían	**tuve** **tuviste** **tuvo** **tuvimos** **tuvisteis** **tuvieron**	**tendré** **tendrás** **tendrá** **tendremos** **tendréis** **tendrán**	**tendría** **tendrías** **tendría** **tendríamos** **tendríais** **tendrían**	**tenga** **tengas** **tenga** **tengamos** **tengáis** **tengan**	**tuviera** **tuvieras** **tuviera** **tuviéramos** **tuvierais** **tuvieran**	**ten (no tengas)** **tenga** tened (**no tengáis**) **tengan**

*Verbs with irregular *yo*-forms in the present indicative

Infinitive / Present Participle / Past Participle	Present Indicative	Imperfect	Preterite	Future	Conditional	Present Subjunctive	Past Subjunctive	Commands
traer *to bring* **trayendo** **traído**	**traigo** traes trae traemos traéis traen	traía traías traía traíamos traíais traían	**traje** **trajiste** **trajo** **trajimos** **trajisteis** **trajeron**	traeré traerás traerá traeremos traeréis traerán	traería traerías traería traeríamos traeríais traerían	**traiga** **traigas** **traiga** **traigamos** **traigáis** **traigan**	**trajera** **trajeras** **trajera** **trajéramos** **trajerais** **trajeran**	trae (**no traigas**) **traiga** traed (**no traigáis**) **traigan**
★venir *to come* **viniendo** venido	**vengo** **vienes** **viene** venimos venís **vienen**	venía venías venía veníamos veníais venían	**vine** **viniste** **vino** **vinimos** **vinisteis** **vinieron**	**vendré** **vendrás** **vendrá** **vendremos** **vendréis** **vendrán**	**vendría** **vendrías** **vendría** **vendríamos** **vendríais** **vendrían**	**venga** **vengas** **venga** **vengamos** **vengáis** **vengan**	**viniera** **vinieras** **viniera** **viniéramos** **vinierais** **vinieran**	**ven** (**no vengas**) **venga** venid (**no vengáis**) **vengan**
ver *to see* viendo **visto**	**veo** ves ve vemos veis ven	**veía** **veías** **veía** **veíamos** **veíais** **veían**	**vi** **viste** **vio** **vimos** **visteis** **vieron**	veré verás verá veremos veréis verán	vería verías vería veríamos veríais verían	**vea** **veas** **vea** **veamos** **veáis** **vean**	viera vieras viera viéramos vierais vieran	ve (**no veas**) **vea** ved (**no veáis**) **vean**

★Verbs with irregular *yo*-forms in the present indicative

Glosario: español-inglés

A

a cuadros plaid, checked
a rayas striped
a fin de que in order that, so that
a la hora on time
a menos que unless
a pesar de despite
¿A qué hora? (At) What time?
A su servicio. You are welcome.
A sus órdenes. You are welcome.
a veces sometimes
abandonar un programa to quit a program
abdomen *m.* abdomen
abogado(a) attorney
abordar to board
Abran el libro en la página... Open your books on page . . .
abrigo overcoat
abril April
abrir to open
abuelo(a) grandfather (grandmother)
aburrido *adj.* bored
acabar de + *infinitive* to have just (done something)
acampar to camp
accesible *adj.* accessible
aceite *m.* oil
¿Aceptan tarjetas de crédito? Do you take credit cards?
aceptar to accept
acomodar to accommodate, to arrange
aconsejar to advise
acordarse (ue) de to remember
acrílico acrylic
activo *adj.* active
aderezo dressing
¡Adiós! Good-bye!
administración de empresas *f.* business administration
administrar to manage, to administer
aeróbicos aerobics
aeropuerto airport
africano *adj.* African

afuera away, outside
agencia de bienes raíces real estate agency
agosto August
agresivo *adj.* aggressive
agricultor(a) farmer
agua water
ahora now
ajo garlic
al cubierto indoors
al lado de next to
alcalde *m.* mayor
alcantarillado sewage system
alcanzar (c) to reach
alegrarse (de) to be glad (about)
alegre *adj.* happy
alegría happiness
alergia allergy
alfombra carpet
álgebra algebra
algo something
¿Algo más? Anything else?
algodón *m.* cotton
alguien somebody, someone, anyone
algún any, some
alimentar to feed
allí there
almacén *m.* store
almeja clam
almuerzo lunch
alojamiento lodging
alquilar to rent
altavoz *m.* speaker
alto *adj.* high, tall
ama de casa housewife
amable *adj.* kind
amar to love
amar el trabajo to love one's work
amarillo *adj.* yellow
amigable *adj.* friendly
amigo(a) friend
amistad *f.* friendship
amistoso *adj.* friendly
amor *m.* love
anaranjado *adj.* orange
aniversario anniversary
anoche last night
antes (de) que before

antibiótico antibiotic
anticipo down payment
antipático *adj.* unfriendly
antropología anthropology
anuncio clasificado classified ad
añorar to long for
apagado *adj.* turned off
apagar to turn off
aparcamiento parking lot
apellido last name
aperitivo before-dinner drink
apoyar to support
aprender to learn
aquél/aquélla that one (over there)
aquéllos(as) those ones
aquí here
Aquí tiene. Here you are.
árbitro referee
árbol *m.* tree
archivo file
arena sand
arete *m.* earring
argentino *adj.* Argentinean
armario dresser
arnés *m.* harness
arquitecto(a) architect
arreglar to fix, to tidy up
arriesgarse to take risks
arroz *m.* rice
arte *m.* art
arvejas peas
artista *m., f.* artist
asiático *adj.* Asian
asiento seat
asistir to attend
aspirar (a) to aspire to; to vacuum
atender (ie) al público to deal with customers
ático attic
atletismo track and field
atún *m.* tuna
aumentar to increase
avión *m.* airplane
ayudar to help
azúcar *m., f.* sugar
azul *adj.* blue

B

baile *m.* dance
bajar de peso to lose weight
bajo *adj.* low, short
bajo techo indoors
baloncesto basketball
banana banana
banco bank
bañador swimsuit
baño bathroom
bar *m.* bar
barato *adj.* cheap
barra bar
barrio neighborhood
basura garbage, trash
basurero garbage hauler
bautizo baptism
beber to drink
béisbol *m.* baseball
beneficencia charity
biblioteca library
bicicleta bicycle
bien well, good, fine, okay
Bien, ¿y tú? Fine, and you? (informal)
Bien, ¿y Ud.? Fine, and you? (formal)
bienes raíces *m.* real estate
bienvenido *adj.* welcome
billete *m.* airline ticket
billetera wallet
biología biology
bistec *m.* beef steak
blanco *adj.* white
blusa blouse
boca mouth
bocadillo sandwich
boda wedding
bola ball
boleto airline ticket
bolígrafo pen
boliviano *adj.* Bolivian
bolos bowling
bombero firefighter
bonito *adj.* pretty, beautiful
borrador *m.* eraser
bota boot
botiquín de primeros auxilios *m.* first-aid kit
brazo arm
brócoli *m.* broccoli
bucear to dive

buena presencia good personal appearance
¡Buenas noches! Good evening!
¡Buenas tardes! Good afternoon!
bueno *adj.* good,
¡Buenos días! Good Morning!
Busco... I am looking for . . .

C

caballo horse
cabeza head
cable *m.* cable
cada each, every
café *m.* coffee; *adj.* brown
caja box
caja de cartón cardboard box
cajero automático automatic teller machine (ATM)
calcetín *m.* sock
cálculo calculus
calentamiento warm-up
calle *f.* street
cama bed
camarón *m.* shrimp
cambiar to exchange
cambio change
caminar to walk
camión de mudanzas *m.* moving truck
camisa shirt
camiseta T-shirt
campesino(a) farmer
campo countryside (field)
cancha court
cangrejo crab
cansado *adj.* tired
cantar to sing
cara face
cargar to load
caridad *f.* charity
carne *f.* meat
carro car
carta menu
carta de presentación cover letter
cartera handbag
casa house
casarse por la iglesia/por lo civil to get married in a religious /civil ceremony
casco helmet
casi nunca almost never

casi siempre almost always
CD *m.* CD-ROM
cebolla onion
ceja eyebrow
cena dinner
centro downtown
centro comercial mall
cerca de near
cerdo pig
cereal *m.* cereal
cerrar (ie) to close
césped *m.* grass, lawn
chaleco vest
champiñón *m.* mushroom
chaqueta jacket
charlar por teléfono to chat on the phone
¡Chau! Bye!
cheque *m.* check
cheque de viajero traveler's check
chícharos peas
chileno *adj.* Chilean
chofer *m., f.* driver
chuleta (de cerdo) (pork) chop
ciclismo bike riding
cien one hundred
cien mil 100.000
cien mil uno/a 100.001
cien mil dos 100.002
ciencias naturales natural sciences
ciencias políticas political science
ciencias sociales social sciences
ciento uno/a 101
ciento dos 102
ciento tres 103
cine *m.* movies; movie theater
cinta tape
cintura waist
cinturón *m.* belt
cliquear to click
clóset *m.* closet
cocina kitchen
cocinar to cook
cocinero(a) cook
coche *m.* car
codera elbow pad
codo elbow
colaborar to collaborate
collar *m.* necklace
colombiano *adj.* Colombian
color naranja *adj.* orange
combatir to combat

comedor *m.* dining room
comer to eat
cómico *adj.* funny
comida food, meal, lunch
como like, as
¿Cómo? How?, What?, Excuse me?
¿Cómo está Ud.? How are you? (formal)
¿Cómo estás? How are you? (informal)
¿Cómo se dice... ? How do you say . . . ?
¿Cómo te va? How are you? (informal)
compañero(a) colleague
compañero(a) de trabajo co-worker
compartir to share
competente *adj.* competent
comprar to buy
comprender to understand
comprometido *adj.* engaged
computadora computer
computadora portátil laptop computer
comunicación *f.* communication
con with
¡Con gusto! You are welcome!, With pleasure!
con tal de que provided that
conectar to plug in
conexión a Internet *f.* Internet connection
confiable *adj.* trustworthy
congestión *f.* traffic congestion; congestion
conocer (zc) to know; to meet
consejo advice
conservar to preserve
construir to build
consumir to consume
contable *m., f.* accountant
contaminación *f.* pollution
contar (ue) con to count on
contento *adj.* happy
contestar to answer
contrato contract
copa wine glass
corazón *m.* heart
corbata tie
corregir (i, i) to correct
correo electrónico e-mail
correr to run
cortar to cut

cortina curtain
corto *adj.* short
cosecha harvest
cosechar to harvest
costarricense *adj. m., f.* Costa Rican
costo de la vida cost of living
cotización *f.* price estimation
creativo *adj.* creative
criar to raise
cuaderno notebook
cuaderno de ejercicios workbook
cuadra city block
cuadro painting
¿Cuál? ¿Cuáles? Which? Which ones?
cualquier any, whatever
¿Cuándo? When?
cuando when
¿Cuánto? How much?
¿Cuántos? How many?
cuatrocientos/as 400
cubano *adj.* Cuban
cubiertos tableware
cuchara spoon
cucharita teaspoon
cuchillo knife
cuello neck
cuenta check
cuerda rope
cuerpo body
cuero leather
cuidar to care for, to watch over, to look after
cultivar to cultivate
cultivo crop
cultura masiva mass culture
cumpleaños birthday
cumplidor *adj.* reliable, trustworthy
cuñado(a) brother-in-law/sister in law
cuota inicial down payment
curar to heal
curita Band-Aid
currículum *m.* résumé

D

dar to give
datos personales personal information
de buen humor funny
de fantasía costume (jewelry)
de lunares/puntos polka-dot

¡De nada! You are welcome!
de un solo tono solid color
de maravilla great
debajo de under
débil *adj.* weak
dedo finger
dedo del pie toe
defender (ie) to defend
dejar to leave, to quit, to stop, to let (allow)
dejar de to quit, to stop (doing something)
delegar parte del poder to delegate power
delgado *adj.* thin
delincuencia (juvenil) (youth) crime
deporte *m.* sport
deprimido *adj.* depressed
derecho law, right
derechos humanos human rights
desafío challenge
desayuno breakfast
descanso rest
desconectar to unplug
desde from, since
desear to want
desempacar to unpack
desenchufar to unplug
despacio slowly
despedida farewell
despertador *m.* alarm clock
después (de) que after
detrás de behind
día *m.* day
dibujo drawing
diciembre December
diente *m.* tooth
diez mil 10.000
diez mil uno/a 10.001
diez mil dos 10.002
difícil *adj.* difficult
digitar to key in
diligente *adj.* diligent
dinero money
dirección *f.* address
disco CD
discriminación *f.* discrimination
diseño design
disgustado *adj.* angry
distraer to entertain, to amuse
divertido *adj.* fun

divorciado *adj.* divorced
divorciarse to get divorced
doctor(a) (Dr.[a]) doctor
documento document
doler (ue) to ache, to hurt
dolor de cabeza *m.* headache
domicilio address
domingo Sunday
dominicano *adj.* Dominican
¿Dónde? Where?
¿Dónde está? Where is?
dorado *adj.* gold
dormitorio bedroom
doscientos/as 200
doscientos/as uno/a 201
doscientos/as dos 202
doscientos/as tres 203
dos millones 2.000.000
duro *adj.* hard, difficult

E

echar de menos to miss
ecología ecology
ecólogo ecologist
economía economy
ecosistema *m.* ecosystem
ecuatoriano *adj.* Ecuadorian
edificio building
educación *f.* education
educación física physical education
efectivo cash
eficiente *adj.* efficient
egoísta *adj.* selfish
elasticidad *f.* flexibility
electricidad *f.* electricity
embalaje *m.* packing
embriagado *adj.* drunk
emocionado *adj.* excited
empacadores *m.* packing staff
empacar to pack
emparedado sandwich
empleado(a) employee
empleado(a) doméstico(a) maid
en on, in, at
en cambio instead
en caso (de) que in case, in the event that
en cuanto as soon as
¿En qué puedo servirle, señor? How can I help you, sir?
enamorarse to fall in love
Encantado(a). Pleased to meet you.

encantar to love, to like something very much
encargarse de + *verb* to be responsible for doing something
encender (ie) to turn on
encendido *adj.* turned on
enchufar to plug in
encima de on, over, above
enero January
enfermarse to get sick
enfermero(a) nurse
enfermo *adj.* sick
enfrentar to face; to confront
enfrente de in front of
enojado *adj.* angry
ensalada salad
enseñar to teach
entrada appetizer
entre between
entremés *m.* appetizer
entretener (ie) to entertain
entrevista interview
enviar to send
envolver (ue) to wrap
equipaje *m.* luggage
equipaje de mano carry on luggage
equipo equipment; team
es dudoso it is doubtful
¡Es fantástico! It's wonderful!
¡Es ideal! It's wonderful!
es importante it is important
es imposible it is impossible
es improbable it is improbable (not likely)
es justo it is fitting
¡Es maravilloso! It's wonderful!
es mejor It is better
es necesario it is necessary
¡Es perfecto! It's wonderful!
es posible it is possible
es preciso it is necessary
es probable it is probable
es urgente it is urgent
escalada libre rock climbing
escalar to climb
escalera stairs
escena scene
Escriban... Write . . .
escribir to write
escritorio desk
escuchar to listen to
escultor(a) sculptor
escultura sculpture
eso(a) that one

esos(as) those (ones)
espalda back
español *adj.* Spanish
espárrago asparagus
especialidad *f.* major
especie *f.* species
especie en vía de extinción threatened species
espejo mirror
esposo(a) husband/wife
esquí *m.* ski
esquiar to ski
esquiar en el agua to water-ski
esquina street corner
estación *f.* season
estación de policía police station
estación de trenes/autobús/metro train/bus/subway station
estacionamiento parking lot
estado civil marital status
estadounidense *adj. m., f.* American (from the US)
estampado print
Están/Son como para chuparse los dedos. They are finger-licking good.
¿Están listos para pedir? Are you ready to order?
estante *m.* bookcase
estar to be
estar dispuesto to be ready (eager)
estar (parcialmente) nublado to be (partly) cloudy
éste(a) this one
estéreo stereo
estimado price estimation
estiramiento stretching
estómago stomach
éstos(as) these (ones)
estrés *m.* stress
estricto *adj.* strict
estudiante *m., f.* student
estudios realizados studies completed
estufa stove
estúpido *adj.* stupid
europeo *adj.* European
evitar to avoid
expediente *m.* file
experiencia laboral work experience
exposición *f.* exposition
extinción *f.* extinction
extinguirse to become extinct

extrañar to miss
extrovertido *adj.* extroverted

F

fácil *adj.* easy
facilidad de expresión *f.* ease of expression, ability to speak
falda skirt
fallarle to fail (not be there)
familia family
famoso *adj.* famous
farmacia pharmacy
fauna fauna, wildlife
fax *m.* fax
febrero February
fecha de nacimiento date of birth
fecha de grado graduation date
feliz *adj.* happy
feo *adj.* ugly
fibra fiber
fiebre *f.* fever
fiel *adj.* faithful
filete de res/salmón *m.* beef/salmon filet
filosofía philosophy
finalmente *adv.* finally
finca farm
firme *adj.* firm
fisioterapia physical therapy
flaco *adj.* skinny
flora flora
formulario application form
fotografía photography
fresa strawberry
frijoles *m.* beans
frito *adj,* fried
fruta fruit
fuerte *adj.* strong
fuerza strength
fumar to smoke
funcionario(a) público(a) public official
fútbol *m.* soccer
fútbol americano football
futuro future

G

gafas protectoras goggles
galería de arte art gallery
galleta cookie
gallina hen

gambas shrimp
ganado livestock
ganar to gain
garaje *m.* garage
garganta throat
gas *m.* natural gas
gato cat
generoso *adj.* generous
geografía geography
geología geology
geometría geometry
gerente *m.* manager
gimnasia gymnastics
gimnasio gymnasium
golpear to hit
gordo *adj* fat
gorra cap
Gracias. Thank you.
gracioso *adj.* funny
graduación *f.* graduation
grande *adj.* big
grasa animal animal fat
gripe *f.* flu
gris *adj.* gray
guante *m.* glove
guapo handsome
guardamuebles *m.* storage
guardaparques *m.* park ranger
guardar to store, to save,
guatemalteco *adj.* Guatamalan
guerra war
gustar to like, to please

H

habitación *f.* bedroom
hablar to talk, to speak
hacer to do, to make
hacer buen tiempo to be good weather
hacer calor to be hot
hacer clic to click
hacer estiramiento to stretch
hacer fresco to be cool
hacer frío to be cold
hacer la cama to make the bed
hacer mal tiempo to be bad weather
hacer realidad to make come true
hacer sol to be sunny
hacer surf to surf
hacer un poco de calentamiento to do some warm-up exercises

hacer un viaje to take a trip
hacer una pregunta to ask a question
hacer viento to be windy
halar to pull
hambre *m.* hunger
hamburguesa hamburger
hasta (que) until
¡Hasta la vista! See you around!
Hasta luego. See you later.
¡Hasta pronto! See you soon!
helado ice cream
hermanastro(a) stepbrother/ stepsister
hermano(a) brother/sister
hijo(a) son/daughter
hipoteca mortgage
historia history, story
hogar *m.* household, home
hoja de vida résumé
¡Hola! Hi! Hello!
hombre de negocios *m.* businessman
hombro shoulder
hondureño *adj.* Honduran
honesto *adj.* honest
horno microóndas microwave oven
hospital *m.* hospital
hotel *m.* hotel
hueso bone
huevo egg
humanidades *f.* humanities

I

idioma *m.* language
iglesia church
ilusión *f.* dream, illusion
imagen *f.* image
impermeable *m.* raincoat
impresora printer
imprimir to print
indiferencia indifference
individual *m.* placemat
infiel *adj.* unfaithful
influenza flu
informática computer science
informe *m.* report
ingeniería engineering
ingeniería multimedia multimedia engineering
ingeniero(a) engineer
inmobiliaria real estate agency

insertar to insert
instalar to install
inteligente *adj.* intelligent
invertir (ie, i) to invest
investigación *f.* research
investigar to research, to investigate
invierno winter
ir to go
irse to leave
isla island

J

jalar to pull
jamón *m.* ham
jarabe *m.* cough syrup
jardín *m.* garden
jefe(a) boss
joven *adj.* young
jubilación *f.* retirement
judía verde string bean
juego game, set
jueves *m.* Thursday
jugador(a) player
jugar (ue) to play
jugo juice
julio July
junio June
juntos together
juzgar to judge

L

lago lake
lámpara lamp
lana wool
langosta lobster
lápiz *m.* pencil
largo *adj.* long
lavandería laundromat
lavar to wash
lavar la ropa to do laundry
lavar los platos to do the dishes
leal *adj.* loyal
Lean... Read . . .
leche *f.* milk
lechuga lettuce
leer to read
legumbre *f.* vegetable
lejos de far
lengua language
lentes de sol *m.* sunglasses

levantamiento de pesas weight lifting
librería bookstore
libro book
licencia profesional professional license
licenciado(a)/Lic(a). (for various professions) licensed
limonada lemonade
limpiar to clean
liso *adj.* straight, solid color
listo *adj.* smart, ready
literatura literature
llamada telefónica phone call
llegar to reach
llegar a ser to become
llevar to wear
llover (ue) to rain
lograr to achieve
los... on (day[s] of the week)
lucha libre wrestling
lugar de interés *m.* landmark
lunes *m.* Monday
luz *f.* light, electricity

M

madrastra stepmother
madre *f.* mother
maíz *m.* corn
maleta suitcase
maletín *m.* briefcase
malo *adj.* bad, mean
mamá mother
manejar to operate, to handle, to drive, to manage
mango mango
mano *f.* hand
manta blanket
mantel *m.* tablecloth
mantener (ie) to maintain, to support
mantenerse en buen estado de salud to keep in good health
mantenerse en forma to keep fit
mantequilla butter
manzana apple; city block
mar *m.* sea
maravilloso *adj.* wonderful
marcador *m.* marker
marcar to label
mareo dizziness
mariscos seafood

marrón *adj.* brown
martes *m.* Tuesday
marzo March
más more
Más despacio, por favor. More slowly, please.
más o menos so so
matemáticas mathematics
material sintético *m.* synthetic material
matrícula profesional professional license
matrimonio wedding
mayo May
mayor *adj.* mature, older
Me llamo... My name is . . .
¿Me podría traer... ? Could you bring me . . . ?
media sock, stocking
medicina medicine
médico(a) doctor
medio ambiente environment
mejillones *m.* mussels
mejor better
mejorar to improve
melón *m.* melon
menaje *m.* household goods, belongings
menor *adj.* younger
mensaje electrónico *m.* e-mail
mentir (ie, i) to lie
mermelada jam, marmalade, jelly
mes *m.* month
mesa table
mesa de centro (mesita) coffee table
mesa de noche/mesa de luz (mesita) bedside table
mesero(a) waiter/waitress
meta goal
metal *m.* metal
mexicano *adj.* Mexican
miel *f.* honey
mientras que while, whereas
miércoles *m.* Wednesday
mil *m.* one thousand
mil uno/a 1.001
mil dos 1.002
millón *m.* one million
mineral *m.* mineral
minifalda mini-skirt
mirar to see, to look at, to watch
miseria extreme poverty
mochila backpack
montaña mountain

montar a caballo to horseback ride
morado *adj.* purple
moreno *adj.* dark-haired
mostaza mustard
mostrar (ue) to show
motor de búsqueda *m.* search engine
movimiento movement (school)
Muchas gracias. Many thanks.
mucho many, much
Mucho gusto. Pleased to meet you.
mudanza move
mudarse to move
muebles *m.* furniture
muestra sample, show
mujer de negocios *f.* businesswoman
mundo world
museo museum
música music
Muy bien, gracias. Very well, thank you.
muy very

N

nacimiento birth
nacionalidad *f.* nationality
nada nothing
nadar to swim
nadie nobody
naranja orange
nariz *f.* nose
natación *f.* swimming
naturalista *m. f.* naturalist
navegar el Internet (la red) to surf the net
negro *adj.* black
nervioso *adj.* nervous
nevar (ie) to snow
nevera refrigerator
ni... ni neither . . . nor
nicaragüense *adj. m., f.* Nicaraguan
nieto(a) grandson/granddaughter
No comprendo. I do not understand.
No funciona. It doesn't work. / It is broken.
nombre *m.* name
Nos vemos el lunes. I'll see you on Monday.
novecientos/as 900
novecientos mil 900.000

novecientos noventa y nueve mil 999.000
noviembre November
novio(a) boyfriend, girlfriend, fiancé(e)
nuevo *adj.* new
nunca never

O

objeto object
obra work
obra maestra masterpiece
obrero(a) construction worker
ochocientos/as 800
octubre October
ocupado *adj.* busy
odio hatred
oficina de correos post office
oficina de turismo tourist office
oído inner ear
Ojalá. I hope.
ojo eye
olvidar to forget
oprimir to push, to hit, to click
ordenador *m.* computer
oreja ear
oro gold
otoño fall

P

paciente *adj.* patient
padrastro stepfather
padre *m.* father
página page
paisaje *m.* landscape
palabra word
pan *m.* bread
pan tostado toast
pana corduroy
panameño *adj.* Panamanian
pantalla screen
pantalones *m.* pants
pantalones cortos shorts
papa potato
papas fritas french fries
para que in order that, so that
parada de autobús/tren/metro bus/train/subway stop
paraguayo *adj.* Paraguayan
paramédico(a) paramedic
parásitos intestinales parasites

parecer (zc) to deem, to consider, to seem, to appear
pared *f.* wall
pariente *m., f.* relative
parlante speaker
parque *m.* park
parqueadero parking lot
pasaporte *m.* passport
pasar hambre to be hungry
pasar tiempo libre/los ratos libres to spend free time
pasear to take a short trip, to go for a walk
pasillo aisle
pasta pasta
pastel *m.* cake
pastilla pill
patatas fritas french fries
patinaje (sobre hielo) *m.* skating (ice skating)
patinaje en línea in-line skating
pato duck
patria homeland
pavo turkey
pedalear to pedal
pedir (i, i) to ask, request
película movie
pelo hair
pelo blanco gray hair
pelo castaño brown hair
pelota ball
peluquería barber shop, beauty parlor
peluquero(a) hairdresser
pendiente *m.* earring
pequeño *adj.* small
pera pear
perder (ie) to lose
perezoso *adj.* lazy
periodismo journalism
periodista *m., f.* journalist
permitir to allow, permit
pero but
perro dog
pescado fish (caught)
peso weight
pez *m.* fish (live)
pie *m.* foot
piel *f.* skin
pierna leg
pimienta pepper
pintor(a) painter
pintura painting
piña pineapple

pizarra blackboard, chalkboard
pizza pizza
planos blueprints
planta baja first floor
plástico de burbujas bubblewrap
plata silver
plátano plantain, banana
plateado *adj.* silver
platillo saucer
plato dish, plate
plato principal entrée (main course)
playa beach
plaza town square
pobre *adj.* poor
poco: un poco some, a little
poder *m.* power
poder (ue) to be able, to succeed
policía *m., f.* police, policeman(woman)
policía vial (de tránsito) traffic police
poliéster *m.* polyester
pollo chicken
por for, on
por ciento percent
por cierto for certain
por ello because of that
por eso because of that
por esto because of this
por favor please
por fin finally
por la mañana in the morning
por la noche at night
por la tarde in the afternoon
por otro lado on the other hand
¿por qué? why?
Por supuesto. Of course.
postre *m.* dessert
pregunta question
prender to turn on
preocupado *adj.* worried, preoccupied
preocuparse to worry about
preparar to prepare
presentar to present, to introduce
presentarse to present oneself, to appear
preservar to preserve
presionar to push, to hit
préstamo loan
primavera spring
primer piso *m.* second floor

primo(a) cousin
producir to produce
producto refinado refined product
profesión *f.* job
profesional *m., f.* professional
profesor(a) teacher
programa *m.* program
programador(a) de computadoras computer programmer
programar to program
promover (ue) to promote
propiedad *f.* property
propina tip
proporción *f.* proportion
proteger to protect
proteína protein
puerco pig, pork
puerta door
puertorriqueño *adj.* Puerto Rican
pulcera bracelet
pulmón *m.* lung
pulsar to push, to hit
puntual *adj.* punctual

Q

¿Qué? What?
¿Qué significa... ? What does . . . mean?
¿Qué tiempo hace? What is the weather like?
quehaceres *m.* chores
¿Quién?, ¿Quiénes? Who?
queso cheese
querer to want, to love
química chemistry
quinientos/as five hundred

R

rábalo bass
radiografía x-rays
raqueta racket
rasgo trait
ratón *m.* mouse
recámara bedroom
recepción *f.* reception desk
receta prescription
recibir to receive
reciclar to recycle
recoger to collect, to pick up
recuerdo memory
recursos naturales natural resources

reducir (zc) to reduce
reforestar to reforest
refresco soda
refrigerador *m.* refrigerator
refugio natural (silvestre) wildlife reserve
regresar to return
regular *adj.* regular, so so
reloj *m.* watch
reparar to fix, to repair
repetir (i, i) to repeat
representar to represent
reserva biológica biological reserve
resfriado cold
resistencia resistance
respetar to respect
respeto respect
respetuoso *adj.* respectful
responder to answer
responsable *adj.* responsible
restaurante *m.* restaurant
reto challenge
reunión *f.* meeting
revisar el buzón to check the mailbox
revuelto *adj.* scrambled
rico *adj.* rich
riesgo risk
río river
rizado *adj.* curly
róbalo bass
rodilla knee
rodillera knee pad
rojo *adj.* red
ropa clothes, laundry
ropa interior underwear
rosado *adj.* pink
rubio *adj* blond(e)
ruido noise

S

sábado Saturday
saber to know (how)
sacar to get, to take out, to obtain
sal *f.* salt
sala (living) room
sala de espera boarding area
salchicha sausage (hot dog)
salir (juntos) to go out, to exit, to leave, (to date)
salón de belleza *m.* beauty parlor
salón de clase classroom

salsa de tomate tomato sauce
salud *f.* health
saludo greeting
salvadoreño *adj.* Salvadorian
salvar to save
sandalia sandal
sandía watermelon
sándwich *m.* sandwich
sección de no fumar *f.*
   non-smoking section
seda silk
seguro de sí mismo *adj.* confident
seiscientos/as 600
selva jungle
semáforo traffic light
semana week
sembrar (ie) to sow
sentido del humor sense of humor
sentir (ie, i) to feel, lament
sentirse mal to feel ill
Señor (Sr.) Sir, Mr.
Señora (Sra.) Madam, Mrs.
Señorita (Srta.) Miss
separarse to get separated
septiembre September
ser to be
ser novios to be dating/going out
serio *adj.* serious
servicios públicos utilities
servicios sociales social services
servilleta napkin
set *m.* set
setecientos/as 700
sicología psychology
siempre always
silla chair
sillón *m.* armchair
simpático *adj.* nice
sobre on, over, above
sobrino(a) nephew/niece
sofá *m.* sofa
solicitar to request
solicitar trabajo to apply for a job
solicitud *f.* application
solidaridad *f.* solidarity
soltero *adj.* single
sombrero de sol sun hat
sopa soup
sótano basement
subir de peso to gain weight
suegro(a) father-in-law/
   mother-in-law
suelo soil

sueño dream
suéter *m.* sweater
supermercado supermarket

T

también also
tampoco neither, either
tarea homework, duty
tarjeta de crédito credit card
tarjeta de embarque boarding pass
taza cup
té *m.* tea
techo roof
teclado keyboard
técnica technique
técnico *m., f.* technician
tejanos blue jeans
tela fabric
teléfono telephone, phone number
televisión *f.* television, TV
televisor *m.* television set
tenedor *m.* fork
**Tenemos una reservación a nombre
   de...** We have a reservation. The
   name is . . .
tener to have
tener calor to be hot
tener constancia to be constant, to
   persist
tener disciplina to be disciplined
tener éxito to be successful
tener frío to be cold
tener ganas de to want, to have the
   desire (to do something)
tener hambre to be hungry
tener miedo (de) to be afraid (of)
tener paciencia to be patient
tener prisa to be in a hurry
tener sed to be thirsty
tener sueño to be sleepy
tener suerte to be lucky
tenis *m.* tennis
teñido *adj.* colored
terminal internacional *f.* international departures terminal
terminar to finish, to break up
términos de financiamiento credit
   terms
ternera veal
tiempo time; weather
tienda store
tienda de ropa clothing store

tierra land, earth, homeland
tijeras scissors
tímido *adj.* shy
tintorería dry cleaners
tío(a) uncle/aunt
tirar to throw
título title
tiza chalk
tobillo ankle
tocino bacon
todos los días every day
tolerante *adj.* tolerant
tomar to take, to drink
tomate *m.* tomato
tonto *adj.* foolish, dull
toro bull
torta cake
tos *f.* cough
trabajador *adj.* hardworking
trabajador(a) worker
trabajador(a) no calificado(a)
   unqualified worker
trabajo social social work
traje *m.* suit
traje de baño swimsuit
transporte *m.* transportation
trasladarse to relocate
traslado relocation, transfer
tratar de to try
trescientos/as 300
triste *adj.* sad
trucha trout

U

ubicación *f.* location
un millón 1.000.000
uña fingernail
uruguayo *adj.* Uruguayan
usar to use, to wear
útil *adj.* useful
utilizar (c) to make use
uva grape

V

vaca cow
valle *m.* valley
vaqueros blue jeans
variedad *f.* variety
vaso glass
vegatales *m.* vegetables
vendedor(a) salesperson

vender to sell
venezolano *adj.* Venezuelan
venta sale
ventana, ventanilla window
ver to see, to look
ver televisión to watch TV
verano summer
verde *adj.* green
verduras vegetables
vestido dress
veterinario(a) veterinary
viajar to travel
vida life
viejo *adj.* old
viernes *m.* Friday
vinagre *m.* vinegar

vincularse to get involved
vino wine
violencia violence
vitamina vitamin
viuda widow
vivir to live
volcán *m.* volcano
voleibol *m.* volleyball
volver (ue) to return
Vuelva pronto. Come back soon.

Y

y and
yeso cast

Z

zanahoria carrot
zapatilla slipper
zapato shoe
zapato alto/de tacones high heel shoe
zapato de tenis sneakers
zumo juice

Glosario: inglés-español

A

a little un poco
abdomen abdómen *m.*
   ability to speak facilidad de expresión *f.*
above sobre, encima de
accept aceptar
accessible accesible *adj.*
accommodate acomodar
accountant contable *m., f.*
achieve lograr
acrylic acrílico
active activo *adj.*
address dirección *f.*, domicilio
administer administrar
advice consejo
advise aconsejar
aerobics aeróbicos
African africano *adj.*
after después (de) que
aggressive agresivo *adj.*
airline ticket billete *m.*, boleto
airplane avión *m.*
airport aeropuerto
aisle pasillo
alarm clock despertador *m.*
alergy alergia
algebra álgebra
allow permitir
almost always casi siempre
almost never casi nunca
also también
always siempre
American (from the US) estadounidense *adj.*
amuse distraer
and y
angry disgustado, enojado *adj.*
animal fat grasa animal
ankle tobillo
answer contestar, responder
anthropology antropología
antibiotic antibiótico
any algún, cualquier
anyone alguien
Anything else? ¿Algo más?
appear parecer (zc), presentarse
appetizer entrada, entremés *m.*
apple manzana

application solicitud *f.*
application form formulario
apply for a job solicitar trabajo
April abril
architect arquitecto(a)
Are you ready to order? ¿Está listo para pedir?
Argentinean argentino *adj.*
arm brazo
armchair sillón *m.*
arrange acomodar
art arte *m.*
art gallery galería de arte
artist artista *m., f.*
as como
as soon as en cuanto
Asian asiático *adj.*
ask pedir (i, i)
ask a question hacer una pregunta
asparagus espárrago
aspire to aspirar a
at en
at night por la noche
attend asistir
attic ático
attorney abogado(a)
August agosto
aunt tía
automatic teller machine (ATM) cajero automático
avoid evitar
away afuera

B

back espalda
backpack mochila
bacon tocino
bald calvo *adj.*
ball bola, pelota
banana banana
Band-Aid curita
bank banco
baptism bautizo
bar bar *m.*
bar barra
barber shop peluquería
bass rábalo
baseball béisbol *m.*
basement sótano

basketball baloncesto
bathroom baño
be ser; estar
be able poder
be afraid (of) tener miedo (de)
be bad weather hacer mal tiempo
be cold tener frío, hacer frío
be constant tener constancia
be cool hacer fresco
be dating/going out ser novios
be disciplined tener disciplina
be glad (about) alegrarse (de)
be good weather hacer buen tiempo
be hot tener calor, hacer calor
be hungry tener hambre, pasar hambre
be in a hurry tener prisa
be lucky tener suerte
be (partly) cloudy estar (parcialmente) nublado
be patient tener paciencia
be ready (eager) estar dispuesto
be responsible for (doing something) encargarse de + *verb*
be sleepy tener sueño
be successful tener éxito
be sunny hacer sol
be thirsty tener sed
be windy hacer veinto
beach playa
beans frijoles *m.*
beautiful bonito *adj.*
beauty parlor peluquería, salón de belleza *m.*
because of that por ello, por eso
because of this por esto
become llegar a ser
become extinct extinguirse
bed cama
bedroom dormitorio, habitación *f.*, recámara
bedside table mesa de noche/de luz (mesita)
beef filet filete de res *m.*
beef steak bistec *m.*
before antes (de) que
before-dinner drink aperitivo
behind detrás de
belongings menaje *m.*
belt cinturón *m.*

better mejor
between entre
bicycle bicicleta
bike riding ciclismo
big grande *adj.*
biological reserve reserva biológica
biology biología
birth nacimiento
birthday cumpleaños
black negro *adj.*
black hair pelo negro
blanket manta
blond(e) rubio *adj.*
blond hair pelo rubio
blouse blusa
blue azul *adj.*
blue jeans tejanos, vaqueros
blueprints planos
board abordar
boarding area sala de espera
boarding pass tarjeta de embarque
body cuerpo
Bolivian boliviano *adj.*
bone hueso
book libro
bookcase estante *m.*
bookstore librería
boot bota
bored aburrido *adj.*
boss jefe(a)
bowling bolos
box caja
boyfriend novio
bracelet pulsera
bread pan *m.*
break (up) terminar
breakfast desayuno
briefcase maletín *m.*
broccoli brócoli *m.*
brother hermano
brother-in-law cuñado
brown marrón, café *adj.*
brown hair pelo castaño
bubblewrap plástico de burbujas
build construir
building edificio
bull toro
bus station estación de autobús *f.*
bus stop parada de autobús
business administration administración de empresas *f.*
businessman hombre de negocios *m.*
businesswoman mujer de negocios *f.*
busy ocupado *adj.*

but pero
butter mantequilla
button botón *m.*
buy comprar
Bye! ¡Chau!

C

cable cable *m.*
cake pastel *m.*, torta
calculus cálculo
camp acampar
cap gorra
car coche *m.*, carro
cardboard box caja de cartón
care for cuidar
carpet alfombra
carrot zanahoria
carry-on luggage equipaje de mano *m.*
cash efectivo
cast yeso
cat gato
CD disco
CD-ROM CD *m.*
cereal cereal *m.*
chair silla
chalk tiza
chalkboard pizarra
challenge desafío, reto
change cambio
charity beneficencia, caridad *f.*
chat on the phone charlar por teléfono
cheap barato *adj.*
check cheque *m.*
check *(bill)* cuenta
check the mailbox revisar el buzón
checked a cuadros *adj.*
cheese queso
chemistry química
chicken pollo
Chilean chileno *adj.*
chores quehaceres *m.*
church iglesia
city block cuadra, manzana
classified ad anuncio clasificado.
classroom salón de clase *m.*
clean limpiar
click cliquear, hacer clic, oprimir
climb escalar
close cerrar (ie)
closet clóset *m.*

clothes ropa
clothing store tienda de ropa
coffee café *m.*
coffee table mesa de centro (mesita)
cold resfriado
collaborate colaborar
colleague compañero(a)
collect recoger
Colombian colombiano *adj.*
colored teñido *adj.*
combat combatir
Come back soon. Vuelva pronto.
communication comunicación *f.*
competent competente *adj.*
computer programmer programador(a) de computadoras
computer science informática
computer computadora, ordenador *m.*
confident seguro de sí mismo *adj.*
confront enfrentar
congestion congestión *f.*
consider parecer (zc)
construction worker obrero(a)
consume consumir
contract contrato
cook cocinar
cook cocinero(a)
cookie galleta
corduroy pana
corn maíz *m.*
correct corregir (i, i)
cost of living costo de la vida
Costa Rican costarricense *adj. m., f.*
costume (jewelry) de fantasía
cotton algodón *m.*
Could you bring me . . . ? ¿Me podría traer...?
cough syrup jarabe *m.*
cough tos *f.*
count on contar con (ue)
countryside campo
court cancha
cousin primo(a)
cover letter carta de presentación
cow vaca
co-worker compañero(a) de trabajo
crab cangrejo
creative creativo *adj.*
credit card tarjeta de crédito
credit terms términos de financiamiento

crime (youth) delincuencia (juvenil)
crop cultivo
Cuban cubano *adj.*
cultivate cultivar
cup taza
curly rizado *adj.*
curtain cortina
cut cortar

D

dance baile *m.*
dark-haired moreno *adj.*
date of birth fecha de nacimiento
date salir (juntos)
daughter hija
day día *m.*
deal with customers atender (ie) al público
December diciembre
defend defender (ie)
delegate power delegar parte del poder
depressed deprimido *adj.*
design diseño
desk escritorio
dessert postre *m.*
develop desarrollar
difficult duro, difícil *adj.*
diligent diligente *adj.*
dining room comedor *m.*
dinner cena
discrimination discriminación *f.*
dish plato
dive bucear
divorced divorciado *adj.*
dizziness mareo
do hacer
do laundry lavar la ropa
do some warm-up exercises hacer un poco de calentamiento
do the dishes lavar los platos
Do you take credit cards? ¿Aceptan tarjetas de crédito?
doctor doctor(a) (Dr.[a]), médico(a)
document documento
dog perro
Dominican dominicano *adj.*
door puerta
down payment cuota inicial, anticipo

downtown centro
drawing dibujo
dream ilusión *f.*, sueño
dress vestido
dresser armario
dressing aderezo
drink tomar, beber
drive manejar
driver chofer *m., f.*
drunk embriagado *adj.*
dry cleaners tintorería
duck pato
dull tonto *adj.*
duty tarea

E

each cada
ear oreja
earring arete *m.*, pendiente *m.*
earth tierra
ease of expression facilidad de expresión *f.*
easy fácil *adj.*
eat comer
ecologist ecólogo
ecology ecología
economy economía
ecosystem ecosistema *m.*
Ecuadorian ecuatoriano *adj.*
education educación *f.*
efficient eficiente *adj.*
either tampoco
elbow codo
elbow pad codera
electricity electricidad *f.*, luz *f.*
e-mail mensaje electrónico *m.*
employee empleado(a)
engaged comprometido *adj.*
engineer ingeniero(a)
engineering ingeniería
entertain distraer, entretener (ie)
entrée (main course) plato principal
environment medio ambiente
equipment equipo
eraser borrador *m.*
European europeo *adj.*
every cada
every day todos los días
exchange cambio
excited emocionado *adj.*
Excuse me? ¿Cómo?
exit salir

exposition exposición *f.*
extinction extinción *f.*
extroverted extrovertido *adj.*
eye ojo
eyebrow ceja
e-mail correo electrónico

F

face enfrentar
face cara
fabric tela
fail (not be there) fallarle
faithful fiel *adj.*
fall otoño
fall in love enamorarse
family familia
famous famoso *adj.*
far lejos de
farewell despedida
farm finca
farmer campesino(a), agricultor(a)
fat gordo *adj*
father padre *m.*
father-in-law suegro
fauna fauna
fax fax *m.*
February febrero
feed alimentar
feel sentir (ie, i)
feel ill sentirse mal
fever fiebre *f.*
fiancé novio
fiancée novia
fiber fibra
field campo
file expediente *m.*
file archivo
finally por fin, finalmente *adv.*
fine bien
Fine, and you? (informal) Bien, ¿y tú?
Fine, and you? (formal) Bien, ¿y Ud.?
finger dedo
fingernail uña
finish terminar
firefighter bombero(a)
firm firme *adj.*
first floor planta baja
first-aid kit botiquín de primeros auxilios *m.*
fish (caught) pescado
fish (live) pez *m.*

five hundred quinientos
fix arreglar, reparar
flexibility elasticidad *f.*
flora flora
flu gripe *f.*, influenza
food comida
foolish tonto *adj.*
foot pie *m.*
football fútbol americano *m.*
for por
forget olvidar
fork tenedor *m.*
french fries papas/patatas fritas
Friday viernes *m.*
fried frito *adj.*
friend amigo(a)
friendly amistoso, amigable *adj.*
friendship amistad *f.*
from desde
fruit fruta
fun divertido *adj.*
funny cómico, gracioso *adj.*, de buen humor
furniture muebles *m.*
future futuro

G

gain ganar
gain weight subir de peso
game juego
garage garaje *m.*
garbage basura
garbage hauler basurero
garden jardín *m.*
garlic ajo
generous generoso *adj.*
geography geografía
geology geología
geometry geometría
get sacar
get divorced divorciarse
get involved vincularse
get married in a religious/civil ceremany casarse por la iglesia/por lo civil
get separated separarse
get sick enfermarse
girlfriend novia
give dar
glass vaso
glove guante *m.*
go ir
go for a walk pasear

go out salir
goal meta
goggles gafas protectoras
gold dorado *adj.*
gold oro
good bueno *adj.*
Good afternoon! ¡Buenas tardes!
Good evening! ¡Buenas noches!
Good morning! ¡Buenos días!
Good-bye! ¡Adiós!
grandfather abuelo
grandmother abuela
grandson nieto
granddaughter nieta
graduation graduación *f.*
graduation date fecha de grado
grape uva
grass césped *m.*
gray gris *adj.*
gray hair pelo blanco
great de maravilla
green verde *adj.*
greeting saludo
Guatemalan guatemalteco *adj.*
gymnasium gimnasio
gymnastics gimnasia

H

hair pelo
hair dresser peluquero(a)
ham jamón *m.*
hamburguer hamburguesa
hand mano *f.*
handbag cartera
handsome guapo *adj.*
happiness alegría
happy alegre, feliz, contento *adj.*
hard duro *adj.*
hardworking trabajador(a) *adj.*
harness arnés *m.*
harvest cosecha
harvest cosechar
hatred odio
have just (done something) acabar de + *infinitive*
head cabeza
headache dolor de cabeza *m.*
heal curar
health salud *f.*
heart corazón *m.*
helmet casco
help ayudar

hen gallina
here aquí
Here you are. Aquí tiene.
Hi! ¡Hola!
high alto *adj.*
high heel shoe zapato alto/de tacones
history historia
hit golpear, pulsar
home hogar *m.*
homeland patria, tierra
homework tarea
Honduran hondureño *adj.*
honest honesto *adj.*
honey miel *f.*
hope esperar
horror horror *m.*
horse caballo
hospital hospital *m.*
hotel hotel *m.*
house casa
household hogar *m.*
household goods menaje *m.*
housewife ama de casa
How? ¿Cómo?
How are you? (formal) ¿Cómo está Ud.?
How are you? (informal) ¿Cómo estás?, ¿Cómo te va?
How can I help you, sir? ¿En qué puedo servirle, señor?
How do you say . . . ? ¿Cómo se dice... ?
How many? ¿Cuántos?
How much? ¿Cuánto?
human rights derechos humanos
humanities humanidades *f.*
hunger hambre *m.*
hurt doler (ue)
husband esposo

I

I am looking for . . . Busco...
I do not understand. No comprendo.
I'll see you on Monday. Nos vemos el lunes.
I hope. Ojalá.
ice cream helado
illusion ilusión *f.*
image imagen *f.*
improve mejorar
in en
in case en caso (de) que

in front of enfrente de
in order that a fin de que, para que
in the afternoon por la tarde
in the event that en caso (de) que
in the morning por la mañana
increase aumentar
indifference indiferencia
indoors al cubierto, bajo techo
in-line skating patinaje en línea *m.*
inner ear oído
insert insertar
install instalar
instead en cambio
intelligent inteligente *adj.*
international departures terminal terminal internacional *f.*
Internet connection conexión a Internet *f.*
interview entrevista
introduce presentar
invest invertir (ie)
investigate investigar
island isla
It doesn't work. No funciona.
It is wonderful! ¡Es fantástico!, ¡Es ideal!, ¡Es maravilloso!, ¡Es perfecto!

J

jacket chaqueta
jam mermelada
January enero
jelly mermelada
job profesión *f.*
journalism periodismo
journalist periodista *m., f.*
judge juzgar
juice jugo, zumo
July julio
June junio
jungle selva

K

keep guardar
keep fit mantenerse en forma
keep in good health mantenerse en buen estado de salud
key in digitar
keyboard teclado
kind amable *adj.*
kitchen cocina
knee rodilla

knee pad rodillera
knife cuchillo
know conocer
know (how) saber

L

label marcar
lake lago
lamp lámpara
land tierra
landmark lugar de interés *m.*
landscape paisaje *m.*
language lengua, idioma *m.*
laptop computer computadora portátil
last name apellido
last night anoche
laundromat lavandería
laundry ropa
law derecho
lawn césped *m.*
lazy perezoso *adj.*
learn aprender
leather cuero
leave salir, dejar, irse
leg pierna
lemonade limonada
let (allow) dejar
lettuce lechuga
library biblioteca
lie mentir (ie)
life vida
light luz *f.*
like como
like gustar
like something very much encantar
listen to escuchar
literature literatura
live vivir
livestock ganado
living room sala
load cargar
loan préstamo
lobster langosta
location ubicación *f.*
lodging alojamiento
long largo *adj.*
long for añorar
look ver
look after cuidar
look at mirar
lose perder (ie)
lose weight bajar de peso

love amor *m.*
love (someone) amar, querer
love (something) encantar
love one's work amar el trabajo
low bajo *adj.*
loyal leal *adj.*
luggage equipaje *f.*
lunch almuerzo, comida
lung pulmón *m.*

M

maid empleado(a) doméstico(a)
maintain mantener
major especialidad *f.*
make hacer
make come true hacer realidad
make the bed hacer la cama
make use utilizar (c)
mall centro comercial
manage administrar, manejar
mango mango
many mucho
Many thanks. Muchas gracias.
March marzo
marital status estado civil
marker marcador *m.*
marmalade mermelada
married casado *adj.*
mass culture cultura masiva
masterpiece obra maestra
mathematics matemáticas
mature mayor *adj.*
May mayo
mayor alcalde *m.*
meal comida
mean malo *adj.*
meat carne *f.*
medicine medicina
meet conocer
meeting reunión *f.*
melon melón *m.*
memory recuerdo
menu carta
metal metal *m.*
Mexican mexicano *adj.*
microwave oven horno microóndas
milk leche *f.*
mineral mineral *m.*
mini-skirt minifalda
mirror espejo
miss echar de menos, extrañar
Miss Señorita (Srta.)
Monday lunes *m.*

money dinero
month mes *m.*
more más
More slowly, please. Más despacio, por favor.
mortgage hipoteca
mother mamá, madre *f.*
mother-in-law suegra
mountain montaña
mouse ratón (mouse) *m.*
mouth boca
move mudanza
move mudarse
movement (school) movimiento
movie theater cine *m.*
movie película
movies cine *m*
moving truck camión de mudanzas *m.*
Mr., Sir Señor (Sr.)
Mrs., Madam Señora (Sra.)
much mucho
multimedia engineering ingeniería multimedia
museum museo
mushroom champiñón *m.*
music música
mussel mejillón *m.*
My name is . . . Me llamo...

N

name nombre *m.*
napkin servilleta
nationality nacionalidad *f.*
natural gas gas *m.*
natural resources recursos naturales
natural sciences ciencias naturales
naturalist naturalista *m., f.*
near cerca de
neaklace collar *m.*
neck cuello
neighborhood barrio
neither tampoco
neither . . . nor ni... ni
nephew sobrino
nervous nervioso *adj.*
never nunca
next to al lado de
Nicaraguan nicaragüense *adj. m., f.*
nice simpático *adj.*
niece sobrina
nobody nadie
noise ruido

non-smoking section sección de no fumar *f.*
nose naríz *f.*
notebook cuaderno
nothing nada
November noviembre
now ahora
nurse enfermero(a)

O

objects objetos
obtain sacar
ocean océano
October octubre
Of course. Por supuesto.
old viejo *adj.*
oil aceite *m.*
older mayor *adj.*
on en, encima de, sobre
on time a la hora
on the other hand por otro lado
one hundred cien
one million millón *m.*
one thousand mil *m.*
onion cebolla
open abrir
Open your books on page . . . Abran el libro en la página...
operate actuar, manejar
orange anaranjado, color naranja *adj.*
orange naranja
outside afuera
over sobre, encima de
overcoat abrigo

P

pack empacar
packing embalaje *m.*
packing staff empacadores *m., f.*
page página
painter pintor(a)
painting cuadro, pintura
Panamanian panameño *adj.*
pants pantalones *m.*
Paraguayan paraguayo *adj.*
paramedic paramédico(a)
parasites parásitos intestinales
park ranger guardaparques *m.*
park parque *m.*
parking lot aparcamiento, estacionamiento, parqueadero
passport pasaporte *m.*

patient paciente *adj.*
pear pera
peas arvejas, chícharos
pedal pedalear
pen bolígrafo
pencil lápiz *m.*
pepper pimienta
percent por ciento
permit permitir
persist tener constancia
perseverance constancia
personal information datos personales
pharmacy farmacia
philosophy filosofía
phone call llamada telefónica
phone number teléfono
photography fotografía
physical education educación física *f.*
physical therapy fisioterapia
pick picar
pig cerdo, puerco
pill pastilla
pineapple piña
pizza pizza
pink rosado *adj.*
placemat individual *m.*
plaid a cuadros
plantain plátano
plate plato
play jugar (ue)
player jugador(a)
please gustar
please por favor
Pleased to meet you. Encantado(a), Mucho gusto.
plug in conectar, enchufar
police policía
police station estación de policía *f.*
policeman(woman) policía *m., f.*
political science ciencias políticas
polka-dot de puntos, de lunares
pollution contaminación *f.*
polyester poliéster *m.*
poor pobre *adj.*
pork puerco
(pork)chop chuleta (de cerdo)
post office oficina de correos
potato papa
power poder *m.*
preoccupied preocupado *adj.*
prepare preparar
prescription receta

present (oneself) presentar(se)
preserve preservar, conservar
pretty bonito *adj,*
price estimation cotización *f.,* estimado
print imprimir
print estampado
printer impresora
produce producir
professional profesional *m., f.*
professional license licencia profesional, matrícula profesional
program programa *m.*
program programar
promote promover (ue)
property propiedad *f.*
proportion proporción *f.*
protect proteger
protein proteína
provided that con tal de que
psychology sicología
public official funcionario(a) público(a)
Puerto Rican puertorriqueño *adj.*
pull halar, jalar
punctual puntual *adj.*
purple morado *adj.*
push presionar, oprimir, pulsar

Q

question pregunta
quit dejar de
quit a program abandonar un programa

R

racket raqueta
rain llover (ue)
raincoat impermeable *m.*
raise criar
reach alcanzar (c), llegar
read leer
Read . . . Lean...
ready listo *adj.*
real estate agency inmobiliaria, agencia de bienes raíces
receive recibir
recycle reciclar
red rojo *adj.*
red hair pelo rojo
reduce reducir (zc)

referee árbitro
refined product producto refinado
refrigerator nevera, refrigerador *m.*
regular regular *adj.*
relative pariente *m., f.*
reliable cumplidor *adj.*
relocate trasladarse
relocation traslado
remember acordarse (ue) de
rent alquilar
repair reparar
repeat repetir (i, i)
report informe *m.*
represent representar
request pedir (i, i), solicitar
research investigación *f.*
research investigar
resistance resistencia
respect respetar
respect respeto
respectful respetuoso *adj.*
responsible responsable *adj.*
rest descanso
restaurant restaurante *m.*
résumé hoja de vida, currículum *m.*
retirement jubilación *f.*
return regresar, volver (ue)
rice arroz *m.*
rich rico *adj.*
right derecho
risk riesgo
river río
rock climbing escalada libre
roof techo
rope cuerda
rude grosero *adj.*
run correr

S

sad triste *adj.*
salad ensalada
sale venta
salesperson vendedor(a)
salmon filet filete de salmón *m.*
salt sal *f.*
Salvadorian salvadoreño *adj.*
sample muestra
sand arena
sandal sandalia
sandwich bocadillo, emparedado, sándwich *m.*
Saturday sábado
saucer platillo

sausage (hot dog) salchicha
save salvar
scene escena
scissors tijeras
scramble revuelto *adj.*
screen pantalla
sculptor escultor(a)
sculpture escultura
sea mar *m.*
seafood mariscos
search engine motor de búsqueda *m.*
season estación *f.*
seat asiento
second floor primer piso *m.*
see mirar, ver
See you around! ¡Hasta la vista!
See you later. Hasta luego.
See you soon! ¡Hasta pronto!
seem parecer (zc)
selfish egoísta *adj.*
sell vender
send enviar
sense of humor sentido del humor
September septiembre
serious serio *adj.*
set set *m.,* juego
sewage system alcantarillado
share compartir
shirt camisa
shoe zapato
short corto, bajo *adj.*
shorts pantalones cortos *m.*
shoulder hombro
show mostrar (ue)
shrimp camarón *m.,* gamba
shy tímido *adj.*
sick enfermo *adj.*
silver plata
silver plateado *adj.*
silk seda
since desde
sing cantar
sister hermana
sister-in-law cuñada
single soltero *adj.*
skating (ice skating) patinaje (sobre hielo) *m.*
ski esquí *m.*
ski esquiar
skin piel *f.*
skinny flaco *adj.*
skirt falda

slipper zapatilla
slowly despacio
small pequeño *adj.*
smart listo *adj.*
smoke fumar
sneakers zapatos de tenis
snow nevar (ie)
so so más o menos, regular *adj.*
so that a fin de que, para que
soccer fútbol *m.*
social services servicios sociales
social sciences ciencias sociales
social work trabajo social
sock calcetín *m.*, media
soda refresco
sofa sofá *m.*
soil suelo
solid color de un solo tono, liso
solidarity solidaridad *f.*
some un poco, algún
somebody alguien
someone alguien
something algo
sometimes a veces
son hijo
soup sopa
sow sembrar (ie)
Spanish español *adj.*
speak hablar
speaker parlante *m.*, altavoz *m.*
specialty especialidad *f.*
species especie *f.*
spend free time pasar tiempo
  libre/los ratos libres
spoon cuchara
sport deporte *m.*
spring primavera
stairs escalera
stepbrother hermanastro
stepfather padrastro
stepmother madrastra
stepsister hemanastra
stereo estéreo
stocking media
stomach estómago
stop (doing something) dejar de
storage guardamuebles *m.*
store almacén *m.*,tienda
store guardar
story historia
stove estufa
straight liso *adj.*
strawberry fresa
street calle *f.*

street corner esquina
strength fuerza
stress estrés *m.*
stretch hacer estiramiento
stretching estiramiento
strict estricto *adj.*
strike huelga
string bean judía verde
striped a rayas
strong fuerte *adj.*
student estudiante *m., f.*
studies completed estudios
  realizados
stupid estúpido *adj.*
subway station estación de metro *f.*
subway stop parada de metro
succeed poder
sugar azúcar *m., f.*
suit traje *m.*
suitcase maleta
summer verano
sun hat sombrero de sol
Sunday domingo
sunglasses lentes de sol *m.*
supermarket supermercado
support apoyar
support mantener
surf hacer surf
surf the net navegar el Internet (la
  red)
sweater suéter *m.*
swim nadar
swimming natación *f.*
swimsuit bañador *m.*, traje de baño
  m.
synthetic material material sintético
  m.

T

table mesa
tablecloth mantel *m.*
tableware cubiertos
take tomar
take a short trip pasear
take a trip hacer un viaje
take out sacar
take risks arriesgarse
talk hablar
tall alto *adj.*
tape cinta
tea té *m.*
teach enseñar
teacher profesor(a)

team equipo
teaspoon cucharita
technician técnico *m., f.*
technique técnica
telecommunications telecomunica-
  ciones *f.*
telephone teléfono
television televisión *f.*
television set televisor *m.*
tennis tenis *m.*
terrible terrible *adj.*
Thank you. Gracias.
that one (over there) aquél (aquélla)
that one eso
there allí
these (ones) éstos(as)
They are finger-licking good.
  Están/Son como para chuparse
  los dedos.
thin delgado *adj.*
this one éste
those ésos(as)
those (over there) aquéllos
threatened species especie en vía de
  extinción *f.*
throat garganta
throw tirar
Thursday jueves *m.*
tidy up arreglar
tie corbata
time tiempo
tip propina
tired cansado *adj.*
title título
toast tostada
toe dedo del pie
together juntos
tolerant tolerante *adj.*
tomato tomate *m.*
tomato sauce salsa de tomate
tooth diente *m.*
tourist office oficina de turismo
townsquare plaza
track and field atletismo
traffic congestion congestión *f.*
traffic light semáforo
traffic police policia vial (de tránsito)
train station estación de trenes *f.*
train stop parada de trenes
trait rasgo
transfer traslado
transportation transporte *m., f.*
trash basura

travel viajar
traveler's check cheque de viajero *m.*
tree árbol *m.*
trout trucha
trustworthy confiable, cumplidor *adj.*
try querer, tratar de
T-shirt camiseta
Tuesday martes *m.*
tuna atún *m.*
turkey pavo
turn off apagar
turn on encender (ie), prender
turned off apagado
turned on encendido

U

ugly feo *adj.*
uncle tío
under debajo de
understand comprender
underwear ropa interior
unfaithful infiel *adj.*
unfriendly antipático *adj.*
unless a menos que
unpack desempacar
unplug desconectar, desenchufar
unqualified worker trabajador(a) no calificado
until hasta (que)
Uruguayan uruguayo *adj.*
use usar
useful útil *adj.*
utilities servicios públicos

V

vacuum aspirar
valley valle *m.*
value valor *m.*
variety variedad *f.*
veal ternera
vegetable verdura, legumbre *f.*, vegetal *m.*
Venezuelan venezolano *adj.*
very muy
Very well, thank you. Muy bien, gracias.
vest chaleco
veterinary veterinario(a)

vinegar vinagre
violence violencia
violet violeta *adj.*
vitamin vitamina
volcano volcán *m.*
volleyball voleibol *m.*

W

waist cintura
waiter/waitress mesero(a)
walk caminar
wall pared *f.*
wallet billetera
want aspirar, desear, querer
want (to do something) tener ganas de
war guerra
warehouse bodega
warm up calentamiento
wash lavar
watch reloj *m.*
watch mirar
watch over cuidar
watch TV ver televisión
water agua
watermelon sandía
water-ski esquiar en el agua
weak débil *adj.*
wear usar, llevar
weather tiempo
wedding boda, matrimonio
Wednesday miércoles *m.*
week semana
We have a reservation. The name is . . . Tenemos una reservación a nombre de...
weight peso
weight lifting levantamiento de pesas
welcome bienvenido *adj.*
well bien
What? ¿Cómo?, ¿Qué?
What does it mean? ¿Qué significa?
What is the weather like? ¿Qué tiempo hace?
(At) What time? ¿A qué hora?
whatever cualquier
when cuando
When? ¿Cuándo?
Where? ¿Dónde?
Where is? ¿Dónde está?

Where to? ¿Adónde?
whereas mientras que
Which? ¿Cuál?
Which ones? ¿Cuáles?
while mientras (que)
white blanco *adj.*
Who? ¿Quién?, ¿Quiénes?
Why? ¿Por qué?
widow viuda
wife esposa
wildlife reserve refugio natural (silvestre)
wildlife fauna
window ventana, ventanilla
wine vino
wine glass copa
winter invierno
with con
With pleasure! ¡Con gusto!
wonderful maravilloso *adj.*
wool lana
word palabra
work experience experiencia laboral
work obra
workbook cuaderno de ejercicios
worker trabajador(a)
world mundo
worried preocupado
worry about preocuparse
wrap envolver (ue)
wrestling lucha libre
write escribir
Write . . . Escriban...

X

x-ray radiografía

Y

yellow amarillo *adj.*
You are welcome! ¡De nada!, ¡Con gusto!, A su servicio. A sus órdenes.
young joven *adj.*
younger menor *adj.*

Z

zero cero

Índice

A

a: + el, 105
abrir, past participle, 314
acabar de + infinitive, 298
activities: daily, 37–38, 41, 116, 128, 156–157, 159–160, 165; past, 184, 195–196, 208–209, 226–227, 235
adjectival clauses: subjunctive in, 388, 498
adjectives: agreement of, 29, 66; comparative, 148–149; demonstrative, 247–248; descriptive, 29–30, 63, 73, 168–169; irregular comparative, 149; irregular superlative, 149; of nationality, 30; possessive, 66; used with **estar,** 73, 168–169; used with **ser,** 168–169; superlative, 148–149
adverbial clauses, 415, 498
adverbs: of frequency, 38, 119; of sequence, 155; of time, 415
advice, giving, 358–359, 362–363, 400, 424, 460, 464, 498
algo/alguien, subjunctive in questions with, 388
-**ar** verbs: commands, 323; conditional tense, 449; daily activities with simple present tense, 37–38;

future tense, 427, 446; imperfect subjunctive, 464; imperfect tense, 227, 489; past participle, 313, 489; present participles of, 145; present progressive, 145; present subjunctive, 359, 362, 498; present tense, 37–38; preterite tense, 184, 488
articles: definite, 16–17; indefinite, 18; neuter, 273
asking questions, 51
aspirations, talking about, 446
averiguar, present subjunctive, 363

B

beber, past participle, 313; present perfect, 313; present subjunctive, 498; preterite, 184
beneficiary of an action, referring to the, 286–287
bueno, 88, 149

C

c → z(c) spelling changing verbs, 165, 498
caber, future tense, 428, 446
caer: imperfect subjunctive, 474; present participle, 225
cantar, past participle, 313; present perfect, 313; present subjunc-

tive, 498
-**car** verbs: commands, 324; present subjunctive, 363, 498; preterite tense, 184
comer: conditional tense, 449; imperfect subjunctive, 464; present subjunctive, 359
commands: formal, 323–324, 327, 400, 424, 498; informal, 403, 424, 498; plural **nosotros,** 424; verbs with irregular **tú** affirmative, 403
comparatives, 148–149
comparing and contrasting, 148–149
condition: expressing, 478; talking about, with **estar** and **tener,** 73
conditional tense, expressions used with, 450; uses of, 449–450, 504
conjecture, expressing, 449
conjunctions, 415, 460, 465
conocer: present subjunctive, 363; present tense, 116, 165; preterite, 251; versus **saber,** 238
corregir, present subjunctive, 363
correr, imperfect tense, 227; present tense, 41
crecer, imperfect subjunctive, 474
cubrir, past participle, 314

D

daily activities, 37–38, 41, 116, 128, 156–157, 159, 165
daily routines, 159
dar: commands, 324; imperfect subjunctive, 474; present subjunctive, 363; present tense, 116; preterite tense, 196, 488
de: + el, 66; to express possession, 66; verbs that require, 298
decir: command form, 403; future tense, 427, 446; imperfect subjunctive, 473; past participle, 314, 489; present subjunctive, 362; present tense, 166
definite articles, 16–17
demonstrative adjectives and pronouns, 247–248
denial, expressing, 385, 464
describing: objects, 168–169; people, 29–30, 168–169
describir, past participle, 314
desire, expressing, 131
destination. *See* location
direct object pronouns, 199–200, 400, 424
directives, giving, 424
dislikes and likes, talking about, 77
dormir: imperfect subjunctive, 474; present subjunctive,